UTB **3148**

Eine Arbeitsgemeinschaft der Verlage

Böhlau Verlag · Köln · Weimar · Wien
Verlag Barbara Budrich · Opladen · Farmington Hills
facultas.wuv · Wien
Wilhelm Fink · München
A. Francke Verlag · Tübingen und Basel
Haupt Verlag · Bern · Stuttgart · Wien
Julius Klinkhardt Verlagsbuchhandlung · Bad Heilbrunn
Lucius & Lucius Verlagsgesellschaft · Stuttgart
Mohr Siebeck · Tübingen
Orell Füssli Verlag · Zürich
Verlag Recht und Wirtschaft · Frankfurt am Main
Ernst Reinhardt Verlag · München · Basel
Ferdinand Schöningh · Paderborn · München · Wien · Zürich
Eugen Ulmer Verlag · Stuttgart
UVK Verlagsgesellschaft · Konstanz
Vandenhoeck & Ruprecht · Göttingen
vdf Hochschulverlag AG an der ETH Zürich

Helge Nowak

Literature in Britain and Ireland:
A History

francke VERLAG

Prof. Dr. Helge Nowak lehrt am Department für Anglistik und Amerikanistik der LMU München.

Für meine Tochter Lara

*Glaub mir: englische Literatur
macht richtig Spaß!*

Bibliografische Information der Deutschen Nationalbibliothek

Die Deutsche Nationalbibliothek verzeichnet diese Publikation in der Deutschen Nationalbibliografie; detaillierte bibliografische Daten sind im Internet über http://dnb.d-nb.de abrufbar.

© 2010 · Narr Francke Attempto Verlag GmbH + Co. KG
Dischingerweg 5 · D-72070 Tübingen
ISBN 978-3-7720-8279-5

Internet: http://www.francke.de
E-Mail: info@francke.de

Einbandgestaltung: Atelier Reichert, Stuttgart
Umschlagfoto Salman Rushdie: Tim Ross
Satz: Informationsdesign D. Fratzke, Kirchentellinsfurt
Druck und Bindung: fgb – freiburger graphische betriebe
Printed in Germany

ISBN 978-3-8252-3148-4 (UTB-Bestellnummer)

Contents

Introduction IX

1   Medieval Literature (up to c.1500)   1
1.1   Literature from Anglo-Saxon England   1
1.2   Middle English Literature.   7
1.3   Celtic Contexts   20
      Guiding Questions and Exercises   25

2   Renaissance Literature (c.1500 – 1660).   27
2.1   Renaissance Contexts   27
      Guiding Questions and Exercises   36
2.2   Theatre and Drama.   36
      2.2.1 The Renaissance Stage   36
      2.2.2 Romans and Roses: Elizabethan History Plays. . .   41
      2.2.3 Tragedies   55
      2.2.4 (Tragi-)Comedies and Humours   70
      Guiding Questions and Exercises   78
2.3   Renaissance Poetry   79
      2.3.1 Poets, Poetic Styles and Themes   79
      2.3.2 The Sonnet Craze   93
      2.3.3 Epic Poetry and Other Long Poems 105
      Guiding Questions and Exercises 112
2.4   *Utopia* and Other Prose Writings 113
      Guiding Questions and Exercises 125

3   The Long Eighteenth Century:
      Neoclassicism and Romanticism (1660 – c.1830). 127
3.1   Literary Communication in Britain between 1660
      and the 1830s 127
      Guiding Questions and Exercises 144
3.2   Performance Culture: Drama, Orality and Oratory 145

3.2.1 Dramatic Genres and Genre Theory. 145
3.2.2 Popular Politics in Songs and Speeches 159
Guiding Questions and Exercises 162
3.3 Neoclassicist and Romantic Poetry. 162
3.3.1 Translations, Imitations, Mock-Epic and
Verse Satire 162
3.3.2 From Gray's "Elegy" to the Odes of Keats, from
the Ballad Revival to the Return of the Sonnet . . 168
3.3.3 Poetry and Gender Relations: 'Love, Honour
and Obey'? 182
Guiding Questions and Exercises 191
3.4 From Manuscript to Print: Adaptation to a
New Medium, and New Forms of Writing. 192
3.4.1 Romantic Poets and the Continuum of Recital,
Manuscript and Print 192
3.4.2 'Letter Writing' in Various Forms. 196
3.4.3 Familiar, Formal and Periodical Essays 200
3.4.4 Writing Lives. 203
3.4.5 The Literature of Travel .207
3.4.6 The Children's Book: Literature for a
New Audience. 216
Guiding Questions and Exercises 221
3.5 'The Rise of the Novel': A Series of Experiments 222
3.5.1 Robinson Crusoe and Its Relation to Individualism,
Religion and Colonialism 222
3.5.2 Male Novelists and Their Female Heroines:
Gender Relations, Materialism and Morality in
Moll Flanders, Pamela, and Fanny Hill 225
3.5.3 The Novels of Fielding and Sterne 230
3.5.4 'Mothers of the Novel': Women Writers before
and beside Jane Austen. .236
3.5.5 Oriental Tales and Gothic Romances: Other
Worlds in an Age of Reason 242
3.5.6 Fiction and Nation-Building in Scott's Historical
Novels 247
Guiding Questions and Exercises 253

**4   The Literature of the Victorian Age and of the
Early Twentieth Century** (c.1830–c.1920) 255
4.1   Authors, Publishers and Readers: The Changing Face
of Literary Communication in Britain and Ireland . . . 255
Guiding Questions and Exercises. 268
4.2   'Victorian Values': Materialism, Morals and Mentalities
in the Literature of the Period 269
4.2.1 Utilitarianism, Darwinism and Religious Belief
in the Victorian Age 269
4.2.2 The Impact of the Empire. 277
4.2.3 'The Angel in the House' vs. the Fallen Woman:
Gender Roles and Their Impact on Literature . . . 291
Guiding Questions and Exercises. 304
4.3   Drama and Performance: From Music Hall and
Melodrama to the Plays of Wilde, Shaw, Yeats and
Synge. 304
Guiding Questions and Exercises. 326
4.4   Poetry from Tennyson to Yeats: Forms and Themes . . . 327
Guiding Questions and Exercises. 350
4.5   The Development of Fiction from Dickens to
Lawrence. 351
4.5.1 Charles Dickens and the Breakthrough of
the Novel. 351
4.5.2 History and Social Realism in Fiction by
Dickens's Rivals and Contemporaries 361
4.5.3 Regional and Sensational Elements in the Novel
from Wilkie Collins and Thomas Hardy to
D. H. Lawrence. 378
4.5.4 Devils, Doubles and Detectives:
The Development of Short Fiction in Ireland,
Scotland and England 390
4.5.5 From Workhouse to Wonderland: The Child in
Fiction, and Fiction for Children 400
Guiding Questions and Exercises. 419

5   Modernism and Beyond (c.1920 to the Present) 421
5.1   New Developments in Poetry. 421
5.1.1 From Yeats's Later Poetry to Radical Modernism. 422
5.1.2 Tradition and the Individual Talent: More
Moderate Forms of Experiment and Innovation . 431

5.1.3 Englishness in English Verse since the 1960s . . . 448
5.1.4 Scottish, Welsh and Irish Poetry since the 1960s 458
5.1.5 Summing Up a Century in Sonnets 465
Guiding Questions and Exercises 468
5.2 Drama and Theatre 469
5.2.1 New Spaces for Performance and New Media . . . 469
5.2.2 Well-Made Plays and Verse Plays 477
5.2.3 Absurdity, Anger and After 486
5.2.4 Irish Drama and Theatre since the 1920s 501
5.2.5 Drama and Theatre since the 1980s 512
Guiding Questions and Exercises 517
5.3 Fiction 518
5.3.1 Mainstream Writing up to the 1960s,
and a Concern with History Well Beyond 520
5.3.2 Forms of Popular Fiction 526
5.3.3 Modernist and Postmodernist Experiments 542
5.3.4 Gender and Region 554
5.3.5 Residues of Empire and Transcultural Fiction in
Britain 566
5.3.6 Intertextuality and Intermediality in
Contemporary Fiction 586
Guiding Questions and Exercises 593

References and Further Reading 595

Subject Index 620

Name Index 623

Introduction

British and Irish poets, dramatists and storytellers have produced Scope a large and immensely rich body of literature, and keep on adding to it. They found their audiences (ranging from the illiterate to the intellectual) in the marketplace and in the playhouse, or when their works were recited to the court, read aloud to the family, or read silently alone. *Literature in Britain and Ireland: A History* surveys that field of literary communication in the British Isles from the beginnings of literature in English in Medieval times up to the present. Such a wide **scope** is justified as authors of great renown from the last two centuries – such as Sir Walter Scott, Alfred Lord Tennyson, Ezra Pound, J.R.R. Tolkien and Seamus Heaney – re-created and revamped the literature of the Middle Ages in works of their own. In various modes of modern dress, Shakespeare has become a cultural hero of the twentieth and twenty-first centuries, too. The actor and screenwriter Ian McKellen turned *Richard III* into a piece of alternate history, in which Britain sees the rise and fall of a Fascist dictator. *A Midsummer Night's Dream* travelled from the fairy kingdom to alternate worlds in Terry Pratchett's works of fantasy and in Neil Gaiman's graphic novels. Such instances of literary response over the centuries are continuously noted in the present survey, and so are the ways in which adaptors, actors and directors, scribes, printers, booksellers and patrons facilitated the production of literature in performance and in print, within a specified period as well as over time. *Literature in Britain and Ireland: A History* attempts to present a balanced account of all phases of development, though in recognition of the needs of students of literature the nineteenth to twenty-first centuries will loom somewhat larger. Innovative tendencies in teaching are recognised, too, through the inclusion of representative contemporary authors and their works, and through a look at popular literature in all periods.

Literary Periods

Literary historians have proposed demarcations and denominations of periods in order to serve a better understanding of literatures in the context of their time of composition. Quite naturally, any such act of construction will remain open to debate. **Periodisation** in the present survey generally follows the conventional practice of teaching the literature of the British Isles, simply because this appears to be most helpful to students in their preparation for classes or for examinations. Where the present survey differs from other literary histories is in its treatment of medieval literature from the fifth to the fifteenth century, of literature between 1660 and c.1830, and from c.1920 to the present, each in one section only. In this way, the linguistic change from Old English, the language of the Anglo-Saxons, to Middle English after the Norman Conquest will appear as part of a wider linguistic and cultural pluralism in the Middle Ages. The likewise comprehensive view of literature between 1660 and c.1830 responds to recent trends in research that speak, as here, of a 'Long Eighteenth Century' reaching across Neoclassicism and Romanticism. Those conventional period denominations will however be discussed as then contemporary literary tendencies. The heading 'Modernism and Beyond' allows for the treatment of the many facets of literature from the twentieth and twenty-first centuries – Modernist and otherwise. The term 'Postmodernism', which is still disputed as a period denomination, is reserved here for a post-1960s form of experimental fiction (akin to the usage in US-American literary history).

Variety of Literary Traditions

That wide angle of vision needs to be supplemented, however, by a closer look at the **linguistic, regional and ethnic differences within and between the literatures of the British Isles.** Quite intentionally, *Literature in Britain and Ireland: A History* takes note of more than one national literature, and of a great variety of literary traditions. The multilingual and multicultural character of medieval Britain and Ireland is pointed out and exemplified in the first part of the survey. Later and under the aspect of regionalisation, Irish, Scottish and Welsh authors and their works may eventually be treated in separate sections. In similar fashion, trans-cultural literature with a focus on ethnic minorities is addressed. In such a way, respective literary traditions are clearly marked out (perhaps more clearly than in other literary histories), and they are kept visible throughout. The same applies for **genre traditions.**

A recurrent series of sections and chapters keyed to theatre and drama, poetry, fiction (the novel as well as the short story) and also non-fictional prose allows the reader to read across the variety of literature within one period, but also to concentrate on the development of major genres over time by following the respective sections one after another. Time and again, starting from the account of medieval literature, reference is made to instances of intertextuality and also intermediality that may establish connections across centuries, genres and the media. **Links in the text** as well as the information provided in the **Index** help to map out such a field of intertextual response. In addition to the treatment of major genres on their own, further chapters of *Literature in Britain and Ireland: A History* are focused on **period contexts**. They address the establishment and changes of forms of literary communication as well as the impact of the media, and they moreover take into account Cultural, Postcolonial and Gender Criticism. **Study Questions** at the end of chapters provide opportunities to rehearse and read on.

When there is no other source given for a quotation, the text cited can be found in one of the comprehensive anthologies listed (together with the abbreviations used) at the beginning of the References section. Capitalisation is used for individual words within a title cited in the text; if not, the title of a poem will be identical with its first line. The chapters on poetry and gender relations throughout the Long Eighteenth Century, and on Victorian Values, may fruitfully be read together with the cultural 'clusters' marked out in *The Norton Anthology of English Literature*, which is just one example for the conscious attempt to link up with this and other widely used anthologies of literature. The **References** section is supplemented by further lists of handbooks and glossaries of literary terms, and by select bibliographies keyed to each period. The reader may also profit by reading *Literature in Britain and Ireland: A History* together with the systematic introduction to literature and literary terminology provided by Michael Meyer's *English and American Literatures* in the *UTB Basics* series. I hope that the combination of canonical with more unconventional features will render *Literature in Britain and Ireland: A History* useful alike as a textbook to be used in class and as an opportunity to discover authors and texts worth reading on their own.

Citation

Reaching Out

A number of people had a share in the genesis of this literary history. Let me begin with two of my former teachers. At school, Günther Schalbruch kindled my interest in the works of Shakespeare as well as Graham Greene. Sadly, he died a few weeks before the completion of this book. At the university, Dieter A. Berger helped me to be on track by widening my horizon and teaching me method. I am very grateful to both of them, and to my students for what I have learnt from our discussions over the years. During the writing of this book, I profited from the professional help of two publisher's readers: Kathrin Heyng, who instigated the whole project and expertly saw it to completion, and Christina Esser, who read and helpfully commented upon large parts of the manuscript in between. To both of them, I owe great thanks, and also to the team at Munich University. Eva Große typed and commented upon some of the early drafts and lent her hand to the index. Christine Mayerhofer, Solomon Winterl and Johanna Marx read the whole book in manuscript and helped me enormously with their suggestions for improvement. Christine Mayerhofer moreover assisted me greatly in compiling the index, while Solomon Winterl searched for suitable illustrations. Thank you all very much for your great effort! My colleague Hans Sauer kindly read and commented upon the chapter on Medieval Literature, for which I am grateful, as this reduced those inaccuracies for which I alone remain responsible. Finally, I want to express my gratitude to my family: thank you, Claudia and Lara, for your great patience during the laborious period of composition. I hope you like the book, as I hope my father does, who asked with a smile, when it will come to an end at last.

Medieval Literature (up to c.1500) | 1

Summary

Medieval Britain and Ireland were oral, multilingual and multi-cultural societies. There existed parallel traditions of literature in Old and Middle English as well as in Gaelic, Latin and Anglo-Norman French. Moreover, we find a variety of forms of expression. While some poets composed alliterative verse, others wrote in rhyming couplets, and perhaps also in iambic pentameter, a tradition handed down over the centuries. There were three types of vernacular drama in the later Middle Ages: mystery plays, miracle plays and morality plays. Popular heroes such as Robin Hood or King Arthur and the Knights of the Round Table appeared in narratives in verse and in prose. The Old English epic *Beowulf*, the Arthurian romances since the twelfth century, the various groups of stories that make up traditional Irish myth, and the work of the fourteenth-century poet and storyteller Geoffrey Chaucer stand out as memorable pieces of medieval literature that have fascinated generations of readers and writers.

Literature from Anglo-Saxon England | 1.1

From a literary point of view, medieval societies in Britain and Ireland and their modern counterparts are characterised alike by **multilingualism, multiculturalism, and multiple media use**. Over the whole medieval period, literary communication was marked by the succession or co-existence of different speech communities, which manifested itself in a variety of linguistic codes. Even before Germanic peoples migrated in large numbers to the British Isles – the beginning of the conquest of Celtic Britons by Angles, Saxons and

Multiculturalism and the Media

Fig. 1.1

British Isles 802

Jutes dates from A.D. 449 – oral and written traditions had existed side by side in the Roman province of Britannia (43–c.420), albeit in Celtic and **Latin**. The conversion to Christianity brought along a new influx of Latin as well as the coming of the book. In the centuries to come, literature in Latin was kept alive in the scriptoria by medieval monks who were engaged in writing and illustrating manuscripts. They were usually collected as a *codex* (a handwritten book), which was an innovation. Arguably the first specimen of prose literature in Celtic Ireland (which had never been a Roman province) is the Latin *Confessio* of St Patrick, who began his missionary work in 432. The beginnings of Anglo-Saxon conversion date back to St Augustine's arrival in Kent in 597, when Canterbury became a centre of Christian culture in England. Bede's *Ecclesiastical History of the English People*, which is also a history of the Anglo-Saxon Conquest, is among the first important non-fictional writings from mainland Britain: it was completed in Latin in 731. As missionaries, Irish monks went abroad to found monasteries on the islands of Iona (in the Inner Hebrides, 563–849) and Lindisfarne (off the coast of Northumberland, 635–875), there to produce superbly decorated *codices*. Two of the most famous **illuminated manuscripts** strikingly exemplify the multicultural and multilingual situation: the decorations of the *Book of Kells* (by monks from Iona, c.800) follow Celtic patterns, while the Latin text of the *Lindisfarne Gospels* (715–21) became accompanied later by glosses providing an Anglo-Saxon translation.

Anglo-Saxon or Old English had developed after the fifth-century Germanic invasion of Britain, which met with a native population of Britons that spoke and wrote in Latin or the Celtic languages Welsh, Cumbric and Cornish. Most of these (and Irish Gaelic, too) remained in use, yet Cumbric became extinct in the twelfth, and Cornish in the eighteenth centuries. The earliest extant examples of Anglo-Saxon or Old English literature are the eighteen half-lines of "Caedmon's Hymn" (c.658/80) preserved in Bede's *Ecclesiastical History*, and also *Beowulf*, a heroic epic that survives in a manuscript from c.1000, but may have been originally composed much earlier. (While the terms are here used interchangeably, *Anglo-Saxon* accentuates the close relations to other Germanic literatures and cultures in medieval Scandinavia and on the Continent – see e.g. *Beowulf*, which takes place among pagan Danes and Geats. The designation *Old English* on the other hand, with hindsight and a more national focus, posits the continuity with successive historical developments in Britain.) From about 800, continuous **Viking invasions** in England and Ireland led to the Viking foundations of Dublin (841), Cork and Limerick, and to the establishment of a Viking kingdom in England, the **Danelaw** (865). What remained of the Anglo-Saxon kingdoms was united under King Alfred the Great of **Wessex** (871–99). His reign went along with a boost for Anglo-Saxon culture and for the manuscript record: translations of major works from Latin into the West Saxon dialect of Wessex were either commissioned or undertaken by the King himself, who ordered that students should be educated in the vernacular. In Ireland, the Southern Irish King Brian Ború achieved a singular supremacy before he died in a battle against the Vikings (1014). His power politics were not associated with a cultural renaissance, though he became the subject of later Celtic eulogies.

This first phase of the history of literature in English was predominantly oral in character, and as such, volatile. Only four Anglo-Saxon poets are known by name: Caedmon, Bede, Alfred and Cynewulf; the others remain anonymous. "Caedmon's Hymn" and *Beowulf* were meant to be sung by a *scop*, perhaps accompanied by a harp. However, it is just the *written* record of what was originally intended for *oral* performance that points to the fact that we deal with a situation that is not only multilingual but also characterised by the principal availability of two media (regardless of the fact that the great majority of Anglo-Saxons will not have known how to write and read). There are four major manuscript collections of Old English poetry that all date from about 1000, and that are either anthologies of poetry (*Junius Manuscript* and *Exeter Book*) or contain a mix of poetry and prose (*Codex Cotton Vitellius A. xv* and *Vercelli Book*).

Anglo-Saxon poetry, of which some 30,000 lines survive, consists of long lines divided into half-lines by a pause or *caesura*.

Old English Poetry

One or both of the two stressed syllables of the first half-line are linked with the first (but not the second) syllable in the second half-line by **alliteration**. A characteristic feature is the **kenning**, a type of poetic imagery that by its formulaic nature (e.g. 'din of spears' for 'battle', or 'the whale's road' for 'sea') enabled the *scop* to compose and memorise his text or to improvise during the performance (Oral-Formulaic Theory). **Riddles** (at times obscene) were part of the oral poetry of the period, as were **mnemonic poems** that helped to memorise lists of names: in *Widsith*, the eponymous *scop* rehearses no less than three such catalogues of rulers, peoples and legendary heroes. Other meditations and laments, such as *The Ruin*, *Wulf and Eadwacer*, *The Wanderer*, *The Seafarer* and *The Wife's Lament*, are referred to as **Old English elegies**. From those elegies, which are independent of the Classical tradition, *Deor* (a pseudo-autobiographical poem mentioning Weland the Smith) sticks out as an exception because of its strophic form. Among the Anglo-Saxon **religious poems** that testify to the influence of Christianisation are paraphrases of the Biblical Books of Genesis, Exodus and Daniel. Longer hagiographies deal with the life of the saints Andreas, Elene, Guthlac and Juliana. Finally, there are original religious poems on a Christian theme such as *The Dream of the Rood*: this is a vision which entails a part in which Christ's crucifixion is emotionally reported by the Cross.

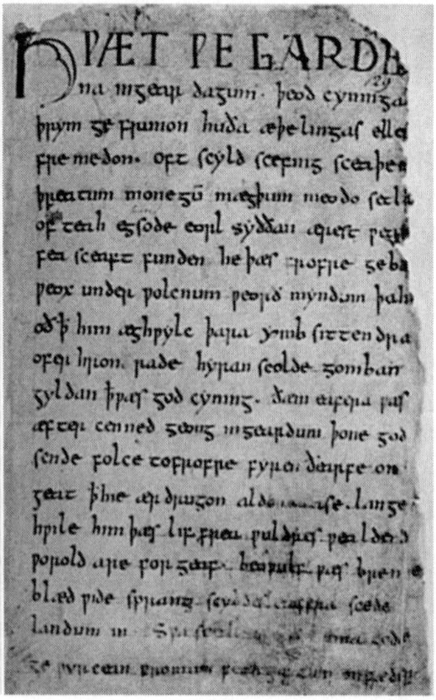
HWÆT WE GARDE
na in geardagum þeod cyninga
þrym ge frunon hu ða æþelingas ellen
fremedon. oft scyld scefing sceaþena
þreatum monegum mægþum meodo setla
of teah egsode eorl syððan ærest wearð
fea sceaft funden he þæs frofre gebad
weox under wolcnum weorð myndum þah
oð þ him æghwylc þara ymb sittendra
ofer hron rade hyran scolde gomban
gyldan þ wæs god cyning. ðæm eafera wæs
æfter cenned geong in geardum þone god
sende folce to frofre fyren ðearfe on
geat þ hie ær drugon aldor(le)ase. lange
hwile him þæs lif frea wuldres wealdend
worold are forgeaf. beowulf wæs breme
blæd wide sprang scyldes eafera scede
landum in

Fig. 1.2 | Original image of the first page of the *Beowulf* manuscript

Apart from a paraphrase of the Biblical story of Judith and Holofernes, the *Codex Cotton Vitellius A. xv* contains the most prominent example of secular **heroic poetry** of the period: *Beowulf*. The narrative, which takes place in Scandinavia (and therefore strictly speaking is no national epic such as the Homeric Epics or Virgil's *Aeneid*), falls into two parts. In the first part, Beowulf the Geat comes to help the Danes resident at the great hall of Heorot by successively and successfully killing two monstrous enemies, first Grendel and then his mother. In a second part, an older Beowulf, now King of the Geats, scores a final victory against a dragon, but dies of the dragon's poison and is given a hero's funeral. Both parts of the story are dramatised by monologue and dialogue. They are also interspersed with flashbacks, repetitive summaries, or the Finnsburg Episode, which takes the form of a heroic poem within the poem performed by a *scop*. Of such an oral context to *Beowulf* altogether, we are reminded by the initial word *hwæt*, an interjection translating as "Listen!" or "Hear!" (Milfull and Sauer 2003: 115–16). However, the question whether this narrative poem of over 3,000 lines originated either from an oral tradition or whether it was first written down by a single poet to be performed later cannot ultimately be decided.

Other, shorter examples of heroic poetry from the period are *The Fight at Finnsburh* (a companion piece to the episode in *Beowulf*) and two tales of the Viking invasions, *The Battle of Maldon* (a fragment of over 300 lines) and "The Battle of Brunanburh". The latter poem is part of *The Anglo-Saxon Chronicle*, an annual account of events begun in the times of King Alfred and continued – in the version known as *The Peterborough Chronicle* – well up to the reign of the Plantagenet kings (until 1154). Together with Bede's Latin *History* of 731, *The Anglo-Saxon Chronicle* is a unique and continuous source of early English history. Moreover, it is a documentary record of the development of the English language over three centuries, and a prominent specimen of Anglo-Saxon prose. (There is no exact counterpart on the Green Isle, yet scholars use the umbrella term *The Chronicle of Ireland* for the various ecclesiastical annals from medieval Ireland.) Further notable examples of prose literature from Anglo-Saxon England are the late ninth-century translations by King Alfred's circle (which included an Old English translation of Bede's *History*) and the **homilies** or church sermons by Aelfric of Eynsham (†c.1020) and Wulfstan of York (†1023).

Old English Prose

The legacy of the literature and culture of Anglo-Saxon England was not lost on later writers. Though the Kingdom of Wessex became extinct after the Norman Conquest of 1066, its name lived on in the regional novels and poems written by Thomas Hardy (1840–1928) towards the end of the nineteenth century (see chaps. 4.4 and 4.5). Other poets did as Alfred had done and

Re-Creations of Anglo-Saxon England

revived the Anglo-Saxon literary record in translations into Modern English. In 1880, the Victorian Poet Laureate Alfred Lord Tennyson (1809–92) produced an alliterative verse translation of the "Battle of Brunanburh" (based upon his son Hallam's preceding prose version). In *Ripostes* (1912), the American Modernist Ezra Pound (1885–1972) – who admonished his contemporaries to 'make it new!' – tried his hand at an alliterative, but otherwise free translation of the first part of *The Seafarer* that inspired him when he went on to compose the first of his *Cantos* (published in 1924). The Orkney poet George Mackay Brown (1921–96) used rhyme instead of alliteration when he turned *Deor* into three-stressed **accentual verse**. (See Heaney and Hughes 1997: 521–22 for the poem, and chap. 5.1 for more contemporary specimens of accentual verse.) Finally, two of the most notable Scottish and Irish poets of the present age tested their mettle against *Beowulf* as the most demanding of Old English texts. Edwin Morgan (*1920), since 2004 established as the *Scots Makar* or National Poet for Scotland, produced a verse translation as early as 1952, to be followed half a century later by the Irish Nobel Prize winner Seamus Heaney (*1939). Heaney had been concerned with the Anglo-Saxon legacy since when he produced the poems "Bone Dreams" (*North*, 1975) and "The Wanderer" (*Stations*, 1975), a poem which is inspired by the eponymous Old English elegy. In 1999, Heaney brought out a new verse translation of *Beowulf*, which had kept him occupied since the 1980s when he got commissioned from the editors of NAEL. Heaney's poem "A Ship of Death" (*The Haw Lantern*, 1987) was a first attempt at translating the initial episode of Scyld Scefing's funeral. In the four-stressed lines of his *Beowulf* translation, Heaney merges the metric and alliterative conventions of Old English poetry with the Modernist revival of accentual verse. Some of the poems in Heaney's successive collection *Electric Light* (2001) owe their inspiration to his *Beowulf* translation. (See Anon. 2000, Milfull and Sauer 2003, and here chap. 5.1.) In addition, *Beowulf* has been adapted for the screen several times in recent years (e. g. by Robert Zemeckis in 2007, to the script of Neil Gaiman and Roger Avary), after the story had been re-told from the monster's point of view by the American writer and critic John Gardner (1933–82) in his experimental novel *Grendel* (1971).

Middle English Literature

After the Norman Conquest, which had begun in 1066 with another invasion and the decisive Battle of Hastings, English society continued to be multicultural (though strictly hierarchical), with a variety of languages spoken. In particular, there was **linguistic coexistence** between English as the language of the people, Latin as the language of learning and the Church, and the Anglo-Norman variety of Old French as the language of the new rulers. (The great survey of England conducted for William the Conqueror and completed in 1086 was recorded in Latin in *The Domesday Book*.) There was moreover **language change**: Middle English began around 1100, and the same twelfth century sees also Scottish Gaelic newly replacing other Celtic vernaculars in Scotland. **Parallel traditions of literature** in different languages existed all over the British Isles, but there were also examples of a **cultural crossover**, either with the same writer or in works on the same theme. Chaucer's friend John Gower (c.1330–1408) produced long moral poems on Man's sinfulness first in French (*Le Mirour de l'omme*, 1376–79) and then in Latin (*Vox clamantis*, 1379–82) before he finally came out with his masterpiece. *Confessio Amantis* (or 'The Lover's Confession', rev. 1393) is a collection of stories on courtly love that despite its Latin title was composed in English. Another striking example for such a crossover is the Arthurian literature, which has easily traversed languages and genres (see below). From the twelfth to the fourteenth centuries, there was an increase in **bilingualism** among speakers of Anglo-Norman French and of what developed as Middle English. The Norman masters had to come to terms with their English-speaking servants, and the English merchants and other citizens required French as a second language for commercial, political and legal transactions. In a military situation when Normandy was lost to France (1204), the Anglo-Norman barons forced King John 'Lackland' to sign the *Magna Charta* (1215), the foundational document of what was to develop into Westminster Democracy. De-

| Fig. 1.3

The Bayeux Tapestry

spite a later series of spectacular victories against the French, the English ultimately lost the Hundred Years War (1337–1453) and their French possessions, but by the late fourteenth century had gained **a new sense of national pride**. From 1362, English began to be used besides French in the Westminster Parliament as well as the law courts. Twenty years later (from c.1380), the first complete translation of the Bible was under way, begun by John Wycliffe and his radical followers, the Lollards. Also during the 1380s, Geoffrey Chaucer turned literature from Continental French and Italian sources into Middle English masterpieces.

Writing Systems

In addition to the variety of languages spoken in the British Isles, several writing systems existed alongside each other. From the Middle Ages throughout the Early Modern Period, texts were encoded in distinctive scripts and types. Latin texts in *Roman majuscule* (capital letters only) were paralleled by the *Ogham alphabet* employed for Old Irish (Gaelic) inscriptions on stone monuments, and by the *runic alphabet* first used to write short Old English (Anglo-Saxon) texts: a version of the report of Christ's crucifixion in *The Dream of the Rood* is preserved, too, in runic alphabet on a monument, namely the eighth-century *Ruthwell Cross*. In the later Old English period, Latin texts were written in the rounded *Carolingian minuscule* (known to the Continent since it had been developed by the English scholar Alcuin of York at Aachen around 800), whereas Old English texts (including Old English translations from Latin) continued to be written in the *insular script* hitherto used in Ireland and Britain. Around 1200, the Carolingian minuscule was further developed into the *Gothic* or *blackletter script*. After the establishment of print – which began when William Caxton (†1492) set up a printing press near Westminster Abbey in 1476 – such scripts survived as a typeface. Some texts signalled their genre true to type: in Britain, blackletter was reserved for the printing of 'blackletter ballads' and popular chapbooks up to

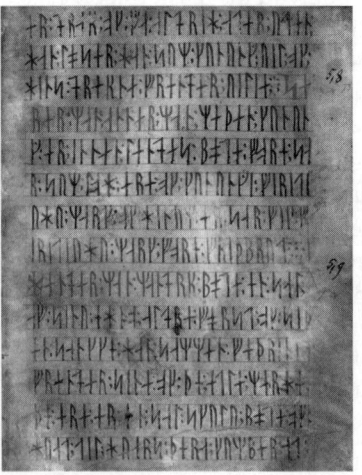

Fig. 1.4

Codex runicus, a vellum manuscript from c.1300

about 1800, while highbrow literature was set and read in a different type. In other cases, type equalled individual distinction: in Ireland, the *Gaelic typeface*, which is based upon the insular script, continued to be used even until the mid-twentieth century to signal cultural autonomy from Britain. Thus, the various scripts and types sent a message of their own, and the seemingly simple act of reading required different skills in decoding them altogether.

A third instance of variety relates to the literary genres that were already available (especially to story-tellers) or that were newly developed. Such **variety of narratives in verse and in prose** can be exemplified with regard to popular heroes such as King Arthur. At the beginning of Arthurian literature, the mythical fifth-century leader of the Britons' backlash against receding Romans and invading Anglo-Saxons frequently appears in a double act together with Brutus, the legendary founder of Britain. Brutus is said to be the grandson of Aeneas, that Trojan figure whom the Roman poet Virgil in the *Aeneid* had likewise brought into connection with the origins of Rome. In his Latin *History of the Kings of Britain* (c.1135), Geoffrey of Monmouth (†c.1155) starts with this foundation myth before he passes over other legendary figures from Celtic Britain such as Gorboduc and Lear (the protagonists of two Renaissance tragedies) to come to Arthur. Earlier Celtic Welsh sources had already credited this leader of steadfast Britons with keeping the Anglo-Saxon invaders in check, for a time, before twelfth-century writers in England (such as Geoffrey) and on the Continent fashioned the myth about King Arthur and the Knights of the Round Table. With *Le Roman de Brut* (1155), Wace (c.1110–80), a Norman writer from the Channel Island of Jersey, produced a translation of Geoffrey's Latin prose history into **rhyming couplets** of French verse. It is Wace who adds the detail of the Round Table where no-one takes precedence, and who presents Arthur and his Knights to an aristocratic audience as their ideal of chivalry. Once more adapted and embellished, Arthur returns in *Brut* (16,000 lines, c.1190) by the English priest Layamon, who transposed Wace's eight-syllable couplets of French verse into a Middle English verse narrative that **revived alliteration** instead of rhyme. From then on, English, French and German writers gave more attention to formerly minor characters such as Merlin the Wizard and Morgan le Fay (Arthur's half-sister, the enchantress) as well as the Knights Gawain, Lancelot and Perceval. Thus, the

The Beginnings of Arthurian Literature

|Fig. 1.5
Woodcut from the *Nuremberg Chronicle*, 1493

original story became fleshed out with more and more details, e.g. Arthur's passing of the kingship test related to the sword in the stone, Lancelot's adulterous liaison with Arthur's Queen Guinevere, and Perceval's quest (search) for the Holy Grail. Such embellishing occurred in the form of (lengthier) **verse romances** and (shorter) Breton lays. Both of them typically fuse a story of love, chivalry and adventure with features of mystery and magic into a narrative that is not bound by the limits of realism. Between 1160 and 1180, the French poet Chrétien de Troyes (c.1140–90) produced a series of five such romances for an aristocratic audience. In addition to her animal fables, the Anglo-Norman poet Marie de France (c.1155–89) became famous for her **Breton lays**: shorter romances in French verse that (perhaps only in her fiction) were related to a minstrel tradition from Celtic Brittany. Marie's *Lanval* is such a Breton lay in eight-syllable couplets (the form of Wace's much longer *Roman de Brut*). It tells of how Lanval, a Knight of the Round Table, is tried first by Queen Guinevere's seductive charm and then tested by her revengeful attempt to discredit him, yet throughout keeps his pledge to his true love. While it is not clear whether the stories of the *Mabinogion* (laid down in fourteenth-century manuscripts of Welsh prose) preceded or paralleled such a development towards romance, they also testify to a wider European interest in Arthurian literature.

Sir Gawain and the Green Knight

The most magnificent Middle English specimen of an Arthurian **romance of chivalry** is the anonymous tale of *Sir Gawain and the Green Knight* (c.1375–1400). Just like Layamon's *Brut*, this romance of over 2,500 lines is part of an **Alliterative Revival**, which however does not strictly copy Old English conventions: *Gawain* is composed in alliterative stanzas that are irregular in length and metre, yet are invariably tailed by a **'bob and wheel'** section of altogether five lines rhyming *ababa*, of which the first line is shortened to two syllables ('bob') and generally followed by (two to) four longer, three-stressed lines ('wheel'). There are four parts to this verse romance, the first of which is set during the Christmas festivities at Camelot during the early years of Arthur's reign. There, a mysterious Green Knight of the Green Chapel arrives to challenge Arthur 'to strike one stroke for another', that is, to deal a possibly deadly blow but to come and stand one in return twelve months later. Gawain, Arthur's nephew and a Knight of the Round Table, agrees to the 'beheading game' in Arthur's stead, and thus the Green Knight leaves the scene with his severed head in his hands. The second and third parts take place a year later at a castle on the way to the elusive Green Chapel, where Gawain's host makes him stand another test. Whereas the host goes out hunting on three successive days, Gawain rests in the castle, where he has to fend off politely the man-hunting of the host's wife. (Both aspects of hunting are related with much gusto.) A third trial awaits Gawain in the last part of the story, when he arrives at the Green Chapel to place himself at the mercy of the Green Knight. There, Gawain ultimately and successfully passes his series of tests, is spared his life, and is able to look behind the Green Knight's incognito. At the end of the romance, the green girdle that Gawain accepted as sole favour from the lady, and then concealed from his host, is related to the Order of the Garter, another emblem of chivalry (created in 1342). But for this green girdle, honest Gawain remained a paragon of virtue and chivalry, tried and tested.

The same apparently cannot be said of Sir Thomas Malory (c.1405–71), who is credited with a criminal rather than chivalric record, and who may have written the most comprehensive of Arthurian *prose* romances during a term in Newgate Prison. The culmination of medieval Arthurian literature in Malory's *Le Morte Darthur* is strikingly illustrated by the fact that his Middle English prose narrative is based on several eponymous predecessors: the French prose romance *Mort Artu* (1210–30) as well as the Middle English poems *Morte Arthure* (c.1360, alliterative) and *Morte Arthur* (c.1400, in stanzas). From these and other sources in more than one language and more than one form, Malory compiled his own comprehensive account which he completed in 1469–70. It survived in a single manuscript (discovered only in 1934) that differs from the more influential version adapted for print by William Caxton in 1485 (who also provided the title). What all of these versions have in common is a more gloomy view on the world of Camelot. This represents no longer an unblemished ideal of chivalry, but a paradise lost to the destructive effects of a love that is more powerful than the conventions of marriage and the ban on incest. The illicit liaison between Tristan and Iseult (Isolde), the wife of his uncle King Mark of Cornwall, is only one example of cuckolding that finds its counterpart in Sir Lancelot's adulterous affair with Queen Guinevere. Arthur's incestuous relationship

Malory to Tennyson, and Beyond

with one of his half-sisters, Morgause, produces a son, Mordred, whose murderous treachery brings about the death of Arthur and the destruction of his Kingdom, though in some versions he is said to be only asleep and awaiting his return.

The myth of Arthur's return became a literary fact as later writers, inspired by Malory, set out to fill the gaps left in his account. Edmund Spenser (1552–99) revived young Arthur in a context of chivalry for his allegorical epic *The Faerie Queene* (1590–96). John Milton (1608–74) likewise pondered the idea of an English national epic based on the Arthurian myth before he turned his attention to a Christian theme and composed *Paradise Lost* instead (1667/74, see chap. 2.3.3). Milton's abortive plans for an Arthurian epic resurfaced in the collaboration of the Restoration Poet Laureate John Dryden (libretto) and the famous composer Henry Purcell (music) on the opera *King Arthur* (1691). Alfred Lord Tennyson, the Victorian Poet Laureate, first wrote the Arthurian poem "The Lady of Shalott" (1832; revised 1842, 1855) before he emulated Milton in *Idylls of the King*. This Arthurian epic began with "Morte d'Arthur" (1833–38, publ. 1842) and finally ran to twelve books in blank verse written over a span of fifty years (publ. 1859–85; see chap. 4.4). In the twentieth century, T[erence].H[anbury]. White (1906–64) extended what began with an account of Arthur's youth in *The Sword in the Stone* (1939) into a quartet of Arthurian novels collectively entitled *The Once and Future King* (1958). They in turn became the basis for the Broadway musical *Camelot* (1960) and for the animated Disney film *The Sword in the Stone* (1963). Malory's focus on the male characters in the story was reset in *The Mists of Avalon* (1982) by the American novelist Marion Zimmer Bradley (1930–99), who combined fantasy and feminism when she looked at the legend from the perspective of Morgaine (Morgan le Fay) and Gwenhwyfar (Guinevere).

Popular Heroes: Robin Hood and Guy of Warwick

Robin Hood and Guy of Warwick are two other popular heroes from the lower ranks of society that have captivated audiences across the ages and across the media. Over several centuries, their literary life ran a course from oral **balladry** over manuscript and blackletter ballads – where they travelled together with the likes of "Barbara Allen", "Sir Patrick Spens" and "Chevy Chase" – to chapbooks, the 'simplified readers' of the Early Modern Age (see chaps. 3.3.2 and 3.4.6). The earliest written record of the legend of Guy of Warwick is an anonymous Anglo-Norman romance (*Gui de Warewic*, c.1232–42), which at the beginning of the fourteenth century was turned into a Middle English romance of some 12,000 metrical lines. To win the heart of his beloved Felice or Phyllis, and to make up for their class difference, poor Guy takes part in a series of tournaments and adventures in order to prove his knight-like qualities. Once successfully married, but dissatisfied with his earlier vio-

| Fig. 1.6

The frontispiece of Howard Pyle's *The Merry Adventures of Robin Hood* (1883)

lent life, Guy leaves again for a pilgrimage to the Holy Land, from which he returns incognito to end his life as a hermit. In several contemporary versions of that romance and in later adaptations, the story of Guy the lover, the knight and the devout Christian became a long seller – in an oral context, in manuscript and in print (see Richmond 1996). Such widespread popularity is likewise true of the Robin Hood legend, only that this has remained vibrant until today. From the first such ballad extant in manuscript ("Robin Hood and the Monk", c.1450) through numerous 'garlands' or collections to Hollywood movies, the antagonism between the Anglo-Saxon outlaw and the Sheriff of Nottingham has symbolised the relationship between 'us' and 'them' under Norman rule. For this reason, Robin Hood and his Merry Men (e.g. Little John, Friar Tuck, and the minstrel Alan-a-Dale) were reserved a place in *Ivanhoe* (1819) too, the historical romance in which Walter Scott attempted to recreate (and romanticise) the cultural clash in Anglo-Norman times (see chap. 3.5.6). Perhaps even more so than his prose fiction, Scott's earlier tales in verse such as *The Lay of the Last Minstrel* (1805) are indebted to the medieval tradition of verse romances and Breton lays.

Apart from those narratives in verse and prose that deal with popular heroes in a predominantly secular context, there is a recurrent concern with religious matter in medieval literature,

Piers Plowman: Politics, Allegory and Satire

and in particular with dream visions and revelations. *The Vision of William Concerning Piers the Plowman* by William Langland (c.1330–87) is an outstanding example in several respects. It is the longest and most thoroughly reworked religious verse narrative in Middle English. The three substantially different A, B and C versions that were composed between c.1366 and 1387 testify to a constant habit of revision (as pronounced as, say, that of the twentieth-century poets W.B. Yeats and W.H. Auden). In its last and longest version, Langland's poem extends to over 7,300 lines of alliterative verse, organised into a "Prologue" and 23 *passus* or books. Together with Layamon's *Brut* and with the works of the *Gawain* poet, we deal here with another prominent specimen of the Alliterative Revival in Middle English poetry. Moreover, just like *Pearl* (one of the *Gawain* poet's further poems of note), *Piers Plowman* is a dream vision, or to be exact: the account of a series of visions by Long Will in which Piers the title character appears only sporadically. The speaker-poet's dreams contain a satirical portrait of fourteenth-century English society. In this "fair field full of folk" ("Prologue", l.17) we witness allegorical characters such as the Seven Deadly Sins and the Lady Holy Church appear together with personifications of Conscience, Reason and 'Saint Truthe' – *truthe* understood to be a form of Divine justice. Will's dreams and debates with the other characters were understood as a call for a reformation of society in a political and a religious sense, and the effects of Langland's poem reached widely when it circulated in manuscript as well as when it was first printed (in 1550). The explicit reference to *Piers Plowman* during the violent Peasants' Revolt in 1381 is a final instance that singles out this long poem as significant. The rebels' singular conquest of the capital London before the suppression of the Peasants' Revolt, the gradual increase in the role of the Westminster Parliament (in particular the House of Commons) from the thirteenth to the fifteenth centuries, and the Wars of the Roses (1455–87) between different factions of the English nobility all testified to a shift in politics. This led to a redefinition of power relations between the monarchy and individual groups of society in the Tudor Period.

With regard to dreams, debates and devoutness, William Langland links up with his contemporary Geoffrey Chaucer (c.1343–1400). Chaucer's early poetic narratives *The Book of the Duchess*, *The House of Fame* and *The Parliament of Fowls* (none composed much later than 1382) are all presented as dream visions, and so is *The Legend of Good Women* (c.1385), a fragmentary catalogue of outstanding women in history and myth. Composed in what was to become Chaucer's hallmark stanza, seven lines of **rhyme royal** (*ababbcc*), *The Parliament of Fowls* (c.1382) moreover belongs to the genre of **debate** between two or more disputants on various topics (here: about love). Chaucer's poetic debate compares well with *The Owl and the Nightingale* (c.1220), a notable earlier example that however was cast in the French form of eight-syllable rhyming couplets. Chaucer's importance lies not least in his decision (in contrast to his friend John Gower) to pass over Latin or Anglo-Norman French and stick to the vernacular instead. While he developed into the major medieval English poet who recited his poetry at court, Chaucer functioned as a royal official, filling several posts (e.g. Controller of Customs in the Port of London). Such positions allowed him to go on official business to Italy twice in the 1370s. There, he acquainted himself with the work of the Italian Renaissance triad of Dante, Petrarch and Boccaccio, whose *Il filostrato* became the basis for *Troilus and Criseyde* (which Chaucer completed around 1385, and Caxton printed in 1485). Chaucer's verse romance is composed in rhyme royal and set before the Classical background of the War against Troy: it tells of the tragic fate of two Trojan lovers who, soon after they have struck a match, are already made to part. When Criseyde, who was forced to leave Troy, gives in to the circumstances and breaks her pledge to remain faithful to Troilus, he seeks death, and Fortune's Wheel has run its course. However, in an epilogue, Troilus sends a message from the heavenly spheres to the young on Earth, to follow Divine love rather than earthly passions. This moral to the story has met with mixed response because it cannot easily be reconciled with a comprehensive interpretation of all aspects of love in this romance. Chaucer's romance inspired Robert Henryson's *The Testament of Cresseid* (see chap. 1.3) and Shakespeare's stage-play *Troilus and Cressida*.

Devoutness is the occasion for *The Canterbury Tales*, which purports to follow 30 pilgrims (including 'Chaucer' as narrator) on their way to the shrine of St Thomas à Becket, the Archbishop of Canterbury whose confrontation with King Henry II ended in his assassination in 1170. (The case was dramatised by Tennyson in 1884 and by T.S. Eliot as *Murder in the Cathedral* in 1935,

|Fig. 1.7
Geoffrey Chaucer

Troilus and Criseyde

The Canterbury Tales

see chap. 5.2.2.) Once more, Boccaccio provided the pattern with his *Decamerone*, in which each of ten narrators tells ten stories. From this, Chaucer developed the plan to have each pilgrim tell two stories on the way to and back from Canterbury, introduced and interlinked by additional prologues and interjections by the other travellers. This scheme of ideally 120 stories is laid out in the **"General Prologue"**, but also laid to rest when Chaucer left his work a fragment of merely 24 stories. Yet what a fragment: in the hands of a master poet, the narrative frame and the individual tales are made to present a remarkably wide variety of memorable characters, poetic genres and forms of verse. Chaucer's realism of characterisation shows in the "General Prologue" as well as in the individual tales and 'links', which add up to a humorous panorama of professions and layers of society. Through its versification alone, the "General Prologue" represents another of Chaucer's poetic legacies to his successors: it is written in **rhyming couplets in iambic pentameter**, a form that will close Shakespearean sonnets from the Renaissance onwards, and that will function – as heroic couplet – as the standard form of Neoclassical verse. In the individual tales, lines of iambic pentameter either followed this model or were combined to patterns of six lines (in the concluding envoy to "The Clerk's Tale"), seven lines (rhyme royal) or eight lines (*abab-bcbc*, a variation upon Boccaccio's *ottava rima* that ends in a couplet, *ababab cc*). "The Tale of Sir Thopas" Chaucer tells himself with self-deprecating humour. Joining form to content, this tale is cast in the seemingly haphazardly constructed verse that came to be called **doggerel**, because it is conceived as a parody of tail-rhyme romances such as Guy of Warwick (which is singled out as an example). "The Franklin's Tale" is a Breton lay, and "The Nun's Priest's Tale" an animal fable. "The Miller's Tale", "The Reeve's Tale" and "The Shipman's Tale" are typical **fabliaux**, complete with

Fig. 1.8 | Scan of Ellesmere manuscript of *The Canterbury Tales*. The first page of "The Knight's Tale"

farcical situation comedy and bawdy humour. "The Wife of Bath's Tale" of her five husbands became famous for its representation of gender relations, and for her repudiation of negative gender stereotypes. The five husbands are mentioned in the prologue to the tale. This is much longer than the tale itself, which has an Arthurian setting: it is about a loathly lady, and the question what women want most. (Gower has another version of the same tale.)

With Chaucer, we also meet with early attempts at **canonisation of writers and their works**, which can take several forms. Chaucer **in person** is honoured by the fact that his burial site marks the beginning of the tradition of the Poets' Corner in Westminster Abbey, in which outstanding poets may continue to be honoured posthumously. Chaucer's friend John Gower (who was mentioned at the beginning of the present section as an author who switched easily between three literary languages) was not only honoured as Poet Laureate during his lifetime, but has also been commemorated with an eye-catching tomb in Southwark Cathedral, much like Shakespeare later with his bust in Stratford's Holy Trinity Church. **In poetry**, Chaucer's impact was freely admitted through imitation of his poetic innovations: Thomas Hoccleve (c.1369–1437) as well as the Scottish Chaucerians took up rhyme royal (see chap. 1.3), whereas John Lydgate (?1370–1449) imitated the rhyming couplets of Chaucer's "General Prologue" when he composed his verse romance *The Siege of Thebes* (c.1421). In his own prologue he even has himself join Chaucer's pilgrims in the tavern. Finally, Chaucer's standing is borne out by the fact that his *Canterbury Tales* and *Troilus and Chriseyde*, just like Malory's *Le Morte Darthur*, were among the first works that appeared **in print**, having been selected by William Caxton for the new medium.

Canon Formation

Pilgrimages and the accounts thereof were among the first instances of travel writing (see Korte 2000), and when a personal travel experience could not be had, fictional travel accounts would serve the purpose. So, European audiences got to know about the world abroad – from the Near to the Far East, with parts of Africa visited *en route* – through *The Travels of Sir John Mandeville*. Though marked out as personal experience starting from a pilgrimage, this is actually a compilation of existing travel accounts that as such attained widespread popularity, counting Christopher Columbus as one of its avid readers. *Mandeville's Travels* was first written down in an Anglo-Norman French version (c.1357–71), but

Mandeville's Travels and Other Medieval Prose

Fig. 1.9
Portrait of Sir John
Mandeville

Medieval Drama

circulated in manuscript in several Latin and English translations, too. (The competing English versions in the Egerton and Cotton manuscripts both date from c.1410–20.) Further than Malory's *Le Morte Darthur*, examples of Middle English prose are rare, and often come with a religious background. One is reminded of Long Will clad 'in the habit of a hermit' ("Prologue" to *Piers Plowman*), and Guy of Warwick at long last falling into such a habit, when reading *The Ancrene Riwle* (Anchoresses' Rule, c.1215), a religious reflection for devout women who have chosen to live the life of a female anchorite or hermit. Julian of Norwich (1342–c.1416) was such a religious recluse who meditated thoroughly about her revelations before she set them down in *A Book of Showings* (1373–93). The meeting between Julian of Norwich and Margery Kempe (c.1373–1438), a laywoman who likewise experienced visions, is related in *The Book of Margery Kempe* (c.1432–38). This spiritual autobiography and travel account is a further work of religious inspection that the illiterate author had dictated to a scribe (the manuscript was discovered not before 1934).

Christianity (rather than Classical precedent) had an impact, too, on the development of literature meant for dramatic performance. In a first stage, Christian liturgy was extended to include Latin plays performed in church, as when Passion and Easter plays dramatised the Passion and Resurrection of Christ, whereas Nativity or Shepherd's plays were made part of Christmas celebrations. From 1311, the newly introduced feast of Corpus Christi provided a fresh opportunity for processions and public spectacle. A second (simultaneous or successive) stage is reached in England through the establishment of religious drama in the vernacular, which deviated from Classical conventions of staging and of genre. Communal plays were put on in open air, yet no longer in arenas or amphitheatres with their theatre machinery (which allowed for the introduction of a *deus ex machina* to facilitate a sudden and surprising change of action). Instead, improvised and simultaneous stages were set up annually for a summer festival in the market place, with the fronts of surrounding houses providing the scenery. The spectators may have followed the action by either viewing a procession of pageants (mobile carts) or by going round from one fixed pageant, tent or booth to the next. Each of them presented one play within a dramatic cycle put up by one of the city's guilds of craftsmen. Naturally, there was a close contact between the audience and the great number of lay actors that were members of the guilds. **Mystery plays** dramatised a succession of memorable Biblical stories from the Creation to Judgment Day: *Le Jeu d'Adam* or *The Play of Adam* is among the first such plays in Anglo-Norman French (thought to date back to the twelfth century), others are called e. g. *Noah's Flood*. Four (nearly) complete sequences or cycles of Middle English mystery plays are extant from the fourteenth and fifteenth centuries: the Chester cycle (25 pageants or plays in rhyming verse, performed c.1350/75–1575), the York Corpus Christi plays (48 plays in various forms of verse, c.1376–1569), the Wakefield or Towneley plays (32 pageants, c.1377–1576), and the N-Town plays that were previously called *Ludus Coventriae* (42 frequently alliterative plays, first produced c.1450/75). The York play of *The Crucifixion* (c.1425) sticks out as a single play because of its stage realism in scenes of cruelty and torture. By contrast, *The Second Shepherds' Play* by the Wakefield Master presents a combination of the religious theme with comic characters and farcical scenes, and moreover exemplifies the nine-line stanza that is a characteristic creation of the Wakefield Master. In distinction from mystery plays that dramatised Biblical stories, **miracle plays** were dramatic hagiographies that enacted the lives of saints. They are more rarely represented (but see chap. 1.3 for an example from Cornwall). Mystery and miracle plays lasted well into the Reformation, but were ultimately suppressed because of their association with Catholic liturgy.

A further distinction concerns **morality plays**, which were no longer conceived as part of a cycle, but as a single play. Moreover, they were no longer bound to Biblical stories or exemplary lives of saints, but dramatised ethical problems, in which an individual is confronted with a moral decision between several options. The allegorical make-up of morality plays consisted of key scenes involving stock characters: the confrontation of Virtues and Vices, the coming of Death, and the conflict between Love and Justice. A personification that is distinct from the Devil is the Vice. Its typical features are black humour and the habit to inform the audience directly about evil intentions and machinations in a Vice monologue – characteristics that translated to Shakespeare's King Richard III and to Iago, the scheming villain in *Othello*. Prominent examples of the genre range from the fourteenth-century morality *The Pride of Life* over *The Castle of Persever-ance* (c.1425) and *Mankind* (c.1473) to *Everyman* (after 1485), the only medieval play to go directly into print. The latter's cast of characters includes God and Death as well as many personifica-tions: facing Death and the day of judgment, Everyman the mer-chant is left alone by Goods, Beauty and Fellowship, but taught by Knowledge to go into the Grave as a Christian, accompanied only by Good Deeds. This allegorical play, which probably stems from a Dutch source, was revived in Hugo von Hofmannsthal's German adaption (1911) to become the opening act of the an-nual Salzburg Festival. More recently, Barry Unsworth (*1930) brought out a historical novel entitled *Morality Play* (1995). Here, a murder mystery serves to evoke the genre as a whole together with the atmosphere of fourteenth-century England ridden by the Plague – which was the major demographic catastrophe of the Middle Ages, claiming the lives of more than a quarter of the European population.

1.3 | Celtic Contexts

England and the Celtic Fringe

Between the twelfth and fourteenth centuries, when the social and linguistic developments towards Middle English were under way, the Celtic Fringe (a Victorian term for England's neighbours) suffered from a **politics of expansion**. Cornwall had been subjugat-ed still in Anglo-Saxon times (936). In 1169, a full century after the Norman Conquest of England, Anglo-Norman nobles began another conquest when they invaded Ireland for the first time, frequently to return. In 1171, the Plantagenet King Henry II per-sonally followed suit and (though in control only of the province of Leinster) assumed the Lordship of Ireland, a claim that his suc-cessors were to uphold until Henry VIII had himself proclaimed King of Ireland in 1541. In 1277–84, Wales had been annexed under Edward I, before that English king turned his attention to Scotland. However, he was less successful in his campaigns (1296–1306) against William Wallace ("Braveheart") and Robert the Bruce, who as King Robert I maintained Scotland's indepen-dence through his victory in the 1314 Battle of Bannockburn (see Table 3 in chap. 2.2.2). After renewed and prolonged conflict, Da-vid II (Robert's son) secured Scotland's independence from Eng-land up to the 1603 union of the crowns under a Scottish king.

The step from an official survey such as *The Domesday Book* (1086) to topographical writing based on personal travel experience was made in the work of Gerald of Wales (c.1146–1223). He wrote as Giraldus Cambrensis, first about Ireland and its Anglo-Norman conquest in *Topographia Hibernica* (1188), and then in companion volumes about his native Wales (*Itinerarium Cambriae*, 1191; *Descriptio Cambriae*, 1194). Although Gerald's Latin writings on the Celtic Fringe are endowed with an Anglo-Norman bias, they are nevertheless telling documents of medieval cross-cultural contact experienced in 'home tours' within the British Isles. As such, they contrast with *Mandeville's Travels* mentioned in chap. 1.2, and may rather be compared to Edmund Spenser's later pamphlet *A View of the Present State of Ireland* (circulating in manuscript from 1598), Daniel Defoe's frequently reprinted *A Tour through the Whole Island of Great Britain* (1724–26), and Samuel Johnson's *A Journey to the Western Islands of Scotland* (1775).

Medieval Irish literature is the earliest and most voluminous among the literatures from the Celtic Fringe, but its English component is least developed. Although intermarriage between Anglo-Norman settlers and native Celts was quite frequent in medieval Ireland, members of each group seem to have kept their literary traditions apart. Between the lives of Gerald of Wales and of Edmund Spenser, there is yet a silence in the written record of Irish literature in English, and this changed only with the influx of English- and Scots-speaking settlers in the seventeenth-century Ulster und Cromwellian Plantations (see chap. 2.1). Before we pass on, though, a few remarks need to be made about traditional Irish myth, which falls into four groups of stories: the Mythological and the Historical Cycle, the Ulster Cycle, and the Fenian or Finn Cycle. Such a body of legend and literature once served the *filí* (the learned poet) and the *bard* (performer), and it was preserved when the Celtic bards later turned hedge schoolmasters (see chaps. 4.1 and 4.5.4). The **Mythological Cycle**, which is set in a world of fighting gods, has a foundational character: the central narrative (*Lebor Gabála Érenn* or 'Book of Invasions') traces the origins of Irish history from before Noah's Flood through the successive influx and displacement of legendary peoples. By contrast, the **Historical Cycle** informs about the genealogy of Irish kings up to Brian Ború (†1014, see above), and in particular contains the legend of Mad Sweeney (*Buile Suibhne*). Mad Sweeney re-appears

Topographical and Travel Writing

Fig. 1.10
The *Domesday Book*

Memorable Irish Myths

in the novel *At Swim-Two-Birds* (1939) by the Irish novelist 'Flann O'Brien' (Brian O'Nolan, 1911–66) as well as in Seamus Heaney's poetic sequences "Sweeney Redivivus" (1984) and *Sweeney Astray* (1983; rev. 2001). In the 'Bog Poems' that were part of his earlier collections *Wintering Out* (1972) and especially *North* (1975), Heaney had already responded to the archaeological findings of the bodies of Iron Age men and women who had been executed or sacrificed. (See chap. 5.1. For the Gaelic tradition, see Deane 1986 and Meid 1997, and for the response to Sweeney moreover Pehnt 1997 and Shields 2000: 175–78.)

The heroic **Ulster Cycle** at times overlaps with the Mythological Cycle. The first tale that is of special interest deals with a tragic triangle of love that compares to the constellation of King Mark of Cornwall, Tristan and Iseult (see chap. 1.2). In *The Exile of the Sons of Uisliu* (*NAEL* I, 129–36), beautiful Deirdre frustrates all the romantic and revengeful efforts of King Conchubar of Ulster by her decisions first to elope with Naoise (or Naisi) rather than marry the King, and then to follow her lover into death rather than marry his murderer. In the character of Fergus mac Róich, a former King of Ulster, this tragic story leads to another and most prominent tale of the Ulster Cycle, the *Táin Bó Cuailnge* or 'Cattle Raid of Cooley', of which the twelfth-century *Book of Leinster* contains the most complete version. This is the story of how a quarrel about two bulls develops into an assault on Ulster, in which young Cú Chulainn heroically defends the region in a series of single combats. Deirdre and Cú Chulainn were popular with poets and dramatists of the early twentieth-century Irish Renaissance such as W. B. Yeats (1865–1939) and J. M. Synge (1871–1909, see chap. 4.3). Under the title *The Táin*, the medieval bull's tale in its entirety was twice revived again in poetic translations for a modern audience: in 1969 by Thomas Kinsella (*1928), and more recently in 2007 by Ciarán Carson (*1948).

The **Fenian or Finn Cycle**, finally, is perhaps the one cycle that has witnessed an uninterrupted history of oral transmission that led to present-day legends and folk tales (see Meid 1997: 63). In the form of *Ossianic lays*, some of the heroic deeds and tales of Finn mac Cumaill and his son Oisín or Ossian were told and re-told over centuries, before they saw print in connection with a spectacular case of literary forgery. In 1762–63, James Macpherson published his spurious 'translations' of such *Ossianic lays*. These fake versions did not only find their way into the *Reliques of Irish Poetry* by Charlotte Brooke (1789), a prominent collection of otherwise authentic versions, but also met with a pre-Romantic spirit and quite impressed Johann Wolfgang Goethe and other European writers. A century later, the *Ossianic lays* were revived again in print in the title poem of Yeats's collection *The Wanderings of Oisin* (1889). In the long run, therefore, such memorable myths continued to be a point of reference for Irish writers from Yeats to Heaney.

Over and above such lays and tales, Celtic bards had made an impact by providing basic features of the Arthurian myth. Arthur is casually mentioned, too, in *Y Gododdin*, an Old Welsh poem that tells of a battle between a Southern Scottish people (the Gododdin) and the Saxons. Ascribed to the sixth-century Welsh bard Aneirin (but extant only in the thirteenth-century manuscript *Book of Aneirin*), *Y Gododdin* is arguably amongst the first examples of either Welsh or Scottish literature. Moreover, this series of heroic elegies (partly rhymed and partly alliterative) on the fallen fightes of the Gododdin is interesting as an early specimen of **syllabic verse**. This form of poetry with a fixed number of syllables is more frequently encountered in the Romance languages, e. g in the above-mentioned Arthurian verse romances in French. (However, see chap. 5.1 for twentieth-century syllabic verse in English.) After the English annexation of Wales, the Welsh bards organised in guilds and met (for the first time in 1450) at an **eisteddfod**. Such poetic assemblies have intermittently preserved the Welsh bardic tradition up to the present day, even though Thomas Gray (1716–71), who pioneered verse translations of old Welsh and Icelandic texts, lamented the demise of that tradition in "The Bard: A Pindaric Ode" (1757). In addition to poetry, there are Welsh tales in prose, gathered in

Medieval Welsh and Cornish Literature

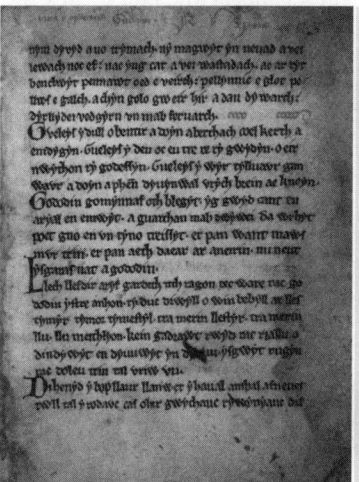

|Fig. 1.11
Page from the *Book of Aneirin*

two fourteenth-century manuscripts that were collectively called *The Mabinogion*. (They are mentioned above in relation to their Arthurian matter.) The literature in Middle Cornish contributed the *Ordinalia* (completed c.1400), a sequence of three mystery plays (*Origo Mundi, Passio Christi and Resurrexio Domini*) amounting to some 9,000 lines of verse. This was complemented by *Pascon agan Arluth* ('The Poem of Mount Calvary', c.1375), a poem on the Passion of Christ, and by a miracle play in verse on the life of a Cornish saint, called *Beunans Meriasek* ('The Life of Meriasek', 1504). All these works testify to the effects of Christianisation on a Celtic region.

The Multilingual
Literature of Scotland

The literature of medieval Scotland was at times as multilingual as its counterpart in Anglo-Saxon or Anglo-Norman England. The most important **Latin** specimen is the hagiographical *Vita Columbae* or 'Life of St Columba' (†597), the founder of the monastery on Iona, written by one of his successors, the abbot Adomnán (†704). **Old French** happened to be a literary language in medieval Scotland, too, and is represented in the *Roman de Fergus*, an Arthurian verse romance written by one Guillaume le Clerk around 1200. **Scottish Gaelic** had developed from Middle Irish to become the language of the Highlands, visibly so in *The Book of the Dean of Lismore* (c.1512–26). That first anthology of medieval bardic poetry contains poems in praise of aristocratic or royal patrons, religious poetry, moral and didactic verse, and mythological poems that take their characters and themes from Irish legends. Such bardic verse continued to be written in the Highlands up to the eighteenth century. With *The Brus* (1375), John Barbour (c.1320–95) created the first major work in **Scots**, the Middle English dialect of Lowland Scotland. Barbour's patriotic epic in (French) eight-syllable couplets about Robert the Bruce and the fight for Scottish independence extended to 20 books or 14,000 lines, and found a companion piece in *The Wallace* (c.1477) by Blind Harry alias Henry the Minstrel (c.1440–92). Paradoxically, it was under English influence that Scottish poetry flowered in the fifteenth and early sixteenth centuries, in the rhyme royal of King James I Stuart (*1394, reigned 1424–37) and in the verse of four other **Scottish Chaucerians or Scots Makars** who wrote for the court. William Dunbar (c.1460–1513) is remembered for his verse satires (which are full of flyting, or rounds of poetic abuse) and for his elegiac *Lament for the Makaris* (poets). With *The Thistle* *and the Rose* (1503), Dunbar produced a dream vision and a nuptial song in Chaucer's rhyme royal on the marriage of James IV Stuart and Margaret Tudor. Gavin Douglas (c.1475–1522) employed rhyming couplets when he freely translated the *Aeneid* into Scots (*Eneados*, 1513), and the poet and diplomat Sir David Lindsay (c.1490–1555) made use of the 'bob and wheel' form known from *Gawain* in his morality play *A Pleasant Satire of the Three Estates* (1540). In *The Testament of Cresseid* (posthumously printed 1593), Robert Henryson (c.1425–1506) had continued *Troilus and Chriseyde* in Chaucer's rhyme royal but with an alternate ending. Henryson moreover wrote shorter love poems on a Classical theme ("Orpheus and Eurydice") and a cycle of *Moral Fables* inspired by Aesop's animal fables (e.g. "The Cock and the Fox"), and perhaps by those of Marie de France. In 2009, Seamus Heaney responded to Henryson's Scots poems with a modern translation of *"The Testament of Cresseid" and Seven Fables* – ten years after the Irish poet's engagement with Old English *Beowulf*, and a full quarter of a century after Heaney had begun a re-circulation of Irish myth with *Sweeney Astray*.

Guiding Questions and Exercises

1. Describe and discuss the ways in which multilingualism, multiculturalism and multiple media use have made themselves felt in Britain and Ireland over the Middle Ages.
2. Point out the main features of Old English poetry and exemplify them with *Beowulf*.
3. Give a short sketch of the development and forms of Arthurian literature.
4. Compare William Langland's *Piers Plowman* with John Bunyan's *Pilgrim's Progress* (1678–84) and with William Blake's prophetical writings around 1800 (see chaps. 3.4.1 and 3.4.5). Please include in your comparison the individual shape of those allegorical works in verse and prose as well as the period context.
5. Discuss the position of Chaucer's *The Canterbury Tales* within the history of short fiction in Britain and Ireland. Sum up the variety of its forms, themes and characters.
6. What are the main currents of medieval drama in Britain?

7. Where are the similarities, and where the differences between English literature and the literatures of the Celtic Fringe?

Renaissance Literature (c.1500–1660) | 2

Summary

The multilingualism of medieval Britain and Ireland extended into the Early Modern Period. Yet between Reformation and Restoration, England and Scotland (more so than Ireland) experienced the gradual establishment of print as a new medium of literary communication. The flowering of Renaissance literature in English is marked out most in drama and in poetry. Shakespeare, Marlowe, Jonson and many other dramatists have written history plays and various forms of tragedy and comedy, in verse and prose, for the first London playhouses as well as for the court. The sixteenth- and early seventeenth-century craze for the sonnet is a prominent feature of the poetry of the period. Spenser and Milton, each in his own way, composed epic poetry on national and religious themes. The prose works of the period reflect not only the cultural learning of the Renaissance, but also the religious and political upheavals of the time of Reformation, as well as the first stage of Empire-building.

Renaissance Contexts | 2.1

The English Renaissance had a very ambivalent relationship with its Continental counterparts.

> The Italian Renaissance took the best part of two centuries to reach England, a little offshore island outside the mainstream of European culture; its founding poets were Petrarch and Boccaccio, the Italian contemporaries of the English poet Geoffrey Chaucer. [...] But English poets continued to treat their European models with a degree of suspicion, even while they borrowed from them, [...]. English writers had grown up within the Reformed Church, under an emergent nationalism that

was both political and religious, that regarded Catholic Europe with distrust and Spain and Italy with something approaching paranoia. A sense of identity as a newly forged Protestant nation fostered a desire to equal or surpass the acknowledged masterpieces of pagan Rome or of modern Catholic nations. (Briggs 1997: 2–3. For a general survey of the period, see moreover Suerbaum 1989.)

Political Confrontation
at Home and Abroad

Between the 1450s and 1660, the British Isles experienced political strife within and between its various regions as well as abroad. **The Wars of the Roses** between rival factions of the English nobility, the House of Lancaster (with its emblem of the Red Rose) and the House of York (White Rose), though they did not exactly amount to civil wars, nevertheless paralysed England between 1455 and 1485. After the death of the last Yorkist King Richard III on the battlefield of Bosworth (1485), and the marriage of the victor Henry Tudor, Earl of Richmond with Elizabeth of York a year later, the **House of Tudor** (1485–1603) could look to the consolidation of its ruling power. A propagandistic part of that endeavour is the **Tudor Myth** about the return to harmonious and peaceful government (see Tillyard 1944 and chap. 2.2.2). The term **Tudor Revolution** has been applied to the more effective form of government (in which the Tudor monarchs relied on a new institution, the Privy Council), rather than to the revolutionary process of separation of the (Protestant) Church of England from the Roman Catholic Church (see below). At about the same time, in 1536, the **Principality of Wales** was formally united with England, and in 1541, Henry VIII became hereditary monarch of the newly established **Kingdom of Ireland**, too. However, English rule in Ireland was basically limited to the control of the harbour towns of Cork and Waterford and of the coastal area around Dublin known as *The Pale*. In the last years of her reign, Elizabeth I had to fight a rebellion in Ireland (1594–1603) led by the Ulster nobleman Hugh O'Neill, the Earl of Tyrone, which did not succeed. One of the English landowners driven from their estates during the rebellion was the poet Edmund Spenser (†1599), who was involved in the administration of Ireland, and who had come out in favour of scorched earth tactics in his pamphlet *A View of the Present State of Ireland*. After the 'Flight of the Earls', the emigration of Irish nobility and their households in 1607, English and Scottish colonisation of Ireland continued with the Ulster Plantation that included a great number of Scottish Presbyterians, laying the ground for sectarian violence centuries later. The Puritan general Oliver Cromwell suppressed renewed rebellion that had begun with the massacre of an estimated 12,000 Protestant settlers in 1641. Cromwell's invasion and conquest of Ireland (1649–50) spawned Andrew Marvell's commendatory verse entitled "An Horation Ode. Upon Cromwell's Return from Ireland" (printed only in 1681), that is at odds with the 1649 massacres of Irish soldiers and civilians after the ending of the sieges of Drogheda and Wexford. The Cromwellian Plantation and the resettlement of Catholic landowners and their households (some 44,000 people) to Connaught in the West consolidated the Protestant Ascendancy as ruling class in Ireland (1652 ff.).

Cromwell's subsequent engagement in Scotland (1650–51) is part of a longer story. **English-Scottish relations** continued to be frosty or even violent, thereby providing Walter Scott with a subject matter for his early nineteenth-century verse narratives and Waverley Novels to rival Shakespeare's English history plays based on the Wars of the Roses (see chaps. 2.2.2 and 3.5.6). Despite his marriage to a Tudor princess, namely Henry VIII's sister Margaret, King James IV of Scotland waged war on England, and fell in the Battle of Flodden Field (1513). Their granddaughter Mary Queen of Scots became a prisoner in England for 18 years, after she had to flee from her kingdom after the Scottish Reformation of 1560, and after a succession of marriages to murderous husbands. However, even in prison she remained the focus of Catholic opposition against the Tudors and was a serious rival to Queen Elizabeth, until Mary Stuart's involvement in a series of plots ended in her execution (1587). Under her son, James VI and (in England) the I, the crowns of both kingdoms fell to the **House of Stuart** (1603–1714), a century before the United Kingdom of Great Britain was formally established in 1707. The Absolutism of the Stuart monarchy and its increasingly Catholic tendency led to confrontation with the Parliament of Westminster, and with Calvinist Protestants in England (Puritans) as well as in Scotland (Presbyterians). A series of **Civil Wars** ensued (1642–51), first between Royalists (Cavaliers) and the parliamentary and Puritan opposition (Roundheads), and then between the English parliamentary forces and their opponents in Ireland and in Scotland. History repeated itself when another Stuart, Charles I, had to lay his head on the block in 1649. During the **Republic** (first called

Commonwealth and then Protectorate, 1649–60), the parliamentary champion Oliver Cromwell usurped the power and ruled England, Scotland and Ireland as Lord Protector from 1653 to his death in 1658. In 1660, the return of King Charles II from his French exile brought about the **Restoration** of the Stuart monarchy and of court culture.

From the ending of the Hundred Years' War with France (1339–1453) to Cromwell's rule two centuries later, political confrontation was not limited to the British Isles but also continued abroad. After 1453, Calais remained England's sole possession in France and its gate to the Continent, until it was lost in a new war with France in 1558, in the year of Queen Elizabeth's accession. However, the first Tudor King Henry VII had already laid the foundations for England's rise as a mercantile and sea power, a development that continued well over the Tudor period. During the reign of Elizabeth I, the new economic rival and political enemy was Spain. English piracy at sea and the execution of Mary Queen of Scots led to open war with this Catholic power-base. Once the threat of invasion had been averted through the defeat of the Armada, in 1588, England emerged as the leading Protestant and maritime power from this conflict, which had also been fought on the Atlantic and in the Caribbean. Key events in the process of a **re-orientation to the New World** are the 'discovery' of the West Indian islands and mainland America by Christopher Columbus (1492–1504); Sir Francis Drake's circumnavigation of the globe (1577–80); the establishment of chartered companies such as the East India Co. (1600), the Virginia Co. (1606) or the Hudson's Bay Co. (1670); and the foundation of colonial settlements and plantations, as in Virginia (1584) and Jamestown (1607 ff., named after the ruling monarchs) as well as in Jamaica (1655). Colonial expansion had mixed results: Drake's cousin, the sea captain John Hawkins, is credited not only with the introduction of the potato and of tobacco into England, but also with pioneering the trans-Atlantic Triangular Trade in slaves. A new intake of the changed outlook on the world was the racial stereotype of the native as cannibal (in one of Montaigne's late sixteenth-century essays) or Caliban (in Shakespeare's *The Tempest*, 1611), which was followed up with the more positive image of the 'noble savage' (as in Aphra Behn's *Oroonoko; or, The Royal Slave*, 1688). The spread of the English language as another long-term effect of colonial expansion broke the ground for 'New English Literatures' in the future.

During the half-century of Elizabeth I's reign (1558–1603), the English nation increased from 3 to 4 million. By 1652, again half a century later and after Cromwell's campaign, Ireland was said to number just 850,000 people. The British Isles on the whole were predominantly rural in character, with one exception. London as a metropolis started into the sixteenth century with a population of 50,000, to reach 100,000 at the time of Elizabeth's accession, and 200,000 by the year 1600. Norwich and Bristol, the next greatest urban centres, had between 10,000 and 15,000 citizens, and others less than half that number. The nucleus of society was the household, which comprised the extended family and all dependants. English society was characterised by a class division that spread from the aristocracy – a nobility that was diminished through the Wars of the Roses, and the landed gentry – over the land-owning bourgeoisie (yeomanry) of merchants, lawyers and other citizens and the tenants down to the steadily increasing number of rural vagabonds and beggars. Upward mobility was possible, to a certain extent, as is evident from Shakespeare's rise from an actor, playwright and shareholder in the theatre business to the station of a prosperous citizen of Stratford. The materialism that went hand in hand with the economic changes during the sixteenth century, when England became a mercantile and naval power of the first order, is the theme of plays such as Marlowe's *The Jew of Malta*, Shakespeare's *The Merchant of Venice* and Jonson's *Volpone*.

Social Context

The worldliness and materialism of the age was countered by a preoccupation with religious matters from monarchs down to the common people. At first, King Henry VIII earned himself the Papal honorific *Defensor fidei* through his repudiation of Martin Luther's Reformist Theses of 1517. When the King however, in want of a legitimate male heir, sought the annulment of the first of his then altogether six marriages, he brought about a revolution from the top. In 1533/34, Henry VIII achieved the separation of the Church of England from the Roman Catholic Church, with the monarch as supreme head of the church replacing the Pope. For his refusal to accept this solution, Henry's Lord Chancellor Sir Thomas More, a leading Humanist and the author of *Utopia*, paid with his life: he was executed in 1535 (as were two of the King's

Religion

six wives). From the dissolution of the monasteries (1536–39) and the redistribution of their land and wealth, the Crown profited together with the landed gentry and yeomanry. The Protestant Reformation of the Church of England happened under the boy-king Edward VI, with the publication of the officially sanctioned (Second) *Book of Common Prayer* in 1552, which regulated Anglican church-service, and in which Thomas Cranmer, the Archbishop of Canterbury, and the Scottish preacher John Knox had a hand. The pendulum swung back and a Catholic backlash occurred in England under Maria Tudor, a fanatical Catholic married to King Philip of Spain, who then became the archrival of her Protestant sister Elizabeth. During the five years of the reign of "Bloody Mary", some 300 Protestants, including Archbishop Cranmer and other bishops, were burned at the stake. With the English Church Settlement of 1559, Elizabeth achieved a lasting compromise in religious matters, though the Catholic and Puritan factions abstained. In the same year, John Knox (c.1510–72) returned from his exile in England and in Geneva and became a Calvinist leader of the Scottish Reformation, which in 1560 succeeded in making the Church of Scotland independent from Rome, and Scotland free from the influence of the French court. The Church of Scotland was reformed along Presbyterian lines, and in 1568, it was Mary Queen of Scots who was forced to go into exile in England, where she found her death (see above).

Renaissance Views of Man and the Universe

The Reformation in England and Scotland is also marked by repeated attempts to translate the Bible and the Psalms into English. At the same time, verse and prose **translations** of 'Classic' works of Greek and Roman literature were produced. With their motto *ad fontes* ('to the sources'), **Humanists** worked their way back to the roots of Classical European culture and brought about its rebirth or re-naissance: in Italy already in the fourteenth, and in England in the sixteenth centuries, with men like More. This programme filtered down when after the dissolution of the monasteries, monastic schools were replaced by secular grammar schools, where laymen provided an education in Classical languages and literatures. Roger Ascham's educational book *The Schoolmaster* (1570) illustrates this development (see chap. 2.4). Apart from the re-discovery of the Classics, our image of the Renaissance is also bound up with an *Advancement of Learning*, as Sir Francis Bacon (1561–1626) formulated in the title of his

1605 review of research (which he reissued in Latin in 1623). Bacon himself is credited with breaking the ground for an **empiricism** based on inductive reasoning, a Baconian Method that proceeds from given facts to interpretation and further to scientific laws. Such empiricism was akin to the new insights Renaissance scholars gained in the fields of **astronomy and anatomy**. Nicolaus Copernicus's revolutionary replacement of a geocentric with a heliocentric universe (1543) was improved upon by the work of Galileo Galilei and Johannes Kepler. The 1543 anatomy book by Andreas Vesalius helped to demystify the human body, and the English physician William Harvey broke with established views when he pointed out the circulation of the blood (1628). At the ending of the period under review, the 'new Philosophy [that] calls all in doubt', as the poet John Donne had written in his *First Anniversary* in 1611, became institutionalised in the Royal Society of London for the Improvement of Natural Knowledge (1660). In Donne's and Shakespeare's time, medieval cosmology and medicine, though out of date, survived in a form that twentieth-century historians of ideas were to describe as *The Great Chain of Being* (Lovejoy 1936) and *The Elizabethan World Picture* (Tillyard 1943). When such models are used with caution – i.e. in awareness of their ideal character (which can never describe the individual disposition of any real Elizabethan) and of their ideological nature (which speaks of a respect for fixed order and hierarchies) – they still retain their usefulness as a compendium of contemporary thought (see Suerbaum 1989: 475–540). Plato and Aristotle were among the first to use the image of a **Chain of Being** to distinguish Chaos from Cosmos, and to describe the Macrocosmos as a hierarchy that sees Man as the link between Earth and Heaven (but also liable to create Chaos). Moreover, Man as a Microcosmos is the sum of four states of being on a scale of degree: more than barely existing like *minerals*, s/he is a living organism like *vegetables*, animated and sensuous like *animals*, yet the only rational one of all, and therefore definitely *human*. In Tillyard's *Elizabethan World Picture*, such vertical hierarchy is supplemented by a series of **Correspondences**, as between Macro- and Microcosmos, or between the human body and the state as a *body politic*. Part of that worldview is the explanation of the human character with recourse to bodily fluids called **Humours** and in combination with the Four Elements and a *psychological disposition*: **Blood**/Air/

|Fig. 2.1

Ptolemy's geocentric and spherical cosmology (from Peter Apian's *Cosmographia*, 1524)

Sanguinic matches **Phlegm**/Water/*Phlegmatic*, **Choler or Yellow Bile**/Fire/ *Choleric* and **Black Bile**/Earth/*Melancholic*. The Humours concept is central to Ben Jonson's satiric stage-plays *Every Man in His Humour* (1598, rev. 1616) and *[...] Out of His Humour* (1599) as well as to Robert Burton's literary *Anatomy of Melancholy* (1621).

Literary Communication

Between Reformation and Restoration, England and Scotland (but not yet Ireland) entered into a **new stage of literary communication**. The beginning of the English Renaissance is marked by the completion of a **language change** that had led to the formation of Early Modern English by about 1500. But as there was no notion of Standard English, spoken or written, Scots remained an acknowledged speech variety throughout the period. The **multilingualism** of medieval Britain and Ireland moreover extended into the Early Modern Period. Even after the Anglo-Saxon and Norman invasions of Britain, as well as the English invasions of Ireland, Latin and most of the Celtic languages retained their literary potential. Latin remained a viable alternative for literature in manuscript and in print until the beginning of the eighteenth century, as can be gleaned from the two versions of Thomas More's *Utopia* and of Francis Bacon's prose writings (see chap. 2.4). Cornish suffered from the massacre of native speakers after the abortive 1549 rebellion against the introduction of the *Book of Common Prayer* and of English as the language of church services; and by the end of the eighteenth century, Cornish had become extinct. Welsh, by contrast, profited from the translation of the New Testament and of the English *Book of Common Prayer* (both by William Salesbury, 1567); and with the translation of the whole Bible into Welsh in the year of the Armada (1588), William Morgan stabilised the Late Modern Welsh language. Scottish and Irish Gaelic continued to be spoken throughout the period, but were to wait for a literary revival until the twentieth century.

A major innovation is the invention of the **printing press**, which arrived at different times in the three kingdoms: William Caxton (†1492) was the first Englishman to set up a printing press in Westminster in 1476; Edinburgh followed in or about 1508, and Dublin in 1550. An edition of Chaucer's *Canterbury Tales* was the first book printed by Caxton in England, after he had printed his own translation of a French romance in Bruges in 1473. Caxton functioned likewise as the first English bookseller. The gradual establishment of print as a new medium of literary communication happened in England up to the middle of the sixteenth century: the publication of *Tottel's Miscellany* in 1557 (which anthologised sonnets that had hitherto circulated in manuscript) and of *The Mirror for Magistrates* in 1559 (which was to have an impact on Elizabethan stage tragedies) are convenient examples. When the Stationers' Company in London secured the English monopoly on printing in 1557, this was at the same time a means for the state to exercise state **control**, as the entry into the *Stationers' Register* of books in print was synonymous with the successful passing of censorship. Between 1500 and 1640, about 20,000 items (from the broadsheet to the Bible) were printed in England alone.

The (First) *Book of Common Prayer*, which had appeared in England in 1549, became the first printed book in Ireland in 1551. This 'book' is not only important for the spread of Protestantism, but also and in several ways significant within a history of literary communication.

- ► **Spreading the word:** the rapid export of the English liturgical book to Ireland testified to the missionary zeal of the Protestant Church of England towards Irish Catholicism, and moreover to the English society's confrontation of the Gaelic community with a politics of linguistic and cultural expansion.
- ► **Code-switching:** as a translation of the liturgy from a privileged foreign language (Latin) into the vernacular, this prayer-book marks a stage in the rising esteem for Early Modern English as a means of communication that entails, in the widest sense, also a literary communication.
- ► **Simultaneity of the media of performance and of print:** as such, part of the *Book of Common Prayer* should be read aloud (and thus 'performed') amongst the congregation, yet it is likewise purposefully produced in the new medium of print to make mass distribution possible.
- ► **Social context:** in terms of composition, the 1549 *Book of Common Prayer* must be seen as a (first and later revised) compromise between various religious factions in Tudor England. Code-switching and the simultaneity of the media explain themselves with regard to the special character of this text, which is seen as fundamental for a Christian society, and therefore is officially sanctioned.

Yet the events in Dublin of 1550/51 notwithstanding, the establishment of print as a new medium of literary communication took much longer in Ireland than in England. Belfast had to wait until 1694 for a printing press to be permanently set up, and the process as a whole was not completed before 1726, when George Faulkner (Jonathan Swift's publisher) began to operate as a printer and bookseller in Dublin.

As the development of the Renaissance stage, as another medium of literary communication, is closely connected to the dramatic production of the period, those two are best seen together (in chap. 2.2.1). The link between selected contextual features of the Renaissance and the prose literature of the period is further explored in chap. 2.4.

Guiding Questions and Exercises

1. Give a short sketch of the social, political and religious development in the British Isles between Reformation and Restoration.
2. What is meant by the term Elizabethan World Picture? Try to discuss E. M. W. Tillyard's representation of the spirit of the age in the light of his critics.
3. What is characteristic of literary communication in the Renaissance as compared to the time before? (You may include the performance context described in chap. 2.2.1.)
4. Sum up the exemplary character of the *Book of Common Prayer* for literary and cultural developments in sixteenth-century Britain and Ireland.

2.2 | Theatre and Drama

2.2.1 | The Renaissance Stage

The Renaissance Stage

Drama on the Renaissance stage differed from its predecessors in Classical Greece and Rome as well as in Medieval England. (See chap. 1 and Meyer 2008: 116–18.) During the sixteenth century, booth stages were replaced by makeshift tavern stages (in London until 1596), before the theatre business became increasingly institutionalised (see Suerbaum 1989, Briggs 1997). Dramatic productions were **popular entertainment** in the sense that they attracted an audience of between 1,000 and 3,000 people to the commercial theatre, six days a week in the season and from all sections of society. Dramatists catered to everyone's taste, as when Shakespeare (in the Porter Scene in *Macbeth*) provides 'comic relief' from a scene of political murder through a comic interlude based on bawdy humour. **'Public' open-air theatres** were concentrated just outside London in the Bankside area that offered bear baiting and further, more disreputable forms of entertainment. This is why the Puritans and some members of the upper classes nursed their moral and social prejudices and abstained. With "The Theatre" in 1576, the actor-manager James Burbage (†1597) had built the first London playhouse (still in Shoreditch), before alternatives sprang up with the "Curtain" (1577), "Rose" (1587), "Swan" (1595), "Fortune" (1600), "Red Bull" (1605) and "Hope" (1613) theatres – "The Globe" (1599–1613, and again 1614–44) being the most famous of all because of its association with the work of William Shakespeare. There were also permanent, **'private' indoor theatres** with artificial lighting – such as the "Blackfriars" (1576), which was also frequented by Shakespeare's troupe – and, from 1605, court theatres such as the "Cockpit-in-Court" built by Inigo Jones (1630) for the production of court masques. In 1637, the first playhouse outside London opened in Dublin. Other than the single sketch of a 1596 performance at "The Swan" or the rebuilding of "Shakespeare's Globe" in London in 1997 may suggest, there is **no prototype of the playhouse**: Renaissance plays were laid out to be staged in very different venues. However, a few essential features are beyond dispute: to stage the famous Balcony Scene from *Romeo and Juliet* one needed a gallery as additional theatrical space, situated over the thrust or 'apron stage' that extended into the audience. In the public theatres, 'Heaven' referred to the painted roof that provided shelter in case of rain for the actors on stage in their elaborate costumes, but not for the 'groundlings' standing in front of the stage in the open-roof playhouse. (In 1599, they paid a penny, which is equal to 10% of an average day's wage for a learned profession. Prices in the indoor theatres started with sixpence.) The theatrical term for the trapdoor centre-stage was 'Hell': this could moreover function as a grave, as in *Hamlet*. Noise made in the [at]tiring-house backstage (if available) usefully signified battles, whereas royalty or other Very Important Persons in the play were announced with a

| Fig. 2.2
The Swan theatre in London, 1596

flourish. Apart from a few prop[ertie]s of an emblematical nature (such as a throne and a map in *King Lear*) and other, smaller ones such as a handkerchief (in *Othello*), daggers (in *Macbeth*), a crown (in *Richard III*) or a skull (in *Hamlet*), the **stage was bare**. The use of tapers and torches in an open-air theatre lit by daylight indicated night scenes or scenes that take place in vaults, as in *Romeo and Juliet*. Costumes e.g. for Roman plays were not historically accurate, but generally colourful and contemporary in character. Scenery and a change of setting were indicated verbally (the German term is *Wortkulisse*). This happened right away as "In fair Verona, where we lay our scene" (*Romeo and Juliet*, 1.1.2), maybe with a pun as in "Now is it Rome indeed and room enough/When there is in it but one only man" (*Julius Caesar*, 1.2.156–57), or in the now proverbial form of "Something is rotten in the state of Denmark" (*Hamlet*, 1.5.90). A special feature of the Renaissance period was that the performance of a play (tragedies included) usually ended in a jig or any other lively dance.

Until 1608, the private theatres used only companies of **boy actors**, which competed with rival **companies of professional actors** under the patronage of courtiers: after 1597, those were limited to the Lord Admiral's Men and the Lord Chamberlain's Men (Shakespeare's troupe, from 1603 called The King's Men). Female roles were played by boys, as **actresses were allowed on stage only after the Restoration**. Obviously, this gives extra fun to 'breeches scenes' and related forms of gender bending where boys acting women disguise as men (as does Rosalind in *As You Like It*). Outside London, plays were also presented by companies of actors touring the provinces or the Continent, e.g. as *Englische Komödianten* in Germany from c.1586. The **repertory system** that was in use meant that the same play was seldom acted on successive nights, and that there was a continuous demand for new plays. This is why so many dramatists collaborated on their plays: the well-known partnership of Beaumont & Fletcher rather states the rule, to which Shakespeare and Jonson are the exception.

Didactic Performances

Plays, on principle, were no longer religious in character, but their popular form of entertainment might include religious satire. This, together with the public nature of the playhouse and their large audiences, was reason enough for monarchs to exercise **stage censorship**. To justify his title of *Defensor fidei*, King Henry VIII repeatedly took measures (in 1533 and 1543) to suppress political as well as religious, anti-clerical satire, such as in the morality play *A Pleasant Satire of the Three Estates* (1540) by Sir David Lindsay. Under Queen Elizabeth, the Master of the Revels read the text of stage-plays in advance and licensed their performance, while other institutions – including the Stationers' Company (from 1557) – governed the publication of playbooks. Censorship had ambivalent effects: Ben Jonson (1572–1637), for instance, profited from the suppression of all satirical pamphlets in prose and verse, in 1599, because this left a loop-hole for satirical stage-plays such as his own. Jonson had a much higher esteem of drama than had most of his contemporaries (who regarded it merely as a form of popular entertainment). This included his own works for the stage, which he published in 1616 in the Folio format that was associated with the Bible. Such a rivalry between the teachings of the pulpit and the stage, between the **didactic performances** of the preacher and the playwright, was keenly felt. Persistent protest from Puritan circles, which Jonson lampooned in *The Alchemist* (1610), against the lack of religious correctness on stage (and the convention of boys acting women alike) eventually led to the **closing of the theatres** between 1642 and 1660 in the times of the Commonwealth and the Protectorate.

The dramatic work of William Shakespeare (1564–1616) will necessarily loom large in this account of Renaissance drama. Two of his friends and fellow-actors collected the first complete edition of his plays that appeared posthumously in Folio format. All earlier and variant editions of individual plays had appeared in the smaller and much less venerable Quarto format, and generally without Shakespeare's blessing. With Shakespeare, the dramatic unit was the scene, not the division into acts (which is more characteristic of the Folio than the Quarto versions of his plays). In the title and the table of contents of the **1623 First Folio**, Shakespeare's work for the stage was subsumed under three categories: *Comedies, Histories and Tragedies*. This generic distinction, though practical, is not always clear-cut: the picture becomes blurred, for instance, in the titles of the First and Second Quarto of *The Tragicall Historie of Hamlet, Prince of Denmarke*, and even in the First Folio, where we find *The Tragedy of King Richard the Third* amidst the Histories, while *Cymbeline King of Britaine* is listed as a tragedy. Among the comedies, subsequent Shakespeare criticism produced further subdivision, again with a logic of its own.

Fig. 2.3
The Chandos portrait of William Shakespeare, c.1610

When Romances are defined by their proximity to fairy tales and myth, then *A Midsummer Night's Dream* is clearly involved, too – and yet it is counted as a Romantic Comedy, not as a Romance. The ambiguous term Problem Play, on the other hand, may have been suggested to late nineteenth-century critics by contemporary work for the stage (see chap. 4.3), if not by the problems they encountered in defining pieces that are neither particularly funny (and thus pure comedy) nor end with the death of their protagonists (as the common denominator for tragedies requires). To see Tragicomedies as a hybrid group of its own seems to be more helpful in this case. While opinion is divided upon the dating of

Table 1 Chronology and Conventional Categorisation of Shakespeare's Works

Period of Composition	(English) Histories	Tragedies (and Roman Plays)	Comedies
1589–92	1,2,3 Henry VI Richard III	Titus Andronicus	(Romantic Comedies:) The Taming of the Shrew The Two Gentlemen of Verona
1592–94	**Narrative Poems:** Venus and Adonis, The Rape of Lucrece; **Sonnets**		
1594/95–98	Richard II King John 1 Henry IV 2 Henry IV	Romeo and Juliet	The Comedy of Errors Love's Labour's Lost A Midsummer Night's Dream The Merchant of Venice The Merry Wives of Windsor Much Ado About Nothing
1599–1602	Henry V	Julius Caesar Hamlet	As You Like It Twelfth Night ('Problem Plays':) Troilus and Cressida
1603			Measure for Measure
1604–07		Othello King Lear Macbeth Antony and Cleopatra Timon of Athens	All's Well That Ends Well
1608 1613	 All Is True [Henry VIII] (with John Fletcher)	Coriolanus	('Romances':) Pericles Cymbeline The Winter's Tale The Tempest The Two Noble Kinsmen (with John Fletcher)

individual plays, too, Table 1 (which is informed by Dobson and Wells 2001) may still allow an overview of Shakespeare's œuvre in its development, and it may moreover help to become familiar with a conventional typology of his work for the stage. In what follows, however, the plays by Shakespeare and by his contemporaries will be treated in a different manner, namely with regard to their historical subject matter (2.2.2), to their tragic features (2.2.3), and to their uses of comedy and tragicomedy for different ends (2.2.4).

Romans and Roses: Elizabethan History Plays

2.2.2

The **English history play** thrived in the second half of the sixteenth century, and died down not long after the death of Queen Elizabeth I in 1603. (See Tillyard 1944; Massai in Dobson and Wells 2001: 203). For Renaissance plays based on English history, there was no Classical precedent. Tudor historians such as Polydore Vergil (*Anglica historia*, 1534), Edward Hall (*The Union of the Two Noble and Illustrious Families of Lancaster and York*, 1548) and Raphael Holinshed (*Chronicles of England, Scotland and Ireland*, 1587) provided the material, whereas dramatic features such as the Vice character (visible in Richard III) derived from English medieval morality plays. There are **three main reasons for the great popularity**, in its time, of the history play as a genre:

- ► Within the **theatre business**, the new dramatic kind was a welcome addition to the bill, as there was a continuously **high demand for new plays** for the public stage.
- ► Elizabethan **dramatists** saw that there was a dramatic potential in staging one of **two conflicting views on history:** (a) the Christian notion of Providence (see Tillyard 1944) and (b) the Humanist (Machiavellian) view of history as source of pragmatic lessons (*historia magistra vitae*, see Ribner 1957).
- ► The **politics of the audience** were marked by a **rise of nationalism** after the Protestant Reformation and during the conflict with Spain. This development climaxed in 1588, with the threat of invasion and the defeat of the Armada.

All in all, William Shakespeare wrote ten English history plays. They fall into **two tetralogies**, which were written in reverse order, and which are framed by a single play each.

Shakespeare's English History Plays

Table 2 Shakespeare's English History Plays

Group	Single Play	Date of Composition	Subject Matter
	King John	Written c.1596	1199–1216 whole reign, yet not including the Magna Charta
Second (Lancaster) Tetralogy	Richard II	Written only in the late 1590s	1415 Hundred Years' War resumes with Henry V's invasion of France; Battle of Agincourt
	1 Henry IV		
	2 Henry IV		
	Henry V		
First (York) Tetralogy	1 Henry VI	Written first, in the early 1590s	1455–87 Wars of the Roses
	2 Henry VI		
	3 Henry VI		1485 Battle of Bosworth Field Accession of Tudor Monarchy
	Richard III		
	All Is True [Henry VIII]	Probably written in collaboration with John Fletcher, c.1613	1533 marriage with Anne Boleyn; birth of Princess Elizabeth

When E. M. W. Tillyard wrote his seminal study on *Shakespeare's History Plays* (1944), he produced a general interpretation of which the major theses bear quotation:

➤ **The Tudor Myth** [...] the Tudors, to suit their ends, encouraged their people to look on the events that led to their accession, in a special way. [...] Henry VII fostered [... the notion] that the union of the two houses of York and Lancaster through his marriage with the York heiress was the providential and happy ending of an organic piece of history. [... This notion is] crucial to an understanding of Shakespeare's Histories (36).

➤ Shakespeare turned the Chronicle Play into an independent and authentic type of drama, and no mere ancillary to the form of tragedy. [...] he expressed successfully a universally held and still comprehensible scheme of history: a scheme fundamentally religious, by which events evolve under a law of justice and under the ruling of God's Providence, and of which Elizabeth's England was the acknowledged outcome. The scheme, which, in its general outline, consisted of the distortion of nature's course by a crime and its restoration through a long series of disasters and suffering and struggles, may indeed be like Shakespeare's scheme of tragedy; but it is genuinely political and has its own right of existence apart from tragedy. (324–25)

➤ Shakespeare's History Plays are political writings [...]. The picture we get from Shakespeare's Histories is that of disorder. Unsuccessful war abroad and civil war at home are the larger theme; victory abroad and harmony at home are the exceptions, and the fear of disorder is never absent. (7, 15)

Tillyard's argument has withstood the test of time, even though it did not remain uncontested because of its Conservative penchant for order and stability.

The outline of Shakespeare's sequence and its historical reference can be gleaned from Tables 2 and 3. Shakespeare's *Richard III* and *Henry V* complement each other in their portrait of power politics. For *Richard III*, Shakespeare found his material (in addition to the chronicles of Hall and Holinshed) in the *History of King Richard III* written by Sir Thomas More (some 30 years before its publication in 1543). True to the Tudor Myth, the later chancellor of Henry VIII portrayed the last king from the House of York as an evil being on the grand scale. To pave his way to the throne, Richard Duke of Gloucester seduces the widow of the former Prince of Wales (Lady Anne) whom he has killed, sees to the murder of his brother (the Duke of Clarence) and his nephews (the 'Two Princes in the Tower'), and to the execution of rival noblemen (including his fellow-conspirator, the Duke of Buckingham). With his considerable charm, this hunchbacked Machiavellian villain manages to deceive the people about him. By contrast, the audience is allowed a look behind the devil's mask. One of Richard's soliloquies starts the play off with a pun ("Now is the winter of our discontent/Made glorious summer by this son [sun] of York," 1.1.1–2), and from then on, the usurper and serial murderer reveals his real self and intentions again and again in his monologues, soliloquies and asides, quite in the tradition of the medieval Vice character. In addition to such thrill and rhetorical power play, *Richard III* is characterised by the frequent use made of curses and of wishes for revenge, as well as by its vivid animal imagery (the usurper is repeatedly compared to a poisonous toad or spider). While the audience may at first be puzzled by the gallery of widowed queens and noble women 'left over' from both the House of Lancaster and of York, their sheer number is a reminder of how much bloodshed and grief has resulted from these wars among the nobility. Shakespeare's history play translated well into the twentieth century, when the actors Laurence Olivier and Ian McKellen starred in two outstanding and very different adaptations for the screen. In the widely-seen 1955 film, directed by Olivier himself two years after the coronation of Elizabeth II, the crown is a potent visual symbol, both of Richard's personal ambition as well as of a patriotic notion of

Fig. 2.4
William Blake,
Richard III and the Ghosts, c.1806

English history in which such murderous monarchs are merely an episode. By contrast, when Ian McKellen wrote the screenplay for the 1996 film directed by Richard Loncraine, he engaged in a piece of alternate history. Unwittingly alike to the 1937 Orson Welles production of *Julius Caesar* (mentioned below), the film transferred the action and the text of Shakespeare's play into an imaginary 1930s Britain, where Richard (McKellen) turns into a fascist dictator. The plausibility of this modern-dress version extends even to Richard's famous last words, "A horse! A horse! My kingdom for a horse!" (5.4.13) even though they are spoken from an armoured vehicle in a battle that involves bombers and tanks.

Fig. 2.5

Henry V, portrait by a Tudor Artist

Just like in the chronicles on which the Histories are based, Shakespeare's stage portrait of Henry V as a model of kingship compares well with the villainous Richard as a negative image for the use of power. There is a longer story behind this though: the King transformed himself from a licentious youth (Prince Hal in *1, 2 Henry IV*) who had frequented taverns together with his friend Sir John Falstaff, into a warrior King who leads the English to victory over France and fires their patriotic spirit. The dramatist moreover supported such patriotism by the inclusion of four captains as personifications of the four major regions in the British Isles: Captains Gower (English), Fluellen (Welsh), MacMorris (Irish) and Janny (Scot) stand for the unity of the realm and for a vision of a United Kingdom in the future. Henry's behaviour is not only mirrored in their discussion, but also in the Chorus's speeches, from the meta-dramatic Prologue to his return at the beginning of each of five acts, in order to summarise the historical action. Just like the Chorus's speeches in *Romeo and Juliet*, the Epilogue spoken in this play takes the form of a sonnet, reminding the audience that what was won by Henry V was lost by his son Henry VI, and that renewed civil wars ensued. Both the King and his future spouse, the French Princess Katherine, are involved in funny scenes that – quite surprising for this patriotic play – are for the most part or fully spoken in French, the language of the enemy (3.4 and 5.2). Yet there is also a darker side to this warrior-king, who during the 1415 Battle of Agincourt orders the French prisoners of war to be killed (4.6, 4.7). The positive qualities of Henry V as a soldier shine so much brighter by contrast with those of Falstaff, who appears in *1, 2 Henry IV* (but not in *Henry V*, where he dies off-stage) as a military braggart. (For Falstaff's career as a lover, see chap. 2.2.4.) The King's two speeches, "Once more unto the breach" (*Henry V*, 3.1) and "This day is called the Feast of Crispian" (4.3.18–67), have become classics of English patriotic rhetoric, and guaranteed the revival of Shakespeare's play in times of war. Once again, Laurence Olivier's film version (1944) bears comparison with a successive adaptation for the screen in a different spirit, namely the one directed by Kenneth Branagh (1989), who also took the lead. The patriotic spirit of Olivier's film, which was released during the 1944 Invasion in Normandy, shows in its dedication to the troops fighting the Germans in France. On the other hand, Branagh's version, produced at the end of the Cold War, was widely received as an anti-war film just because of its uncompromising, brutal realism in the depiction of war's atrocities.

Successive dramatists, screenwriters and film directors have completed and corrected the historical record on stage and screen (see Table 3). Beginning with Christopher Marlowe's *Edward II* and the anonymous *Edward III*, in which Shakespeare might have had a hand, too, they produced stage-plays and films that are situated around Shakespeare's dramatic sequence, and that focus on the history of the medieval Plantagenet kings as well as the Tudor monarchs Henry VIII and Elizabeth I. When Irish and Scottish playwrights added to the picture, they usually abstracted from the Tudor Myth, and generally also from an English perspective – much more so than Shakespeare did when he turned to Scotland for *Macbeth*. The plays about the French heroine Jeanne d'Arc (written over three hundred years later by G.B. Shaw) and about Mary Queen of Scots (Liz Lochhead) are good examples. Many of those later stage-plays listed will be treated in more detail in chaps. 3.2, 4.3 and 5.3.

The cycle of plays about English history had come to its (ideo-) logical end when the action approached the beginning of the Tudor monarchy, a few years before the throne went to the Scottish House of Stuart (1603). At about this time, Shakespeare and his fellow-dramatist Ben Jonson turned to Rome in Antiquity and produced **historical plays with a Classical setting and a tragic plot**. As such subject matter continued to fascinate later dramatists, novelists, historians and film directors, a synopsis is useful to point out the historical reference and contents (see Table 4). The best-known

Roman Plays

Table 3 English and Scottish History in History Plays and in Film

Date	Historical event	Year	Author / Director	Work / Film
1154–1399	the **Plantagenets** on the throne			
1154–89	Henry II, married to Eleanor of Aquitaine (the former wife of the French king), rules over half of France, too	1966 1968	James Goldman Anthony Harvey (Dir.)	*The Lion in Winter* film version, starring P. O'Toole, K. Hepburn, A. Hopkins
1183–89	death of Prince Henry leads to rivalry and rebellion of other sons	2003	A. Konchalovsky (Dir.)	film version, starring G. Close
1154–70	Thomas Becket: 1154–62 Chancellor, then Archbishop of Canterbury, falls out with Henry II and is murdered in the cathedral	1884 1935	Alfred Lord Tennyson T.S. Eliot	*Becket* *Murder in the Cathedral*
1189–99	Richard I "Lionheart"	1938 1952	Michael Curtiz (Dir.) Richard Thorpe (Dir.)	*Robin Hood*, starring E. Flynn *Ivanhoe* (after Walter Scott's novel)
1199–1216	reign of John "Lackland", who loses the possession of Normandy	c.1596/ 1623	William Shakespeare	*The Life and Death of King John* (not mentioning the Magna Charta)
1215	**Magna Charta**	1965	J. Arden and M. D'Arcy	*Left-Handed Liberty*
1296–1306	campaigns of the English King Edward I in **Scotland** against William Wallace ("Braveheart") and Robert the Bruce	1995 1593/94	Mel Gibson (Dir.) Christopher Marlowe	*Braveheart*, starring M. Gibson *The Troublesome Reign and Lamentable Death of Edward II*
1306–29	King Robert I of Scotland			
1307–27	turbulent reign of Edward II of England, deposition and murder	1991	Derek Jarman (Dir.)	film version
1314	Battle of Bannockburn secures Scotland's independence	1924	Brecht/Feuchtwanger	*Leben Eduards II.* (adaptation)
1327–77	reign of Edward III	1596	Anonymous (Shakespeare ?)	*The Reign of Edward III*
1337	begin of the **Hundred Years' War**: campaigns in France			
1399	deposition and abdication of Richard II, the last Plantagenet King	1595 1596–98	W. Shakespeare	**Second Tetralogy:** *The Tragedy of King Richard II* *1, 2 Henry IV* (with Falstaff)
1413–22	reign of **Henry V**	1600	W. Shakespeare	*Henry V*
1415	the Hundred Years War resumes with Henry's invasion of France Battle of Agincourt: English victory; massacre of French prisoners	1944 1989	Laurence Olivier (Dir.) Kenneth Branagh (Dir.)	film version, starring L. Olivier film version, starring K. Branagh
1420	Henry V is effectively in command of all of France			
1429	**Jeanne d'Arc** rises from peasant girl to leader of the French army; with her help, the siege of Orléans is lifted, an English army defeated, and the French *dauphin* crowned king of France	1801 1923	Friedrich Schiller G.B. Shaw	*Die Jungfrau von Orléans* *Saint Joan*
1431	capture, trial and execution of Jeanne d'Arc as a witch	1623	W. Shakespeare	**First Tetralogy:** *1 Henry VI*
1920	Jeanne d'Arc canonised as Saint Joan by the Church of Rome			
1455–87	**Wars of the Roses** between the Houses of Lancaster and York	1594–95	W. Shakespeare	*2, 3 Henry VI*
1478	trial and murder of the Duke of Clarence (of the House of York)	1593/97	W. Shakespeare	*The Tragedy of Richard III*
1483	Duke of Gloucester becomes first Protector, then King **Richard III**; disappearance (and murder?) of the 'Two Princes in the Tower'			
1485	execution of opponents, among them the Duke of Buckingham Battle of Bosworth Field: Richard III dies, Henry Tudor succeeds	1955 1996	L. Olivier (Dir.) R. Loncraine (Dir.)	film version, starring L. Olivier film version, starring I. McKellen

Date	Event	Year	Author/Director	Work
1485–1603	the **Tudor Dynasty**			
1520	meeting of the English and French court in France; peak of Wolsey's career as Chancellor under **Henry VIII** (1509–47)	1613	W. Shakespeare (?) and John Fletcher (?)	*All is True [Henry VIII]* (first performance results in the destruction of the Globe Theatre by fire)
1529/30	Wolsey loses office; arrest and death	2007–09	Michael Hirst	*The Tudors* (TV series)
1533	Henry's (bigamous) marriage to Anne Boleyn, birth of Elizabeth	2008	Justin Chadwick (Dir.)	*The Other Boleyn Girl* (adapt. of Philippa Gregory's 2002 novel)
1534	Act of Supremacy: Henry VIII head of the new **Anglican Church** trial and execution of Thomas More (Chancellor since 1529)	1960 1966	Robert Bolt Fred Zinnemann (Dir.)	*A Man for All Seasons* film version
1553–58 1558–1603	"Bloody Mary" (Tudor) Queen of Engld.: persecution of Protestants **Elizabeth I**	1998	Shekhar Kapur (Dir.)	*Elizabeth*
1542–67 1565–67 1567	**Mary** (Stuart) **Queen of Scots**, also heir to the English throne second marriage to Lord Darnley (murdered) third marriage to the supposed assassin, Lord Bothwell; rebellion: Mary's imprisonment and abdication: James VI succeeds	1800/01 1958 1987 1970/72 1987/89	Friedrich Schiller Robert MacDonald Robert Bolt Liz Lochhead	*Maria Stuart* first produced in England *"Mary Stuart" by Schiller* (adapt.) *Vivat! Vivat Regina!* *Mary Queen of Scots Got Her Head Chopped Off*
1568 1586/87	Mary's escape is followed by arrest in England after a series of conspiracies, Parliament enforces Mary's execution			
1588	defeat of the Spanish Armada	1731 2007	George Lillo Shekhar Kapur (Dir.)	*The London Merchant; or, The History of George Barnwell* [domestic tragedy, no history play] *Elizabeth: The Golden Age*
1576 1583 1590s	James Burbage begins building of the first playhouse in London formation of The Queen's Players to stage royal performances Shakespeare's history plays; Globe Theatre (1599–1613)	1998	John Madden (Dir.)	*Shakespeare in Love*
1593–1603 1607ff.	rebellion in **Ireland**, led by the Earl of Tyrone, fails to succeed English colonisation of Ireland	1988/89	Brian Friel	*Making History*
1603–1714	with James I and VI, accession of the **Stuart Dynasty**			
1642–51 1649–60	**Civil Wars** execution of King Charles I; England a **Republic** (Commonwealth) under Oliver Cromwell as Lord Protector	1970	Ken Hughes (Dir.)	*Cromwell*

Table 4   Roman History in Literature and in Film

B.C.				
5th cent.	Rome under attack from Italian rivals > Coriolanus legend	1608/09	W. Shakespeare	Coriolanus (stage-play)
73–71	slave revolt under Spartacus, quenched by Pompeius	1960	S. Kubrick (Dir.)	Spartacus (film)
63/62	Cicero uncovers Catilina's conspiracy Cato argues (against Caesar) for the execution of the conspirators	1611	Ben Jonson	Catiline His Conspiracy (stage-play)
58–51	Caesar's armies conquer Gaul: surrender of Vercingetorix	51 B.C. 1959/61	Caesar Goscinny & Uderzo	De bello Gallico (prose account) Astérix le Gaulois (comic)
55 and 54	the Romans in Britain (twice): Caesar's armed reconnaissance, surrender of British over-lord Cassivelaunus	1980	Howard Brenton	The Romans in Britain (stage-play)
49–45	Civil War: Caesar wins against Pompeius (†48) and against Cato (†46, commits suicide after battle of Thapsus)	1713	Joseph Addison	Cato (stage-play)
48–47	Egypt: Caesar meets Cleopatra; they have a child (Caesarion)	1901/06 1946 1963	G.B. Shaw Gabriel Pascal (Dir.) J.L. Mankiewicz (Dir.)	Caesar and Cleopatra (stage-play) film version Cleopatra (film)
44–27 44 (March) 43–36 42	power-struggle, turning the Roman Republic into a monarchy Cassius, Brutus and other conspirators kill Caesar in the Senate 2nd triumvirate (Octavius Caesar, Antonius, Lepidus); proscriptions Antonius wins over both Cassius and Brutus (battle of Philippi)	1599 1953	W. Shakespeare J.L. Mankiewicz (Dir.)	Julius Caesar (stage-play) film version
36 32 31/30	Antonius and Octavius Caesar rule each in their own right Antonius moves to Egypt and lives with Cleopatra: children Octavius Caesar arranges for war declared on Cleopatra battle of Actium; both Antonius and Cleopatra commit suicide	1607–09 1678	W. Shakespeare John Dryden	Antony and Cleopatra (stage-play) All for Love (stage-play)
c. A.D. 10	legendary over-king Cunobelinus rules in SE-England (†c.41)	1610/11	W. Shakespeare	Cymbeline (stage-play)
30	trial and crucifixion of Jesus Christ in Jerusalem trial and execution of L. Aelius Seianus, who fell from high offices after rumours of his alleged conspiracy to become Princeps	1603	Ben Jonson	Sejanus His Fall (stage-play)
41–54 43–44 48, 54	Emperor Claudius: the Romans in Britain (again): Britain is made a Roman province Claudius has his first wife executed, and is poisoned by the second	1934 1976	Robert Graves H. Wise (Dir.)	I, Claudius and Claudius the God (historical fiction) I, Claudius (TV series)
54–68	Emperor Nero; fire of Rome (64); rebellion and suicide (66–68)	1895/96 1951	Henryk Sienkiewicz Mervyn Le Roy (Dir.)	Quo Vadis (fiction, Polish original) film version, starring Peter Ustinov
79	eruption of the Vesuv: destruction of Pompeii and Herculaneum	1834 2003	E. Bulwer Lytton Robert Harris	The Last Days of Pompeii (fiction) Pompeii (fiction)
81–96	Emperor Domitian: ruthless rule and incest rumours	1626	Philip Massinger	The Roman Actor (stage-play)
161–80	Emperor Marcus Aurelius	1776–88	Edward Gibbon	The History of the Decline and Fall of the Roman Empire (historiogr.)
180–92	Emperor Commodus, his son	1964 2004	Anthony Mann (Dir.) Ridley Scott (Dir.)	Fall of the Roman Empire (film) Gladiator (film)

Roman tragedies from the Renaissance are Shakespeare's *Julius Caesar* and *Antony and Cleopatra*.

The action of *Julius Caesar* (1599) takes place within a short span of time (44–42 B.C.), but one of great importance, as it marks the turning point between Republic and Monarchy, or – as characters in the play suggest – the point where a state of liberty might be turned into tyranny and despotism. With its **debate on liberty**, Shakespeare's play strikes a key note which will be heard more often in the following centuries (see chap. 3.2.1). For his play, Shakespeare assembled a large cast that consists, in addition to the historical elite of military leaders and statesmen, of individuals such as the Soothsayer and the poet Cinna, and also of the people in the streets of Rome, who function as some sort of chorus. Yet Rome is no real democracy: the common people are deceived and bribed, and willing to be treated like that. The overall conception that transpires as a result is that History is made by Great Men: in this play, Shakespeare has allowed only minor roles for women. C. Julius Caesar, as a famous and likewise ambiguous character in history, presented Shakespeare with a whole range of complex options. Because of his many-faceted personality and fallibilities, Caesar could be presented

|Fig. 2.6

Brutus and the Ghost of Caesar (Engraving by Edward Scriven from a painting by R. Westall, 1802)

1. as the man of noble birth who fought for the popular party, as the statesman who re-organised Rome (e.g. through the Julian Calendar), and as an extra-ordinarily successful military strategist;
2. as the power politician and imperialist: the conqueror of Gaul, the invader of Britain as well as Egypt, and the victor in the Civil War who was tempted to accept the crown (and while he did not become a monarch himself, still left his name as a title for kings and emperors to come);
3. from a personal angle: as the man who once fell for Cleopatra, and as a mighty man who suffered from the falling sickness, i.e. epileptic fits.

Whereas successive dramatists such as Joseph Addison, G.B. Shaw and Howard Brenton decided for one of the latter two possibilities, all three of them are represented in Shakespeare's play in which Caesar however features only as the title character. The real protagonist is Marcus Junius Brutus, who contrasts with two further important characters, namely his fellow-conspirator Cassius and their opponent Mark Antony. And yet, the judgment on Brutus as an 'honourable man' is inextricably linked to one's view of Caesar. If Caesar (whose offices included that of 'dictator') is seen as a tyrant, then his assassination can be justified as being 'honourable', and in the best interest of the state. However, if the conspirators cannot state their case convincingly, their deed will bring (in the understanding of Renaissance England) just that disorder and calamity which they decry. Therefore, how is the historical subject matter presented?

Shakespeare's principal source is Plutarch's complementary series of *Lives of the Noble Grecians and Romans* in the translation of Sir Thomas North (1579), and *Julius Caesar* can be said to be an adaptation of Plutarch's biographies for the stage. Shakespeare closely follows, concentrates and compresses Plutarch's account that is spread over the individual biographies of Caesar, Brutus and Antony. However, Shakespeare can also be seen to deviate from received historical wisdom and to alter events when it suits his dramatic purposes better: at the beginning of the play, he brings the festival of the Lupercal and the Ides of March together, although they actually are a month apart; and the battle of Philippi at the end of the play "was actually two battles, the deaths of Cassius and Brutus separated by 20 days rather than the few hours which seem to intervene in the play" (Dobson and Wells 2001: 229). In terms of genre, Shakespeare chose to cast his play on an episode from Roman history into the form of a tragedy, and thus chose a Classical form for a Classical subject matter. This brings up, again, the question of the tragic hero: Caesar and/ or Brutus? Indeed, the play shows two climactic scenes, and not just one, as the fall of Brutus (in the fifth act) follows upon the fall of Caesar (3.1). The **Forum speeches** made at Caesar's funeral occur between those two climactic developments. Those monologues of Brutus and of Antony are Shakespeare's own invention, and they are regarded as one of his masterpieces. With the staging of their debate, Shakespeare was to shape cultural memory, and not only to re-enact it. (See Table 5 for more detail.) In addition, several features of Shakespeare's Roman tragedy – namely murder, blood and the corpse (on stage and as a verbal image), the ghost scenes and Antony's role as avenger of Caesar – may have reminded an Elizabethan audience of the special Renaissance form of the revenge tragedy (see chap. 2.2.3). Conformity

Table 5 William Shakespeare, *Julius Caesar*, 3.2: the Forum Speeches

	Brutus (3.2.12–53, one pause and a longer interruption)	Antony (3.2.57–242, several pauses = interruptions)
form	prose (12–39) blank verse (47–53)	blank verse throughout
pose	a Roman patriot, and a champion of liberty	a friend of Caesar, mourning him "I come to bury Caesar, not to praise him" (66) "I am no orator, as Brutus is, But [...] a plain blunt man That love my friend" (207–9)
prominent rhetorical features	parallelism (= syntactic repetition) rhetorical questions	Caesar's corpse and mantle as 'props': effect verbal repetition ("honourable men") irony ("honourable men") rhetorical question as finish
rhetorical structure/ line of argument	act of justification, asking public for verdict love for Caesar vs. love for Rome respect for death for his Caesar's virtues ambitious will and glory (= tyranny) is prepared to die under the same law	Caesar ambitious? – no, he was generous (providing money and relief for the poor), and he refused the crown (69–93) reminds the Romans of their former feelings towards Caesar (94–119) Caesar's testament: a document of his generosity (120–51, 225–42) Caesar's end: a bloody spectacle < the mantle and the corpse (160–88) treason Antony himself is not ambitious (200–20)

with an 'Elizabethan World Picture' may be seen in the fact that disorder is finally overcome, and that poetic justice necessitates the death of conspirators, but also includes their eulogy.

In the light of what was said about Caesar's ambivalence and the importance of the political theme, the **performance history** of *Julius Caesar* is of special interest. Individual productions of *Julius Caesar* have accentuated certain parts of plot and characterisation, and may thereby have changed Shakespeare's original meaning. To stage the assassination of a monarchic ruler was already difficult in the times of Shakespeare and of Queen Elizabeth, and did not become easier after the execution of King Charles I by the Puritans. Yet perhaps because the story was well known from school, the play was popular in the seventeenth century. As was said before, the evaluation of Brutus hangs in the balance, as it depends on one's view of Caesar. Antony, on the other hand, appears in Shakespeare's text not only as a loyal follower of Caesar and in every sense endowed with the purest motives, but also as an opportunist politician with a sense of power. In the 'proscription scene' (4.1), he strikes a deal with the other members of the new triumvirate, Octavius Caesar and Lepidus, and thereby sacrifices his own nephew for political purposes. This scene disappeared from productions on the London stages in the nineteenth century, between 1812 (John Philip Kemble at Covent Carden) and c.1915 (William Bridges-Adams at the Shakespeare Memorial Theatre). In the early twentieth century, *Julius Caesar* gained renewed interest. The production directed by Orson Welles in New York in 1937, which was subtitled "Death of a Dictator", stressed the parallels to the contemporary Fascist dictators and presented Caesar as such – and thereby exonerated Brutus. The post-war film version of 1953 is particularly strong in its representation of the Forum speeches (where director Joseph L. Mankiewicz pitted actors James Mason and Marlon Brando against each other).

Antony and Cleopatra
"[N]ext to the story of Julius Caesar, the story of Antony and Cleopatra was perhaps the prerogative Roman theme among the dramatists of the sixteenth century", Munro MacCallum wrote in his early, but seminal study on *Shakespeare's Roman Plays* (1910: 309–10). The general interest in this historical love affair has never decreased. To an English audience, Egypt meant an even more exotic, luxurious, and decadent setting than Rome, and thus gave dramatists (and film directors) a good opportunity to produce a costume piece together with a moral. The combination of a power struggle with a love interest made for a suspenseful plot, and in Cleopatra – an alluring woman whose physical charms first enchanted Julius Caesar and then Marcus Antonius – history provided an attractive specimen of a *femme fatale*. Cleopatra is the rare example of a woman in the political arena, and in order to survive in this arena, the pharaoh-queen had to fall back on her personal charms. This was done first to secure her throne (with the help of Julius Caesar) against her rival brother, and later to defend her realm and her rule (with the help of Mark Antony). In the present age, her fate may have acquired an additional interest, as Cleopatra is a potential symbol with regard to issues of race, culture and power:

► Cleopatra symbolises the non-Roman (and possibly non-White) ethnic groups;

- she stands for the ancient culture of Egypt and of Greek Hellenism, which spread to Egypt just like her own royal family
- even as a queen, she is part of all those who were overcome by Imperial Roman rule.

The last point is also obvious with regard to our image of Cleopatra, which depends first of all on accounts written by Roman historians. With them, she generally had a bad press. Roman historians saw her as a *femme fatale* who led otherwise virtuous Roman generals astray, to follow personal interests, passion and lust rather than reason and virtue – and virtue here included the military and political interests of Rome. That our image of Cleopatra today is a more complex one is largely due to the efforts of playwrights such as Shakespeare, Dryden and Shaw.

The story of *Antony and Cleopatra* (see Table 4) is a continuation of events related in *Julius Caesar*: both plays together form Shakespeare's Roman sequence. The compression of a greater span of time (some ten years) led in consequence to a continuous change of setting, which is a peculiar hallmark of Shakespeare's play. However, such change was criticised in the times of Neoclassicism, and it presents difficulties for stage productions of the play even today. In the medium of film, on the other hand, such as in *Cleopatra* (1964) with Elizabeth Taylor and Richard Burton, such an abundance of distinct and possibly exotic locations is no longer an obstacle, but rather has special appeal. A comparison in great detail of Shakespeare's relationship to Plutarch, and a discussion of his deviation from this source in particular, can be found in Thomas (1989: 93–119). He improves upon MacCallum (1910: 335–39), who had pointed out, though, that Antony's military glamour in Shakespeare's play rests in part on the fact that the dramatist omitted Antony's military failures. Minor omissions from the historical record concern both Cleopatra's child with Julius Caesar (Caesarion) and her children with Antony, and also Antony's children with Octavia: the effect is a concentration of the attention on the two lovers. Compared with Plutarch's account, Shakespeare's Antony and Cleopatra are made more sympathetic (by glossing over their faults). Octavius, on the other hand, is presented as more calculating and more manipulative, and as one who never shares a joke or enjoys a personal friendship. Among the minor characters, the qualities of his sister Octavia, and her loyalty to Antony, her unloving husband, are painted over, while Enobarbus, whom Plutarch mentions just in passing, is developed into a recognisable character by Shakespeare. Enobarbus's account of Cleopatra's arrival in a splendid barge at her first meeting with Antony (2.2.198–225) – a passage where Shakespeare used exoticism to great effect – is taken nearly word for word from Plutarch. In terms of **race**, Shakespeare had a lasting effect on the common perception of Cleopatra, who in all historical probability was White (she descended from the Greek House of the Ptolemies), yet is said by Shakespeare's Philo to have "a tawny front [... like] a gypsy" (1.1.6, 10), while she considers herself to be Black (1.5.27–28). In other matters, Shakespeare did not resort (like Dryden) to a simplified characterisation in black and white. Paul Cantor denied for Shakespeare any simple equation of Antony and Cleopatra with love, and Octavius with politics: these two themes were combined, rather (see Cantor 1976: 127), as the protagonists could not make a difference: "Their inability to keep their public and private roles clearly separate is in fact almost a defining characteristic of Antony and Cleopatra" (Cantor 1976: 194). Neither should the audience make a distinction between their behaviour in public and in private, and it is here that the **theme of liberty vs. despotism** comes up once again. In Cantor's words:

> the element common to their love and rule is an attempt to do without law. [...] It is characteristic of Antony and Cleopatra as rulers that [...] they never appeal to law or custom in making or announcing their decisions. [...] The same absoluteness that makes Antony and Cleopatra look glorious as lovers makes them appear despotic as rulers, even though they pursue the same goal in rule that they do in love, namely, to bring reality into accord with their own desires, to have their world exactly the way they want it, without compromise (Cantor 1976: 201–2).

Indeed, compared to the "loveless marriage" of Antony and Octavia, the interethnic and transcultural relationship between the Roman and the Egyptian is a "marriageless love", and moreover a "marriage-in-death" (Cantor 1976: 158, 169). In this way, the lovers are also opposed to **Roman custom and culture.** Seen in a different way, this lack of typically Roman traits in the behaviour of Shakespeare's characters may also explain the enduring appeal of the love-story that is at the bottom of the play.

In this respect, too, Shakespeare's *Antony and Cleopatra* makes for good comparison with two further 'Cleopatra plays': Dryden's *All for Love* (1677) as well as Shaw's *Caesar and Cleopatra* (1901/06).

Tragedies

| 2.2.3

With regard to tragedy as a dramatic representation of a serious action that turns out disastrously for the protagonist, Renaissance playwrights had to begin anew. Aristotle's *Poetics*, the Classical Greek primer of genre theory in this respect, had been available again in Latin only from 1481, and it is uncertain, for instance, whether it came to Shakespeare's knowledge. Because of their Christian basis, the religious plays of the Middle Ages offered no conceptual model for the representation of individual tragic 'fate' or 'fortune' (which in themselves are non-Christian concepts). The term tragedy even had lost its original meaning, as it had sometimes been applied to verse narratives such as Chaucer's "The Monk's Tale". Such 'tragedies' translated into the Renaissance via compilations of exemplary stories from high life, as in Giovanni Boccaccio's *De Casibus Virorum Illustrium* (completed 1373), in John Lydgate's *The Fall of Princes* (1431–38) and in its continuation in *The Mirror for Magistrates* (first edited by William Baldwin in 1559 and then continuously enlarged). From such tales of the rise and fall of mighty persons, the image of Fortune's Wheel stuck, and the related type of **De Casibus tragedies** developed, of which Marlowe's tragedies and Shakespeare's *Macbeth* are good examples.

|Fig. 2.7
Fortune's Wheel: book illustr., 1467

Christopher Marlowe (1564–93), who shared his year of birth with Shakespeare and his last lodgings with the dramatist Thomas Kyd, enjoyed only a brief life whose incomplete record, just like Shakespeare's, left enough room for later critics and novelists to fill it with their imagination (see chap. 5.3.6). Within a few years, Marlowe produced a series of tragedies that impressed contemporary audiences by their overreaching protagonists (acted by Edward Alleyn, the star actor of the Lord Admiral's Men) and by a use of blank verse that until then was unheard of on stage. Taken together, this made up for Marlowe's loosely constructed plots. *Tamburlaine the Great* (1587/88) is a historical tragedy that stretches over two full-length plays: the first charts the rise to power of this fourteenth-century nomadic shepherd and Mongol warrior, who scores victories against Persian, Turkish and Egyp-

|Fig. 2.8
Portrait, supposedly of Christopher Marlowe, 1585

tian rulers. The second play depicts the end of Tamburlaine's love to the beautiful Zenocrates, and then his fall. Both in his monologues full of pathos and in his various acts of cruelty, Tamburlaine appears as a monomaniac character who proudly says of himself that he aspires to

> [...] triumph over all the world:
> I hold the Fates bound fast in iron chains,
> And with my hand turn Fortune's wheel about;
> And sooner shall the sun fall from his sphere
> Than Tamburlaine be slain or overcome. (*Tamburlaine Part I*, 1.2)

Such aspirations are likewise characteristic of the protagonists in *The Jew of Malta* (see below) and *The Tragical History of Doctor Faustus*, a play that Marlowe must have composed at any time between 1588 and his death in 1593, and which is extant in two versions: the A-Text in 13 scenes (printed 1604) and the B-Text in 20 scenes (1614) which later editors divided into five acts. Like Goethe's *Faust*, Marlowe's tragedy in blank verse and in prose (reserved for its farcical scenes) transforms a German popular legend that appeared in print in 1587 into the portrait of an individual whose boundless thirst for knowledge (and the power derived from such knowledge) oversteps the limits set by a Christian world order. This is pointed out to the audience by a Chorus that speaks a prologue and an epilogue to the play, which sees Faustus enter into a pact with the Devil: enticed by Mephastophilis (as spelt in the A-Text), Faustus sells his soul to Lucifer to learn Black Magic, but is then deceived. Marlowe's rhetorical gifts come out best in Faustus's soliloquies – when he is first seen alone in his study, and later when he contemplates his last hour on Earth – as well as in Faustus's monologue praising the beauty of Helen of Troy.

"There is no such thing as Shakespearian Tragedy: there are only Shakespearian tragedies", the critic Kenneth Muir stated famously in 1972. (Muir's quip at the title of A.C. Bradley's seminal study of 1904 is cited in the comprehensive introduction of Dieter Mehl, 1983: 10. For preceding criticism of Shakespeare's tragedies over the ages, see my chaps. 3.2.1, 3.4.3 and 4.2.1.) Indeed, Shakespeare's tragedies – unlike Marlowe's – cannot be said to follow a common pattern and, rather than being lumped together, are therefore more usefully compared to similar plays by other writers. *Macbeth* is a good example of a tragedy of the *De Casibus* type,

Fig. 2.9

Macbeth seeing the Ghost of Banquo by Théodore Chassériau (1819–56)

and moreover one that has suggested itself for classroom usage because of its shortness and regular design. After the cycle of English history plays had run to its end, the new Stuart King James I may have been pleased to see – supposedly in a first production at court in 1606 – Shakespeare's play about a Scottish King: *Macbeth* catered to the King's personal interest in witchcraft and demonology, and it addressed him directly in the witches' conjuration of eight Scottish Kings – his ancestors (4.1.112–24). Driven by the ambiguous prophecies of those three witches, by his own will to power and by the encouragement of his no less ambitious wife (for which communion Bradley coined the term "*egoïsme à deux*", 1905: 350), Macbeth turns from loyal general to regicidal usurper of the Scottish throne. "To be thus is nothing, but to be safely thus" (3.1.47): to stay in power, Macbeth must continue murdering anyone he regards as a rival, including his former fellow general Banquo and the entire family of Macduff. Macbeth's monologues and soliloquies show him torn between a cold conscience ("I am in blood/Stepp'd in so far, that, should I wade no more,/Returning were as tedious as go o'er", 3.4.135–37) and the foreboding that he will never again sleep peacefully (2.2.34–42). He is haunted by Banquo's Ghost indeed (Banquet Scene, 3.4) yet keeps on fighting to his end, while Lady Macbeth descends from manliness ("Unsex me here", 1.5.41) into madness before she takes her own life. *Macbeth*, like *Richard III*, is a study in Evil, but there is a limit to the analogies between the Scottish King and that Son of York: Macbeth is a man susceptible to the persuasions of Evil, but he is no Vice. There is a fight in his conscience (memorably expressed in his soliloquies) between scruples and ambition, Fair and Foul. If there is a moral to what is no morality play, it is the simple message better to play fair, not foul, as the price paid for the latter could be the destruction of many lives – at first those of others, and in the end one's own.

In *Macbeth*, there is a certain overlapping of features from *De Casibus* tragedies and those of the Senecan type. The influence of Seneca (c.4 B.C.–A.D. 65), whose tragedies appeared in English translation in 1581, generally makes itself felt in sensational stories of murder and revenge, incest and adultery. Senecan five-act tragedy is moreover characterised by a dominance of *telling* over *showing*, as is evident from the use of epic features such as Chorus

Seneca's Impact upon Revenge Tragedies

parts, extended monologues and messenger's reports. *Gorboduc* (1561), the collaboration between Thomas Sackville (1536–1608) and Thomas Norton (1532–83), is the first proper example of a Senecan and blank verse tragedy in English. The action of this five-act play – which centres on the ill-advised decision of the legendary British King Gorboduc to divide his realm during his lifetime – looks ahead to Shakespeare's *King Lear*. Each act sets in with a summary of the action in form of a **dumb show** or pantomime, and ends in a Chorus's interpretation. Seneca's impact is also felt in the mother of all Renaissance **revenge tragedies**: *The Spanish Tragedy* by Thomas Kyd (1558–94), which was produced and published in 1592 (but composed six years earlier), tells the story of a father's revenge for the murder of his son (Horatio). The Ghost of an earlier victim (Don Andrea), together with the personification of 'Revenge', shares in the function of a Chorus that comments upon each act. The appearance of a ghost, an avenger (Horatio's father Hieronymo) and a Vice-like villain (Lorenzo), in combination with such typical features as the protracted process of revenge, scenes of madness and a play within the play, are to be found again in Shakespeare's *Hamlet* (which tells of a son's revenge for the murder of his father). The sensational potential of such stories as well as the dilemma that blood revenge is sanctioned neither by Christian doctrine nor the state, is exploited further in *Antonio's Revenge* (1600), a play by John Marston (1576–1634) that shows numerous affinities to *Hamlet*. One could moreover mention *The Revenger's Tragedy* (printed in 1607 and now ascribed to Thomas Middleton rather than Cyril Tourneur) as well as *The White Devil* (1608) and *The Duchess of Malfi* (c.1614), both by John Webster (c.1580–1625). In these last revenge tragedies, there is a return to the spectacularly drastic scenes of brutality that were characteristic of Shakespeare's earlier *Titus Andronicus* (1594), but now those acts of brutality were committed *on stage*, in view of the audience. The revenge tragedy remained a prominent period piece – it still informs *'Tis Pity She's a Whore* (1633), a tragedy by John Ford (1586–?1640) about an incestuous love between brother and sister – but just like the English history play, this genre died out well before the end of the Renaissance.

As *Hamlet* (1599/1600) is one of the best-researched pieces of world literature, it may suffice here to comment upon three features only, namely Hamlet's motivation, his famous monologues and soliloquies, and the meta-dramatic qualities of Shakespeare's play. Proper revenge tragedies, just like successive eighteenth-century Gothic romances, are usually located in a Catholic and Mediterranean setting. To make for an even greater contrast with English moderation, such a setting was moreover associated (in a common stereotype that looked for analogies between climate and character) with hot-blooded people, as passionate in love as cruel in murder. Therefore, as a revenge tragedy, *Hamlet* is an exception: because it is set in Northern and not Southern Europe, and because the Prince of Denmark seldom acts as heedlessly as in his stabbing of Polonius (in the Closet Scene, 3.4), thereby unwittingly killing the father of Ophelia, who is in love with him. For this act of rashness alone, Hamlet cannot be said to be an irresolute person. Still, he does not avenge himself on his sly uncle, King Claudius, when he chances upon him alone immediately after Claudius's confession of the fratricide committed on Hamlet's father (Prayer Scene, 3.3). However, here as elsewhere, there is indeed reason in Hamlet's 'madness'. Hamlet wants to make sure that his revenge sends the murderer directly to Hell, therefore (and that is the explicit logic of his thinking) it were unwise to attack the culprit in a possible act of repentance – in a knock on Heaven's door. Hamlet knows that his father, just because he was killed before he could be absolved from his 'imperfections' (1.5.79), was denied entrance into Heaven and forced into the intermediate existence of a Ghost, in which state he had called on his son to avenge himself on callous Claudius (1.5). A second grievance nurtured by both Hamlet Senior and Junior against the new King and Queen Gertrude is their 'incestuous' marriage: very rashly (albeit innocent of the murder), the Queen married her former husband's brother. From a psychoanalytical point of view, the nature of her son's hurt feelings was interpreted as an Oedipal desire, first by Freud himself and then by his biographer Ernest Jones in the 1940s. This view inspired the actor and director Laurence Olivier in his 1948 adaptation of the stage-play for the screen, which moreover depicts Elsinore Castle as a claustrophobic setting in black and white.

'**Comic relief**' – a term that was first applied to the Porter Scene following upon the regicide in *Macbeth* – is provided by the Graveyard Scene of *Hamlet* (5.1), but only as long as the Prince

| Fig. 2.10
Edwin Booth as
Hamlet, c.1870

Hamlet's Monologues
and Soliloquies

talks to the clownish gravedigger. (He prepares the burial of Ophelia, who was seen deranged at first and found drowned later.)
Then, in an emblematic moment within the same scene, Hamlet
takes the skull of Yorick, the former court-jester, from the grave
and talks to his friend Horatio upon death and decay. For the
audience, this ties in with Hamlet's earlier thoughts on suicide
within his series of six monologues. Those long speeches – called
soliloquies when the character speaks his mind not in the presence
of others, but when being alone – have different functions (see
Clemen 1964 and Pfister 2001), and frequently, like in this case,
they can stand as a blank verse poem on their own (which is another way of saying that they are altogether less well integrated
into the dramatic action than their counterparts in *Macbeth*). In
a first soliloquy (1.2.129–58), Hamlet already touches upon 'self-
slaughter' when he criticises the rashness of his mother's remarriage ("Frailty, thy name is woman"). Suicide is then the topic of
his most famous soliloquy: "To be, or not to be, that is the question" (3.1.56–88). To enhance an understanding of the nuances
of Hamlet's argument, Shakespeare's artful blank verse may
profitably (albeit momentarily) be transposed into free verse. The
answer Hamlet gives to himself is that it was "the dread of something after death/the undiscover'd country,/from whose bourn/
no traveller returns, [that] puzzles the will" (ll. 78–80) and that
ultimately decides against taking one's own life.

Table 6 "To Be, or Not To Be" Transposed: Argument and Rhetoric
Structure of Hamlet's Soliloquy (Shakespeare, *Hamlet*, 3.1.56–88)

To be, or not to be, that is the question:	topic: suicide as alternative
Whether 'tis nobler in the mind to suffer the slings and arrows of <u>outrageous</u> fortune, or to take arms against a sea of troubles and by opposing end them.	capricious
To die – to sleep, no more; and by a sleep to say we end the heart-ache and the thousand natural shocks that flesh is heir to: 'tis a <u>consummation</u> devoutly to be wish'd.	pro: death as end of suffering final ending
To die, to sleep; to sleep, perchance to dream –	contra: fear of the 'after-life'

ay, there's the <u>rub</u>: For in that sleep of death what dreams may come, when we have <u>shuffled off</u> this mortal coil, must give us pause – there's the respect that makes <u>calamity</u> of so <u>long</u> life.	<u>obstacle</u> <u>got rid of</u> <u>disaster</u> <u>long-lived</u>
For who would bear the whips and scorns of <u>time</u>, th'oppressor's wrong, the proud man's contumely, the pangs of <u>dispriz'd</u> love, the law's delay, the insolence of office, and the spurns that patient merit of th'unworthy takes when he himself might his <u>quietus</u> make with a bare <u>bodkin</u>?	<u>our time</u> <u>unvalued</u> <u>quittance</u> <u>stiletto</u>
Who would <u>fardels</u> bear, to grunt and sweat under a weary life, but that the dread of something after death the undiscover'd country, from whose <u>bourn</u> no traveller returns, puzzles the will and makes us rather bear those ills we have than fly to others that we know not of?	<u>burdens</u> <u>boundary</u>
Thus conscience does make cowards of us all, and thus the <u>native</u> hue of resolution is sicklied o'er with the <u>pale</u> cast of thought, and enterprises of great <u>pitch</u> and moment with this regard turn awry and lose the name of action.	 <u>(red)</u> <u>(white)</u> <u>height</u>

In such pondering of suicide as a viable alternative and as a way of escape, in his (unquestioning, this time) stance towards blood revenge, and in his pessimistic view on life-after-death, Hamlet seems not much troubled by Christian doctrine. Hamlet's melancholic disposition, together with a medieval or Elizabethan worldview, comes out well in a prose monologue that culminates as follows:

> What piece of work is a man, how noble in reason, how infinite in faculties, in form and moving how admirable, in action how like an angel, in

apprehension how like a god: the beauty of the world, the paragon of animals – and yet, to me, what is this quintessence of dust? Man delights not me – nor woman neither (2.2.303–09).

The pendulum swings even further to the negative in a later soliloquy, which sets out from the proposition that Man was "A beast, no more." (4.4.35). The two remaining speeches – a soliloquy that aptly sets in with the phrase "Now I am alone" (2.2.543–601) and a monologue addressed to Horatio (3.2.57–74) – are more deeply interwoven into the action, as they address the role of the play within the play in Hamlet's plan of revenge.

Meta-Dramatic Elements

In *Hamlet*, Shakespeare's recurrent theme of appearance vs. reality, which includes Hamlet's feigned madness, too, moreover expresses itself in meta-dramatic form. The arrival of a company of strolling players occasions the characters in the scene to refer to contemporary stage practice (2.2.336 ff.). The fashion of boy actors is the topic of Hamlet's conversation with courtiers Rosencrantz and Guildenstern (both of whom will reappear as death-marked characters in Tom Stoppard's stage debut of 1966, see chap. 5.2.3). Afterwards Shakespeare, tongue in cheek, has Polonius spell out the full variety of dramatic genres imaginable: "tragedy, comedy, history, pastoral, pastoral-comical, historical-pastoral, tragical-historical, tragical-comical-historical-pastoral, scene individable, or poem unlimited" (2.2.392–96). The scene is rounded off by the principal Player's rehearsal of a stilted blank verse passage based upon a Classical legend which Shakespeare may have intended to sound either serious or satiric (2.2.448ff.; see the editor's note 1982: 478–81). The touring company of actors becomes part of the Prince's plan to confront the King with his own deed, and thus to denounce him in public, by presenting him with a stage-play that shows obvious similarities to the murder of Hamlet's father (3.2). The play within the play that deals with "The Murder of Gonzago" is entitled *The Mousetrap* (which gave a cue to Agatha Christie for her long-running criminal play, see chap. 5.2.1), and it has the intended effect: the King, 'frighted with false fire', leaves before the end of the performance. Interestingly, the production mimics Elizabethan stage-practice in that the staged play is preceded by a Prologue figure and by a dumb show with an advance summary of the action.

Marlowe's Jew of Malta as a Machiavellian Villain

Outside the revenge tragedy proper, revenge as a theme is noticeable, too, in Shakespeare's *Richard III* and *Julius Caesar* (see chap. 2.2.2), in *Romeo and Juliet* as well as in *Macbeth*, and moreover in Marlowe's *The Famous Tragedy of the Rich Jew of Malta*. The similarities between Marlowe's tragedy and Shakespeare's tragicomedy *The Merchant of Venice* (see chap. 2.2.4) are explained with common sources (Italian novellas, and a play that is lost). *The Jew of Malta* was quite popular when first produced in 1589 or 1590 as well as in its 1633 revision by the dramatist Thomas Heywood. In the play, Barabas (the title character) seeks revenge for the confiscation of his wealth by the governor of Malta to meet the Turkish demands for tribute, and – knowing no bounds to his wrath – turns into a serial killer. He murders, first, most of the guests at a banquet, including the Christian lover of his daughter Abigail, then poisons her after she turned her back on him and went into a nun's convent, before he goes on to kill two monks to whom Abigail had confessed her father's crime. Subsequently, Barabas manages the take-over of Malta by the Turks, who make him governor, whereof he avenges himself on the Turks, until he is finally found out and dies in his own trap. *The Jew of Malta* shows all the qualities as well as the loose construction of Marlowe's work, and it is moreover characterised by an anti-Semitism that relied upon the dissatisfaction of contemporary English audiences with the material success of Jewish moneylenders. Such audiences may have relished the play's anti-Catholicism, too, which is related to the appearance of the Italian political philosopher Machiavelli as the person who speaks the prologue. Through *Il Principe* (1532), his treatise on the pragmatics of power, Niccolò Machiavelli (1469–1527) became in Elizabethan times a household name for diabolic nihilism, amorality and evil – qualities that are found in Marlowe's Barabas as well as in Shakespeare's portrait of Richard III.

"In fair Verona, where we lay our scene,/[…]/Where civil blood makes civil hands unclean./[…]/A pair of star-crossed lovers take their life,/[…]/Doth with their death bury their parents' strife." In these first lines from the Prologue to *Romeo and Juliet* (1.1.2–8, first printed in 1597), Shakespeare does several things at once. The advance summary of the action is modelled on the convention associated with Elizabethan dumb shows (see above). Here, the lines come from a Chorus who, together with the theme of blood revenge, is reminiscent of the Senecan tradition. The Chorus reappears to introduce the second act, likewise with an

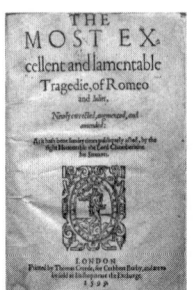

Fig. 2.11

Title page of William Shakespeare's play *Romeo and Juliet* (1599)

English sonnet – an Elizabethan form of love poetry in which Shakespeare the sonneteer had a hand himself (see chap. 2.3.2). Critics have looked for more sonnets hidden in the text of the play, though Shakespeare refrained from using the Chorus after this stage, perhaps because he had second thoughts on the play's overall design. (The short epilogue is spoken by Prince Escalus.) The stark contrast between the nature of the 'star-crossed lovers' (a positive image taken from astrology) and their unavoidably unhappy ending makes for the heartrending effect of this romantic tragedy. Like so many of Shakespeare's tragedies and comedies, this one, too, is based upon Italian novellas in French or English translation, and moreover an **adaptation** for the stage of Arthur Brooke's epic entitled *The Tragical History of Romeo and Juliet* (1562). In the world of Elizabethan theatre with its tight production schedules, and generally in pre-Romantic times, such imitation or adaptation that brought an improvement was appreciated rather than scolded for a lack of inventiveness and originality, and did not count as plagiarism. For his *Romeo and Juliet*, Shakespeare devised a symmetrical constellation of characters: on the one side we find the Montagues, with Romeo as the only son and heir, together with his cousin Benvolio and with Balthazar as Romeo's servant; on the other side the Capulets, with their only daughter Juliet, her Nurse, and Juliet's fiery cousin Tybalt. The patrician nobles of Verona are situated between both enemy camps, ranging from Prince Escalus over County Paris (who nurtures an unrequited love for Juliet, and therefore is Romeo's rival) down to witty Mercutio. Among the minor characters – citizens, soldiers, watchmen, servicemen and musicians – the churchmen Friar Laurence and Friar John stand out. Rosaline, Romeo's unattainable beloved before he passionately falls in love with Juliet, should be noted as an off-stage character with a contrastive function. From a legal point of view, the plot hinges upon three cases of manslaughter – Mercutio dies in a fight instigated by Tybalt, whom Romeo then stabs in retaliation (3.1) before he later sends his rival Paris to death in another fight (5.3) – followed by a simulated death and two suicides: when Juliet's feigned death is taken by Romeo for a real one, he poisons himself, whereupon she takes her life when she awakes to find him dead beside her (5.3). What elevates this tragedy of love above such suspenseful plot devices is its **element of romance in combination with Shakespeare's**

use of imagery, which comes out best in three scenes before the climactic finale. On the way to the Capulet's party – just before Romeo first chances upon Juliet – Mercutio delivers his **Queen Mab Speech** (1.4.51–93). This exuberant monologue about a Fairy Queen (with a pun on a second meaning, that of a promiscuous woman or a prostitute) is extraneous to the plot of this tragedy, though its supernatural imagery ties in perfectly well with the fairy world of *A Midsummer Night's Dream* (a comedy which Shakespeare supposedly wrote at about the same time). The famous **Balcony Scene** (2.1.44ff.), in which Romeo successfully woos Juliet, sets in with an extended cosmological comparison. Finally, the scene on the morning after the consummation of their love starts off with what is perhaps Shakespeare's most memorable specimen of animal imagery – "It was the nightingale, and not the lark,/That pierced the fearful hollow of thine ear." (3.5.2–3) – reserved for the point of dawn where their only night of love turns into one of their last days alive. The tragic lovers have lived on in adaptations for the stage and for the screen (Franco Zeffirelli's 1968 film makes for a good comparison with Baz Luhrmann's 1997 version) as well as in the musical *West Side Story*, which premiered on Broadway in 1957 before it was made into a movie, too (in 1961, again with Stephen Sondheim's lyrics and Leonard Bernstein's music). The star-crossed lovers easily translated from sonnet to pop song in the Dire Straits' "Romeo and Juliet" (1980).

In *Othello* (1604), we move from Verona to Venice for another romantic tragedy of passionate love, which counts alike as an early example of a **domestic tragedy**. This genre becomes more prominent in the eighteenth century, with George Lillo's *The London Merchant* (1731) and with G. E. Lessing's concept of *bürgerliches Trauerspiel* (see chap. 3.2.1). When comparable Renaissance tragedies are defined as "heavily moralized stories about unruly passions destroying ordinary families" (Braunmuller and Hattaway 1990: 113), this might just include *Romeo and Juliet*, but generally we deal with tales of adultery in a non-aristocratic setting. The anonymous blank verse tragedy *Arden of Faversham* (first printed 1592), whose stage realism contrasts starkly with Shakespeare's verbal virtuosity, dramatises a true case of 1551, in which an adulterous love triangle ended in the death of all concerned: after several unsuccessful attempts which are part of the tragedy,

Othello as a Domestic Tragedy

Alice Arden and her lover Mosbie manage to murder her (generally less sympathetic) husband Thomas, only to be caught and executed. In *A Woman Killed with Kindness* (1603), the prolific dramatist Thomas Heywood (?1573–1641), who later had a hand in the 1633 revival of Marlowe's *Jew of Malta*, started from a similar *précis* but ended in heavy moralising: when John Francford returns his wife Ann's extra-marital affair with kindness, she repents her adultery that she had committed out of weakness rather than passionate love, and ends her life in a hunger strike against her sinful self. In *Women Beware Women* (c.1625) by Thomas Middleton (1580–1627), the villain in the piece is a woman called Livia. In the main plot, she takes an active part in the seduction of a young woman; and in a sub-plot, she moreover enables her brother and her niece to start an incestuous affair. What is even more provocative, in terms of sexual morality, is that in both cases, the young women are hardly to be called innocent. Once more, like in his satirical comedy *A Game at Chess* (1624), Middleton used chess as a metaphor and as a plot device. In *Women Beware Women*, Middleton moreover combined domestic realism with other stage conventions: towards the ending, a **court masque** (that is, a highly stylised and allegorical play) functions as a play within the play that, just like in a revenge tragedy, ends in killing off the guilty part of the cast. *The Changeling* (1622), a collaborative effort of Middleton and William Rowley (c.1585–1626 or 1642), has been compared to *Othello*, both because of similarities of plot and its similar necessity of development. *The Changeling* is set in Spain, in Alicante, where the governor's daughter Beatrice attempts to get rid of her fiancé in order to live her passionate love to a Spanish knight. Her fiancé is indeed killed by her father's scheming servant De Flores, who is infatuated with Beatrice and blackmails her into loving him. Beatrice tries to cover this up by sending her maid in her stead into her lover's bed, but her bluff is called. Afterwards, De Flores kills first Beatrice and then himself.

Shakespeare's *Othello* is a story of a great love across the ethnic divide that ends tragically because the machinations of a villain turn the husband's pride of honour into murderous jealousy. Three features of Shakespeare's tragedy are of special interest: (1) the issue of race, (2) the role of the villain in the piece, and (3) Shakespeare's verbal imagery. (1) **Race**: it is not only Postcolonialist Critics that have been interested in Othello's Otherness, and in the exact meaning of Shakespeare's subtitle "The Moor of Venice" (see Bradley 1905: 198–206; Shakespeare 1999a: 14–31). A closer reading reveals a greater ambivalence than in the case of Aaron, the 'coal-black' Moor in *Titus Andronicus*. Othello's characterisation as "black" (1.3.291, 3.3.267 and 390) and, derogatively, as "thicklips" (1.1.65) contrasts with other references to "Barbary" and "Barbarian" (1.1.110, 1.3.356), which may be taken as a hint at another possible meaning of Moor in the sense of Arab or Berber (as in Salman Rushdie's 1995 novel *The Moor's Last Sigh*). What is at stake here is the degree of Otherness, and therefore possibly offensiveness, that is seen in the love relationship between Othello and Desdemona. The Romantic poet and critic S.T. Coleridge is on record with the racist remark that "it would be something monstrous to conceive this beautiful Venetian girl falling in love with a veritable negro. It would argue a disproportionateness, a want of balance, in Desdemona", an argument that A.C. Bradley (1905: 201–02) cited yet confuted through Shakespeare's text. Moreover, Bradley rightly stressed that it is actually Desdemona's character that is a matter of concern here, and that for this reason the ethnic divide bridged by their (and particularly her) love should rather be accentuated than diminished. (2) Critical opinion was divided, too, upon **the nature of Iago** and on the extent of Othello's shortcomings. Once again, Bradley challenged Coleridge on his view of Iago as a Vice figure, and of his monologues and soliloquies as the 'motive-hunting of a motiveless malignity'. This provided Bradley with the occasion to engage in a piece of **character criticism** (1905: 207–37) for which he was in turn lambasted by F.R. Leavis (1952), a critic that is related to the text-centred **New Criticism** of the 1930s to '60s. Leavis saw no reason for a positive view of the 'noble Moor' when compared to scheming Iago. To round the story off, one should mention Stephen Greenblatt's essay on the theme of adultery in *Othello* (1980) which is typical of Greenblatt's **New Historicism** in that it is less interested in an interpretation of textual ambivalence than in a concern with contextual features and power relations in then contemporary society. (3) Over and above their function as a means of contrastive characterisation, the great number of Othello's as well as Iago's monologues and soliloquies testify to Shakespeare's **verbal dexterity** (see Shakespeare 1999a: 78–89). Ensign Iago, who makes

General Othello doubt his wife's constancy, is full of jealousy himself: over Cassio's promotion to Lieutenant and over Othello's prowess as a lover. The playwright's use of imagery in relation to Iago stretches from the Ensign's bawdiness (when referring to the sexual act as 'making the beast with two backs', 1.1.116) over his sexual jealousy and fear to have been cuckolded by his superior ("I hate the moor/And it is thought abroad that 'twixt my sheets/He's done my office. I know not if't be true," 1.3.385–87) to Iago's materialism (which comes out when he repeatedly admonishes Roderigo to "put money in thy purse", 1.3.301–403). In the Moor's speeches, by contrast, we find what G. Wilson Knight (a New Critic) in a 1930 essay called **"The Othello Music"**. This can be heard in Othello's initial story of his life's adventures and love conquest (1.3.77–94, 129–71) as well as in the speeches in the final act of the drama: from his last words to Desdemona, before he kills her out of jealousy, over the moment when he recognises his mistake up to his last words of justification, before he kills himself, too (5.2.1–83, 258–79, 336–57). In the alternation between prose and the metrical forms of blank verse and rhyming couplets, *Othello* (1.3.180–228, just like *Hamlet* 2.2.115–601) is a suitable example for Shakespeare's general use of dramatic language. *Othello* appealed to composers such as Rossini (1816) and Verdi (1887), who turned Shakespeare's stage-play into operas, as well as to actors and directors who produced adaptations for the screen, such as Orson Welles (1950–52), Laurence Olivier (1965) and Kenneth Branagh (1995).

King Lear

With *King Lear* (1606), Shakespeare tested his critics' belief in the possibilities of the Renaissance stage. The tragedy sets off from the King's partition of his realm amongst his three daughters during his lifetime, and his later recognition that he had been utterly deceived in the love of those two daughters, Goneril and Regan, who shared in the power, and likewise in his arrogant dismissal of his third daughter, loyal Cordelia. The action in the main plot is mirrored and reinforced in a sub-plot that deals with the Earl of Gloucester's relations to his sons Edgar and Edmund (a Vice figure). Right in the centre of the tragedy, we find the Heath Scenes (3.1–4.1) in which the King, naked as a beggar, is out on a heath in a storm, utterly thrown upon himself when not accompanied by his Fool and by Edgar, the Earl of Gloucester's son. Whereas the Romantic critics Charles Lamb and William Hazlitt pronounced the tragedy to be great art, but for those tempestuous Heath Scenes unfit and unintended to be staged, Bernard Shaw's friend the director Harley Granville-Barker argued to the contrary in one of his *Prefaces to Shakespeare* (1930). Under the influence of Samuel Beckett's plays (*Endgame*, 1957) and the Theatre of the Absurd, the Polish critic Jan Kott made a connection with Shakespeare's bare stage and stage imagery and post-war forms of staging Existentialism and the grotesque ("King Lear or Endgame", in *Shakespeare Our Contemporary*, 1964). Finally, when Stephen Greenblatt the New Historicist concerned himself with Lear's and Edgar's behaviour on the heath, he typically turned away from questions of the text (which exists in two versions that are quite distinct, of which the Folio version lacks Lear's mock-trial, 3.6.15ff.) as well as from problems of its staging. Instead, Greenblatt related those scenes to Samuel Harsnett's 1603 pamphlet on exorcism, to discuss exorcism as a public spectacle and the play's relevance to this issue (Greenblatt 1988; see also Greenblatt 1990).

Apart from the varied criticism drawn from the Heath Scenes, three further features shall be mentioned: first, the function of Lear's Fool, then the significance of Cordelia's fate and, finally, the tragic ending. **The Fool** is part of a group of fellow jesters such as Touchstone in *As You Like It* and Feste in *Twelfth Night* as well as Lavatch the clown in *All's Well that Ends Well*. Paradoxically, it is Lear's Fool who talks reason to the King in his riddles and prophecy (1.4, 1.5, 2.4, 3.2), having Lear look like a real fool in his relations to his children. Cordelia's tragic fate – the only loyal of Lear's daughters is hanged in her cell towards the ending of the play – is the more significant because it is utterly devoid of poetic justice, as is the similar fate of Romeo's Juliet and Othello's Desdemona. The lack of mercy in each case has these entirely innocent victims point to the non-Christian character of **Shakespeare's tragic cosmos**. Such feature is further stressed by Gloucester who, after his blinding by the hands of Regan's husband, sums up human life in the words "As flies to wanton boys, are we to th' Gods;/They kill us for their sport." (4.1.36–37. Gloucester's sarcasm was not lost on the Victorian novelist Thomas Hardy, who attached these words to his novel *Tess of the d'Urbervilles*. See chap. 4.5.3.) However, Shakespeare's intentions with regard to the Fool and Cordelia's execution were overruled by Nahum

Tate's 1681 adaptation of *King Lear* as a tragicomedy: this version, which had no place for the Fool but ended happily, was the only one available to English audiences in the theatre for the 150 years between the Restoration and the 1830s.

2.2.4 | (Tragi-)Comedies and Humours

Tragicomedy

The Renaissance knew no fixed delimitation of comedy as a genre: comedy comprised all plays that were neither histories nor tragedies. One can still distinguish different types: the playbill of Renaissance theatres regularly offered romantic as well as satiric comedies, arguably already early examples of the comedy of manners, and also tragicomedies. (For their definition, see Meyer 2008: 108–15.) When Shakespeare introduced his 'star-crossed lovers' Romeo and Juliet with a positive image taken from astrology and at the same time left no doubt about their ultimately tragic fate, he intentionally blocked a stage production of the play as a tragicomedy. Apart from proper tragedies, the Renaissance playhouses frequently offered such tragicomedies, i.e. serious plays in which a looming catastrophe can just be avoided. In his last works for the stage, Shakespeare collaborated with John Fletcher (?1579–1625), who also clarified the term (which derives from one of Plautus's Classical comedies). Fletcher's definition can be found in an address "To the Reader", which he wrote for the printed text (c.1609) of his play *The Faithful Shepherdess*, where he states: "A tragie-comedie is not so called in respect of mirth and killing, but in respect it wants deaths, which is inough to make it no tragedie, yet brings some neere it, which is inough to make it no comedie". Such a generic mix (which was already advertised in Polonius's speech in *Hamlet*, 2.2.392–96, quoted above) posed less of a problem for Renaissance dramatists like Fletcher than for those successors that more strictly observed the Neoclassicist doctrine of the purity of genres. Together with Francis Beaumont (1584–1616), Fletcher wrote popular plays for The King's Men (Shakespeare's troupe) at the Blackfriars Theatre, such as *The Knight of the Burning Pestle* (a comedy, c.1607), *The Maid's Tragedy* (c.1610) and the tragicomedy *Philaster* (c.1609).

The Merchant of Venice

Shakespeare's Problem Plays belong to this category of tragicomedy, yet the earlier *Merchant of Venice* and the later Romance of *The Tempest* are also usefully seen within this context. In *The*

Merchant of Venice (produced before 1600), Bassanio's successful courtship of Portia, the heiress of Belmont, is achieved against other rivals and in spite of his own financial straits by choosing from three caskets the right one which includes the portrait of his beloved. Shakespeare combined this romantic strand of the plot with another, potentially tragic one: in order to financially support his friend Bassanio, the Venice merchant Antonio strikes a deadly deal which entitles Shylock, the Jewish moneylender, to cut a pound of the merchant's flesh when his loan is not punctually repaid. Shylock is an ambivalent character: he harbours spite against Christians in general, to whom he lost his daughter Jessica, and he is vengeful towards Antonio in particular. However, Shylock has a tragic aura, too: the (slightly inconsistent) story that the generous merchant of Venice once gave free rein to his anti-Semitism and spat on Shylock points to the social ostracising of him and other Jews. When the unforeseen occasion arises, debtor and creditor meet before the Duke of Venice, a climactic scene that compares to a similar confrontation at the beginning of *Othello*. At the last moment, Antonio's life is spared, and Shylock's revenge frustrated, when Portia (who has arrived disguised as a male advocate) discovers a legal loophole, so that the play can end without bloodshed, and thus on a 'happy' note, albeit not for Shylock. Shylock's ambivalence has led to contrary realisations of Shakespeare's character on stage as well as on screen (such as in Michael Radford's 2004 movie), and in Arnold Wesker's 1977 rewriting *The Merchant* (see chap. 5.2.3).

The dramatic mix in Shakespeare's *The Tempest* (1611) also has led to a very varied response that either stresses the play's magical features or its racial and colonial sub-text. At the centre of the plot we find Prospero, a magician and former Duke of Milan who was deposed by his own brother and driven into exile, to reside on a remote island together with his daughter Miranda. Bereft of his political powers, Prospero has used his magic might first to subdue the island's native inhabitants before he now proceeds to summon his opponents. Shipwrecked in a tempest that was raised by Prospero, they land on 'his' island, there to lose the power struggle and eventually be pardoned by Prospero. These strands of the plot find a happy ending in the prospective marriage between Miranda and Ferdinand (one of the shipwrecked noblemen) and in the envisaged return of Prospero to his duke-

| Fig. 2.12
John William Waterhouse, *Miranda – The Tempest* (1916)

dom. In a meta-dramatic epilogue, Prospero (and, in a biographical reading, Shakespeare, too) says farewell to the magic arts and urges the audience to set him free. With the advent of Decolonisation and of Postcolonial Criticism in the 1950s, a notable shift in the response occurred. Writers and critics increasingly abstracted from seeing *The Tempest* in terms of comedy and Romance and devoted their attention instead to the colonial and racial subtext that involves the island's native inhabitants. They consist of Sycorax, an evil witch and off-stage character said to have died before Prospero's arrival, of her deformed son Caliban, and of Ariel, an 'airy spirit'. Shakespeare's constellation of Prospero, Caliban and Ariel came to be regarded as a graphic, if unwitting, expression of interethnic encounters right at the beginning of the period of colonialism and trans-Atlantic slavery. In such a view, Prospero's newly acquired position of power abroad and his enslavement of Caliban matters as much as the latter's abortive rebellion against Prospero's rule. Shakespeare's characterisation of Caliban (just like that of Shylock) is ambivalent: the dark, deformed and monstrous appearance of the savage, together with his name (which suggests the then fresh expression 'cannibal') and his lust after, and attempted rape of, a White woman such as Miranda, all conform to racial stereotypes. However, Caliban's speeches about the nature of his servitude and about his close connection to the nature of the island present the native in a much more sympathetic light (1.2.332ff., 3.2.40–103, 135–43). From this cue, twentieth-century poets, dramatists and novelists proceeded to flesh out such minor characters and to present them from a new (but seldom comic) angle. (See the note on Auden's "The Sea and the Mirror" in chap. 5.1, chaps. 5.2.3 and 5.3.6, and Shakespeare 1999b: 73 ff.)

The Origins of Renaissance Comedy

The really funny plays from Renaissance times show the **influence of Latin comedies** by Plautus (c.245–184 B.C.) and by Terence (c.195–59 B.C.), which were read and produced in grammar schools. Plautus's plot element of a 'comedy of errors' is developed in Shakespeare's eponymous 1594 play as well as in his romantic comedies. Stock characters that derive from plays by Plautus comprise those speaking either a Prologue (as in *Romeo and Juliet* and in *Henry V*) or an Epilogue (Rosalind in *As You Like It*) or the girl that masquerades as a boy (once more Rosalind, together with Viola in *Twelfth Night*). Plautus's type of the *miles* *gloriosus* finds its expression in the title character of *Ralph Rois-ter Doister*, a comedy written (perhaps for a school production in 1552) by Nicholas Udall (?1504–56), the headmaster of Eton and Westminster schools. Shakespeare's Falstaff (see chap. 2.2.2) developed from such a military braggart into one of the most popular comic characters from the Renaissance – indeed so well beloved by Queen Elizabeth I that (as rumour has it) she asked to see Falstaff again as a lover in *The Merry Wives of Windsor* (1597, see Berger 2008: 45 ff.). The additional impact of the **Italian Com-media dell'Arte**, which involves further stock characters in impro-vised scenes, can be detected in the minor plots and characters of Shakespeare's comedies. A third and home-grown tradition of English stage comedy is related to the **interludes**, which entertained their audiences by pointed verbal exchange. Once separated from the context of morality plays (around 1500), such staged debates on worldly themes between some four or five characters repre-sented the first utterly secular drama in England. John Heywood (c.1497–c.1580) is considered to be the master of the form, e.g. in *The Play of the Weather* (1533), which also includes a Vice character. The continuum of comedy in Tudor times spread from such plays that had a popular appeal – not only when they talked about the weather – to the learned comedies of courtly love, produced by John Lyly (1553/54–1606) for an aristocratic audience well versed in Classical history and mythology. In *Campaspe* (1580/81), the focus is on Alexander the Great, who is presented not only in conversation with the philosopher Diogenes at Athens but also as a military leader who ultimately pursues the state's interest rather than his love for the beautiful Theban captive Campaspe. Just like his prose narratives (*Euphues; or, The Anatomy of Wit*, 1578; *Euphues and his England*, 1580), Lyly's comedies are marked by an elaborated rhetorical style that itself became the butt of humour already in the 1590s.

Parts of *A Midsummer Night's Dream* (produced before 1598) are likewise set at the court of Athens, yet Shakespeare demands less Classical learning while he offers much more comic enter-tainment. There is a sharp contrast between the soberness at court – the setting of the frame story that deals with the upcom-ing political marriage between Duke Theseus and Hippolyta, the vanquished Queen of the Amazons – and the magic world of the forest in which three further groups of characters interact during

Fig. 2.13

H. Füssli, *Midsummer Night's Dream* Act IV Scene I, 1796

a Midsummer Night. There is the mixed band of four lovers from Athens – Hermia, Helena, Demetrius and Lysander – who are easily mistaken for one another. The fairy kingdom is represented through Oberon together with his queen Titania, whose infatuation with an Indian boy puts a strain on their marriage, as well as their servant Robin Goodfellow alias Puck (an airy spirit similar to Ariel later in *The Tempest*). The last group consists of six mechanics around Nick Bottom the weaver who go into the forest to rehearse, after a fashion, the tragedy of Pyramus and Thisbe. Oberon is a princely magician much like Prospero, but less in control of events. Via Puck, Oberon plans to exert his magic on his unruly wife as well as on the runaway lovers, but Puck gets it wrong. Under the magic spell and as if in a dream, the lovers swap partners, while Titania falls madly in love with Bottom regardless of the fact that he now wears a donkey's head. When all is set right again in the morning, the lovers return (sorted out and sober) to Athens, there to witness the mechanics perform their tragedy during the marriage celebrations at court. This concluding play within the play mirrors the themes and situations in *A Midsummer Night's Dream* and gives ample opportunity for meta-dramatic comedy.

Romantic Comedy between Farce and Comedy of Wit

Just like *The Tempest*, the tragicomic Romance with which it shares the magic aura, *A Midsummer Night's Dream* drew a huge response from adaptors, artists and composers over time. Moreover, both plays altogether bear similarities to Shakespeare's popular **romantic comedies** *As You Like It* (produced around 1600) and *Twelfth Night; or, What You Will* (1602). "Sweet are the uses of adversity" (2.1.12–16): part of the plot of *As You Like It* hinges on a deposed duke driven into exile by an usurper, and there is once again a dichotomy between 'civilisation' (or rather artificiality) at court and a more natural life in the Forest of Arden. The power struggle between the dukes is however overshadowed by a complex romantic plot that is built upon the at times farcical, at other times witty representation of several kinds of love. One love triangle, which involves the shepherdess Phoebe and the shepherd Silvius, serves for poking fun at a **pastoral tradition** that was seriously concerned with idealised love in an idyllic setting. (For another instance of the pastoral in Shakespeare's plays, see *The Winter's Tale*, 4.4.) Phoebe's turn from Silvius to "Ganymede" is mistaken, because this incognito is actually the assumed character of Rosalind, the exiled duke's daughter. Such cross-dressing helps reasonable Rosalind to keep her passions in check and to put her lover Orlando to the test, with whom she fell in love at first sight. Another triangle sees Audrey the goatherd having the choice between William, a countryman, and Touchstone, the court jester, who is ultimately successful in his down-to-earth way. Touchstone's bawdy humour, together with the travesty that involves a boy actor cast as a woman character (Rosalind) that then dresses like a man (Ganymed) to go on and impersonate a woman (Rosalind) in the role-play with Orlando, are ready instances of **farce**. In *Twelfth Night*, Shakespeare's prevailing theme of illusion and reality finds its expression in a circle of love, and once again in a travesty. Here, Duke Orsino of Illyria woos Countess Olivia, who falls in love with the page Cesario, the incognito of the protagonist Viola, who in turn woos and wins Duke Orsino. (On gender roles in Shakespeare, see Schabert 2000: 319–21, 885–87.) *Twelfth Night* makes much use of stock characters: its cast includes the epitome of a sourpuss Puritan (Malvolio) as well as a foolish rustic (Sir Andrew Aguecheek), and with the clown Feste, it sports a companion of Touchstone the jester and likewise of the Fool in Shakespeare's tragedy *King Lear*. The verbal fencing matches between Viola and Feste in *Twelfth Night* (3.1) and between Rosalind and Orlando in *As You Like It* (particularly their rehearsal of love and their mock wedding, 4.1.35–184) find their extension in Shakespeare's *Much Ado About Nothing*. Because of the frequency of such bantering and **repartee** between Beatrice and Benedick, this play (which may likewise have been produced before 1600) can be regarded as an early example of the **comedy of wit and manners** – a type of play that was to become the fashion when the theatres re-opened after the Restoration (see chap. 3.2.1). Together with gender relations and marriage as a theme, such repartee is also found, quite early in Shakespeare's career as a playwright, in *The Taming of the Shrew* (?1592), but here once again in a farcical context.

When *As You Like It*, much like Jane Austen's novel *Pride and Prejudice*, ends happily with 'Four Weddings and No Funeral', the odd one out is Jaques, a melancholic. Before this denouement, he is made to speak a memorable monologue that is based upon the *theatrum mundi topos* and the idea of the Seven Ages of Man ("All the world's a stage,/And all the men and women merely players."

Ben Jonson's Satirical Comedy of Humours

2.7.139–66). Through such imagery and as a type, Jaques reflects the spirit of the age: together with the other usual suspects – Malvolio and the melancholic Prince of Denmark – he is the rare instance of a comic humour character in Shakespeare. Such a conception is generally more closely related to the work of Ben Jonson (1572–1637, see chap. 2.1). The "Prologue" to *Every Man in His Humour* (1598, rev. 1616) is not only a record of contemporary stage practice (ll. 1–20) but also a good indication of what Jonson set out to do with his **Comedy of Humours**: to conceive of a dramatic realism in terms of characters, action, and language in order to laugh at 'human follies' and 'popular errors' with the ultimate moral purpose of improving mankind (ll. 21–30). Jonson's moralistic conception, which he followed up first in *Every Man Out of His Humour* (1599) and then in **satirical comedies** that could do without humours altogether, contrasted markedly with Shakespeare's 'romantic' comedies as well as Romances. With them, *Volpone; or, The Fox* (1605) shared at least an Italian setting, and with the revenge tragedies moreover the view of Italy as a seat of vice. Generally speaking, however, Jonson devotes himself to a mix of urban realism, allegorical characters and a plot that is informed by (Neo-)Classical notions of dramatic unity and poetic justice. The action of *Volpone* is limited to one day in the Venice of the day, and the play's didactic purpose is to brand avarice and legacy hunting as materialist forms of perversion. Jonson's characters bear telling names that are derived from the animal fable as a Classical genre of satire. Volpone (the fox), a wealthy Venetian, teams up with his wily servant Mosca (a type of fly) for a confidence trick. By talking about his impending death, they lure three prominent citizens – the lawyer Voltore (vulture), the miserly Corbaccio (crow) and the merchant Corvino (raven) – into parting with some of their fortune, or their wife, in order to be accepted as Volpone's heir. When Volpone and Mosca (unsuccessfully) turn from probing morality to material pursuit, and turn against each other, they overreach themselves: the cycle of deceived deceivers has run full circle, and Jonson's stage satire ends on a note of poetic justice. In *The Alchemist* (1610) and *Bartholomew Fair* (1614), the playwright made the final step from urban Italy to contemporary London. *The Alchemist* centres on two enemies of the theatre that eventually might bring about the closure of the playhouses: the plague (which broke out again in London when the play was premièred) and the Puritans. For *The Alchemist*, Jonson devised a constellation of characters that includes Puritans of an opportunist (Tribulation Wholesome) and a fanatic mould (Deacon Ananias), together with a greedy materialist who searches for the Philosopher's Stone (Sir Epicure Mammon) but falls prey to another confidence trickster (Face) allied with an alchemist who clearly is a cheat (Subtle). *Bartholomew Fair* is a comparatively milder branding of middle-class materialism when seen against *Volpone*. In such plays with or without humours, Jonson established a satirical kind of Renaissance comedy that was to be re-born in different form. In the mid-eighteenth century, when he had ultimately lost the competition with Shakespeare for the position of England's pre-eminent dramatist, Jonson's spirit was revived in Henry Fielding's 'comic epic poems in prose', which are likewise informed by a Classical tradition of satire (see chap. 3.5.3).

Together with the designer Inigo Jones, with whom he collaborated from *The Masque of Blackness* (1605) to *Chloridia* (1631), Ben Jonson was also the major creative force behind the **court masque**. This spectacular form of entertainment at the Stuart court consisted of a mix of scenic presentation, music and dance, in which masked courtiers engaged with professional actors who impersonated allegorical figures. In the course of the collaboration between Jonson and Jones, the designer introduced some major innovations on stage (such as moveable and perspective scenery). The poets Samuel Daniel (†1619) and Thomas Campion (†1620) wrote court masques, too. Further notable contributions to the genre include the masque incorporated as a play within the play in Thomas Middleton's *Women Beware Women* (c.1625), and *Comus* (or *A Masque Presented at Ludlow Castle 1634*) by the poet John Milton (1608–74).

Jonson's impact is moreover felt, in a more realistic fashion, in late Elizabethan and Jacobean 'city comedies' as the last subgenre to be mentioned here. With *The Shoemaker's Holiday; or, The Gentle Craft* (1600), Thomas Dekker (?1572–1632) was one of the first to offer a comic view on life in London, rather than in Italian cities. Dekker's city comedy celebrates the 'gentle craft' of shoemakers, and in particular Simon Eyre, a real historical character that rose from shoemaker to London's mayor. In the play, Simon Eyre sees to a happy ending for a love across class barriers,

Court Masques

|**Fig. 2.14**
Design for *The Masque of Blackness* by Inigo Jones

City Comedies

and moreover secures Shrove Tuesday as a holiday for his fellow shoemakers. For the social realism involved, it actually does not matter much that Dekker's play is situated in fifteenth- rather than sixteenth-century England. Dekker is said to have collaborated with John Webster (c.1580–1625) on *Westward Ho!* (1604), another city comedy that drew a parody (*Eastward Ho*, 1605) from the team of Ben Jonson, George Chapman (c.1559–1634) and John Marston (1576–1634). Because of its anti-Scottish tendency, this stage parody offended the new King James I so that Jonson and Chapman landed in jail for a time. With Thomas Middleton (1580–1627), Dekker collaborated on *The Honest Whore*, a drama about a reformed prostitute confronted with double standards. The two full-length parts of this play (published in 1604 and 1630) veer between tragic and comic action both in its main plot and in a farcical sub-plot. Middleton took an interest in various dramatic genres, as became evident in the remarks made in chap. 2.2.2 on *The Revenger's Tragedy* (1607), *A Game at Chess* (1624) and *Women Beware Women* (c.1625). Middleton's *A Chaste Maid in Cheapside* (1613) is a Jacobean city comedy and satire of bourgeois society that, in its crass depiction of sexual greed and amorality, looks ahead to the Restoration comedies of manners, yet lacks their wit combats (see chap. 3.2.1). *A New Way to Pay Old Debts* (c.1625), with its memorable part of the greedy moneylender Sir Giles Overreach, and *The City Madam* (1632) are plays by Philip Massinger (1583–1640) that belong to the same genre of stage satire. *Hyde Park* (1632) is a milder example by James Shirley (1596–1666), the last renowned dramatist active before the Puritans closed the theatres.

Guiding Questions and Exercises

1. Provide a short sketch of the development of drama and the theatre during the Renaissance, from the staging of Tudor interludes to Stuart court masques. What are the main currents?

2. Give a summary review of those Renaissance plays that deal with historical subject matter. What part of historical reality is selected? How is it presented? For whom, to what purpose, and to what effect? What is the overall conception of history that transpires as a result? In how far is the literary text (or its

adaptation for the screen) and the historical picture presented in a fresh and original manner, or related to pre-conceived
notions and forms of presentation?

3. Describe the structure of the argument and the rhetorical
form of the speech of King Henry V to the Governor of the
French town Harfleur in Shakespeare's *King Henry V*, 3.3.1–43.
How is the king characterised in this monologue? How does
this relate to his role and that of the eponymous play within
Shakespeare's cycle of Histories? On the basis of this passage,
point out the major features of Renaissance views on kingship and on the nature of war.

4. Point out some distinctive features of the dramatic work of
Marlowe, Shakespeare and Jonson.

5. List the features that distinguish proper revenge tragedies
from other plays in which revenge is a theme. Provide some
illustration from the drama of the period.

6. Define the various types of Renaissance comedies, and illustrate them with relevant examples.

7. Try to account for the productive response to Renaissance
drama in adaptations for various media.

Renaissance Poetry

| 2.3

Poets, Poetic Styles and Themes

| 2.3.1

There was a flowering of poetry in the Tudor period, ranging
from the epigram to the epic. Media usage began with the recital
and other oral performances of poetry and then extended over
the circulation of verse in manuscript to the publication of song-
books and of other poetry in print. (For individual poets' use of
the media, see Elsky 1989, Love 1993 and Marotti 1995.) The variety of songs that could be heard (and perhaps for the first time
read in manuscript) comprised **folk songs** like "Greensleeves", **popular ballads** such as "Barbara Allen", "Sir Patrick Spens", "Guy of
Warwick" or "Chevy Chase" (see chaps. 1, 3.3.2 and 4.4), and also
carols, in particular Christmas carols. Among the poems that were
set to music (e. g. by William Byrd, John Dowland and Thomas
Morley) were the **madrigal** (to be sung by three to five voices that
observe counterpoint) and, after 1600, the **air** (which by contrast

Songs and Other Forms
of Oral Poetry

is a strophic poem sung by a soloist). The English courtier Sir Thomas Wyatt (1503–42), who lived and died under Henry VIII, composed madrigals as well as sonnets (see chap. 2.3.2). So did William Drummond of Hawthornden (1585–1649), a Scots poet who chose Standard English for his *Sonnets, Songs, Sextains, Madrigals* (1616, see *OAEL*), and who lived long enough to witness the Civil Wars, when he published pamphlets for the Royalist cause and against the Presbyterians.

"My lute, awake!" is one of Wyatt's frequently anthologised songs, and more such lute songs (together with their musical setting) are included in *A Book of Airs* (1601) by the poet and composer Thomas Campion (1567–1620), e.g. "When to her lute Corinna sings". Campion was a champion of Classical Latin poetry. In his own poems in Latin (*Poemata*, 1595) as well as in English ("Rose-cheeked Laura", 1602), he imitated the **quantitative verse** of Latin poetry (see chap. 2.4). "There is a garden in her face" (1617) evokes the time-honoured *topos* or patterned image called *hortus conclusus* which refers to an enclosed garden like e.g. the Biblical Garden of Eden. Campion's love songs can be more down-to-earth: "I care not for these ladies" (1601) contrasts those women "That must be wooed and prayed" (l. 2) in the manner of Petrarchism (see chap. 2.3.2) to "Amaryllis,/The wanton country maid" (3–4) who at first says "Forsooth, let go!" but then "never will say no" (chorus). A song by Catull, translated by Campion as "My Sweetest Lesbia" (1601), also inspired Ben Jonson (1572–1637) to write his "Song: To Celia" (1616, beginning with the line "Drink to me only with thine eyes"), which was still popular in eighteenth-century bar rooms. Jonson made a mark also with songs from his stage-plays (e.g. "Slow, slow, fresh fount", "Queen and huntress" and "Clerimont's Song"), as did William Shakespeare (1564–1616) with some of his, e.g. "Take, o take those lips away" and "Under the Greenwood Tree" (a song which in 1872 provided the title for Thomas Hardy's first Wessex Novel). Further, still anthologised songs from the Renaissance include "Why so pale and wan, fond lover?" by Sir John Suckling (1638), "Ask me no more where Jove bestows" by Thomas Carew (1640), "Go, lovely rose!" by Edmund Waller (1645) and "A Song to Amoret" by Henry Vaughan (1646).

The airs "Go and catch a falling star", "Break of Day" and "Sweetest love, I do not go" are three of the "Songs and Sonnets" by John Donne (1572–1631) that for some time circulated in manuscript before they were first printed in a posthumous 1633 collection of his poems. Such a circulation of verse in manuscript occurred within the poets' circles that gathered around Sir Philip Sidney (†1586) and Ben Jonson (†1637). It also occurred among the law students at the Inns of Court (where John Donne found an audience), and at the royal courts of the Tudor and Stuart monarchs. Queen Elizabeth herself occasionally, but quite competently, composed verse, as can be gleaned from the "Verse Exchange between Elizabeth and Sir Walter Ralegh" (c.1587, on Ralegh's fear to lose the Queen's favour to the Earl of Essex, printed ?1600). Ralegh (or Raleigh, 1552–1618) is remembered as a shining courtier, as an early coloniser of Virginia and leader of expeditions to South America (who sought the gold of El Dorado, but more memorably came back with the potato and tobacco), and as a poet. Ralegh's "What is our life?" (1612) reflects on the life of man in terms of 'all the world's a stage' (*theatrum mundi topos*). Together with Sidney and Marvell, Ralegh and Donne are prominent examples of poets who generally shied away from print, but who were involved in the circulation of **answer poems** as typical expressions of the 'manuscript system' (see chap. 3.3.3). "The Passionate Shepherd to His Love" is a good example. This popular poem by Christopher Marlowe (†1593) was sung in Shakespeare's *The Merry Wives of Windsor* (1597) before it was published posthumously in 1599. Thereafter, Marlowe's poem occasioned first "The Nymph's Reply to the Shepherd" by Ralegh (1600), and then "The Bait" by Donne (1633), who introduced angling as a different source of imagery. "The Lie" (1608), Ralegh's satire on the various estates (ranks and institutions) in a hierarchical society, elicited many replies, too. The habit of circulating verse is moreover illustrated by Ben Jonson's verse letter "To Lucy, Countess of Bedford, with Mr Donne's Satires" (1616), which is addressed to his own patron and that of John Donne, and moreover by the example of Donne himself. The only poem to survive in Donne's own hand is one of his many verse letters ("A Letter to the Lady Carey, and Mistress Essex Rich, from Amiens", rediscovered not before 1970), and merely seven of Donne's poems were printed during his lifetime. Under such circumstances, to ascertain the exact date and order of composition of individual poems is impossible. However, Donne's verse is extant in some 45 contemporary manuscripts, and there were seven posthumous

Circulation in Manuscript

collections of his poetry published between 1633 and 1669: both of these facts attest to the poet's popularity (see Donne 1986: 13).

Canonisation in Poetry

"Of English Verse" (1693), a poem by Edmund Waller (1606–87), is a good reminder of how difficult it still was for English poets to be acknowledged in comparison to their Classical predecessors. Waller proclaims:

Poets that lasting marble seek,
Must carve in Latin, or in Greek;
We write in sand, our language grows,
And, like the tide, our work o'erflows. (ll. 13–16, *OAEL* II, 635–36)

There was yet no national canon. Chaucer is the only poet Waller mentions by name, but even he is said to be metrically awkward (to which the *OAEL* editors appended the note: "Even in Waller's time, it was not understood that Chaucer's verse was iambic pentameter."). However, Renaissance **elegies and other commemorative verse** attest to the esteem of the poets of the day. Both Ben Jonson and John Milton published poems on Shakespeare; Jonson moreover wrote a poem on Donne's *Epigrams*, and he even composed an "Ode to Himself", defying his critics. From Thomas Carew (1595–1640) we have a reply to Jonson's ode as well as a funeral elegy on Donne, and Robert Herrick (1591–1674) added "His Prayer to Ben Jonson". Poets were grouped together in thematic **anthologies**: what *Tottel's Miscellany* (1557, see chap. 2.3.2) had done for the love sonnets by Sir Thomas Wyatt, by the Earl of Surrey and by further 'courtly makers', *England's Helicon* (1600) continued to do for pastoral poetry such as "The Passionate Shepherd to His Love" and "The Nymph's Reply". **Style manuals** such as Thomas Wilson's *The Art of Rhetorique* (1553, 8th ed. 1585) and George Puttenham's *The Art of English Poesie* (1589) contributed their share to pave the way for today's canon of Renaissance poets. Moreover, these and later critics have distinguished different styles in poetry as well as in prose. To write in a **plain style**, that is comprehensibly, was an ideal that was proclaimed by the sixteenth-century Humanists as well as by Sir Francis Bacon and the new scientists of the seventeenth century (see chap. 2.4). Such an ideal does not cover the archaisms in the poetry of Edmund Spenser and likewise the 'metaphysical' conceits or imagery in the poetry of John Donne. Spenser, however, could also switch to an **eloquent**

style that is again distinct from the **grand style** as practised by John Milton in *Paradise Lost*.

Among those who fell victim to the process of canonisation, there are two sixteenth-century and three seventeenth-century poetic stars whose light has markedly waned. John Skelton (c.1460–1529) was the leading poet under Henry VIII, and courageous enough to attack Cardinal Wolsey, the powerful Lord Chancellor, in his satires of 1521/22. Yet Skelton's switching of registers, in combination with his unconventional metre (lines of 2–4 stresses and varying length called *Skeltonics*), was more than critics with a penchant for Classical decorum could bear. (By contrast, Skelton is perhaps more favourably seen in the light of modern performance poetry.) George Gascoigne (1539–78), Skelton's successor as the leading poet of the early Elizabethan age, likewise experimented with versification, but experienced a career break through censorship: Gascoigne's collection of erotic poems was banned twice (in 1573 and again after his revision of 1575). In a similar manner, Abraham Cowley (1618–67, a Royalist poet who in his own time overshadowed Milton, his political opponent), Sir John Denham (1615–69) and also Edmund Waller himself (who together with Denham was once esteemed as an early master of the heroic couplet: see chap. 3.3.1), lost their audiences during the eighteenth century, and today are anthologised only with a couple of poems, if at all. Other poets than Cowley and Denham are more fondly commemorated in **Poets' Corner**: this last and prominent instance of the formation of a national canon properly set in when Edmund Spenser was buried next to Chaucer in Westminster Abbey in 1599.

|Fig. 2.15

Poets' Corner, Westminster Abbey

Edmund Spenser (1552–99) was a Humanist with a Protestant education who became a member of Sidney's circle of poets called *Areopagus*, and later Ralegh's friend and neighbour on an estate in Ireland that he lost during the rebellion in Ulster (see chap. 2.1). Sir Philip Sidney (1554–86) had distinguished himself as a critic with *An Apology for Poetrie* (or alternatively *Defense of Poesie*, 1595), as a poet with the Petrarchan sonnet sequence *Astrophil and Stella* (1591), and as a prose writer with *Arcadia* (1590). That romance was brought out (like all of his major works, posthumously) by his sister, the Countess of Pembroke, with whom Sidney had also collaborated on a translation of the Psalms (see chaps. 2.3.2 and 2.4). Spenser likewise aspired to become a *poeta*

Major Poets of the Renaissance: Sidney and Spenser

doctus or learned poet who measured himself against his predecessors in a variety of genres, but in contrast to Sidney, he regularly gave his work to the printers. *The Shepheardes Calender* (1579, dedicated to Sidney) set the Renaissance vogue of **the pastoral** in motion, which looked back to the pastoral poems or eclogues of Theocrit and Virgil, and which found its expression also in drama and in prose narratives (see chaps. 2.2.4 and 2.4). For each month of *The Shepheardes Calender*, Spenser assigned one eclogue, built around the characters of Colin Clout (the poet), his beloved Rosalind, his friend Hobbinol (Gabriel Harvey) and a rival. In his pastoral poem, Spenser experimented with various metres, and his mix of poetic registers includes **archaisms** modelled on the language of Chaucer. *Colin Clouts Come Home Againe* (1595) is another and more refined pastoral poem. His sonnet sequence *Amoretti* (1595, see chap. 2.3.2) is endowed with an innovative rhyme link and an unconventionally happy ending. The sequence celebrates Spenser's second marriage, and it is concluded by an "Epithalamion" or wedding song that the poet had written for the occasion (again modelled on a Classical Greek tradition). For his *Four Hymns* (1596) in praise of love and beauty, Spenser let himself be inspired by Plato and by Petrarch. While in Ireland, he composed his national and Arthurian epic *The Faerie Queene*, which he began to publish in 1590 (together with a prefatory letter to Ralegh; see chap. 2.3.3), and which he left as a monumental fragment. The **Spenserian stanza** devised for this epic consists of nine lines, first of iambic pentameter but ending in a final *hexameter* (six-stressed line) or *Alexandrine* (12-syllable line), and rhyming *ababbcbcc*. The poet's continued esteem in later centuries can be measured through the great number of Spenserian imitations up to Byron's *Childe Harold's Pilgrimage* (1812–18), all written in the stanza that bears his name (see chaps. 3.1 and 3.5.5).

Christopher Marlowe (1564–93), William Shakespeare (1564–1616) and Ben Jonson (1572–1637) are three major verse dramatists that also distinguished themselves as proper poets. During the time when the theatres had closed because of the Plague, both Marlowe and Shakespeare composed shorter epics, and the latter moreover is renowned for his sonnets (see chaps. 2.3.2 and 2.3.3). By contrast, Jonson was a Classicist who wrote (in addition to the "Song: To Celia" and the songs for his plays mentioned above) epistles or verse letters, elegies, epigrams in

Marlowe, Shakespeare, Jonson

the plain style, an "Ode to Himself" as well as on others ("To the Immortal Memory and Friendship of That Noble Pair, Sir Lucius Cary and Sir H. Morison"), not to forget one of the earliest country-house poems in the language ("To Penshurst", see chap. 2.3.3). "Why I write not of love" is a self-critical piece on the limitations of a poet who famously chided Shakespeare for his 'little Latin, and less Greek'. Jonson published his dramatic and poetic *Works* in Folio in 1616 and assumed a prominent role in the Stuart court (for which he wrote court masques). Together with Shakespeare, Beaumont and Fletcher, Jonson held regular meetings in a London tavern. Later, he assembled a poets' circle called the 'tribe of Ben' and 'sons of Ben', or the Cavalier Poets (which included e.g. Thomas Carew, Robert Herrick and Sir John Suckling, see below).

John Donne (1572–1631) was a London poet born in the same year as Jonson, but into a Roman Catholic family with a record of persecution, who became a royal chaplain after his conversion to Anglicanism. (Meanwhile, Jonson had first converted to Catholicism and then returned to the Church of England.) Donne and Jonson shared a fondness for the epigram (see Donne's rhyming couplet on "Manliness"), and in company with Joseph Hall (1574–1656), Donne revived the Classical form of verse satire in the 1590s (see chaps. 2.4 and 3.3.1). There are three further sides to his work: a religious, an amorous and a cosmological. Together with George Herbert and John Milton, Donne is the foremost **religious poet** of the Renaissance. In addition to his sermons and other religious prose, Donne wrote two sequences of *Holy Sonnets* and four religious hymns that were published posthumously after they had circulated in manuscript (see below as well as chaps. 2.3.2 and 2.4). Donne's social network, and the patronage of his verse, is apparent from the epithalamions that he wrote even on royal marriages, from his funeral elegies, and from the many verse letters he sent to aristocratic persons of rank (e.g. to the Countesses of Bedford, of Huntingdon and of Salisbury). However, Donne is also a poet who, even though he became a figure of the establishment – as an MP and as the Dean of St. Paul's Cathedral (from 1621) – continued to write uncommonly direct love poems that break with the conventions of Petrarchism:

John Donne and the Metaphysical Poets

|Fig. 2.16
John Donne

> In most sixteenth-century love poetry the mistress is remote, unattainable, approached by the poet from time to time only to be rebuffed, at which point he laments his misfortune [...], and finds continuing inspiration from his frustration. Donne breaks with all this. Where other poets place their mistress on a pedestal, he puts her in bed, next to him. [...] Where other poets use the pronouns 'I' and 'she', implying a distance between man and woman, [...] Donne fuses both pronouns into 'we', 'us', 'our'. [...] The lovers form a unit outside time, outside the world, in one sense above it. One of the great insights of Donne's new attitude to love is that a love-relationship constitutes an experience knowable only by the two people involved in it. Other people's judgements are of no relevance (Brian Vickers in Rogers 1987: 171).

Outside the funeral elegies that are in many editions assembled in a section called "Epicedes and Obsequies", Donne wrote some twenty "Elegies" that are **poems on heterosexual love** inspired by the Classical example of Ovid's *Amores*. In the centre of "Love's Progress" (Elegy 18), we find a *blazon* or catalogue of beauty (see chap. 2.3.2) that is couched in a metaphoric journey (with much *double entendre*) on a sailing ship along a woman's body, from top to toe, with the desire to anchor (rather than shipwreck) in between. "To His Mistress Going to Bed" (Elegy 19), a companion poem which likewise fell victim to censorship in 1633, engages in the wishful thinking of the female lover's striptease before the male speaker's eyes, up to the final couplet which bluntly states: "To teach thee, I am naked first, why then/What needst thou have more covering than a man." Donne's "Songs and Sonnets" contain a good number of equally outspoken poems. Some startle the reader or listener because of the (at times, aggressive) directness of address in the very first lines. In "The Canonization", this applies to the act of love ("For God's sake hold your tongue, and let me love"), in "The Sun Rising", to the morning after ("Busy old fool, unruly sun/Why dost thou thus,/Through windows, and through curtains call on us?"). This compares to the beginning of Donne's air "Break of Day", where the same situation of an impending parting of the lovers is wittily expressed in the form of a rhetorical question, posed by her to him:

> Why should we rise, because 'tis light?
> Did we lie down, because 'twas night?
> Love which in spite of darkness brought us hither,
> Should in despite of light keep us together. (ll. 3–7, Donne 1986: 45)

In many further of Donne's poems, the appeal lies in their fusion of two quite separate semantic fields into one complex image, often called **metaphysical conceit**. The "Songs and Sonnets" section contains four farewell poems entitled "A Valediction", of which "A Valediction: forbidding Mourning" is best known. The poem's couplets in alternating rhyme contain the startling (but on second thought, convincingly apt) comparison of the temporary parting of a loving couple with a pair of compasses:

> Our two souls therefore, which are one,
>> Though I must go, [...]
>
> If they be two, they are two so
>> As stiff twin compasses are two
> Thy soul the fixed foot, makes no show
>> To move, but doth, if th'other do.
> (ll. 21–22, 25–28)

The speaker continues the conceit first with a vision of (and the hint of a sexual pun related to) the reunion of the lovers, and then ends with a circle as the symbol of perfect unity, fostered by the firmness in love shown by the partner who stayed at home (the "fixed foot"):

> And though it in the centre sit,
>> Yet when the other far doth roam,
> It leans, and hearkens after it,
>> And grows erect, as that comes home.
>
> Such wilt thou be to me, who must
>> Like th' other foot, obliquely run;
> Thy firmness makes my circle just,
>> And makes me end, where I begun.
> (ll. 29–36, Donne 1986: 84–85)

In the poem "The Flea", the insect that partook of the blood of both lovers is turned into a symbol of their sexual communion: "This flea is you and I, and this/Our marriage bed, and marriage temple is;" (ll. 12–13, Donne 1986: 59). The **cosmological aspect** of Donne's verse – his regular references to medieval notions of, and post-Copernican challenges to, a geocentric and spherical universe – extends into all poetic genres, but comes out best in the two long *Anniversary* poems discussed further below (*An Anatomy of the World*, 1611, and *Of the Progress of the Soul*, 1612;

see chap. 2.3.3). Over and above his conversational directness, his original use of imagery and his cosmological outlook, Donne distinguished himself as a particularly inventive poet who created individual stanza forms rather than imitate given models. All this did not endear him and other **Metaphysical Poets** to successive critics with a Neoclassical taste like Samuel Johnson, who lamented that in such conceits, 'the most heterogeneous ideas are yoked by violence together' (which is why actually quite diverse poets such as Donne, George Herbert and Andrew Marvell were lumped by violence together because their imagery is alike out of the ordinary). However, Donne made a positive impact on the Modernist poetry of T.S. Eliot (e. g. "Prufrock") after he had been rediscovered at the turn to the twentieth century. Eliot acknowledged the inspiration, and furthered the revival, in several influential essays written on seventeenth-century poetry (see chap. 5.1).

John Milton

The last major poet of the age, John Milton (1608–74), prepared himself through extensive studies for his vocation as a learned poet who put himself to the test of a variety of genres (much like Spenser, or later Keats and Auden). In his hymn "On the Morning of Christ's Nativity" (1629) and in his elegy *Lycidas* (1638), the Puritan poet combined the Classical and the native tradition of pastoral poetry with the Biblical narratives of shepherds. Milton's companion poems "L'Allegro" and "Il Penseroso" (1631) were inspired by Italian poetry, and he returned to the Petrarchan form for the sonnets he wrote up to 1658 on personal, political and religious matters. Together with *Comus: A Masque* (presented 1634), the Biblical tragedy *Samson Agonistes* (a closet play, 1671) represents a dramatic interlude in Milton's work. From the beginning of the Civil Wars and throughout the period of the Commonwealth and Protectorate, which he actively supported as a Puritan and as a democrat, Milton published prose pamphlets, most famously in the cause of free speech (*Areopagitica*, 1644). Although by 1652 he had lost his eyesight completely (which is reflected in his sonnet "When I consider how my light is spent"), Milton continued to work for Oliver Cromwell's government, assisted by his friend, the poet Andrew Marvell (see below), who also saved him from threats against his life after the Restoration of the monarchy. During this time, and as a blind man who dictated to his daughters, Milton composed his masterwork in **blank**

verse (i.e., unrhymed iambic pentameter): the ten (later twelve)
books of his Christian epic *Paradise Lost* (1667), to which he added
Paradise Regained (1671). By comparison with other poets, Milton's
'grand style' is characterised by a Latinate syntax. (See also the
remaining chapters in this section.)

In contrast to Spenser's *Four Hymns* (1596), which are devoted   Poetic Themes: Religion
to abstract concepts, Milton's 1629 Nativity hymn as well as Don-
ne's four hymns – "A Hymn to Christ" (1619), "A Hymn to God the
Father" (1623), the funeral "Hymn to the Saints, and to Marquis
Hamilton" (?1625), and "A Hymn to God my God, in my Sickness"
(written on the poet's deathbed in 1631) – are religious odes and
a testimony of Christian faith. There were more poets than Donne and Milton who wrote Christian verse in a period of religious
sectarianism. Sidney's friend and biographer Fulke Greville, Lord
Brooke (1554–1628) adorned his closet (reading) play *Mustapha*
(1633) with a chorus of priests. This "Chorus Sacerdotum" begins
with an antithetical definition of Man as the prominent but also
problematic link in the Chain of Being connecting Heaven and
Earth:

> O wearisome condition of humanity!
> Born under one law, to another bound:
> Vainly begot, and yet forbidden vanity,
> Created sick, commanded to be sound:
> What meaneth Nature by these diverse laws?
> Passion and reason, self-division cause.
> (ll. 1–6; *OAEL* II, 151)

The poem ends in a couplet that predates Romantic notions of
true wisdom: "Yet when each of us, in his own heart looks,/He
finds the God there, far unlike his books." (ll. 23–24). Further religious poems by Thomas Nashe (1567–1601) and Robert Southwell (1561–95), two writers from Shakespeare's and Marlowe's
generation, are still anthologised. Nashe, too, conceived of "A
Litany in Time of Plague" as part of a play (a comedy entitled
Summer's Last Will and Testament, which was acted in the Archbishop of Canterbury's palace at Croydon in 1592, and published
in 1600). Despite its shortness and outward simplicity, Nashe's
"Litany" compares to Donne's *First Anniversary* (see chap. 2.3.3),
because it is likewise based on the Classical **sic transit gloria mundi topos** and thus laments the world's decay. Southwell's "The
Burning Babe" (1602), on the other hand, links Donne's 'meta-

physical' poetry to Milton's Nativity hymn. Southwell, a Catholic, first joined the Jesuits in France and then, in 1586, returned to minister the English Catholics in the wake of the execution of Mary Queen of Scots, and of the Armada. In 1592, Southwell (like some of Donne's Catholic relatives) was taken into prison, tortured, and executed for treason three years later. Despite its formal regularity (16 lines of *Septenar*, i.e. 14 syllables, and rhyming couplets), "The Burning Babe" shares some features with the 'metaphysical' imagery and strong expression of Donne's poetry. Southwell's vision of Christ's Nativity (which differs starkly from Milton's and Crashaw's successive hymns) is that of a child born from fire, burning brightly.

By comparison with Southwell the Martyr and Donne the Dean, George Herbert (1593–1633) was a devout Anglican and a country parson (in the last years of his life) who wrote 'sacred poems' in the plain style. "The Altar" and "Easter Wings" are two of the more than 160 poems in the collection *The Temple* (1633) that stick out as **shaped verse**: on the printed page, each poem takes a form that illustrates itself. Such a union of content and design in the medium of print is reminiscent of the pattern poem "Wings" by Simias of Rhodes in the Classical *Greek Anthology*, and it looks ahead to twentieth-century examples of **concrete poetry** (see chap. 5.1). Crashaw, Vaughan and Traherne were likewise ranked as Metaphysical Poets, because their religious verse is either reminiscent of Herbert's or closely resembling that of one another. The vicissitudes of an era of Reformation and Counter-Reformation are strikingly illustrated by the life and verse of Richard Crashaw (c.1613–49), who began his poetic career (like Donne) as a Roman Catholic convert turned priest in the Church of England, to end it with a return conversion to Catholicism during his exile with the Stuart court in France. As a poet, Crashaw followed in Herbert's *Steps to the Temple* (1646, rev. 1648), a collection that included the poet's translations of his celebrated Latin epigrams (1634). Crashaw's posthumous collection *Carmen Deo Nostro* (1652) contains his own pastoral hymn "In the Holy Nativity of Our Lord God: A Hymn Sung as by the Shepherds". Henry Vaughan (1621–95), a Welshman like Herbert, is remembered for his 1650 collection *Silex Scintillans* (i.e., The Flashing Flint, enlarged 1655) which takes its title from the image of a flint-like heart struck by God's lightning, and which abounds in imitations of Herbert's poetry. When the religious prose (*Centuries of Meditation*, 1908) and poetry of the Church of England parson Thomas Traherne (1637–74) were rediscovered in 1896/97, they were in turn mistaken for Vaughan's. Quite understandably so: in their imagery and visionary outlook, Traherne's "Wonder" (1903) and "On Leaping over the Moon" (1910) indeed correspond to Crashaw's finest poem entitled "The World" (1650), which is a Christian vision that reiterates a medieval, geocentric and spherical universe. By contrast, Crashaw's poems on childhood as a period of innocence in which Man is next to Nature (e.g. "Regeneration" and "The Retreat") anticipate the views of Romantic poets such as Blake or Wordsworth.

The religious and metaphysical features of seventeenth-century poetry are balanced out by more worldly concerns that become apparent e.g. in John Donne's elegies of love, and also in the love sonnets of the Renaissance (see chap. 2.3.2). Such concerns also characterise the work of Milton's friend Andrew Marvell (1621–78), whose love poetry spans the whole continuum from pastoral verse in the line of Spenser, Marlowe and Ralegh to the libidinous poems of Donne, with whom he also shared a preference for the distribution of verse by manuscript circulation. Such habit obscured not only the exact dating of Marvell's poems (many of which might have been composed in c.1650–52, though they were published only in 1681), but also affected Marvell's authorship, in particular of the post-Restoration verse satires directed against the Stuart court. "The Nymph Complaining for the Death of Her Fawn", a lament for the death of a pet, is reminiscent of the pastoral tradition, as is "The Garden", a poem that features the personification of Love and Beauty as well as the *topos* of *hortus conclusus*. Those two pastoral poems are cast in couplets of iambic tetrameter, as is Marvell's country-house poem "Upon Appleton House" (see chap. 2.3.3). For "The Definition of Love", Marvell made use of alternating rhyme, of personifications (Love and Fate, Hope and Despair), and of 'metaphysical' conceits taken from geometry (parallels of love) as well as astronomy (the conjunction and opposition of the stars). With "To His Coy Mistress" (again in couplets of iambic tetrameter), Marvell wrote the most celebrated poetic illustration of the *topos* of **carpe diem** as well as an early example of a dramatised monologue (see also chap. 4.4). This poem is a tongue-in-cheek

Carpe Diem and a Cavalier Attitude to Love in Poems by Marvell and his Contemporaries

|Fig. 2.17
Andrew Marvell
(1621–1678)

advice given by the male lover to his coy mistress to 'seize the day', here and now ("Now let us sport us while we may", l. 39), as the span of human life is limited, and there will be no opportunity for love thereafter: "The grave's a fine and private place,/But none, I think, do there embrace." (ll. 31–32). Such a view of life and love principally owes more to Classical precedent (Ovid) than to Christian precepts, though the limits of time are pointed out with Biblical references: "I would/Love you ten years before the Flood,/And you should, if you please, refuse/Till the conversion of the Jews." (ll. 7–10). This broad view of world history is complemented by a *blazon* that likewise plays with a panoramic vision:

> An hundred years should go to praise
> Thine eyes, and on thy forehead gaze;
> Two hundred to adore each breast,
> But thirty thousand to the rest:
> An age at least to every part,
> And the last age should show your heart. (ll. 13–18)

This increasingly hyperbolic praise of love and beauty – in quite physical rather than metaphysical terms – is one of the most striking features of Marvell's poem, which thus follows up on Catull's "Vivamus mea Lesbia" (*Carmen* 5) and Donne's "The Computation". In equally sensuous verse that shows a cavalier attitude to love inspired by Catull and Ovid, the **Cavalier Poets** in Ben Jonson's circle justified their label (which also refers to their Royalist politics). With "To the Virgins, to Make Much of Time", the country parson Robert Herrick (1591–1674) offered another striking variation upon the *carpe diem topos*. "Delight in Disorder" and several poems in praise of Julia are further amorous poems that stick out from Herrick's vast collection *Hesperides* (1648). "A Ballad upon a Wedding" (1646) and "Out upon It!" (1659) by Sir John Suckling (1609–42) as well as "Love Made in the First Age. To Chloris" by Richard Lovelace (1618–57, from the enlarged 1659 collection entitled *Lucasta*) also belong into this context. The long and lustful poem entitled "A Rapture" (1640) by Thomas Carew (1595–1640), which sets in with the lines "I will enjoy thee now, my Celia, come/And fly with me to love's Elysium." before it tours the female body, is perhaps the most outspoken period example – outspoken, too, in its rejection of marriage in favour of casual affairs – ahead of the libidinous poems of John Wilmot, Earl of Rochester (1647–80).

While male poets such as Spenser and Donne celebrated the legal act (rather than the consummation) of marriage in their epithalamions, women poets frequently took a more critical look at gender relations. The case of Queen Elizabeth (*1533, reigned 1558–1603) is certainly exceptional, yet "On Monsieur's Departure", composed by the Virgin Queen after breaking off marriage negotiations with the French Duke of Anjou (c.1582, published not before 1823), commands attention as a poem on unfulfilled love by a person with limited choice in matters of the heart. Female poets other than the Queen addressed misogynistic stereotypes as well as the legal and economic restrictions imposed on women. Aemilia Lanyer (1569–1645) was the mistress of the Queen's Lord Chamberlain (and Shakespeare's patron), as well as a poet. Although *Salve Deus Rex Judaeorum* (1611) remained her single volume of poetry, it is nevertheless a starting point for the female tradition of poetry in English. With "Eve's Apology in Defense of Women", it contains, couched into a Biblical frame of reference, a correction of conventionally male-centred views on gender relations. (For Lanyer's "The Description of Cookham", see chap. 2.3.3). Isabella Whitney (*fl.* 1567–73) is a recent discovery who hitherto unknown, is now being anthologised with "Will and Testament" (1573). The altogether 364 lines of Whitney's poem show a regular alternation in rhyme and in their number of (seven and eight) syllables. From the mouth of a *persona*, the poet made a stand and satirised the legal situation that prohibited women from passing on their possessions by making a will. In "A Married State", Katherine Philips (1632–64) continued such a decidedly female stance with regard to the marriage settlement. (Read on in chap. 3.3.3.)

Gender Issues in Women Poets' Verse

The Sonnet Craze

| 2.3.2

The sonnet is one of the major poetic innovations of the Renaissance, when it was available in various media. Because of their shortness and strophic design, those 14-line poems lent themselves to performance in form of a recital. Single or in sequences, sonnets moreover circulated in manuscript and were distributed in print. Historically speaking, the sonnet is a good indicator of the gradual spread of the Renaissance throughout Europe. After its conception in the thirteenth century and a flowering in

The Two Principal Forms of the Sonnet

fourteenth-century Italy with Dante Alighieri (c.1265–1321) and Francesco Petrarca or Petrarch (1304–74), the genre wandered North across France to Britain, where it arrived in the middle of the sixteenth century. The **Italian or Petrarchan sonnet** consists of two quartets or one octave in embracing rhyme (*abba abba*), and two tercets or a sestet that allows for variation (e. g. *cde cde*). The richness of sound, and therefore also the abundance of rhyme words, is generally greater in the Italian language, which is why experimentation with the sonnet form occurred in England until the turn to the seventeenth century. The apparently unauthorised publication of Shakespeare's *Sonnets* (1609) signalled the conventionalisation of a second type of sonnet: the **English or Shakespearean sonnet** is made up of seven rather than five rhymes, and falls into three quartets in alternating rhyme and a final couplet (*abab cdcd efef gg*). Common to both types is therefore a **bipartite form**, and moreover a conventionalised pattern of sound. The major difference, apart from the different realisation of the rhyme scheme, lies in the place of the *volta* or **turn** from one side of the argument to the other within the poem: in Petrarchan sonnets, the *volta* is met in the middle of the poem (after line 8), whereas in a Shakespearean sonnet, the turn (which is often signalled by the word 'but') occurs only two lines before its ending. Thus, any poet after Shakespeare that is aware of both types, can suit the form to his or her intentions: while the Italian sonnet lends itself to a weighing of two argumentative positions, the English sonnet heads for a bombshell, perhaps in the form of a paradoxical conclusion.

Petrarchism

Petrarch's *Il Canzoniere* (printed under the alternate title *Rime* in 1470) merits a closer look, because its design and imagery became the pattern for English poets, too. With both Petrarch and Shakespeare, single sonnets are part of a **sonnet sequence**, and at least with *Il Canzoniere*, there is also a consistent narrative plot. This is the short version: (a) boy meets girl, (b) look, don't touch: the girl is married, (c) Death strikes home: exit girl, (d) the boy funnels his lovesickness into love poetry. It is tempting to spot an autobiographical subtext to this unhappy romance, yet one should note that the element of plotting in this love story extends further. According to the poet's account, his first encounter with Laura and her death 21 years later have occurred, strangely enough, on the same day, namely 6 April. (The poet himself is similarly said to have made his life come full circle, by dying merely two days before his birthday.) An attempt to match poetic fiction to reality is even more conspicuous in the fact that *Il Canzoniere* contains a total of 366 poems, and thus as many as there are days in a leap year (and 1348, the year of Laura's death, was a leap year). In order to present Madonna Laura as an ideal of womanhood, Petrarch makes recurrent use of the **blazon** or catalogue of beauty (from the French *blason du corps*), which extends from Laura's golden hair, dark eyes and white complexion over her red lips and pearl-white teeth to her graceful neck. Amor's darts of love are sent through the eyes of the two lovers, and the lyrical speaker's painful feelings for this female angel are conveyed through a paradoxical imagery that includes 'fire and ice' as a *concetto* or **conceit**. With later sonneteers, such patterns of Petrarchism first became fashionable, and then worn out.

At the court of Henry VIII, poets like Wyatt and Surrey experimented with the Petrarchan form. Their sonnets, which they recited and circulated in manuscript, were freely translated imitations of Petrarch rather than original poems. For *A Book of Songs and Sonnets* (1557, 7th ed. 1584), the bookseller Richard Tottel collected and edited the sonnets of those 'courtly makers'. *Tottel's Miscellany*, as the popular anthology was more commonly called, provided ready examples for later manuals such as George Puttenham's *The Art of English Poesie* (1589). Much like Geoffrey Chaucer in Petrarch's generation, the Tudor poet Sir Thomas Wyatt (1503–42) came into contact with the poetry of the Italian Renaissance on diplomatic missions, which is reflected in his own madrigals and his use of Italian forms of verse. Chaucer's **rhyme royal** (*ababbcc*) is revived in Wyatt's "They flee from me": a reflection on the fickleness of love and lust, and one of Wyatt's poems edited for *Tottel's Miscellany*. For his three satires in the tradition of Horace and the Italian poet Alamanni, Wyatt combined Chaucer's iambic pentameter with Dante's **terza rima** (*aba bcb cbc*). Wyatt's poems in **ottava rima** (*abababcc*), a form pioneered by Boccaccio, are less conspicuous than its more prominent revivals in the poetry of Lord Byron (*Don Juan*, 1819–24) and of W.B. Yeats ("Sailing to Byzantium", 1927). In sonnets such as "I find no peace" and "My galley charged with forgetfulness", Wyatt adapted the Petrarchan model and imagery to English (see *Rime* 134 and 189). The personal tone is deceptive: "Whoso list to hunt" looks

Wyatt and Surrey

|Fig. 2.18
Sir Thomas Wyatt by Hans Holbein, c.1535–37

like a sonnet on Wyatt's alleged love affair with Anne Boleyn, Henry VIII's mistress and queen whom Wyatt knew from childhood, but in fact is a translation of one of Petrarch's sonnets, too (*Rime* 190). Wyatt's "Farewell, Love", on the other hand, is an original that begins as an Italian sonnet but ends in a quatrain and a couplet. Such a **hybrid form**, which exemplifies an intermediate stage in the development from the Petrarchan towards the Shakespearean type of sonnet, is more frequently encountered in the poetry of Henry Howard, Earl of Surrey (1517–47). "Alas! So all things now do hold their peace" (*Rime* 164) and "The soote season" (*Rime* 310) – two of Surrey's sonnets that also found their way into *Tottel's Miscellany* – are good examples of such a hybrid form. Compared with Wyatt's poetry, Surrey's sonnets appear more regular and more melodious, which is borne out when Wyatt's "The long love that in my thought doth harbour" is seen against Surrey's "Love, that doth reign and live within my thought" (a complementary version of *Rime* 140). Over and above his role in the development of the sonnet, Surrey introduced **blank verse** (unrhymed iambic pentameter) to English poetry and drama through his translation of the second and fourth book of the *Aeneid* (posthumously published 1554–57, see chap. 2.4).

Sidney and Spenser

The composition of sonnets continued during the reign of Elizabeth I, in whose glorification as Gloriana and The Virgin Queen politics met with poetry. A climax of the development was reached in the 'Sonnet Craze' of the 1590s, which produced a number of famous **sonnet sequences** circulating in manuscript (some of which continued to be revised and published after 1600). Sir Philip Sidney (1554–86) made a start with *Astrophil and Stella*, a sequence of 119 poems (108 sonnets and eleven songs) printed in 1591. This takes up the Petrarchan convention of passionate love yet unsuccessful courtship to a married woman who is not free. As conventional are the telling names and the idealised features of the two sweethearts roaming the galaxy of love, the star-like Stella and her star-struck suitor. In the initial sonnet to the sequence, Astrophil ('star-lover') protests his true love and also his intention to strive for originality, though such a pose is quite conventional, too. However, it is memorably expressed in the concluding admonition not to copy from other poets' verse: "'Fool,' said my Muse to me, 'look in thy heart and write.'" Sidney's poetic gifts show also in "I never drank of Aganippe well" (no. 74), a hybrid sonnet that combines Classical mythology and Christian imagery as well as features of both the Italian and the English sonnet. Some poems that appeared outside the original sequence in a collection entitled *Certain Sonnets* (1598), such as "Thou blind man's mark" and "Leave me, o Love" (nos. 31 and 32), were appended to *Astrophil and Stella* in later centuries. Over and above all convention and craftsmanship, the fact that Astrophil is a courtier and poet like Sidney wet the curiosity of a contemporary audience for the autobiographical content of the sequence (i.e. to get to know about Sidney's exact relations to Lady Penelope Rich). During Sidney's lifetime, a poets' circle called *Areopagus* developed around him. This included his biographer Fulke Greville, Lord Brooke (1554–1628) and also the poet Edmund Spenser (1552–99), as mentioned above. Greville followed in Sidney's footsteps when he produced *Caelica* (which includes 41 sonnets among a total of 109 poems published in 1633). His sonnet "The earth with thunder torn, with fire blasted" (*Caelica* 29/86) is a good illustration of Elizabethan thought on the Four Elements and on Man. Spenser's sequence *Amoretti* (1595) is special for two reasons. Spenser introduces a new element in that he tells the story of a successful courtship ending in marriage (namely to the widowed poet's second wife), which is why the sequence of 89 sonnets is concluded by an "Epithalamion" (a wedding song in a Classical Greek tradition). Spenser's second innovation is one of form: the **Spenserian sonnet** is a variant of the English type that employs a rhyme link to provide the sonnet with more cohesion. Spenser thus can make do, like Petrarch, with just five rhymes instead of seven (*abab bcbc cdcd ee*). Some of Spenser's sonnets are variations upon Petrarchan originals and their imitations by Wyatt alike (*Amoretti* 34, 67: see the Questions and Exercises section at the end of the present chapter). "One day I wrote her name upon the strand" (75), the best-known sonnet from Spenser's sequence, proposes that human mortality and worldly decay may be overcome through commemoration in an eternal work of art, such as the poem under review. This *aere perennius topos* is found at the end of Ovid's *Metamorphoses* (XV 871–79) and also in Shakespeare's thematically related sonnet no. 60, "Like as the waves make towards the pebbled shore". "Of this worlds Theatre in which we stay" (54) elaborates upon the *theatrum mundi topos*, and thus compares with Jaques's monologue in Shakespeare's *As You Like It* (see chap. 2.2.4) as well as with the short poem "What is our life?" (1612) by the courtier and poet Sir Walter Ralegh. Outside Sidney's circle, Ralegh (or Raleigh, 1552–1618) produced a couple of single sonnets that are still anthologised: "Methought I saw the grave where Laura lay", an English sonnet on Petrarch's lady (1590), and "Three things there be" (c.1600), a piece of advice intended for the poet's son.

Daniel's and Drayton's Sonnet Sequences

Fig. 2.19
Michael Drayton, 1619

The circulation of poems in manuscript entailed the possibility of misattribution. The 1591 edition of Sidney's *Astrophil and Stella* contained 30 sonnets by Samuel Daniel (1562–1619) that were thus published a year before Daniel came out with a sonnet sequence of his own entitled *Delia*, which he continued to revise and expand. Daniel's sonnet "Let others sing of knights and paladins" (*Delia* 46), is built upon the *aere perennius topos*, too, and moreover declares love poetry (read: sonnets) to be superior to romances of chivalry. (For Daniel's literary criticism, see chap. 2.4, and for his and Drayton's long poems, see chap. 2.3.3.) Michael Drayton (1563–1631) is another member of Daniel's and Shakespeare's generation who constantly revised his published poems, which thus exist in different versions. Drayton was a published poet between 1591 and 1630 (a long span!), open to all kinds of poetry, which he himself collected twice, in 1605 and 1619. *Idea: The Shepherds' Garland* (1593) is a pastoral sequence inspired by Spenser's *Shepheardes Calender* (1579). Drayton's sonnet sequence *Idea's Mirror* (1594) saw five revised versions published up to 1619. The introductory poem "To the Reader of These Sonnets" (*Idea* 1, 1599) compares to Sidney's initial sonnet to *Astrophil and Stella* in its higher estimation of individual creativity than of imitation and uniformity. Drayton professes, proudly and patriotically: "My verse is the true image of my mind,/[…]/And as thus to variety inclined,/[…]/My muse is rightly of the English strain,/That cannot long one fashion entertain." (ll. 9–14, *NAEL* I, 999–1000). The sixth sonnet in the sequence entitled "How many paltry, foolish, painted things" combines such fashion bashing with the timeless *aere perennius topos*. "Since there's no help, come, let us kiss and part" (*Idea* 61), Drayton's finest sonnet that was likewise added in 1619, deals with the separation of two lovers. (For good? The paradoxical formulation in the concluding couplet hints at an open ending.)

The early phase of experimentation culminates in William Shakespeare (1564–1616), who established his type of sonnet as the second major variety in the literatures in English. The few factual details known about the poet's life led, perhaps even more so than in the case of other sonneteers, to biographical speculation based on his poems. However, an interpretation that approaches his *Sonnets* (1609) as the record of actual experience runs into more problems than it solves. Such problems with the poems arise, first, from uncertainties connected with their composition and publication; they extend, second, to the possible plot of the sequence; and they concern, third, the exact nature of the relationship between the characters mentioned. The *Sonnets* are thought to have been composed and circulated in manuscript during the 1590s, perhaps until a couple of them were published in a different collection in 1599, a full ten years before they were brought out altogether. The 1609 edition is prefaced by a dedication "To the onlie begetter of these insuing sonnets, Mr W.H.", yet apparently appeared without Shakespeare's consent. This contains less of a mystery (exploited for comic purposes by Oscar Wilde in his essay "The Portrait of Mr W.H.") when the dedication is read together with the signature "T.T." as written by the bookseller and printer, Thomas Thorpe, and not by the poet. Following this argument, whoever Mr W.H. was, it is no longer obligatory to see in the *publisher's* patron the same person as the male friend addressed by the lyrical speaker, and arguably by the *poet*, in the first 17 sonnets of the sequence. As interesting as clue-puzzles are, there is no compelling evidence to read an autobiographical subtext into the characters appearing: the lyrical speaker (not necessarily identical with Shakespeare), a male friend (and not necessarily more than an intimate friend), the capricious Dark Lady who keeps the speaker spellbound (but not necessarily the poet alike), and a rival poet and lover (who does not have to be, say, Christopher Marlowe).

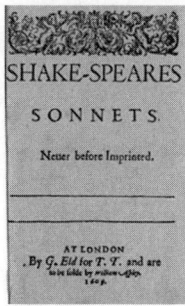

Fig. 2.20
Title page of Shakespeare's *Sonnets* (1609)

This first group of poems is conventionally labelled **'procreation sonnets'** because they deal with principally two options available to the friend in order to outlive his own lifespan. To create a more durable existence, there is, first, the option to father a child, as "nothing 'gainst Time's scythe can make defence/Save breed, to brave him when he takes thee hence." (no. 12, "When I do count the clock that tells the time", ll. 13–14). The second option, *aere* *perennius*, is to have oneself commemorated in the poet's verse: "But were some child of yours alive that time,/You should live twice, in it and in my rhyme." (no. 17, "Who will believe my verse in time to come", ll. 13–14). Precisely because those 'procreation sonnets' evidently fall into a group of their own based on an extended line of thought, they raise questions with regard to the order, cohesion and possible plot of the printed collection. First of all, those 154 sonnets are not Shakespeare's only ones: the Epilogue to his history play *Henry V* is a sonnet, and so are the Chorus's speeches introducing each of the first two acts of the tragedy of *Romeo and Juliet* (with critics pointing to yet more sonnet-like structures in the dialogue of this play). Does the fact that those few sonnets from plays have been omitted say that the poems printed together form a single cohesive sequence with a dramatic action of their own? One will hesitate to answer in the affirmative on every point and without any qualification. There is indeed no conclusive evidence to think that the 1609 edition represents authorial intention rather than the joint venture of the printer and the booksellers mentioned in the imprint. Indeed, the random order of the remaining sonnets within the volume, and the rather loose connection amongst and between further thematic groups and seemingly single sonnets, does not rule out the possibility that the design of the collection is the work of the moment rather than a planned sequence with a proper plot. (Note that in the second, 1640 edition, Shakespeare's sonnets were rearranged.)

This entails significant consequences for the interpretation of the exact nature of the relationship between the characters. Although sonnet no. 18 (famously pondering the question "Shall I compare thee to a summer's day?") directly follows upon the first group of sonnets addressed to a *male* friend, those poems and their addresses may in fact be unrelated. There is no proper reason, therefore, to think of sonnet no. 18 as homoerotic verse when it might also be seen as a beautifully phrased eulogy on an idealised *female* person. Other than this, Shakespeare's adherence to genre conventions extends to the use of the *topos* of *aere perennius* in the final couplet of this sonnet. (The same *topos*, and the same ambivalence of address, is found again in sonnets no. 55, "Not marble, nor the gilded monuments", and no. 60, which was mentioned above in connection with Spenser.)

The eulogy in sonnet no. 18 contrasts well with Shakespeare's sonnet no. 127 in praise of black beauty ("In the old age black was not counted fair,/[...] But now is black beauty's successive heir", ll. 1–3), which introduces the group of sonnets referring to a Dark Lady (e.g. 130–32, 147). Their juxtaposition with other, seemingly self-referential sonnets (see the poet's pun on the name William in "Whoever hath her wish, thou hast thy 'Will'," no. 135) increased the speculation about Shakespeare's personal involvement in a love triangle (42, 133–34) that might also have included a rival poet (76–86). Where Shakespeare deviates even more from conventional idealisations of womanhood is in his parodies on "the blazon of sweet beauty's best,/Of hand, of foot, of lip, of eye, of brow," here in sonnet no. 106 (ll. 5–6) and also in the famous anti-Petrarchist sonnet no. 130. There, the poet parodies the *blazon* or catalogue of beauty by representing it as a checklist of negatives: "My mistress' eyes are nothing like the sun;/Coral is far more red then her lips' red:" and so forth. Far from flattery, indeed; yet the point of such exercise in negativity is reached after the turn, in the final couplet, where realism is rated higher than conventional praise: "And yet, by heaven, I think my love as rare/As any she belied with false compare." To see such poems merely as a clue to Shakespeare's individual life and sexual inclinations is clearly reductive. There are two further sonnets that profit from a comparison. Sonnet no. 116 celebrates everlasting love and its consummation within marriage: "Let me not to the marriage of true minds/Admit impediments. Love is not love/Which alters when it alteration finds," (ll. 1–3). By contrast, sonnet no. 129 turns from love to lust. The initial, laid-back definition of the sexual act as "The expense of spirit in a waste of shame/Is lust in action" (ll. 1–2) is extended in the course of the poem into a breathless and passionate lecture on the joys and discomforts of lustful love. While this is a far cry from Petrarchism, it finds its companion pieces in the love poetry (though not the sonnets) of John Donne.

Donne (1572–1631) is remembered for the striking (and sexually quite uninhibited) use of imagery in his love poetry, which was first assembled under the title "Songs and Sonnets" in the second posthumous (1635) edition of his poetry. "Sonnet. The Token" is however the single proper (Shakespearean) example within this group, while "Witchcraft by a Picture" is a variation

Donne's Holy Sonnets

(rhyming *ababccc dedefff*), and Donne did not set out to write a sonnet sequence on courtship. Instead, the future Dean of St. Paul's turned from secular to **religious love**, and thus broadened the subject matter of the sonnet, when he composed his *Holy Sonnets* in c.1608. Under this general title (albeit in variant order of the poems), Donne's posthumous editors, beginning with the 1633 first collection of his poetry, assembled two sequences and a couple of single sonnets. "La Corona" is a 'crown' of seven religious sonnets, each of which begins with the last line of its predecessor, with the last sonnet coming round to the initial line of the first ("Deign at my hands this crown of prayer and praise"). The second sequence of 19 "Divine Meditations" stands out for Donne's display of ingenuity in finding fresh expressions for his cosmological and 'metaphysical' subject matter. One sonnet cites the medieval view of the Earth as a disk, but paradoxically seems to square the circle, when it begins with the words "At the round earth's imagined corners, blow/Your trumpets, angels, [...]" (no. 4/7). In another sonnet, the speaker first defines Man as a Microcosm and as a sinner, before he elaborates upon this conventional cosmological view:

> I am a little world made cunningly
> Of elements, and an angelic sprite [i.e., spirit],
> But black sin hath betrayed to endless night
> My world's both parts, and, oh, both parts must die.
>
> You which beyond that heaven which was most high
> Have found new spheres, and of new lands can write,
> Pour new seas in mine eyes, that so I might
> Drown my world with my weeping earnestly,
> (no. 14/5, ll. 1–8, Donne 1986: 310–11)

The second quartet is addressed either to the souls of the blessed, ascending to new heavens beyond the known spheres, or to those recent astronomers since Copernicus who have come up with a new design of the Universe. That link between religion and science is developed into an even more complex image which contains references alike to the Biblical Flood and to voyages of discovery. In a telling way, Donne's sonnet thus pinpoints the ambivalence of his age, hovering between hitherto established religious beliefs and a more secular outlook. Two further *Holy Sonnets* stand out for Donne's peculiar use of imagery. "Batter my heart, three-personed God" (no. 10/14) does not only invite the Christian Trinity bluntly "to break, blow, burn, and make me new" (l. 4), but also concludes with the paradoxical statement that "I/Except you enthral me, never shall be free,/Nor ever chaste, except you ravish me." (ll. 12–14) – a drastic fusion of religious longing and of rape understood as a form of making love. The other outstanding sonnet anticipates the theme of 'Don't fear the Reaper' (the 1976 hit record by the rock band Blue Öyster Cult); Donne's words, though, are directly addressed to Death: "Death be not proud, though some have called thee/Mighty and dreadful, for, thou art not so,/[…]/One short sleep past, we wake eternally,/And death shall be no more, Death thou shalt die." (6/10, ll. 1–2, 13–14, 1986: 313). Again, Donne's final couplet ends in a paradox, this time drawing on the Christian notion of Resurrection. A glance at Shakespeare's sonnet no. 146 (that ends in the couplet: "So shalt thou feed on Death, that feeds on men,/ And Death once dead, there's no more dying then.") and further at George Herbert's "Death" as another contemporary poem on the same theme, but with a different emphasis, helps to see the extraordinary features of Donne's manner in stronger relief. His *Holy Sonnets* are marked by their lively tone and the frequent use of **enjambment or run-on lines**, and moreover by Donne's persistent use of the **hybrid form** *abba abba cdcd ee*, for which Wyatt's "Farewell, Love" and similar sonnets by Surrey and Sidney were early specimens. Seen from a different angle, one could say that Donne sums up the formal experiments of his predecessors.

"A Sonnet to the Noble Lady, the Lady Mary Wroth" by Ben Jonson (1572–1637), Shakespeare's friend and rival as a playwright, exemplifies well the circulation in manuscript that is so typical of Donne's verse. The addressee of Jonson's only sonnet, Lady Mary Wroth (née Sidney, 1587–?1651), was the exception from the rule in that she was a female poet who composed a sonnet sequence (*Pamphilia to Amphilanthus*, 1621) which included another *corona* ("A Crown of Sonnets Dedicated to Love"). Further minor sonneteers from the sixteenth and early seventeenth centuries have some interest with regard to their **treatment of region and of gender**. The Scotsman William Drummond of Hawthornden (1585–1649) is notable not only for his madrigals (see chap. 2.3.1), but also as the composer of one of the last proper Petrarchan sonnet sequences. His *Flowers of Sion* (1623) includes religious sonnets such as "Saint John Baptist" and "For the Magdalene". Drummond's poetry is moreover telling for the general literary development at that time just because he tried to weed out any Scots feature in his verse. By comparison, the names of his fellow Scottish sonneteers Alexander Scott (c.1525–85) and Alexander Montgomerie (?1556–c.1611) are known among literary historians only. In their stead, recent editions of the NAEL include the very minor poet Richard Barnfield (1574–1627), because his sonnet sequence Cynthia (1595) exceptionally addresses male homosexual rather than heterosexual desire.

Milton's Sonnets

"Prayer (1)" (a series of metaphors without connection to a main verb) and all further single sonnets by George Herbert (1593–1633) are devoted, like Donne's Holy Sonnets, to his Christian faith. The last major poet that tried his hand at the sonnet before it fell into neglect during the Neoclassical period was John Milton (1608–74). Though he was certainly familiar with Shakespeare's Sonnets, Milton returned to the original Italian form (and occasionally even turned to the Italian language) in his 24 single sonnets composed between 1630 and 1658. They deal with personal matters, with religion and with politics, and in particular with his **topical political sonnets**, Milton, too, extended the subject matter of the genre in the time of the Commonwealth and the Protectorate. "To the Lord General Cromwell, May 1652" praises the Puritan leader and at the same time speaks out against proposals for an established church and a paid clergy. Milton's "On the Late Massacre in Piedmont" (written in 1655) denounces the slaughter of Protestants by troops of the Catholic Duke of Savoy, and calls for revenge. In addition to such poems on worldly matters, Milton wrote two moving sonnets on personal loss. "When I consider how my light is spent" was probably written in 1652, the year when Milton lost first his wife, Mary, and then his eyesight completely – which appeared to bereave him of all his poetic talents and training before he could properly set out to "justify the ways of God to men". In 1658, soon after he had begun to compose his religious epic Paradise Lost, which sets in with those words (l. 26), Milton lost Katherine, his second wife. The sonnet and dream vision "Methought I saw my late espousèd saint", written in that year, reflects the death of either Mary or Katherine. In addition to their note of personal grief, those two sonnets composed at turning points of Milton's life are memorable, too, for the manner in which Milton makes the bipartite form of the Italian sonnet forget through his use of enjambment and of lines of verse running from the octave directly into the sestet. As a sonneteer and as a visionary, Milton inspired the Romantic poets, particularly Wordsworth and Blake (see chaps. 3.3.2 and 3.4.1).

Epic Poetry and Other Long Poems

John Milton, the last major sonneteer of the period, achieved his masterwork in the form of poetry that enjoyed highest esteem: the epic. During the Renaissance, Homer's *Iliad* and *Odyssey*, Virgil's *Aeneid* and Ovid's *Metamorphoses* as Classical examples of poetic narrative became available in verse translations by e.g. Surrey, Golding and Chapman (see chap. 2.4). Characters from Greek and Roman mythology reappeared moreover in shorter epics that were composed by the dramatists Marlowe and Shakespeare in the interval when the London theatres were temporarily closed because of the Plague. *Hero and Leander*, the tragic story (first told by the poet Musaios) about two lovers that ends with his accidental death and her subsequent suicide, was taken up by Christopher Marlowe not long before his death (1593) and turned into a highly eroticised tale. In 1598, Marlowe's fragment was first published on its own and then reissued together with the continuation and completion by George Chapman (1559–1634). Around the same time, Shakespeare wrote and published another verse tale of lustful love and tragic death, based upon Ovid and older sources: in *Venus and Adonis* (1593), the goddess fails to seduce the beautiful young man, and is left to mourn him when he dies at the tusks of a wild boar. Shakespeare followed this up with the Roman tale of *The Rape of Lucrece* (1594), written in Chaucer's *rhyme royal* (*ababbcc*). Michael Drayton (1563–1631) trailed behind with the minor epic *Endimion and Phoebe* (1595), which he revised as *The Man in the Moon* (1606, 1619).

Apart from his constantly revised and expanded sonnet sequence *Idea* (1593–1619, see above), Michael Drayton is also known for a number of such longer poems that were likewise subjected to his habit of reworking. *Poly-Olbion* (1612, and again 1622), a historical and topographical poem of 30,000 lines, is his *magnum opus*. Composed in rhyming couplets of hexameter or *Alexandrines*, this is a poetic memorial to the history of all the

2.3.3

Shorter Epics of the 1590s

Fig. 2.21

Title page of Christopher Marlowe's *Hero and Leander*

Drayton's and Daniel's Long Poems

Fig. 2.22

Title page of Drayton's *Poly-Olbion*, 1622

Horatian and Pindaric Odes

Donne's *Anniversaries*

counties of England and Wales as well as a travel guide to their sights. Though hardly a profitable enterprise, this was a great poetic effort indeed, as was Samuel Daniel's historical epic *The Civil Wars Between the Two Houses of Lancaster and York* (8 vols. in *ottava rima*, 1595), which however remained a fragment after 15 years of work. When Michael Drayton composed his historical epics – *Robert of Normandy* (1596, revised 1605 and 1619), *The Baron's Wars* (1603) and *The Battle of Agincourt* (1627) – he shared the source Shakespeare used for his historical plays, namely Holinshed's *Chronicle*. In 1627, *Nimphidia*, Drayton's sequence of fairy poems inspired by Shakespeare's *A Midsummer Night's Dream*, came out to much acclaim.

Drayton's earlier collection of *Poems Lyric and Pastoral* (1606) contains the first imitations of Horace's odes brought out by an English poet, such as the "Ode to the Virginian Voyage" celebrating the early colonisation of New England (see chap. 2.4). Andrew Marvell's "An Horatian Ode Upon Cromwell's Return from Ireland" (1650) is another example of this homostrophic type that makes use of just one stanza form throughout. In 1629, Ben Jonson had set out to write both the Horatian "Ode to Himself" and another ode that closely imitates the tripartite Pindaric type: Jonson's "To the Immortal Memory and Friendship of That Noble Pair, Sir Lucius Cary and Sir H. Morison" (1640–41) translates the original Pindaric sequence of *strophe*, *antistrophe* and *epode* into "The Turn", "The Counterturn" and "The Stand" (a third section designed differently). In 1656, Abraham Cowley (1618–67) likewise published his Horatian "Ode of Wit" alongside other, irregular odes such as "In Praise of Pindar". Cowley bequeathed such an understanding of Pindaric odes as basically irregular in design to Wordsworth and other Romantic poets (see chap. 3.3.2). In further odes on Thomas Hobbes the philosopher and on William Harvey the physician (who had 'discovered' the circulation of the blood) and also in a later ode written in praise of Sir Francis Bacon and addressed "To the Royal Society" (1667), Cowley acknowledged the impact of Renaissance philosophy and science.

Such an impact was felt, too, in two long poems written and published by John Donne in 1611 and 1612 on the anniversaries of the death of a young girl from a wealthy London family. Both in his funeral elegies and in his *epithalamions* or marriage songs, Donne (like Edmund Spenser in the 1595 "Epithalamion" on his own second marriage) had proved that he could furnish occasional verse with lasting value. Just so with those sombre poems which may originally have been commissioned as funeral elegies by the parents of Elizabeth Drury, and which Donne turned into *An Anatomy of the World: The First Anniversary*, and into a meditation entitled *Of the Progress of the Soul: The Second Anniversary*. Both poems reflect medieval views on a geocentric universe as well as on Man as a Microcosm, and they bring the Classical *sic transit gloria mundi topos* together with the Christian notion of the whole world in decay since the Fall.

> This man, so great, that all that is, is his,
> Oh what a trifle, and poor thing he is!
> If man were anything, he's nothing now:
> [...]
>
> Then, as mankind, so is the world's whole frame
> Quite out of joint, almost created lame:
> For, before God had made all the rest,
> Corruption entered, and depraved the best:
> (*First Anniv.*, ll. 169–71, 191–94; 1986: 275)

The First Anniversary is moreover spiced with references to the revolutionary impact of the new, heliocentric universe envisaged by astronomers since Copernicus (see chap. 2.1), which entailed more than blotting out the outermost sphere related to one of the Four Elements:

> And new philosophy calls all in doubt,
> The element of fire is quite put out;
> The sun is lost, and th' earth, and no man's wit
> Can well direct him where to look for it.
> And freely men confess that this world's spent,
> When in the planets, and the firmament
> They seek so many new; they see that this
> Is crumbled out again to his atomies.
> 'Tis all in pieces, all coherence gone;
> All just supply, and all relation:
> Prince, subject, father, son, are things forgot,
> (ll. 205–15, 1986: 276; see also ll. 249–304)

The impact of Renaissance science and social change on the hierarchical order of Christian society and the medieval cosmos is recorded by Donne, but also accorded the dangerous quality of a descent into chaos.

Country-House Poems

Fig. 2.23
Penshurst Place, 2008

The hierarchical character of society in Renaissance England is moreover mirrored in a minor though telling genre of long poems written on the estates and country-houses of the nobility and the landed gentry. The very first of such place poems, which thereby implicitly acknowledge the aristocratic patronage of verse, are "The Description of Cooke-ham" by Aemilia Lanyer (1569–1645) and "To Penshurst" by Ben Jonson (1572–1637). In the Classical and pastoral tradition of Virgil's first *Eclogue*, Lanyer's country-house poem (210 ll., 1611) bids farewell to an estate where the poet enjoyed the patronage of her art. Jonson's "To Penshurst" (1616), at half that length yet of much greater impact, is addressed to, and speaking of the estate of a younger brother of Sir Philip Sidney, who was born at the manor. "At Penshurst" (1645), a companion poem by Edmund Waller (1606–87), pales beside "To Saxham" (1640) by a member of Ben Jonson's circle of poets, namely Thomas Carew (1594/95–1640), and beside "Cooper's Hill" (1642) by Sir John Denham (1615–69). Most of those country-house poems were composed in **heroic couplets** (of iambic pentameter), the standard metre of successive Neoclassical verse, which is why in particular "Cooper's Hill" enjoyed a longer shelf-life that lasted well into the eighteenth century. Carew's "To Saxham" is an exception from the rule, as it is cast in rhyming couplets of iambic tetrameter (rather than pentameter), and this pertains also to the major and likewise the longest example of the genre: "Upon Appleton House" by Andrew Marvell (1621–78) runs to altogether 97 octets or 776 lines. Marvell's long poem was composed in 1651, while the poet lived on the estate of his patron, General Fairfax. The former parliamentary general, to whom John Milton had dedicated a sonnet ("On the Lord General Fairfax at the Siege of Colchester", written in 1648), had retired rather than join Cromwell in his campaign in Scotland. By showing the reader round the estate, Marvell's poem consummately celebrates its beauty as a modern Garden of Eden (a pastoral note), together with the history of both the great house and the Fairfax family.

Spenser's Epic *The Faerie Queene*

The longest and most ambitious praise poems of the Renaissance were the epics composed by Edmund Spenser (1552–99) and by John Milton. With his Arthurian epic *The Faerie Queene*, Spenser attempted to emulate the success that the Italian Renaissance poets Ariosto (*Orlando furioso*, 1516–32) and Tasso (*Gerusa-*

lemme liberata, 1581) had had with their epics full of chivalrous Christian knights and crusaders. Most of *The Faerie Queene* was written during Spenser's stay in Ireland (which is reflected in the poem). There, he had been rewarded with an estate bordering on Sir Walter Ralegh's for assisting the Queen's deputy in Ireland, who with extraordinary ruthlessness and brutality attempted to break Irish resistance to the extension of English rule (a political goal that the patriotic English poet endorsed). Spenser's original plan for his epic, as laid down in his explanatory letter addressed to Ralegh (1590), conceived of "a continued Allegory, or darke conceit" in twelve books *à* twelve cantos (epic songs), peopled by a great number of personifications and other allegorical characters. Spenser completed only six books in two instalments, printed in 1590 (I–III) and 1596 (III–VI) respectively, that were trailed by two Mutability Cantos published posthumously in 1609. Yet even in its fragmentary state, *The Faerie Queene* is three times as long as Milton's *Paradise Lost*, which is the consummate achievement in this genre. In addition to repeating his habit of writing back to Chaucer with deliberately archaic spelling and wording (first shown in *The Shepheardes Calender*, 1579), Spenser came up with an original nine-line stanza of his own invention, which was frequently imitated in successive centuries (see chap. 2.3.1). Each book of Spenser's allegorical epic is dedicated to one virtue (e.g. Temperance, Chastity and Friendship), and relates the adventures of one of Arthur's Knights of the Round Table, as told on one of twelve successive days of an annual feast in fairyland. When Arthur makes his appearance, he is considerably younger than the character in Malory's *Le Morte Darthur* (1485, see chap. 1), and he is moreover presented as infatuated with Gloriana, the Fairy Queen, to the point where their marriage becomes a future option. Such a union between the glorious Queen Elizabeth (in the letter to Ralegh, Spenser flattered his monarch with such an allegorical interpretation of Gloriana) and the legendary Briton symbolised the unbroken bond of British history and the English nation. Such a connection met with the Tudor Myth as a political ideology (see chap. 2.2.2; quite programmatically, Henry VII, the first Tudor monarch, had named his first-born son Arthur). That link is further stressed in Book II, where the tenth canto follows up a eulogy on Queen Elizabeth with an epic list of the Kings of Britons right to the ending of the canto. The twelfth canto con-

| Fig. 2.24
Prince Arthur and the Faerie Queene, by J. H. Füssli, c.1788

tains another celebrated passage dealing with what looks like an earthly Paradise or *hortus conclusus*, but turns out to be a place of sexual allure and temptation. In the tellingly named Bower of Bliss (II.12, st. 42ff.), the knight Sir Guyon is first teased by 'two naked Damzelles' (st. 63–68) before he meets Acrasia the witch, a *femme fatale* and seductress of numerous knights (who, once discarded, are transformed by her into wild beasts). Acrasia's name signifies intemperance or the incontinence of desires – vices that are exactly opposed to the virtue of Temperance celebrated in Book II, and this is why Sir Guyon finally destroys this palace of the senses. The whole passage owes something to the description of the garden of Armida in Tasso's *Gerusalemme liberata*, and it foreshadows the ballad "La Belle Dame sans Merci" by the Romantic poet John Keats. When Spenser's national and allegorical epic is uncommonly tinged with eroticism, here and in the comparable tale of Venus and the Garden of Adonis (III.6), it begins to resemble the manner of the minor mythological epics penned by his contemporaries Marlowe and Shakespeare.

Milton's *Paradise Lost*

Fig. 2.25

Satan, book ill. by Gustave Doré, in Milton's *Paradise Lost*, c.1866

About half a century later, John Milton (1608–74) decided against another Spenserian national epic based on Arthurian literature (which had been his original intention), and committed himself to a religious epic instead. Milton's sonnet "When I consider how my light is spent" is related to the strenuous composition of his masterwork, which the blind poet had to dictate to his daughters. *Paradise Lost*, a Biblical epic on the Fall and on Satan the Fallen Angel, appeared in 1667, at first in ten books and then (in the 1674 revision) in twelve books, trailed by the four books of *Paradise Regained* (1671) that concern themselves with the temptations of Christ. In the meantime, three Royalist poets had come out with epics of their own: Sir William Davenant (or D'Avenant, 1606–68) with an epic of chivalry called *Gondibert* (1650–51), Samuel Butler (1612–80) with *Hudibras*, a mock-chivalrous epic and a satire against Puritan rule (1663–84), and Abraham Cowley with the fragment of a Biblical epic entitled *Davideis* (1656). It is a mark of Milton's mastery that none of these rival poetic narratives has endured, despite the criticism that now and then has been directed against the Latinate syntax of Milton's 'grand style', which does not always sound habitual to English ears. The poetic force of Milton's blank verse can be felt, however, right from the beginning. The first two epic books are set in Hell, where Satan the "apostate Angel" and "Arch-Fiend" (I.125, 156; Milton 1966: 215–16) holds counsel with Beelzebub and other devils shortly after they have been hurled from Heaven. The epic narrator's **invocation** to his muse Urania (I.5–26, 376, VII.1), the initial description of Satan in the form of an extended, **epic simile** (I.196–210, see also 284 ff.), the review of Satan's legions together with the long list of his fellow-fighters' names (I.376ff.) and the later account of the **heroic battle** between God's Arch-Angels and his Arch-Fiends (V–VI) all belong to the defining features of the genre. Satan's speeches to his peers resemble the **Vice monologues** in Renaissance stage-plays (e. g. I.156–91), and the description of Pandemonium, Satan's palace in Hell, is as striking an instance of **the Sublime** in poetry, as the Garden of Eden is of **the Beautiful** (I.670ff., IV.205ff.; see chap. 3.1). In the Arch-Angel Raphael's account of the Creation, related to Adam in Paradise, the pre-Copernican, geocentric and spherical universe is once more evoked (VII). Its harmonious beauty and simplicity was certainly much easier to reconcile with a belief in Divine Creation, which is why this cosmological conception, though at that time already obsolete, best served Milton's overall rhetorical intention, that "I may assert Eternal Providence,/and justify the ways of God to men." (I.25–26). In order to facilitate such purpose, Milton prefaced each book of verse by a prose summary of "The Argument", which for Book VIII simply states: "Adam inquires concerning celestial motions, is doubtfully answered, and exhorted to search rather things more worthy of knowledge." (1966: 355). Adam's enquiries into cosmological details mark his incipient thirst for more knowledge than is allocated to him, and lead directly to the climactic story of the Fall (IX). The epic narrative is rounded off with God's punishment inflicted upon the devils (X), and with a vision of history beyond the Flood to the Second Coming of Christ, granted by the Arch-Angel Michael to Adam before he leads Adam and Eve out of Eden (XI–XII).

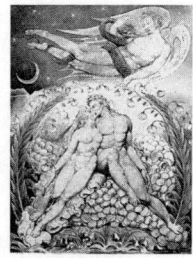

| Fig. 2.26
William Blake,
Satan Watching the Caresses of Adam and Eve, 1808

A forlorn couple of first lovers amidst heroic fights between guardian angels and evil fiends in a scenery part Beautiful and part Sublime, all of it orchestrated by a Divine monarch presiding over Creation and the Fall: as effective as *Paradise Lost* is as a poetic embellishment of the Bible, this is not what Milton actually meant by 'justifying the ways of God to men'. In order to do so, the poet who served Cromwell's Protectorate had to begin explaining those ways to the Puritan, Republican and Democrat in himself. Milton evidently looked for a solution to a personal dilemma that opened up for him between his Republican scepticism towards an Absolutist monarch ruling by Divine Right (his own), his Democratic ideals of free will and individual choice, and the Calvinist creed of Predestination (which leaves no room for such choice). In the encounters first between God the Father and the Son (III), and then between Adam and Eve in Paradise before the Fall (IX.204ff.), Milton tried to deal with his conflicting religious and political beliefs, and to negotiate Faith and Reason (see in particular IX.343–56). Such concerns and ideals were also addressed and negotiated in the prose writing of the period.

Guiding Questions and Exercises

1. Sum up the development of poetry during the Renaissance with regard to individual genres. Moreover, try to account for the usage of the media and the parallel channels of distribution: recital and performance, the circulation of poetry in manuscript, and the publication in print.

2. Petrarch's sonnet "Passa la nave mia colma d'oblio" (*Rime* 189) was freely translated first by Sir Thomas Wyatt as "My galley charged with forgetfulness", and then by Edmund Spenser as "Lyke as a ship that through the Ocean wyde" (*Amoretti* 34). Compare the three poems with regard to their make-up and treatment of the theme. To extend the comparison with another group of related poems, take a further look at the form and imagery of Petrarch's "Una candida cerva sopra l'erba" (*Rime* 190), Wyatt's "Whoso list to hunt" and Spenser's "Lyke as a huntsman after weary chace" (*Amoretti* 67).

3. At the turn to the twentieth century, the American poet Edwin Arlington Robinson (1869–1935) became famous for his sonnets. "Another Dark Lady" is included in Robinson's *The Man Against the Sky* (1916) and in his *Collected Poems* (New York: Macmillan, 1944, 41–42). Discuss this poem in the light of the sonnet tradition, with particular reference to Shakespeare's Dark Lady sonnets. You may extend the discussion to the anonymous fifteenth-century poem "Of his Ugly Lady" (Clark and Healy 1997: 9) and to related poems written by Shakespeare's contemporaries (reprinted in Meller 1985: 42–55).

4. C. S. Lewis (1898–1963), who wrote *The Chronicles of Narnia* (1950–56), was also a Renaissance specialist at Cambridge University, and a poet. Lewis's sonnet "As the Ruin Falls" is included in his *Poems*, ed. Walter Hooper (London: Geoffrey Bles, 1964) and in Noçon (1983: 138–39). Rehearse the argument in this poem and then discuss it, too, in the light of the sonnet tradition.
5. Compare Milton's *Paradise Lost* to Spenser's *The Faerie Queene* with regard to the poets' use of epic conventions for their ideological purposes.
6. Take a look at chap. 2.4 and compare thematically related works of Renaissance poetry and prose.

Utopia and Other Prose Writings

| 2.4

The European Renaissance (literally: re-birth) is a period of religious reformation, geographical exploration, scientific discovery, and cultural rediscovery. Part of the Protestant Reformation in England and Scotland was the renewed effort put into the **translation of the Bible into English**, following upon the first complete translation produced by John Wycliffe and his followers after 1380. The translations of the New Testament (1525) and of sections of the Old (1534) by William Tyndale (c.1490–1536) were considered heretical and could only be published abroad. Tyndale himself died at the stake in 1536, but his work found its way into the *Great Bible* (in Folio format), the first authorised version of the English Bible, which in 1539 was required to be placed in every English church. Its successor, the *Geneva Bible* of 1560, remained an influential Protestant English Bible even after King James I had ordered a revised translation. The *Authorised Version* or *King James Bible* (1611) had a **lasting effect on English prose style**, and so had *The Book of Common Prayer*, which regulated Anglican church-service. The first edition of 1549 was revised in 1552 by Archbishop Thomas Cranmer, who died as a Protestant martyr in 1556. A companion-piece in verse can be seen in the poetical translations of the Psalms that were begun by Sir Philip Sidney (1554–86) and completed (c.1595) by his sister Mary Herbert, the Countess of Pembroke (1562–1621). With 107 out of 150 poetic

Translations of the Bible and the Psalms

translations, hers was the greater contribution to a widely circulated volume of great impact on other religious poets.

Sermons and Religious Tracts

Apart from the Bible, the numerically strongest category of printed books in the Renaissance were sermons, which were considered part of literature. A characteristic feature of the *96 Sermons* (1629) by Lancelot Andrewes (1555–1626) is the close reading of the Biblical text. John Donne (1572–1631), poet and Dean of St. Paul's in London, left some 160 sermons for publication (1632), including "Death's Duel", which in fact became his own funeral sermon. In addition to his weekly sermons, Donne composed 23 meditative *Devotions upon Emergent Occasions* (1624). Sir Thomas Browne (1605–82) wrote further notable books of religious prose in which he told about his life and opinions on various matters (*Religio Medici*, 1643), or meditated at length about death (*Hydriotaphia; or, Urn-Burial*, 1658). The poet Thomas Traherne (1637–74) later followed suit with *Centuries of Meditations* (the manuscript of which turned up only in 1896–97). Another group of religious tracts was concerned with the relation between individual Christians and the Church. William Tyndale's *The Obedience of a Christian Man* (1527) belongs into this category, and so does *Of the Laws of Ecclesiastical Polity* (8 books, 1593–1662), in which Richard Hooker (1554–1600) defended the doctrine and the hierarchy of the Anglican Church against Catholics and Calvinists (Puritans as well as Presbyterians) alike. In *The Reason of Church Government* (1642), the Puritan poet John Milton (1608–74) returned to that issue, arguing against Hooker that any church government can only be based on the Bible.

Topographical and Travel Literature

Further prominent features of the Renaissance period are the **voyages of discovery** that led to a widening of the horizon of Europeans, and to commercial and intercultural contacts under the sign of colonialism and slavery. Reports written during or after such exploratory voyages were compiled by Richard Hakluyt (c.1552–1616) in *The Principal Navigations, Voyages, Traffics, and Discoveries of the English Nation* (1589; rev. and expanded ed. 1598–1600), and read all over Europe in translations. *A True Discourse of the late Voyages of Discovery* (1578) tells the story of Martin Frobisher's three voyages to the Arctic in search of the Northwest Passage to China (1576–78). *The Famous Voyage of Sir Francis Drake into the South Sea, and therehence about the whole Globe of the Earth,* is an account written by Francis Pretty, a member of the crew who joined Sir Francis Drake (1540–96) on this (second) circum-navigation of the Globe (1577–80). Drake was hindered by Queen Elizabeth to write the report himself, as his own material about his dealings with the Spanish colonies was classified a state secret. Sir Walter Ralegh (or Raleigh, 1552–1618), another of the Queen's favourite courtiers and explorers, was able to personally relate the story of his 1595 expedition to the West Indies and South America in *The Discovery of the Large, Rich and Beautiful Empire of Guiana* (1596). Ralegh had been involved in the founding of **Virginia, the first English colony** in North America, named after the 'Virgin Queen' Elizabeth. *A Brief and True Report of the New-Found Land of Virginia* (1588) is a contemporary report by Thomas Hariot (c.1560–1621). During his imprisonment for treason under Elizabeth's successor James I, Sir Walter Ralegh attempted to write *The History of the World* (1614; published 1628), but was hindered to complete it through another voyage to South America, and his subsequent execution. In addition to those prose writings, there exist poetical remembrances of the beginnings of the British Empire. Michael Drayton (1563–1631) composed the "Ode to the Virginian Voyage" (1606) for the establishment of a permanent settlement in Jamestown, Virginia. In the 1650s, Andrew Marvell (1621–78) wrote a song (in rhyming couplets) on the Bermuda Islands, sung by English sailors rowing a small boat. Marvell's "Bermudas" (published posthumously 1681) is a poem in praise of God for the creation of this island paradise.

In addition to its 'discovery' of New Worlds abroad, Tudor and Stuart Britain re-discovered the Ancient World and its cultural heritage. William Tyndale could base his prose translation of the New Testament on the Greek and Latin versions prepared by Erasmus of Rotterdam (†1536) who was, together with his close friend Sir Thomas More, one of the public faces of **Renaissance Humanism** (see chap. 2.1) While Humanists like More continued to write in Latin, major works of Ancient Greek and Roman literature for the first time appeared in English **translations** in verse and prose. The original Latin hexameter of Virgil's *Aeneid* was translated into English by the printer Wiliam Caxton (*Eneydos*, 1490) and the Scottish poet Gavin Douglas (*Eneados*, 1513), before the Earl of Surrey (1517–47) experimented with blank verse in his translation of the second and fourth book of the *Aeneid* (1554–57). Arthur Golding (1536–1605) came out with his verse translations of Ovid's

Re-Discoveries of the Past

| Fig. 2.27
Sir Walter Raleigh by Nicholas Hilliard, c.1585

Metamorphoses (1565–67) before George Chapman (1559–1634) followed suit with his translations, in different forms of verse, of Homer's *Iliad* (1611) and *Odyssey* (1614–15, in 'heroic couplets'). 'Chapman's Homer' was to impress the Romantic poet John Keats a full two centuries later (see chap. 3.3.1), even though Chapman had created such a powerful effect by working from a Latin translation instead of the original Greek. Thomas North's prose translation of Plutarch (1579) was likewise based on the French translation of Jacques Amyot. By such re-discovery, through the editing of past masters and by publishing works of their own, Renaissance Humanists profoundly influenced their contemporary literature. North's translation of Plutarch, for example, proved useful to Shakespeare in the composition of his Roman Plays. In similar fashion, *The Mirror for Magistrates* (1559), with its account of the fall of princes, had a great impact on Elizabethan history plays. So did the Latin and English **chronicles** of Tudor historians such as Polydore Vergil (*Anglica historia*, 1534), Edward Hall (*The Union of the Two Noble and Illustrious Families of Lancaster and York*, 1548) and Raphael Holinshed (*Chronicles of England, Scotland and Ireland*, 1587), not to forget the partisan *History of King Richard III* written by Sir Thomas More in Latin and in English (c.1513–20, publ. in English 1557; see chap. 2.2.2).

Utopia, another work of More (1478–1535) that was written at about the same time, is the most prominent example of English literary Humanism. This fictional travel narrative was given a Greek title and setting, but it was composed and published in Latin prose (1516). It is cast in the form of a philosophical dialogue between More as well as further real historical persons, and an invented traveller called Raphael Hythlodeus (which translates as 'nonsense-pedlar'). Book I, which was completed in London in 1516, contains a 'talk within the talk' that Hythlodeus remembers to have had with the Lord Chancellor, Cardinal John Morton (†1500), and in which the traveller laments the social grievances in contemporary England. Then, More juxtaposes such social criticism with a general discussion of Utopian Communism. This however values the interests of society higher than the freedom of the individual. In the exchange between More and Hythlodeus on the make-up and manners of Utopia, this island-state emerges as an **alternate world** in which Reason is written large. The dialogue in Book II was written in Antwerp a year earlier. It deals with the

Fig. 2.28

Sir Thomas More by Hans Holbein the Younger, 1527

non-materialist attitude of the Utopians (evident from their con-
tempt for gold and private property), with their sexual morality
(which punishes premarital intercourse and adultery but allows
for divorce) and their toleration of religious beliefs. *Utopia* (which
appeared in English translation in 1551) soon became a foundational text for Utopian literature as a genre, even though critical
opinion was divided upon the extent to which the dialogue can
be said to reflect either More's own views, or a mere fiction (the
Greek word *utopia* means 'no place'), or even a positive ideal (*eu-
topia*).

In England, the Humanist ideal of the fully developed individual became extended by the ideal of a nobleman with a Humanist education who looked to additional fulfilment in the
service of the state. Two basic texts for the new creed were *Il
Libro del Cortegiano* (1528) by Baldassare Castiglione (1478–1529),
a philosophical dialogue that appeared in the translation by Sir
Thomas Hoby (1530–66) as *The Book of the Courtier* (1561), and
The Book Named the Governor (1531) written by Sir Thomas Elyot
(c.1499–1546). True to such a **Gentleman ideal**, English Humanists
and other learned writers were not at all averse to holding public offices – for which some of them paid with their lives. After he had published his *Utopia*, Sir Thomas More, for example,
served King and country as Lord Chancellor until he met with
the executioner for his conscientious objections to Henry VIII's
religious policy. (For Robert Bolt's pertinent play *A Man for All Seasons*, see chap. 5.2.3.) Two other distinguished authors who were
also prominent courtiers – namely the Earl of Surrey (†1547) and
Sir Walter Ralegh (†1618) – were executed for political reasons,
too. Those writers that survived the political hotbed of the Tudor
and Stuart courts include the soldiers and sailors Sir Philip Sidney and Sir Francis Drake as well as the poet Edmund Spenser
(who was involved in political business in Ireland). The Humanist Roger Ascham (1515–68) was the childhood tutor and Latin
Secretary of Queen Elizabeth, before he continued in the vein
of Castiglione, Hoby and Elyot by writing his educational treatise *The Schoolmaster* (1570) in two volumes, the second of which
is wholly dedicated to the teaching of Latin. In the 1650s, John
Milton (1608–74) and Andrew Marvell (1621–78), two famous poets and friends, followed in Ascham's footsteps when they assisted Cromwell's Puritan government as Latin Secretaries. Before

The Gentleman in Ideal
and Practice

the Commonwealth period, Ben Jonson (1572–1637) supported royal representation by his regular supply of court masques for the Stuart court. Sir Francis Bacon (1561–1626), much like Sir Thomas More, distinguished himself as Lord Chancellor under James I and as the author of a **scientific utopia**. For the publication of *The New Atlantis*, Bacon translated his English manuscript into Latin. *Nova Atlantis* (published posthumously in 1627) is informed by the empirical method that is connected with Bacon's name (see chap. 2.1), in particular when Bacon comes to speak on Salomon's House as a model institute of science. Bacon chose to publish his methodological treatise *Novum Organon* in Latin (1620), but his famous *Essays* in English (1597/1625, see below).

In **Scotland**, where Humanism was generally less visible, George Buchanan (1506–82), the childhood tutor of Prince (later King) James, stuck to Latin for his works of history, poetry and drama, but later fell out with his former pupil. In two works on Scottish law and history (*De jure apud Scotos*, 1579, and *Rerum Scoticarum historia*, 1582), Buchanan claimed the people's right to depose those monarchs that are unfit to rule. King James banned Buchanan's books (1586) before he answered with *Basilikon Doron* (Greek for 'royal gift'), a treatise in the form of a confidential letter (in English) to the King's son on effective monarchical rule. In this treatise, which was published first in Edinburgh (1599) and then in London (1603), King James argued for an unrestricted Absolutism based on the Divine Right of monarchs – a view that became heavily contested in the seventeenth-century Civil Wars and up to the Glorious Revolution of 1688.

Life Writing and Speeches

An **increased interest in the individual**, in life as well as in art, has generally been associated with the Renaissance. It is borne out in *The Life of Sir Thomas More* (written by his son-in-law William Roper in the 1550s, though printed only in 1626) and in two of several biographies from the pen of Izaak Walton (1593–1683): *The Life of Dr John Donne* (1640) and *The Life of Mr George Herbert* (1670). John Foxe (1516–87) catered to the interest in the last words and full lives of exemplary churchmen or Christian martyrs other than More. "Foxe's *Book of Martyrs*", a compilation of news on the persecution of Protestants in the 1540s and '50s, was first written and published in Latin (Strasbourg, 1554). In 1563, Foxe published his own translation as *Acts and Monuments*, and Elizabeth's government ordered the 1570 reissue of that massive Folio

volume of over 2,000 pages to be placed in churches throughout England, and thus next to the Bible and the Anglican *Book
of Common Prayer*. Recent editions of the *NAEL* include an extract
pertaining to Anne Askew, the female martyr who was tortured
and burned at the stake in 1546.

Of course, royalty stood a higher chance to have their public
and private pronouncements preserved for posterity, especially
so in an age that lost not only leading statesmen to the executioner's block and blade, but also royal consorts (two of Henry VIII's six queens) and even monarchs (Mary Queen of Scots
and her grandson Charles I). The greatest impact was achieved by
a purported spiritual autobiography of Charles I that appeared
right after the beheading of the King (*Eikon Basilike: The Portraiture
of His Sacred Majesty in His Solitudes and Sufferings*, 1649). To counter
its effect of raising sympathy for the 'royal martyr' and the mon-
archists' cause, the Puritan Parliament commissioned the poet
John Milton to write a reply, which appeared within the same
year (but with less success) under the title *Eikonoklastes* ('The Icon-
Breaker'). The *NAEL* section "Women in Power" shifts the focus
to female royalty and assembles relevant manuscript letters, diaries and speeches, all of which eventually were to be distributed
in print, too. They belong or refer to Catholic Queens such as
"Bloody Mary" Tudor (*1516, reigned 1553–58) and Mary Queen
of Scots (1542–87) as well as to their Protestant antagonists, Lady
Jane Grey (*1537, who sat on the throne for merely nine days
after a coup in July 1553 and was executed in 1554) and Queen
Elizabeth (*1533, reigned 1558–1603). The *NAEL* section extends
to Elizabeth's rousing "Speech to the Troops at Tilbury" (1588)
and also to "The Golden Speech" delivered in Parliament (1601).
The first is a famous piece of patriotic rhetoric from the moment
when the threat of the Armada and a Spanish invasion loomed
large, whereas the latter speech (which was recorded by one MP
and revised by the Queen for publication) is used by Elizabeth
to sum up her use of royal power as well as the relations to her
subjects during her long reign.

Among the variety of **political writings** from the period, a few
further prominent examples stand out. The Communist features
of *Utopia* came alive in the time of the Civil Wars in the radical action taken by the so-called **True Levellers or Diggers** that challenged rural enclosures and the private ownership of land by

Areopagitica and
Leviathan

Fig. 2.29
Frontispiece of
the *Leviathan* by
Thomas Hobbes,
1651

digging up and cultivating wasteland. Those Christian Communists represented the most radical Puritan end of the religious and political continuum. Their programme is contained in the political tracts with Biblical overtones that were published by Gerrard Winstanley (1609–?76) between 1648 and 1652. The poet John Milton (1608–74) was a true but more considerate supporter of the Puritan cause and of Oliver Cromwell's Protectorate. In a tract called *The Tenure of Kings and Magistrates* (written and published in 1649, after the execution of Charles I), Milton reiterated Buchanan's views on the limitations of sovereignty in the light of the political theory of *covenants* or pacts between men on the powers of the sovereign. In *Areopagitica* (1644), on the other hand, Milton belaboured his fellow-Puritans in Parliament to believe in the superior value of the **freedom of the spoken and printed word** over the politicians' interest in censorship. Milton thus famously argued for a right of the individual that was at stake in Utopia as well as in seventeenth-century England, and since. At the Royalist end of the political continuum, we find in Thomas Hobbes (1588–1679) another prominent writer besides Milton who was not wholly carried away by his political sympathies. Hobbes followed the Royalists into their exile in Paris, where he tutored the future Charles II during the period of Puritan rule over Britain. However, his major work of political philosophy, *Leviathan* (1651/68), could have been claimed by Royalists and Republicans alike for their cause. Hobbes's conception of Leviathan or the State is expressed, in typical Renaissance fashion, by means of an extended analogy of Microcosm (the human body) and Macrocosm (the 'body politic', see Hobbes's introduction to his work). In the position of the sovereign head of state and absolute ruler, a hereditary monarch is as imaginable as a successful usurper like Cromwell, because Hobbes's philosophy defends any might as right. Hobbes declared the life of man to be "solitary, poor, nasty, brutish, and short" (Chap. 13), and regarded the human condition as a war of everyone against everyone with the (to Hobbes, legitimate) intention to win **superiority** over one's fellow human beings. Hobbes's principal belief in human egotism as a fact of life is summarised in his phrase "*homo homini lupus est*" (each man is another's wolf or enemy). As a **materialist philosopher**, Hobbes moreover states that "there is no conception in a man's mind which hath not at first, totally or by parts, been begotten upon the organs of sense" (Chap. 1). When he denies the existence of a spirit outside matter and sensory perception, Hobbes contradicts the radically Christian beliefs of Puritans like Milton as well as Diggers like Winstanley.

Political dissent could also be vented in satirical form. The 1590s saw a great increase in satires in prose (by e.g. Thomas Nashe and Thomas Lodge) and in verse, by the poet John Donne, the dramatist John Marston, and by Joseph Hall, all of whom looked back to the Classical models of Horace, Juvenal and others. (For the various forms of satire, see chap. 3.3.1.) When the Archbishop of Canterbury (whose powers then extended to the censorship of literature) in 1599 ordered the banning and burning of printed satires in prose and verse, this gave a new impetus to satirical stage-plays such as Ben Jonson's. Joseph Hall (1574–1656), who had already distinguished himself by composing the first proper Juvenalian satire in English (*Virgidemiarum*, 9 editions between 1598 and 1639), is also known for his *Characters of Virtues and Vices* (1608). This is the first collection of such **character sketches** that were to have an impact in the next age on essayists such as Addison and Steele, Goldsmith and Lamb, and on novelists who delighted in creating odd characters, such as Fielding, Smollett and Sterne.

Over and above such satires and sketches, there existed a variety of prose narratives that preceded the rise of the novel, and they came in a variety of styles. In *Euphues; or, The Anatomy of Wit* (1578) by John Lyly (1553/54–1606), the plot serves mainly as a peg on which to hang the fruits of the author's Humanist education and moral reflections. It was only for a brief period that Lyly's elaborated rhetorical style found favour with the (aristocratic) reading public. This however allowed Lyly to produce a sequel (*Euphues and his England*, 1580), and Thomas Lodge (c.1558–1625) to follow it up with an imitation entitled *Rosalynde: Euphues Golden Legacy* (1590). This in turn influenced Shakespeare's treatment of the pastoral in his comedy *As You Like It* (c.1600, see chap. 2.2). In *Arcadia*, Sir Philip Sidney (1558–86) moved beyond Lyly's stilted style. *Arcadia* is a combination of a **pastoral prose romance** (complete with loving and happily united shepherds and shepherdesses in an idyllic setting) and a romance of chivalry, in which the arrival of shipwrecked princes evokes a storm of passion and a spell of danger to the royal family ruling over Arcadia. Sidney's romance

Satires and Early Forms of Prose Fiction

circulated in manuscript after 1580 (in a version scholars call *Old Arcadia*) and was heavily revised by Sidney two years later, yet left as a fragment (*New Arcadia*), before Sidney's sister fused both versions into what appeared in 1590 as *The Countess of Pembroke's Arcadia*. Their niece, Lady Mary Wroth (née Sidney, 1587–?1651), honoured her uncle's romance through an imitation (*The Countess of Montgomery's Urania*, 1621).

For *The Unfortunate Traveller; or, The Life of Jack Wilton* (1594), the satirist Thomas Nashe (1567–1601) tried out a different combination of subject matter. His protagonist and first-person narrator, Jack Wilton the page, tells a tale of travel and adventure set in the times of Henry VIII (1509–47) amidst historical persons and events. True to the type of the **picaresque narrative**, Wilton first enjoys himself as rascal (the Spanish word is *picaro*) in military campaigns on the Continent, before he becomes acquainted with characters from different sections of society. In the company of the English sonneteer Henry Howard, Earl of Surrey, Wilton travels from Rotterdam to Rome and meets the Humanists Erasmus and More, the Reformer Martin Luther, and the scandalous Italian poet Pietro Aretino. Further popular authors from the 1590s who were likewise committed to more realistic forms of fiction are Thomas Deloney (c.1543–1600) and Robert Greene (1558–92). Deloney's tale *The Gentle Craft* (1597–98) about Simon Eyre, the shoemaker who turned mayor of London, gave the cue for Thomas Dekker's city comedy *The Shoemaker's Holiday* (1600, see chap. 2.2.4). The way that Deloney celebrated the success stories of real and prominent craftsmen such as Eyre and the weaver *Jack of Newbury* (1597) mirrors the self-esteem and social aspirations of a late Elizabethan middle-class audience that liked to read and hear about themselves. On the other hand, Greene's **cony-catching pamphlets** (1591–92) warn their readers against a danger for their property. In order to prevent them from being caught by confidence tricksters like conies (rabbits), Greene tells exemplary (and sometimes ironical) tales about the various tricks rogues use to dupe their victims. Those pamphlets are early instances of cheap fiction and of crime stories appearing in the new medium of print.

Bacon's *Essays*

For different forms of advice, readers around 1600 turned to *The Essays; or, Counsels, Civil and Moral* by Sir Francis Bacon (1561–1626), which first appeared in 1597, later to be revised and enlarged (1612, 1625). Classical precedents notwithstanding, the new form originated in the French writer Michel de Montaigne (1533–92). Montaigne's *Essais* (1580), his major work, are of the **informal** kind: highly personal, unsystematic and increasingly lengthy reflections about any given topic, and in the last resort about the author's self. John Florio's celebrated 1603 translation of Montaigne's *Essais* made them more widely available in Britain. Bacon's essays, by contrast, though to him only a minor project besides his scholarly writings (*The Advancement of Learning*, 1605; *Novum Organum*, 1620) and his scientific utopia *The New Atlantis* (see above), pioneered a second tradition of the genre. Bacon's essays are informed by Classical rhetoric, and they are **formal** – that is, impersonal and systematic – in the way that Montaigne's essays are not. Among the stylistic means that Bacon forcefully employs are

- ► sententious diction: "It were better to have no opinion of God at all than such an opinion as is unworthy of him" ("Of Superstition", 1612/25),
- ► antithetical syntax: "It is generally better to deal by speech than by letter, and by the mediation of a third man than by a man's self. [...] It is better dealing with men in appetite, than with those that are where they would be" ("Of Negotiations", 1597/1625),
- ► the rhetorical figure of the *tricolon*: "Studies serve for delight, for ornament, and for ability. [...] To spend too much time in studies is sloth; to use them too much for ornament is affectation; to make judgment wholly by their rules is the humour of a scholar" ("Of Studies", 1625 version).

Subjects and tone of the examples quoted show that *The Essays; or, Counsels, Civil and Moral* by Lord Chancellor Bacon address the gentleman and the statesman, and aim at a wise conduct in society. The two parallel traditions of the formal and the informal essay became increasingly marked out over the Long Eighteenth Century (see chap. 3.4.3), where they were also used for literary criticism.

Renaissance literary criticism extended from style manuals such as Thomas Wilson's *The Art of Rhetorique* (1553, 8th ed. 1585) and George Puttenham's *The Art of English Poesie* (1589) to the spirited *Defense of Poesie* by Sir Philip Sidney (written in

Literary Criticism

1581–83 and published posthumously 1595 under this and the alternate title *An Apology for Poetrie*). With *Observations in the Art of English Poesy* (1602), Thomas Campion started a **debate about the use of rhyme** in which he proposed quantitative verse in the tradition of Latin poetry as a superior model (though using rhyme himself). Samuel Daniel, a fellow poet, answered with *A Defence of Rhyme* (1603), before the debate was continued after the Restoration in John Dryden's *An Essay of Dramatic Poesie* (1668, see chap. 3.2.1). But there were also other concerns. A by-product of Thomas Hobbes's views on superiority in human relations is his **theory of comedy**. For Hobbes, humour does not arise from a comic *incongruity*, but from a feeling of *superiority*, which is why Hobbes centres on the manner of laughing *at* rather than *with* other people (*Leviathan* I.6). Hobbes's view on laughter is illustrated by the Restoration comedy of manners, whereas the latter notion of a sympathetic laughter based on incongruity became more popular in the advent of the eighteenth-century idea of Benevolence (see chaps. 3.2.1, 3.5.3 and Berger 2008: 14 ff.).

Burton's *Anatomy of Melancholy*

One may easily conclude this chapter with *The Anatomy of Melancholy* (3 vols., 1621) by Robert Burton (1577–1640), as this book contains elements of many of those categories of prose literature mentioned so far rather than any one of them alone. The title suggests a comprehensive medical treatise on a prominent aberration from the norm related to one of the four humours or bodily fluids. However, the seemingly systematic design of Burton's *Anatomy* is broken up by digressive essays on a variety of topics. The "Digression of Air" (2.2.3), placed within a treatment of the cure of melancholy, extends into a long and informed (if haphazard and biased) discussion of Copernican cosmology together with the work of Kepler and Galilei, but ends in the personal (and quite melancholic) statement: "*Nihil est sub sole novum* [there is nothing new under the sun]. But my melancholy spaniel's quest, my game, is sprung, and I must suddenly come down and follow." It is a testimony to the long popularity of Burton's work that the eighteenth-century novelist Laurence Sterne did not only follow Burton's example in indulging in long digressions in his novel *Tristram Shandy*. He also quoted directly and at length from the *Anatomy* (see e.g. Sterne's chap. V.1 for the tongue-in-cheek way in which he deals with plagiarism and imitation), pointing to Burton's own load of quotations from Scripture as well as Classical and Elizabethan authors.

1. Sum up the variety of Renaissance prose literature, and provide relevant examples.
2. Discuss the role of translations and transnational relations in Renaissance literature. To extend the discussion to other literary periods, have a look at the treatment of translations in chaps. 1, 3.3.1, 4.4 and 5.1.
3. Discuss the role of politics and religion in the prose writing of the period under review.
4. Queen Elizabeth's "Speech to the Troops at Tilbury" awaiting the Armada (1588) looks forward to those of Prime Minister Winston Churchill's wartime speeches in the House of Commons that were moreover broadcast to a nation facing a German invasion, e.g. "Blood, Toil, Tears and Sweat" (13 May, 1940) and "Their Finest Hour" (18 June, 1940). (See *Winston S. Churchill: His Complete Speeches 1897–1963*. Ed. Robert Rhodes James. 8 vols. New York: Chelsea House Publishers, 1974. VI, 6218–6220; 6231–6238.) Compare this and perhaps also other pieces of patriotic rhetoric in times of war (such as Admiral Lord Nelson's signal to the fleet before the 1805 Battle of Trafalgar, "England expects every man to do his duty") with King Henry's two speeches in Shakespeare's history play *Henry V*, "Once more unto the breach" (3.1) and "This day is called the Feast of Crispian" (4.3.18–67). What are the rhetorical means that were employed for the desired effect? Where are the similarities, and where the differences?

The Long Eighteenth Century: Neoclassicism and Romanticism (1660–c. 1830)

Summary

As a single phase in literary history, the years between 1660 and the 1830s are marked by an overlapping of seemingly opposed aesthetic tendencies, and by a new relationship between authors, booksellers and readers. The theatrical scene within the United Kingdom of Great Britain as well as abroad was concentrated on just two London playhouses: the Theatre-Royal in Drury Lane and the Duke's Theatre. Initially, their programme pitted Restoration comedies of wit and manners against Roman and heroic tragedies. Over the years, stage satires, sentimental comedies and domestic tragedies were added to the bill. Neoclassicist and Romantic poets alike favoured the forms of verse letters, satires, odes and elegies, yet there also occurred a ballad revival and the return of the sonnet. Major innovations in prose fiction are the children's book as well as the adult novel (of adventure, of character and manners, or of history), yet the more exotic Gothic romance, the literature of travel and the periodical essay are further characteristic features of the period.

Literary Communication in Britain between 1660 and the 1830s

At the end of the period here under review, the concept of periods as compact and definable units of history gained a new momentum. In general, delimitation and labelling of periods are attempts to bring order into at first confusing variety. All such efforts are connected with the attempt to catch what William Hazlitt the critic and John Stuart Mill, the liberal political theorist, likewise called *The Spirit of the Age* in their series of es-

Periods as Constructs

says published under that title. (Hazlitt's collection came out in 1825, Mill's series in 1831.) Around the same time, the German historian Leopold von Ranke (1795–1886), one of the founders of modern narrative historiography, stressed the discrete and unique characters of individual periods. However, since periods are now generally understood not as given in reality, but as methodological constructs, it will not surprise that the concept of individual periods, their label and delimitation are bound to change. Literary histories and other handbooks offer a number of labels for sub-sections of this time span, for instance *Restoration* for the time after 1660, *Augustan Age* for the early years of the eighteenth century, and *Age of Sensibility* or *Pre-Romanticism* for the later years of that century. In handbooks dealing with the history of the arts and especially with architecture, moreover, one comes across the designation *Georgian Period* for "the reigns of the first four Georges (1714–1830)". This is the definition of the term given by the *Oxford English Dictionary* that is generally helpful, too, in charting changes pertaining to the denomination and delimitation, and thus the concept of individual periods.

Over and above the sub-sections just mentioned, the **Long Eighteenth Century** is usually presented, in terms of literary and cultural history, as the succession of two distinct periods, one of which is labelled the Age of Neoclassicism or the Age of Enlightenment, the other called the Romantic Age. These periods are not only seen as distinct, but are also addressed separately. The **Age of Neoclassicism** is said to set in with the year 1660, and to come to an end with some in the 1780s, with others in the year 1798. The designation **Romantic Age**, then, is used for the successive period of time up to about 1830. The conventional view of Neoclassicism sees it as a long and stable period, as a relatively consistent understanding of life and art, which was characterised by a deferential attitude of authors, critics, readers and publishers towards the literature of ancient Greece and Rome. However, when 'Neoclassical' and 'Romantic' tendencies in the Arts have been discussed in recent years, such a unified and uniform character of periods has been put into question. And such a harmonising view is indeed not without problems, as there were not only parallels and continuities, but also inconsistencies and ruptures. Moreover, there was an overlapping of seemingly opposed tendencies, both at the beginning, in the middle and at the end of the time span here under review. With a look, first, at critical concepts and artistic practice, and then at further aspects of literary communication between authors, publishers and readers in Britain, it makes sense to view the years between 1660 the 1830s as a single phase in literary history.

There is without doubt a reverential attitude towards a golden age of Classical literature prevailing in Britain in the late seventeenth and throughout most of the eighteenth century. This is however not the whole story. There is not only the retrospective glance at past masters, but also a look out for native, national competitors. Moreover, there is a turn towards the possibility of doing it even better, towards progression and a general idea of progress. This is visible for instance in the so-called *Querelle des Anciens et des Modernes*, i. e. the wide-ranging quarrel between those that held the Classical masters supreme vs. those that admitted more modern authors and texts to be equal, if not even superior. The prominent contribution to that debate in Britain was Jonathan Swift's *A Full and True Account of the Battle Fought Last Friday, Between the Ancient and Modern Books in St. James's Library* (written in the 1690s and published in 1704), a fable which is built on a parody of epic conventions. Swift takes (as usual) a conservative view, and argues for the supreme virtue of the Classical canon, in contrast to the deficiencies of 'modern' critics. The contrary view, which allows for modern masters to be put on an equal footing with their ancient forebears, is visible in the increasing reverence paid to 'native' writers like Chaucer, Spenser, Shakespeare and Milton, around whom a national canon is beginning to be constructed. John Dryden had also and much earlier contributed to the debate with his *Essay of Dramatic Poesy* of 1668, which is much more tolerant towards modern authors. In his best-selling and long-selling edition of *Fables, Ancient and Modern* (1700; luxurious re-issue 1797), Dryden included, apart from Ovid's *Metamorphoses*, also selections from Boccaccio's *Decamerone* and from Chaucer's *Canterbury Tales*. **Imitations of Edmund Spenser** and his Renaissance epic *The Faerie Queene* abound in the eighteenth century. There is even an early one of Pope: "The Alley. An Imitation of Spenser" (*NOBEV* 87–88) is a mock-epic, parodistic London poem in Spenserian stanza. And the mock-epic vogue can also be seen as a reverence paid to Milton and his *Paradise Lost* as the greatest epic in the native, English language (for mock epic see chap. 3.3.1).

Critical Concepts and Artistic Practice

Ancients vs. Moderns

Last but not least, it is of course **Shakespeare** who is granted a prominent place in the national canon, and who is increasingly being seen as an equal to his Classical predecessors. The turning point is reached in the 1760s, at the latest, and that is in the middle of the period under review. Then, David Garrick organised the first festival at Shakespeare's birthplace Stratford-upon-Avon (1769), and Samuel Johnson, the foremost Neoclassicist critic of his time, introduced his edition with a famous "Preface to Shakespeare" (1765), defending the bard against the negative criticism of other Neoclassicist critics. Johnson was rather willing to stretch the 'rules' to admit Shakespeare's rule-breaking style of writing, than to do without Shakespeare as a matter of principle. This is a clear instance not only that a dogmatic adherence to 'rules' and 'unities' as aesthetic corner-stones was coming to an end, but also that there were always inconsistencies, for instance when a stout Classicist like Johnson asked for more flexibility in aesthetic criteria.

But overlapping, inconsistency and the simultaneity of old and new are also visible at the end of this phase of literary communication. Once again, this should be a caveat, a warning sign not to ground periodisation on matters of style or critical doctrine alone, if at all. A few examples may suffice: Thomas Love Peacock could see the 'Romantic' poetry of Wordsworth and Coleridge only as degeneration from former golden and silver ages of modern poetry (i.e. the Renaissance and the age of Neoclassicism, from Dryden up to Collins and Gray). In his essay "The Four Ages of Poetry", published in 1820, he implicitly argued for a continuous adherence or a return to Classicism. Lord Byron was most outspoken against the latest contemporary fashion, and for a continuous orientation on Renaissance and Neoclassicist forebears. Near the end of the first canto of his mock epic *Don Juan* (published in 1819), Byron's epic narrator holds forth thus:

> Thou shalt believe in Milton, Dryden, Pope;
>   Thou shalt not set up Wordsworth, Coleridge, Southey;
> Because the first is crazed beyond all hope,
>   The second drunk, the third so quaint and mouthey:
>   [...]   (*Don Juan* canto 1, stanza 205, ll. 1633–36).

Indeed, Jerome McGann's revisionist anthology, *The New Oxford Book of Romantic Period Verse*, is built on the explicit premise that there is a continuous tradition of poetry aligned with Neoclassicism written and published throughout the so-called Romantic Age, contradicting conventional views of the aesthetic development at that time.

And yet, even if one does not want to uphold conventional views, one is of course well advised to inform oneself on the self-characterisation and ideology promulgated in key documents of both a 'Neoclassicist' and a 'Romantic' tendency, and on critical pronouncements of later years. The following programmatic pronouncements confront 'Neoclassicism' with 'Romanticism', and they will be illustrated and discussed further by way of poetic examples: Key Texts in the Debate

a) Alexander Pope's *Essay on Criticism* (1711) – a didactic poem in the manner of the Roman poet Horace and his *Ars Poetica*;
b) Edmund Burke, *A Philosophical Enquiry into the Origin of Our Ideas of the Sublime and Beautiful* (1757);
c) Samuel Johnson's "The Preface to Shakespeare" (1765);
d) William Wordsworth, "Preface" to the second edition of the *Lyrical Ballads* (1800), enlarged for the third edition (1802);
e) Samuel Taylor Coleridge, *Biographia Literaria* (1817);
f) Thomas Love Peacock, *The Four Ages of Poetry* (1820);
g) and, with reservation, Percy Bysshe Shelley, "A Defence of Poetry" (an answer to Peacock written in 1821, but not available to a larger audience at that time, as it was published only in 1840).

Writers, critics and readers of a Neoclassicist set of mind upheld, first, the notions of a **purity and hierarchy of genres**, with tragedy and the epic ranking highest in their respective fields, and comic "after-pieces", burlesques on stage and on the page, ballads and other songs ranking much, much lower. And yet, we will see that an interest in oral literature such as folk songs and folk tales is apparent already in the early decades of the eighteenth century, not just in more 'Romantic' times. Such an interest manifests itself in the collections of Scottish, Irish and English ballads and songs, of which Bishop Percy's *Reliques of Ancient Poesy* are the best known. Moreover, this is apparent from 'ballad' operas such as Gay's *Beggar's Opera*, or from adaptations of folk tales such as that of Tom Thumb in Fielding's *The Tragedy of Tragedies*. The mock epic both underlines and undermines the reverence in which the Genres epic is held. However, a genre mix occurs prominently only in later years, for instance in the odes of Keats and Shelley.

The **conception of art** changes fundamentally over these years. While ideal Beauty to poets like Pope means regularity, symmetry, perfection and closure, the so-called 'Romantic movement' allows for ruptures and for fragments. The former conception is addressed in Pope's *Essay on Criticism*:

The Ideal Work of Art:
Regularity vs. Rupture

> In wit, as nature, what affects our hearts
> Is not the exactness of peculiar parts;
> 'Tis not a lip, or eye, we beauty call,
> But the joint force and full result of all.
> Thus when we view some well-proportioned dome
> (The world's just wonder, and even thine, O Rome!)
> No single parts unequally surprise,
> All comes united to the admiring eyes:
> No monstrous height, or breadth, or length appear;
> The whole at once is bold and regular. (1.243–52)

The artistic product here is conceived of as a harmonious whole that is balanced out. In 'Romantic' poems, ruptures and fragments are acceptable, either because the work of art made such imperfections a theme (such as in Shelley's sonnet "Ozymandias"), or because the work itself remained a fragment (such as Coleridge's "Kubla Khan", Wordsworth's *The Prelude*, Byron's *Don Juan* or even Shelley's "A Defence of Poetry"). As a result of the creative process, an 'open' nature of the work of art is clearly tolerated, and sometimes consciously attempted.

And whereas Wordsworth's famous definition in his preface to *Lyrical Ballads* runs, "all good poetry is the spontaneous overflow of powerful feelings", Pope, to the contrary, had advised restraint:

> Be sure yourself and your own reach to know,
> How far your genius, taste, and learning go;
> Launch not beyond your depth, but be discreet,
> And mark that point where sense and dullness meet.
>   Nature to all things fixed the limits fit,
> And wisely curbed proud man's pretending wit. [...]
>   Avoid extremes; and shun the fault of such
> Who still are pleased too little or too much.
>   (Pope, *Essay on Criticism* 1.48–53; 2.384–85)

With Pope, mere effect should be avoided: an overabundance of emotion as well as the dominance of some parts over others.

Perhaps surprisingly, not just 'Romantic' poets, but already the Classically minded writers put a strong stress on Nature as poetic theme. Pope's commandment runs:

> First follow Nature, and your judgment frame
> By her just standard, which is still the same;
> Unerring Nature, [...]
> At once the source, and end, and test of art.
> Art from that fund each just supply provides,
> Works without show, and without pomp presides.
>
> (Pope, *Essay on Criticism* 1.68–75)

This overall theme, '(Human) Nature' can be represented either through **mimesis**, or through the imitation of other, excellent works, or through adherence to Classical 'rules' or doctrines.

> Those rules of old discovered, not devised,
> Are Nature still, but Nature methodized;
>   [...]
> Learn hence for ancient rules a just esteem;
> To copy Nature is to copy them.
>
> (Pope, *Essay on Criticism* 1.88–89, 139–40)

With Wordsworth, to the contrary, 'rules' are definitely not regarded as vital elements in the act of composition, nor is the description of nature seen as an end itself. External nature functions rather as a stimulus for an author's creative response:

> I have said that poetry is the spontaneous overflow of powerful feelings: it takes its origin from emotion recollected in tranquillity: the emotion is contemplated till by a species of reaction the tranquillity gradually disappears, and an emotion, kindred to that which was before the subject of contemplation, is gradually produced, and does itself actually exist in the mind. In this mood successful composition generally begins, and in a mood similar to this it is carried on; (Wordsworth, "Preface", *NAEL* II, 273).

Poetry, thus understood, is not primarily a representation of 'Nature', or reality, but rather the representation of the poet's mind at a given moment.

What are the functions and the qualities of an author according to these pronouncements? Where do authors differ from

[margin note: Imitation of Nature]

[margin note: Authorship between Refined Taste and Original Genius]

other, 'ordinary' people? With Wordsworth, the difference lies in the extraordinary sensibility of the artist, and thus seems to be an innate quality:

> What is a poet? [...] He is a man speaking to men: a man, it is true, endued with more lively sensibility, more enthusiasm and tenderness, who has a greater knowledge of human nature, and a more comprehensive soul, than are supposed to be common among mankind; [...]

> Among the qualities which I have enumerated as principally conducing to form a poet, is implied nothing differing in kind from other men, but only in degree. [...] the poet is chiefly distinguished from other men by a greater promptness to think and feel without immediate external excitement, and a greater power in expressing such thoughts and feelings as are produced in him in that manner. (Wordsworth, "Preface", *NAEL* II, 269, 272)

With Pope, this is not a matter of sensibility, but a question of education, rather, and the difference lies in the degree of learning and of discipline:

> A little learning is a dangerous thing;

> True ease in writing comes from art, not chance,
> As those move easiest who have learned to dance.

> True wit is Nature to advantage dressed,
> What oft was thought, but ne'er so well expressed;
> (Pope, *Essay on Criticism* 2.215, 362–63, 297–98)

Pope's didactic verse essay contains the idea that by learning and by an acknowledgement of a fixed set of rules and skills **taste** is formed, and works of art are created. With Pope, poetry is an art that can be learned; with Wordsworth, it is the impression of a moment, filtered through memory. Wordsworth however refrains from seeing authors as quasi-superhuman beings, as genius. This view was promulgated – again, already long before 'Romanticism' is properly said to have set in – by Edward Young's *Conjectures on Original Composition* (1759). Here, the keywords are **originality** (as opposed to imitation) and **genius** (as opposed to learning).

Rules and the Role of
the Imagination

Pope, who clearly advocated the adherence to 'those rules of old', nevertheless allowed deviations from them in exceptional cases, as a poetic 'licence':

> Great wits sometimes may gloriously offend,
> And rise to faults true critics dare not mend;

From vulgar bounds with brave disorder part,
And snatch a grace beyond the reach of art,
   [...]
But though the ancients thus their rules invade
(As kings dispense with laws themselves have made)
Moderns, beware! or if you must offend
Against the precept, ne'er transgress its end;
Let it be seldom, and compelled by need;
And have at least their precedent to plead.

(Pope, *Essay on Criticism* 1.152–55, 161–66)

A slow process of **liberation from the adherence to rules** is visible in the programmatic statements over this period of time. When Samuel Johnson came to justify Shakespeare's non-conformity with later doctrines of the three unities (of time, place and action) in his "Preface to Shakespeare", Johnson did not only continue Pope's line of argument, but spoke out clearly against the usefulness of at least two of these rules, those of time and place. With Wordsworth then, and his view of poetry as a "spontaneous overflow of powerful feelings", an adherence to rules clearly is no longer in view. Wordsworth and other Romantics confuted Pope's conception of acquired taste and artistic creation and referred to the artist's individual **imagination** instead. However, the definition varies with each writer. At the end of his long autobiographical poem *The Prelude; or, Growth of a Poet's Mind*, the lyrical speaker (i. e. Wordsworth) attempts a definition of

[...] Imagination, which, in truth,
Is but another name for absolute power
And clearest insight, amplitude of mind,
And Reason in her most exalted mood.
This faculty hath been the feeding source
Of our long labour: [...]

(Wordsworth, *The Prelude* 14.189–94).

This passage, and the whole poem, was available to the reading public only after the poet's death, in 1850. Wordsworth's collaborator in the project of the *Lyrical Ballads*, Samuel Taylor Coleridge, had earlier on published his definition of 'imagination' in a similar text. Coleridge's *Biographia Literaria*, which came out in 1817, is also meant to be an account of the 'Growth of a Poet's Mind', if only presented in prose. Coleridge circles the term 'imagination' and distinguishes it implicitly from reason on the one hand, and explicitly from another and seemingly similar faculty, 'fancy' (chaps. 4, 13–14) on the other hand. 'Imagination' is presented to be the more creative faculty, by which existing objects are first taken apart and then re-created anew; whereas 'fancy' is just conceived to be the act of choice. It deals only with objects and materials that are already made, brings them in connection, but does not create something that has not existed before.

Another poet that prominently dealt with 'imagination' as a concept was Percy Bysshe Shelley in his "Defence of Poetry" (published posthumously, too). Here again we find the view that "Poetry, in a general sense, may be defined to be 'the expression of the 'Imagination'" (NAEL II, 838). However, with Shelley, this is defined to be a 'sympathetic imagination', something that binds the individual artist back to his society, and does not leave him a solitary being (II, 844). Shelley, who sees all creative persons as 'poets', closes his "Defence" unabashedly with the words "Poets are the unacknowledged legislators of the World" (II, 850).

To sum up: while Wordsworth, Coleridge and Shelley all view the poet's 'imagination' as prime mover of his art, the exact definition varies with each poet. There are two complex aspects of the literary theory of the Long Eighteenth Century that remain to be addressed. The first complex is concerned with the aesthetic concepts of the Sublime, the Beautiful and the Picturesque, and with certain conventionalised presentations of Nature and of landscape in particular that resulted from them as a consequence. This aspect of the literary theory of the day can serve once again to stress the overlapping or continuity between 'Neoclassicist' and 'Romantic' tendencies in art and literature. The second complex, on the other hand, is related to a programmatic break with traditions of 'poetic decorum', visible in markedly different views held by Pope and by Wordsworth on the language that is appropriate to poetry.

Any visit to a gallery of paintings from the seventeenth to the nineteenth centuries will come up with an experience of two conventionalised, even stereotypical presentations of landscape. **The Beautiful** deals with idyllic, pastoral landscapes that show Man in harmony with the beauties of Nature. The panoramic view may create a sense of infinite distance, which is however never threatening, never closing down on the observer. The other tradition of **the Sublime** consists of the depiction of wild and desolate natural scenes, and of natural forces that dwarf the individual human figure and, by extension, the observer: mountain scenery, glaciers, torrents or waterfalls, the endlessness and power of oceans etc. come into view.

From the last decades of the eighteenth century onwards, the contrast between the Beautiful and the Sublime is dissolved by a third term, **the Picturesque**. This, by way of compromise, was an attempt to bring about a new concept, midway between the two others, and with a penchant for 'noble ruins'.

The French painter Claude Lorrain (1600–82) has been regarded as a master of the Beautiful and of the Picturesque. The origins of the Sublime style are usually seen in the work of the Italian painter Salvatore Rosa (1615–73), Claude's contemporary, but visually his antagonist. Both painters and their imitators were immensely popular in eighteenth- and nineteenth-century Britain, and so you find their works today in many collections and galleries. Later, such conventions of landscape presentation were to be developed further by the Romantic painters Caspar David Friedrich (1774–1840), William Turner (1775–1851) and John Martin (1789–1854). You find these aesthetic concepts also in landscape gardening, and of course in literary theory and in literature proper.

In *OAEL* (III, 632 ff.), the history of the opposition between Sublime and Beautiful in English literature can be traced from Joseph Addison's series of essays on "The Pleasures of the Imagination" (1712) through Edmund Burke's relevant treatise of 1757 (which was read all over Europe and stimulated a response by Immanuel Kant) to the poetry of Wordsworth and other Romantic poets. In Addison's essays, the Sublime is discussed in relation to a religious experience, to the mystical apprehension of a Divine Maker, and then brought – more pragmatically – into connection with contemporary fashions of landscape gardening. The mystic, religious experience triggered by contact with a Sublime scenery is also documented in a letter from Thomas Gray to his friend Richard West, after having crossed the Alps in 1739 together with Horace Walpole, the prime minister's son: "In our little journey up to the Grande Chartreuse, I do not remember to have gone ten paces without an exclamation that

|Fig. 3.1

The Sublime: Caspar David Friedrich, *The Wanderer above the Sea of Fog,* 1818

there was no restraining: not a precipice, not a torrent, not a cliff, but is pregnant with religion and poetry. There are certain scenes that would awe an atheist into belief without the help of other argument" (*OAEL* III, 636). Key works by William Wordsworth, Percy Bysshe Shelley and Lord Byron, which were all inspired by personal experience of the Swiss Alps, testify to the continuity of thought from the Augustan to the Romantic Age. For those later poets, the Sublime opened up a possibility to escape the restrictions prescribed during Neoclassicism to govern literary form. The Sublime cannot be confined; wildness cannot be subjected to 'rules'. As examples for the other two concepts, that of Beauty and that of the Picturesque, the following texts are of interest: Alexander Pope's poem "Windsor Forest" (1713; see ll. 7–43), William Gilpin's *Three Essays: On Picturesque Beauty; on Picturesque Travel; on Sketching Landscape* (1792), and the two satirical poems, "Picturesque: A Fragment" by John Aikin (1791, *NOBEV* 776–78) and the book-length *The Tour of Dr Syntax in Search of the Picturesque* by William Combe (1809, illustrated by Thomas Rowlandson).

Poetic Diction

From continuity all over the Long Eighteenth Century, we will now move to a theoretical field where **a conscious break with tradition** was strongly advocated. The subject in question is 'decorum', or to be more exact: **the kind of language suitable for poetry**. The contrast here is between the Neoclassicist notion of a stylised, highly artistic but also highly artificial 'poetic diction' on the one hand, and on the other hand a programmatic turn to a 'language really used by men' as a key feature of the Romantic tendency. For a justification and a prominent example of the use of **poetic diction**, we turn once more to Thomas Gray, who wrote in another letter to his friend Richard West in 1742: "the language of the age is never the language of poetry" (Jones 1961: 265–66). Richard West died later that year, and Thomas Gray's "On the Death of Mr Richard West" (*ECP* 324) – an elegy brought into sonnet form – is a good example of poetic diction in practice. Its key features are *personification* (l. 2: "redeeming Phoebus" means the sun), *periphrasis* (l. 9, where "the busy race" means either birds or men), *stock phrases* (as in l. 6: "green attire") or *Latinate diction* (l. 3: "amorous descant" means love song). For another example of 'poetic diction', see the periphrastic expression "finny Prey" for fish in Alexander Pope's *The Rape of the Lock* (ll. 2.26). This mock-heroic

poem is also a good example of the handling of another prominent formal device of Neoclassical poetry, namely the heroic
couplet.

To Gray's dictum, that "the language of the age is never the
language of poetry", that artistic use of language deviates from
ordinary speech patterns, Wordsworth formulated the opposite
in his "Preface" to the *Lyrical Ballads*. Here, Wordsworth quoted
Gray's poem in full as a specimen of that 'curiously elaborate
[...] poetic diction', against which he set his own postulates of
a "a selection of **language really used by men**". Wordsworth's own
concept met with heavy criticism from Peacock in *The Four Ages
of Poetry* (1820), and even from Coleridge in *Biographia Literaria*
(chap. 17). The poetry of Robert Burns (1759–96), who had died
shortly before the publication of the "Preface", already exemplified key features of Wordsworth's poetic concept (and perhaps
much better than many of Wordsworth's own poems). Because
of his farming background, Burns was hailed as the model of a
'rustic' genius and of a 'ploughman poet'. He became deeply im-
mersed in projects that aimed at the collection of popular oral
literature, of Scottish songs and their music – an experience that
inspired him in terms of subject matter as well as stanza form
(see the treatment of ballads in chap. 3.3.2). Burns himself became a famous songwriter who either reworked existing songs
("Auld Lang Syne") or wrote original songs that became popular ("A Red, Red Rose"). Already his first collection *Poems Chiefly
in Scottish Dialect* (which was published by subscription in 1786),
and most prominently his verse tale "Tam O'Shanter" (1791), signalled Burns's turn to dialect – and thus to a language register
which is actually given much less prominence in Wordsworth's
own poems (s. tab. next page).

No survey of the literature of this period is complete without
a closer look at the development of a new relationship between
authors, publishers and readers during the Long Eighteenth
Century. For scholars doing research on the **history of the book** as
a medium of (literary) communication, those years are synonymous with 'the period of the expansion of print' (Willison 1991;
see also Watt 1963 and Rogers 1982). The central player in this
context was the 'bookseller', who in those days combined the
functions of patron, publisher and retailer of works of literature.
Royal patronage became visible e.g. during the Restoration in

New Relations between
Authors, Publishers and
Readers

The Bookseller as
Patron

A Synopsis of Tendencies in Literature and the Arts over the Long Eighteenth Century
(based on Abrams and Harpham 2005: 183 ff.)

'(Neo-) Classicism'	'Romanticism'
general features:	**general features:**
• great respect for Classical Antiquity (Greece and Rome) • strong traditionalism • distrust of radical innovation	• strong interest in the Middle Ages and in medieval art • favours innovation over adherence to conventions • French Revolution first seen as a promise of a renewal of society and of new individual possibilities
world view and view of Man:	**world view and view of Man:**
• Newtonian laws; universal hierarchy: *Great Chain of Being* • reason as guide: *Age of Reason or Enlightenment* • reasonableness: restraint, acceptance of limited means of man, avoidance of extremes	• endeavour to overreach the limits and to advance towards superhuman areas (*the Sublime*)
conception of art:	**conception of art:**
• ideal *Beauty* = regularity, symmetry, perfection, closure • product = a balanced harmonious whole • avoiding mere effect: an over-abundance of emotion or the dominance of some parts over others	• fascination of *Beauty*, but also the *Sublime* and the *Picturesque* • acceptance of ruptures and of fragments as results of the creative process: 'open' nature of the work of art • 'spontaneous overflow of powerful feelings'
conception of literature and of authorship:	**conception of literature and of authorship:**
• theme: '(Human) Nature', represented through *mimesis* or through *imitation* of other, excellent works • literary work and authorship seen in a social context: art for humanity's sake; didacticism; representativeness • abstraction from personality of the author • ideals: professionalism, craftsmanship, correctness; an art that can be learned, *taste* is formed • adherence to a fixed set of *rules* and a defined set of skills • purity and hierarchy of genres stressed; *decorum* (propriety) • *heroic couplet* as the standard form of verse	• (external) Nature as stimulus for author's creative response, imaginary, fantastic worlds • autonomy of the artist: seen as a solitary, isolated figure: art for art's and for the artist's sake • authors and their experience may be subjects themselves • cult of *genius*: emphasis on the authors' individual *imagination*, on their *originality* and *spontaneity* • (sterile) rules no longer seen as binding • purity and hierarchy of genres subverted: genre mix • poetry in a variety of forms, including fresh and original ones

the new position (usually for life) of the **Poet Laureate**, with John Dryden as the first occupant (1668–88, †1700).

However, this remained the exception to the rule. For mid-eighteenth century authors, their bookseller's commission to write a certain text had taken the place of aristocratic patronage – quite certainly in the case of those poorly paid **Grub Street Hacks** who had to produce whatever was just in demand. The change is strikingly documented in the further use of letters of dedication, which had hitherto been appended to printed works as acknowledgment of patronage received. In his letter to Lord Chesterfield, the scholar and critic Samuel Johnson famously rejected such a belated and insubstantial offering downright (7 February 1755, see *NAEL*). Shortly afterwards, such a dedication served Laurence Sterne for no more than a jest in his comic novel *Tristram Shandy* (1759–67), and towards the end of the eighteenth century, the great historian Edward Gibbon roundly stated in his *Memoirs of My Own Life*:

|Fig. 3.2
John Dryden

> I cannot boast of the friendship or favour of princes. The patronage of English literature has long since been devolved on our booksellers, and the measure of their liberality is the least ambiguous test of our common success. (Fragment published posthumously in 1796, and reprinted in *OAEL* III, 751.)

One of these influential London booksellers (whose number increased from about fifty at the time of Dryden's Laureateship to about 200 when Gibbon wrote those lines) was Jacob Tonson the elder (1655/56–1736). He secured the copyright in Shakespeare's works that his family business then held throughout the eighteenth century, when the first critical editions of the plays began to appear, and he furthered the canonisation of Milton's *Paradise Lost* through a lavish folio and many more editions. To meet the costs of printing this expensive folio (1688), Tonson took up the innovative idea of publishing by **subscription**, i.e. by securing advance payment from the smart set. Dryden and Pope were to use this method successfully for their (in any sense of the word) precious translations from the Classics. Tonson published the works of Dryden since before his Laureateship, and he co-opted Dryden into regularly editing and promoting Classical or Classicist poetry that set the tone (*Tonson's Miscellany*, 1684–1709). With Joseph Addison's tragedy *Cato* (1713) as well as his *Spectator* essays,

Tonson also had a leading Neoclassicist of the next generation on his list. Other notable booksellers operating in the period include George Faulkner, whose setting up business in Dublin in 1726 helped to create a new infrastructure, and John Newbery, who from 1744 paved the way for the children's book. The names of further publishers and retailers such as Longman (from 1724), John Murray (from 1768) and W.H. Smith (from 1792) are still well known today.

Developments in Publishing and Criticism

The 'expansion of print' came but slowly. Up to about 1750, roughly 100 new titles per year were printed per hand on Gutenberg presses in Britain, a figure that rose to 600 by 1825, at the time when the steam engine entered the print shop, and then to 6,000 before about 1900. In the 1770s, the first run of an average novel comprised 500 copies, with best sellers in the range of a few thousand copies sold. Some publishers created a new medium with long-running **literary reviews and literary magazines**. Over nearly a decade, Daniel Defoe single-handedly wrote the tri-weekly *Review* (1704–13), which however was more of a newspaper with political commentary in the 'editorial'. The essayists Joseph Addison and Richard Steele collaborated on *The Spectator*, a magazine that had a great impact considering its short original run (1711–12; see chap. 3.4.3). While *The Gentleman's Magazine* (from 1731) still presented a mixed bag of information on literature, literary reviewing set in with the *Monthly Review* (from 1749) and the *Critical Review* (from 1756). John Dennis (1657–1734) became the first professional **literary critic** in England. His prominent status was inherited first by Samuel Johnson (1709–84) and then by Francis Jeffrey (1773–1850), the first editor of the *Edinburgh Review* (1802–1929), a quarterly periodical that combined conservative aesthetics with liberalism in politics. It was inaugurated by Archibald Constable, another publishing genius, and then run by Longman. Other early nineteenth-century additions include the more conservative *Quarterly Review* (1809–1967) that came from the press of John Murray, the publisher of Byron, who sent his works also to *The Examiner* (1808–80), a more radical periodical edited by Leigh Hunt. The prominent yet short-lived *London Magazine* (1820–29) included essays by Charles Lamb, William Hazlitt and Thomas De Quincey, while the monthly *Blackwood's [Edinburgh] Magazine* ('Maga', 1817–1980) regularly featured Gothic short stories that were to be an influence on Edgar Allan Poe.

In 1707, the hitherto separate kingdoms of England and Scotland had become a **United Kingdom of Great Britain**. Two years later, with the **1709 Copyright Act** – the first worldwide – the relations between publisher and author began to be set on a new basis, too, albeit only in the long run. The lapsing of the Licensing Act in 1695 had ended pre-publication censorship for printed matter, but had also created a loophole for book piracy.

Authors on the Way to Autonomy in a United Kingdom

The Act of 1709 was meant as a protection of booksellers' investment rather than authors' invention against piracy, which continued to be a profitable business in Ireland over the century until 1801, when the 'United Kingdom' and its 'Union Jack' incorporated Ireland, too. The 1709 Act had also made copyright a commodity with a sell-by date. The 1814 and 1842 Copyright Acts prolonged the period of protection from the original span of 14 years to at least the author's lifetime. Usually, authors sold their copyright right away to the publishing bookseller, and negotiated a lump sum for the first and subsequent editions. Thus, Jonathan Swift's overall profit from *Gulliver's Travels* (1726, see chap. 3.4.5) was the sizeable sum of £200, yet this compared less well with his annual salary as Dean of St. Patrick's in Dublin of £700. Compiling a history book from other sources was more lucrative than composing an original work: half a century after Pope, Tobias Smollett sold the copyright in his novel *Humphry Clinker* (1771) for £210, after he had earned £2,000 from copies sold of his *Compleat History of England* (1755–58), while David Hume made over £3,000 from his rival *History of England* (1754–61). The royalty system (which made authors partake in best-selling books) had not yet been adopted on a general basis, and advance payment was first being offered to the Gothic novelist Ann Radcliffe (see the figures mentioned in chap. 3.5.5) and later to the poet and historical novelist Walter Scott. The first poets and novelists who made themselves financially independent by their own writing were Scott, Lord Byron, his friend the Irish poet and songwriter Thomas Moore, and then Charles Dickens.

Books remained expensive, and became really affordable only when bought in sheets or wrappers, i.e. unbound, or when lent from one of the many **circulating libraries** that were established as new institutions during the period. In his groundbreaking study on the eighteenth-century novel, Ian Watt estimated that

Book Prices in Relation

novels were in the medium price range. [...] *Tom Jones*, for example, cost more than a labourer's average weekly wage. [...] The price of a novel [...] would feed a family for a week or two. This is important. The novel in the eighteenth century [...] was not, strictly speaking, a popular literary form. (Watt 1963. 43)

In 1832, the year of Scott's death, the price of one of his historical novels – now in three-decker (three-volume) format at 31½ shillings – would still roughly equal the weekly wage of compositors as the highest-paid craftsmen (36 shillings).

Reading Revolutions

Another economical alternative were the **chapbooks** that presented a story in a condensed version accompanied by woodcut illustrations. Such simplified and illustrated chapbooks, which compare to today's books for young children or graded readers in the foreign-language classroom, took note of the high degree of **illiteracy**, too. In the 1750s, two thirds of women and one third of men could not sign their name, and more than 70% remained illiterate in some rural areas of Ireland in 1841. In the absence of universal and compulsory state schooling (which became law in England and Wales only with Forster's Education Act in 1870), significant if still not satisfactory change in elementary education was effected from the 1780s by the **Sunday school movement**, i.e. in classes associated with Protestant churches. This laid the grounds for a mass readership and for mass literature after 1830. The writer and reformer Hannah More is renowned for her involvement with the movement, which led her to write 50 "Cheap Repository Tracts" for the poor between 1795 and 1798, i.e. 'moral tales' which already sold in millions of copies. Moreover, there were **two other 'reading revolutions'** in this still largely oral society: the first marked the turn from reading aloud and collectively to the habit of individual, silent reading, while the second implied the change from a repeated reading of a few texts (notably the Bible) to the single reading of many.

Guiding Questions and Exercises

1. Contrast the critical pronouncements of Alexander Pope with those of William Wordsworth as being representative of the tendencies of Neoclassicism and Romanticism.

2. Summarise the developing new relationship between authors, publishers and readers during the Long Eighteenth Century. Try to account for

- the implications of the new copyright law and of other innovations in publishing,
- the role of periodicals or circulating libraries as new institutions in the field of distribution,
- and the gradual replacement of 'reading aloud' in a collective setting by forms of reading which are the norm in our own times.

Performance Culture: Drama, Orality and Oratory | 3.2

Dramatic Genres and Genre Theory | 3.2.1

Post-Renaissance drama is characterised by a number of changes relating to actors and audiences, to the management of theatres and to the form of the stage. However, there is also a **continuity of state control over stage culture**. Various acts of licensing and censorship affected theatre and drama between the Restoration and the year 1843. The re-opening, in 1662, of the theatres closed by Puritans two decades earlier resulted in a **monopoly**, as only **two playhouses** were granted royal patent and patronage: the Theatre-Royal in Drury Lane enjoyed the patronage of King Charles II, and the Duke's Theatre (from which the present Royal Opera House in Covent Garden originated) was patronised by his brother, the Duke of York and future James II. Both playhouses were built or re-built first by Sir Christopher Wren, the famous architect of St. Paul's Cathedral, to provide for audiences of up to 1,200 people, and then were re-built again at intervals throughout the eighteenth and well into the nineteenth centuries, until their extensions sufficed to provide space for 3,000 to 3,600 people. Such figures from the 1790s approach again those of Shakespeare's time, when drama indeed was a public spectacle (usually outdoors). By comparison, Restoration drama began as an entertainment for the court, but already during this period, the social circle widened to admit the middle to upper-middle classes, until the (indoor) theatre again became a microcosm of society, where everyone could find a seat, or at least place to stand. The social

Continuity and Change in the Theatre

division within the auditorium however showed in the common reference to **'box, pit, and gallery'**, which were priced differently. "The boxes were the preserve of the upper classes and gentry, the pit was the realm of the middling and professional orders, while the gallery belonged to the artisans, the servant class, soldiers, and sailors" (Russell 1999: 226) – not to forget the girls selling oranges, and often not only this fruit, in the vicinity of the stage. In this matter, royal 'patronage' extended to **actresses** (and mistresses) such as Nell Gwynn, which together with ballet-dancers provided a lasting change for the hitherto exclusively male profession of acting. Actors and actresses formed companies at a permanent theatre, or travelled in troupes to perform in the provinces or in the colonies, perhaps on a temporary stage, but in more extravagant and historically accurate costumes than before.

The wide but also unpredictable appeal of the theatres (and not simply their sexual allure, on stage and backstage) was the reason why the stage continued to be regulated by the state. Theatres and plays were a rough equivalent to today's talk shows, in which public opinion is formed and expressed, with possibly dramatic results for the government of the day. Often an attempt to raise ticket prizes sufficed to rouse the public (which rioted in 1792, and for 66 nights in 1809). In addition to the two 'patent houses' in London, an increasing number of provincial 'Theatres-Royal' were established in other prominent cities, and also minor playhouses with a different bill. The **1737 Theatre Licensing Act** of the Walpole government (which was satirised on stage in John Gay's *The Beggar's Opera* and in Henry Fielding's *Tom Thumb the Great*) extended the monopoly of the 'patent houses' by their exclusive right to perform 'legitimate drama', which means tragedies and comedies, interludes and after-pieces, 'melodrama' (a combination of song and recitative) and fully-sung operas. A typical evening of several hours in such a licensed theatre included a double or triple bill of **varied genres**, with 'legitimate drama' as a main-piece (often introduced by a 'Prologue'), then a musical interlude and finally a farcical after-piece or ballet. At the minor playhouses, a genre mix developed which produced playlets such as the 'burlesque' (a stage parody), the 'burletta' (a lighter form of musical comedy which is otherwise structurally similar to melodrama) or the 'pantomime', all of which retained their popularity in the nineteenth century (for instance in form of the 'Christmas pantomime').

The London playhouses were often managed by men of the theatre who had acquired the patents, such as the playwrights Sir John Vanbrugh, Sir Richard Steele and Richard Brinsley Sheridan. Famous actor-managers included Colley Cibber, David Garrick and John Philip Kemble (all at the Drury Lane Theatre). **David Garrick** (1717–79) was influential in several respects: as the **leading actor of his age**, he became known for his naturalistic and expressive impersonation of dramatic characters. His breakthrough performances of Richard III and of Hamlet in 1741 and 1742 were immortalised by his friends Hogarth and Fielding (in *Tom Jones*, XVI.5). Garrick deviated from the conventional and more formal style of declamation in order to make emotions visible. As a **promoter of Shakespeare**, over and above his acting, Garrick furthered the (pre-)Romantic cult of the National Bard by organising the 1769 Jubilee, the first Shakespeare festival at Stratford. And as a **manager**, Garrick cleared the stage from spectators, and introduced new lighting in the theatre (in 1765). By darkening the audience, he also educated spectators to concentrate on the action on the lighted stage. The protruding stage of Shakespeare's times had by then given way to the **picture-frame stage** which originated from opera houses and is still in use today, together with curtain and moveable scenery as other innovations of this period. In all his roles, Garrick established a more respectful atmosphere in the theatre and ensured that drama was acknowledged not only as pure entertainment, but also as a form of art.

| Fig. 3.3
W. Hogarth, *Garrick in the Character of Richard III* (1746)

Three performances of a play constituted the minimal success (which meant the beginning of earnings to a playwright), "six was quite a good showing, and nine a hit" (Bevis 1988: 36). The plays which follow were successful on these terms, and they can be summarily discussed with regard to their genre affiliations (which shows the influence of the French drama of the period, albeit with modifications). The Restoration comedies of manners contrasted with the 'heroic plays' of the period. After 1700, both kinds were replaced by domestic tragedies, by satirical farces and sentimental comedies, and by intermedial hybrids such as the ballad opera or the melodrama.

The **Restoration comedy of manners** is built on a pattern which includes typified characters and their mannerisms, plots full

Restoration Comedy of Manners

of sexual intrigue and cuckoldry, and verbal fencing-matches (certainly enjoyed by 'box' and 'pit') as well as much bawdy humour (catering, but not exclusively, to the 'gallery'). The constellation of characters includes as protagonists and role-models first a **'rake-hero'** who is celebrated for his ingenuity, but whose male-chauvinist attitude is matched and tempered by the self-confident quick-wittedness of his female partner (to be impersonated by an actress, and no longer by a boy actor). And a loose partnership of **'true-wits'** – rather than 'a marriage of true minds' (as envisaged in Shakespeare's sonnet no. 116) – is what such comedies foresee as a 'happy' ending for the **'gay couple'**. This couple of stylish, aristocratic, urban London youth of both sexes triumphed easily over *ingénue* characters whose only fault is their *naïveté* (which is exploited), over either **'wit-woulds'** which are snobs and fops of fashion or 'country bumpkins' devoid of any wit, and over an older generation which has not become any wiser but only more voracious, but whose material and sexual greed ultimately meets with no gratification. Telling names such as Sir Wilfull Witwoud, Sir Fopling Flutter or Lord Foppington, Horner and Freeman (for a rake), Lady Cockwood and Lady Fidget (for an elderly, but easily enticed woman), or Marjorie Pinchwife (for a 'country-wife' and, initially, an *ingénue*) help the audience to identify the respective types. However, the Restoration comedy of fops and follies is endowed with an altogether less satirical urge than, for instance, Ben Jonson's comedy of humours; it does not bite the hand that feeds it. The seemingly harmonious union of the 'gay couple' is usually achieved after much verbal in-fighting, of 'wit combats' peppered with instances of **repartee** or answering back, in particular on the side of the heroine, who thus can prove herself as a truly witty successor to Shakespeare's Kate in *The Taming of the Shrew*, Beatrice in *Much Ado about Nothing*, or Rosalind in *As You Like It*.

Among the court wits who wrote comedies of manners was Sir George Etherege (1635–91). It was perhaps his wide experience as a courtier and diplomat which helped him to create aristocratic fops and fools such as Sir Frederick Frollick (in *The Comical Revenge; or, Love in a Tub*, 1664) or Sir Fopling Flutter and also rakes such as Dorimant (both in *The Man of Mode*, 1676) that sent audiences asking for more. They were duly served in *The Country-Wife* (1675) by William Wycherley (1640–1716), and in *The Rover; or, The Banished*

Cavaliers (two parts, 1677–81) by Aphra Behn (c. 1640–89). This play by a female author testifies both to her Stuart leanings and to her gender politics, and in this is perhaps exceptional among the Restoration comedies. With the male protagonist, Willmore (built, like Dorimant, on John Wilmot, Earl of Rochester, a notorious womaniser and profligate poet), Behn presents a rake and rover, i. e. one of the Royalist Cavaliers living in exile during the Puritan Interregnum. Moreover, Behn dedicated the second part of *The Rover* to the future James II (at a time when he was in voluntary exile). However, Behn sets her rake-hero against two women who are his match: against the courtesan Angellica Bianca, who can choose her sexual partners on her own terms, and also against quick-witted Hellena, the heroine which excels in repartee and succeeds in bringing him to marry her (who had not enjoyed the same sexual liberties before). In *The Rover, Part II*, both qualities are to be found united in one woman, the witty courtesan La Nuche.

The first wave of Restoration comedies was followed up on by dramatists of the 1690s, who were writing after the death of Charles II (1685) and the deposition of his brother James II in the Glorious Revolution of 1688/89. However, the times were a-changing indeed, and with the two successful plays of Sir John Vanbrugh (1664–1726), *The Relapse; or, Virtue in Danger* (1696) and *The Provok'd Wife* (1697), the Restoration comedy already veered towards its end. After the churchman Jeremy Collier had attacked the moral lapses and provocative hedonism of Restoration comedy in his influential pamphlet *A Short View of the Immorality and Profaneness of the English Stage* (1698), Vanbrugh shifted his creativity to work as an architect rather than as a playwright. The work of George Farquhar (1678–1707), who was born in Ireland, and of William Congreve (1670–1729), who had grown up in this island, marked the end of this phase of the comedy of manners and of wit, before another Irishman, Oscar Wilde, was going to revive the genre two centuries later. Due to its verbal humour, later critics have singled out Congreve's *The Way of the World* (1700) as the finest example of Restoration comedy. It is also the last proper one, and it conspicuously failed to convince its contemporary audience, although the 'proviso scene' (IV.5), in which hero and heroine debate their terms of marriage, presents a compromise between aristocratic hedonism, bourgeois morals, and female

Fig. 3.4
William Congreve

emancipation. Farquhar's more successful plays *The Recruiting Officer* (1706) and *The Beaux Stratagem* (1707) centre again on love intrigues and bedroom farce, but are altogether less given to verbal virtuosity, and to sexual hedonism, too.

In the long run, this more bourgeois and even more 'bowdlerised' version (see below) translated into another genre, namely in Jane Austen's witty novel of manners. The aristocratic cynicism of Restoration comedies had sparkled once again before, in *Les Liaisons dangereuses* (by Pierre Choderlos de Laclos, 1782). The French novel, which depicted the pre-Revolutionary court at the end of the *Ancien Régime*, compares well with the English stage-plays a century earlier which had preceded another, the Glorious Revolution. Generally speaking, however, the comedy of wit and of manners as a kind of stage drama fell into disrepute until Oscar Wilde (1856–1900) and Noël Coward (1899–1973) revived it, but in a bourgeois spirit. The revived kind directed the audience to laugh at (and no longer with) aristocratic snobs, and it was ultimately shorn of sexual indecencies and of flagrant amorality. Wilde's plays in particular have come to over-shadow their predecessors on the stage, but the Restoration originals or their period atmosphere have been revived repeatedly in recent times. The historic fact that Farquhar's *The Recruiting Officer* became the first play to be staged 'down under', by convicts landed in the colony of New South Wales in 1789, lies at the heart of Thomas Keneally's novel *The Playmaker* (1987), which in turn was adapted by fellow-Australian writer Timberlake Wertenbaker in her bicentennial stage version *Our Country's Good* (1989). Both the hedonistic Stuart court and the Christian-fundamentalist world of a Jeremy Collier resurfaced in Rose Tremain's rewarding historical novel *Restoration* (1989), which was adapted to the screen (1995). Finally, *Les Liaisons dangereuses*, too, was reworked successfully first for the stage by Christopher Hampton (*Dangerous Liaisons*, 1985) and then for the screen, in the rival film versions of Stephen Frears (1988, based on Hampton's play and screenplay), and of Milos Forman (*Valmont*, 1989).

Forms of Tragedy

By comparison, the heroic tragedies from the Restoration period have lost their audiences much earlier, and for good. Like so many revenge tragedies of the Renaissance, those plays were often given a Mediterranean or even more exotic setting, and just like their predecessors, they usually lasted for no more than one generation. The **heroic play** (just like a heroic poem) tells of an epic contest, in which stage battles, impressive sets and extravagant costumes make for a bombastic form of entertainment. The best-known of these period pieces, which were set in the two centuries before and up to the Restoration, presented a tale of endurance, strife and conquest in times of war, and staged a moral conflict between love and honour. Heroic action, not historical accuracy, is what counts in plays such as Sir William D'Avenant's *The Siege of Rhodes*, a 'melodramatic' verse tragedy with music which shows Christian soldiers holding out against the Turks. This proto-operatic play in two parts (1656–61) could be performed because musical drama alone was allowed to be staged during the Puritan Interregnum (see Bevis 1988: 19). John Dryden (1631–1700) excelled in more exotic scenery, but also conspicuously chose **heroic couplets** for *The Indian Emperor; or, the Conquest of Mexico by the Spaniards* (1665) and *The Conquest of Granada by the Spaniards* (two parts, 1670–71). For *Aureng-Zebe; or, The Great Mogul* (1675), which was set in the vicinity of the Taj Mahal in India in 1660, Dryden turned from rhymed heroic plays to **blank verse**, an alternative which he had discussed at length in *An Essay of Dramatic Poesie* (1668). Dryden also wrote a (rhymed) prologue to Thomas Otway's blank-verse tragedy *Venice Preserv'd; or, A Plot Discovered* (1682). In its presentation of a Catholic conspiracy, Otway's play contained topical allusions to just such a 'Popish Plot' many Protestant Englishmen in 1678 had suspected the future James II to be involved in (which was why he chose to reside way from London when Otway's tragedy and Behn's *The Rover, Part II* were produced).

In addition to heroic plays, audiences were presented with **Roman tragedies in Neoclassicist fashion** in which the foremost authors and critics of the day either imitated or attempted to improve on Shakespeare. In December 1677, John Dryden's play *All for Love; or, The World Well Lost: A Tragedy, [...] Written in Imitation of Shakespeare's Style* (i.e., in blank verse) was premiered in Drury Lane. On the same spot, but a quarter of a century later, followed *Cato* (1713) by Joseph Addison (1672–1719), another blank-verse tragedy with a prologue contributed by Alexander Pope (the only part of the play written in heroic couplets). Both plays are showpieces of 'Augustanism', that is the effort to model the England of the **Augustan Age** on the ideal of Augustan Rome (see

Bevis 1988: 136). The two Roman tragedies look back to the Classical past as a glorious period, in the history of politics as well as of art. In the choice of historical subject matter and theme, *Cato* paralleled *Julius Caesar*, while Dryden's tragedy adapted Shakespeare's *Antony and Cleopatra*. What adds to this glorification of the past is the presentation of the subject matter in a Neoclassicist fashion that observes critical doctrines of the day which refer back to Aristotle in Greece or Horace in Rome. Dryden's "Preface" to *All for Love* is a good example and key document in this regard, as he speaks at length about the critics of Classical Antiquity and of French Neoclassicism. The notion of **decorum** required that the treatment of theme ('noble', i. e. dealing with grave and serious matter), of characters (presented as moral examples) and of language (polished, **poetic diction** in blank verse or heroic couplets) should fit the occasion. Besides decorum, both tragedies are also informed by the critical doctrine of the **three unities** (of time, of place, and of action), and it is here that they try to improve on Shakespeare's craftsmanship by cutting down on the span of time, on the number of locations, of characters and of sub-plots.

Dryden, Addison and Pope perceive and present their historical subject matter in a moral and ideological framework: there is a clash between Good and Evil, honour and treason; public commitment is set against the pursuit of personal pleasures (Antony and Cleopatra), and pure virtue (Cato) is set against sheer power (Caesar). In this sense, we are dealing here with some sort of 'drama of ideals'. The Neoclassicist doctrine of **poetic justice** is part and parcel of this moral framework: this is why not only various traitors, but also Antony and Cleopatra have to die. (The virtuous Cato has to commit suicide, too, but this violation of the rule of virtue rewarded is being justified as an exceptional act of Roman Stoicism.) Dryden's and Addison's Roman plays are also patriotic plays: their didacticism moreover extended to the politics of the day, and to notions of **Englishness**. In a second preface of *All for Love*, namely his long "Dedication" of the printed text (1678) to the Lord High Treasurer of England, Dryden had struck a patriotic and also a government-friendly note. He attempted to reconcile the virtues of the Roman Republic with post-Commonwealth, Restoration times, and flattered a Government which has all the Advantages of Liberty beyond a Commonwealth, and all the Marks of Kingly Sovereignty without the danger of Tyranny. Both my Nature, as I am an *Englishman*, and my Reason, as I am a Man, have bred in me a loathing to that specious Name of a *Republick*: that mock-appearance of a Liberty ("Dedication", Dryden 1984: 6).

Later, when the Glorious Revolution had done away with the monarchical Absolutism of the Stuart *régime* (yet stopped short of re-introducing a Republic) and when Great Britain had been united in one kingdom (1707), Pope's "Prologue" to Addison's *Cato* urged patriotic Britons to behave like the great Republican by defending the cause of freedom – here perceived as a hallmark of Britishness. Moreover, a patriotic audience should consciously 'buy British', as a late twentieth-century slogan ran: they ought to shun foreign plays and operas ("French translation, and Italian song", l. 42) and call for more such truly British plays instead.

This was the cue for Nicholas Rowe (1674–1718), the editor of the first critical edition of Shakespeare's works, who added to the subject matter of the English history plays with *The Tragedy of Jane Shore: Written in Imitation of Shakespeare's Style* (1714). The subtitle refers again to Shakespeare's use of blank verse as a dramatic idiom, instead of the rhyming couplets which prevailed in the Heroic Plays; both of which were gradually replaced by prose, as in *The London Merchant; or, The History of George Barnwell* (1731). This Neoclassicist play by George Lillo (1693–1739) is set in the days of the Armada (1588), but not concerned with affairs of state. As a **domestic tragedy** of love and murder in the private realm, Lillo's play followed up on *Othello* (here, young and innocent Barnwell is seduced by a *femme fatale*, indeed with fatal consequences). With its cast of typified characters taken from the middle classes, and bearing telling names such as Thorowgood or Trueman, this moralistic piece testified to the more bourgeois and didactic tendencies after 1700, and it was marked out by G. E. Lessing as a forerunner of the Continental kind of *bürgerliches Trauerspiel*.

To see that Henry Fielding's *The Tragedy of Tragedies; or, The Life and Death of Tom Thumb the Great* (1730) is a **mock-heroic play**, and thus a parody of the genre, one has to look no further than its title. The play was first conceived as a farcical after-piece, and then rewritten into an anti-tragedy in three acts. Fielding's burlesque involves a switching between registers of speech: he violates de-

Dramatic Parody and Satire

corum and peppers the dialogue which is usually rendered in blank verse (and occasionally in heroic couplets) with more colloquial expressions. The play's intertextual frame of reference extends to the medieval legends about the court of King Arthur (which provides the play's setting), to the folk stories about Tom Thumb the Giant-Slayer (Fielding's small-sized anti-hero), and to conventional characters of the heroic play, all of whom are shown to be deficient in comparison to the model. All the romantic and 'tragic' conflicts are solved by a series of revenge murders, which kill off most of the cast, but in slapstick fashion. When Walpole's 1737 Theatre Licensing Act effectively barred this playwright and political opponent from the stage, Fielding transferred his mock-heroic gifts to novels like *Joseph Andrews* and *Tom Jones*.

John Gay (1685–1732) was highly critical of Walpole, too, and *The Beggar's Opera* (1728) likewise is a parody of literary genres. The "Introduction" and prologue to this **ballad opera** – a conversation between two characters, the Beggar and the Player – sizes up, in ironical manner, the artificiality of the Italian opera (fashionable since Handel's arrival in England). In another exchange between the same two characters as a kind of epilogue, the concept of **poetic justice** is ridiculed. Indeed, if "Through the whole piece you may observe such a similitude of manners in high and low life"

Fig. 3.5 |
W. Hogarth, *Beggar's Opera* (1728)

(III.16), then why – such is Gay's suggestive question – should gangsters like Macheath and Peachum be punished, when a corrupt politician like Walpole can get away with it scot-free? With Peachum, the receiver of stolen goods, Gay drew a hardly flattering portrait of Walpole, and with Lockit, the head of prison, a caricature of another member of the government. There are two themes in *The Beggar's Opera*: first, corruption and crime; and second, gender relations, or the complex of love, sex and marriage. To begin with the second complex: gender relations are shown to be governed either by sexual greed (in men) or by materialist intentions (in women). Just like a Restoration rake, Macheath sets himself no limits to sexual freedom, and shows only a thief's morality by fathering children so as to save their mothers from the gallows, by enabling them to 'plead their belly'. Macheath avoids marriage at all costs, or handles it unconventionally, by entering on bigamous relations with Polly Peachum and with Lucy Lockit, indiscriminate of their fathers' position. Love marriages are a thing to laugh at; and Polly Peachum is taught soon to elicit favours by promising sex in return, and to see the ultimate aim of a prudent marriage in the comfortable existence of living as "a rich widow" (I.10). Gay's cynical presentation of gender relations continues where the Restoration comedies left off; however, his cast of characters comes from a very different section of society. *The Beggar's Opera* is set in London's gang-land, in the subculture of thieves, prostitutes and prison-wardens – with more polite society said to behave in the same way, but remaining off-stage (or in the auditorium). Man's nature – in all classes – is seen to be that of an animal of prey, following the summary definition of the English political philosopher Thomas Hobbes: "*homo homini lupus est*" (in *Leviathan*, 1651/68). There is no justice to keep such egotism in check; and judicial sentences are shown throughout to be a matter of bargaining.

The Beggar's Opera is a literary parody, and it is a satire of contemporary politics and of materialism in society. This musical drama is also an interesting case of **intermediality**, and a storehouse of popular, oral culture. In Gay's ballad opera, recitative is replaced by dialogue in prose, interspersed with songs which provide fresh texts to well-known tunes. Among the popular ballads which are thus given a new twist, are classic examples such as "Chevy Chase", "Greensleeves" and "Lilliburlero" (see the treatment in chap. 3.2.2). The blending of 'high' and 'low' culture is surely one reason why Gay's play experienced an immediate success (and could not be censored): there was a record of 63 performances in 1728 in London, before the play was soon produced all over the British Isles, on the Continent, and in the colonies. Five years after its première, a touring company acted the play in Jamaica, to make it the first recorded production on the island (Hill 1992: 74–75). Gay's play spurned a sequel of his own, *Polly* (which Walpole immediately suppressed, because of its political satire); a series of similar plays in his time (called Grub Street Operas); and the bicentennial adaptation by Brecht and Weill, *Die Dreigroschenoper* (1928; *The Three-Penny Opera*). Their famous song "Mackie Messer/Mack the Knife" is being 'covered' again and again, yet there were even more adaptations by notable writers of script and score (produced for instance in connection with the coronation of Queen Elizabeth II in 1953).

Sentimental Comedy

Gay's sequel, *Polly*, nods towards the **sentimental comedy** that had developed after Jeremy Collier's indictment of the sexual morals of the Restoration comedy. The best-known example of the new kind is *The Conscious Lovers* (1722) by Sir Richard Steele (1672–1729), who was Addison's partner as an essayist and also a theatre manager. Like Addison's Roman tragedy *Cato*, Steele's comedy shows first of all a Neoclassicist spirit: it is intertwined with the Roman playwright Terence's comedy *Andria*, whole passages of which are here included in translation. With the social setting and morality of his play, Steele, however, clearly targeted a contemporary middle-class audience. The dramatic conflict in *The Conscious Lovers* confronts the marriage of convenience with the love match. The arranged marriage between Bevil and Lucinda, a merchant's daughter, runs against both their love interests: Lucinda is in love with Bevil's best friend, and Bevil loves Indiana, an orphan whom he protects in gentlemanly fashion against the material interests of her official, but untrustworthy guardian. The dramatic conflict involves rival candidates and a bout of jealousy, and the conflict management includes Bevil's virtuous refusal to fight it out in a duel with his best friend – a refusal to an obsolete aristocratic code of conduct which is presented by Steele as a moral example. The play ends with two love marriages, and with a surprise twist which clears up family connections in a way that guarantees a bourgeois life-style for both

Fig. 3.6
Sir Richard Steele

the merchant's daughter and the orphaned girl. By comparison with Restoration comedy, Steele's play and later sentimental comedies do not deal with sexual trysts and innuendo, but with true love and innocence; their protagonists are a virtuous pair of 'conscious lovers', not a 'gay couple'; and their interaction shows more of an exchange of inside views than of wit. With Steele and his imitators, stage dialogue is used not for witty repartee, but for the (often tearful) revelation of the lovers' conscientiousness and state of emotions.

Sentimentalism will be found outside the theatre, too, in novels from Richardson to Austen (see chap. 3.5). On stage, Steele's sentimental comedy was followed up on by Richard Cumberland's *The West Indian* (1771), which chose the owner of a West Indian plantation as a sentimental hero (instead of a more likely slave, as in Aphra Behn's tragic story of *Oroonoko*, which could still be seen in Thomas Southerne's stage adaptation of 1695). It was not only the growing movement for the Abolition of Slavery which put an end to sentimentalism of this kind, but also the indignation of two Irish dramatists, Oliver Goldsmith (?1730–74) Oliver Goldsmith and Richard Brinsley Sheridan (1751–1816). With both "An Essay on the Theatre; or, A Comparison Between Laughing and Sentimental Comedy" (1773) and his prose comedy *She Stoops to Conquer; or, The Mistakes of a Night* from the same year, Goldsmith meant to curb excessive sentimentalism and to set a different example. His comic treatment of the complex theme of love and (arranged) marriage hinges on a practical joke and a resulting comedy of errors, when the shy protagonist Charles Marlow (a namesake of the narrator of Joseph Conrad's famous tales) is duped into meeting his prospective spouse and parents-in-law as barmaid and inn-keepers at their private home turned into a public house. In their attempts to reform the stage, both Goldsmith and Sheridan were supported by actor-manager David Garrick, who wrote a fitting prologue each for *She Stoops to Conquer* and for Sheridan's *The School for Scandal* (1777), which followed upon his first work for the stage, *The Rivals* (1775). In their use of stock characters (with telling names such as Surface, Careless or Lady Sneerwell) and in their witty dialogue, Sheridan's plays recall the comedies of humours and of manners. With the character of Sir Lucious O'Trigger in *The Rivals*, the Irish playwright pleased his London audiences with another version of the (drunken and swearing)

stage Irishman, and he created another enduring comic character with Mrs Malaprop, who is both fond of hard words and always so much at odds with them as to coin **malapropisms**. In contrast to their forebears, however, Sheridan's plays are set – like Goldsmith's comedy – in provincial society, and they join wit and sentiment in a fresh manner: in *The School for Scandal*, both malicious wits (Lady Sneerwell) and sentimental hypocrites (Joseph Surface) are unfavourably contrasted with true-wits who are trustful and benevolent (Charles Surface).

Shakespeare Cult

In addition to the interest these eighteenth-century plays merit in their own right, they are also indicative of the renewed and **strong appeal of Shakespeare**. The seeds for what turned into a cult of the National Bard (verging on 'bardolatry') were laid during the Long Eighteenth Century. This development can be traced from self-proclaimed 'imitations of Shakespeare's style' such as Dryden's *All for Love* (1677/78) and Rowe's *Jane Shore* (1714); through the preface of Fielding's mock-heroic *Tom Thumb* (1730), which claimed that the play was allegedly written by Shakespeare; and further on through homage paid to the Bard in the initial letter of dedication to Lillo's *The London Merchant* (1731) and in the epilogue of Goldsmith's *She Stoops to Conquer* (1773), which paraphrases the "All the World's a Stage" monologue of Jaques in *As You Like It*. David Garrick's role as promoter of Shakespeare was already mentioned, and in his productions of Shakespeare's plays, he shows the conflicting tendencies of his age, veering between *Werktreue* and a liberal adaptation which involves sometimes drastic changes. Garrick's abortive attempt to stage the original form of *A Midsummer Night's Dream* in 1763 ties in well with the return to Shakespeare's own words in the first critical editions edited by Nicholas Rowe, Alexander Pope and Samuel Johnson. These editions, which attempted to fix the performance text in print, became the material to work upon for critics such as Johnson himself (in his "Preface" of 1765), and later for enthusiastic Romantic critics such as Charles Lamb (*On the Tragedies of Shakespeare*, 1811) or William Hazlitt (*Characters of Shakespeare's Plays*, 1817). But there is also a counter-tendency to *alter* the texts for stage and print. This is apparent in the many adaptations of Shakespeare's plays from the Restoration onwards, including Nahum Tate's adaptation of *King Lear* (1681) with its happy ending, or the reworking of *Midsummer Night's Dream* into an opera such as *The Faeries* (1755), which was produced with Garrick's libretto, but without Shakespeare's mechanics. Some adaptations in book form proved so popular as to be read when the Long Eighteenth Century was long over, such as Thomas (and Henrietta) Bowdler's *The Family Shakespeare* (1807, ²1818), which 'bowdlerised' out the Bard's many indecent puns, or Charles and Mary Lamb's *Tales from Shakespeare* (1807), fictionalised for a juvenile audience.

When the Long Eighteenth Century phased out, theatre and drama again underwent significant changes. In the wake of the-atre riots at the turn to the nineteenth century, audiences from the middle classes upwards abstained for some decades from the playhouses and turned to private performances for the se-lect few, or to play-reading as an alternative and more intimate form of enjoyment. This coincided with a predilection, among Romantic poets as well as among critics such as Lamb or Hazlitt, to see plays primarily as dramatic poems, as **closet plays** and not as proper stage-plays. Lord Byron's *Manfred* (1817) and Percy Bysshe Shelley's *Prometheus Unbound* (1820) are notable examples of this turn of a public art into both a more intimate spectacle and an introspection of the individual mind. Those who continued to visit the playhouses saw features of the sentimental plays survive in the popular **melodrama**, which however really flowered in the Victorian Age (and therefore will be mentioned later).

Changes after 1800

Popular Politics in Songs and Speeches

3.2.2

Performance culture in the Long Eighteenth Century extended also to literary works connected with orality and oratory. Just like stage-plays, together with their prologues and prefaces, songs and speeches, too, served to popularise political views and to proclaim notions of **Englishness and Britishness**. This shall be pointed out first with a few songs which have become part of an oral tradition, regardless if they can be ascribed to an individual poet and composer (who are often known only to historians). Such is the case with "Lilliburlero" (Friedman 1961: 286–88). In 1688, when the opposition against Stuart absolutism turned into the Glorious Revolution and the deposition of James II, this song (for which the famous composer Henry Purcell is credited with the tune) became so very popular that it was said even then to have driven the king out of his three kingdoms. "Lilliburlero" is

Lilliburlero

deeply ironical: the lyrics (attributed to the Marquis of Wharton) are rendered in Irish English and purport to be an exchange between two Catholic Irishmen, who are apparently so enraptured by James's decision to appoint another radical 'Teague' as his deputy in Ireland as to revel in fantasies of a murderous Catholic backlash. The song's chorus ("Lilliburlero, burlen a-la") is less nonsensical than it seems, because it revives a watchword used in the massacre of Protestants in Ireland in 1641. The song dramatises just such a Popish Plot which had been feared by liberal-minded English Protestants for some time, and thus helped to bring about the Glorious Revolution.

From the point of view of a political opportunist, "The Vicar of Bray" continued the satirical account of political upheavals up to the accession of the House of Hanover in 1714. In each reign – from "good King Charles's golden days" after the Restoration over the rule of James II, when "popery grew in fashion", and through the reigns of William of Orange and Queen Anne up to George I – the unprincipled vicar continuously adjusted his outspoken religious and political beliefs to the order of the day, and always secured his post. The anonymous song concludes with the turncoat's ironical oath of allegiance:

> For in my faith and loyalty
> I never once will falter,
> But George my lawful King shall be
> Except the times should alter. (ll. 53–56)

Both songs continued to be so popular that they were incorporated into *The Beggar's Opera* and other *ballad operas* of the period. "Lilliburlero" even found a place in individual editions of Sterne's novel *Tristram Shandy*, as Tristram's Uncle Toby is said to be constantly whistling the tune, which moreover has been used as a signature by the BBC since the Second World War. In James Thomson's "Ode: Rule Britannia" (1740), the satirical mask is shed for patriotic sentiment. Thomson's ode to unerring beliefs rather than unprincipled behaviour was immediately seized by the public, and the (perhaps too well-known) chorus, "Rule, Britannia, Britannia rule the waves,/Britons never, never, never will be slaves", has been sung, often less ceremoniously, by patriotic Britons up to the present day, whenever there is something to celebrate. Apart from its obvious power politics, the chorus alone is interesting for its silent acceptance of the Union of Great Britain (1707) and for its proclamation of liberty, which was pointed out already with regard to the drama of the period. Such a self-proclaimed image of Britain and its empire as a realm of the free, however hollow it must have sounded to the colonial subjects and slaves, was ingrained in the minds of the British over the ages until it was resonantly rephrased in the war-speeches of Winston Churchill, in order to foster a spirit of endurance and an unwavering belief in the ultimate victory over dictatorship.

Churchill's predecessors were the **politicians and great orators** from the latter half of the Long Eighteenth Century: eloquent war-time ministers and prime ministers like William Pitt the Elder and the Younger, leaders of the opposition like Charles James Fox, influential politicians such as William Wilberforce (who greatly contributed to the movement for the Abolition of Slavery) or Henry Grattan (who dominated Irish politics before the parliamentary union with Westminster in 1801), and rhetorical talents such as Edmund Burke. Burke (1729–97) was born in Ireland and delivered memorable performances, in and out of the House of Commons, in speeches on a number of issues. In relation with the American War of Independence, which shattered the first British Empire, Burke discussed the ideas of political union and liberty in his speeches on the taxation of the American colonies (1774) as well as on conciliation with the American rebels (1775); speeches which had deserved the same hearing with the British government than they got on the other side of the Atlantic. With his highly self-critical approach to the British administration of India, which was just being turned into the 'jewel in the crown' in a second phase of colonialism, Burke's speech on the East India Bill (1783) compares well with a more imperialist counterpart that was delivered half a century later (1833) by Lord Macaulay, a Victorian historian and another rhetorical talent, who had also written an essay on the performance of William Pitt the Younger in parliament. (For all the texts mentioned in this paragraph, see Gross 1998.)

Outside parliament, in the lecture-halls of London and in the provinces, another Victorian institution began to be institutionalised, namely the **public lecture series** (which later might be collected as essays and published as a book). Samuel Taylor Coleridge, the Romantic poet and critic, is a good and early example with his lectures on Shakespeare and other literary matters, which he delivered from 1808 onwards. His successors in the next age are Carlyle, Dickens or Ruskin.

Guiding Questions and Exercises

1. Point out the main features of development of theatre and drama in the period between 1660 and c. 1830. Make note of the continuity and changes within the theatrical context, and of the influence of Neoclassicist thinking on the drama of the period.
2. Give a summary account of the kinds of drama staged during the specified period: of the various types of comedy and of tragedy produced, of heroic and of mock-heroic plays, and of intermedial hybrids such as the ballad opera.
3. Compare any of the Restoration comedies of manners to Shakespeare's *As You Like It*, *Much Ado About Nothing*, or *The Taming of the Shrew* with regard to their theme and form.
4. John Dryden's *All for Love* can be seen as a rewriting of Shakespeare's Roman tragedy *Antony and Cleopatra* in a Neoclassicist spirit. Compare the individual treatment of historical subject matter within the playwrights' period context.

3.3 | Neoclassicist and Romantic Poetry

3.3.1 | Translations, Imitations, Mock-Epic and Verse Satire

"The Choice", a very popular poem that was published in the year 1700, serves well as an introduction to **Neoclassicism** in life and art (see chap. 3.1.2). The poem is the first specimen in Roger Lonsdale's revisionist anthology *The New Oxford Book of Eighteenth Century Verse* (*NOBEV* 1–4), which looks beyond the conventional canon of works from that period and rediscovers forgotten texts that are able to produce a fresh impression. The poem by John Pomfret (1667–1702), a minor but nevertheless representative poet, is presented as a kind of wishful thinking, as the vision of an ideal life and life-style. The first location that comes into view is a country house. The whole building argues for moderation and against excess (ll. 5–12): it is a model of Neoclassical architecture in its regularity and restraint ("Built uniform, not

little, nor too great"); it avoids "needless pomp" and instead consists only of things which are "useful, necessary, plain". The park
outside again shows the ideal of an English landscape garden
(ll. 13–16), and "At th'end of which a silent study placed/Should
be with all the noblest authors graced" – those of the Classical
canon (ll. 17–22): Horace (the writer of regular odes), Virgil (epic),
Juvenal (satire) and Ovid (love 'elegies'). The aesthetic ideals of
Neoclassicism show up, too, in Pomfret's use of the **heroic couplet**, rhyming couplets in iambic pentameter, a poetic convention which derived from the 'heroic play' of the period (see
chap. 3.2.1) and became the standard form of Neoclassicist verse.

The poetical efforts of other and better-known authors look
at a Classical ideal, too, which is evident from their translations,
'imitations', satires and parodies. The high esteem in which Classical literature and especially the works of the first Augustan
Age were held in Britain around 1700 shows prominently in
the efforts directed towards **translations**. In this way, the works
of Classical authors were made part of English-language literature, and were once more integrated into the national canon.
The renowned poets of the late seventeenth and early eighteenth
century who worked as translators continued the work begun
in the Renaissance, but they differed from their predecessors in
their attempt to polish the originals in their translation, to render them in a congenial form which bore the marks of their own
standards of good writing (see Sühnel 1984).

Translations from the Time of the Renaissance and of Neoclassicism

Homer, *Iliad* and *Odyssey* (both epics)	George Chapman – 1611 – 1614–15	Alexander Pope – 1715–20 – 1725–26
Virgil, *Aeneid* (epic)	Gavin Douglas 1513	John Dryden 1697
Plutarch, *Lives* (biography)	Thomas North 1579	John Dryden (contrib.) 1683–86
Lucretius, *De rerum natura* (didactic poem)		Thomas Creech 1682 John Dryden 1692
Juvenal and Persius (satires)		John Dryden 1693
Ovid, *Metamorphoses* (mythological, epic and didactic poem)	Arthur Golding 1567	John Dryden, *Fables*, 1700

Dryden and Pope, the most famous poets of their time, devoted
much energy to their translations (Pope for instance spent ten

years in bringing Homer into English). The translations were published by subscription, either by Jacob Tonson (in Dryden's case) or by Pope and booksellers, and they made both Dryden and Pope financially independent.

However, when we look at translations, the break with characteristic tenets of Neoclassicism comes out, too. Writing a century after Pope's translations of the Homeric epics were published, in about 1820, both John Keats and Percy Bysshe Shelley, two of the younger Romantic poets, spoke out against these endeavours to transport Classical literature into English, and to even improve stylistically upon the original in translation. In the sonnet "On First Looking into Chapman's Homer", the starting-point of his fame as a poet (1816), the young John Keats returned to the Renaissance version of Homer in English, and renounced later translations in Neoclassical diction. And shortly afterwards, in 1821, Percy Shelley argued in his "Defence of Poetry" against the whole endeavour as such:

> the language of poets has ever affected a certain uniform and harmonious recurrence of sound, without which it were not poetry, and which is scarcely less indispensable to the communication of its influence, than the words themselves, without reference to that peculiar order. Hence the vanity of translation; it were as wise to cast a violet into a crucible that you might discover the formal principle of its colour and odour, as seek to transfuse from one language into another the creations of a poet. The plant must spring again from its seed or it will bear no flower – and this is the burthen of the curse of Babel. (*NAEL* II, 841)

If Keats wanted to break with Neoclassical diction, Shelley wished to do away with translations altogether, and thus with the attempt to fuse foreign (Classical) and native literature by making them available in the same language – one of the efforts of outstanding poets like Dryden or Pope.

Forms of Satire

Characteristic for the high esteem in which Classical literature was generally held at that time is moreover a second group of works entitled **'imitations'**. These are adaptations of poetic forms, i.e. efforts to combine a classical form with more topical contents. (For the vogue of imitations of the work of the Renaissance English poet Edmund Spenser, see chap. 3.1.2.) A characteristic feature of poetry in the Long Eighteenth Century is the creation of new satires, in verse and in prose. Satire has been understood as a form of **didactic literature**: as a corrective of human vice and folly in general, and of a deplorable political state of affairs in particular, which should be remedied. In awareness of Classical models, two main types (and some sub-types) have been distinguished (see Abrams and Harpham 2005: 284–88, Jack 1952 and Preminger 1993). **Indirect satire** (which is also called Menippean or Varronian satire, in honour of its Classical masters) takes the form of a fictional narrative about ludicrous characters or events. Jonathan Swift's prose narrative *Gulliver's Travels* (1726) and John Gay's drama *The Beggar's Opera* (1728) are considered prime examples of indirect satire, because they are (among other things) veiled forms of criticism of government politics in general and in particular of Robert Walpole, the first British prime minister. **Formal or direct satire** replaces the narrative of events by a more dramatic situation: it has the structure of a dialogue, or rather of a satirical monologue of the 'masked' speaker (*persona*), who addresses himself to another character or directly to the reader (as an *adversarius*). The satiric voice can belong either to a serious moralist (as in the satires of Juvenal) or to a more amused, relaxed and tolerant speaker (as in the satires of Horace).

The imitators of Classical **verse satires** before 1700 include the Earl of Rochester (1647–80), a notorious womaniser and provocative poet whose "A Satire Against Mankind" (1680) undermined the optimistic Enlightenment belief in the power of Reason. (Rochester's Juvenalian verse satire survived the period to provide the Caribbean poet Derek Walcott three hundred years later with the cue for his own satire on the politics in postcolonial Trinidad, entitled "The Spoiler's Return", 1980.) John Dryden (1631–1700) wanted to stick closer to the original tradition, and thus occupied himself with translations rather than imitations of Roman satirists. The prefaces to these translations and his "Discourse Concerning the Original and Progress of Satire" (1693) are important documents in the history of the genre in Britain. Well-known verse satires from the eighteenth century come from the pens of Pope and Johnson. Alexander Pope (1688–1744) published three volumes of *Imitations of Horace* (1734, 1737–38), both of verse satires and of verse letters (epistles). "The First Satire of the Second Book of Horace" has the structure of a dialogue, in which the speaker/poet "P." (inspired by the Horatian original, this refers to Pope) is interrupted now and again by the addressee "F." (which stands for William Fortescue, Pope's legal adviser). The imitation

John Dryden

includes topical, satirical quips at contemporary *literati* and at politicians such as prime minister Walpole. In his satirical verse letter, Pope rounds on his critics, among them Lady Montagu (see chap. 3.3.3). With regard to satire of the Juvenalian kind, Pope found a worthy successor in Samuel Johnson (1709–84), the great lexicographer and leading critic of his day. From his pen came first "London" (1738) and then *The Vanity of Human Wishes* (1749), in which he imitated the third and tenth satires of Juvenal, respectively. – In addition to the models imitated, verse satire can take other forms as well, e. g. the short form of the satiric **epigram**, of which Matthew Prior (1664–1721) and once again Pope were acknowledged masters.

Verse satire is also closely related to the form of the **mock-epic or mock-heroic poem** that was initiated by Dryden's *Mac Flecknoe* (1682), his personal invective directed against Thomas Shadwell, a rival colleague. Dryden's poem combines a trivial subject with a formal and elevated language, and with allusions to other conventional features of the epic (which, together with tragedy, ranked highest in the Neoclassicist hierarchy of genres). The imaginary coronation of Shadwell, "who never deviates into sense" (l. 20), as successor to the throne of dullness is the occasion which gives Dryden every opportunity to show both his own poetic craftsmanship and a deprecating sense of humour.

After Dryden, the species flowered under the hands of Alexander Pope, who expertly handled the heroic couplet for comic purposes: ranging from simply funny statements over those of a more witty kind to pointed, personal remarks. (For Swift's related fable *The Battle of the Books*, see chap. 3.1.2.) The importance of this genre in Pope's *oeuvre* is recognisable in the fact that Pope revised and enlarged his two famous mock-epics, so that there is more than one version of them. "The Rape of the Locke" (1712) was considerably enlarged from two 'cantos' (epic songs) to five when it was published in book form and with slightly altered title as *The Rape of the Lock* (1714). The second version was the one preferred by the poet and his contemporary public. In his 'heroi-comical poem', Pope takes a trivial event (the cutting off of a lock of hair) and presents it both in mock-epic fashion and with sexual overtones, as if it were the rape (abduction) of Helen of Troy or the rape (sexual abuse) of Lucrece, as in Shakespeare's epic of that title. In the extended version of *The Rape of the Lock*,

Fig. 3.7
Alexander Pope

Pope increased his substitution of epic conventions with more trivial counterparts: Belinda's morning toilet replaces the conventional arming of the epic hero (1.121–39); 'Ombre', a game of cards, is the equivalent of a battle scene (3.25–100); and the 'machinery' of epic gods is replaced by the Sylphs and Gnomes of Pope's invention, of which one by name of Ariel functions as the narrator. His name is a reminiscence of Shakespeare's 'airy spirit' in *The Tempest*, and amongst other things, Pope was also an editor of Shakepeare's works. Pope's mock-epic is therefore more of a genre parody than a sharp satire of 'polite society'. In fact, the poet – himself a Catholic, and conscious of belonging thus to a religious minority with a political handicap – sought to reunite in mirth two warring families of the Catholic nobility. In his other great mock-epic, *The Dunciad* (Books 1–3, 1728; Book 4, 1742/43), Pope sang a song of fools (dunces), and revenged himself bitterly upon his critics.

A century later, William Wordsworth tried to follow up Milton's *Paradise Lost* with a serious epic of his own entitled *The Prelude; or, Growth of a Poet's Mind* (1850), while the Romantic poet Lord Byron (1788–1824) proved to be the true successor to Pope, a Neoclassicist whom he held in high regard (see the quotation in chap. 3.1.2). Byron's verse satire *English Bards and Scotch Reviewers* (1809) explicitly continued in Pope's vein: in the heroic couplet as the chosen form as well as in the manner of criticising the critics, and of attacking rival poets (Wordsworth, Coleridge and Southey). Robert Southey, the Poet Laureate, is lampooned in true mock-epic fashion in Byron's *The Vision of Judgment* (1822). The protagonists of *Childe Harold's Pilgrimage* (1812–18) and *The Corsair* (1814) are exceptional characters outside social norms that fascinated a contemporary audience through their *mélange* of melancholy, *Weltschmerz*, and slumbering passion. With ambivalent heroes like these, a fascinating personality of his own, and exceptional poetic gifts, Lord Byron became *the* best-selling English poet at the end of the Long Eighteenth Century – and fittingly one of both Neoclassicist and Romantic credentials. His greatest effort was directed towards the comic epic *Don Juan* (1819–24), a long poem cut short only by Byron's death. It is characterised by elements of love romance and by a comic reversal of the traditional view of Don Juan as a woman's man. In addition, there is ongoing, topical political comment, in which Byron, a

Fig. 3.8
Lord Byron

Byronic Hero

British aristocrat long fascinated by the Emperor Napoleon and living in Mediterranean exile, made himself a champion of Liberty and an enemy of the reactionary politics of his fellow-peers of the realm, and of the monarchs on the continent. (See also chaps. 3.4.5 and 3.5.5.)

3.3.2 | From Gray's "Elegy" to the Odes of Keats, from the Ballad Revival to the Return of the Sonnet

Apart from epic and verse satire, there are two further Classical genres of poetry which were highly esteemed since the Renaissance, namely elegy and ode. The understanding of an **elegy** was at times flexible, so that the designation was applied to poems as diverse as the meditative long poems "The Wanderer" and "The Seafarer" in Anglo-Saxon times, and love poems such as John Donne's "Elegies" in the Renaissance. Towards the beginning of the Long Eighteenth Century, however, the term became limited to "a formal and sustained lament in verse for the death of a particular person, usually ending in a consolation" (Abrams and Harpham 2005: 77), and in this way it continued to be used up to the present day for poems such as Shelley's *Adonais* (1821), Tennyson's *In Memoriam* (1850), Auden's "In Memory of W.B Yeats" (1939), or Derek Walcott's "Eulogy to W.H. Auden" (1983), all of which commemorated friends or fellow poets. In a likewise

Fig. 3.9

Thomas Gray

manner, Thomas Gray (1716–71) had mourned the death of his personal friend Richard West in an elegiac sonnet (*ECP* 324), while in his "Elegy Written in a Country Churchyard", Gray was concerned with 'the common man' in general. In Gray's elegy, the two tendencies of Neoclassicism and Romanticism converge: in its strict formal regularity (quatrains made up of alternately rhymed lines of verse in iambic pentameter), Gray's *memento mori* observes Neoclassicist taste, but with its evening setting, its sympathy for simple country-folk and its self-reflexive meditation on the melancholy speaker (in the concluding "Epitaph"), this elegy is a good example of nascent Romanticism. If their material circumstances had not "repressed their noble rage,/and froze the genial current of the soul" (ll. 51–52), any of these peasants and field labourers in their lifetime might also have become a politician like Cromwell, or a poet like Milton; and yet their simple life was also less endangered by temptation, just because they lived

"Far from the madding crowd's ignoble strife" (l. 73, a phrase that was to provide Thomas Hardy with the title for the first of his Wessex novels). No wonder then that this peculiar lament and consolation for the death of common people brought instant fame and popularity to Gray, and continued to be his best-known poem. Its only rival in the period is Percy Bysshe Shelley's *Adonais* (1821), his commemoration of the fellow poet John Keats in a **pastoral elegy** which is second only to Milton's *Lycidas* (1638), and which similarly observes the Classical decorum of shepherds and mythological characters.

The impact of Gray's "Elegy" is visible in two poems by Charlotte Smith (1749–1806). The first companion-piece (because of its setting) is her "Sonnet Written in the Church Yard at Middleton in Sussex", the second an "Elegy" of her own. Both poems were first published in 1789 and are now available in *ECP* (514–18; the "Sonnet" alone can be found in other anthologies, too). Smith's elegy is both set in a country churchyard and rendered in Gray's stanza form, yet its supernatural elements point rather to Goethe's "Erlkönig" or foreshadow "Tam O'Shanter" by Burns (1791). These companion-pieces attest, first, to the great impact of Gray's "Elegy" on a Romantic sensibility; second, and more specifically, they are examples of women's answer poems in response to the work of male writers, and often enough also to male stereotypes. (This intertextual category will be discussed in chap. 3.3.3.) Finally, the sonnet mentioned is typical of the work of Charlotte Smith, who is credited with the revival of the sonnet at the outset of Romanticism.

The distinction between the elegy and another form of praise poem, namely the ode, is not always easy, in particular when such odes are also written in commemoration of individual persons, such as Ben Jonson's **ode** on Lucius Cary and Henry Morison (1640–41), John Dryden's "To the Pious Memory of the Accomplished Lady, Mrs Anne Killigrew" (1685) or William Collins's ode on the death of James Thomson (1749), the poet of *The Seasons* and of "Rule Britannia", itself an ode. However, Classically-educated (even if Romantically-inclined) poets and their public would have distinguished between various characteristic subtypes. Andrew Marvell's "An **Horatian Ode** Upon Cromwell's Return from Ireland" (1650) has a Classicist appeal due to its formal regularity (through the use of one stanza form throughout) and its balanced

Horatian and Pindaric Odes

view of both Charles I, "the royal actor" ending on the "tragic scaffold" (ll. 53–54), and of Oliver Cromwell, who defeated in quick succession first the Royalists and then the Irish. With its recurrent stanza and chorus, Thomson's "Ode: Rule Britannia" (1740), which was mentioned in chap. 3.2.2, is another example of the Horatian type. Apart from his Horatian ode on Thomson, William Collins (1721–59) provided a kind of blank-verse specimen (with alternating pentameter and trimeter lines) in his "Ode to Evening" (1746; revised 1748). Formal regularity and poetic diction mark it as a piece of Neoclassicism, while its imagery of time and place has it appear as a pre-Romantic poem, just like Gray's "Elegy". One of the personified abstractions that are a hallmark of Neoclassicist poetic diction is used for the evening itself, which is addressed as Eve, a nymph. The lyrical speaker asks Eve first to teach him how to sing a song of *beauty* (ll. 15–28), and then to lead him through a *sublime* landscape (ll. 28–40), before he ends (by a juxtaposition of imagery) on a *picturesque* note with a vision of eternity, a praise of Eve(ning) which will last as long as the seasons run.

It would be too simplistic to make the distinction between Neoclassicist and Romantically-inclined poets solely on their stance towards a regular type of ode. With his "Ode to Duty" (1807), the Romantic poet William Wordsworth (1770–1850) produced a Horatian ode on a Classical (and quite un-Romantic) maxim, which found its memorable, but more epigrammatic expression in the phrase: "England expects every man to do his duty" (Admiral Lord Nelson's signal to the fleet before the Battle of Trafalgar, 1805). Neoclassicist poets, on the other hand, were also drawn to the **Pindaric ode**, which either makes use of more than one stanza form, or avoids any regularity short of free verse. The original odes by the Greek poet Pindar consisted of a succession of *strophe*, *antistrophe* and *epode* (a third section showing a different make-up). In deviation from this original pattern, the term 'Pindaric' had come to be used more loosely since the seventeenth century, as an equivalent to an 'irregular ode', which comes in verse paragraphs of different length and structure. John Dryden's ode on the female poet Anne Killigrew (1685) is a case in point, and so is his "Alexander's Feast" (1697). William Wordsworth provided another prominent (and properly Romantic) example with his irregular "Ode: Intimations of Immortality from Recollections of

Fig. 3.10
William Wordsworth by B. Haydon, 1842

Ode: Intimations of Immortality

Early Childhood" (1807). Here, the lyrical speaker attempts to reverse the loss of imaginative powers in advanced age by jumping back in time to the creative potential available in childhood, a phase in human life which is seen as nearest to God and to divine inspiration (section V). In this paradoxical sense, "The Child is Father of the Man", as Wordsworth quotes himself in the motto to the ode (which is taken from his short poem "My heart leaps up", 1802), and in this same sense the apostrophe is to be understood which follows later in the poem:

> Thou little Child, yet glorious in the might
> Of heaven-born freedom on thy being's height,
> Why with such earnest pains dost thou provoke
> The years to bring the inevitable yoke,
> Thus blindly with thy blessedness at strife? (8.121–25)

Wordsworth's ode is a model of his own Romantic credentials (which are summarily expressed in his "Preface" to the *Lyrical Ballads*; see chap. 3.1.2). They come out first in the use made of both the Sublime and the Beautiful (1.19–35) in his presentation of Nature, both in its local and its abstract sense, as a testimony to the existence of a Supreme Being. Moreover, his general view shows in his idealisation of the child (of nature) together with the belief that "poetry is the spontaneous overflow of powerful feelings; it takes its origin from emotion recollected in tranquillity". His continuous self-inspection is also characteristic, together with the self-consciousness of his role as a poet, and thus as an extraordinarily sensitive, imaginative and creative individual. However, for his further programmatic statement that "ordinary things should be presented to the mind in an unusual way", albeit "in a selection of language really used by man", Wordsworth's ballads are perhaps a better example than his "Intimations of Immortality".

"Dejection: An Ode" (1802) by Samuel Taylor Coleridge (1772–1834) compares well with other odes of that time. It was directly inspired by Wordsworth's "Intimations of Immortality" and presents itself likewise in an irregular shape. (For the details of composition, see chap. 3.4.1.) In its depressed mood, it finds a counterpart in the "Ode on Melancholy" (1820) by John Keats. It shares its theme – engagement with Nature as a form of consolation for a lamentable loss of artistic powers – with Wordsworth's "Intimations of Immortality" and Shelley's "Ode to the West Wind".

|Fig. 3.11
S. T. Coleridge

Coleridge's night-thoughts likewise include an apostrophe to the wild west wind, which as an expression of the Sublime in Nature is less influential than Joy, the personification of vitality and inward happiness (ll. 40–75, 130–39).

When Percy Bysshe Shelley (1792–1822) wrote his "Ode to the West Wind" (which was published in 1820), he provided this counterpart with a less circumstantial argument. Here, the lyrical speaker leaves no doubt about the superior, "uncontrollable" powers of the "Wild Spirit", who is simultaneously "Destroyer and Preserver" (ll. 47, 13–14). Each of the first three sections of the poem is dominated and interlinked by one image from Nature: fallen leaves, rain-clouds and waves of the ocean. By the fifth and ultimate section, when the three visual elements have been first called up together (ll. 43–45, 53) and then complemented by an allusion to fire as a fourth ("an unextinguished hearth", l. 66), the consummate reference to the four elements from medieval and Renaissance cosmology is complete, and thus a unified structure of images achieved (see chap. 2.1). Once more, childhood is perceived as a stage of superior visionary and creative faculties, an artist's paradise which was lost and might eventually be regained through communion with the Sublime. The shape of Shelley's "Ode to the West Wind" is clear-cut and at the same time more complex. It is subdivided into five sections of fourteen lines each. Shelley incorporates, by unmistakable reference, the sonnet. In this, he follows the precedent of Thomas Gray. The sonnet-like sections of his ode follow neither the Petrarchan nor the Shakespearean pattern, but come up with an original scheme based on *terza rima* and rhyming couplets. Thus, Shelley's ode is regular, but not strictly homostrophic. Originality, the buzzword of Romanticism, is the note sounded here in a piece of poetical showmanship, and a clever play with the reader's conventional expectations (in particular about Horatian odes).

And in this, Shelley sides with John Keats (1795–1821), on whom Shelley will later write an elegy (*Adonais*). In the spring of 1819, Keats began to compose a series of odes, some of which are considered to be the finest of their kind in the English language. Like Shelley, Keats blended the ode with the sonnet in an undogmatic and original fashion. Nearly all his odes are of the homostrophic type, and their ten-line stanza is, generally speak-

Fig. 3.12

P. B. Shelley

Ode to the West Wind

ing, a clipped Italian sonnet, lacking the first quatrain. In each ode, this form is tested out with regard to metrical rhythm and rhyme. The "Ode to a Nightingale" conforms to the general pattern, and is Keats's contribution to a series of **reflective poems with an evening and/or graveyard setting**. This line of tradition, which is a characteristic part of the poetry of the Long Eighteenth Century, set in with Edward Young's popular *Night Thoughts on Life, Death and Immortality* (1742–46) and continued with Collins's "Ode to Evening", Gray's "Elegy", Charlotte Smith's "Sonnet Written in the Church Yard at Middleton in Sussex" and Coleridge's ode "Dejection". "[T]ender is the night" in Keats's "Ode to a Nightingale" (l. 35, a phrase which provided F. Scott Fitzgerald with a title for one of his novels), and the lyrical speaker finds in the beautiful song of the "immortal Bird" (l. 61) some consolation for his own mortality and morbidity. "Ode on a Grecian Urn" continues with the juxtaposition of the mortality of mankind with the eternity of beauty and art. The characters depicted on this Greek vase are frozen in motion, but nevertheless immortal – a "Cold Pastoral!" (l. 45) indeed, but also an image of everlasting beauty, of an eternal state of being and of an ultimate truth otherwise unattainable to mankind. At the end, as an answer to a series of rhetorical questions by the lyrical speaker, the ode sends out this half-consoling message (ll. 49–50): "'Beauty is truth, truth beauty' – that is all/Ye know on earth, and all ye need to know." This view is both a denial of the Rationalism and empirical science of the Age of Enlightenment (which sought truth through reason and experiment) and a foreshadowing of the late-nineteenth century Aestheticism of Walter Pater and Oscar Wilde.

|Fig. 3.13
John Keats

Closely related to the ode is the hymn. Both ode and **hymn** were originally sung as praise poems. Objects of praise were either gods or sometimes heroes and abstractions – and this holds true for both forms, which does not make distinction easier. However, the original Pindaric ode is usually remembered as a form of praise sung for the victorious sportsmen in the Olympic Games, and thus has a more secular character, while the hymn is much more closely connected to forms of religious worship. The translators of the Old Testament used the words *hymnos* and *psalmos* as equivalents of Hebrew expressions for praise songs. In the sixteenth and seventeenth centuries, there were many attempts (by Milton and others) to render the Biblical hymns and

Evangelicalism and
the Hymn

psalms in English. The writing of original, new hymns (in the religious sense of the word) however was an eighteenth-century phenomenon.

The revival of the hymn for liturgical purposes is connected with the names of Isaac Watts, of the Wesley brothers and of William Cowper, and it is indicative of a cultural development, namely the attempt at a renewal of Christian belief and worship. Isaac Watts (1674–1748) was the son of a Nonconformist minister, and became one himself (that is, he was a member of a Protestant group of Dissenters besides the Anglican Church). Watts promoted the practice of hymn singing in Nonconformist congregations and wrote original, new hymns for that purpose. His principal collections are *Hymns and Spiritual Songs* (1707) and *Divine Songs* (1715), which is also the first book of hymns for children. (For the children's book as another eighteenth-century innovation, see chap. 3.4.5.) Not much later, the Anglican Church was affected by a wave of religious fundamentalism that is generally referred to as **Evangelicalism**. An initiating factor and later on a prominent element in this grass roots attempt to renew and strengthen Christian belief in a sceptical Age of Reason is the Methodist movement, which was founded by the brothers John (1703–91) and Charles Wesley (1707–88). Both brothers "recognized the value of hymns in worship as a method of instruction and a channel for religious fervour" (Head 2006: 1186). Charles Wesley composed thousands of hymns, many of which are still sung and not only in Methodist chapels, for instance "Jesu, lover of my soul" (Jain and Richardson 1994: 395–98), a poem that combines the features of religious and of secular love songs, in the tradition of the Biblical "Song of Solomon", or John Donne's "Batter my heart, three person'd God". An early collection of Charles Wesley's hymns came out in 1749 (*Hymns and Sacred Poems*). The third poet to be linked with the liturgical hymn is William Cowper (pronounced 'Cooper', 1731–1800). Under the influence of an Evangelical surrounding, Cowper funnelled his emotional and psychological instability early on into the writing of hymns (see his contribution to the *Olney Hymns* edited by the Evangelical pastor John Newton, 1779). Like the hymns by Isaac Watts and by Charles Wesley, Cowper's hymns are indicative of the fundamentalist turn in eighteenth-century Protestantism which paved the way for the moral framework of 'Victorian values'. The writing of religious hymns in great number continued in the nineteenth century, and new hymns are still being composed to the present day.

Beside the liturgical hymn, there has also been a more secular tradition, visible in the Renaissance for instance in the *Four Hymns* (1596) by Edmund Spenser, which praise love and beauty in a more philosophical and literary manner that is inspired by Plato and by Petrarch. Specimens of a much more mundane and indeed satirical character are Daniel Defoe's "Hymn to the Pillory" (1703) and "A Hymn to the Mob" (1708). Spenser's understanding of the hymn as a poem in praise of abstract concepts, sometimes personified by mythological deities outside the Christian canon, shows again in "A Hymn to the Seasons". James Thomson (1700–48) added this hymn to the first collected edition of his sequence of four nature poems, *The Seasons* (1730) – a blank-verse counterpart to Vivaldi's famous Baroque concerto under the same title (*Le Quattro Stagioni*, 1725). Relevant examples from later poets include the "Hymn to Apollo" by Keats, the hymns of Apollo and of Pan by Shelley, and above all Shelley's "Hymn to Intellectual Beauty" (1817).

While the genres which have been looked at so far (epic, verse satire, elegy, ode and hymn) can all trace their history back to Classical antiquity, there is also recognisable a characteristic turn to medieval genres, and it is increasingly in evidence from the second half of the eighteenth century onwards. Thomas Gray's "The Bard: A Pindaric Ode" (1757) is one good example of the turn to medieval subject matter and oral literature. Gray was also a pioneer in producing verse translations of old Icelandic and Welsh texts. Sensational cases that testify to a fashionable interest in the Middle Ages are the actual **forgeries** of allegedly medieval literature undertaken independently from each other by James MacPherson (1736–96) and by Thomas Chatterton (1752–70). MacPherson fabricated 'translations' of epic poetry of a third-century Scottish bard by name of 'Ossian'; Chatterton 'discovered' (that is, invented) a fifteenth-century poet of Bristol, 'Thomas Rowley', and even wrote fake Anglo-Saxon poetry. (A fictional account of the tragic life of the forger himself followed two centuries later with Peter Ackroyd's novel *Chatterton*, 1987.)

Further striking examples of medievalism are the anthologies of English, Irish and Scottish ballads – such as Bishop Percy's

Medievalism

Ballad Revival

Reliques of Ancient English Poetry (1765), Charlotte Brooke's *Reliques of Irish Poetry* (1789) or Walter Scott's *Minstrelsy of the Scottish Border* (1802–3; 1833) – and similar collections of songs from Scotland and Ireland in which Robert Burns and Thomas Moore were involved. A 'ballad' opera such as John Gay's *Beggar's Opera* (1728) speaks of the same fascination with the poetry of the common people. There are three basic types of ballads. The **popular ballad** (such as "Barbara Allen", "Sir Patrick Spens", "Guy of Warwick" or "Chevy Chase") is a tragic, romantic or heroic narrative from the oral tradition, and it is to be performed. With its topical and often comical content, the **street ballad or broadside ballad** functions as the poor people's newspaper, and it is distributed simultaneously in two media: it is both sung in the streets and sold in form of printed broadsides (cheap pamphlets). Finally, **literary ballads** (such as the ones written by Wordsworth, Coleridge or Keats) are modelled on the other types, but are the creation of an individual artist and are circulated in manuscript or in print. Like his Irish contemporary Thomas Moore (1779–1852), the Scottish poet Robert Burns (1759–96) rewrote folk songs, or provided existing tunes with a new text. The most common **ballad metre** is named after its occurrence in the ballad "Chevy Chase", and consists of a quatrain of alternating lines of iambic tetrameter and trimeter, of which only the second and fourth lines rhyme (*abcb*).

The Rime of the Ancyent Marinere

Coleridge used both the same traditional ballad metre and the typical feature of **incremental repetition** (the repetition of key elements in slightly varied form) in his long poem "The Rime of the Ancyent Marinere, In Seven Parts". A first, pseudo-medieval version in archaic spelling and with much alliteration takes pride of place in the *Lyrical Ballads* (1798; ²1800) which Coleridge wrote in collaboration with Wordsworth. Later, the spelling was modernised and the poem was further revised, but also enlarged by marginal glosses (1817). At a wedding – i.e. in a frame-story (1.1–24, 7.651–58) – one of the guests is approached by an old sailor who tells him a tale of the Supernatural. The embedded tale proceeds with a series of views or visions of death: first, the mariner shoots an albatross, but is made to wear the dead bird around his neck by the superstitious crew; then a "spectre-ship" appears with a naked beauty ("Life-in-Death") and a skeleton; shortly afterwards the rest of the crew dies, only to rise again and to sail the ship back to the harbour, where the ship sinks. The mariner is the only one left to tell the tale, which he compulsively does wherever he goes. In his ballad, Coleridge fuses elements of Gothic literature (see chap. 3.5.5) with the legends of the Wandering Jew or the Flying Dutchman, and moreover with the theme of life as a journey – a theme which could be read in a religious sense as an allegory or a parable, as the way from crime to punishment and further to redemption.

In his ballad "La Belle Dame sans Merci" (which was like so *La Belle Dame sans* many of his sonnets and odes written in the memorable spring *Merci* of 1819, and published in the following year), John Keats shifts a deadly female figure centre-stage. This tale of love and lust has the form of an embedded story, too, told by a badly shaken knight-of-arms to a passer-by (the narrator of the frame story). The pale knight was one of the victims of a *femme fatale* who offered passionate love to her suitors in her 'elfin-grot', only to suck their life-essence out of them while they were asleep – but it is certainly less the sexual moral of the tale that has fascinated readers than its combination of medievalism and melodrama. Once more, Keats acknowledges, but does not strictly adhere to genre conventions. The last line of his ballad stanza is stressed twice only – a poetic license which is also in evidence in Robert Burns's ever-popular song "Auld Lang Syne" (1796).

Although the work of Burns is once again a reminder that Romantic tendencies preceded the publication of the *Lyrical Ballads* (1798), this joint venture has been rightly regarded as programmatic – not least because of the ballad revival signified by its title. For William Wordsworth, the volume also provided an occasion to come out (in his preface to the second edition of 1800) with a manifesto of the 'Lake School' of poets, as Wordsworth, Coleridge and Southey were referred to at the beginning of their career, after their residence in the picturesque Lake District. The designation 'Romantic' was commonly applied only towards the end of Wordsworth's life, his most productive phase lasting from 1797 to 1807, and its beginning being marked by his ballads or ballad-like compositions. "We are Seven" (1798) consciously makes use of the traditional ballad metre, shows indeed more of a language register used by simple folk, and of the naïve world-view of children. This ballad gives the theme of Life and Death another twist: here, the lyrical speaker meets 'a simple child' for whom a dead sister and brother are nevertheless present in the life of the family that continues to number seven children. Although written in a different pattern, "Simon Lee, The Old Huntsman" (1798), a simple tale of an individual's show of humanity contrasting with the common lack of gratitude, corroborates well Wordsworth's self-interpretation that "Low and rustic life was generally chosen, because in that condition, the essential passions of the heart [...] speak a plainer and more emphatic language" ("Preface"). Another poem, "I wandered lonely as a cloud" (1807, better known under the title "Daffodils"), is a set-piece of Wordsworth's aesthetic of "emotion recollected in tranquillity" ("Preface"). It comes from the end of his most creative phase, when he was less concerned with ballads and took part instead in the revival of just another genre usually slighted by Neoclassicists, namely that of the sonnet.

Sonnet Vogue

The last great practitioner of the sonnet before this period was Milton, who bypassed Shakespeare for Petrarch and wrote his **sonnets in the Italian form**. Thereafter, the sonnet fell into neglect. Poets of a Neoclassicist turn of mind, such as Dryden or Pope, clearly avoided to be seen in connection with this genre of medieval origin. After the Restoration, and up to the last decades of the eighteenth century, there are hardly any sonnets to be found. Thomas Gray's "On the Death of Richard West" (*ECP* 324) is the exception, and even this poem, although written in 1742, was not published during Gray's lifetime. However, the revival of the sonnet is traditionally not associated with Gray's singular specimen, but with the Romantic poets, and especially with Wordsworth and Keats. Actually, the return of the sonnet occurred earlier – a fact which was readily admitted by poets such as Wordsworth and Coleridge, and which is now again beginning to be acknowledged in our own day. In *Biographia Literaria*, Coleridge explicitly refers to the sonnet collections of William Lisle Bowles (1762–1850), such as *Fourteen Sonnets, Elegiac and Descriptive* (1789), revised and enlarged in the same year as *Sonnets, Written Chiefly on Picturesque Spots, Written During a Tour*. Coleridge also admired Charlotte Smith, who is now seen as the poet instrumental in that revival. Her collection *Elegiac Sonnets* – note the continuity of the combination with a melancholy mood of mourning – first came out in 1784, and was enlarged in later editions. In recent years, the contribution of women poets to the revival of the sonnet form before Wordsworth and Keats has been rightfully stressed, and individual sonnets from the sequences *Sappho and Phaon* (1796) by Mary Robinson (1758–1800) or of *Original Sonnets* (1799) by Anna Seward (1742–1809) have found again entrance into relevant anthologies that map the period.

The few sonnets Samuel Taylor Coleridge wrote himself have not entered the canon (although his self-parody "On a Ruined House in a Romantic Country" of 1797 shows an unexpected, humorous awareness of the clichés of nascent Romanticism). Yet of the altogether more than 500 sonnets that his friend William Wordsworth composed on a diversity of subjects, some have become the most famous examples of the revival: there are "Poems Dedicated to National Independence and Liberty" (1807) in the manner of Milton as well as topographical sonnet sequences which follow the example of Bowles, such as "The River Duddon" (1820) or the "Ecclesiastical Sonnets" (1822) written on the cathedrals of England. Moreover, there are individual sonnets celebrating landscape and the Sublime, such as "It is a beauteous evening, calm and free" or "The world's too much with us"; there are others that praise the beauty of the cityscape (such as "Composed upon Westminster Bridge, September 3, 1802"); and there are still others which inspect the genre itself, such as the meta-sonnets (i. e. sonnets on the sonnet) "Nuns fret not at their convent's narrow room" or "Scorn not the sonnet, critic". A striking example for the influence of Milton on Wordsworth is "London, 1802", which is a political rather than a topographical poem. A personal apostrophe in the first line of the sonnet – "Milton! thou shouldst be living at this hour" – evokes the predecessor as a kind of demigod who should provide for a return of traditional values, as a Messiah who should "return to us again;/And give us manners, virtue, freedom, power" (ll. 7–8) instead of individual selfishness and political stagnation. Over and above personal esteem and political content, the influence of Milton shows also in Wordsworth's similar penchant for the Petrarchan instead of the Shakespearean form in this as in his other sonnets. In "Scorn not the sonnet, critic" (1827), Wordsworth comments directly on preceding sonneteers and on a history of artistic achievement from Petrarch over Spenser and Shakespeare to its culmination, once again, in Milton.

Among the younger Romantic poets, John Keats and Percy Bysshe Shelley stick out with their interest in the sonnet, which they adopt and adapt with even greater independence of mind and originality. Keats is the less unruly of the two. Like John Milton before him, John Keats purposefully concerned himself with a variety of poetic genres, to achieve mastery in each – an approach best exemplified by his corpus of sonnets. Like Wordsworth, he fell back first on the original Italian pattern, which he practised in "On First Looking Into Chapman's Homer" (1816). This early example already signals Keats's engagement with literature itself, and – in extension – art, as his prominent subject matter. In this sonnet, reading the Homeric epics in translation is compared to a voyage of discovery, with the reader taking the place of a conquistador. That Keats did not check his historical facts when wrongly crediting Cortez in the poem with Balboa's 'discovery' of the Pacific does only underline the spontaneity of his response as a reader, and the Eurocentric perspective on the 'new planet' may be forgiven, too. Yet another incongruity shows this poem clearly to be a first attempt: while Keats's lyrical speaker compares the rough manner of the Renaissance translator and poet George Chapman positively to the translations of Neoclassicist successors such as Alexander Pope (who is clearly meant even if not mentioned by name), he himself falls back on just that poetic diction which is so typical of Pope. "On Seeing the Elgin Marbles" (1817), his poem following on the purchase of the marble statues and friezes of the Parthenon in Athens for the British Museum, shows Keats once more to be a Petrarchan/ Wordsworthian sonneteer, a Neoclassicist in spirit, and a lover of artistic perfection. (The poem makes for good comparison with Lord Byron's *The Curse of Minerva*, a verse satire that presents Lord Elgin in an entirely different light.) With "On Sitting Down to Read *King Lear* Once Again" (1818), Keats varies his theme of inspiration by art and tries his hand now at the hybrid of the Petrarchan and Shakespearean species (a pattern which was favoured for instance by John Donne in his *Holy Sonnets*). This intertextual poem is another reverential tribute and one more step into his direction of mastery of the genre. In "When I have fears that I may cease to be" (composed nine days later, but published not before 1848), Keats shows a very different anxiety, but also comes up with a proper Shakespearean sonnet, and thus finally breaks with Wordsworth's habit. Paradoxically, the *English* sonnet is also applied to Keats's response to a piece of *Italian* literature, "A Dream, after reading Dante's Episode of Paolo and Francesca". In the same spring of 1819 which produced "A Dream", there is only one move further to be made to a proper meta-sonnet, and this is achieved in "If by dull rhymes our English must be chained". Here, Keats matches content and form, and frees the sonnet from the fixed patterns to which it was chained one way or another: his sonnet eschews the conventional, 'dull rhymes' which are deplored for a fresh, irregular pattern of Keats's own making. After this final step, there is nothing further to be gained along this road, and Keats redirects his efforts to attain artistic mastery to another genre, the ode (see above).

The sonnets by Percy Bysshe Shelley are even more radical in their approach. Shelley's "England in 1819" countered the apparently ongoing stagnation of the country with a more revolutionary appeal than Wordsworth's "London, 1802". This finds its proper expression in the form of Shelley's sonnet that turns convention on its head, by opening with a sestet. Even more radical in the attempt to match form and content is Shelley's "Ozymandias" (1817). The sonnet centres on the fragmentary and shattered remains of a colossal statue of Ozymandias – that is pharaoh Ramesses II – in the desert and gives a new twist to the *sic transit gloria mundi topos* so often used since the Sonnet Craze in the Renaissance by presenting itself in a state of artful disintegration. The rhyme scheme is devised in an original as well as irregular fashion, and the poet sometimes makes use of up to three different metres in a line of verse ("Stand in the desert. … Near them, on the sand," l. 3). The intricate structure of this poem foreshadows Shelley's original use of the sonnet in his "Ode to the West Wind", which ties in with his overall rejection of Neoclassicist dogma, including the notion of the 'purity' of genres. Altogether these poems attest to Shelley's radical self-fashioning: he was neither given to obey social conventions in his way of life nor to simply follow given rules in his work of art. In this uncompromising stance, he was not alone, as the consideration of women poets of the period (such as the Countess of Winchilsea, Lady Mary Wortley Montagu or Anna Laetitia Barbauld) shows.

3.3.3 | Poetry and Gender Relations: 'Love, Honour and Obey'?

When men have written poems on women or on the relationship of the sexes (such as the Renaissance poet Andrew Marvell in "To His Coy Mistress"), these poems are very often, and not surprisingly, endowed with a distinctively male point of view, a 'male gaze' (Mulvey 1975). Women poets turning to the same subject matter did not only adopt the literary or cultural conventions they found (including the 'male gaze' involved), but also have shown themselves adept at 'answering back'. Extra-literary occurrences apart, this phenomenon of having one's say by answering back is known, as a dramatic set piece, from dialogue in comedies by either men or women. Female characters in Shakespeare's plays such as Kate in *The Taming of the Shrew*, Beatrice in *Much Ado about Nothing*, or Rosalind in *As You Like It*, had already been connected with early examples of **repartee**, before it flourished later in the 'wit combats' of Restoration comedies, including those by Aphra Behn (c. 1640–89). With "The Disappointment", Aphra Behn also provided a poetic equivalent to repartee. To well-versed contemporaries of Behn, her outwardly mock-pastoral, but nonetheless outspoken poem on male impotence must have appeared most of all as a companion-piece to "The Imperfect Enjoyment" by the Earl of Rochester (a Restoration rake if ever there was one outside the comedies of that period). In Rochester's poem, the embarrassing situation was dealt with from a male perspective only, and in not too delicate garb. In Behn's rendering, however, more stress than in either of its predecessors was laid, too, on the Other, on Woman's experience of such male malfunction. That particularly Behn's and Rochester's poems were seen as companion-pieces, indeed, comes out clearly in the fact that Behn's poem was first printed not under her own name, but – well within her life-time – in the posthumous collection of Rochester's poetry, as one of his. Through publication of both Behn's and Rochester's poems together in a collection of his poetry, any notion of female maliciousness was blurred. If only in this coincidence, the example shows that such a give-and-take, however pointedly expressed, may not be seen by definition as an indication of a spirit of retaliation between the sexes: this may sometimes come into it, but must not necessarily always be the case. While Behn does not explicitly refer to Rochester by name in her companion-

Fig. 3.14 |
John Wilmot, 2nd Earl of Rochester (c. 1665–70)

piece, the **answer poems** that follow show a directly personal and   Answer Poems
intertextual response. These answer poems took up a given text,
either on its own terms or because it dealt with gender-related
matters such as a male stereotype of women, women at work,
marriage and rights within marriage, or women's rights in general.

There are a number of women's answer poems from the
eighteenth and from later centuries, which were sent in return
to male writers, usually the literary lions of the period (which
may also explain why the poetic replies have been preserved).
In *NAEL*, readers find the exchanges of semi-private, semi-public
epistles or letters in verse between Lady Mary Wortley Montagu
(1689–1762) and Jonathan Swift (1667–1745), or between Alexander Pope and a series of women poets: the Countess of Winchilsea
(1661–1720), Viscountess Irwin (?1696–1764) and Mary Leapor
(1722–46). This exchange of poetic letters (*NAEL* I, 2585–2603; see
also *NALW* 165–66, 179–80, 197–202; *BWP* 23–24, 469–70) exemplifies the general character of literary communication in polite
society at that time, yet there is also a dramatic story about the
breakdown of personal relationships involved. In the course of
this increasingly bitter retaliation between the sexes, some members of polite society shed all masks of 'politeness'.

Alexander Pope followed up the first version of "The Rape of
the Locke" (1712) with an "Impromptu to Lady Winchilsea: Occasioned by Four Satirical Verses on Women Wits, in *The Rape of
the Lock*". This *impromptu* was already a poetic answer, evidently
composed in response to the Countess of Winchilsea's (no longer documented) criticism of his lines of verse in question. However, when Pope seemed to make amends for what could have
been read as a personal criticism of Lady Winchilsea's writings,
he did so by paying Her Ladyship a patronising compliment. In
depicting her as the glorious exception to an otherwise intellectually handicapped female sex, Pope only restated his general
prejudice – and promptly received an answer poem to hold such
alleged male superiority in check. In "The Answer (To Pope's *Impromptu*)", Pope the poet is compared to the singer Orpheus, who
had also mocked the other sex in his songs, and ended up by being torn to pieces by wild women, the maenads. In a bantering
spirit, Mylady described how the head of Orpheus rolled on, before she assured Pope that he could still rely on the admiration of

his female readers: "You need not fear his [Orpheus's] awkward fate:/The *Lock* won't cost the head." (ll. 27–28)

Twenty years later, another such exchange of verse letters occurred that appeared less as a bantering form of parody and polite conversation than rather as the poetic equivalent to a boxing match with either side punching below the belt. Again, Pope had opened the fight by including in one of his ambitious 'imitations' a few couplets that were seen as an invective against Lady Mary Wortley Montagu. She had fallen out with Pope, who had been in love with her before. Within a few weeks, Lady Mary had composed "Verses Addressed to the Imitator of the First Satire of the Second Book of Horace" (1733; *ECP* 188–91): an extended personal satire, which saw in the physical deficiencies of the Imitator (Pope) a symbol for his diseased mind. The answer poem reached its climax in the characterisation of Pope as an "angry little Monster" (ll. 76). At about the same time, Lady Mary also engaged in a second bout, by rounding on another literary lion of the age that also condescended to the female sex in his poetry, namely Jonathan Swift. In his notorious satire on female vanity, "The Lady's Dressing Room" (1732), Swift had stooped so low as to make his misogynistic point by extended reference to the contents of a chamber pot. Lady Mary's incrimination of this 'excremental poem' is found in "The Reasons That Induced Dr. Swift to Write a Poem Called 'The Lady's Dressing Room'" (1734). This satirical answer poem offered to tell the whole story, by sending "the Doctor" to a prostitute where he proved himself unable to achieve his purpose, then blamed the uncomfortable state of her room and promised to take revenge in the poem he was to write. However, both as a character in the answer poem and in poetic confrontation with Lady Mary, Swift came up against women who answered back and had the last word. In both the metric form and the stark language of her satirical reply, Lady Mary proved herself to be Swift's equal, and she did not forget to include also a deprecating aside on Pope:

> Poor Pope philosophy displays on
> With so much rhyme and little reason,
> And though he argues ne'er so long
> That all is right, his head is wrong. (ll. 45–49)

Pope's predictable reaction, and the opening of Round Three, came in a verse letter entitled "Of the Characters of Women" (1735). In this epistle, addressed to one of his closest female friends, Pope satirised the female sex in general and once more incorporated lines that read as a defamation of Lady Mary Wortley Montagu. As Lady Mary's second in this round, her friend, the Viscountess Irwin went into the ring with "An Epistle to Mr. Pope, Occasioned by his *Characters of Women*" (1736). To Pope's contention, given out as the opinion of his female friend, "Nothing so true as what you once let fall,/'Most women have no characters at all.'" (ll. 1–2), Viscountess Irwin replied in a memorable fashion:

> By custom doomed to folly, sloth and ease
> No wonder Pope such female triflers sees.
> But would the satirist confess the truth,
> Nothing so like as male and female youth,
> Nothing so like as man and woman old,
> Their joys, their loves, their hates, if truly told.
> Though different acts seem different sex's growth,
> 'Tis the same daring principle impels them both.
> [...]
> In education all the difference lies;
> Women, if taught, would be as bold and wise
> As haughty man, improved by art and rules;
> Where God makes one, neglect makes twenty fools.   (ll. 1–8, 33–36)

Viscountess Irwin, too, proved her point by writing back to Pope on his own terms, beginning her answer with a motto taken from Horace's *Art of Poetry* and continuing in heroic couplets throughout. And this is not yet the end of answer poems to Pope or Swift: some years later, "An Essay on Woman", written by Mary Leapor (†1746), added further proof by showing that one did not need to have an aristocratic education to do what a gardener's daughter could achieve as well.

This first group of answer poems represents more than merely poems written on the occasion of another's verse: they are endowed with a special significance, over and above all personal strife. First of all, this poetic correspondence is evidence of the final stages of the gradual change from the **'manuscript system'** towards print as a dominant form of publication and distribution. These poetic repartees, which were often cast in the form

Poetical Exchange in a Time of Change

of verse letters, hover between the personal correspondence and the semi-public letter which circulates either in manuscript or which reaches its equally select audience in form of a book published by subscription. The ambivalent nature of this correspondence comes out in different forms of address, as when the correspondent is sometimes intimately addressed as "Alexander" (in the Countess of Winchilsea's answer), sometimes more formally as "Pope" or "the Doctor" (in the poems by Lady Mary Wortley Montagu and Viscountess Irwin).

With regard to **gender concepts**, too, these answer poems are evidence of a time of change. In recent years, scholars sketched a long-term development in the history of mentalities by which an older construct, the so-called 'one-sex model' which saw Man – in every sense of the word – as the crowning achievement of creation, was replaced at the turn to the eighteenth century by a 'two-sex model' which no longer conceived of women merely as a kind of 'lesser man', but as intellectually equal (see Laqueur 1990 and Schabert 1997: 24 ff.). This egalitarian understanding of the Enlightenment period is mirrored in the poetic counter-discourse here under review. Even though a certain degree of role-playing must be granted, the respective poems by Pope and Swift clearly smack of the older, condescending and misogynistic attitude, and it is exactly this attitude that impelled the female aristocrats to answer back, again and again. In their replies, they confront this fading concept with the new, egalitarian understanding of gender and intellectual abilities. To make this point, it was perhaps helpful not to break with poetic conventions such as the heroic couplet in order to get a sympathetic hearing. The progressive spirit of Enlightenment is indeed found in these answer poems, but it is also bound to a conventional form of presentation.

Feminist Answers

The improvement of society through a **vindication of the rights and the work of women** is the theme of a second, differently orientated, but equally egalitarian group of answer poems from the latter half of the eighteenth century. Mary Collier (?1690–1762) and Anna Laetitia Barbauld (1743–1825) produced relevant examples. Mary Collier's *The Woman's Labour: An Epistle to Mr Stephen Duck* (1739) was written in reply to Duck's poem "The Thresher's Labour" (1730) which conveyed a realistic portrait of the working year of rural labourers, but at the same time showed a rather deprecating attitude towards women's labour (see *ECP* 249–62). Collier strove to set this right: her answer poem was a graphic depiction of, for instance, the hard work of washerwomen like herself. The dialogic context is now that of print and the marketplace, but this kind of social realism was achieved once more in heroic couplets and through the use of poetic diction. When Anna Laetitia Barbauld took up this theme later in her poem "Washing-Day" (1797), she turned to blank verse. There is an ambivalent effect, because such poetic decisions may either appear as having the hardship of woman's labour recognised in the dignity of verse, or they may appear as a form of literary mimicry which still abides by the rules made by male poets and critics.

However, abiding by convention was not the stance that was generally taken in women's answer poems over the centuries. Discussion of the rights of women long went together with a consideration of their **rights within marriage**, and a fresh view of wedlock is therefore documented in form of answer poems, too. For centuries, women had found themselves conventionally addressed either as a muse or in the form of a Petrarchan paragon of beauty and virtue. With women put on pedestals, as in Renaissance sonnet sequences, marriage did not always appear within easy reach, but nevertheless it was equally conventionally presented by male sonneteers as the desirable state of union for members of either sex. This abstract ideal of gender roles and gender relations long persisted as a norm, at least within the realm of poetry. By the eighteenth century, at the latest, it called for a reply. In "The Rights of Woman" (perhaps composed around 1795, but only published in 1825), Anna Laetitia Barbauld took the step from woman's labour to 'women's lib', in an answer poem that replied to the work of another woman, namely Mary Wollstonecraft's classic feminist treatise *A Vindication of the Rights of Woman* (1792). In this treatise, one of Barbauld's poems was criticised as showing women in a position smelling of weakness, instead of arguing for strength (see *ECP* 481), and Barbauld can here be seen to make amends, to sound a call to arms in the battle of the sexes. While every effort is made to show women as equally powerful, it is not victory of one sex over the other that is the ultimate aim. What is envisaged as a vision of the future is a world of 'mutual love'.

In its ultimately conciliatory view of the union of the sexes, Barbauld's poem was moreover an exception in a period when women writers usually spoke out against the institution of marriage. A very early, seventeenth-century example (which however did not unequivocally specify its addressee) was "An Answer to Another Persuading a Lady to Marriage" by Katherine Philips (†1664, *WSO* 63), and more examples were to follow. Lonsdale's revisionist anthology *Eighteenth-Century Women Poets* opens right away with a poem that in more than one sense showed women answering back. *The Ladies' Defence* (1701) by Mary, Lady Chudleigh (1656–1710), had been written, as Lonsdale noted, "in response to *The Bride-Woman's Counsellor* (1699), a sermon preached at a wedding at Sherborne by the Nonconformist John Sprint, which advocated total subordination of women to their husbands" (*EWP* 1). Lady Chudleigh's answer, a response both to Sprint and in the spirit of Mary Astell's early feminist tract *Some Reflections on Marriage* (1700), moreover reflected the dialogic situation in that it was in itself shaped as a debate on this issue. This is how Melissa, the poetic *persona*, protests against the subordination of women to male prejudice and prerogative, to a 'male gaze':

> 'Tis hard we should be by the men despised,
> Yet kept from knowing what would make us prized;
> Debarred from knowledge, banished from the schools,
> And with the utmost industry bred fools;
> Laughed out of reason, jested out of sense,
> And nothing left but native innocence;
> Then told we are incapable of wit,
> And only for the meanest drudgeries fit;
> Made slaves to serve their luxury and pride, (*EWP* 2).

To change this situation, Melissa advocates, in best Enlightenment tradition, a rigorous course of education for women to achieve equality on all levels (*EWP* 2–3). In other words: instead of continuing to be a laughing stock, Woman should rather turn into a bluestocking. In 1703, Lady Chudleigh added another pointed address "To the Ladies" – and likewise a general answer to Mylord. In this poem, the explicit comparison of slavery and the marriage bond was continued, but on an even more sarcastic note, and the words were no longer put into the mouth of a poetic *persona*.

WIFE and servant are the same,
But only differ in the name:
For when that fatal knot is tied,
Which nothing, nothing can divide,
When she the word *Obey* has said,
And man by law supreme has made,
Then all that's kind is laid aside,
And nothing left but state and pride.
Fierce as an eastern prince he grows,
   [...]
Who, with the power, has all the wit.
Then shun, O! shun, that wretched state,
And all the fawning flatterers hate.
Value yourselves, and men despise:
You must be proud, if you'll be wise. (*EWP* 3, ll. 1–9, 20–24)

In a curious way, one hears in the last lines – "Value yourselves, and men despise:/You must be proud, if you'll be wise" – more than an appeal to womanhood to catch up with any man's wit. Indeed, these lines anticipate the phrases in which, towards the end of the century, Immanuel Kant was to answer a question he put to himself, namely as how best to define Enlightenment: "Habe Mut, dich deines e i g e n e n Verstandes zu bedienen!" (Kant 1784/1922–23: IV, 169).

Understandably, marriage as an issue continued to be of interest for women poets in later centuries. The "Song: Woo'd and married and a'" (1822) by the Scottish writer Joanna Baillie (1762–1851) was originally written as part of a stage-play. Inspired by her Scottish colleague Robert Burns, Baillie's song shows the 'language really used by *women*': in 60 lines of vernacular verse in Scots, the poem tells the story of a wilful bride who longs for an extravagant dress, and therefore is in a bad mood, but overcome by her bridegroom's love. A fresh view of marriage, and a memorable example of an answer poem of a different kind was written by Una Marson (1905–65), a twentieth-century Jamaican feminist who spent most of the 1930s and '40s in London, where she became private secretary of the Ethiopian emperor Haile Selassie. As perhaps the first important woman poet from the colonial West Indies, Una Marson became known in particular for her blues poems and for the use of Jamaican Creole as a fresh language of poetry – in short: for a self-assured break with conventional forms of poetic discourse. However, in her poetic reply "To Wed or Not to Wed" (Burnett 1986: 161), she used the language of the Bard to write right back to the colonial centre, and to engage in a dialogue over the centuries. Writing back, but not with a vengeance (to quote Salman Rushdie's resonant phrase): the Jamaican feminist's reply to Hamlet's famous soliloquy was clearly both a reverential tribute to the Bard and a considered engagement with the topic at hand. If this unexcited answer poem by a twentieth-century feminist can be said to be in any way paradigmatic for long-term developments, gender relations clearly had come a long way since the days of Lady Chudleigh and others.

Una Marson's reply to Shakespeare leads to a last group of relevant poems, namely those which, irrespective of gender issues, centred on the work of male writers, of the present and the past. Here, the answer poem functions primarily as a form of a **female reader's response and literary criticism**. When these answer poems addressed then contemporary colleagues such as Coleridge, their response usually took the form of great praise. The shift in attitude from serious praise to more comic appraisal is in evidence in the otherwise continuous dialogue over time with the two Romantic poets Wordsworth and Coleridge. "To the Poet Coleridge" by Mary Robinson (1758–1800) is an early eulogy on the "Spirit divine" and "Genius of Heav'n-taught poesy" (ll. 2, 27; 52), written in the sublime manner of his "Kubla Khan" and interspersed by frequent verbatim references to the yet unpublished poem that Robinson had read in manuscript in 1797. Mrs Barbauld's "To Mr. C[olerid]ge" is a frequently anthologised companion-piece from the same year. This allegorical blank-verse poem was written after Barbauld had received a visit from the much younger Romantic poet, who is appraised less enthusiastically and warned not to get lost in a 'grove of enchantment, midway up the hill of science':

> Youth beloved
> Of Science – of the Muse beloved, – not here
> Not in the maze of metaphysic lore,
> Build thou thy place of resting! (*EWP* 311, ll. 32–35)

When some 160 years later, Stevie Smith wrote down her "Thoughts about the Person from Porlock" (1962, in Smith 1985:

385–86), who had allegedly interrupted Coleridge's dream-vision of Kubla-Khan's pleasure-dome, the time-lapse changed also the nature of her answer poem. It still served as a piece of literary criticism, but moreover functioned as a vehicle of cultural memory, and as one that struck (for most of the poem) a comic note, not the least by focusing on the visitor rather than on the visionary.

> As the truth is I think he was already stuck
> With Kubla Khan.
> He was weeping and wailing: I am finished, finished,
> I shall never write another word of it,
> When along comes the Person from Porlock
> And takes the blame for it.
> [...]
> I felicitate the people who have a Person from Porlock
> To break up everything and throw it away
> Because then there will be nothing to keep them
> And they need not stay. (ll. 7–12, 38–41)

Wendy Cope proceeded further on this way in her series of answer poems to both Wordsworth and T. S. Eliot, which will be mentioned later in chap. 5.1.

Guiding Questions and Exercises

1. Point out various forms of comic and satiric verse with reference to individual examples from the Long Eighteenth Century.
2. Can you summarise the development of the ode from Andrew Marvell to John Keats?
3. Compare P. B. Shelley's "Ode to the West Wind" with the thematically related twentieth-century poems "Why east wind chills" by Dylan Thomas and "Facing North" by Tony Harrison (on the North Wind, 1984). Please include in your comparison the individual shape of those poems and the period context.
4. Give a short sketch of the ballad revival that took place during the eighteenth and early nineteenth centuries.
5. Try to account for another revival – that of the sonnet – by a summary discussion of individual poets and poems.

6. Take another look at the work of women poets in the period, and in particular at their poetical response to their male colleagues. What are the main currents?

7. In "To Wed or Not to Wed", the twentieth-century Caribbean woman poet Una Marson rewrote the famous soliloquy from Shakespeare's *Hamlet*. Derek Walcott, another famous Caribbean poet, based his own satire on the situation in Trinidad, "The Spoiler's Return" (1980), on "A Satire Against Mankind" (1680) by the Earl of Rochester, a Restoration poet. Describe the ways in which the original texts have been used in a feminist and a postcolonial context.

8. With "A Kumquat for John Keats" (1981), Tony Harrison wrote a long answer poem to the "Ode on Melancholy" by Keats. Compare the two poems with regard to their theme and form.

3.4 | From Manuscript to Print: Adaptation to a New Medium, and New Forms of Writing

3.4.1 | Romantic Poets and the Continuum of Recital, Manuscript and Print

Women's answer poems from the Long Eighteenth Century present a fascinating record of the individual experience of gender relations and of their general development over time. Moreover, even though Pope saw to his own ambitious poems being printed, the answer poems altogether point to a system of literary communication in which the **circulation of manuscripts** was the norm – and the misattribution of authorship sometimes the consequence, as in the case of the Earl of Rochester and Aphra Behn. Even after the introduction of print, and well into the eighteenth century, literary communication in verse clearly had not severed its links with the 'manuscript system'. The end of its heyday fell together with the Age of Neoclassicism (see Love 1993; Marotti 1995; Speck 1998: 31–47). The impact of the 'manuscript system' cannot only be detected in those poems (such as a number of Rochester's) that might have had to seek a clandestine form of publication for reasons of obscenity or political partisanship, but also in the eighteenth-century vogue for the **'epistle'**. Such artful yet artificial letters in verse looked back to the Classical tradition of Horace, who had cast his literary criticism in epistolary form (*Epistula ad Pisones* = *Ars Poetica*), and of Ovid, who had centred on mythological heroines (*Epistulae Heroidum*). Prominent eighteenth-century examples were Alexander Pope's *Epistle to Dr Arbuthnot* (1735) and his *Essay on Man* (1733–34), a philosophical poem in four epistles in which Pope summed up the thinking of his age on mankind.

The most prominent Romantic poets occasionally recited their poems to one another and they also continued, if not to compose verse letters, then to circulate and **to criticise verse *in* letters**. As a direct response to listening to Wordsworth's recital of a first draft of his "Ode: Intimations of Immortality", Coleridge composed what was to become "Dejection: An Ode" in the form of a verse letter. He then revised the verse letter and sent it to others than the original addressee. Coleridge generally circulated versions of his poetry in manuscript long before they went into print. In this way, Mary Robinson in 1797 could write a poetical reply to "Kubla Khan" before this poem was published, together with *Christabel*, in 1816 (see the preceding chapter). At that time, Walter Scott had been acquainted with *Christabel* for already more than a decade, in which the metrically experimental poem continued to be revised by the poet and transcribed by different hands. Coleridge's decision to print the poem was taken at the urgent request of Lord Byron, who had also come to know *Christabel* in a manuscript version. Byron had left Britain in disgrace shortly before the publication of Coleridge's poems, never to return. Some grisly part of *Christabel* Byron recited from memory to Percy Bysshe and Mary Shelley at their meeting at Lake Geneva in the summer of 1816, when the party entertained themselves by telling ghost stories to one another around the fireplace – which laid the germ for Mary Shelley's *Frankenstein* (1818). Byron, a constant traveller and a copious and witty correspondent, went on to live in Italy and Greece, and thus had to keep up his relations with his friends and with his London publisher John Murray via letters, which he used to send and to discuss his own poems as well as to comment on poetry by contemporaries such as Shelley or Keats. So did Keats, whose letters to his relatives and friends might include a fresh sonnet or a piece of aesthetics, such as his thoughts on the concept of 'negative capability' and on the role of the imagination. The letters of Byron (†1824) were first published in 1830 (by his friend and fellow-poet Thomas Moore, and then in 12 vols. in 1973–82), the letters of Keats (†1821) followed in 1848 and 1878. (For selected letters from Byron and Keats, see *NAEL*)

The lingering influence of the 'manuscript system' is also evident from the manner in which William Blake (1757–1827) laid out and distributed his poetry. Medieval manuscript-books clearly had an impact on Blake's conception of **'illuminated printing'** from plates he had etched himself. Both his lyrical *Songs of Innocence and Experience* (1789–94) and his prophetic poems of epic length were conceived as an intermedial work made up of text and illustration. The handwritten poem was illustrated with engravings that the artist and his wife Catherine were then to colour individually on the printed page – thus making each of the limited set of editions a unique version. Blake was a singular exception in retaining complete control over all laborious stages of production and distribution of his literary works of art – for which the truly original poet paid the price of remaining largely unknown during his lifetime.

Fig. 3.15
William Blake, "The Tyger"

What added to such obscurity were the prophetical yet idiosyncratic character and the experimental form of his epic prose poems such as *The French Revolution* (c. 1791), *The Marriage of Heaven and Hell* (1790–93), *The Visions of the Daughters of Albion* (1793), and *Jerusalem* (1804–20). This last 'prophecy' should not be mistaken with the short poem "And did those feet in ancient time" that actually prefaces his visionary poem *Milton* (1803–08), but which has also been entitled "Jerusalem" when sung as a hymn. It ends with the following patriotic vision:

I will not cease from Mental Fight,
Nor shall my Sword sleep in my hand,
Till we have built Jerusalem
In England's green & pleasant Land. (*NAEL* II, 124–25).

During the laborious work spent on each of his 'prophecies', Blake developed his personal view of Christianity into an individual cast of mythological characters, in which Albion represents Man(kind) or England, Urizen a despotic God, and Orc his enemy and a champion of revolution. This appears to be a reversal not only of the Biblical point of view, but also of the characterisation in Milton's *Paradise Lost*. Indeed, in a section from *The Marriage of Heaven and Hell*, "The Voice of the Devil" contests that "The reason Milton wrote in fetters when he wrote of Angels & God, and at liberty when of Devils & Hell, is because he was a true Poet and of the Devil's party without knowing it." (*NAEL* II, 113). Beginning with its title and with an introductory sentence such as "Without Contraries is no progression.", *The Marriage of Heaven and Hell* is run through with paradoxes and pairs of opposites. In constant alternation with the visionary prose sections entitled "A Memorable Fancy", readers are confronted not only with the Devil's voice, but also with "Proverbs from Hell" (e. g. "The road of excess leads to the palace of wisdom" and "Prisons are built with stones of Law, Brothels with bricks of Religion") and with a concluding vision of revolutionary upheaval in "A Song of Liberty".

Blake's *Songs of Innocence and Experience: Shewing the Two Contrary States of the Human Soul* (1789–94) appear to be inspired by folk songs, and to be much more accessible than the 'prophecies'. Once again, the pairing of opposites is the principle underlying this collection of **contrary poems**, some of which are headed by identical titles. The "Introduction" to the *Songs of Innocence* highlights the process from piping or singing a song to the writing down of the text, i. e. the way from orality to scripture. Its counterpart in the *Songs of Experience* is tinged again by prophetic overtones ("Hear the voice of the Bard!"). In seemingly simple terms, the two contrary poems "The Lamb" and "The Tyger" treat no less than Theodicy, i. e. the problematic reconciliation of the idea of Divine Benevolence and Omnipotence with the existence of Evil. The animal symbolism in these contrary poems sets the Christian image of the *agnus Dei* against a symbol of the Sublime.

Songs of Innocence and Experience

"The Divine Image" and "The Human Abstract" come to speak on the nature of Man in general terms, while in both poems entitled "The Chimney Sweeper", and even more so in "London", where the working children turn up once more besides young prostitutes, the grim reality, un-naturalness and corruption of the urban world are addressed in graphic detail.

Over the century following upon his death, William Blake transcended the obscure status he had held among his contemporaries. With the 'illuminated printing' of his works, Blake clearly influenced the Pre-Raphaelite poet and painter Dante Gabriel Rossetti. In the longer run, he had an impact on the likewise intermedial and dystopian character of *Lanark* (1981) by the Scottish novelist Alasdair Gray, and perhaps also on more contemporary 'graphic novels' or comic books. The visionary power of Blake impressed itself, too, on W. B. Yeats and his apocalyptic *A Vision* (1926). Yeats, together with e. g. Gerard Manley Hopkins, is also a good example for the fact that the habit of circulating poetry in manuscript for quite a time before printing did not entirely end with the Romantic poets, but was kept up in the later nineteenth and early twentieth centuries (see chap. 4.4).

3.4.2 | 'Letter Writing' in Various Forms

Fig. 3.16
Horace Walpole

As could already be gleaned from the examples of poetry circulated in letters, the Long Eighteenth Century witnessed the ubiquity of the letter as a varied sort of text hovering between the media of manuscript and print. Usually understood as a form of personal communication between two persons only, letters became adapted over time to various other forms of literary communication in public, in print, and occasionally even in prose (as mentioned above). **Personal correspondence** was greatly enhanced by the union of the postal services of the three kingdoms in 1711, which ensured a surprisingly fast transport of often two deliverances a day. With men and women of letters, the personal correspondence often assumed a semi-public (and unquestionably literary) status, and was frequently published as a collection later in life. Alexander Pope saw the publication of his letters from the start as an ultimate end, so that he asked correspondents to return his letters to enable him to edit them as part of his works (1737, †1744). Jonathan Swift, too, published his own letters within his lifetime (1741, †1745), while the *Turkish Embassy Letters* (see below) by the extravagant Lady Mary Wortley Montagu (†1762) had to wait until after her death (1763, with her remaining correspondence published not before 1803). Posthumous publication likewise occurred in the case of the Earl of Chesterfield's *Letters to His Son* (1774, †1773), although this widely read book on education promised less scandalous news. Horace Walpole (1717–97; see chaps. 3.1 and 3.5.5) was not only exceptional in that he was the son of the first prime minister. He went on the Grand Tour, i.e. the traditional journey through France and Italy, together with Thomas Gray, whose *Odes* (1757) Walpole printed at his own press at Strawberry Hill, Twickenham, his model country house in the Gothic style. In literature, Horace Walpole set down this new fashion in the first Gothic romance entitled *The Castle of Otranto* (1764), but he was esteemed as a letter-writer more than for everything else. Walpole had planned his copious correspondence purposefully: like Pope, he wrote his letters on a variety of topics with an eye to publication, asked his correspondents to return them, and even annotated his letters for future editors. To keep them occupied, Walpole left altogether over 4,000 letters to be collected in nearly fifty volumes (1937–83). To compare: Lord Byron, another good but generally more spontaneous correspondent, managed to leave as much as 3,000 letters from an itinerant life of merely 36 years.

Besides their semi-public correspondence first circulating in manuscript, the *literati* wrote a variety of letters for different ends, though always meant for publication in print. The **letter of dedication** prefixed to a literary text was a significant expression of the patronage system, with Samuel Johnson's famous letter of refusal marking the anti-type (see chap. 3.1). The arrival of the periodical press inaugurated the convention of the public, and often political, statement made in a **'Letter to the Editor'**, sent anonymously or signed to be printed in a newspaper or magazine. An extended use of such freedom of 'speech' was made in those **political pamphlets** that presented the voice of the political opposition. *Cato's Letters* were actually written by Thomas Gordon and John Trenchard, yet published anonymously in 1720–23, and then again as a book (4 vols., 1724). *Cato's Letters* were directed against the Walpole government, but also had a great impact on public opinion in the American colonies in the half-century before the American War of Independence. Perhaps even more famous are the *Letters of Junius*, which appeared anonymously in *The Public Advertiser* from 1769 to 1772, and in book form in 1772. Even today, the author is still unknown, but was tremendously successful with this piece of effective rhetoric: the "Letter to the King" [George III] found more than 100,000 readers, and the series of letters helped to bring about the downfall of the Bute government. Both series of printed letters testify to a (Neo-)Classical tradition with their reference to Cato the Roman censor, and to Junius as the successful rebel against the monarchy, who brought about Republican Rome.

Prominent writers used the form for political satire, too, and to promote regional autonomy from London. By donning the satirical mask or *persona* of 'M. B. Drapier' of Dublin, Jonathan Swift presented the public with a series of seven *Drapier's Letters* distributed as broadsheets (1723–24, 1735). With his ultimately successful attempt to avoid the introduction of a new and less valuable currency for Ireland – a significant expression of how the Green Isle actually rated in the City of London – the Irish satirist had provided a model for another such series in Scotland a century later. In the first months of the year 1826, three long *Letters of Malachi Malagrowther on the Proposed Change of Currency* were sent to the editor of the *Edinburgh Weekly Journal*. By this means and by defending the right of Scottish banks to issue their own banknotes (in 1826 the only form of currency and credit in Scotland), Walter Scott – a prominent figure of the Scottish literary and legal establishment – issued a general protest against the English domination of Scotland.

In some cases, formal and political letters were not just reprinted in book form, but conceived as a **book-length essay** right from the start, as in the case of *A Letter Concerning Toleration*, in which the philosopher John Locke (1632–1704) marked out the separate spheres of the state and of the Anglican and Nonconformist churches, and tried to negotiate between them. Edmund Burke (1729–97) regularly used the letter – as well as the speech – for political purposes (see chap. 3.2.2). It is therefore no coincidence that Burke's *Reflections on the Revolution in France* (1790) is cast in the form of one long letter. This influential Conservative manifesto was answered, also in form of letters addressed to Burke, within the same year by two women writers who were more sympathetic to the revolutionary and Republican cause. Catharine Macaulay (1731–91) replied in her *Observations on the "Reflections"*, and Mary Wollstonecraft (1759–97) in *A Vindication of the Rights of Man*, which spurned Wollstonecraft's feminist treatise, *A Vindication of the Rights of Woman* (1792, see chap. 3.5.4).

The **epistolary novel**, or novel in letters, was a characteristic development within the Long Eighteenth Century, and (singular exceptions notwithstanding) remained restricted to that period. English writers could build on a French literary tradition of **prose romances**. The anonymous *Letters of a Portuguese Nun* (*Lettres portugaises*, 1669), the *Histoire du Chevalier des Grieux et de Manon Lescaut* by Abbé Prévost (1731) and *La Vie de Marianne* by Marivaux (1731–42) were known to an English audience either in the original French or in English translation. An early attempt to produce an English equivalent to such love romances was made by Aphra Behn in *Love-Letters between a Nobleman and his Sister* (1684–87), before Samuel Richardson took up the form in a more realistic vein. Richardson was a well-versed writer of letters before he turned into a novelist, as is evident from his *Familiar Letters* (1741), a non-fictional conduct book in the form of letters written as an example for the common reader. Richardson's epistolary novels conveniently mark out the two main types of the novel in letters. *Pamela; or, Virtue Rewarded* and its sequel (1740, 1742) exemplify the first (unilateral and univocal) type that is focused on a single letter-writer and principally rendered in his or her voice alone, even though the narrative may be framed by a preface or other matter given to a fictional editor. By contrast, *Clarissa* (1747–48) consists of an exchange of more than 500 letters sent by two male and two female characters, and thus is characteristic of the second (multilateral or plurivocal) type which allows for a change of point of view. John Cleland's *Memoirs of a Woman of Pleasure* (better known as *Fanny Hill*, 1749) imitates the first type, while Tobias Smollett's *The Expedition of Humphry Clinker* (1771, plurivocal) and Frances Burney's *Evelina* (1778, multilateral) are further examples of the second type. (For more information on these epistolary novels, see chap. 3.5.)

Romance and Novel in Letters

3.4.3 | Familiar, Formal and Periodical Essays

The essay is regarded as a characteristic feature of British literary history. Its flexible form has been adapted to a wide variety of subjects. The two types of essays that were marked out during the Renaissance by Montaigne and by Bacon (see chap. 2.4) developed into separate lines of tradition over the next centuries. Montaigne's type, because of its tone variously designated as **informal, personal or familiar essay**, resurfaced in Abraham Cowley's *Several Discourses by Way of Essays, in Verse and Prose* (1668) and in Sir William Temple's *Miscellanea* (1680–1701) before it was taken up again by Lamb, Hazlitt and de Quincey in the 1820s. Bacon's type of the **formal essay** offered the model for a number of book-length philosophical writings of renown. John Locke's *Essay Concerning Human Understanding* (1690) was one of the greatest works of the Age of Reason and, with its discussion of the Association of Ideas, of considerable influence on Laurence Sterne's novel *Tristram Shandy* (1759 ff.). The 3rd Earl of Shaftesbury's *Characteristics of Men, Manners, Opinions, Times* (1711) propagated the principle of Benevolence which found its literary impersonation for example in Sterne's Uncle Toby and in Fielding's Mr Allworthy (see chap. 3.5.3). David Hume's *Essays, Moral, Political, and Literary* (1742) highlighted the Scottish Enlightenment, following close upon Alexander Pope's *Essay on Man* (in epistles, 1733–34) mentioned at the beginning of this chapter. Finally, the *Essay on the Principle of Population* (1798) by Thomas Robert Malthus proved to be of considerable influence not only to the theory of economics, but also in political practice, leading to the first national census in England and Wales (1801), and to a discussion of social welfare reforms. By speaking of "the struggle for existence", Malthus provided Charles Darwin with a key concept for his thinking on evolution that found its way into *The Origin of Species* (1859).

The arrival of the literary magazine and the literary review (see chap. 3.1) provided the **periodical essay** with a new medium and a new forum. The collaboration of Joseph Addison (1672–1719) and his fellow-dramatist Richard Steele (1672–1729) on *The Tatler* (1709–11) and *The Spectator* (1711–12) far exceeded in importance any initial expectation. When the sharing of copies in the coffee-houses is taken into account, Addison's guess at a contemporary audience of 60,000 Londoners (a tenth of the capital's population) for the daily numbers of *The Spectator* may indeed not be too far off the mark. Collected in multi-volume editions, *The Spectator* continued to adorn the bookshelves of public libraries and private households throughout the eighteenth and nineteenth centuries. Instead of topical news, readers were offered topics for polite conversation, moral instruction, a manual of elegant style, and a primer in Neoclassicist aesthetics (e.g. on "The Pleasures of the Imagination", including the Beautiful and the Sublime as a pair of opposites, see chap. 3.1). Most of this was related to the experience and observation of a small group of idealised male representatives of the middle classes. In the initial numbers, 'Mr Spectator' introduced first himself as a cultured observer of men and manners, and then the other six members of the Club: the country-squire and benevolent patriarch Sir Roger de Coverley; the merchant and free-trader Sir Andrew Freeport; Capt. Sentry, a retired soldier and man of honour; Will Honeycomb, a gallant cavalier and man of fashion; an unnamed lawyer and literary critic; and a man of the church. For the sake of illustration, a small selection of related essays should suffice. London was mapped twice by the essayists, but in different ways: Steele took readers on a day's journey by boat and coach from Richmond to the City and to Covent Garden (no. 454), while Addison's essay 'On the Cries of London' (no. 251) charted the urban microcosm by listening to the milkman's, vendors' or watchman's calls from morning to night. In further essays that focused on the character of Sir Roger, Addison addressed the differences between town and country (no. 106, 112, 122, 517). His ironical account of the manners of the age can be found in the uneventful diary of an ordinary citizen (no. 317) and in a letter on the ladies' 'Exercise of the Fan' (no. 102). Such letters to 'Mr Spectator' can be seen as non-political variations upon the convention of the 'Letter to the Editor'.

Oliver Goldsmith (?1730–74) looked at Britain from a foreigner's point of view in his collection of 119 'Chinese letters' published under the title *The Citizen of the World* (1762) – an ideal of humanity which Goldsmith defended, in one of those essays, against "National Prejudices". In another piece, and in good-humoured fashion, Goldsmith presented "The Man in Black" as a paragon of Benevolence. Later essayists continued to come up with sketches of odd but memorable characters. Under the pen name of 'Elia', Charles Lamb (1775–1834) wrote familiar essays for the *London Magazine* such as "The Old Benchers of the Inner Temple" (1821), "The Praise of Chimney-Sweepers" and "A Dissertation upon Roast Pig" (1822). "Mrs Battle's Opinions on Whist" (1821, in Lamb 1903–5) are interesting as much for what they reveal about her character as for their general view on life. She who was "none of your lukewarm gamesters" and always played with passionate enthusiasm, had decided on Whist, a precursor of Bridge, likewise played by four persons and to her superior to other card-games such as Ombre (though she revered Pope for giving Ombre a prominent part in his *Rape of the Lock*). In Sarah Battle's opinion, "man is a gaming animal" – a view that was greatly extended by the cultural historian Johan Huizinga in his 'Essay on Man' entitled *Homo Ludens* (1938). For aptly named Mrs Battle (and later for Huizinga), "cards are war, in disguise of a sport [...] The hostile feeling is weakened by multiplying the channels. War becomes a civil game." Like Lamb's other familiar essays, this one is marked by nostalgic overtones and by an elevated style, featuring syntactic parallelism and paratactic sentences. In his essay "On Familiar Style" (from the collection *Table Talk*, 1822), Lamb's friend William Hazlitt (1778–1830) enlarged upon the subject, continuing a meta-literary strand of the genre that also includes "Of Essay Writing" (1742) by David Hume (1711–76).

Meta-essays apart, the genre served for writing **literary criticism** of a more general nature. Neoclassicist aesthetics were formed by John Dryden's *Of Dramatick Poesy: An Essay* (in prose, 1668) and by Alexander Pope's *Essay on Criticism* (in verse, 1711). Henry Fielding (1707–54) used the introductory chapters to each part of his novels *Joseph Andrews* (1742) and *Tom Jones* (1749) to instruct his readers in an entertaining fashion on literary matters (see chap. 3.5.3). For the same purpose, Samuel Johnson (1709–84) used his own periodical *The Rambler* (1750–52). A good example for Johnson's treatment of a non-literary topic in a light vein is his essay on 'the causes of disagreement in marriage' (no. 45). In further essays, written in a more elaborate style full of abstract nouns, Johnson praised the merits of biography as a genre (no. 60), yet spoke out against any biographical form of criticism (no. 14). He also compared the novel as a novelty favourably to the established form of the romance, and pronounced judgment

Fig. 3.17
Samuel Johnson

on the achievement of Richardson and Fielding, criticising the latter for his morally ambivalent and thus questionable character Tom Jones (no. 4). In his *Letters on Chivalry and Romance* (1762), Richard Hurd continued the discussion in an essay in letters.

Several notable essays significantly advanced the course of **Shakespeare criticism**, beginning with Johnson's *A Preface to Shakespeare* (1765). In his essay "On the Tragedies of Shakespeare" (1811), Charles Lamb saw the dramatic works – in truly Romantic fashion – only as closet plays that allegedly would lose in a performance on stage. Hazlitt shared Lamb's view, and with *Characters of Shakespeare's Plays* (1817) Hazlitt gave the cue to the 'character analysis' in A. C. Bradley's influential lectures on *Shakespearean Tragedy* (1904). Finally, the essay "On the Knocking at the Gate in *Macbeth*" (1823) by Thomas De Quincey (1785–1859) is still regarded as the *locus classicus* for the discussion of Shakespeare's use of 'comic relief' to check the psychological effect of cruel and tragic action. In *Confessions of an English Opium-Eater* (1821, rev. 1856), De Quincey had turned the psychoanalytical approach to himself, to tell the story of his addiction and his nightmarish dreams. This autobiographical essay caught a dark Romantic mood (just like E. A. Poe's short stories of the 1830s and '40s), and it spoke, too, of a more general interest in writings about individual lives.

Writing Lives | 3.4.4

The seventeenth century – that is the century preceding the period here under review – was marked already by a **strong interest in individual lives**. (Note the related occurrence of portrait painting, for which particularly British painters became famous.) Such an interest manifested itself in various forms of prose writing. They, too, tell of the lingering influence of the manuscript in a time of transition to print as a dominant medium of literary communication outside the performance context. Turning from those kinds of prose more closely connected with manuscript as a medium to others purposefully written for publication in print, the list includes

- ► the **letter**, which was seen to hover between the private and the public domain;
- ► the personal, perhaps even intimate account of one's individual experience in a **diary**, narrated close to the events or

reflections and usually addressed to the writer as reader, but occasionally meant as part of literary communication with someone else;

► **autobiography** as the writing of one's own life-story, usually with hindsight;

► and **biography** as the story of another one's life, again written from a certain distance.

The comprehensive understanding of 'poesy' within the period comprises all of these life-writings in prose, which were regarded as proper works of literature, regardless of whether they were concerned with men and women of letters or not. Moreover, such real life-stories became the models for the novels of Defoe, Fielding and Sterne, which were given out as fictional biographies and autobiographies (and therefore often called *History* or *Memoir*). In each instance, a few notable examples may suffice.

As **diaries** recorded the trivialities of everyday life and manners, of customs and costumes, they became important documents of social and cultural history, too. The two most famous early diaries are those of two friends and men of the world, who were still alive at the beginning of the eighteenth century. John Evelyn (1620–1706) was a *virtuoso* who was fascinated by the new natural sciences, and who became one of the founders of the Royal Society of London for the Improvement of Natural Knowledge in 1660. His diary records events between 1631 and 1706, and was published under the title of *Memoirs* in 1818. Even though it comprised a much shorter span of time (1660–69), the diary of Evelyn's friend Samuel Pepys (pronounced 'Peeps', 1633–1703) has remained better known for several reasons. His diary is a record of the Restoration and of the pompous entry of King Charles II in London; it is an eyewitness account of the Fire of London, which destroyed the city in 1666; and it is last but not least much more intimate than Evelyn's diary, telling us in detail about Pepys's love affairs. Perhaps also for this reason, the diary was written in stenographic notes, and when it came to sex scenes, moreover in a secret code. The diary of Pepys apparently was not meant for the public, yet was widely read in print after 1825.

Among eighteenth-century diaries, Jonathan Swift's *Journal to Stella* (written 1710–13, published 1766) and Laurence Sterne's *Letters from Yorick to Eliza* (written 1767, published 1775) likewise secured public interest in private affairs, as they tell of amours, too. Traveller's tales with a humorous note are Henry Fielding's *Journal of a Voyage to Lisbon* (1755) and James Boswell's *Journal of a Tour to the Hebrides* (1786) on which he had embarked together with Samuel Johnson in 1773. Johnson and the actor David Garrick also entered the diaries and letters of the sentimental novelist Frances 'Fanny' Burney (1752–1840), which were first addressed to 'No-body' yet published nevertheless (1842–46; 1889). Not only Burney's years at court and in Napoleonic France, but also her account of her breast removal provides for an intimate as well as intense reading experience. (Burney survived her mastectomy to live for another 28 years.) The journals of Dorothy Wordsworth (1771–1855) have been read for what they say about the Lake District and about the 'Lake Poets' (her brother William and S. T. Coleridge). The same applies to William Hazlitt's autobiographical sketch "My First Acquaintance with Poets" (1823). For different reasons, the diary of John Wesley (1703–91) is regarded as a key document of the period. Wesley, the founder of Methodism who travelled extensively to spread the Word, wrote his diary between 1735 and 1791, and published a first extract already in 1738 to further his cause.

Autobiographies, too, served as a means of (religious) introspection and a search for self. In *Grace Abounding to the Chief of Sinners* (1666), the Nonconformist preacher John Bunyan (1628–88) deals with his religious experiences, conversion and doubts, all of which fed into his religious allegory *The Pilgrim's Progress* (1678–84, see chap. 3.4.5). The Scottish philosopher and essayist David Hume finished his work *Life Written by Himself* in the year of his death (1776, to be published a year later), while the enlightened and enlightening *Memoirs of the Life and Writings* of Edward Gibbon (posthumously published in 1796; complete edition 1896) remained in a fragmentary state. Each of the surviving six drafts tells a slightly different version of the life of Gibbon (1737–94), who had achieved lasting fame as a rationalist historian and as a prose stylist with *The History of the Decline and Fall of the Roman Empire* (6 vols., 1776–88). As if warned, the poet and critic Samuel Taylor Coleridge published his *Biographia Literaria* in middle age (1817), while William Wordsworth again took a lifetime to complete his autobiography of epic dimension and in blank verse, entitled *The Prelude; or, Growth of a Poet's Mind* (1850, see chap. 3.1).

Literary biographies of note that followed upon Fulke Greville's *Life of Sir Philip Sidney* (1625) included Izaak Walton's biographies of the poets John Donne (1640) and George Herbert (1670) as well as Gilbert Burnet's account of the deathbed confession of the Earl of Rochester, a notorious womaniser (1680). The most widely read, literary biographies were James Boswell's *Life of Samuel Johnson* (1791) and John Gibson Lockhart's *Life of Sir Walter Scott* (1837–38), to which one might add a Poet Laureate's story of a naval hero – Robert Southey's *Life of Nelson* (1813). When Virginia Woolf's father, Sir Leslie Stephen, embarked on the monumental project of compiling a *Dictionary of National Biography* (1885 ff.), he could build on **biographical dictionaries** such as *Fuller's Worthies* (i.e. Thomas Fuller's *History of the Worthies of England*, 1662) and John Aubrey's *Brief Lives* (the manuscript of which was printed only in 1889, long after it had been a source for *Athenae Oxonienses* by Anthony à Wood, 1691–92). Samuel Johnson's influential *Lives of the English Poets* since Cowley (1779–81) was supplemented by Anna Laetitia Barbauld's biographical notes to her reprint series *The British Novelists* (50 vols., 1810 ff.). Such biographies and reprint series testify of course to who was 'in' and who was 'out' of the then-contemporary **canon**.

Special Focus: Black Britain

Among those who began to make their way 'in' were Black British authors. The Long Eighteenth Century was the time, too, when Black people in Britain found their own voices. In their extant autobiographies and letters, the "Black" experience was documented authentically and for the first time (in distinction from recreations of that experience by White writers in e.g. *Othello* or *Oroonoko*). By the middle of the eighteenth century, an estimated 15,000 Black people lived in London: servants, sailors, former slaves and their families. The first published work of a Black writer in English, entitled *A Narrative of the Uncommon Sufferings and Surprising Deliverance of Briton Hammon, a Negro Man* (1760), was an oral account transcribed by a White scribe. The patriotic and therefore aptly named Briton Hammon served as a sailor on British warships, saw action and was wounded in battle. His narrative centres on the demonstration of Divine Providence in that he is finally (and joyfully) reunited with his beloved master. The episode describing Hammon's capture by American Indians bears resemblance to the **captivity tale** as a genre. The first authentic account in English from a former slave's own hand,

and thus a proper and prominent **slave narrative**, was the *Life* of
Olaudah Equiano (1745–97). Equiano's memoirs of his childhood
in Africa, his enforced migration, enslavement and liberation,
were published in the year of the French Revolution, and this
best-selling book was a boost to the Abolitionist Movement that
gained momentum in the 1780s. The *Letters* (1782) of Ignatius
Sancho (1729–80) turned out to be a further important contribution to the Movement that was ultimately successful in outlaw-
ing the Slave Trade within the British Empire in 1807, and in
bringing about the Emancipation from Slavery during the 1830s.
In his own person, Sancho belied all the conventional prejudices against intellectual disabilities of Blacks. From his birth on a
slave ship to his employment as a butler in a Duke's household,
Sancho became well educated and well acquainted with such
eminent people as the actor Garrick, the painter Gainsborough
(to whom he sat for a portrait), and the writers Laurence Sterne
and Samuel Johnson. Sancho's correspondence (for instance with
Sterne, but also with more ordinary people) was esteemed for its
versatility and wit. What it meant to be Black and female could
be read only at the ending or well after our period. *The History of
Mary Prince, a West Indian Slave* (another transcript of an oral narrative, 1831) and *The Wonderful Adventures of Mary Seacole in Many
Lands* (1857) are perhaps the only two books published by Black
women in Britain during the nineteenth century. (For extracts
and further information on the texts mentioned, see e.g. *NAEL*,
Gates 1987, Edwards and Dabydeen 1991, Caretta 1996, Kitson
and Lee 1999, and Innes 2004.)

The Literature of Travel | 3.4.5

The literature of travel is a hybrid genre that again hovers between the media, comes in many forms, and has been adapted
to a variety of purposes. In a wider sense, the literature of travel
spans the whole range from travel guidebooks as a form of non-
fictional prose over journals (originally in manuscript) of authentic individual journeys to fictionalised travel narratives in verse
or prose – in short: from travellers to 'travel liars' (see Adams
1962 and Korte 2000). **Pilgrimage as a theme** can be found across this
continuum of texts. During the Middle Ages, guidebooks were
written for pilgrims, followed up by reports of their travels af-

ter the event. In the fourteenth century, Geoffrey Chaucer made pilgrimage the basis for his generically varied and sometimes bawdily humorous *Canterbury Tales* in verse. John Bunyan used the theme for *The Pilgrim's Progress: From this World to That Which is to Come* (in two parts, 1678–84), which again is not an authentic account, but a dream vision and a **religious allegory** in prose. Informed by Bunyan's personal history of persecution as a Nonconformist preacher in Restoration times, *The Pilgrim's Progress* follows Christian, the protagonist, his wife Christiana and some other allegorical characters on a flight and pilgrimage. Some stations on the way to the Celestial City are named the Valley of Humiliation, Doubting Castle, kept by the Giant Despair, and Vanity Fair (which provided the title for the Victorian novel by W. M. Thackeray). Bunyan's religious allegory became one of *the* long sellers of English literature, whereas Lord Byron won overnight fame for *Childe Harold's Pilgrimage* in 1812. This best-selling **travelogue** in verse (to be completed with the fourth canto in 1818) fused a travel narrative with a monological commentary. Here, Byron combined his actual travel experience in the Mediterranean – unavailable to most other Britons during the Napoleonic Wars – and his personal observations with a fictional form and a Byronic Hero of his own invention (see chap. 3.3.1).

Fig. 3.18
Lord Byron in Albanian Dress

What is more typical of the Long Eighteenth Century, however, are three other forms of travel narratives, namely those tied up with voyages of discovery, then others that were related to the Grand Tour, and finally those which marked an increasing interest in travelling to the sights of the newly United Kingdom. **Voyages of discovery** – to new worlds, or around the world – were linked with the expansion of European rule and the development of a global economy in the context of colonialism and slavery. The 'Improvement of Natural Knowledge' was a prominent purpose of later explorations that were made under commission and financial support of scientific institutions such as the Royal Society (in the founding of which the diarist John Evelyn had been involved in the year of the Restoration). While only 49 % of the earth (and 32 % of its land surface) were known to Europeans around 1600, after Sir Francis Drake's circumnavigation of the globe, such figures compared to the knowledge of 83 % (60 %) around 1800, after the three voyages of James Cook. Accounts of such explorations that met with great interest among readers include William Dampier's *A New Voyage round the World* (1697), trailed by the *Voyage round the World* of George Baron Anson (1748). There are several accounts of James Cook's second voyage, yet the most widely read was *A Voyage round the World*, written and illustrated by Georg Forster (1777, German original 1778–80). Further notable examples are *Travels in the Interior Districts of Africa* (1799) by Mungo Park and Charles Darwin's *Voyage of the "Beagle"* (1839).

Between the sixteenth and the nineteenth centuries, a new kind of pilgrimage took place, however towards different shrines. The **Grand Tour** through France and Italy was a journey with an educational purpose, yet not a voyage of discovery made by setting out to new and foreign parts of the world. Instead, it was a *Bildungsreise* to locations that were already known and widely held in reverence – the 'classic' sites of Mediterranean culture – and as such, an adequate expression of the general tenets of Renaissance Humanism and of Neoclassicism. The sites to be seen comprised for instance the Forum and the Colosseum in Rome, and later in the eighteenth century also the excavations of Pompeii near Naples. By visiting these picturesque ruins and remnants of Classical civilisation, the modern traveller participated in and profited from such antiquities by improving his (and occasionally her) personal taste and style. *Remarks on Several Parts of Italy* (1705) by Joseph Addison were the fruit of such an educational journey, and throughout his travel account, Addison paralleled his own views on the landscape with relevant quotations from Classical authors. Further and more patriotic remarks that centre on the politics of the day compare despotism in Italy unfavourably to liberty at home. Although soon outmoded in its bookish approach, Addison's *Remarks* remained a 'must read' for the rest of the century, not least for its stylistic precision.

The Grand Tour had a general impact in matters of cultural transfer, visibly for example in Georgian architecture, in the galleries of paintings with their depictions of the Beautiful or the Sublime, and in the vogue for Italian opera, together with its repercussions on drama and playhouses in the British Isles. In and outside their novels, the best-known novelists of the day were involved in writing about travels, too. The Grand Tour featured in different ways in travel accounts by Tobias Smollett and by Laurence Sterne, both of whom actually embarked on their jour-

Fielding, Smollett and Sterne as Travel Writers

neys for reasons of bad health and in the attempt to cure it in a more hospitable climate. So had Henry Fielding – but in vain: he died during a journey to Portugal. However, in his *Journal of a Voyage to Lisbon* (1755), Fielding sounded a personal and a humorous note, and, much like in his novels, he prefaced the travel account with a critical essay on the genre as a whole. Indeed, the further reflections of the traveller resemble a series of essays on different subjects, as the journey as such was bare of adventures. Much of the narrative was given to a continuous criticism of deplorable affairs, in the course of which Fielding abstracted from the miseries of travels to address general evils in society.

In his *Travels through France and Italy* (1766), Tobias Smollett presented himself as an eccentric character who always found fault with something, which was also the occasion for humour, especially in the description of mishaps with which he was confronted as a traveller. In this, he was no greenhorn: Smollett had already sailed to Jamaica as a surgeon to the Royal Navy (1740–41, an experience that was funnelled into his novel *Roderick Random*, 1748). Moreover, he had collected and reviewed a great number of travel accounts before he went on the Grand Tour together with his family. Much like his later novel in letters, *The Expedition of Humphry Clinker* (1771, see below), Smollett's personal tour report was brought into the fictional form of fabricated letters, most of which were written after his return from the journey. 'Home, sweet home': a patriotic point of view was recognisable throughout in Smollett's presentation of France and the French that (much like contemporary Italian politics in Addison's view) compared negatively with the domestic situation. In this way, the reader gets the impression (which is part of the comic design) that the traveller should rather have stayed at home.

Laurence Sterne's *Sentimental Journey* (1768) was based on two actual journeys of the novelist, and likewise very subjective. It was marked, too, by the same episodic and digressive style as his novel *Tristram Shandy*, which had included a different version of the journey to France (in vol. VII, published three years earlier). Sterne, like Fielding before him, made some summary remarks on the literature of travel in a preface that he, typically enough, inserted into the running text (Sterne 1975: 33–37). Moreover, Sterne took a minor character from *Tristram Shandy* as the writer's *alter ego* and as the first-person narrator of *Sentimental Journey*, namely the parson Yorick, who travelled in the company of his servant La Fleur. Sterne's pre-Romantic travel narrative was an attempt to correct Smollett's account in a fresh fashion. The new angle, and the difference to the conventional Grand Tour and the accounts thereof, lay in the manner and motivation of travel: in his own words, Yorick had embarked on "a quiet journey of the heart in pursuit of NATURE, and those affections which arise out of her, which make us love each other – and the world, better than we do" (Sterne 1975: 109). The *Sentimental Journey* was one of the heart and not of the head, and the travel account was directed primarily at the description of the traveller's feelings during the journey, with Benevolence as an overriding sentiment. This was the reason why Yorick (Sterne) criticised 'Smelfungus' (Smollett) in his text as a learned yet miserable traveller whose account reeked of the sour smell of frustrated expectations (1975: 51–53). In contrast to him, Yorick went out to explore and find – not the France and Italy of his imagination – but ultimately himself (which is why it did not matter much that the traveller never reached Italy). Notwithstanding the fragmentary character of Sterne's travel narrative, that just like *Tristram Shandy* was cut short by the writer's ill health and finally his death, *Sentimental Journey* had a great impact on the cult of Sentimentalism in Britain and on the Continent.

For a long time, only men of the upper classes embarked upon the Grand Tour and on other travels to the Mediterranean. This is why *The Turkish Embassy Letters* by Lady Mary Wortley Montagu (1763, †1762), a cousin of Fielding, are so exceptional. Only a few literary works of Lady Mary were printed during her lifetime – the satiric answer poems mentioned in the previous chapter are such exceptions – but transcriptions of her letters from Turkey, like the rest of her poetry, had been available to her aristocratic friends. From 1716 to 1718, Lady Mary had stayed in Turkey as the wife of the British Ambassador. The actual letters she sent home were later reworked by Lady Mary herself and circulated in manuscript. Publication in print, and under one's own name, was still considered bad taste within the smart set, but Lady Mary had seen to posthumous publication of *The Turkish Embassy Letters*, which then made her famous throughout Europe (see Bode 1997: 13–48). The ambivalence of the Orient explained the special appeal of Mylady's travel account to her contemporary readers: up

Lady Mary Wortley Montagu

to the Siege of Vienna (1683), Turkey had been a dangerous political opponent, yet the exotic Otherness of the East had also
given rise to a fashionable Orientalism in literature and the other
arts (see chap. 3.5.5). For today's readers, the letters are still of
interest in their attempt at an understanding of a foreign, Islamic culture. The unique feature of Lady Mary's correspondence is
the fact that she could provide first-hand experience otherwise
unavailable. She, who could communicate with Turkish people
(albeit of her own social circle) in their own language, went out
in Turkish costume and disguised behind veils, and as a woman
was able to visit locations of which very many men dreamed but
which they were forbidden to enter under threat of execution. In
a paradoxical way, however, it was just with the women in the
Turkish Bath and in the Harem that Lady Mary found 'women's
lib'. She praised their liberty from marital restraints and from
the social constraint on Western European women to squeeze
their bodies into corsets, so as to be locked up in a machine only
their husband was able to open (see Bode 1997: 24–27). Such
passages reflect the subjective character of Lady Mary's travel
account, but also her independent mind. In politics, Lady Mary
proved herself to be a patriot and the true daughter and wife
to liberal Members of Parliament. She brandished every form of
oppressive rule: the 'Oriental despotism' of the Turkish rulers
and the Absolutism of German princes alike, both of which were
compared unfavourably (once again) to the liberty at home. With
regard to intellectual freedom, Lady Mary opposed the Church
of Rome as an institution that she saw as irreconcilable with an
Age of Reason and Enlightenment. In their views on the Self and
on the Other, *The Turkish Embassy Letters* tell of the spirit of the
age; and while this travel account may not easily be reclaimed
for a feminist tradition, it will remain an impressive example of
cultural contact and cultural exchange.

Other travel accounts by female travellers of note are *A Journey
Made in the Summer of 1794 through Holland and the Western Frontier
of Germany* by the Gothic novelist Ann Radcliffe (1795) and *Letters
Written During a Short Residence in Sweden, Norway and Denmark* by
Mary Wollstonecraft (1796). The Wars with Revolutionary and
Napoleonic France and the Continental Blockade effectively hin-
dered Britons (except e. g. Lord Byron) in travelling to Continen-
tal Europe. After Waterloo, this kind of *Reiselust* set in with new

vehemence, and now involved more women, too. However, the old ideal of the *Bildungsreise* – which indeed for young males may not always have been the single most important aim to venture abroad – was less and less a reason to travel. The 'Grand Tour' (first occurrence of the term in 1670) bore the 'tourist' (1780), who has increasingly been seen – not least by travel writers – as a negative counterpart to the 'traveller'. A funny approach to the new vogue for the Picturesque at home and abroad was taken in *The Tour of Dr Syntax in Search of the Picturesque* (1809, followed up by two more tours, 1819–21, and many imitations). For this comic narrative, the caricaturist Thomas Rowlandson (1756–1827) provided plates that were illustrated by the verse of William Combe (1741–1823).

In addition to the Grand Tour, a new development properly set in during the eighteenth century, which is sometimes called the **Home Tour** (Korte 2000). The best-known such travel account from the beginning of the century is Daniel Defoe's *A Tour through the Whole Island of Great Britain* (1724–26), which is not the account of one single journey, but a synthesis of several of Defoe's travels, always seen with a merchant's eye. A best seller in its day and a long seller throughout the period, Defoe's account was revised and reissued several times by other writers, of which the novelist Samuel Richardson is the best known. Defoe's *Tour* is an early example of literary (and economic) **nation-building**, of the way in which the 'United Kingdom' – meaning the formal union of the hitherto separate English and Scottish kingdoms in 1707, and the enlarged union of 1801, which was to comprise Ireland, too – was constructed in literature.

While Defoe had informed in detail on the economic side and not the tourist sights of the Union, later examples of literary Home Tours accentuated the diversity of regional cultures. Christopher Anstey's *New Bath Guide* (1766), a fictional travel account in verse letters about the fashionable centre of English Neoclassicism, inspired the Scottish novelist Tobias Smollett to attempt the same in prose and on a larger scale. In its general make-up as a comical novel in letters, *The Expedition of Humphry Clinker* (1771) went out from Smollett's *Travels through France and Italy*, yet headed towards different shores. *The Expedition of Humphry Clinker* follows the valetudinarian Welsh squire Matthew Bramble and his entourage to Bath, London and up to Edinburgh. They pay

Defoe and the Home Tour

visits to seaside resorts and less fashionable cities in between and pick up Humphry Clinker on the way. The letters were written from various points of view and sometimes in phonetic spelling, which surely made this an instructive as well as delightful experience for actual armchair travellers in England. Readers also got to know many details about the manners of the 'North Britons' – as these citizens of the Union were designated here in a friendlier manner than in the periodical *The North Briton*, edited by the radical politician John Wilkes (1762–63).

Both Samuel Johnson (*A Journey to the Western Islands of Scotland*, 1775) and James Boswell (*The Journal of a Tour through the Hebrides*, 1786) catered to the same *Sassenach* or *Southron* (English) audience in the complementary accounts of their 1773 journey together to the wild Northwest of the United Kingdom. By the turn of the century, the tourist mapping of the United Kingdom was completed: summary guidebooks such as *The British Tourists; or, Traveller's Companion through England, Wales, Scotland and Ireland* (by William Mavor, 6 vols. 1798–1800) and *The Modern British Traveller; or, Tourist's pocket directory. Being an accurate and comprehensive history and description of all the counties in England, Scotland, and Wales, as also the adjacent islands* (by George Alexander Cooke, 47 vols. 1802–10) remain on the British Library shelves.

When the various possibilities of relating of travels within the British Isles, through Continental Europe and in the Mediterranean, and even around the world seemed exhausted, there was still one possibility left for a writer: to tell about Utopia. Still one of the best known among the 'travel liars' (Adams 1962) from the period is Jonathan Swift's Captain Lemuel Gulliver. The fantastic tale of his *Travels into Several Remote Nations of the World* (1726) fits into several categories of narrative. Not only for this reason, the account of *Gulliver's Travels* has been read avidly, but in very different ways by successive generations of readers. In its numerous adaptations as a humorous children's book, *Gulliver's Travels* was usually cut down to the first two of altogether four voyages, telling of his experiences with the dwarfish inhabitants of Lilliput and the giant people of Brobdingnag. Other and older readers today may approach the text as a utopian novel that tells of further voyages to the Flying or Floating Island of Laputa as well as to the Academy of Projectors at Lagado (part III), and also to the Country of the Houyhnhnms and the Yahoos (part IV). To his own

Fig. 3.19
Jonathan Swift

Gulliver's Travels

contemporaries, however, Swift (1667–1745), the Dean of St. Patrick's Cathedral in Dublin, was known as a political pamphleteer (*The Conduct of the Allies*, 1711) and as a parodist and satirist in verse and prose. He was the author of *The Battle of the Books* (1704) and of the *Drapier's Letters* (1723–24, see chaps. 3.1 and 3.4.2), and later came out with *A Modest Proposal* (1729) to improve the economic problems of Ireland – namely by feeding the children of the Irish poor to 'persons of quality and fortune' elsewhere in the United Kingdom. Here, in the mask of a 'projector', Swift applied his training in Classical rhetoric to turn the Enlightenment ideals of Progress and Benevolence on their head, and to deal with the political and economic dependency of Ireland in a most sarcastic way.

Swift's contemporaries therefore read the complete *Gulliver's Travels* as a **prose satire** from the mouth of a *persona* (Gulliver), aiming at three objects altogether: first, the vogue for travel writing; then, the role of projectors and the natural sciences in the context of the Enlightenment; and finally, contemporary British politics. Especially with regard to the last two points, Swift's satiric narrative was marked throughout by a steadily increasing bitterness in tone, though the individual parts were written in a different order. (For more detailed information and interpretation of Swift's satire, see Real and Vienken 1984 and Weiss 1992.) In a literary context, *Gulliver's Travels* is directed against conventions of the literature of travel apparent in both the 'circumstantial style' of narration in Defoe's *Robinson Crusoe* (see chap. 3.5.1) and in travel accounts such as the one by William Dampier (Gulliver refers to him as his cousin in a letter added as a postscript in 1735). The introductory letters as well as the maps and dates included in the text protest and at the same time undercut the truthfulness of Gulliver's account. In an Enlightenment context, part III is of special interest with its science fiction of the Flying Island and its satire on speculative thinking and on scientific projects. Political satire and references to controversies and deficiencies at home are to be found throughout the text: in the disputes between rivalling religious and political factions in Lilliput (part I, chap. 4), in the rebellion at 'Lindalino' (meaning Dublin, III.3) and in the political projects discussed at Lagado (III.6). To the same satirical effect, the King of Brobdingnag (II.6–7) and the rational horse-race of the Houyhnhnms (IV.4–7) are made to compare critically both the political systems and the political practice at home and abroad. At the end of his travels, Gulliver first turns Man alone, and then turns against Mankind. The patriot who was once so proud of life and liberty in Britain now has come to doubt if any historical and political progress has been made since Antiquity (III.7–8), and he has come to despise not just the humanoid Yahoos but moreover all of humanity (IV.10–12). Such was the pessimistic and misanthropic moral of the tale, and in this complete version, Gulliver's travel account, although otherwise known as a classic children's book, was indeed no book for children.

3.4.6 | The Children's Book: Literature for a New Audience

A new phenomenon, the children's book, was also born into the Long Eighteenth Century. If we borrow the classic definition of literature by Horace, claiming that literature should both teach and entertain (*prodesse et delectare*), a definition which was so dear to Neoclassicists, then we will be able to distinguish between four ideal types of literature relevant to children outside (1) the oral and folk tradition. These further types can be differentiated with a view to their intended audience and their intended purpose, and by the extent to which they accentuate instruction or delight. There is didactic literature written either (2) for adults on the bringing-up of children, or (3) more directly for children and adolescents. Moreover, there are (4) those entertainments written especially for children and adolescents, and there are (5) other entertainments written for adults that were read by or adapted for children. This distinction, though useful as a first classification, is of course an artificial one, as especially entertainments for a young audience may often be endowed with a didactic purpose, a 'moral of the tale'. Moreover, a sixth and very different category might consist of those works that either have children as protagonists (such as Blake's songs on chimney-sweepers and Wordsworth's poems on Lucy Gray) or that have childhood as a theme (such as Wordsworth's "Ode: Intimations of Immortality from Recollections of Early Childhood"). This interesting, sixth category can only be mentioned here, so as to stress the increased interest in the child's experience as a notable development within the period and especially around the turn to the nineteenth century; in the discussion of nineteenth-century literature, such

texts will feature more prominently. (For the period here under review, see Gaull 1988: 50–80; Dabundo 1992; McCalman
1999).

Let us therefore turn to the first categories mentioned above. A
philosophic and **didactic concern with the bringing-up of children (2)** was
a characteristic expression of the Age of Enlightenment. With
Some Thoughts concerning Education (1693), the rational philosopher
John Locke wrote a popular treatise that was to influence in turn
Émile; ou, De l'éducation by Jean-Jacques Rousseau (1762), which
showed a more Romantic understanding of education through
Nature rather than Society. Another pedagogic classic from the
Enlightenment (with more than 120 editions in 60 years, compared to 22 of Richardson's best-selling novel *Pamela*) were the
collected *Letters to His Son* by the Earl of Chesterfield (1774, †1773).
The title of this book already signals a shift in the intended audience from adults to an adolescent. But what was actually read to
children? Folk stories, fairy tales and other favourites from the
oral tradition (1) were the precursors of the children's book. The
first collections of such oral literature came out in print during the eighteenth century, and they were evidence of a concern
with popular literature and the culture of the common people
that was older than Romanticism (which usually has been credited with it). The first collections of **nursery rhymes** featuring popular heroes such as Tom Thumb and Jack the Giant Killer were
Tommy Thumb's Song Book and its sequel (both printed in 1744;
see also Fielding's farce mentioned in chap. 3.2.1). These were
trailed by the collection of Mother Goose rhymes in *Mother Goose's
Melody; or, Sonnets for the Cradle* (advertised for 1780). However,
those first collections met with opposition. In *Émile*, Rousseau
famously declared that all literature apart from *Robinson Crusoe*
should be banned from the nursery. Rousseau's successors spoke
out particularly against **fairy tales**, which were suspect on several
grounds. With their 'superstitious' elements, fairy tales (which
were so dear to Romantics) stood in the way of teaching children
the 'true religion' (which explains the oppositional stance from
Enlightenment philosophers and Protestant churchmen alike).
Moreover, their supernatural elements (witches, goblins etc.) were
said to unduly frighten children. In their stead, children should
hear or read more relevant tales about their domestic surrounding.

As a consequence, allegedly more suitable didactic fiction was written for children, e. g. by Mrs (Anna Laetitia) Barbauld (*Lessons for Children* in 3 vols., 1778–79), by Mrs (Sarah) Trimmer (*Fabulous Histories* of talking animals, 1786) and by Mrs Edgeworth. Together with her father Richard Lovell Edgeworth, the Irish novelist Maria Edgeworth brought out a book on *Practical Education* (1798) and followed it up on her own with a collection of *Moral Tales for Young People* (1801). By 1800, these **moral tales (3)** "were the predominant genre of children's books in England" (Carpenter and Prichard 1984: 358), and with *The Guardian of Education* (1802), Sarah Trimmer edited a magazine that carried the first regular reviews of children's books and thus monitored the book market. Three such moral tales may serve as illustration. Hannah More's "Betty Brown, the St. Giles's Orange Girl" was one of the *Tales for the Common People* (1801, in More 1830), and like her earlier "Cheap Repository Tracts" suitable for the Sunday school movement in its fight against still widespread illiteracy among adults and children (see chap. 3.1). The didactic story tells of fall and rise. The miseducation of orphaned Betty Brown by the hands of Mrs Sponge (whose telling name signals that she thrives on what she can squeeze out of other people) turns Betty into a petty criminal. However, the re-education by the wife of a justice fends off the danger that the orange girl might end her life as a streetwalker. This pious lady makes Betty aware of Good and Evil, instils a religious sense in the girl, provides for her Sunday school education, and thus paves the way for an honest existence. The commentary of the heterodiegetic narrator guides the reader throughout this moral tale, as in the likewise longish tale "The Grateful Negro" from Maria Edgeworth's collection of *Popular Tales* (1802, in Edgeworth 1893). Here, the distinction between Good and Evil is set within the contemporary discourse on Slavery and its Abolition, with Edgeworth taking a more paternalistic view than Hannah More, who was one of the prominent Abolitionists. The last moral tale to be mentioned was written by the essayist Charles Lamb in collaboration with his sister Mary for a collection of stories connected by a school frame: *Mrs Leicester's School; or, The History of Several Young Ladies, Related by Themselves* (1809, in Lamb 1903–5). "Elinor Forester: The Father's Wedding-Day" is a story of development, told by a girl in the first person, which stresses (as e. g. in Defoe's novels) the truthfulness of the account. The child opens up her mind and describes how she learned to overcome mistakes and misconceptions until she finally came to terms with her father's second marriage, her new step-mother and her step-sister. (Note that behind the acceptance of the new situation within the family lurks another, less harmonious interpretation, in which the older child and narrator is sent to Mrs Leicester's school just because it will then be out of the way when the new love-child arrives.) The accents falling on education and sensibility place the tale within the Age of Enlightenment, while its character as didactic fiction and the focus on the child's own experience are more Romantic features. The negotiation of the concepts of biological family and 'patchwork family' is certainly no less topical today than it was two centuries ago. (For the contextualisation of these moral tales within the history of short fiction, see Korte 2003: 55–62.)

The same set of writers of moral tales was also influential in adapting classic adult literature for the nursery, and in producing the first **entertaining books written especially for children and adolescents (4)**. In 1744, the publisher John Newbery (1713–67) had begun to create a new market for cheap, illustrated and didactic books for children by bringing out *A Little Pretty Pocket Book*, which contained rhymes, stories and children's games (plus 'a ball and a pincushion' as a free gift). By the turn to the nineteenth century, children had all kinds of literature (not just moral tales) created especially for them. There were collections of stories such as *Hymns in Prose for Children* by Anna Laetitia Barbauld (1781) or *The Parent's Assistant; or, Stories for Children* by Maria Edgeworth (1796–1800). Later, Edgeworth added *Little Plays for Children* (1827). Charles Lamb composed *Poetry for Children* (1809) as well as an acceptable fairy tale in verse, entitled *Prince Dorus* (1811). *The Comic Adventures of Old Mother Hubbard and Her Dog* (by Sarah Catherine Martin, 1805) and "Twinkle, twinkle, little star" from Jane Taylor's *Rhymes for the Nursery* (1806) soon became popular favourites.

In addition to the new and original children's books, the younger readers were entertained by **adaptations of stories that had once been created for an adult audience (5)**. From the sixteenth to the nineteenth centuries, in an age of still widespread illiteracy, most readers were acquainted with legendary figures such as Sir Guy of Warwick or Robin Hood through **ballads** or illustrated

Fig. 3.21
chapbook

12   THE HISTORY OF   SIMPLE SIMON.   13

He went to shoot
A wild duck,
But the wild duck flew away,
Says Simon I cant
Hit him,
Because he would not stay.

Simon was sent
To market,
To buy a joint of meat,
He tied it to
His horses tail,
To keep it clean and sweet.

chapbooks. (See chap. 3.1, Rogers 1985, and for Guy of Warwick, see Neuburg 1968: 8–11, 81–104.). These truly 'cheap books', which could be bought for a few pennies from wandering ped-lars or chapmen, contained a simple tale that was illustrated with woodcuts, and in this way resembled the picture books for children we are used to today. However, some stories told in those booklets (perhaps an adaptation of an adults' novel such as *Robinson Crusoe* or *Moll Flanders*) were of a more sensational and sometimes quite cruel nature. No wonder then that chapbooks met with the same opposition from devoutly Protestant and from Enlightenment circles of didactic writers, who produced instead adaptations from the classics that were made suitable for children. In *The Family Shakespeare* by Thomas and Henrietta Bowdler (1807, ²1818), "those words and expressions are omitted which cannot with propriety be read aloud in a family" (subtitle). In their fictionalisation of the plays as *Tales from Shakespeare: Designed for the Use of Young Persons* (1809), Charles and Mary Lamb made *A Midsummer Night's Dream* into a tale of fairies but no longer of mechanics, too, and – alas, poor Yorick! – Hamlet had to make do without a gravedigger. A couple of years later, Charles Lamb went on to rewrite *The Adventures of Ulysses* (1811). Soon enough, the rougher elements of the chapbook tradition had been tamed, too. In 1795, Joseph Ritson had edited the first scholarly collec-tion of 'Robin Hood Garlands', and when the second edition of this collection of ballads about the legendary outlaw and his Merry Men appeared in 1820, parents were being assured in a note that the book could be read by children without harm being done. The year before, in 1819, Walter Scott had included Robin Hood (as 'Locksley') and Friar Tuck in his historical novel *Ivanhoe* (see chap. 3.5.6). Even a revival of the chapbook occurred with The Catnach Press (in operation 1813–c. 1883), which then specialised in chapbooks for children.

Rousseau's recommendation of *Robinson Crusoe* for the nursery – where it regularly rubbed shoulders with *The Pilgrim's Progress*, *Gulliver's Travels*, or *Ivanhoe* – spurned rewritings that were to be translated into many languages and to rival the original, such as J. H. Campe's *Robinson der Jüngere* (1779/80, by 1894 in its 117th German edition) and *The Swiss Family Robinson* by J. D. Wyss (itself continuously rewritten by other hands since its original German publication 1812). What was Defoe's novel actually about? This will be discussed in the next chapter.

Guiding Questions and Exercises

1. Point out the various ways in which older conventions of oral transmission and of the circulation of manuscripts have made themselves felt in literature in an age of print.
2. William Blake's "London" (1794) and Wordsworth's poem "Composed upon Westminster Bridge" share the same urban setting, while Wordsworth's "London, 1802" compares with P. B. Shelley's "England in 1819". Discuss all these poems with regard to their theme and form. If you want to enlarge the field of comparison, then you should have a look at *London Poems*, ed. Adolf Barth (Stuttgart: Reclam, 1988), and at *The Oxford Book of London*, ed. Paul Bailey (Oxford: Oxford UP, 1995).
3. Distinguish between various types of essays and summarise their development. Take a collection of essays and try to find and discuss examples that are thematically related.
4. Try to account for the various ways of writing about one's own and other people's lives by a summary discussion of individual writers and texts from the period under review.
5. There are many gaps in the historical record of the Black experience in the British Empire before the Emancipation from Slavery. Late twentieth-century novelists such as Caryl Phil-

lips (*Cambridge*, 1991; *Crossing the River*, 1993), Fred D'Aguiar (*Feeding the Ghosts*, 1997) and David Dabydeen (*A Harlot's Progress*, 1999) have attempted to fill those gaps through fictional re-creations. Compare these contemporary 'neo-slave narratives' to their authentic predecessors from the eighteenth and nineteenth centuries.

6. The literature of travel takes many forms. Single out relevant examples from the period for comparison.

7. Give a short sketch of the early development of the children's book. Discuss relevant examples within the contexts of Enlightenment and of Romanticism.

3.5 | 'The Rise of the Novel': A Series of Experiments

3.5.1 | *Robinson Crusoe* and Its Relation to Individualism, Religion and Colonialism

Fig. 3.22 |
Daniel Defoe

Among the famous early examples of novels in the English language, most of which were already best sellers in their own time, *The Life and Strange Surprising Adventures of Robinson Crusoe, of York, Mariner* (1719) is certainly the one with a global outlook and an incessantly global appeal. Daniel Defoe's first novel, written in the 60th year of his life, tells as much of the penchant for travel narratives and exotic settings in a period of European colonial expansion as of the lingering spirit of grass roots Protestantism. The novel was built on the model of voyages of discovery in the footsteps of Sir Francis Drake and Sir Walter Raleigh (such as William Dampier's *A New Voyage round the World*, 1697), and on the authentic story of one mariner in particular (that of Alexander Selkirk, one of Dampier's sailors who had held out on an uninhabited island for several years). However, there was something that set Defoe's narrative apart from others with an exotic setting – like Aphra Behn's *Oroonoko; or, The Royal Slave* (1688), which was also placed near the Orinoco River. This extra quality was indeed – in Walter Scott's words – the 'circumstantial style', the detailed and plausible manner in which Robinson's singular story of survival was told and likewise justified as seemingly true – as *vraisemblable* (a period term) and therefore as 'realistic' as any fictional account can ever be.

Defoe (1660–1731) was at pains to present Robinson's travel account as a "just history of fact" not only through a fictional editor's preface (who cannot observe "any appearance of fiction in it", Defoe 1986, 25), but also throughout the fact-ridden narrative in the first person. Defoe's solution to the novelist's problem of narrative point of view was simply to have the title-character tell his own life-story in episodic form, unqualified by any other character. This generally took the form of a retrospective autobiography told in old age and thus with hindsight, but incorporating passages in which the immediate experience is laid down in detail and in a journal with exactly-dated entries. The inconsistencies in Robinson's dating of events, and therefore in the actual time-frame of the novel, are due to his creator's habitually fast (and eventually hasty) manner of composition: within a year, Defoe had followed up on the success of *The Life and Strange Surprising Adventures* with a second and a third Robinson novel, combining entertainment and instruction by first presenting Crusoe's *Farther Adventures* (1719) and then his *Serious Reflections* (1720). Notwithstanding such minor inconsistencies and also the parody of Defoe's particularity of description included in Swift's prose satire *Gulliver's Travels* (1726), Ian Watt was therefore principally right to see in Defoe's plausibly-told story of an average individual in trouble (and not in Aphra Behn's romance ending in the unbelievably stoic and heroic death of her Royal Slave) the first instance of the realistic novel on record in the English language. Such **'formal realism'** Watt saw defined by a believable temporal and spatial setting, by a plausible plot and characterisation and by a language ringing true (Watt 1963).

How can a shipwrecked person evade dying of hunger? Simply by feeding on the remaining dry provisions in the wreck, by killing wild animals, and by making the lucky find of grains of corn, enough to ensure the cultivation of barley and later the baking of bread. How can a single man survive in a hostile surrounding? By gathering from the wreck those Old World tools needed to build a fortified 'settlement' in the New, and by making use of fire-arms to defend himself against wild beasts and native 'savages'; in short: by taking it easy, and by making use of superior European technology. Finally, how can a single unfortunate human being survive in an 'Island of Despair'? By rediscovering the consolations of Christianity and by soothing the troubled mind with a trust in the blessings of Providence; by regulating the apparently endless time alone with the help of a Christian calendar; and of course by extending Christian brotherhood in lending help to and making a convert of the next person to arrive, Man Friday. In this way, the traveller's tale of shipwreck and adventure turned into another Puritan autobiography and spiritual self-discovery (such as John Bunyan's *Grace Abounding to the Chief of Sinners*, 1666), and into a religious parable which professed to be 'useful' and instructive indeed also for those Christian fundamentalists who were accustomed to listen only to the lessons of the Bible.

Moreover, the name of this sole survivor has become a synonym: for an existentialist view of Man Alone as well as for the capitalist belief in economic individualism and for that imperialist ideology of White Supremacy which was attacked by Black and Postcolonialist critics. All of this, too, critics have associated with Robinson Crusoe, the white man who sailed on a slave-trading ship, became shipwrecked on a desert island in the New World and survived for more than 25 years thrown back on his individual self, before human society ultimately returned in the shape of a black servant whom Robinson saved from becoming a victim of cannibalism, christened Man Friday and duly taught Christianity, but first of all to kneel down and address his white saviour as 'Master'. The peculiar blend of religious and economic individualism, of Calvinism and Capitalism, which the sociologist Max Weber marked out as characteristic of Early Modern economic history is also evident from Robinson's diary, in particular from the manner in which the shipwrecked merchant ponders the 'Good' and 'Evil' aspects of his forlorn state and presents the conflicting arguments "very impartially, like debtor and creditor", in a balance-sheet (Defoe 1986: 83–84).

In contrast to Aphra Behn's *Oroonoko; or, The Royal Slave*, which is focused on a 'noble savage' as protagonist and tragic hero, Defoe's novel centres on a slave-trader who manages to turn his misfortune into his profit. When he starts to build his New World settlement, complete with 'castle' and 'country-house', Robinson cannot help but "to think that this was all my own, that I was king and lord of this country indefeasibly, and had a right of possession; and if I could convey it, I might have it in inheritance as completely as any lord of a manor in England"

(Defoe 1986: 114). After his rescue, he continues to draw money first from the lease and later from the sale of his 'colony' and 'plantation' to other colonists. It cannot surprise, therefore, that postcolonial critics and writers – such as the Caribbean poet and dramatist Derek Walcott (*Pantomime*, 1978) or the South African novelist J.M. Coetzee (*Foe*, 1986), not to forget the French novelist Michel Tournier (*Vendredi*, 1967) – have drawn repeatedly on the character constellation of Robinson and Man Friday as the most illustrative example of colonialism and slavery in English literature, besides that of Prospero and Caliban in Shakespeare's *Tempest*.

Beyond such rewritings, there is of course the long history of rewriting Defoe's novel into a proper children's book (see chap. 3.4.6), or into a thematically related instance of the *Robinsonade* type, such as R.M. Ballantyne's *Coral Island* (1858) or William Golding's *Lord of the Flies* (1954).

Male Novelists and Their Female Heroines: Gender Relations, Materialism and Morality in *Moll Flanders*, *Pamela*, and *Fanny Hill*

3.5.2

In the eighteenth century, novels as such had a low status and were widely considered as entertainment fit for servants only. The best-known novelists however aimed at raising the general esteem of fiction by presenting works that were realistic and frank and which provided their readers with a positive example. This applied also to the complex of gender relations, materialism and morality.

The eponymous heroine of Defoe's novel *Moll Flanders* (1722) is the first female protagonist that stands out in this respect. True to the type of novel that Defoe had established with *Robinson Crusoe*, this novel as well as *The Fortunate Mistress* are fictional autobiographies written from a retrospective point of view, at the end of the protagonist-narrator's life. Although he chose to set all three novels in the 1680s, Defoe was not much interested in historical particularities (the historical novel proper still had to wait for Walter Scott) but in personal stories of out-of-the-way lives. Each of them was introduced by a fictional editor and second narrator, who guaranteed that the protagonist's account was true to life and provided moral instruction – which had required in the case

Moll Flanders

of Moll Flanders, this editor said, some effort to purify language and life from the most indecent elements. A reader hooked on by this preface and by the title page of the novel's first edition, which was made up in the sensational style of a street ballad, read the story of a girl born in Newgate prison, who makes one career as a thief, and another as a prostitute, serial wife, incestuous and bigamous lover; who is (just like her mother) sentenced to death and transported to the plantations in colonial America, only to return as a repentant sinner, and to end her life happily and in affluence. Fellow-novelist E. M. Forster later singled out *Moll Flanders* as his "example of a novel in which a character is everything and is given freest play" (Forster 1976: 68), but other critics have found fault with the episodic structure, the continuity, and the moral of the story. In taking up Forster's further **distinction between 'story' and 'plot'**, critics of Defoe have said that he did not manage to integrate the individual episodes of the 'story' into a proper 'plot', linked in each case by (for instance) cause and effect instead of purely chronological sequence. Defoe, a learned journalist, was used to writing fast and to moving swiftly from one text to the next, and this acquired habit may explain some inconsistencies and discontinuities of the narrative (see Watt 1963: 103). Finally, the happy ending and the overall moral of the story is not easily brought in line with the didactic concept of **poetic justice**, and with Christian notions of honest repentance, in distinction from a mere feeling of remorse. Indeed, at the end of her life, Moll – a mother and thief who prior to her penitence had neither shown much parental feelings for her own children nor refrained from robbing and threatening others – has not only escaped punishment, but has also achieved her consistent aim, namely to rise to the status of a gentlewoman and to live in material comfort.

The uneasiness of critics is related to the ambivalence of Defoe's novel, which – artistic merits and Christian morals disregarded – also reads well as an undaunted woman's story of sexual emancipation and success. Once Moll has been seduced, as a young woman living in a foster family, she soon learns to manipulate men into marriage, and thus to secure her own share of their material wealth. Moving from one partner to the next, she rarely reports their names, but never forgets to mention how she profited from the relation. This combination of matter-of-

factness and materialism continues in Defoe's later novel *The For-*
tunate Mistress [...] Being the Person known by the Name of Lady Roxana   *Roxana*
in the time of Charles II (1724), which shows many parallels in form
and theme (see Sherbo 1969: 150–67), but takes the story of upward mobility of a 'material girl' even into the highest sections
of society. The heroine and narrator is a Frenchwoman who lives
alternately on the Continent and in Restoration England, and
her story of a woman's sexual emancipation is even more firmly
set in a material context. Sex is seen as a commodity that can be
consciously exchanged for a rise from rags to riches. The series of
love affairs and sexual trysts that are to follow on an early marriage, at the age of 15, to a London brewer who went bankrupt,
lead from an adulterous liaison with the landlord to the role of
mistress to a French prince. When the courtesan returns to England, she hosts a masked ball for high society and suggests that
this secured her in consequence the favour of King Charles II.
Although in the ultimate sentences of Defoe's novel, the fortunate mistress tells also of her downfall and repentance, this appears to be no more than a last-minute attempt on the author's
side to adjust the moral ambivalence of his story with a dash of
poetic justice. Roxana will find a true successor, albeit in an altogether different moral climate, in Becky Sharp, the protagonist
of Thackeray's *Vanity Fair*.

Samuel Richardson (1689–
1761) professed to provide
a better example of moral
instruction with *Pamela; or,*
Virtue Rewarded (1740). Once
more, the title page and a fictional editor testify to both
truthfulness and didacticism
of the narrative, which however this time comes – and
this is Richardson's innovation – in the form of a novel
in letters. Pamela Andrews is
a young servant-maid who
has to defend herself against
the sexual harassment of her
master, even to endure a pe-

| Fig. 3.23
Book illustration of
Pamela

riod of captivity, until she is able to bring about the moral reformation of the rake she loves. The reward for retaining her virtue (which implicates also her virginity) and for turning the squire into a gentle man is a marriage that provides Pamela with a loving husband, and with the status of a gentlewoman. Richardson gave more room to psychological insight and to the expression of emotions: through Pamela's letters (and a diary written during her captivity) the reader can follow events and sentiments more closely than in the retrospective form of Defoe's memoir-novels. Right from the first letter, Richardson attempted to dramatise his single story of courtship:

> I have been scared out of my senses; for just now, as I was folding up this letter, in my late lady's dressing-room, in comes my young master! Good sirs! how I was frightened! I went to hide the letter in my bosom, and he, seeing me tremble, said smiling, 'To whom have you been writing, Pamela?' (Letter 1, Richardson 1985: 44)

Such postscripts were 'written to the moment' in order to provide (not altogether successfully) a clear moral tale with additional variety and suspense. In *Clarissa* (1747–48), Richardson went on to tell the story of a rape and its consequences, extending the form to include letters by more than one character, and also letters in return. (For a typology of the epistolary novel, see chap. 3.4.2.)

Richardson's first sentimental novel and moral tale was an instant success in Britain and elsewhere, even though some critics complained that the didactic value of *Pamela* was marred by its sexual overtones. While Richardson continued to revise and refine his text, others attempted to cash in on his best seller with continuations and adaptations, until the author produced (like Defoe in the case of *Robinson Crusoe*) a sequel of his own, as the only effective way, in these early days of copyright history, to keep artistic control over one's original creations. And yet, two of these spin-offs that are also literary parodies ultimately overshadowed Richardson's own sequel. In *Joseph Andrews* (1742), Henry Fielding purported to tell the history of Pamela's brother, both to set the record of Richardson's ultra-virtuous heroine straight and to come up with an alternative conception of the novel (see below). As a gifted writer of farcical plays, Fielding had also the authorship of *An Apology for the Life of Mrs Shamela Andrews* (1741) attributed to him: this spoof on Richardson's heroine retained the form of an epistolary novel complete with 'writing to the moment', but gave full rein to bedroom farce in order to satirise the alleged moral hypocrisy of *Pamela*. Shamela is far from being an *ingénue* and a conscientious objector against sexual harassment: in her letters, she reveals herself instead as a well-experienced and fully emancipated man-hunter, and as an extreme version of the smart material girl. While Defoe's counterparts are altogether more colourful, the protagonist of the parody is distinguished by a ruthless manner barely covered by her righteous mask. Shamela's innocence as well as her principles are indeed no more than a sham, and serve only to strike a better bargain on the marriage market, and to sell her 'virtue' at the highest price.

In his 'circumstantial description' of the sexual adventures *Fanny Hill* of Fanny Hill, John Cleland (1710–89) was even more drastic than the author of *Shamela* and than Defoe – who actually had turned out to be quite prudish in that regard. Cleland's *Memoirs of a Woman of Pleasure* (1748–49) tells the story of a poor country-girl who is driven to the city, first to be deceived and then to receive a sexual education which leads her (quite willingly) to work as a prostitute. The *Memoirs*, too, are presented as a novel in letters which purports to be founded on facts – right from the beginning of Fanny's first letter, the reader is left with no doubt that "Truth! Stark naked truth, is the word". In this case, the self-proclaimed realism serves as pretence to depict a variety of sexual practices, often with a 'male gaze' (Mulvey 1975) and from a keyhole perspective. *Memoirs of a Woman of Pleasure* is however more than a classic of its kind, namely the epistolary novel of the pornographic type; and Fanny Hill is more than an outright sexual *picaro*, involved with men of all classes. The response to Cleland's novel was also an indication of the sexual morality of the age. The first edition of the *Memoirs* comprised two scenes where Fanny observes homosexuality between men, and it were just these scenes that were considered to be particularly offensive by churchmen and politicians in Cleland's day. In the nineteenth century, the novel became an underground classic in Britain, but was banned for obscenity in the USA, until it was cleared by the US Supreme Court in 1966. British courts had initially upheld the ban, but the novel was finally allowed to appear, and this development – like the groundbreaking clearance of D. H. Lawrence's indicted novel *Lady Chatterley's Lover* in the Old

Bailey in 1960 – was a further sign of relaxing sexual morals in the Swinging Sixties. In 1980, *Fanny*, the accomplished rewriting of Cleland's novel by the American novelist Erica Jong became a best seller. The ultimate seal of approval for the classical status of the *Memoirs* came in 2007 when the BBC broadcast a prime time TV series commissioned from the acclaimed screenwriter Andrew Davies, who had already adapted *Moll Flanders* (1996) and *Pride and Prejudice* (1995).

3.5.3 | The Novels of Fielding and Sterne

Fig. 3.24|
Henry Fielding

It was Walpole's Theatre Licensing Act that directed the former playwright Henry Fielding (1707–54) to his career as a novelist. He came out with a novel that turned out to be more than a parodistic sequel to Richardson's novel about the virtues of Pamela Andrews. In the ongoing process of experimenting with the concept and form of the novel, both *The History of Joseph Andrews* (1742) and *The History of Tom Jones, a Foundling* (1749) marked a new stage by turning away from the limited first-person point of view of an eye-witness and experiencing self to a more distanced and panoramic perspective. Fielding's models were the Classical epics and the comic novel *Don Quixote* (1605–15) by Cervantes, all of which were presented from a reliable third-person or hetero-diegetic point of view, and divided into meaningful parts such as 'books' or chapters (not just individual letters) – a manner which is even commented upon in one of the introductory chapters of *Joseph Andrews* (II.1: "Of Divisions in Authors").

The fun with Fielding already begins with quirky chapter headings that may summarise the action in phrases like "Containing five pages of paper" or "Containing little or nothing" (*Tom Jones* IV.1, III.1). In both *Joseph Andrews* and *Tom Jones*, the former playwright knows how to keep his audience entertained with a series of comical 'battles' (pub quarrels) and farcical bedroom scenes, with scenes of seduction (in which usually the female characters take the initiative) and with surprise twists of the story, which may not only involve the protagonist's narrow escape from the gallows, but sometimes have "The Reader's Neck brought into Danger", too (*Tom Jones* I.4). The plot of Fielding's masterwork *Tom Jones* is made up of several sub-plots with a causal connection: there is a mystery-plot concerning the nature and discovery

Tom Jones

of the foundling's parents; there is also his half-brother Blifil's intrigue to estrange Tom from his foster-father's favour and fortune; then we find the love-plot centring on Tom and Sophia Western, another squire's daughter; and finally there are Tom's relations to a series of other women along the way. In order to present a panoramic view of eighteenth-century England, Fielding painted on a large canvas, and yet there is a coherent pattern. Of altogether eighteen 'books', six are set in the county of Somerset, in the West of England; another six relate the adventures of both Tom and Sophia on the road to London (in inns, in coaches and in confrontation with highwaymen); while the last six 'books' present life in the metropolis, from high society down to the prison cell.

Among eighteenth-century British novelists, Fielding was the only proper Neoclassicist, as is already evident from the well-balanced design of *The History of Tom Jones*; but Fielding wore his learning lightly and turned it to comic ends. Just like Pope in his narrative poem *The Rape of the Lock* (1712/14) and true to his own burlesque play *The Life and Death of Tom Thumb the Great* (1730), Fielding called up Classical and Neoclassical precedents in a mock-heroic manner. Fielding's **stylistic parody of poetic diction** switches between elaborated and colloquial speech registers, as in this instance: "Aurora now first opened her casement, *Anglicè*, the day began to break" (*Tom Jones* IX.2, Fielding 1986, 440; similar cases of *periphrasis* are found at the opening of X.2 and X.9).

In a more general sense, Fielding famously defined his **concept of the novel** as "a comic epic poem in prose" ("Preface" to *Joseph Andrews*). However, such comedy masked a serious didactic purpose: the satiric treatment of social evils such as hypocrisy and affectation was meant to bring about a *catharsis* through laughter (instead of pity or fear, as in Aristotle's concept of tragedy). The Neo-Aristotelian overtones are no coincidence: Fielding, like Aristotle before him, tried to raise the esteem of literary art by pointing to its social and didactic usefulness, and by defending it not only against Puritans, like Defoe in his prefaces, but ultimately against Plato's equation of fiction with fraud, of literature with lies. It is not difficult to see why Fielding entitled and conceived of his novels as 'histories': just like a historian, the 'author' (read: narrator – which is principally of the same kind in all his novels) protests the usefulness and truthfulness of his account, and purposefully relates the story of an individual life in order to talk about 'Human Nature' in general (*Tom Jones* I.1, VIII.1, IX.1). In the eighteenth century, this was still widely believed to be invariably the same in all places and at all times. "The same hypocrisy, the same fraud; in short, the same follies and vices, dressed in different habits. [...] human nature is everywhere the same" (VIII.15, 1986: 430): these are the words given to an admittedly misanthropic stranger in conversation with Tom Jones, but they still reflect Fielding's own social mission, who has "endeavoured to laugh mankind out of their favourite follies and vices" ("Dedication" to *Tom Jones*). Fielding's concept of the novel and his literary criticism are to be found in the prefaces to his 'histories' of *Joseph Andrews* and of *Tom Jones* (1749), and in the introductory chapters to each of their 'books'. Altogether, they form a running series of essays in criticism parallel to the comic action, in order both to entertain and to educate the reader (V.1). Fielding's 'author' occasionally compares the world to a stage (*theatrum mundi*) and the novel to a stage-play (VII.1), where he is acting as a master of ceremonies: he welcomes the reader of *Tom Jones* with a "Bill of Fare to the Feast" (I.1) and continues in this convivial tone throughout the novel, until he amiably bids the reader farewell at the end (XVIII.1). However, the 'author' lets the reader know, too, that he wants himself to be seen as an enlightened monarch, and (in a colonial metaphor reminiscent of Defoe's *Robinson Crusoe*) as

> the founder of a new province of writing, so I am at liberty to make what laws I please therein. And these laws, my readers, whom I consider as my subjects, are bound to believe in and to obey; [...] I shall principally regard their ease and advantage in all such institutions: for I do not, like a *juro divino* tyrant, imagine that they are my slaves or commodity. I am, indeed, set over them for their own good only (II.1, 1986: 88).

Apart from the political wording, this passage is also interesting for its philosophical overtones, namely for the idea of **Benevolence**, which is personified by Tom's foster-father, the aptly named Squire Allworthy. In distinction from materialists such as Moll Flanders, Mr. Allworthy is said to be "a human being replete with benevolence, meditating in what manner he might render himself most acceptable to his Creator, by doing most good to his creatures." (I.4, 1986: 59). Another eighteenth-century character that springs to mind in this context is Uncle Toby from *The Life and Opinions of Tristram Shandy, Gentleman*, who will rather escort an annoying fly out of a room than kill her on the spot (II.12). In this voluminous novel published in instalments (9 vols., 1759–67) – a form of publication which looks towards Victorian novelists such as Dickens – Laurence Sterne (1713–68), a Yorkshire parson born in Ireland, summed up and at the same time hilariously parodied the experimental process set in motion by his predecessors. As in Defoe's fictional autobiographies, Sterne's Tristram Shandy is made to review and relate his own life in detail; yet for the sake of completing the record he cannot be content with the 'circumstantial description' of his own conception (beginning literally *ab ovo*), but finds himself required to dig even further into the family's history and give much room to other relatives. Therefore, it could well be said that the readers of Sterne's novel are presented with the life of Uncle Toby, together with the opinions of Walter Shandy (Tristram's father). As in Richardson's epistolary novels, the narrative of events is seasoned with instances of 'writing to the moment'; yet Tristram is prone to give such free rein to the Association of Ideas – a concept which Sterne had borrowed from the philosopher John Locke and brilliantly illustrated throughout his own novel – that the result of this radical form of psychological realism is a haphazard and endlessly digressive form of narration. Sterne's most prominent stylistic device therefore seems to be his recurrent use of dashes to indicate yet another digression:

Tristram Shandy

> the machinery of my work is of a species by itself; two contrary motions are introduced into it, and reconciled, which were thought to be at variance with each other. In a word, my work is digressive, and it is progressive, too, – and at the same time. [...] Digressions, incontestably, are the sunshine; – they are the life, the soul of reading; – take them out of this book for instance, – you might as well take the book along with them; – [...]
> what jovial times! – but where am I? And into what a delicious riot of things am I rushing? I – I who must be cut short in the midst of my days, and taste no more of 'em than what I borrow from my imagination – peace to thee, generous fool! and let me go on. (*Tristram Shandy* I.22 and VII.14, Sterne 1983: 95, 473).

It is therefore difficult to summarise this non-linear narrative neatly, which is held together primarily by Tristram's train of thought, even though there are distinctly recognisable strands of the plot. There are the stories about Tristram's mother in labour, the midwife and Dr. Slop, the 'man-midwife' blundering Tristram's birth; about the philosophising of Walter Shandy and his great enlightened project, the *Tristra-paedia* (V.16 ff.); and about the life and sermons of Parson Yorick (named after old Hamlet's court-jester, I.10 ff., II.15 ff.). Tristram's own life turned out to be a series of mishaps: his nose was crushed when he was born; he was christened on the name of Tristram only through another accident; and his masculinity was severely impaired at the age of five. That might also be feared of his uncle, Captain Toby Shandy, who had received an obscure 'wound in the groin' during the early eighteenth-century wars against France. For the rest of his life, Uncle Toby rides a peculiar 'hobby-horse' (one of the key metaphors and a prominent device of characterisation in Sterne's novel, I.7–9, 24 ff.): together with his erstwhile comrade and present servant, Corporal Trim, Uncle Toby keeps the war experience alive (but closes the painful wound) by memorising every tiny little detail about the campaign in Flanders. The novel ends on the hilarious scene when Widow Wadman, out of a personal interest as eager for detail as Uncle Toby, enquires as to *where exactly* he was so fatally wounded (IX.16 ff.) ...

When compared with their Victorian successors, the novels by Fielding and Sterne stand out by their rather uninhibited presentation of sexual matters (a fact which was deplored by the Victorian novelist W. M. Thackeray in his lectures on *The English Humourists of the Eighteenth Century*, 1851–53). In *Tom Jones*, Fielding presented a hero who is regularly giving in to the seductive charms of women until he becomes happily married to virtuous Sophia Western in the end. **Sexual comedy** involves scenes of bedroom farce (V.5, X.2–7, XV.7), but Fielding's narrator regularly refrains from spelling out possibly indecent language (including that of Sophia's outspoken father, Squire Western), and he presents seductive scenes in a mock-heroic manner (e. g. the 'battle of the sexes' in IX.5). Sterne's Tristram, who is generally less dedicated to *decorum*, thrives on his many sexual puns and jokes, but again does not attempt to rival the "stark naked truth" of Fanny Hill's account.

It was through the comparison of Fielding and Sterne with their predecessors that Wayne C. Booth developed his **typology of**

narrators (see Booth 1952; 1991). Like Fielding's 'author', Tristram is a **dramatised, self-conscious and intrusive** narrator who converses with the reader throughout; and yet, his endeavour to establish and explain the causal connection between individual episodes brings him to narrate them in an utterly whimsical sequence, and in an ultimately **unreliable** fashion. Tristram leaves out some parts of the story (IV.24) and transposes others (IX.18–19, 25), including the "Dedication" (follows on chap. I.8) and the "Preface" (inserted only in chap. III.20). Tristram's birth does not occur before the third volume (III.22), although the day of birth has been circumstantially specified already in the first (I.5). There are tales inserted which are superfluous to the action, but may nevertheless be presented even in a bilingual version (III.11, IV); and there is the continuous promise – which is actually never fully kept – to include chapters of highly important but also seemingly indecent nature (in relation to the significance of noses, of chambermaids and of button-holes, III.31–38, IV.14, V.8). Moreover, there are typographic oddities like the two black pages inserted to commemorate a deceased character (Parson Yorick, I.12), the blank page providing the reader with space to paint another character to his own liking (Widow Wadman, VI.38), and the marble pages inserted to underline the 'motley' character of the whole narrative (III.36). In addition, the far-from-linear nature of the unconventional narrative is graphically and self-critically illustrated, too, by a series of curved lines (VI.40).

Tristram Shandy became an instant success all over Europe. Through its peculiar humour, its psychological interest and its non-linear structure, it has inspired several other unconventional writers, such as the Enlightenment thinker Denis Diderot (who paid him a tribute with the novel *Jacques le Fataliste*, 1796), the fellow-Irishmen and Modernist writers James Joyce (*Ulysses*, 1922) and Flann O'Brien (*At Swim-Two-Birds*, 1939), the Postmodernist American short story writer and novelist Donald Barthelme (*The Dead Father*, 1975), and the postcolonial fabulist Salman Rushdie, who rewrote both Shakespeare and Sterne in his short story "Yorick" (included in the collection *East, West*, 1994). Parson Yorick had become a kind of *alter ego* to Parson Sterne, who used his character's name as a pseudonym when publishing his own sermons, and who made both Yorick and Tristram travel to the Continent in his own footsteps. The story of how the adult Tristram narrowly escaped Death by flying first to and then travelling through France (*Tristram Shandy* VII) does not only mirror the author's own search for health, but also finds its parallel in Sterne's only other novel, *A Sentimental Journey through France and Italy. By Mr. Yorick* (1768), where the parson returns as a sentimental and benevolent traveller. **Sentimentalism** as the other side of the Age of Reason (see chaps. 3.2.1, 3.3.2 and 3.4.5) is also evident in the sentimental comedy of the age as well as in Samuel Richardson's novels of the 1740s, in Henry Mackenzie's novel *The Man of Feeling* (1771), in Frances ('Fanny') Burney's *Evelina* (1778), and in Jane Austen's comic concern with conscious lovers who ponder *Sense and Sensibility* (1811).

3.5.4 | 'Mothers of the Novel': Women Writers before and beside Jane Austen

In her essay *A Room of One's Own* (1929), the novelist and feminist Virginia Woolf marked out the middle-class women writers of the Long Eighteenth Century as initiators of an alternative tradition:

> And with Mrs Behn we turn a very important corner on the road. We leave behind, shut up in their parks among their folios, those solitary great ladies who wrote without audience or criticism, for their own delight alone. [...] Mrs Behn was a middle-class woman [...] forced by the death of her husband and some unfortunate adventures of her own to make her living by her wits. She had to work on equal terms with men. She made, by working very hard, enough to live on. The importance of that fact outweighs anything she actually wrote [...]. Without those forerunners, Jane Austen and the Brontës and George Eliot could no more have written than Shakespeare could have written without Marlowe [...]. For masterpieces are not single and solitary births; they are the outcome of many years of thinking in common, [...]. Jane Austen should have laid a wreath upon the grave of Fanny Burney [...]. All women together ought to let flowers fall upon the tomb of Aphra Behn, [...] for it was she who earned them the right to speak their minds. (Woolf 2000: 58–60).

Were it not for her non-conformity to Ian Watt's criteria of 'formal realism' (see chap. 3.5.1), a case could be made indeed to see the poet, playwright and prose writer Aphra Behn (?1640–89) as the first novelist writing in English, and as a predecessor to both Defoe and Richardson (though all of them had to fall back on something else than prose fiction to earn a living). Behn's

Love-Letters between a Nobleman and his Sister (1684–87) brought the French tradition of epistolary fiction to England, and thus preceded *Pamela* by over 50 years. However, Behn's narrative (though based on an authentic incident) assumes the manner of a romance. In *Oroonoko; or, The Royal Slave: A True History* (1688), Behn had dealt with the issues of race and colonialism through a 'noble savage' and in a Caribbean setting well before the publication of *Robinson Crusoe*, and yet again, her claim to plausibility is ultimately less well-founded than Defoe's. Both the West African prince Oroonoko and his beloved Imoinda are sold into slavery by a rival suitor, and although the lovers meet again on a plantation in Guyana, they are doomed to die tragically in the cause of a slave revolt. The lovers' names, their idealised behaviour in the conflict between love and honour and the exotic settings (first the Gold Coast and then Guyana – today's Ghana and Surinam) point back to the tradition of the heroic play – or even further to Shakespeare's Moor of Venice – rather than forward to the experiments with a novel form of fictional realism. Behn's story was indeed adapted as a heroic play (by Thomas Southerne in 1695), and through its continuous stage presence helped to further the movement for the Abolition of Slavery.

|Fig. 3.26
Aphra Behn

Feminist critics writing in the wake of Woolf and arguing for a canon revision (e. g. Spencer 1986; Spender 1986; Todd 1989) have come up again with the names of further women writers between Aphra Behn and Jane Austen which had been successful in their time. Even though they may not always have attempted to rival the radical experiments of their canonised male colleagues, it is nevertheless interesting to see how closely all of them were involved with each other's work (so much so that it begs the question if we can really speak of two parallel lines of tradition). Eliza Haywood (?1693–1756) collaborated with Defoe on *The Life of Mr Duncan Campbell* (1720) and, besides writing numerous other novels, adapted Fielding's mock-heroic stage-play *Tom Thumb the Great* as a comic opera (1733). She also edited *The Female Spectator* (1744–46), which looked back to the famous collection of essays by Addison and Steele. For *The Adventures of David Simple* (1744–53), Sarah Fielding (1710–68) could enlist the help of her brother Henry, who contributed prefaces to individual volumes of her popular narrative in between the publication of his own novels *Joseph Andrews* and *Tom Jones*. Henry Fielding's admiration for Cervantes's *Don Quixote* is borne out, too, in *The Female Quixote; or, The Adventures of Arabella* (1752) by Charlotte Lennox (1720–1804), which the writer herself adapted for the stage (this time under the title *Angelica; or, Quixote in Petticoats*, 1758). In this parody on romances (and later in Austen's *Northanger Abbey*), the heroine mistakes the world of fiction, and its image of male lovers, for the real world.

Frances Burney

Half way between Richardson and Austen, also in terms of genre, lies the novelistic work of Frances ('Fanny') Burney (1752–1840, see chap. 3.4.4). With *Evelina; or, The History of a Young Lady's Entrance into the World* (1778), Burney came out with a sentimental novel in letters as well as a **female novel of development** (*Bildungsroman*), a sub-genre to become popular with later women novelists such as Charlotte Brontë, George Eliot, Kate Chopin or Toni Morrison. In addition to her epistolary novel *Evelina*, Burney has been increasingly esteemed for her private letters and diaries, too.

Fig. 3.27

Mary Wollstone-
craft

Because of their thematic concerns, some other contemporaries of Jane Austen can be sorted into pairs. There are, first, Mary Wollstonecraft (1759–97), the wife of one novelist (William Godwin) and the mother of another (Mary Shelley), and Hannah More (1745–1833), an educational writer with a different cause. Mary Wollstonecraft became famous for her classic feminist treatise *A Vindication of the Rights of Woman* (1792), which she followed up (posthumously) with *The Wrongs of Woman* (1798), a reworking of her ideas presented in the form of a novel. By contrast, Hannah More dedicated herself to educate the poor and the barely literate coming out of the new Sunday Schools, for whom she wrote a series of 50 "Cheap Repository Tracts" (1795–98), which sold in millions of copies. Her best-selling and yet only novel *Coelebs in Search of a Wife* (1808: 11 editions in 9 months) is marked by Hannah More's deeply religious stance (which also made her support the cause of Abolition). The great success of this piece of literary Evangelicalism signals the gradual change of mentality towards 'Victorian values'. (For Evangelicalism, see chap. 3.3.2, and for the two writers, see also chaps. 3.4.2 and 3.4.6.)

A second pair of women writers can be seen, despite the generation gap, in Ann Radcliffe (1764–1823) and in Wollstonecraft's daughter, Mary Shelley (1797–1851). Both Radcliffe and Shelley became famous for Gothic romances such as *The Mysteries of Udolpho* (1794) and *Frankenstein; or, The Modern Prometheus*

(1818) – and for just that reason are treated together in the next chapter. A third pair consists of two Irish women writers, namely Maria Edgeworth (1767–1849) and Sydney Owenson, Lady Morgan (?1775–1859). Maria Edgeworth wrote books on education as well as children's books, but she is today best known as the first writer of **regional novels of manners**. In the year which saw the union of the realms and parliaments of Great Britain and Ireland (1801) and the concentration of the power in London, Edgeworth published *Castle Rackrent: An Hibernian Tale, Taken from Facts, and from the Manners of the Irish Squires, before the Year 1782* (the year which had gained the Irish parliament a sovereign, yet short-lived independence from Westminster). This novel of manners about the decline of the Irish landed gentry is presented by the Rackrents' steward, Thady Quirk, a narrator-observer who barely mentions the fact that this story of a family's degeneration over three generations is closely linked with the gradual rise to affluence and final take-over of the estate by his own offspring. Thus, Thady Quirk becomes the next prominent example of an unreliable narrator (Booth 1991) after Tristram Shandy. For non-Irish readers, Edgeworth's footnotes and her glossary presented a wealth of information on a bygone age and culture. Edgeworth's novel *The Absentee* (1812), though told by a heterodiegetic narrator, had otherwise much in common with Lady Morgan's earlier novel of letters *The Wild Irish Girl: A National Tale* (1806) in that both are regional novels in which the protagonists (and likewise the average English reader) start from England on an educational journey to Ireland, and back again. In this design, Walter Scott found a model for *Waverley* (1814), the first of his series of regional and historical novels dealing in likewise manner with the rift between Scotland and England. In the Irish novels by Maria Edgeworth and Lady Morgan, *John Bull's Other Island* (as Shaw was to call it a century later in the title of his stage-play) is purposefully chosen as a setting in order to confront existing stereotypes against Irish Catholics, and thus to explain a region of the United Kingdom to Protestant English readers such as Jane Austen who must have regarded it as a wild and essentially foreign country.

Jane Austen (1775–1817) is the last major novelist treated in Ian Watt's seminal study *The Rise of the Novel* (1957), where she is seen as following in the line of Defoe, Richardson, Fielding, and

Maria Edgeworth

Lady Morgan

Frances Burney. And quite rightly so: although Austen's novels in their finalised form were published between 1811 and 1818, work on them had already begun in the 1790s. A first draft of *Pride and Prejudice* was then called 'First Impressions', and one of Austen's earliest fictional attempts was an (unpublished) novel in letters called 'Lady Susan', whose cynical plot and tone seems indebted to both Richardson's *Clarissa* and to *Les Liaisons dangereuses* by Pierre Choderlos de Laclos (1782). Both Austen's lineage and her limitations can be exemplified by a series of variations upon a single ironical sentence. "It hath been observed by wise men or women, I forget which, that all persons are doomed to be in love once in their lives." – this is Fielding writing, and here again: "It hath been observed by some man of much greater reputation for wisdom than myself, that misfortunes seldom come single." (For both quotations, see *Tom Jones* I.11, III.9; 1986: 77, 144.) From such initial intrusions, Austen fashioned her most popular piece of irony, namely the following, first impression of *Pride and Prejudice* (1813): "It is a truth universally acknowledged, that a single man in possession of a good fortune, must be in want of a wife." This introductory sentence has become proverbial, and recognisable even in further variation such as here: "It is a truth universally acknowledged, that Jane Austen chose to ignore the decisive historical events of her time. Where, it is still asked, are the Napoleonic wars: the real current of history?" Raymond Williams (1973: 113), the famous Cultural Materialist critic, is right: some settings and themes are simply not being talked about in Austen's novels. What about the Celtic Fringe of Britain? (This is left to Lady Morgan, Maria Edgeworth and Walter Scott.) What about Colonialism, Slavery and the Abolitionist Movement? There is no more than a casual reference to the Slave Trade, and a passing acknowledgment of the fact that the social life of *Mansfield Park* is being financed through the profits reaped from a West Indian plantation (I.3, II.3). What about such topics as industry and the working classes, London and the slums? (They remain to be addressed by Charles Dickens or Elizabeth Gaskell.)

Ian Watt's treatment of Jane Austen centres both on her technical achievements as a writer and on the rather restricted picture of society that she presents – in her own words: "the little bit (two Inches wide) of Ivory on which I work with so fine a Brush, as produces little effect after much labour" (from a letter to J.E. Austen, 16 Dec. [1816]). What all of Austen's published **novels of manners** have in common is their setting in the middle classes and the landed gentry of turn-of-the-century, provincial, Southern England. Their comic plots usually deal with match-making and marriage in the Home Counties, leaving out the spheres of working life, of politics (then and now), of sexuality and death. Austen's restriction to a partial view of society, history and human life comes out, perhaps unwittingly, in the initial sentence of her novel *Emma* (1816), which introduces the protagonist in these terms: "Emma Woodhouse, handsome, clever, and rich, with a comfortable home and a happy disposition, seemed to unite some of the best blessings of existence; and had lived nearly twenty-one years in the world with very little to distress or vex her." The comic conflicts in the novel arise out of Emma's 'benevolent', but clearly self-serving and blundering attempts to make matches for others and for her own; and they are only solved when Emma recognises her failures, and finds her 'Mr Right' in Mr Knightley. As in Austen's other novels, a series of dinner-parties, a ball and even a picnic provide the means to bring the characters together and to present them in a context of well- (or ill-) mannered behaviour and polite conversation, in which the observance of 'propriety' and 'decorum' serves as a bench mark for good manners.

Emma

Whereas *Janeites* have been taken in rather by comic types such as the ever-prattling Miss Bates, and altogether much more by *Pride and Prejudice* than *Emma*, Austen's twentieth-century academic critics have frequently taken up the latter to point out her achievement, for instance in managing to elicit sympathy for an egotistical Emma instead of gentle Jane Fairfax, another character who clearly has much more potential for a virtuous and likeable heroine (which has been exploited in 1990 by Joan Aiken in her complementary and complimentary novel *Jane Fairfax*). Austen achieves her aim by the frequent use of **Free Indirect Discourse** to grant the reader psychological insight into Emma's mind but not that of Jane Fairfax, who is seldom seen, and never overheard in her thoughts.

Moreover, this and other novels by Austen are characterised by a heterodiegetic narrator-observer (in the terminology of Genette and of Booth) in combination with a dominantly scenic presentation and with dramatic irony.

> She dispensed with the participating narrator, whether as the author of a memoir as in Defoe, or as a letter-writer as in Richardson [...]; instead she told her stories after Fielding's manner, as a confessed author. Jane Austen's variant of the commenting narrator, however, was so much more discreet that it did not substantially affect the authenticity of her narrative. (Watt 1963: 309)

Pride and Prejudice

To rephrase Watt in terms of Booth: Austen's narrator is not as actively involved as Defoe's or Richardson's protagonists, and altogether less intrusive than the narrator in Fielding's novels. The famous first sentence apart, this is also true of *Pride and Prejudice*, whose plot nowadays looks like 'Four Weddings and No Funeral'. However, there is a moral to this tale of manners: not all matches and marriages are agreeable alike. Austen clearly wanted her readers to see the difference between the two extremes of (first) a mere marriage of convenience, which may unite a single man and heir to a fortune with a material girl (as exemplified by Reverend Mr Collins and Charlotte Lucas), and (second) a passionately 'romantic' love which, for its reliance on 'first impressions' only and for its breach of decorum, must lead to unhappiness and a decline in social and financial status (as in the case of Lydia Bennet and Mr Wickham, and also of Mr and Mrs Bennet). The way to happiness, Austen suggested, lay middle of the road, in a match that saw emotion controlled by reason, and thus was to unite, in the telling title of her earlier novel, *Sense and Sensibility*. The loving marriage of Jane Bennet and Mr Bingley presented such a positive example, and the author had another happy union in store for the protagonists. Elizabeth Bennet is an outspoken and headstrong middle-class girl, whereas Mr Darcy is aristocratic and rather reserved. In the ballroom scene (chap. 18) where the conversation between Elizabeth and Darcy first breaks down, and then is resumed with a good amount of repartee, Austen can be seen to provide the missing link between the Restoration comedy of manners and the witty comedies of Oscar Wilde.

3.5.5 | Oriental Tales and Gothic Romances: Other Worlds in an Age of Reason

Orientalism

Audiences in the Long Eighteenth Century continued to be enthralled by exotic settings, from the Guyana of Aphra Behn's *Oroonoko; or, The Royal Slave* (1688) to the Oriental tales as well as the Gothic romances of the period. When Western European societies had no longer to worry about the Ottoman Empire as a constant political threat (after the Siege of Vienna, 1683), Orientalism became a literary and an aristocratic fashion. Montesquieu's satirical and epistolary novel *Lettres persanes* (1721) found its English equivalent in the collection of 'Chinese letters' in *The Citizen of the World* (1762) by Oliver Goldsmith (1728–74), which also looked at Europe from an extraneous point of view, and this was closely followed by the posthumous publication of *The Turkish Embassy Letters* of Lady Mary Wortley Montagu (1763, †1762; see chaps. 3.4.3 and 3.4.5). The mode of the **Oriental tale** started around the same time with *The History of Rasselas, Prince of Abyssinia: An Asiatic Tale* (1759) set in Cairo, which served its author Samuel Johnson (1709–94) as a vehicle for moral and melancholy reflections about life, luck and the pursuit of happiness.

Vathek: An Arabian Tale by William Beckford (1759–1844) is an altogether different matter. The text hovers between languages (the English translation by Samuel Henley was published prior to Beckford's French original in 1786, and later revised by the author) and between genres: it is affiliated with both the Oriental tale and the Gothic romance, yet not without humour either, despite its cruel and supernatural features. Caliph Vathek enters into a Faustian pact with the satanic ruler of the underworld, organises a slaughter of children in order to gain enlargement of his knowledge as well as of his sensual experience, and embarks on a journey full of adventures and further sadistic crimes. In this Arabian tale, the Oriental setting is exploited mainly for exoticism and excess.

Vathek continued to exert its influence on Romantic writers, even though they turned to Oriental tales in verse. Such exotic romances were often built around stereotypes (such as the harem, a cruel Turk, a female Christian slave and an avenging hero) and supplied a wider public with elements of sensation and suspense. Lord Byron (1788–1824) was enormously successful with six Turkish tales (1813–16): his third, *The Corsair*, sold 10,000 copies on the day of its publication in 1814 alone, and a total of 25,000 copies in its first year. With such a success, which is partly due to his creation of a **Byronic Hero** (see chap. 3.3.1), Byron eclipsed the fame of Walter Scott as a storyteller in verse, who then turned to writing historical novels and romances instead (see below). Byron used Mediterranean and Oriental settings also for his travelogues, *Childe Harold's Pilgrimage: A romaunt* (4 cantos in Spenserian stanzas, 1812–18) and *Don Juan* (16 cantos in *ottava rima*, 1819–24). In those comic epic poems, Byron continued in the eighteenth-century vein of the *Lettres persanes* by blending ex-oticism with satire striking home, but did so in a manner of his own. In such verse narratives, the poet who loved to clad himself in exotic fashion could feed upon his own travel experience. This however could not have included the Sultan's harem – just the place for his character Don Juan to join the ladies, escape the Sultan's notice by appearing before him disguised as a woman, and then let himself be seduced by the Sultana Gulbeyaz (V–VI). When Byron stopped writing Oriental tales proper, his friend Thomas Moore (1779–1852) stepped in successfully with one of his own, *Lalla Rookh: An Oriental Romance* (1817; 15th ed. 1829).

Gothic romances, too, often took their readers to an exotic Medi-terranean setting; however, their stories were also located in the remote past. The term 'Gothic' signals a re-appreciation of the Middle Ages which already makes itself felt within the Age of Neoclassicism: in *Tom Jones* (1749), the house of Mr. Allworthy's is marked out as the most noble example of the "Gothick stile of building", complete with "an old ruined abbey" (I.4), and at the time of publication of Fielding's novel, Horace Walpole (1717–97, see chaps. 3.1 and 3.4.2) had set the new fashion when he had himself built just such a deliberately irregular model home, Strawberry Hill at Twickenham (1748 ff., prompting William Beckford to commission the Gothic mansion of Fonthill Abbey). In 1764, Walpole turned his efforts at a Gothic revival to writ-ing fiction and came out with *The Castle of Otranto: A Gothic Story*, the first romance of its kind that also provided a pattern. The fantastic tale of love and intrigue is placed in a medieval, Medi-terranean and Catholic setting of haunted castles and gloomy cloisters – the exact opposite to the world in which the major-ity of English readers would have felt comfortable at that time. Subconscious fears and suspense are key features, and this is oc-casionally brought off by the intrusion of the supernatural (such as a ghost or a gigantic helmet falling from the sky). The plot hinges, too, on a love triangle and involves an *ingénue* who is pursued by an aristocratic, villainous brute, yet adored and saved by a braver and kinder specimen of masculine values. *The Cham-*

pion of Virtue was therefore an apt title for Clara Reeve's romance (1777), which was then re-titled to appear as *The Old English Baron: A Gothic Story* (1778). It came with a preface in which Reeve critically reviewed Walpole's romance and promised to improve on him in terms of credibility, and with the expressed intention to blend the Gothic romance into the sentimental novel.

The more sensational (Walpole) as well as the sentimental and yet more sober style (Reeve) each became better delineated in the Romantic Age, which marked a (first) high tide of Gothic fiction. Ann Radcliffe (1764–1823) was one of the woman writers who did not really need to be rediscovered by feminist literary history. Radcliffe was the highest paid author in 1790s Britain, earning an advance of £500 for *The Mysteries of Udolpho: A Romance* (1794), and even topping that sum a few years later when she received £600 for *The Italian [...]: A Romance* (1797) – while Jane Austen was paid only £10 for *Northanger Abbey*, her parody on Gothic romances. Ann Radcliffe continued to think and write along Reeve's lines and came up with the time-honoured distinction between the 'terror' and 'horror' variety of the Gothic:

|Fig. 3.29
Ann Radcliffe

> Terror and horror are so far opposite, that the first expands the soul, and awakens the faculties to a high degree of life; the other contracts, freezes, and nearly annihilates them. [...] the great difference between horror and terror [... lies] in the uncertainty and obscurity, that accompany the first, respecting the dreaded evil ("On the Supernatural in Poetry", published posthumously 1826).

One could be tempted to apply the twentieth-century term 'magic realism' (which has designated authors such as Günter Grass, Gabriel García Márquez and Salman Rushdie) already to the late eighteenth-century romances of Ann Radcliffe, who used but also explained supernatural features in her fiction ('terror'). However, even when her own distinction between 'terror' and 'horror' is granted, it is nevertheless clear that 'formal realism' was not an object in her description of Sublime settings, stereotyped characters and shock effects. As far as the principal setting, the constellation and the motivation of her characters were concerned, Radcliffe's romances observed the already established pattern. What distinguished them from their precedents, apart from Radcliffe's handling of the Supernatural, were the frequent and extended descriptions of Beautiful, but especially Sublime scenery. These exemplify the conceptualisation of Nature in the period very well. Together with Emily St. Aubert, the sentimental heroine and damsel in distress, readers of *The Mysteries of Udolpho* embark on a Grand Tour of Terror through France and Italy, taking in the impressive mountain ranges of the Pyrenees, the Alps and the Apennines, to meet the villain Montoni in his labyrinthine and spooky castle of Udolpho, which finds it Gothic French pendant later in Chateau-le-Blanc, where the romance ends in proper style. Montoni's characterisation as an aloof, passionate, but also melancholy person (II.3) makes him a Byronic Hero before its time.

A further escalation in terms of anticlericalism, sex and crime happened with the publication of *The Monk: A Romance* (1796) by Matthew Gregory Lewis (1775–1818). With its lusty monk, a seductive nun and black magic woman who sells her soul to the Devil to circumvent the inquisition, and the appearance of the devil in person, Lewis's Gothic romance presented a steamy version of convent life, and an orgy of seduction, rape and incest.

Fig. 3.30
Matthew G. Lewis

Compared with this sensational specimen of Gothic 'horror', the sexual inhibition of later novelists like Jane Austen and Walter Scott, and also their Victorian successors, becomes more apparent. The Faustian theme, which could already be seen in *Vathek* and *The Monk*, returned in *Melmoth the Wanderer: A Tale* (1820) by the Irishman Charles Robert Maturin (1780–1824), as did the anti-Catholic sentiment in the description of the cloister and the Inquisition. The title character is another version of the Wandering Jew type – just like Coleridge's Ancient Mariner. Much in *Melmoth* is part of the Gothic pattern, but what will strike today's reader as ahead of its time is Maturin's plan to integrate six individual tales, each focused on another character, into one complex plot.

Such a multiple point of view is also characteristic of *Frankenstein; or, The Modern Prometheus* (1818; revised in 1831) by Mary Shelley (1797–1851), which has turned into a modern myth indeed. Thus, the story may appear too well known to need any introduction, yet any simple plot summary will reveal that Mary Shelley's romance is often enough different from the popular film versions (with the exception of the 1994 adaptation *Mary Shelley's Frankenstein*, which remained generally true to its source but was to become a box office flop). First of all, the focus in Shelley's romance is mostly on the scientist Victor Frankenstein and not on

Fig. 3.31
Mary Shelley

the Monster that he created in an overreaching manner, out of human remains; a Monster that holds him in thrall, yet thwarts all of his scholarly ambition when it turns into a serial killer. Secondly, the life of Frankenstein is revealed through a series of inter-related stories, and in the form of a novel in letters: the polar explorer Robert Walton provides the epistolary frame narrative which includes Victor Frankenstein's report, which in turn includes others. Such a Chinese box structure points forward to Emily Brontë's *Wuthering Heights* and to Modernist novels.

Mary Shelley's romance was the best-known result of a ghost-story telling session that took place in Switzerland in the summer of 1816 between Mary and Percy Shelley, fellow-poet Lord Byron, Byron's lover (and Mary's stepsister) Claire Clairmont and Byron's physician, Dr John Polidori (1795–1821). Polidori's contribution then was "The Vampyre" (1819), which paved the way for other vampire stories by the Irish writers Sheridan Le Fanu ("Carmilla", 1872) and Bram Stoker (*Dracula*, 1897). In the meantime, this extraordinary group session has inspired further novelists like Reinhard Kaiser, and also the film-maker Ken Russell (*Gothic*, 1986). However, at this time, the first wave of Gothic fiction had already reached its crest, which is also evident from the two parodies that appeared within the same year 1818. In *Northanger Abbey* by Jane Austen (†1817), the heroine Catherine Morland is spoilt by reading too many of Radcliffe's romances, while *Nightmare Abbey* by Thomas Love Peacock (1785–1866) makes fun of both the Gothic genre and of the Romantic poets Byron and Shelley (and of Coleridge, too). Publishers like the Minerva Press continued to supply Gothic romances as a staple product, until they went out of fashion in the 1820s, by which time historical novels and romances had been successfully established as new forms of narrative looking to the past.

Gothic fiction

Fiction and Nation-Building in Scott's Historical Novels | 3.5.6

Sir Walter Scott (1771–1832) is credited with having created the new genre of the **historical novel** – a plausible, realistic form of narrative centred on events in the past, which met an immediate success with the reading public. Authors and readers of *The Mysteries of Udolpho*, *The Monk* or *Melmoth the Wanderer* had been more interested in a tale of terror or in a horror story than in

Fig. 3.32

Sir Walter Scott

an authentic recreation of past events and of the culture and society of another age. With Scottish history, and more particularly with the relationship between the Scots and the English in history, Walter Scott had found a theme of his own. Since 1603, when the crowns of England and Scotland were united under a Scottish monarch, and even more so since 1707, when an Act of Union established a "Great Britain" symbolised by the "Union Jack", the struggle of England and Scotland against each other had given way to a common journey. Or so it seemed. Again and again (in 1690, 1715, 1719 and 1745–46), there were unsuccessful attempts to undo the Glorious Revolution and achieve a second Stuart Restoration, the last of which, the 1745 Jacobite Rising, proved fatal. 'Bonnie Prince Charlie', grandson to James II and the last Stuart Pretender to the throne, managed to raise an army and march from the Scottish Highlands to the English Midlands. Unable to raise more support, the rebel army was forced to retreat to Scotland and finally beaten at the Battle of Culloden (1746). The English backlash saw to the destruction of the Stuart powerbase in the Highland clans, and to the suppression of the peculiar Highland culture.

Scott became first known as a translator and then as a collector of narrative ballads (*Minstrelsy of the Scottish Border*, 1802–03). Afterwards, Scott made his name as a poet of Romantic verse tales of his own, such as *The Lay of the Last Minstrel* (1805), *Marmion: a Tale of Flodden Field* (1808), *The Lady of the Lake* (1810) or *Rokeby* (1813). It was already in these verse narratives that Scott showed his interest in historical subject matter, and particularly in decisive moments of Scottish history. Moreover, the Scottish writer already tried out a formula that he was to take up later in his novels: he devised a love plot between fictional characters of his own invention and related this to a narrative centred on historical struggles and actual, 'very important persons' of a bygone age.

Scott was quite successful as a poet. He was not only offered the post of Poet Laureate (which he declined in 1813), but at a time when the reading public is estimated between 80,000 persons (by Edmund Burke for the 1790s) and some 200,000–220,000 persons (the educated guess of the critic Francis Jeffrey in 1812), Scott could sell 20,000 copies of his *The Lady of the Lake* in its first year after publication. And yet, he was to be eclipsed soon as a writer of verse tales by an even more successful contemporary,

Lord Byron, whose exotic, Turkish tales sold even better (see above). This, then, made Scott alter his course, and begin work as a writer of historical narratives in prose.

In the same year when Byron installed himself successfully as a poetic rival, Scott came out with *Waverley*, his first historical novel and the first of its kind at all. In the remaining 18 years of his life, besides editing other works, Scott wrote close to 30 historical novels and romances, which can be subsumed under two or three different thematic groups. There are (1) those like *Waverley* (1814), *Rob Roy* (1817) and *The Heart of Midlothian* (1818) – by far the majority – that are related to the history of Scotland and its turbulent relationship to neighbouring England from the eighteenth back to the sixteenth centuries. Then there are (2) the couple of novels such as *Quentin Durward* (1823) and *Anne of Geierstein* (1829) which take readers back to fifteenth-century France and Switzerland; and (3) those which are set in England, in Palestine and even in Constantinople in the Middle Ages, at the time of the Crusades, and of which *Ivanhoe* (1819) is the earliest and still best-known specimen.

Waverley

Rob Roy ('Red Robert') has often been called 'the Scottish Robin Hood', because this Highlander likewise became famous for stealing from the rich to provide for the poor, but in contrast to the legendary English outlaw, Robert Roy MacGregor (1671–1734) was an actual historical person, and not only a hero of folk tales and ballads. According to the historical records, he was a drover (a cowboy) and a cattle-dealer who became a cattle-thief, offering protection to his neighbours and clansmen from other cattle-thieves. (Scott returned to this rural world in his thematically related short tale "The Two Drovers", 1827.) However, Rob Roy's sympathy for the oppressed and his temporarily anti-government stance brought him fame as a freedom fighter. When the Duke of Montrose, one of the leading Scottish noblemen, seized Rob Roy's property as a payment for a debt, a quarrel between both men ensued, in which Rob Roy enjoyed the protection of the pro-English Duke of Argyll. As a result of this quarrel (which began around the time of the 1715 Jacobite Rising, and lasted into the 1720s) Rob Roy was imprisoned, but later pardoned, and died in peace at his family home.

Rob Roy

In Scott's historical novel, the outlaw's moral ambivalence remains visible, but he does not dominate the scene, and the historical details of his personal life are interwoven with the affairs of state and the Stuart cause. In many ways, *Rob Roy* is similar to *Waverley* that had centred on the ultimate 1745 Jacobite rebellion (which only four years after the event had featured in *Tom Jones* VII–XII, but seen from an English point of view). Moreover, the reader of both novels will also detect again the pattern that Scott had tried out in his earlier verse narratives. Scott's historical novels, too, are set at a moment of crisis in national history, and told retrospectively, perhaps by a fictional eyewitness and narrator such as Francis Osbaldistone who lays down the outlaw's story in his 'memoirs'. (In *Rob Roy*, Scott is clearly referring back to Defoe a century earlier, both in his general handling of point of view and in the motto prefixed to chap. 16, which quotes Robinson Crusoe's discovery of Friday's footprint.) Further authentication is achieved through the appearance of a few, powerful historical personages (noblemen or royalty) as minor characters in the novel. The protagonist (usually no real historical person, but an invented character) remains a **neutral hero**, an Englishman who is granted access – and likewise introduces the English reader – to all the parties in the conflict (as before in Lady Morgan's *The Wild Irish Girl* and in Maria Edgeworth's *The Absentee*). In a cross-cultural sense, too, the protagonist assumes the function of a go-between and cicerone, and this function explains also the bipartite structure of *Rob Roy*. The first half of Scott's novel is set in Northumbria and narrates Osbaldistone's experiences with his uncle's family (all of them Jacobites), centring on the growing love relationship with his cousin Diana Vernon and the mounting antagonism to his other cousin Rashleigh Osbaldistone, who also has a love interest in her. After such a slow start, the scene moves first to Lowland Glasgow and then to the Scottish Highlands; the novel's action moves at a faster pace, including much sword-fighting; and characters such as Nicol Jarvie, a *bailie* (judge) from Glasgow, and Rob Roy the Highlander (who had hitherto appeared only in disguise) come into the fore. These two memorable characters lend a hand to thwart Rashleigh's intrigues, which are central to the complex plot. Rashleigh's vile and vengeful schemes are first of all directed against a love match between his cousins Francis and Diana as well as against the Osbaldistone family fortune (I.17). Then, Rashleigh's dealings – including outright robbery, still committed together with an impoverished

and embittered Rob Roy – both sully Francis's reputation and implicate financial difficulties for the chiefs of the Highland clans
(I.7–10). Ultimately, such dealings of Rashleigh, a Jacobite agent,
accelerate the move towards a Stuart rebellion (II.9). This is suppressed also with the help of Francis Osbaldistone and of Rob
Roy, who has got to know his real enemies and turned his back
on the Jacobites, and who is to kill Rashleigh in a fight – which
paves the way for a happy ending.

Rob Roy, which had been written by Scott on his publisher's
suggestion in just eight months, came out as a **three-decker** (three-
volume) **novel** on New Year's Eve 1817/18, and thus signalled the
dominant form of publication of novels in Britain during the remainder of the nineteenth century. Aesthetical flaws apart, this
novel is also a good indicator of Scott's commercial success and
enduring fame: 10,000 copies were printed of the first edition,
before the novel was soon turned into a stage-play (1819). It was
accompanied by a musical overture (composed by Hector Berlioz,
1838), then adapted as a full-length comic opera (*Rob Roy; or, The
Thistle and the Rose* by Reginald de Koven, Detroit 1894) and afterwards turned repeatedly into films (1911, 1913, 1922, 1953). The
film version directed by Michael Caton-Jones in 1995 (starring
Liam Neeson as Rob Roy) fed on the popularity of the Highlander's story, but was not meant to be a proper adaptation of Scott's
novel – it attempts to be more true to the personal record, and
it is generally less interested in the then-contemporary political
background than in Family Values as a cultural theme.

However, the Gothic romance was not completely eclipsed by   *Ivanhoe*
historical novels such as *Waverley* (1814), *Rob Roy* (1817) or *The
Heart of Mid-Lothian* (1818). Walter Scott blurred the distinction
himself when he chose the subtitle *A Romance* for *Ivanhoe* (1819),
his attempt at translating his new formula to the Middle Ages. In
this clash of (Anglo-Saxon, Norman and Jewish) cultures in the
past, at the time when Richard Lionheart is away on the Third
Crusade (1189–92), the neutral hero is Sir Wilfred of Ivanhoe, a
Saxon nobleman who supports King Richard against Prince John.
He is also a man who is loved and nursed by the daughter of a
Jewish merchant (Rebecca), while he in turn loves and wins a
Saxon lady (Rowena) courted by Norman noblemen. With Robin
Hood and his Merry Men, Scott – a truly Romantic novelist –
also included characters from folklore and legend in his cast.

Moreover, Scott did comply with audiences won over from the Gothic romances in the character of Ulrica of Torquilstone, who is said once to have been the cause for a Norman nobleman to kill his father, and who is then seen, in one of the novel's climactic scenes, as instrumental in the capture and destruction of the Norman castle of Torquilstone. This old 'madwoman in the attic' (Gilbert and Gubar 1979) that sets fire to a castle and perishes in the flames looks forward to both Charlotte Brontës's Victorian novel *Jane Eyre* and to its postcolonial rewriting in the novel *Wide Sargasso Sea* by Jean Rhys – but this is already another story.

Scott's Use of Language   *Ivanhoe* was Scott's first historical narrative that was set outside Scotland throughout, and moreover much further in the past than in his other novels. Historical accuracy, and a truthful rendering of facts, was therefore much more difficult to achieve. This time, Scott could not rely on his great knowledge of documents about the details of Scottish history, and this is one reason why from the third edition of 1822 onwards, *Ivanhoe* was published as part of a collection entitled **Historical Romances**. Indeed, when departing from his initial conception of a setting two or three generations ago (the subtitle of *Waverley* describes the distance between its readers and the historical events depicted as *Sixty Years Since*), Scott had to make concessions, for instance with regard to language. While the Scottish group of 'Waverley Novels' is distinguished by an attempt at narrative realism with regard to the characters' speech – many of them speak varieties of Scots, the regional dialect, in a manner that can be understood by 'South Britons' – this will not do for the presentation of medieval characters. Instead of "writing the dialogue of the piece in Anglo-Saxon or Norman-French", Scott explicitly addressed the multilingualism of the period in the first two chapters of the novel, and then settled for a compromise, a kind of "modern Gothic" half way between the Middle Ages and his own time ("Dedicatory Epistle", Scott 1937: xlvii, lii). The speech of Saxon and Norman characters alike was generally modernised, yet peppered with **archaisms** from Early Modern English. The words in which Prince John addresses 'Locksley' (i.e. Robin Hood) may serve as an illustration: "'Fellow,' said Prince John, 'I guessed by thy insolent babble thou wert no true lover of the long-bow, and I see thou darest not adventure thy skill among such merry-men as stand yonder.'" (chap.13, 1937: 180–81).

Sir Walter Scott remained one of the best-selling authors all over Europe throughout the nineteenth century. With both his historical novels and his romances, he was a strong influence on all those interested in the revival of cultural memory. Some writers of historical fiction, such as Edward Bulwer-Lytton (*The Last Days of Pompeii*, 1834), wrote back in time to Antiquity even, while others applied the pattern to different regions, such as James Fenimore Cooper (*Leatherstocking Tales*, 1823–41), Victor Hugo (*Nôtre-Dame de Paris*, 1831) and Alexandre Dumas *père* (in the cloak-and-dagger romance *Les trois mousquetaires*, 1844), or Lew Tolstoy (*War and Peace*, 1869). The success of *Ivanhoe* is also mirrored in its adaptations. Apart from being followed up by a parodistic sequel (W. M. Thackeray's *Rebecca and Rowena: A Romance upon Romance,* 1850), this historical romance, too, was adapted as an opera (by Giacomo Rossini in 1826, and by several other composers). In Hollywood, Scott's novel informed not only *Ivanhoe* (1952, dir. Richard Thorpe and starring Robert Taylor), but also *The Adventures of Robin Hood* (1938, dir. Michael Curtiz and starring Errol Flynn).

Guiding Questions and Exercises

1. Relate Daniel Defoe's *Robinson Crusoe* (1719) to either Aphra Behn's *Oroonoko* (1688) or J. M. Coetzee's *Foe* (1986) with regard to their theme and form.

2. Characterise Fielding's conception of the novel. In which way does his narrative technique differ from that of his predecessors Defoe and Richardson?

3. Compare either the adaptation to the screen of *Tom Jones* by Tony Richardson (1963, with a screenplay by John Osborne) or the TV series made of *Moll Flanders* by David Attwood (1996, based on a script by Andrew Davies) to their originals. What are the specific characteristics of each version, and how does their individual historical context show?

4. Explain the difference between the 'Terror' and the 'Horror' type of Gothic romance.

5. Relate Jane Austen's *Pride and Prejudice* to Helen Fielding's *Bridget Jones's Diary* (1996) and its sequel with regard to its form and the presentation of gender relations. Moreover, include the BBC TV adaptation of Austen's novel (directed by

Andrew Langton, 1995) and the film versions of Fielding's novels (by Sharon Maguire, 2001 and Beeban Kidron, 2004, which are also based on screenplays by Andrew Davies) in your discussion of intertextual and intermedial relations.

6. Walter Scott is regarded as the creator of the historical novel. Describe the political and cultural context of the *Waverley Novels*. Point out the main features of the historical novel, in distinction from historical romances and Gothic romances. To what extent can Scott's novels be called 'Romantic'?

7. Compare Walter Scott's *Waverley* (1814) or *Rob Roy* (1817) to either Lady Morgan's *The Wild Irish Girl* (1806) or Maria Edgeworth's *The Absentee* (1812).

The Literature of the Victorian Age and of the Early Twentieth Century (c. 1830–c. 1920)

Summary

Victorian Values, e. g. those connected with gender relations and female stereotypes, show in 'three-decker' (three-volume) novels from Dickens to Hardy as well as in the non-fictional prose of the period, and also in the banning of provocative books from circulating libraries. Dickens, the best-selling novelist, dominated the literary world in his lifetime, and thus came close to the artist's ideal of autonomy. Dickens was involved in crucial developments within the manner of literary communication – from the social problem novel as a new type of serialised fiction to changes in copyright law – which is why he is put centre-stage. There, he often found himself as one of the first writers to offer public readings from his works. Professional dramatists such as Oscar Wilde and G.B. Shaw excelled in witty comedies; others who wrote for the London and Dublin stages engaged in melodrama, in well-made (problem) plays and in peasant plays. The Dramatic Monologue is an innovation in the varied poetry from Tennyson to Yeats.

Authors, Publishers and Readers: The Changing Face of Literary Communication in Britain and Ireland

Although Queen Victoria (1819–1901) and Charles Dickens (1812–70) met only once, when the monarch granted the novelist a private interview three months before his death, both were seen as figureheads of their respective realm for the greater part of the period here under review. The career of Dickens, the pre-eminent Victorian novelist, is in many ways a good example for the development of authorship and artistic autonomy, of pub-

Book Illustration: An
Example of Collabora-
tive Production

lishing and copyright, and of reading and the response to fiction in the Victorian Age. At the time of Victoria's accession in 1837, Dickens, aged 25, was already England's most popular and best-paid author, who could change publishers when he thought it fit to do so. After John Macrone (*Sketches by 'Boz'* 1836) and beside Richard Bentley (*Oliver Twist*, 1837–39), Dickens went to publishers Chapman and Hall, first for *The Pickwick Papers* (1836–37) and then for *Nicholas Nickleby* (1838–39), to stay there up to the publication of *A Christmas Carol* (1843).

Together with Dickens, Chapman and Hall established the illustrated serial novel in monthly parts at the cost of one shilling. In contrast to their modern paperback reprints, Victorian novels were frequently accompanied by illustrations that were produced during composition (see Harvey 1970; Ray 1976; Steig 1978). Dickens was at first singled out to produce stories to go with a visual sequence. He soon reversed that relationship, however, in his close collaboration with illustrators such as George Cruickshank (1792–1878) on *Sketches by 'Boz'* and *Oliver Twist*, with 'Phiz' (Hablot K. Browne, 1815–82) from *The Pickwick Papers* to *A Tale of Two Cities* (1859), and with John Leech (1817–64) on *A Christmas Carol*. Leech's successor as principal cartoonist for the comic weekly *Punch* was John Tenniel (1820–1914), who was chosen by Lewis Carroll to illustrate the *Alice* books (see chap. 4.5.5). Dickens's contemporary and competitor, the novelist W.M. Thackeray (1811–63), also worked for *Punch*, which serialised his combination of satirical prose and pictorial sketches that became *The Book of Snobs* (1846–48). Thackeray provided vignettes and full-page illustrations for the individual chapters of his novel *Vanity Fair* (1847–48), which he brought out in the form of illustrated monthly parts pioneered by Dickens (see Shillingsburg 1992). There were more writers than just Thackeray who were their own illustrators: Edward Lear (1812–88) drew sketches for his travel writing, limericks and nonsense verse; Dante Gabriel Rossetti (1828–82) embellished his own Pre-Raphaelite poetry as well as Tennyson's verse; and Beatrix Potter (1866–1943) famously illustrated her own children's books. At a time when the professional illustrator Aubrey Beardsley (1872–98) created Aestheticist and provocative designs alike for editions of Alexander Pope's *Rape of the Lock* and of Oscar Wilde's *Salome*, Rossetti's friend, the writer and designer William Morris (1834–96), set up a **small in-**

dependent press in order to regain artistic control over such collaborative forms of production. Like Morris, who instigated the Arts and Crafts Movement and who produced beautiful books at The Kelmscott Press (1891–98), Virginia and Leonard Woolf also aimed at such independence from publishers when they set up The Hogarth Press (1917 ff., see chap. 4.4).

In some instances, the illustrations themselves had a lasting impact, as when Sidney Paget (1860–1908) contributed his share to the recognisable physiognomy of Sherlock Holmes in *The Strand Magazine*. In other instances, contradictions between narration and illustration allowed for a distinctly different interpretation of the whole. In Cruickshank's quite independent portrait of "Fagin in the Condemned Cell", from the ending of *Oliver Twist*, the master criminal appears as a judicial victim rather than a person singled out for poetic justice. In a visual image at the ending of *Vanity Fair*, by contrast, we are presented with a surprise, and a murderer in disguise. In Thackeray's own sketch of "Becky's second appearance in the character of Clytemnestra" and its caption (chap. 67), Becky's complicity in the death of Jos Sedley is much more hinted at than in the narration, where this is merely a possible reading between the lines. (See Gilmour 1982: 55–61, Maack 1991: 79–86.)

Dickens's contract with Chapman and Hall was solicited by his friend John Forster (1812–76), who is of interest himself because he functioned variously as literary adviser to the publishers, as Dickens's literary agent (and eventually his biographer), and as a literary critic. The new function of a **publisher's reader and literary adviser** called for sound judgment on both the literary and the commercial value of manuscripts submitted for publication. Edward Garnett (1868–1937) proved valuable to a series of publishers, and most influential for the career of novelists Joseph Conrad, John Galsworthy, E. M. Forster and D. H. Lawrence. The list of leading **publishing companies** included those of long standing such as Longman (1724 ff.) and also Blackwood (1804 ff.), who had contracted in George Eliot one of Dickens's main competitors. In addition, others whose names are still well known today, albeit as academic publishers, set up rival business during the Victorian Age. George Routledge launched his company at the beginning of Dickens's career, in 1836, and made money with a Railway Library series of cheap reprints. Macmillan followed in

Publishers and
Publisher's Readers

1843, first with Evangelical literature and soon also with a profitable list of children's books (including *Tom Brown's Schooldays* and *Alice's Adventures in Wonderland*), before the family firm gained from the work of Thomas Hardy and Rudyard Kipling.

Literary Periodicals

Dickens's move to Bradbury and Evans (printers to his former publishers) in 1844 marked a further step on the way to autonomy as an artist, as did his return – but on different terms – to Chapman and Hall in 1857 for the rest of his life. In 1850, Dickens became the editor of the **family journal** *Household Words*, a medium in which he could publish both his own novel *Hard Times* and the fiction of Elizabeth Gaskell and Wilkie Collins in weekly instalments (an experiment which had been successful with *Oliver Twist*, although it failed with successive novels in 1840–41). After his break with Bradbury and Evans, Dickens terminated *Household Words* and started a new weekly journal, *All the Year Round* (1859–95), which he published independently on his own, and which became the medium for the serialisation of *David Copperfield* (1849–50), *Bleak House* (1852–53) and *Great Expectations* (1860–61). During Dickens's lifetime, the circulation of *All the Year Round* increased from 120,000 to 300,000. New and notable, monthly magazines besides *Blackwood's 'Maga'* (1817–1981) included *Bentley's Miscellany* (1837–68), *Macmillan's Magazine* (1859–1907) and the *Cornhill Magazine* (1860–1975). The famous comic magazine *Punch* appeared weekly (1841 ff.), and from 1880, the weekly *Illustrated London News* (1842 ff.) included serialised fiction, too. For *The Strand Magazine* (1891–1950), the Sherlock Holmes stories ensured a circulation of 500,000 copies. To counter the effect of pulp fiction in 'penny dreadfuls', a younger audience was being served by the Religious Tract Society (an Evangelical publisher) with less sensational fare in weeklies such as *The Boy's Own Paper* (1879–1967, starting with a circulation of 200,000) and its sister publication *The Girl's Own Paper* (1880–1965; see Turner 1948, Carpenter and Prichard 1984). In addition to the continuously influential *Edinburgh Review* (Longman, 1802–1929) and *Quarterly Review* (John Murray, 1809–1967), new **reviews** sprang up to become influential for their literary criticism, such as *The Athenaeum* (1828–1921), the *Saturday Review* (1855–1938), *The Fortnightly Review* (Chapman and Hall, 1865–1954) and the *Times Literary Supplement* (1902 ff.). The reviewers now took fiction seriously, as Dickens and his competitors had achieved a breakthrough

Fig. 4.2
The Strand Magazine

for the consideration of novels as literary forms of art. (See Ford 1955, Altick 1957, Webb 1980.)

While literary agents and publisher's readers gave their advice to writers and publishers, it was the reviewers who provided guidance to a steadily increasing number of readers. This increase can be explained not just with demographic developments (e.g. the rise in the population of England and Wales from 9.2 millions in 1801 over 13.9 millions in 1831 to 32.5 millions in 1901), but also with a parallel **increase in literacy**, which however could differ markedly in terms of region, class and gender. The available statistics for the year 1841 show that in many parts of Ireland, more than 70% of the population were *illiterate*, while in England and Wales, 67.3% of males and 51.1% of females counted as *literate*. At the end of the Queen's reign, in 1900, the level of literacy among her subjects in England and Wales had reached about 97% for males and females alike. (See Altick 1957: 171; Edwards 1973: 226–29; Moody et al. 1984: IX, 70; Flint 1993.) However, the figures need to be treated with some caution, and the exact nature of the impact of **educational reforms** is also a matter of debate. But there is no doubt that the fight against illiteracy had top priority for the various attempts to improve elementary education, beginning with the eighteenth-century Sunday school movement and the rural Irish hedge schools (where barns were converted into classrooms). The replacement of hedge schools by English-language National Schools in Ireland in 1831 not only led to the creation of Irish National Readers as textbooks, but was turned into a literary theme: already within the 1830s in William Carleton's tales, and again in 1980 in Brian Friel's stage-play *Translations* (see chaps. 4.5.4 and 5.2.4). In late Victorian times, the state became more involved in elementary education in Britain. Forster's Education Act (1870) for England and Wales was followed by a similar act in Scotland (1872) that went even further by making elementary education compulsory. This was adopted in England and Wales in 1880, after English elementary schools had introduced 'Eng. Lit.' as a subject in 1876. Being a best-selling novelist himself, Victoria's Prime Minister Disraeli certainly approved of such a development, and it was accidentally within the same year that he created the new title of Empress of India for the Queen, and thus signalled a Greater Britain. The expanding **Empire** was indeed also affected by changes in the educational system. With his

New Readers and
Old Reading Habits

1835 "Minute on Indian Education", the historian and politician Thomas Babington Macaulay succeeded in persuading the government to adopt the English language in colonial schools in India. This helped to spread British literature abroad, for educational and recreational purposes, and arguably implanted the Empire in the heart of the children. The publishing company of Thomas Nelson and Sons made a significant impact in that direction: by the 1850s, they were the largest printing and publishing house in Scotland, known to be the publisher of R.M. Ballantyne's classic tale of adventure, *Coral Island* (1858), and later also of the Bible. After the 1870/1872 Education Acts, the company moved into the new and expanding markets linked to education and Empire, and became the major supplier of textbooks for Britain and its colonies. Nelson's Royal Readers and related series replaced the Irish National Readers of the 1830s that had also been used in Canada, Australia and New Zealand, but were found to be unsuitable. After 1900, the company's name was moreover linked to their cheap reprint series Nelsons Sixpenny Classics (later renamed Nelsons Classics), which included novels by Dickens, too.

In a period in which the reading public showed a marked increase in literacy and in extent, 'reading a novel' very often meant reading aloud in the family circle or to another audience. George Henry Lewes, the influential Victorian reviewer and partner of the novelist George Eliot, moreover recommended such a reading habit as a critical exercise. He reflected on "what a severe test that is, how the reading aloud permits no skipping, no evasion of weariness, but brings both merits and defects into stronger relief by forcing the mind to dwell on them" (Lewes 1859/1968: 151 – a view that might today be applied to audiobook versions). In Lewes's own experience, by the way, Jane Austen's novels passed the test of reading aloud well even on a fourth turn, while Henry Fielding's *Tom Jones* and Charlotte Brontë's *Jane Eyre* allegedly disqualified themselves immediately (151–52). This impression, however, might also have to do with a certain lack of gentility in those two novelists in their representation of gender relations. One function of Victorian reviewers such as Lewes was to indicate to middle-class families exactly which reading matter was not harmful, but 'useful' and genteel.

> This almost universal habit of reading aloud had its effect upon the books that were being produced. The test of a really good book became,

for a number of people, its fitness for being read aloud in the family circle, and this caused a certain class of writers to show an excessive carefulness in avoiding the mention of anything that could be called indelicate or improper. (Cruse 1930: 17)

In this way, reading as a performance affected the response to fiction as well as its creation, and it also pertained to *The Family Shakespeare* and other 'bowdlerised' editions (see chap. 4.5.5).

Old habits die hard indeed. "Reader, I married him": this is a singular example (from the last chapter of *Jane Eyre*) of a narrator who intimately addresses a *single* reader – perhaps in a railway compartment. In how far the railways and a new sense of time did affect not only the distribution and reading of literature, but also produced a new 'railway style' of prose markedly different from Neoclassical syntax, was a question that was already raised by contemporary critics (see Breen 1857: 141, cited in Davis 2002: 213). What cannot be disputed is that reading changed over time in that more books were (a) read less often, and (b) often alone. A few statistics may be helpful here to see Dickens in a general context. One of the noticeable developments in the publishing sector in Britain was the **steady increase of new titles** per year, from roughly 100 up to about 1750, to 600 by 1825, rising to 6,000 titles before about 1900. They could now be printed in larger editions. The mass production of literature for a mass audience was made possible by the introduction of the steam engine into the print shop (the first steam press was used to print *The Times* in 1814). It has been estimated that during Queen Victoria's reign (1837–1901), some 3,500 novelists published a total of over 40,000 novels in Britain. Dickens alone contributed 15 novels and 5 Christmas Books within the first 34 years of that reign. Dickens continued to dominate the scene throughout, until the first decades after his death. His record sales testify to the considerable enlargement of the audience, and to the esteem in which novels were held. The usual **size of editions** in the nineteenth century amounted, on average, to around 750 copies for a serious book, while the ordinary circulating library novel, throughout the century, seldom had an edition of more than 1,000 or 1,250 copies. Bestselling exceptions from the rule were e.g. Dickens's *A Christmas Carol* (1843: 6,000 sold on publication day, and a total of 15,000 within a year), George Eliot's *The Mill on the Floss* (1860: 6,000 in 3 months), *Tom Brown's Schooldays* by Thomas Hughes (1857: 11,000 in 9 months), Rider Haggard's *King Solomon's Mines* (1885: 31,000 in 15 months), and *Dr Jekyll and Mr Hyde* by R.L. Stevenson (1886: 40,000 in 6 months). With both serialised novels and cheap reprints, the numbers were even higher. A reprint of Charlotte Brontë's 1848 novel *Jane Eyre* sold 35,000 in 2 years (1857–58), and when a reissue of R.D. Blackmore's historical romance *Lorna Doone* (1869) was due to appear in 1897, the exceptional number of 100,000 were ordered. By comparison, in 1838–39, the monthly numbers of *Nicholas Nickleby* had sold 50,000 copies, and though there were less successful novels in between, the first part of Dickens's last and unfinished novel *The Mystery of Edwin Drood* reached the same figure at the time of his death. As a matter of fact, nineteenth-century fiction could not compete with either religious texts nor with self-help books: in 1881, the Revised Version of the New Testament sold 1 million copies on publication day, and a reprint of Mrs Beeton's *Book of Household Management*, which had first appeared in 1859, sold 2 million copies between 1861 and 1870. Still, the overall figures for Dickens's work remain exceptional:

> In 1871, the "penny edition" of *Oliver Twist* (weekly numbers, monthly parts) sold 150,000 in three weeks; *David Copperfield* sold 83,000 in an equal period. In 1882 it was reported that the total sale of Dickens' works, in England alone, in the twelve years since his death amounted to 4,239,000 volumes. (Altick 1957: 384, with further reference. For comparison, see also Altick 1969, 1986; Patten 1978.)

Circulating Libraries and Censorship

Fiction reviewed and possibly recommended was available in **circulating libraries** such as Mudie's (1842–1937). W.H. Smith's, a leading retailer (bookseller) with a monopoly in railway bookstalls since 1848, also ran a lending library (1860–1961). Three volumes were the norm for first editions of novels between Scott's *Ivanhoe* (1819) and Hardy's *Tess of the D'Urbervilles* (1891). At a time when the weekly wage of compositors (as the highest-paid craftsmen) was set at 36 shillings, their work's product, the so-called **'three-decker novels'** were sold at 31 shillings and sixpence. Due to pressure from the circulating libraries, both the format and the initially high price remained fixed until 1894. By comparison, an annual subscription of 21 shillings gave Mudie's clients the right to borrow one volume of a novel at a time. Seen the other way round, the individual tomes of any 'three-decker' could be lent to three clients simultaneously, maximising the profit for the commercial library, and the output of the publishing industry, too (see above). Circulating libraries, just like critics, were institutions that could make or break a writer's career. By 1861, Mudie's purchased 180,000 volumes a year, and could thus exercise strict control on the contents and their conformity with Family Values. When Mudie's in 1859 objected to the frank treatment of sexuality in *The Ordeal of Richard Feverel*, and banned the book from their library shelves, they did fatal damage to the sales of the novel, and to Meredith's reputation (see Sutherland 1989: 481). Banned by Mudie's – with a few (bracketed) additions, a counter-canon of taboo-breaking novels and their offensive topics looks like this:

Banned by Mudie's: a counter-canon of taboo-breaking novels and their offensive topics

1859	George Meredith	*The Ordeal of Richard Feverel*	Sexual frankness
1870	Wilkie Collins	*Man and Wife*	Criticism of British marriage laws
1873	Wilkie Collins	*The New Magdalen*	Prostitution
1879	Wilkie Collins	*The Fallen Leaves*	Prostitution
1885	George Meredith	*Diana of the Crossways*	New Woman before the term was coined; divorce
1885	George Moore	*A Mummer's Wife*	Wife's adultery and divorce
1886	Wilkie Collins	*The Evil Genius*	Wife's adultery and divorce
1891	Thomas Hardy	*Tess of the D'Urbervilles*	Seduction of innocent girl, single motherhood, lay baptism
1894	George Moore	*Esther Waters*	Seduction, single motherhood, sexual frankness
1895	Thomas Hardy	*Jude the Obscure*	Anti-marriage tendency
1895	Grant Allen	*The Woman Who Did*	New Woman: sexual liberty
(1890s	'Walter'	*My Secret Life*	Pornography)
1909	H.G. Wells	*Ann Veronica: A Modern Love Story*	New Woman
(1912/1971	E.M. Forster	*Maurice*	Male homosexuality)
1913	D.H. Lawrence	*Sons and Lovers*	Sexual frankness
1915, 1920	D.H. Lawrence	*The Rainbow* and *Women in Love*	Sexual frankness
(1916	Ada Leverson	*Love at Second Sight*	Wife's adultery and divorce)
1922	James Joyce	*Ulysses*	Sexual frankness
1928	D.H. Lawrence	*Lady Chatterley's Lover*	Sexual frankness
1928	Radclyffe Hall	*The Well of Loneliness*	Female homosexuality

In line with the views of 'Mrs Grundy' (the personification of Victorian Prudery and conventional morality), the candid treatment of sexuality, but also the portrayal of a wife's adultery and of divorce were reasons to ban a book from the lending library. Such unofficial **censorship of literature** added to the provisions of the 1857 Obscene Publications Act. This was accompanied by the discrimination of homosexuality under the Criminal Law Amendment Act, which was in force between 1885 and 1967, and which played a crucial role in the trial of Oscar Wilde in 1895. (See chap. 4.2.3.)

Cut-Price Offers Made to a Mass Readership

Apart from lending libraries and the serialisation in (two-penny) weekly instalments or monthly (shilling) parts, **cheap reprints** meant a further opportunity for readers to strike a bargain. In the 1830s, Richard Bentley's reissue of novels from the Long Eighteenth Century were part of a canonisation process that was continued later with Nelsons Classics and Everyman's Library (J. M. Dent, 1904 ff.). With his series of Standard Novels (1831 ff.), Bentley moreover set an example for the republication of more recent fiction, for instance also in the Tauchnitz Edition (1841 ff.) produced in Leipzig for the Continental market. A best-selling historical romance by a friend of Dickens, Bulwer Lytton's *The Last Days of Pompeii*, is a good example: originally published by Bentley (1834), the novel came out with Chapman and Hall when they began to issue cheap editions of Dickens's and of other novels (1847). Later, Routledge bought the copyright for a reissue (1854) in the Railway Library, a reprint series that sold 1,300 volumes between 1848 and 1898. By buying back his copyrights from Bradbury and Evans in 1861, Dickens gained control over all the cheap reprints of his novels, which had further consolidated his popularity with the reading public, and turned out to be a profitable business for all sides concerned. Cheap reprints made up as 'railway novels' or 'yellowbacks' (the precursors of our paperbacks) were sold for one or two shillings and appeared in one volume – a format which in 1895 became the norm also for hardback first editions. In that year, Hardy's scandalous last novel *Jude the Obscure* became one of the first successful examples (selling 20,000 in three months). The old as well as the new format of publication had been dictated by the commercial lending libraries such as Mudie's and W. H. Smith's to the publishers. For them, new rivals arose with civic institutions such as the London

Library (co-founded by Dickens and Carlyle in 1841) or Dublin's Central Catholic Library (established in 1922), which offered the same services, often at reduced costs or free of charge. In the bookshop, the slashed introduction price of 6 shillings for the new one-volume format remained constant for the first half of the twentieth century. Together with the institutionalisation of business relations in the Society of Authors (1883) and the Publisher's Association (1895), such stability was achieved through the **Net Book Agreement** between publishers and booksellers. The NBA effectively ruled out price dumping while it lasted (1900–97), and thus protected individual publishers and booksellers, and small businesses in general, against ruinous discounts by their rivals.

From such a stability of the British book market, authors profited, too (and they had done well before): facing a growing number of readers eager for new fictional objects of instruction and recreation, the authorship of fiction became a profitable business.

Authors' Earnings

Dickens's independence from his publishers can already be seen in the fact that he retained the entire copyright for *Nicholas Nickleby*, and only agreed to lease it to the publishers Chapman and Hall for five years following serialisation. Copyright continued to be a vexed question. The sensational success of *The Pickwick Papers* (1836–37), Dickens's first serial publication, can also be measured from the many instances of plagiarism, imitations, and adaptations for the stage, all of which testify to the shortcomings of **copyright law in Britain** before the passing of the 1842 Copyright Act, in which Dickens had a vested interest. The period of protection was prolonged from 28 years (and the rest of the writer's life, 1814 Copyright Act) to 42 years (or eventually life plus 7 years). It was only with the 1911 Copyright Act that the period of protection was further extended to an author's lifetime plus 50 years. **International Copyright** was a different matter altogether. After the American Independence – including the independence from British copyright legislation – separate editions of English-language books were published and distributed in Britain (and its Empire) and in the USA. This led to different spelling and punctuation as a result of the publishers' individual **house-styling**, and, more importantly, to book piracy on both sides of the Atlantic. (Short stories and novellas presented less of a problem when they were made available in magazines for audiences on either side simul-

Copyright Law, and a Note on Anglo-American Literary Relations

taneously.) On his 1842 tour of America, Dickens pointed to the lack of protection of best-selling British books in the USA, which however pertained also to Routledge's cheap pirated reprints of *Uncle Tom's Cabin* in 1852. (Of this top seller of the century, 1,500,000 copies were bought in the first year in Britain and its Empire.) Trade relations went normal only with the passing of the 1891 US Copyright Act (Chace Act) that protected the rights of non-American authors. Frances Hodgson Burnett, the author of the juvenile novel *Little Lord Fauntleroy* (1886; see chap. 4.5.5) who had moved to Tennessee, brought about a British equivalent and legal precedent that *vice versa* secured American authors the control over the publication of their work in Britain.

While the British and the postcolonial American markets for printed literature increasingly separated from each other during the nineteenth century, there were still transatlantic connections, old and new. As far as oral literature was concerned, traditional ballads such as "Barbara Allen" were sung on both sides of the Atlantic (for different versions, see Friedman 1961). Several notable American writers crossed the Atlantic and made an impact in Britain and Europe. James Fenimore Cooper (1789–1851) adapted Walter Scott's concept of the historical novel to colonial America in his *Leatherstocking Tales* (1823–41), and struck a personal friendship with Scott during an extended stay in Europe (1826–32). Henry Wadsworth Longfellow (1807–82) twice travelled to Europe at the same time (1826–29, 1835), to become one of the most celebrated poets of the age on both sides of the Atlantic. Harriet Beecher Stowe (1811–96) went even three times during the 1850s, after the phenomenal success of her anti-slavery novel *Uncle Tom's Cabin* (1851–52), and made friends with the British women writers Elizabeth Barrett Browning and George Eliot. From 1867, Mark Twain (1835–1910) was celebrated on a series of visits to Europe, which resulted in *The Innocents Abroad* (1869) and in his parody of medieval myth, *A Connecticut Yankee at King Arthur's Court* (1889). Another American writer of fiction, Henry James (1843–1916), did not only settle in Britain for good, but also created his hallmark **'international theme'** from the experience of innocent Americans abroad, such as the eponymous heroine of the novella *Daisy Miller* (1879). In a funny manner, the international or transatlantic theme informs also Oscar Wilde's "The Canterville Ghost" (1887; see chap. 4.5.5). In the twentieth century, the American Modernist poets Ezra Pound and T. S. Eliot followed the example of Henry James, to settle permanently in Europe, and with Eliot likewise becoming a naturalised Briton.

When British writers crossed the Atlantic in the reverse direction, money was usually the incentive. It was Charles Dickens who set an example in this field, too. In 1842, Dickens – already a man of transatlantic fame – toured the USA and Canada privately for the first time, and was at first favourably received. He published his impressions as *American Notes* within the same year, and reworked his experience into the American episodes in his novel *Martin Chuzzlewhit* (1843–44). The lack of International Copyright, which was to his disadvantage on the American book market, and the personal observation of Southern slavery, however, added a bitter note to his published account, which in turn caused some resentment in the USA. Dickens returned once more in 1867–68, this time it took the form of a reading tour with more than 70 public readings from his work. To the writer's satisfaction, the American tour ended with the handsome profit of £19,000. In Britain, Dickens had staged his first public readings (from *A Christmas Carol*) in 1853 as part of adult education. In addition to the occasional 'charity' reading, Dickens started to give 'paid' readings in 1858, and went on an extended tour through England, Scotland and Ireland. Three years later, with the beginning of regular tours that lasted until the writer's death, the novelist embarked *de facto* on a second successful career as a performer, with altogether 472 public readings to his credit. In 1869, after his return from the second American tour, Dickens added "Sikes and Nancy" (based on *Oliver Twist*) as the last new item to his repertoire – a strenuous piece of performance, which may have hastened his death. (See Schlicke 1999: 482–86, Collins 1975, Andrews 2006.)

Public Readings and Lectures

|Fig. 4.3
Dickens Giving a Public Reading

The enthusiasm over Dickens's dramatised public readings was certainly exceptional. However, the fact that the general public endorsed such communal forms of storytelling over and above the convention of reading aloud, and approved of such intermediality, is also borne out by the great number of stage adaptations of his and of Scott's novels. Even in an age of mass publications, and of the common reader who could read for himself (Altick 1957), such audiences clearly did not only endorse reading aloud, but also wanted to see prose narratives *performed*, too (see Ford 1979; Bolton 1987, 1992). For a gifted amateur actor like Dickens, therefore, such public readings turned out to be a financially more remunerative alternative to those public lectures that were first delivered at academic institutions in Britain and then published as a book (see chap. 4.2.1). However, in the USA, he had made use of the public lecture circuit that had become established in the nineteenth century for a general audience, and that also attracted other writers from Britain with a promise of easy money. After the success of *Vanity Fair* (1847–48), W. M. Thackeray gave a series of literary lectures on writers such as Swift, Fielding and Sterne (*The English Humourists of the Eighteenth Century*, 1851), which he then delivered on his first American tour (1852–53). He followed this up with a second and likewise profitable tour to the USA, this time lecturing on the eighteenth-century Hanoverian Kings of Britain and the history of the Georgian Age (*The Four Georges*, 1855–56, publ. 1860). The next to exploit the American lecture circuit after Dickens's death were Wilkie Collins (1824–89 and Oscar Wilde (1854–1900). Collins toured America in 1873–74, when his friend Dickens was no longer a competitor for him as a writer of sensational fiction. Wilde was at the beginning of his literary career when he embarked on a lecture tour of the USA and Canada throughout most of the year 1882, with great success. This was the occasion when Wilde is said to have given an example of his spontaneous conversational wit by replying to the question of a customs official, "Do you have anything to declare?" – "Only my genius". Wilde went on to become one of the most witty and fashionable of Victorian playwrights, but likewise one of the most famous victims of Victorian Values (see chaps. 4.2.3 and 4.3).

Guiding Questions and Exercises

1. Rehearse the main stages in Dickens's way to autonomy as an artist, and point out the general significance of each move.
2. Point out the roles and influence of illustrators, publishers, periodicals, lending libraries and the state for literary communication in the period under review.

3. In which way did new technology such as the steam engine and the railways make an impact on the network of printing, publishing and distribution?
4. How did older and oral conventions make themselves felt in literature in an age of the expansion of print?

'Victorian Values': Materialism, Morals and Mentalities in the Literature of the Period | 4.2

Utilitarianism, Darwinism and Religious Belief in the Victorian Age | 4.2.1

Victorian Values and a Victorian world-view are documented in the non-fictional prose of the period and its immediate aftermath. In various series of public lectures and essays, Victorian and Edwardian scholars and critics formed general views on individual and society, nature and culture that still exert a great influence on our contemporary understanding of the world. (Useful surveys include Young 1977, Houghton 1957, Altick 1973, Reed 1975, McMurtry 1979 and Thomson 1988.) Literary and academic criticism is part of that picture. With the prestigious post of Oxford Professor of Poetry (1901–06), A[ndrew]. C[ecil]. Bradley (1851–1935) crowned his career as one of the first professors of 'Eng. Lit.'. In his *Oxford Lectures on Poetry* (1909), and more particularly in the preceding series of lectures published under the title *Shakespearean Tragedy* (1904), Bradley brought a century of Shakespeare commentary and 'character criticism' to a close (see chaps. 3.2.2 and 3.4.3). He elaborated on the topics covered in Samuel Taylor Coleridge's lectures (1808 ff.) as well as in the essays on Shakespeare as a dramatic poet by other Romantic critics such as Lamb, Hazlitt and De Quincey. In its special interest, Bradley's *Shakespearean Tragedy* contrasts with the lecture and essay *On the Idea of Comedy and of the Uses of the Comic Spirit* (1877) by the novelist and poet George Meredith (1828–1909). In his thoroughgoing analysis of the tragedies, Bradley was far from reducing his approach to unscholarly questions such as "How Many Children Had Lady Macbeth?" as successive New Critics in the 1930s and '40s alleged in order to detract from Bradley's close reading. In those instances where he showed himself not averse

Character Criticism

to performance criticism, Bradley was indeed much more up to date than they were, and he is still read today with profit. Yet it is in his concern with the individual merit of Shakespeare the dramatist, and with the individualism of his literary characters, that Bradley can be seen to epitomise a distinctive (post-)Romantic tradition that also includes Carlyle.

Cultural Criticism in Lectures and Essay Series

The Scottish historian, essayist, lecturer and critic Thomas Carlyle (1795–1881) was a champion of **Individualism**, and he was one of the great nineteenth-century mediators between Britain and Germany in the fields of literature and history. In the 1820s, Carlyle's essays on German literature, together with his biography of Schiller and his translations from the works of Goethe, paved the way for the reception of then-contemporary German authors in Britain. *The History of Frederick the Great* (1858–1865) was read by a wide readership both in Britain and in German translation. This monumental study about the King of Prussia further exemplified the views on history that Carlyle had expounded in his influential series of lectures delivered and published under the title *On Heroes, Hero-Worship, and the Heroic in History* (1837–40, publ. 1841). In these lectures, Carlyle had generalised a Romantic idea of genius and proclaimed the development of universal history to be the 'history of great men' and their actions (to be executed by ordinary men serving with an ideal of duty). For his gallery of Great Men in history, Carlyle singled out, rather idiosyncratically, heavyweights in the art of literature (Dante, Shakespeare, Samuel Johnson, Jean-Jacques Rousseau and Robert Burns) in addition to religious leaders (acknowledging the prophet Mohammed alongside the Protestant reformers Luther and John Knox) as well as powerful heads of state (Cromwell and Napoleon). Clearly, such a conception of the historical impact of superhuman individuals was radically opposed to the Communist theory of history as a series of class struggles that Karl Marx developed in his London exile at about the same time (1849–83), let alone any Feminist view on 'herstory' (i.e. history written from a woman's point of view) and gender relations (such as patriarchy). Such opposition notwithstanding, Carlyle was during his lifetime regarded as a moral institution and as a sage. With two further works written in his typically oratorical prose, he indeed exerted a great influence on contemporary British novelists. *The French Revolution: A History* (1837) inspired Dickens when he dealt with the 1790s Reign of Terror in his historical novel *A Tale of Two Cities* (1859). Taken together, those two books reinvigorated conservative Britons in their conventional view of individual freedom at home, and in their abhorrence of radical political change as practiced on the Continent. However, in his negative comparison of Victorian to medieval England in *Past and Present* (1843), Carlyle had scratched away at an all too complacent view, and argued for a reform of society (tellingly enough, through the extraordinary leadership of 'Captains of Industry'). In this way, Carlyle exerted an influence on the social realism of the 'Condition of England novels' of the 1840s, being – like Dickens – an outspoken critic of the prevailing Utilitarianism.

The social philosophy of **Utilitarianism** in the tradition of Jeremy Bentham (1748–1832) aims at the greatest possible happiness for the greatest number of people. Each individual has to make himself useful, and should not become a burden to society for long. This thinking, which led to the New Poor Law in 1834, set limits to individual freedom. To further the public good and thereby his or her own, the individual may have to toe the line. For Charles Dickens, such Utilitarian work ethics found their worst expression in the workhouse system, which he openly criticised in *Oliver Twist* (see chap. 4.5.5). John Stuart Mill (1806–73) supported but also qualified Bentham's rigorous views by trying to account for its possible consequences (which e. g. would otherwise not allow to subsidise minority art forms). Grossly simplified, John Stuart Mill could be said to have stood for everything that Carlyle did not – including a lucid prose style. Rather than on Great Men, Mill spoke on women's suffering and on women's suffrage (in the 1869 essay *The Subjection of Women*, see chap. 4.2.3). In addition, Mill confronted Carlyle directly on the issue of Emancipation from Slavery, which he applauded in a public letter known under the title "The Negro Question" (1850). *Principles of Political Economy* (1848) soon became a standard textbook in free-market economics that sidelined the works of Adam Smith (*The Wealth of Nations*, 1776) and of Thomas Robert Malthus (*Essay on the Principle of Population*, 1798). Mill's influential essays *On Liberty* (1859) and on *Utilitarianism* (serialised two years prior to its publication as a book in 1863) negotiated between the individual and society by keeping in check the rights and the 'tyrannical' tendencies of each of the two. In Mill's Utilitarian ethics, it is the usefulness of the consequences of an action that decide on the moral justification of its means. As a result, Mill's views can be cited today to oppose the censorship of free speech, but also to allow for a foreign intervention on (allegedly) humanitarian grounds.

While Mill justified Liberalism in theory, Thomas Babington Macaulay (1800–59) described its historical development: *The History of England from the Accession of James the Second* (5 vols. and still a fragment, 1848–61) is a classic example of what Herbert Butterfield in his 1931 study criticised as **The Whig Interpretation of History**, as a story of steady progress. In his constitutional history, the Whig (Liberal) MP Macaulay asserted and assiduously documented the foundational character of the Glorious Revolution (i. e. the overthrow of King James II) and the Bill of Rights (1688/89) for the constitutional monarchy and for political culture in Britain. With his memorable character sketches and through other rhetorical elements of style that he had refined as a parliamentarian orator, Macaulay deeply impressed his readers and his publisher. The sales figures for his immensely popular *History of England* (26,500 copies of the third and fourth volumes sold out in ten weeks after publication in 1855) rivalled the publication record of the novels of Scott and Dickens. Moreover, they earned Macaulay an advance of £20,000, which far exceeded the sums paid to either Walter Scott or Ann Radcliffe forty to sixty years earlier. Macaulay's *History* was brought up to date, in a more casual style, by the novelist W. M. Thackeray in *The Four Georges* (1855–56, publ. 1860), a series of lectures on the Georgian Age delivered on his second tour to the USA. (For such lectures, public readings and other aspects of transatlantic relations, see chap. 4.1) Apart from his political oratory and his work as a historian, Macaulay's name is closely connected with the "Minute on Indian Education" (1835), a memorandum on administrating the Empire that breathed the spirit of Imperialism. Macaulay advised on creating an anglophile class of native *Mimic Men* (as V. S. Naipaul characterised them in his eponymous, postcolonial novel in 1967), disparaging not only native Indian languages and literatures, but also Western cultures other than English.

Two other complex issues – the role of (elite) culture in an age of massive increase of the populace, and of religious faith in the face of Evolution Theory – became the subject of debate, and the name of Matthew Arnold (1822–88) is involved in both. The Victorian critic and poet was the son of Thomas Arnold (1795–1842), the headmaster who made Rugby School (1828–41) into a model for the English public-school system. (He was affectionately portrayed by his former pupil Thomas Hughes in the best-selling school novel *Tom Brown's Schooldays*, 1857.) For Thomas Arnold, who later excelled at Oxford as an editor of Thucydides and as a historian of Rome, a sound classical education and a religious training served to develop a sense of duty. Arnold junior continued in his father's footsteps: he became an inspector of schools (1851–86) as well as an Oxford don, as **Oxford Professor of Poetry** (1857–67). Apart from A. C. Bradley, an academic in his own right, this prestigious professorship has been given since to other notable poets such as W. H. Auden, Robert Graves, James Fenton, Seamus Heaney and Paul Muldoon. This post requires the incumbent to give a series of lectures. The published lectures of Matthew Arnold centred on Classical literature (*On Translating Homer*, 1861), on the non-English literatures of the British Isles (*On the Study of Celtic Literature*, 1867) and, most famously, on culture as an antidote against the defects of Victorian society (*Culture and Anarchy*, 1869). For such deficiencies, which were aggravated by Manchester Capitalism and industrialisation, members of all classes had to take responsibility – 'Barbarian' aristocrats, the 'Philistine' middle classes and the unlearned 'Populace' alike. Therefore, the antidote Arnold prescribed had less to do with class but with a classical canon – that is, with the study of Great Books rather than Great Men.

In poems such as "Dover Beach" (see chap. 4.4), which, though written beforehand, was conveniently published in the same year as Darwin's *Origin of Species* (1859), Arnold lamented an increasing lack of **religious faith** among his contemporaries (for which he might have cited Carlyle, Mill or Darwin as examples). Such a decrease in faith, which would have precluded an end to the Evangelical revival that in many ways was foundational for Victorian morals (see chap. 3.3.2), the clergyman and historian Charles Kingsley (1819–75) attempted to reverse in both his lectures and his novels. Today, Kingsley is read primarily out of historical interest: as a proponent of Christian Socialism as the answer to the pitfalls of industrialisation, as a champion of the theory of Evolution among the clergy (he was presented with an advance copy of Darwin's *Origin of Species*), and as one of the first writers

Religious Faith in the Face of Evolution Theory

of fantasy fiction for children (see chap. 4.5.5). At the time when Arnold concerned himself with the legacy of the Celts, Kingsley delivered a series of lectures on *The Roman and the Teuton* from the chair of Regius Professor of Modern History at Cambridge (1860–69). In the year of publication (1864), Kingsley – who was not only a professor, but also a professed Protestant – personally attacked the leading English Catholic of his time, thus inciting John Henry Newman (1801–90) to defend himself with *Apologia Pro Vita Sua*. Newman's religious autobiography (serial publication, 1864–65) is an important document of faith in Victorian times, and his controversy with Kingsley, as well as Newman's earlier conversion, tells of the relationship between Anglicans and Catholics three hundred years after they went their separate ways. Like Kingsley, Newman had risen in the Church of England, yet he had supported the **Oxford Movement** which looked for a *via media*, a middle way between Anglican and Catholic beliefs after the **Catholic Emancipation** of 1829. (From this repeal of acts from the Restoration period, Nonconformists profited, too. The long process of liberalisation, which also involved Jews, ended in 1890.) In 1845, Newman spectacularly converted from Anglicanism to Roman Catholicism, where he exerted an enormous influence as a preacher and was elevated to Cardinal (1879). A series of programmatic lectures on education and *The Idea of a University* (1852; 1873) was delivered at the Catholic University of Ireland, an institution that Newman had helped to establish and that later became University College Dublin.

From Divinity to Darwin

There was a further event that proved to be of far more general impact than Newman's conversion. In 1859, after twenty years of deliberation, Charles Darwin (1809–82) published his *magnum opus* which turned into a best-selling book of science. All 1,250 copies of the first edition of *On the Origin of Species* sold out on the first day; and there were five more editions to follow within Darwin's lifetime. The sixth and cheaper edition appeared under the shortened title *The Origin of Species* in 1872, selling at the rate of 250 copies per month. 150 years after the event, **Darwinism** is received wisdom all over the world. There are three points of interest in this successful example of a popularisation of science that have to do with Darwin's *rhetorical skills*, with his initial *reticence* to publish, and with the mixed *response* to the book, once published.

Fig. 4.4|

Charles Dawin

The popular success of *The Origin of Species* was prepared by Darwin's much earlier and highly readable account of his sailing expedition to the Galapagos Islands and then around the world, as laid down in his published *Journal of the Voyage of the "Beagle"* (1839). In addition, Darwin drew his theoretical inspiration from the revolutionary *Principles of Geology* by Charles Lyell (1830–33) as well as from the socio-economical *Essay on the Principle of Population* by Thomas Robert Malthus (1798), who provided the idea of 'the struggle for existence'. This inspiration is clearly stated in the introduction and third chapter of Darwin's book, and it is also evident from its full title: *On the Origin of Species by Means of Natural Selection; or, The Preservation of Favoured Races in the Struggle for Life*. However, over and above all these insights and inspirations, a main reason for Darwin's success rested in the rhetorical skills he used to render his argument persuasive.

The readability of Darwin's scholarly prose even for a non-specialist audience was enhanced for instance by its empirical basis and rhetorical structure. Darwin began his argument with more widely known examples and effects of man-made or *artificial selection*, as visible in cattle breeding or in the variety of domestic pigeons (including those amenable to pigeon-post) that all have descended from one species. Then, on a more abstract level, Darwin advanced to the general implications of his theory of *natural selection*, which sees spontaneous but useful variation gradually develop into distinct species. Prior to publication, Darwin had studied animal husbandry in detail and had tested his theory in experiments. Moreover, Darwin's honesty in dealing with his predecessors (who are mentioned in a review of research entitled "An Historical Sketch") as well as his critics (who occasioned many additions and revisions to later editions, not all of them improvements) was also clearly conducive to the persuasiveness of his argument.

Darwin's initial reluctance to publish had as much to do with his empirical thoroughness as with the knowledge that his theory of **Evolution** disproved the story of Creation in the Book of Genesis as a credible explanation of facts, and that it left no room for a detailed and determinate Divine design in natural history. To the contrary, Darwin's theory of Evolution laid the stress on the lasting effects of spontaneous change (which, when transferred to the politics of the Age of Revolutions 1789–1848, was also not akin to a Conservative tendency directed towards long-term stability and a fixed hierarchical order). Darwin was proved right in his forebodings. Indeed, a controversial discussion set in about the compatibility of Biblical and biological theories of natural history that is still with us today: in the Bible Belt of the USA, Darwin's book is not found on the syllabus, but on the index of banned books. (For the debate, see *NAEL* II, 1538 ff.: "Evolution".)

Another glance at the full title of *The Origin of Species* reveals some misconstructions. The more widely noted yet likewise more notorious expression 'survival of the fittest' was not coined by Darwin himself (though he made use of it from the fifth edition onwards) but was provided by the sociologist and **Social Darwinist** Herbert Spencer (1820–1903) who applied Darwin's theory to competitive societies. "Neither of the two terms with which Darwin's name is chiefly associated, 'evolution' and 'survival of the fittest', occurs in early editions of *The Origin*, where his key ideas are expressed by the words 'mutability' and 'natural selection'." (Burrow in Darwin 1982: 27). It should also be said that Darwin's own use of terms like 'favoured races' and 'natural selection' was quite innocent of racial prejudices, e. g. ideas of White Supremacy. In fact, when Darwin came to extend the theory of Evolution to the human sphere, he looked into a different direction than race and class, and conspicuously entitled this book *The Descent of Man, and Selection in Relation to Sex* (1871).

Ruskin's Criticism of Art and Culture

This is very different from the treatment of sexual and gender relations by John Ruskin in the collection of Manchester lectures entitled *Sesame and Lilies* (1865, see chap. 4.2.3). Ruskin (1819–1900) belonged to the same generation as Arnold and Kingsley, and was a friend of both Carlyle and Lewis Carroll. The foremost art critic of his age, Ruskin was also a popular spokesman on more general matters of culture. Even before he had become the first Slade Professor of Fine Arts at Oxford (1869–79), Ruskin had championed Pre-Raphaelite painters and poets such as Dante Gabriel Rossetti (*Pre-Raphaelitism*, 1851), and *Modern Painters* (1843–60) such as J. M. W. Turner. Ruskin also encouraged a 'modern Gothic' style (in *The Stones of Venice*, 1851–53) that became a hallmark of Victorian architecture. In his critical essays and his academic lectures on architecture and design, Ruskin came out likewise as a nostalgic Conservative and as an Ecologist far ahead of his times. His strong views on the patina and the historical preservation of old buildings found their counterpart in his rejection of industrial standardisation and division of labour, as epitomised for him in the innovative iron and glass structure of the Crystal Palace that was built to house the 1851 Great Exhibition. In *Unto This Last* (1860), Ruskin extended his cultural criticism to the field of Political Economy (that is, John Stuart Mill's sphere) to speak out for an organic and co-operative society, and for Christian Socialism. Ruskin's views did not only inspire William Morris, the late nineteenth-century Arts and Crafts Movement and the National Trust, but also paved the way for the Labour movement. Ruskin even influenced Mahatma Gandhi, who translated *Unto This Last* into Gujarati. It is therefore ironical that Ruskin's Inaugural Lecture (1870, in Boehmer 1998) was likewise a lecture in Imperialism, encouraging students to serve the cause of that British Empire that Gandhi later was so keen to dismantle.

The Impact of the Empire

4.2.2

Dickens and the Empire

When it had reached its greatest extent in the 1920s, the British Empire comprised more than a quarter of the world's land surface, and embraced about a third of the world's people. The colonial experience manifested itself in different forms. From a White British point of view, the family of Charles Dickens illustrates well the personal impact of the Empire. Of the ten children born before the separation from his wife (1858), five sons went to the colonies. Charles (the eldest, born in 1837, the year of the publication of *Oliver Twist*) went into banking and, after the separation of his parents, moved to Hong Kong (1859–61). Walter (*1841) joined the army and went to India at the age of sixteen (to die in India six years later). Francis (*1844), too, went to India at the age of twenty, to join the Bengal Mounted Police during his stay of six years, before he served a further twelve years with Canada's Northwest Mounted Police. Alfred (*1845) left at the age of 20 for Australia, and stayed there for 45 years. Finally, Edward (*1852), too, went to Australia at the age of sixteen, to become an MP in New South Wales in 1902, and died there. Of course there was also "Colonisation in Reverse", but such immigration into Britain from the erstwhile colonies, just like that wittily entitled poem by the Jamaican performance poet Louise Bennett itself (1966; Burnett 1986: 32 f. and *NAEL* II, 2472 f.), became pronounced only after the Second World War.

Travel Writing in an Age
of Expansion

Migration includes travel, and over the nineteenth century, travelling abroad underwent an expansion as well as a democratisation. The age of mass tourism had begun. As a consequence, Baedeker's tourist guidebooks began to appear from 1829 (soon also in other languages than German). Since 1845, Thomas Cook's travel agency offered organised 'Cook's Tours'. Soon, steamship lines were to follow, as symbolised by the passenger liner *Titanic* that sank on its maiden voyage in 1912. As more and more people undertook a journey abroad, a terminological distinction becomes necessary. The **tourist** who follows well-trodden (and maybe out-trodden) paths to see what he has been advised to look at, and what all others will see as well, should be distinguished from the **traveller** who seeks an *individual* experience and who discovers something for himself, and also from the **explorer** who discovers something new to all.

The aristocratic **Grand Tour** (i. e. travelling to the classic sites of Mediterranean culture in France and Italy) was further opened up for the 'mass tourism' of the middle classes. However, there were still notable accounts of individual travellers that compared with their eighteenth-century predecessors. After the publication of his *American Notes* in 1842, Charles Dickens issued some other "Travelling Letters" as *Pictures from Italy* in 1846. Edward Lear (1812–88), who is best known for his limericks and nonsense poetry, wrote a series of travel books on Italy (1846–75), based on his own journals. As he was also a landscape painter, he could illustrate himself the accounts of his Grand Tour. Hilaire Belloc (1870–1953) – who is noted for his "Tarantella" poem (see chap. 4.4) – went on the Grand Tour, too, and the route taken is mirrored in the titles of his travel books: *Paris* (1900), *The Path to Rome* (1902) and *The Pyrenees* (1909).

Other writers of travel accounts went further. The Victorian novelist Anthony Trollope (1815–82) followed in the footsteps of his mother Frances Trollope (1780–1863), who had made her name, and very much money, too, with travel books such as the best seller *Domestic Manners of the Americans* (1829). In addition to his novels, Anthony Trollope came out with a number of travel books that systematically explored the Anglophone world, such as *The West Indies and the Spanish Main* (1860), *North America*

(1862), *Australia and New Zealand* (1873) and *South Africa* (1878). He also wrote a number of essays on travellers and travelling. Robert Louis Stevenson (1850–94), his Scottish fellow-novelist, is a prime instance of the **individual traveller**, for whom the manner of the journey becomes the ultimate goal. *An Inland Voyage* (1878) tells of Stevenson's tour of France and Belgium by canoe, while a headstrong donkey gains prominence in *Travels with a Donkey in the Cévennes* (1879). Like so many eighteenth-century novelists before him, Stevenson left England for reasons of bad health (1888), never to return. On the South Sea island of Samoa, he wrote novellas and other literature. Half a century later, bad health also played a role in the decision of the novelist D[avid]. H[erbert]. Lawrence (1885–1930) to travel abroad. After Lawrence had stayed in Germany (1912–14) together with his wife Frieda (von Richthofen), the couple travelled first to Italy (1919–22) and then to Ceylon, Australia, New Mexico and Mexico (1922–26). D.H. Lawrence's travel books comprise *Twilight in Italy* (1916), *Sea and Sardinia* (1921) and *Etruscan Places* (1932) as well as *Mornings in Mexico* (1927).

Charles Darwin's *Journal of the Voyage of the "Beagle"* (1839) to South America and the South Pacific is a classic account of a **scientific exploration**; accounts for which the Orientalist (Sir) Richard Burton (1821–90) became famous, too. In his childhood, this explorer – who is not to be mixed up with the twentieth-century actor Richard Burton – had already made wanderings through France and Italy before he became known for reports of his more adventurous and exotic journeys. Burton's great gifts in travelling abroad were mimicry and his talent for learning foreign languages. When stationed as a soldier in India in the 1840s, Burton successfully "went native" in disguise. In 1853, he made the pilgrimage to Mecca masked as a Pathan (i.e., Afghan), and thus became one of the first Englishmen to enter the Muslim sanctuary (thereby risking his life, as Mecca is still off-limits to non-Muslims). Burton's *Personal Narrative of a Pilgrimage to Al-Madinah and Meccah* (1855–56) is distinguished by the account of his desert experience, and by precise observations of Arabian customs. From 1858, Burton explored Africa on commissions by the Foreign Office. Together with fellow-explorer and rival John Speke, Burton discovered Lake Tanganyika in East Africa, and he himself also travelled in West Africa. After his scientific explorations – for which he has recently been remembered in Iliya Trojanow's biography *Nomade auf vier Kontinenten* (2007) and in Trojanow's novel *Der Weltensammler* (2006) – Burton famously transferred his linguistic talent to translations of Oriental erotic tales such as *The Kama Sutra* (1883) and *The Arabian Nights* (1885–88).

There are a number of travellers and explorers who followed in Burton's footsteps. The reports of the African journeys of David Livingstone (*Missionary Travels*, 1857) and Henry Morton Stanley (*How I Found Livingstone*, 1872) became best sellers, and Stanley's manner of addressing the lost missionary in the heart of Africa a proverb: "Dr Livingstone, I presume?" *Travels in West Africa* (1897) by Mary Kingsley (1862–1900) provided further information. The niece of novelist Charles Kingsley had travelled to West Africa on a scientific commission (and thus with financial support) from the British Museum in 1893. T[homas]. E[dward]. Lawrence (1888–1935), better known as Lawrence of Arabia, began as an archaeologist, then turned secret agent and soldier. In 1911, T. E. Lawrence travelled to the Middle East, to join the intelligence section of the (colonialist) Arab Bureau after the beginning of the First World War. 'Going native' in 1916, he organised the revolt of Arabs against the Osmanic Empire (i. e. the Turks) which led to the founding of Saudi-Arabia. *The Seven Pillars of Wisdom* (which appeared in different editions between 1919 and 1935) is a personal account of those war years. The legendary hero is the original of 'Sandy Arbuthnot' in John Buchan's spy thriller *Greenmantle* (1916), and the protagonist of a monumental movie (*Lawrence of Arabia*, 1962, based on the screenplay by Robert Bolt).

Performances of Empire

Imperialism as an idea was promoted via oratory, poetry and print. Elleke Boehmer's anthology of *Empire Writing* (1998) and the relevant section in *NAEL* (II, 1607 ff.) include pertinent political speeches such as Prime Minister Benjamin Disraeli's "Crystal Palace Speech" (24 June 1872) as well as other speeches or toasts by Colonial Secretary Joseph Chamberlain (1897) or by the Viceroy of India, Lord Curzon (1906). The academic world was affected, too, as John Ruskin's Inaugural Lecture as Oxford Professor of Fine Art (1870) and John Seeley's Cambridge lecture on *The Expansion of England* show (1883; both in Boehmer 1998).

The Impact of the Empire on Poetry

From his office as Poet Laureate, Alfred Lord Tennyson (1809–92) celebrated British heroism and the Empire. In "The Defence of Lucknow" (1880; Boehmer 1998: 59–64), the scene is a British garrison under siege during the 1857 Indian Mutiny – the rebellion of Indian soldiers (*sepoys*) against their British masters that led to atrocities on both sides. Readers will find obvious similarities to "The Charge of the Light Brigade" (1854; see chap. 4.4), already so because Tennyson lifted memorable phrases from his earlier narrative poem to use them in the latter. Moreover, the Poet Laureate once again made an effort to have a military catastrophe appear as a shining example of heroic endurance – for which the continuous flying of the Union Jack or "Banner of England" becomes a symbol. Tennyson's commissioned poem on the "Opening of the Indian and Colonial Exhibition by the Queen" (1886; *NAEL* II, 1626 f.) is a hymn on the second British Empire, admonishing its listeners never to repeat the mistakes that led to the downfall of the first, when the American colonies were driven to rebellion and independence. Instead, the new imperial spirit passed on by the 'mother'(-country) to her 'sons' should look to patriotic harmony within, and to a defensive attitude without:

> 'Sons, be welded each and all,
> Into one imperial whole,
> One with Britain, heart and soul!
> One life, one flag, one fleet, one Throne!'
>   Britons, hold your own! (ll. 36–40)

For the coronation of Queen Victoria's successor in 1902, A[rthur]. C[hristopher]. Benson (1862–1925) wrote an even more triumphant and enduringly popular hymn (likewise set to music) that defined Britain as "Land of Hope and Glory, Mother of the Free". The text of this seemingly second national anthem was revised and expanded in time for the outbreak of the First World War, to show – apart from the perennial self-image as land of the free – an even more Imperialist attitude in the following chorus:

> Land of Hope and Glory, Mother of the Free,
> How shall we extol thee, who are born of thee?
> Wider still and wider shall thy bounds be set;
> God, who made thee mighty, make thee mightier yet. (Benson 1978)

These lines do no longer give offence, but are usually sung or hummed – not only by Britons – in a cheerful spirit (e. g. on the Last Night of the Proms). By comparison, other once proverbial verse that Kipling wrote as an unofficial 'Poet of Empire' has been viewed more critically.

Fig. 4.5|
Rudyard Kipling

During the first thirty years of his life, Rudyard Kipling (1865–1936) shuttled between India and England. Born in Bombay, Kipling – just like Thackeray – was sent to Britain to receive an education, but returned to India to work as a journalist for seven years. In 1889, a year after the publication of his collection of short stories entitled *Plain Tales from the Hills*, Kipling returned to London to find over-night fame as a poet, and later as the first English writer to receive the Nobel Prize for Literature (1907). "The Ballad of East and West" (1889) is remembered for its pointed opening line, "Oh, East is East, and West is West, and never the twain shall meet," which provoked writers from E. M. Forster (*A Passage to India*, 1924) to Salman Rushdie (*East, West*, 1994) to come up with a qualified response. This and other *Barrack-Room Ballads* (1892; see chap. 4.4) were followed by "Recessional" and "The White Man's Burden", two poems that were conceived around the time of Queen Victoria's Diamond Jubilee in 1897. Once popular and still anthologised for their historical significance (Boehmer 1998; *NAEL*), they testify, moreover, to Kipling's inspiration through popular songs (seen in the adaptation of the Chevy Chase ballad stanza for "The White Man's Burden") and through Wesleyan hymns (as in the title of "Recessional", which refers to such a Protestant hymn sung at the end of a church-service). Perhaps unexpectedly for a Jubilee hymn, the tone of "Recessional" (1897) is quite pessimistic, as the poem is written on the theme of *sic transit gloria mundi* ('Thus passes the glory of the world') and envisages a time in the future when Britannia no longer rules the waves (l. 13). Should the British transfer their power-worship from the Almighty to their mighty Empire, the present British "Dominion over palm and pine" (l. 4) was doomed to decline like other empires in history. It was not this vision of doom but the occasional reference to "lesser breeds without the Law" (l. 22) that later made this poem notorious for racism (even though the awkward Biblical phrasing is used to make a religious rather than an ethnic distinction). By comparison, "The White Man's Burden" (1899) achieved notoriety for the image in the title, which is hammered home through repetition at the beginning of each new stanza. In its call to shoulder the burden and to provide leadership rather than liberty for "[t]he silent, sullen peoples" (l. 47), the topical poem actually did not refer to the British Empire, but to the US-American colonisation of the Philippines. However, "The White Man's Burden" soon became generalised as a catchphrase for the belief in White Supremacy and an Imperialist mission.

The great impact of Kipling's 'good bad poems' (Orwell 1942) that were popular but soon also seen as prime examples of **Jingoism** in poetry, i.e. as extremely nationalist and Imperialist propaganda-pieces, made itself felt even when they drew an anti-colonial response. With "The Dominant White" (1919), Claude McKay (1889–1948), the Black Jamaican poet who was on the way to become one of the leaders of the Harlem Renaissance, wrote an answer-poem that drew on both of Kipling's incriminated poems altogether. In McKay's rejoinder, the lyrical speaker addresses the White Man only to disprove him.

During the first half of the nineteenth century, Britain's colonial empire had showed up in fiction, too, though only occasionally. To give but a few examples: in Jane Austen's *Mansfield Park* (1814), Sir Thomas Bertram leaves his eponymous English estate for his West Indian slave plantation; in W. M. Thackeray's *Vanity Fair* (1847–48, chap. 43), there is a temporary change of location to India, where the novelist was born; and with Abel Magwitch in *Great Expectations* (1860–61), Charles Dickens includes a character who is first transported as a convict and then thrives as a sheep farmer in Australia. After about 1870, when the high phase of Imperialism had set in, the Empire increasingly coloured the setting, characters or themes of fiction. While Thomas Hardy worked out in detail the regional cosmos of his Wessex novels – to which William Morris or H. G. Wells provided a change with more utopian or dystopian settings (see chap. 4.5.3) – novelists of Empire such as H. Rider Haggard, G. A. Henty, Rudyard Kipling and Joseph Conrad carried off their readers to more exotic regions of the English-speaking world. In this context, the principal distinction between **colonial, colonialist and anti-colonial(ist) fiction** (Boehmer 1995) is helpful for discussion, even though the categories become blurred with individual writers, or there is disagreement upon them among critics. For reasons of local colour and the writer's belonging, *The Story of an African Farm* (1883), which the South African novelist and feminist Olive Schreiner (1855–1920) published during her stay in London, is a good example of co-

Imperial Romances and other Fiction

Fig. 4.6

G.A. Henty

lonial fiction, when understood as a neutral term for literature from or about the colonies.

By comparison, the more than 80 children's books that the former war correspondent G[eorge]. A[lfred]. Henty (1832–1902) wrote in the 34 years between 1868 and 1902, clearly belong to the colonialist type that conveys the ideology of imperialism. Henty's patriotic books were extremely popular, but also full of clichés:

> [I]t is estimated that some 25 million copies of his books had been sold by 1914. They were read all over the English-speaking world. [... They are] full of racial (and class) stereotypes, with the English officer class at the top of the pecking order. (Carpenter and Prichard 1984: 245–46).

Seen together, Henty's historical novels of adventure for a young audience span British history from the time of the Norman Invasion in 1066 to the end of the Victorian Era. Henty's juvenile adventure fiction was written to a certain formula, and mainly for boys, as the following titles (all of which featuring a military 'hero') show: *Under Drake's Flag* (1883), *With Clive in India* (1884), *With Wolfe in Canada* (1887), *With Roberts to Pretoria* (1902), *With Kitchener in the Soudan* (1903). To get the exotic flavour of Henty's fiction, one could start with "A Pipe of Mystery" (1890, in Boehmer 1998: 149–61). This Christmas ghost story (just like Tennyson's poem "The Defence of Lucknow" mentioned above) addresses the 1857 Indian Mutiny or Sepoy Rebellion from a British perspective, and it is moreover full of Orientalisms such as ruined temples, wandering fakirs and tiger hunts. (For further fiction on this theme, by both British and Indian writers, see chap. 5.3).

Henty's juvenile, historical and adventure fiction that celebrates the British Empire is closely related to the likewise bestselling fiction by H[enry]. Rider Haggard (1856–1925). The major difference between the two contemporary writers is that Rider Haggard's **imperial romances** abstract from history to include elements of love romance, and moreover some hardly-veiled sexual allure. (For a closer look at the imperial romance, see Patteson 1978, Katz 1987 and Chrisman 2000.) After his residence in South Africa (1875–82), Rider Haggard won a bet that he could equal the success of R.L. Stevenson's *Treasure Island* (1883) with an adventurous (young and old) boys' story of his own, and indeed made his name with *King Solomon's Mines* (1885). The exemplary character of *King Solomon's Mines* as an imperial romance certainly does not rest on the occasional reference to "an imperial smile" (Haggard 1989: 114), but also on its plot, theme and characterisation. There are three strands to the plot. In one, Sir Henry Curtis searches for his brother George, who is missing in Southern Africa (in the 1950 adaptation for the screen, it is Elizabeth Curtis who is in search of her husband Henry). The second consists of the search for King Solomon's (gold or diamond) mines, undertaken by Sir Henry Curtis and Capt. John Good with the help of the hunter and adventurer Allan Quatermain, who is also the narrator of the tale. In Southern Africa, the band of White explorers and mine-hunters enter foreign territory together with their Black servants. The third strand concerns the search for and restoration of the rightful heir to the Kukuana throne, which turns out to be Umbopa alias Ignosi, the Zulu warrior who had accompanied and fought with the Whites. Altogether, they intervene successfully to dispose the brutal regime of Twala, the usurper-king of Kukuanaland, of his son Scragga, and of the evil witch-doctoress Gagool. Just as in *Robinson Crusoe*, the Whites' possession and use of firearms ultimately decides the power-struggle, together with their sense of duty, which – apart from material greed – becomes an overriding theme (e. g. 199, 213–18). The characterisation is not only remarkable for the exceptional virtues (and the funny eccentricities) of the Whites, but also for the period usage of racial terms for Black people. Noticeable, too, is the sexual (and arguably sexist) allure of the South African landscape: in their search for King Solomon's Mines, the fortune hunters cross the twin mountains called Sheba's Breasts to find and explore a treasure spot whose description resembles female private parts (85–86, 104–09).

However, there are also elements that do run against a colonialist interpretation of this narrative. Rider Haggard uses several means to acknowledge the multicultural and multilingual situation in Southern Africa, for instance through isolated instances of lexical borrowing from African languages, including the Afrikaans of the Boers, or by including a full letter in Portuguese (28). Glossing, i. e. an explanation of such borrowing, may be included in the text, or occasionally in footnotes. Elsewhere, the use of languages other than English may be signalled by having the characters speak either archaic forms of English (in the case of Umbopa, a Zulu), or an ungrammatical form of 'broken English' (for the Kukuanas). Interestingly, the deposition of the usurper-king does not lead to the establishment of White Supremacy, but to the restoration of a legitimate Black ruler, who gracefully but self-confidently ushers his White friends out of the country, and announces to forbid the influx of other Whites – a move that the narrator presents respectfully, even though it runs against the grain of colonialist fiction.

Rider Haggard followed up his success first with *She* (1886–87) as another and still popular, spellbinding narrative about a *femme fatale*, and then with sequels to both best sellers, entitled *Allan Quatermain* (1887) and *Ayesha: The Return of She* (1905). Numerous adaptations to the screen secured an enduring popularity for *King Solomon's Mines*, and so did the series of *Indiana Jones* movies that were clearly inspired by Rider Haggard's imperial romances.

Rudyard Kipling was a friend of Rider Haggard and of arch-imperialists such as Cecil Rhodes and Sir Alfred Milner, both of whom extended British colonial power in Southern Africa, where Kipling served as a war correspondent in 1900. Yet in his fiction, Kipling added exoticism with an Oriental rather than African flavour. His *Jungle Books* (1894–95, see chap. 4.5.5) are perhaps the best-known example. Kipling's earlier short story "Beyond the Pale", which is set in an unspecified Indian city, opens with a 'Hindu Proverb' on love as a motto and later prominently refers to a love song from the *Arabian Nights*. On a first reading, this story from Kipling's *Plain Tales from the Hills* (1888; Korte 2002: 202–6) looks like a plain moral tale (see chap. 3.4.6). When the Englishman Trejago 'goes native' and makes love to Bisesa, a flirtatious Indian teenage widow, both have to learn the hard way that interethnic love relationships seem doomed. In a shocking climax, Trejago is attacked, and Bisesa cruelly mutilated by a resentful Indian male. The ending seems to prove the sententious rule spelt out at the beginning – "A man should, whatever happens, keep to his own caste, race, and breed. Let the White go to the White and the Black to the Black." – a rule that foreshadowed the theme of racial segregation in the author's "Ballad of East and West" a year later. However, the fact that not only Trejago – who is able to converse in the vernacular – but also the narrator have 'gone native' – visibly so when he casually introduces words and

concepts from Hindi into his tale, as often as not without glossing them – undercuts the seemingly plain moral of the tale.

In his only yet successful novel *Kim* (1900–01), Kipling likewise *Kim*
shows such ambivalence, and also attempts a cultural translation, with the protagonist acting as a go-between for the reader
'at home' in the colonial metropolis. Kim is introduced as another English person that has 'gone native', and as a problem
case rather than a propaganda model for Imperialism:

> Kim was English. Though he was burned black as any native; though he
> spoke the vernacular by preference, and his mother-tongue in a clipped
> uncertain sing-song; though he consorted on terms of perfect equality
> with the small boys of the bazar; Kim was white – a poor white of the
> very poorest. (Kipling 1987: 1)

His development and search for identity takes three consecutive
stages (of five chapters each). In the first stage, Kimball O'Hara,
nicknamed 'Little Friend of all the World', gets to know about
his Irish father, a soldier in the Indian Army. In addition, two
paths in life open up for the streetwise teenager: on the one hand
through assisting the cunning Afghan horse-dealer and British
agent Mahbub Ali (a Sufi Muslim) in his espionage activities, and
on the other by coming into contact with Buddhist philosophy
in the person of Teshoo Lama, an unworldly Tibetan. After an intermediate stage where Kim receives (but barely accepts) an English education in India, he enters a third stage of development
which takes him to adulthood, and to a forking of the paths that
have run parallel for him so far. Kim has accompanied the Lama
on his quest for a legendary river, and he has also taken part
in counter-espionage activities of the Colonial Secret Service
against the Russians on the Afghan border. In this 'Great Game'
of espionage, which makes *Kim* the **first proper spy novel in English**,
Colonel Creighton acts as one more father figure and possible
role model for Kim. At the point of decision for his further path
in life – either as a Buddhist apprentice or as a British Imperial agent – there is an open ending. Kipling does not disclose
whether (and how) his 'Little Friend of all the World' decides
between East and West, and whether he follows a career as Sahib
or as Sage. In addition to such ambivalence which does not af-
firm Kipling's notorious image as an Imperialist and a Jingoist,
there are other features of *Kim* that speak of the novelist's love
for India and of his respect for the variety of its peoples. Both the

Grand Trunk Road in Northern India and the Himalayas feature largely in the novel, and this panoramic vision is also extended to the cast of characters: apart from an assimilated Bengali agent, the semi-serious surveyor Hurree Chunder Mookerjee, there are also several emancipated women. With such sympathetically delineated 'New Women' as the 'Widow of Kulu' and the 'Woman of Shamlegh', Kipling once more proved his critics wrong. Altogether, as controversial as Kipling was as 'Poet of Empire', his fiction has given less offence than, say, Helen Bannermann's *The Story of Little Black Sambo* (1899), a children's picture book that was also set in India. Once widely popular, the original version is now often discredited as racist in view of its title and of the illustrations by the author.

Even though he was of the same generation as Rider Haggard and Kipling, had perhaps travelled even more widely, and had likewise published fiction full of adventures in exotic settings, Joseph Conrad (1857–1924) had to wait for success until the two other authors had stopped publishing major works. One explanation is to be found in the extraordinary story of his life. Józef Konrad Korzeniowski was born in the Russian-controlled area of Poland, which he left for France when still a teenager. In Marseilles, he joined the Merchant Navy to work as a sailor for 19 years, first on French and then on British vessels, sailing to the West Indies, India, Singapore, Borneo and Australia, and travelling on a steamboat on the Congo River. A naturalised Briton from 1886, and a published author in English from 1895, 'Joseph Conrad' – who had learned the foreign language from the literary classics – wrote serialised fiction and thus for the market. However, he remained in financial debts and therefore indebted to his literary agent J.B. Pinker for most of his writing life. Indeed, debts had nearly cost him his life in an early attempt at suicide, and it was only with the publication of *Chance* as a book in 1914 (after serialisation in 1912) that Conrad's writing became really popular. Coincidentally, this was also the last time that Conrad used (Charles) Marlow as minor character and narrator in his fiction, as he had done earlier in the novellas "Youth" and "Heart of Darkness" (serialised 1899), which were published together as a book (1902), and in the novel *Lord Jim* (serialised 1899–1900 before book publication). Today, Conrad's critical estimate rests mainly on these early works, and perhaps also on the

Fig. 4.7

Joseph Conrad

novels *Nostromo* (1904, set in South America) and *Under Western Eyes* (1910–11, set in Russia). However, today's critics are usually less interested in Conrad's seascapes and exoticism (that link his fiction with e.g. that of the American novelist Herman Melville), but in his anti-colonial outlook and in his affinities with Modernism in fiction – perhaps two more reasons why Conrad had to wait for a wider audience until after 1914.

In the view of Hans Ulrich Seeber (2004: 318 ff. and also in Borgmeier 1984: IX, 289 ff.), Conrad's fiction is characterised, *first*, by a radical questioning of the ideals of progress and civilisation, and of related professional ethics and social morality, all of which are tested out in extreme situations. Often enough these ideals are then found wanting in individuals, and sometimes they turn out to be no more than a thin veneer upon the darker sides of human nature. Were it not for those darker elements, Conrad's narrative technique could well be said, *secondly*, to resemble an Impressionist painting that creates atmospheric setting and delineates characters by many suggestive details rather than one bold stroke. This ties in with a *third* noticeable feature of Conrad's fiction, namely the relinquishing of an authoritative narrative voice and of an omniscient point of view in favour of partial views – Marlow's being one of them – within an atmosphere of oral communication.

The plot of *Lord Jim* is made up of two related parts: the *Patna* and the Patusan episodes. Marlow begins by telling of a gross example of unprofessional conduct at sea in relation to the steamship *Patna* that was chartered to transport 800 Muslim pilgrims from East Asia to Mecca. Being afraid that the old vessel might sink, the white crew abandons ship and passengers in order to save their own skin. When the *Patna* is later found to have moved on, the crew is taken to court for neglect of duty. Marlow follows the inquiry and relates his conversations with the Captain and with Jim, the chief mate. Moreover, Marlow can tell that the Captain committed suicide, failing his own standards of professional conduct, while Jim got his certificate cancelled as a result of the inquiry. Over the years, Marlow meets Jim again and follows his career through the reports of others. Sent as a company representative in the global trade network to the (fictitious) South East Asian island of Patusan, the former mate 'goes native' and first makes up for his former lack of leadership. Thus rehabilitated, he is revered by the native population and rises to the position of Tuan (Lord) Jim – as if Conrad wanted to illustrate Thomas Carlyle's 1841 lectures on heroes and hero worship. However, Tuan Jim is (as Marlow regularly reminds the reader) only "one of us", and as a personification of benevolent White Supremacy, he is toppled when other, greedy and malicious Whites arrive. Hesitant in the face of ruthlessness, Jim loses the power struggle, to perish in an act of sacrifice for his renewed failure as a 'hero' and as a friend.

White Supremacy, both in cross-cultural relations and in connection with a global network of trade and exploitation, together with a look into the dark sides of human nature, is also the composite theme of Conrad's novella "Heart of Darkness". At the outset, Marlow's tale of his journey on the Congo River is once more embedded within a narrative frame established by a second, extradiegetic and heterodiegetic narrator. Marlow's river journey (which echoes Conrad's own) is an exploration in more than one sense – into Central Africa and into the subconscious mind of Man. At the journey's end, at "An Outpost of Progress" (such is the title of a related 1898 Congo short story by Conrad), Marlow finds in Kurtz another personification of White Supremacy and colonialism, but this time in the shape of a brutal White savage among native Africans. "Mistah Kurtz – he dead": this moribund embodiment of Evil dies with the words "The horror! The horror!" (Conrad 1984: 149–50). Into their ambivalence, one can read (with Marlow) a final act of penitence and repudiation of Evil, or, less optimistically, a pronouncement on life in general by someone who has looked into the abyss of the human soul. Conrad's novella had a mixed response, eliciting praise from literary critics for its psychological and anti-colonial features, but also drawing oppositional criticism. In his polemical essay "An Image of Africa: Racism in Conrad's *Heart of Darkness*" (1977), the famous Nigerian novelist Chinua Achebe attacked Conrad for creating a stereotyped, colonialist and racist image of the Dark Continent. Indeed, Achebe can point to the many instances when Marlow or other characters in Conrad's novella refer to Africans as "savages" or "niggers" – which however does not necessarily imply Conrad's approval. To the contrary, when the film director Francis Ford Coppola adapted Conrad's novella for the screen at about the same time under the title *Apocalypse Now* (1979; extended Redux version 2001), he paid much importance to the anti-colonialism and the complex psychology of his source, which he updated to set the action in 1969 during the American War in Vietnam. Here as in some of the other cases mentioned, the exact distinction between colonial, colonialist and anti-colonial texts leaves room for argument – and thus underlines rather than undermines their historical significance.

'The Angel in the House' vs. the Fallen Woman: Gender Roles and Their Impact on Literature

4.2.3

The economic changes in the wake of the Industrial Revolution had strong repercussions on family life. The factory system relieved working-class homes from being a workplace for 'home-made products', too. Moreover, in "Of Queens' Gardens", one of two lectures delivered at Manchester in 1864 and published a year later in the widely read collection *Sesame and Lilies*, the cultural critic John Ruskin even celebrated the private (middle-class) home as a safe haven:

Home, Sweet Home

> This is the true nature of home – it is the place of Peace; the shelter, not only from all injury, but from all terror, doubt, and division. In so far as it is not this, it is not home, so far as the anxieties of the outer world penetrate into it, and the [...] hostile society of the outer world is allowed [...] to cross the threshold, it ceases to be home [...]. But so far as it is a sacred place, a vestal temple, a temple of the hearth watched over by Household Gods, [...] so far it vindicates the name, and fulfils the praise, of Home (Ruskin 1900: 108–09; *NAEL* II, 1588).

The social impact of the middle classes – urban *bourgeoisie* as well as landed gentry – increased with their prosperity, and thus paved the way for some typically Victorian gender concepts. Fleshed out in the works of middle-class writers, they were seized, too, by working-class audiences that looked up to 'their betters'. The 'perfect lady' was one such role model:

> Once married, the perfect lady did not work; she had servants. She was mother only at set times of the day, even of the year; she left the heirs in the hands of nannies and governesses [...]. Her status was totally dependent upon the economic position of her father and then her husband. In her most perfect form, the lady combined total sexual innocence, conspicuous consumption and the worship of the family hearth (Vicinus 1972: ix).

Submissiveness or (to put it more friendly) modesty was the most prominent characteristic of this Victorian ideal of femininity. It was seen as linked up with women's inferiority by nature, "mentally, physically, and morally. Education, therefore, would be wasted upon them; responsibility would overwhelm them, and work made them ill. They must be sheltered, protected, and indulged" (Strachey 1928: 16). Fictional characters such as Rosamond Oliver in *Jane Eyre* and (though more perversely) Estella in *Great Expectations* exemplify this concept of womanhood. In many ways, the best example for a 'perfect lady' who satisfied herself with "a guiding, not a determining, function" (according to Ruskin 1900: 106) was Queen Victoria herself – a woman who ruled in name only, and who spoke out privately against

> this *mad, wicked folly* of 'woman's rights' [...] Woman would become the most hateful, heartless – and disgusting of human beings were she allowed to unsex herself! Where would be the protection which man was intended to give to the weaker sex? (Letter to Sir Thomas Martin, 29 May 1870, quoted from Young 1977: 99–101).

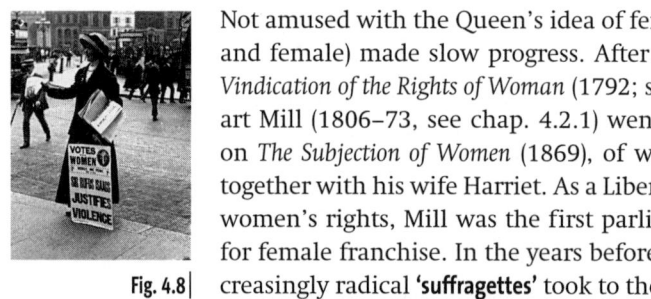

Not amused with the Queen's idea of femininity, feminists (male and female) made slow progress. After Mary Wollstonecraft's *A Vindication of the Rights of Woman* (1792; see chap. 3.5.4), John Stuart Mill (1806–73, see chap. 4.2.1) went on record for his essay on *The Subjection of Women* (1869), of which Mill had conceived together with his wife Harriet. As a Liberal MP and an advocate of women's rights, Mill was the first parliamentarian to speak out for female franchise. In the years before the First World War, increasingly radical **'suffragettes'** took to the streets. When universal suffrage became law in 1918, women finally got the vote.

Fig. 4.8

A British suffragette (c.1910)

With **"The Angel in the House"** (1854–62), of which he sold 250,000 copies during his lifetime, the minor poet Coventry Patmore (1823–96) effectively presented a middle-class version of the 'perfect lady' as a domestic saint. Perhaps to lay that Victorian concept of femininity to rest, the Modernist novelist and feminist critic Virginia Woolf had to make her 1931 essay "Professions for Women" read like an obituary:

> You may not know what I mean by the Angel in the House [...] She was intensely sympathetic. She was immensely charming. She was utterly unselfish. She excelled in the different arts of family life. She sacrificed herself daily [...] she never had a mind or a wish of her own (Woolf 1967: II, 285).

By contrast, John Ruskin had contributed to the idolisation of this Household God in his 1864 essay "Of Queens' Gardens" (see the above quotation), and he had elaborated on the domestic duties of husband and wife: "Now the man's work for his own home is [...] to secure its maintenance, progress, and defence; the woman's to secure its order, comfort, and loveliness" (Ruskin 1900: 130). Mrs (Isabella) Beeton's best-selling *Book of Household Management* (1861) provided help where needed. This binary opposition in gender roles and gender relations is clearly marked out in one of Tennyson's poems, too:

> Man for the field and woman for the hearth:
> Man for the sword and for the needle she:
> Man with the head and woman with the heart:
> Man to command and woman to obey;
> All else confusion.   (Alfred Tennyson, "The Princess", 1847)

In Victorian literature, 'angel in the house' characters were also referred to as 'Griselda' (see Reed 1975: 37–40) and presented in a Romanticised fashion. A more realistic treatment occurred only when Nora, Henrik Ibsen's dramatic heroine, crossed the threshold of *The Doll's House* (Oslo 1880; London première 1889) in the opposite direction, and slammed the door upon her husband. Such an oppositional, late-Victorian ideal of an emancipated **'New Woman'** was also promoted through Grant Allen's popular novel *The Woman Who Did* (1895), and through the plays of G. B. Shaw. (For the context, see Cevasco 1993.)

In the words of a feminist historian, women in Victorian Britain were either "the wives, or the mothers, or the daughters of some man; that was their description and the real justification of their existence" (Strachey 1928: 16). Unmarried or sexually emancipated, independent or intellectually ambitious women were not publicly approved of; and to match the ideals of femininity mentioned, there was a range of negative gender stereotypes. One may begin with the **'old maid'** as a stock character in comedies and novels of manners. Miss Bates in *Emma* (1816) is a prime example, but she is also the object of a more detached observation on the marriage market made by Jane Austen (a celibate herself) in the voice of her heroine:

> I shall not be a poor old maid; and it is poverty only which makes celibacy contemptible to a generous public! A single woman, with a very narrow

income, must be a ridiculous, disagreeable, old maid! the proper sport of boys and girls; but a single woman, of good fortune, is always respectable, and may be as sensible and pleasant as anybody else. (Chap. 10. Austen 1983: 109)

A well-off but vengeful example such as Miss Havisham in Dickens's *Great Expectations* (1860–61) might be cited to refute that statement. In any case, the comic stereotype grossly misrepresents the fact that some 29% of women aged over 20 were celibate according to the 1851 Census, and that "the numbers of bachelors and spinsters were just about equivalent" (Mason 1994: 238–39). Intellectual ambition in women was likewise ridiculed in the **'bluestocking'**, which turned the attempt at a female educational network in the second half of the eighteenth century (an Enlightenment circle which included the writers Frances Burney and Hannah More) into a misogynistic stereotype. To counter such negative typecasting, of which she was keenly aware, the novelist George Eliot chose heroines that were positive examples of female learning and ambition, such as Maggie Tulliver in *The Mill on the Floss* (1860) and Dorothea Brooke in *Middlemarch* (1871–72). They can be contrasted with, once again, the conventional view of John Ruskin, who pontificated that the ideal woman was the one who showed herself to be "instinctively, infallibly wise – wise, not for self-development, but for self-renunciation" (Ruskin 1900: 109; *NAEL* II, 1588). Such thinking translates also to the field of sexual morality, and of female sexuality in particular.

The Depiction of Sexuality in Fiction: 'Prudery', 'Hypocrisy' and 'The Other Victorians'

'Victorian prudery' is as notorious as **'Victorian hypocrisy'**, that is the sexual double standard for men and women in the period, which was characterised by giving (married) men the opportunity to choose among a record number of prostitutes, while any wife with a pre- or extra-marital record of lovers was ostracised as a fallen angel in the house. However, a reconsideration of the facts as well as the myths about Victorian sexuality has taken place since the 1960s, and a more complex picture has emerged (see Marcus 1964, Pearsall 1969, Mason 1994). Moreover, many *Eminent Victorians* (as Lytton Strachey in 1918 entitled his collective and iconoclastic biography) did not care too much for convention in their private lives. The Prince of Wales openly enjoyed the life of a (married) playboy, with a string of mistresses extending into his reign as King Edward VII. Such libertinism was not a royal prerogative, but was shared by the anonymous 'Walter', one of *The Other Victorians* who filled 11 volumes of his candid memoirs with his erotic pursuits (*My Secret Diary*, 1888–95; see Marcus 1964). The unconventional woman writer George Eliot hid under a male pseudonym, but spoke of herself as the wife in her lasting but informal union with the critic George Henry Lewes, while his legal spouse was engaged in one of her extramarital liaisons. The more 'sensational novelist' Wilkie Collins lived in a *ménage à trois* with two mistresses, whereas his friend and rival Charles Dickens was more discreet. The degree of intimacy between Dickens and the actress Ellan 'Nelly' Ternan, before and after the novelist's separation from his wife, was as much the subject of private gossip as the exact nature of the relationship of two successive royal servants, the Scotsman John Brown and the Indian Abdul Karim, to Queen Victoria during her forty years as "The Widow of Windsor" (see Kipling's poem and the 1997 film *Mrs Brown*). On the other hand, there were eminent men of letters who enjoyed Platonic friendships, such as John Stuart Mill, who for 21 years remained husband-in-waiting to Harriet Taylor, and others who even lived in Platonic marriages, as did Thomas Carlyle or John Ruskin. But there were also those who struck (likewise Platonic) friendships with teenage girls, as did Ruskin or Lewis Carroll, or who sought out teenage rent boys for a very different kind of Platonic love, as did Oscar Wilde. In one of the most sensational trials of the outgoing century, Wilde was punished for his homosexuality (a term that began to be first used in 1869). Among those fellow male writers who had engaged in close same-sex friendships, but luckily escaped Wilde's fate, are Cardinal Newman, the poets Lord Tennyson and John Addington Symonds, or the critics Edmund Gosse and Walter Pater.

In view of the anecdotal as well as the scholarly evidence, one should therefore be careful to read the literary discourse on sexuality dating from the period as a literal representation of social reality. Undeniably, however, the *literary* representations are indicative of conventional morality in Victorian Britain, or the views of **'Mrs Grundy'**. In his novel *Vanity Fair* (1847–48, chap. 36), Thackeray had paid ironical homage to this personification of Victorian morals, but when he subsequently gave the last of his lectures on *The English Humourists of the Eighteenth Century* (1851–53), he himself sounded very much like Mrs Grundy:

> There is not a page in [Laurence] Sterne's writing but has something that were better away, a latent corruption – a hint, as of an impure presence.
>
> Some of that dreary *double entendre* may be attributed to freer times and manners than ours [...]. I think of these past writers and of one who lives amongst us now, and am grateful for the innocent laughter and the sweet and unsullied page which the author of "David Copperfield" gives to my children. (Lecture VI: "Sterne and Goldsmith")

Comparison to French Fiction

It takes nothing more than a look across the Channel to observe that not only eighteenth-century British readers, but also contemporary French audiences were dished up with (and mostly relished) more sensual fare. French readers could choose between a tragic tale of passionate love centring on an exotic *femme fatale* (Mérimée: *Carmen*, 1845) and novels about middle-class women who try to spice up the staleness of provincial life with adultery (Flaubert: *Madame Bovary*, 1856; Feydeau: *Fanny*, 1858), not to forget Zola's *Nana* (1879–80), a novel about the varied life and loves of a *demi-mondaine* or kept mistress in higher society, including her Lesbian affair. Such eroticism and characters as the *femme fatale* were displayed in British fiction only towards the *fin de siècle*, e. g. in Bram Stoker's *Dracula* (1897) and – with more of a colonial exoticism – in Rider Haggard's *She* (1886–87). Before that time, most of these topics were taboo to writers and readers in Britain. The critic Ella Westland later explained why, when she elaborated upon Thackeray's point about Dickens in relation to the notorious 'Victorian prudery':

> Dickens [...] never forgot his own responsibility to the family circle. He policed his magazines carefully, revealing the sensitivity of his editorial antennae when a regular contributor to *Household Words* got 'so near the sexual side of things as to be a little dangerous to us at times' (to W.H. Wills, 6 October 1854). [...] Sexuality is normally controlled through a MORAL scheme based on marriage. Dickens's novels strictly enforce a Victorian version of morality. [...] Sexuality is not one of the themes Dickens does best, but the darker side is done brilliantly. Yet Dickens passed himself off as a family writer always mindful of the young person. His contemporaries, and for a hundred years his critics, rarely focused on how he got 'so near the sexual side of things' as to be a little dangerous at times. (Westland, s. v. "Sexuality and gender" in Schlicke 1999: 533–36)

In his treatment of sexuality, Dickens the family writer was sometimes *risqué*, indeed. So far, the female stereotypes called up, positive and negative ones alike – the perfect lady as well as the angel in the house, the old maid as well as the bluestocking – have all been asexual ones. They were matched, over the nineteenth century, with a number of – always negatively connoted – images of sexual women that contrasted with a closely related set of ideals such as modesty and purity, virginity, chastity and fidelity. The above-mentioned Miss Havisham in Dickens's *Great Expectations*, who was denied marital bliss and forced into chastity against her expressed desire, has turned sour from sexual frustration. With this specimen of a **'Madwoman in the Attic'** (Gilbert and Gubar 1979), Dickens imported a literary stereotype from Gothic and other romances, following upon the example of Scott's Ulrica of Torquilstone in *Ivanhoe*, and Charlotte Brontë's Bertha Mason/Rochester in *Jane Eyre*. Brontë moreover delineated her character so as to represent the stereotypically fatal eroticism of exotic females. In its aspect of social marginalisation, this literary stereotype is also sadly indicative of actual nineteenth-century treatments of post-natal stress syndrome, female depression and 'hysteria' (as in the case of Thackeray's wife Isabella, or the American writer Charlotte Perkins Gilman, who wrote about her experience with 'rest therapy' in the 1892 short story "The Yellow Wall-Paper"). With the character of Lady Dedlock in *Bleak House*, Dickens had already presented the tragic story of a **'woman with a past'**, that is, a seemingly perfect lady then discovered to be 'unchaste', due to a premarital affair and a child born out of wedlock. This was a theme that was also exploited by dramatists (see below), yet **adultery and divorce** remained taboo topics in fiction. In reality, this was one of the most striking examples of 'Victorian hypocrisy', and of the link between materialism and mentality:

> There is a curious connection between the offenses against property and adultery. Adultery of the man was, of course, of no consequence; however, adultery of a married woman was different. The correspondent was treated as if he had, indeed, committed an offense against property, a wife (a *feme covert*) being in law a possession of the wronged husband. [... There was a] double standard of morality enshrined in the 1857 Matrimonial Causes Act (a husband could only be divorced if adultery was combined with something else or unless it was adultery in the highest, i.e., incestuous adultery, a woman could be divorced for adultery alone) (Pearsall 1969: 181, 186).

There is also a story of progress, as a series of Married Women's Property Acts (1870–1908) were drawn up in order to improve the situation. And yet, adultery and divorce were generally shunned, with the exception of W. M. Thackeray's *The Newcomes* (1853–55; chap. 58), George Meredith's *Diana of the Crossways* (1885) and Thomas Hardy's *Jude the Obscure* (1894–95), all of which deal with divorce. The result is that Victorian literature lacks a real counterpart to novels such as Flaubert's *Madame Bovary* (1856) and Tolstoy's *Anna Karenina* (1873–77).

The Great Social Evil
When they dealt with extra-marital affairs, British novelists were far more concerned with 'The Great Social Evil' of prostitution. With regard to **'fallen women'** and **'Magdalen(e)s'** (a Biblical term for reformed prostitutes), Dickens proved his social commitment in- and outside his fiction, but showed an ambivalent attitude. The prostitute Nancy in *Oliver Twist* is depicted in a positive light – but Dickens nevertheless signed up to conventional morality in blocking a happy ending for her as for the other female characters mentioned. On the other hand, Dickens, just like the Liberal politician and later Prime Minister William Gladstone, was from the 1840s onwards actively involved in 'rescuing' streetwalkers and seeing them into 'Magdalen homes' (see Westland in Schlicke 1999: 475–77).

The social novelist Elizabeth Gaskell was very much concerned with the topic, too. In *Mary Barton* (1848), poverty breeds prostitution: Esther, the protagonist's aunt, first vanishes and then re-appears as a streetwalker to tell a fallen woman's tale, and to die of exhaustion (chaps. 1, 10, 14, 38). In *Ruth* (1853), the stress falls differently. At first, Gaskell's novel reads like the story of Richardson's *Pamela* gone wrong. The seduction of Ruth, an orphaned working-class girl, by a country gentleman named Mr Bellingham results in her teenage pregnancy and single motherhood. Mr Benson, a Methodist minister, and his sister Faith help Ruth by providing her first with a new identity – as the widow 'Mrs Denbigh' – and then with an employment as a governess to the Bradshaw family. Bellingham, the father of Ruth's child, also has assumed a new identity as a local politician, and now offers marriage and money as a compensation, which Ruth rejects. When Mr Bradshaw, a stern and righteous patriarch, finds out about Ruth's single motherhood, he dismisses her as a sinner. A second attempt at re-integration into society is made. Ruth redeems herself by working bravely as a sick-nurse during a typhus epidemic. In the melodramatic ending to the novel, however, Ruth just manages to save her former lover's life, only to die a martyr's death. Gaskell's Victorian novel, which attacked hypocrisy and intolerance from a Christian point of view, became topical again in a new context: in view of the many teenage pregnancies in Britain today, the novel was adapted as a play for the classroom by Robert Leeson (2000).

The decidedly negative reaction of the public to Gaskell's *Ruth* and to Thomas Hardy's much more acerbic novel *Tess of the D'Urbervilles: A Pure Woman Faithfully Presented* (1891, see chap. 4.5.3), which also deals with the complex theme of seduction, single motherhood and social ostracism, is a literary and historical fact in itself. *Jude the Obscure* (1894–95) brought an increase in Hardy's provocation and in the critical backlash alike, which made Hardy turn away from fiction for good. Yet in "The Ruined Maid", one of the first poems he had written (in 1866) and published (in 1901), one finds once again treatment of the topic of the fallen woman and the Great Social Evil.

In drama, too, conventional morality and the notorious combination of 'Victorian prudery' and 'hypocrisy' show in the handling of the **complex theme of 'the woman with a past' together with the 'fallen woman' and the prostitute**. Alexandre Dumas *fils* had set an example when he successfully dramatised his own novel *La dame aux camélias* as a melodrama (1848/52), to be adapted once more and on the spot by Giuseppe Verdi into the famous, realistic opera *La traviata* (1853). Common to all versions was the story of the honourable (!) courtesan who relinquished her former way of life for the man she loves, but who went on to die – tragically, not as an instance of poetic justice – of tuberculosis. In 1884, the combination of tragic melodrama and social realism reached the English stage with *Saints and Sinners: A New and Original Drama of Modern English Middle Class Life* by Henry Arthur Jones. Seen from today, the moral outlook of this play – which shows a linear development from the seduction of a girl over the ostracised position of a 'fallen woman' who tries to make good by works of charity, and further to her death – appears to be quite conventional, and to bear some resemblance to the plot of Elizabeth Gaskell's novel *Ruth*. However, these works of both Jones and Gaskell implied criticism of a double standard and of

Dramatic Treatments

a hollowness of religious observance, which may explain why Jones's venture into seriousness and the problem play was at first rejected in the theatre and in the press, and made him return to melodrama. In domestic melodramas such as *The Dancing Girl* (1891) and *The Case of Rebellious Susan* (1894), Jones addressed (and confirmed) the sexual double standard for men and women in the Victorian Era.

A decade later, Arthur Wing Pinero (1855–1934) was more successful with *The Second Mrs Tanqueray* (1893), one of a number of *fin de siècle* plays that were conceived around that complex theme. In Pinero's **problem play**, a woman marries but keeps her new family in the dark about her premarital record. However, when her stepdaughter wants to become engaged to one of Paula Tanqueray's former lovers, the truth comes out. There is apparently no way to escape from the past, and the promise of a fresh start into domestic happiness appears to be no more than an illusion. When the full extent to which her family is being ostracised because of her makes itself felt, and when she is rejected by her stepdaughter, Paula becomes so desperate that she sees no other solution than to take her own life, and commits suicide. The tragic ending of Pinero's problem play shows a different moral outlook than *Saints and Sinners*; however, this playwright, too, is apparently more interested in dramatic effect than in social change.

Lady Windermere's Fan　　In *Lady Windermere's Fan: A Play About a Good Woman* (1892), Oscar Wilde approached the theme of 'a woman with a past' from a different angle and in the form of a **comedy of manners**. Mrs Erlynne and Lord Windermere are often seen together, a matter of gossip that Lady Windermere complains about first to her husband, on the day she comes of age, and then later to Lord Darlington, whom she visits instead of taking part in her own birthday party. Lord Darlington in turn confesses his love to Lady Windermere, and asks her to elope with him. The scandal that would arise from the fact that Mylady's fan was found in Lord Darlington's lodgings, suggesting that those two were there together unchaperoned, can be averted when Mrs Erlynne shifts the blame to herself. Mrs Erlynne is an ambivalent person, who just saved Lady Windermere from scandal, but who hitherto has blackmailed Lord Windermere to finance Mrs Erlynne's lifestyle. When a dissatisfied Lord Windermere rounds on Mrs Erlynne and reproaches her not only for her alleged relationship to Lord Darlington, but also for having run away with a lover, twenty years earlier, from a husband and a child, it transpires that this child is Lady Windermere (who is ignorant about all this) – and it also becomes evident that the designation 'Good Woman' in the title actually refers to Mrs Erlynne, whose maternal instinct has not left her for good. For Oscar Wilde, the playwright who usually subscribed to the view of 'Art for Art's Sake' rather than social realism, the play ends on a sober note. The two prominent female characters in the play strike it together. Mrs Erlynne's dictum: "Ideals are dangerous things. Realities are better. They wound, but they're better." (Wilde 1893: 124) is confirmed a short while later in Lady Windermere's verbal rejection of conventional morality:

> There is the same world for all of us, and good and evil, sin and innocence, go through it hand in hand. To shut one's eyes to half of life that one may live securely is as though one blinded oneself that one might walk with more safety in a land of pit and precipice. (Wilde 1893: 130)

Oscar Wilde's plays of the early 1890s exemplify the extent to which a playwright's concern with sexuality still resembled a tightrope walk. Both *Lady Windermere's Fan* and *Salomé: A Tragedy* proved controversial, but where Wilde's comedy of manners found approval with 'Mrs Grundy', his rewriting of the well-known Biblical story ran him into difficulties. His version of the Biblical story differed from other late nineteenth-century treatments in literature or in painting in that it is Salomé who stands out, and not her mother Herodias (as in Flaubert's tale of 1877). Salomé feels both attracted and provoked by the prophet Jokanaan (St. John the Baptist) who has condemned the decadence at court, and who has refused to have any intimacy with her. Salomé plans to revenge herself on him ("I will kiss thy mouth, Iokanaan", Wilde 1894: 24). She entices Herod, the Tetrarch of Judaea, by a Dance of Seven Veils in strip-tease fashion, until Herod complies with her demand and orders the decapitation of Jokanaan. When she is brought the severed head of the prophet on a plate, Salomé lustfully kisses the dead lips – an act that makes a shuddering Herod order her execution, too. *Salomé* was written in French in 1891, but was refused a license in England through the Lord Chamberlain's Examiner of Plays a year later when the

| Fig. 4.9
Salomé by Titian, c.1515

famous actress Sarah Bernhardt was already in full rehearsal for the role. The reason given for this act of censorship (which to all evidence was widely approved) was that Wilde's piece did not observe an English law that forbade the depiction of Biblical characters in stage-plays. This however can only partly explain why the refusal was upheld for another forty years. The first time that Wilde's one-act tragedy could or wanted to be seen by a larger audience in Britain was in 1931 (not counting a private, club-like production of 1905). In the meantime, Sarah Bernhardt had finally acted the title role in France (from 1896), several silent film versions had come out of Hollywood (the first in 1908), and Richard Strauss had adapted Wilde's play as an opera, highlighting the eroticism of Salomé's dance and the final scene. The opera could be staged in London two years after its 1905 premiere, but with alterations, and the real reason for the reserved attitude of British audiences and institutions towards Wilde's stage-play appears to be its peculiar combination of eroticism, cruelty and murder – a combination which was more popular at other times with the audiences of revenge tragedies or Gothic romances. Wilde was helped in the English translation of his French tragedy by his friend Lord Alfred Douglas ('Bosie'), who was also involved in the *cause célèbre* that led to Oscar Wilde's trial because of homosexuality in London in 1895. As a result, Wilde was sentenced to hard labour, a punishment that broke his health. (He wrote about his experience in his moving poem "The Ballad of Reading Gaol" and in his long autobiographical letter *De Profundis*.)

Mrs Warren's Profession   With *Mrs Warren's Profession*, George Bernard Shaw went one step further than Wilde and Pinero, and ran into direct conflict with stage censorship, too. Shaw's play on a prostitute, and on prostitution, was written in 1893 and published as one of three *Plays Unpleasant* in 1898. However, in another act that testified to the moral climate of late Victorian society, the Examiner of Plays considered Shaw's play to be immoral and denied public performance. Thus, *Mrs Warren's Profession* could only be staged in a private production in 1902, which was followed by the German and American premieres in 1904 and 1905, respectively, while the first public performance in Britain did not take place before 1925. Shaw's title character is shown to run a chain of brothels in European capitals, and to see prostitution as an economic consequence of a Capitalist society, which was silently accepted, regardless of moral pretensions to the contrary. Mrs Warren's matter-of-fact view brings her into conflict with her daughter – another emancipated woman, but of a different mould. Vivie Warren exemplifies the New Woman of the *fin de siècle* in that she holds a Cambridge degree and has an independent mind, but she is shocked nevertheless when she is informed about the sources of her mother's economic independence, and she cannot share her mother's materialist outlook. The dramatic conflict of the play, and the debates between mother and daughter, revolve around this issue in a manner that is typical of both Shaw's non-dogmatic socialist beliefs and of his conception of a **drama of ideas**. A decision on the matter of debate is due when Vivie gets the opportunity to choose between three different suitors, and thus between three future roles for herself: first, to live a domestic life free of financial sorrows, but tainted by the fact that her aristocratic husband-to-be Sir George Croft is a stake-holder in her mother's business; second, to accept instead Frank Gardner's offer of an emotionally satisfactory, romantic union; and third, to choose Praed the architect's promise of a life devoted to 'Art for Art's Sake', but likewise devoid of professional fulfilment. In the end, Vivie sets down to work honourably, and remains alone.

'Victorian values' as a concept were by no means limited to England, but stretched out to Ireland, too. Irish audiences protested repeatedly against Synge's iconoclasm in relation to moral institutions and his indifference towards sexual morality. The negative portrait, in *The Tinker's Wedding*, of a Catholic priest who haggles over the fees for a marriage and later is bundled into a sack, ensured that this early play (written 1902/03) had to wait until it could be premiered after Synge's death, in London and not in Dublin (1909). When Nora, the female protagonist of Synge's *In the Shadow of the Glen* (1903), quite like her famous namesake in Ibsen's *A Doll's House*, shuts the door on her husband to seek freedom and emotional fulfilment outside her marriage and on the road, part of the Dublin audience on the first night protested audibly against this disillusioning portrait of the purity and chastity of Irish womanhood. For the same reason, spectators attending the premiere of *The Playboy of the Western World* (1907) reacted with outrage at the word "shifts" in a passage towards the ending of the play:

CHRISTY: It's Pegeen I'm seeking only, and what'd I care if you brought me a drift of chosen females, standing in their shifts itself, maybe, from this place to the eastern world?   (Act III. Synge 1961: 106)

This image of Irish women, near naked and paraded like prostitutes, was such an assault on sexual morality that the 'Playboy Riots' lasted for a whole week, with repercussions felt even in the USA (see chap. 4.3).

Guiding Questions and Exercises

1. What is meant by Victorian Values? Summarise the main features of the contemporary moral code.
2. Discuss the impact of religion and of science on Victorian Literature.
3. In what manner did Imperialism and the colonial Empire affect the literature of the period?
4. Comment upon the literary representation of gender roles and gender relations within the period under review.

4.3 | Drama and Performance: From Music Hall and Melodrama to the Plays of Wilde, Shaw, Yeats and Synge

Melodrama was a popular form of dramatic entertainment which dominated the English stage up to the end of the nineteenth century, but which had its origin in France. *Mélodrames* like Rousseau's *Pygmalion* (1770) consisted of a combination of spoken words (drama) and musical accompaniment (melody), and thus were an intermedial form somewhat akin to early opera. The rise of melodrama – just like that of the music hall – was a result of the restrictive laws governing stage performance, which left a loophole for musical drama (see chap. 3.2.1). The **1843 Theatre Regulation Act** abolished the monopoly of the 'patent houses', but kept the powers of the Lord Chamberlain, a court official who in his function as Examiner of Plays exercised **pre-censorship** of the stage. Between 1807 and 1870, the number of London theatres operating increased from 10 to 30, and the middle classes were represented again in the audience as well as in the stage-plays. Among those powerful **actor-managers** who followed in the

footsteps of David Garrick and John Philip Kemble, likewise by
excelling in the plays of Shakespeare and by reforming theatrical production, were Madame (Lucia) Vestris, first at the Olympic
Theatre and later at the Lyceum and at Drury Lane (1831–54),
William Charles Macready at the patent theatres of Covent Garden and Drury Lane (around 1840), Samuel Phelps at Sadler's
Wells (after 1844), the famous actress Ellen Terry's partner (Sir)
Henry Irving at the Lyceum (1878–1902) and – in a more experimental vein – Harley Granville-Barker at the Royal Court Theatre, after the turn of the century. At that time, Edward Gordon
Craig (Ellen Terry's son) called for the actor-manager to be replaced by the stage director as the person in charge of a production that aimed at artistic unity (*The Art of the Theatre*, 1905), while
J. M. Barrie and G. B. Shaw reserved their authorial play-rights
by confronting actors and directors with unusually detailed
stage directions. (The three tendencies were later dubbed 'actor's theatre', 'director's theatre' or 'total theatre', and 'writer's
theatre'.)

Until 1843, the licensing
law of the time had restricted 'legitimate' (i.e. spoken)
drama at first only to the two
patent theatres, and then
also to the Haymarket Theatre and various provincial
Theatres-Royal. All other venues had to rely on something
else: on instantly recognisable types and on spectacular
action. The British music hall
(the equivalent in the United
States was called 'vaudeville')

Fig. 4.10
1875 The Oxford
Music Hall

originated from the music room annexe in public saloons to become an institution of its own, catering at first to a male working-
class audience and then also to the middle classes. In the heyday
of 'music hall and variety' (c. 1850–1920), these venues for popular musical and comic entertainment employed dancers, jugglers
and acrobats, singers (like Marie Lloyd and Harry Lauder), actors
(including the male impersonator Vesta Tilley) and comedians
(such as Dan Leno). Music hall and variety are sometimes more,

sometimes less nostalgically remembered in T.S. Eliot's obituary essay on Marie Lloyd (1922), in plays by John Osborne (*The Entertainer*, 1957) and by Trevor Griffiths (*Comedians*, 1975), and in novels such as J.B. Priestley's *The Good Companions* (1929) and Peter Ackroyd's *Dan Leno and the Limehouse Golem* (1994).

Melodrama

Contemporary, lively and humorous accounts of the nature and experience of **melodrama** in performance in London and New York can be found in Dickens's *Oliver Twist* (1837–38, chap. 17) and in *Maggie: A Girl of the Streets* (1893, chap. 8) by the American writer Stephen Crane. One can distinguish two types of melodrama: (1) the domestic melodrama and (2) those plays that are based on actual or invented crime stories. Especially in pieces of the latter type, an improbable, but suspenseful plot is built around the moral theme of virtue in distress: unusually virtuous protagonists are put in peril by monstrous vice and villains, and therefore have to survive frightening experiences, which makes for sensational special effects. The plot hovers on the brink of tragedy, as the defeat of the good side often can be averted only narrowly, yet there is no essentially tragic conflict or theme. Melodrama in this sense has more to do with the sensational fiction of the time, and with the timeless traditions of romance literature, than with music-hall entertainment or with today's musicals.

The first English play to be billed as melodrama, *A Tale of Mystery* (1802) by Thomas Holcroft (1745–1809), was suitably enough an adaptation of a French play (*Coelina* by Guilbert de Pixérécourt, 1800). Douglas Jerrold became the next notable playwright in this line with *Black-Eyed Susan* (1829), which is set in the sailors' milieu. Biographical details may give an impression of the worldliness and topicality of the new dramatic kind, and of the versatility and prolific output of its first notable practitioners. Both Douglas Jerrold (1803–57) and Tom Taylor (1817–80) were employed as **house dramatists** before they went on to have another career in journalism. Jerrold worked for the Surrey Theatre before he joined the staff of the comic magazine *Punch* in 1841 and then became editor of *Lloyd's Weekly Newspaper* (1852–57). Taylor taught English at the university in the 1840s and then worked simultaneously for the London Board of Health (1850–71) and as house dramatist at two London theatres (1853–70), of which the Olympic Theatre relied heavily on melodrama. Taylor ended his working life as editor of *Punch* (1874–80), but he is best remembered as a prolific playwright with (according to various estimates) 80 to 100 plays to his credit. In addition to further adaptations of French plays, but also of novels such as *Uncle Tom's Cabin* and of *A Tale of Two Cities*, Taylor wrote farcical comedies such as *Our American Cousin* (the play attended by President Lincoln at the time of his assassination), historical verse drama about Jeanne D'Arc and Anne Boleyn, and melodrama such as *The Ticket-of-Leave Man*. Bob Brierly, the protagonist of the latter play, is a convict released on ticket-of-leave. He restores his reputation by bringing a gang of criminals to justice, together with Hawkshaw, a detective in disguise and precursor of Sherlock Holmes. With this piece (which was adapted from *Le Retour de Melun* and premiered at the Olympic Theatre in 1863), the connection between stage melodrama and popular fiction building on crime, such as the Newgate Novel (1830s), the Sensation Novels (1860s) and detective fiction, becomes evident. Indeed, the histories of melodrama and the novel in this period were closely intertwined, with typical and topical elements of plot and characterisation travelling both ways. There are obvious similarities between Taylor's main characters Brierly and Hawkshaw and their Dickensian counterparts like Inspector Bucket in *Bleak House* and the returning convict Abel Magwitch in *Great Expectations* (himself a highly melodramatic character). Both Taylor and Dickens, who collaborated on the stage adaptation of *A Tale of Two Cities* in 1860, knew how to put melodrama to good effect (see Schlicke 1999: 380–82).

The most prominent representative of stage melodrama is the Irish playwright, actor and theatre manager Dion(ysius) Boucicault (1820–90). He is moreover interesting because his life and career span the English-speaking world. Boucicault was born in Dublin and made his name on London stages in the 1840s with adaptations of French plays. After his emigration to the USA (in 1853), Boucicault embarked on an equally successful career with melodramatic pieces. Of the more than 200 plays to his name, *Jessie Brown; or, The Relief of Lucknow* (1858) was a topical piece referring to the 1857 Indian Mutiny, while *The Octoroon* (1859), produced shortly before the outbreak of the US Civil War, dealt with slavery on the Southern plantations. The titles of Boucicault's adaptation and likewise of its source (*The Quadroon*, 1856, a novel by Capt. Mayne Reid, an author famous for his juvenile adven-

| Fig. 4.11
Dion Boucicault,
ca. 1862

ture stories) refer to the racial classification of 'hybridity' among the slave population. M'Closky, the villain in the piece, tries to get hold of both a plantation and of Zoe, the female protagonist. She is the illegitimate daughter of a slave woman and the former owner of the plantation, and now lives as a freed slave. Her father's relatives try to hinder M'Closky and to save Zoe from his machinations, but to no avail: Zoe finally kills herself. Interestingly however, in order to please his British audiences who had objected to a lack of poetic justice, Boucicault had to change the melodramatic ending for performances in Britain, where Zoe was seen to survive.

In the USA, Boucicault (the first British dramatist to receive a royalty payment) was instrumental in the passing of the 1856 copyright law that increased the protection of American playwrights. He also wrote Irish romantic melodramas that surely spoke to those Irish emigrants in the audience who had left the Green Isle in great numbers after the potato famine of the 1840s. With *The Colleen Bawn* (premiered in New York in 1860), Boucicault once more came out with an adaptation, this time of the crime novel *The Collegians* published by his fellow-Irishman Gerald Griffin in 1829. The title *The Colleen Bawn* – an Anglo-Irish expression for 'fair girl' – characterises the protagonist Eily O'Connor, a poor but virtuous girl, who is secretly married. However, her husband actually needs to marry an heiress in order to make up for the decrease in the family's fortunes, and so he plans to have honest and innocent Eily killed by a servant. Yet the murder is averted by Myles, a vagabond who loves Eily truly, but who nevertheless seems satisfied in the end when Eily is restored to her repentant husband. Boucicault made good use of romance elements – such as the improbable plot linking the *ingénue* as protagonist with a reformed rake as a husband – and of other stereotypes, too. With Myles the *shaughraun*, he presented a new version of the **stage Irishman**, and in his later melodrama *The Shaughraun*, such a vagabond went centre-stage. *The Shaughraun* (first performed in New York in 1874, with Boucicault acting in the title role) combines romance with recent Irish political history. Robert Ffolliott has been transported as a convict to Australia, just like Abel Magwitch in *Great Expectations*, but for different reasons: Robert was formerly a member of the Fenian movement, an underground organisation fighting against British rule. Conn the Shaughraun helps Robert

Ffolliott to escape, and Robert plans first to return to Ireland (for romantic reasons), to see again his beloved Arte O'Neal, and then to flee to the USA. However, Robert is betrayed by a villainous friend and arrested again, coincidentally by an English officer who is in love with Robert's sister. When the Shaughraun once more arranges for Robert's escape, Conn is shot (yet not killed) in the attempt ... only to observe his own wake (a boisterous Irish custom which features also in Joyce's novel *Finnegan's Wake*). During the wake, the villains are exposed, and poetic justice is procured together with a happy ending. This involves no longer a funeral, but three weddings instead: there are marriages in view for Conn to his own sweetheart, of Robert to Arte O'Neal, and of Robert's sister to the English officer.

The last notable, but no less prolific writer of melodramas was Henry Arthur Jones (1851–1929), who wrote 45 full-length plays that were staged in London and New York between 1878 and 1917. In *The Silver King* (premiered in London in 1882, to frequent revivals), the plot was based, again, on crime. Wilfred Denver, the protagonist, is made to believe that he has committed a murder, and as a consequence abandons his family and runs away to America. There, he has better luck, comes from rags to riches and makes a fortune as 'the Silver King'. Upon the news that his family is starving in England, he returns in disguise and reveals his true identity only after he has discovered both his own innocence and the real murderer. The play ends with a prayer, just like Holcroft's *A Tale of Mystery* 80 years earlier.

Besides melodrama, which was to exert its influence in (Hollywood) movies and television drama, the playbill of nineteenth-century theatres featured a number of other dramatic genres that also presented an intermedial combination of spoken words and music. There were playlets such as the **burletta** (a lighter form of musical comedy), the **burlesque** (a stage parody) or the **extravaganza** (a spectacular and brilliantly costumed dramatic entertainment). Both burlesque and extravaganza entertained with verbal wit in songs, but they were distinguished in that the burlesque parodied a popular play or the production of a play (as in J. M. Barrie's *Ibsen's Ghost*, 1891), while an extravaganza was based instead on a story from mythology or folklore. The librettist W[illiam]. S[chwenck]. Gilbert (1836–1911) and the composer Arthur Sullivan (1842–1900) developed these two forms into 'Savoy operas' such as *H. M. S. Pinafore* (1878), *The Pirates of Penzance* (1879) and *The Mikado* (1885) – so-called after the Savoy Theatre that had been built in 1881 as an exclusive venue for Gilbert and Sullivan's popular comic operas (it was the first theatre in Britain to replace gas lighting by the much brighter electric stage lighting). Extravaganzas were gradually introduced on Boxing Night (26 December), just like **Christmas pantomimes** which then catered to a family audience and often continued running up to March. Among the goodies predominantly produced were *Cinderella* and *Robinson Crusoe* pantomimes and also *Peter Pan* by J[ames]. M[atthew]. Barrie (1860–1937). In J. M. Barrie's children's play about *Peter Pan; or, The Boy Who Wouldn't Grow Up* the escapist fantasy is sustained – and this boy has never stopped (in and outside pantomime) flying with his beloved Wendy Darling to the Never Land of fantasy, where they meet the pixie Tinker Bell and the Lost Boys as well as their enemy, the villainous pirate Captain Hook. The convention, dating back to Nina Boucicault (Dion's daughter) in the premiere (1904), to select distinguished actresses to play Peter Pan in a breeches role (or rather in tights, providing them with the opportunity to show their legs) may have helped in making this piece palatable for older children, too. In the likewise popular *Charley's Aunt* (1892), Brandon Thomas (1856–1914) had developed cross-dressing and gender travesty into a full-length **farce**. This is his only play of note, about an aristocrat who dresses up as a woman to facilitate the matchmaking of his friends. *Charley's Aunt* has been regularly revived in theatres around the world and in adaptations for the screen up to the 1970s, when it received a modern touch in thematically related films such as *Tootsie*, 1982.

Fig. 4.12|
Cover of 1915 edition of *Peter Pan*

Charley's Aunt

The (rather derogatory) designation **well-made play** was used for a tightly plotted piece, beginning *in medias res* and ending in a climax shortly before the final curtain's fall. As just one more period term that originated from a French dramatic tradition (*pièce bien faite*), it was applied to both humorous and serious pieces. The plays written by Arthur Wing Pinero (1855–1934) stood out in both categories. Like W. S. Gilbert and later G. B. Shaw, Pinero was no house dramatist but the rare example, in this period, of a playwright exercising control over all aspects of his dramatic production. Farce was well represented in the 1880s and 1890s by his shorter, one- or two-act pieces (e. g., *The Magistrate*, 1885), and it can likewise be detected as an element in the plays of Oscar Wilde. Pinero's meta-theatrical comedy *Trelawney of the 'Wells'* (1898) includes an affectionate portrait of the playwright Thomas William Robertson (1829–71), whose domestic pieces of the 1860s had paved the way for a revival of serious drama. While being in a more serious mood, both Wilde and Pinero wrote plays that confronted Victorian values with the theme of 'the woman with a past' (see chap. 4.2.3). In *The Second Mrs Tanqueray* (1893) and similar problem plays, Pinero found another form congenial to him besides farce. As a somewhat belated counterpart to the Victorian social novel, the **problem play** tackled social and moral issues of the day. The term gained wider currency in the 1890s, when it began to be applied to a group of Shakespeare's plays, too (which created additional problems of its own, see the above chapter on Renaissance tragicomedies). Of major influence was the Norwegian playwright Henrik Ibsen, who was part of a general tendency towards **Naturalism** visible in European and American literature in the nineteenth century, characterised in general by a concern with realism in representation and by a disillusioned view on individual fate as determined through the social milieu. *A Doll's House* (1879), Ibsen's famous play about gender relations and marriage, was adapted as *Breaking a Butterfly* (1884) by Henry Arthur Jones and Henry Herman. When he did not write melodrama, H. A. Jones continued in this vein, for instance in *Saints and Sinners* (1884), but his plays, by general agreement, lack the philosophical basis that were to distinguish G. B. Shaw's. Another notable writer of **Naturalist problem plays** was John Galsworthy (1867–1933), who is perhaps better known as a novelist of manners and creator of family sagas (*The Forsyte Saga*, 1906–22). In his problem plays, Galsworthy questioned social justice: *The Silver Box* (1906) denounces inequality before the law of rich and poor by contrasting two families of different social standing. *Strife* (1909) centres on the difficulty of labour relations, as exemplified by a strike. *Justice* (1910) tells the story of a clerk who is imprisoned for forging a cheque and broken through his experience of solitary confinement. When re-integration into society seems to be impossible, the former prisoner is driven into suicide – and the audience is made fully aware of the sarcastic overtones of *Justice*. In direct response to seeing Galsworthy's play, Winston Churchill, then in his first week as Home Secretary, felt the urge to reform the English prison system.

Sadly, Oscar Wilde (1854–1900) was implicated in a similarly ambivalent enforcement of 'justice' after one of the trials of the century, yet his literary fame is connected moreover with a successful revival of the **comedy of manners**. Wilde, an Irishman born in Dublin, had made his name at Oxford University as a poet and prominent representative of the **Aesthetic Movement** proclaiming the slogan 'Art for Art's Sake' (as opposed to Realism and Naturalism). In addition to his poetry (the first collection of which was published in 1881), he wrote one adult novel (*The Picture of Dorian Gray*, 1890, which shows an influence of melodrama) and several fairy-stories for children. Starting with the scandal around his play *Salomé: A Tragedy* (see chap. 4.2.3), he enjoyed a short, but significant period of success as a playwright (1892–95). Wilde was lionised in fashionable society as a dandy, as a trendsetter, and above all as a person of *esprit*, of wit in conversation. He was a master of the *bon mot* (see the example given at the ending of chap. 4.1). Wilde became famous for these same qualities in his plays, which revived the comedy of manners of the Restoration Era, a type of drama which – both at the end of the seventeenth and at the end of the nineteenth centuries – was deeply connected with the French comedies of the times. No wonder then that Wilde felt also at home in Paris, and that the qualities which are made out in his plays are most often expressed with French terms: *bon mot, aperçu, esprit, charme*.

The Importance of Being Earnest: A Trivial Comedy for Serious People (premiered in London in 1895) is widely regarded as Wilde's masterpiece. Apart from Wilde's hallmark, the verbal comedy that shows already in the punning title, this well-made comedy (which is also known under the alternative title *Bunbury*) is characterised by its use of comic situations and twists of the plot. It is one of the best-known modern examples of a 'comedy of errors': two friends, John ('Jack') Worthing and Algernon Moncrieff, try to cover their secret adventures with an alibi or with an alias. Algernon the Londoner says he visits his sickly friend Bunbury in the country, while 'Jack' leaves his manor house to go to town, travelling under the assumed identity of his invented brother 'Ernest'. Both men are guardians of young women:

Fig. 4.13

Oscar Wilde, New York, 1882. Picture taken by Napoleon Sarony

Algernon of Gwendolyn Fairfax, his cousin in town, and 'Uncle Jack' of Cecily Cardew, his ward in the country. In the course of the play, matches are made between the female adolescents and the aliases. Gwendolyn is infatuated with the name of 'Ernest', so much so, that Jack is even willing to change his name in earnest. Meanwhile Algernon, to poke fun at his friend, pays a visit to Jack's country seat, poses there as the invented brother Ernest Worthing to Cecily, and falls in love with her. When Algernon sheds his mask, it comes out that Jack Worthing – who began his life as a foundling left in a handbag in a railway station – is in fact Algernon's elder brother, and his real name is … Ernest Moncrieff. Thus, the happy ending also spares him another change of his name in order to please Gwendolyn. The minor characters featuring in the subplots of Wilde's play may be memorable just because they belong to types that have peopled other works in the British comic tradition, too: the elderly aunt, the old maid and staid governess, and the irreverent Reverend. Algernon's aunt and Gwendolyn's mother, Lady Bracknell, exemplifies the comic type of elderly person with conventional manners and morality that may stand in the way of the younger lovers. Miss Prism, who had been Jack's short-sighted nanny prior to becoming Cecily's governess, fully justifies her punning name when it transpires that she had mistakenly left baby Jack instead of the manuscript of a novel in a bag at the station. However, when all is out, Miss Prism successfully unites with the learned 'womanthrope' she loves, the Reverend Dr Chasuble, in the third romantic union of the piece.

Apart from the Dublin-born Oscar Wilde (and Dion Boucicault earlier on in that period), there were three other Protestant Anglo-Irish playwrights that went from success – and *succès de scandale* – in the London and Dublin theatre-world to world-literary fame: G. B. Shaw (Nobel Prize 1925), W. B. Yeats (Nobel Prize 1923) and J. M. Synge. There are in fact some similarities, but also some telling differences between George Bernard Shaw (1856–1950) and Oscar Wilde, who was two years his senior. Shaw likewise was a Dubliner who found his fame on the London stages; however, he did not belong to the 'Protestant Ascendancy' (like Wilde, Yeats and Synge, all of whom were born into the Anglo-Irish social elite). Shaw came from a poor background and worked his way out of it. Shaw began his career as a critic of stage-plays

G.B. Shaw and the Drama of Ideas

Fig. 4.14
G. B. Shaw

and of music drama (*The Quintessence of Ibsenism*, 1891; *The Perfect Wagnerite: A Commentary on "The Ring of the Nibelungs"*, 1898) before he turned to writing for the stage. With his provocative plays – which he liked to gather into groups such as *Plays Pleasant*, *Plays Unpleasant* (both 1898) and *Three Plays for Puritans* (1901) – he immediately came into conflict with stage censorship. Only a year after the scandal around Wilde's highly eroticised *Salomé: A Tragedy* (1892), the Examiner of Plays considered *Mrs Warren's Profession*, Shaw's play about a prostitute, not just 'unpleasant' but 'immoral' and denied public performance (see chap. 4.2.3). While Shaw's mix of education and entertainment was also concerned with society, his plays were looking at it from a different point of view than those of Wilde. Shaw was a non-dogmatic socialist and (since 1884) a leading member of the intellectual and reformist movement called the Fabian Society, as well as an effective orator at Speaker's Corner in Hyde Park. When he embarked on his career as a dramatist, he did so as a disciple of Ibsen, and not as a follower of the Aesthetic Movement (like Wilde and Yeats). Finally, 'G. B. S.' likewise became famous for his communication skills and for his intellectual humour, yet he was not content with a *bon mot* on bad manners: where Wilde entertained with smart talk on the smart set, 'Shavian wit' was directed towards social change in earnest. Shaw, who found the English stage dominated by melodrama and by the well-made play or problem play when he began his career, successively opened it up to intellectual debate.

With his own type of a **drama of ideas**, Shaw has influenced dramatists as various as Bertolt Brecht ("Ovation für Shaw", 1926) and Friedrich Dürrenmatt. Shaw's plays, written over a span of nearly 50 years (from *Widower's Houses*, 1892, to *In Good King Charles's Golden Days*, 1939), were defined through common features. These included, on the level of dramatic idiom and plotting, the occurrence of anticlimax, of paradoxical twists and turns, and of verbal and dramatic irony. The dialogue resembled a debate on stage, in which the characters personified an individual point of view or one side of an argument, which expressed itself in monological statements or in a discussion of an issue. Moreover, there were actually two communicative situations: Shaw addressed not only the performers and the audience in the theatre, but also the readers at home who read the book edition (in some cases long before the play could ever be staged). The plays published in book form showed an unusually great extent of extra-dramatic prose, and thus a tendency towards the closet play: in addition to the performance text, there were long notes which exceeded the conventional notion of a stage direction, and long prefaces which turned into essays of its own. All this was of course related to the intellectual character of Shaw's plays, the text of which could bear a re-reading.

In some of his plays, Shaw treated gender relations and power *Man and Superman* politics by giving a modern twist to myth (*Man and Superman*; *Pygmalion*) or to history (*Caesar and Cleopatra*; *Saint Joan*). *Man and Superman* is a "drama of ideas" (as the playwright called it in his first stage direction) that shows Shaw under the philosophical influence of Friedrich Nietzsche and Henri Bergson. The plot of this funny but not-too-well-made play on gender relations is based – like Lord Byron's long poem *Don Juan* (1819–24) – on an ironical reversal of the story of Don Juan (as dramatised by Tirso de Molina, Molière or Mozart). The long and autonomous "Don Juan in Hell" scene, an *entr'acte* in the third of four acts influenced by Mozart's *Don Giovanni*, was premiered on its own (1907) after the rest of the play (1905) and long before they were first performed together (1915). In his "Epistle Dedicatory" to the critic who suggested the theme, Shaw wrote: "Don Juan is a full century out of date for you and for me [...]. You would laugh at me if at this time of day I dealt in duels and ghosts and 'womanly' women. [...] And so your Don Juan has come to birth as a stage projection of the tragic-comic love chase of the man by the woman; and my Don Juan is the quarry instead of the huntsman." Don Juan Tenorio properly appears only in the *entr'acte*, a dream vision accompanied by Mozart's music and set in hell, where he meets first his former lover Doña Ana and then the Devil (who is characterised in the stage direction as "enormously less vital than the woman"). After an exchange of Shavian pleasantries (of the sort of "An Englishman thinks he is moral when he is only uncomfortable."), all three argue at length about Man and Nature, about the institution of marriage, and about the superiority of a Life Force over Death and Degeneration. Here, Darwin's theory of evolution and Bergson's notion of *élan vital* reappear in Shaw's conception of a sort of 'creative evolution' and of a 'life force' determined to produce an *Übermensch*, a Superman (in terms of Nietzsche). In one of Shaw's paradoxical twists, the leading agent behind this evolutionary step towards a human being with superior brains is said to be (New) Woman, not Man. Don Juan as the playwright's mouthpiece attempts to harmonise feminist notions with the worship of female beauty and with a cult of the mother, but Doña Ana contradicts his views on marriage. Contrastive characterisation helps to further the argument, both in hell and on earth. In the rest of the play, set in or around London and Granada, the part of Don Juan Tenorio is given to John Tanner (first played by Harley Granville-Barker), a gentleman-revolutionary who is arguing his case with Mendoza (the Devil's alter ego and a philosophical robber), with Roebuck Ramsden (a pseudo-Socialist who is not by accident presented as statuesque in hell), and with his ward Ann Whitefield/Doña Ana. She is characterised by the playwright on her first entrance as "a cat", as "one of the vital geniuses" and as "a perfectly self-controlled woman". The cast is completed, for the sake of the argument, by other typified characters such as an Irish-American capitalist (Mr Malone) and a Cockney servant turned into a modern man of technology ('Enry Straker). The play subtitled *A Comedy and a Philosophy* ends in what John Tanner does explicitly deny to mean a happy ending for him, but admits to follow from his own views on the Life Force: Ann Whitefield chooses him to be her husband. During the play, Tanner is said to have laid down his views in "The Revolutionist's Handbook", which together with other "Maxims for Revolutionists" had been presented to readers as a long after-word to the play when it was published as a book (1903) a couple of years prior to the first of its first performances. Here, Shaw had further opportunities to illustrate his thinking with jibes against "matrimonomaniacs" and with aphorisms such as "In heaven an angel is nobody in particular", "He who can, does. He who cannot, teaches" or "Take care to get what you like or you will be forced to like what you get."

With a Cockney servant such as 'Enry Straker, and with the playwright's initial characterisation of Ann as someone who would also succeed as a flower girl – "strike all aitches out of her speech, and Ann would still make men dream" – Shaw had already laid the grounds for his famous play *Pygmalion: A Romance*. The Greek myth about a sculptor who falls in love with a statue he has created had been adapted by Rousseau as a melo-drama (1770) and by W.S. Gilbert as a "Mythological Comedy" in blank verse (*Pygmalion and Galatea*, 1871) before Shaw turned it into the story of an experiment in educational perfection. In Shaw's play, Professor Henry Higgins (the modern Pygmalion) and Colonel Pickering attempt to turn the Covent Garden flower girl Eliza Doolittle into a lady, to give her a new social identity by teaching her to shelve her customary Cockney dialect (which provides much of the play's comedy) and to speak more politely. This scheme is, in other words, the attempt to overcome class barriers by cultural adaptation. Here, Shaw could give full rein to his Socialist views as well as to his life-long concern with the divergent pronunciation and spelling of the English language. He himself spelt out the problem in his "Preface: A Professor of Phonetics" and left a legacy for anyone who would bring about a radical change of English usage. The printed text of Shaw's plays frequently shows a simplified spelling, and is therefore proof of his reforming spirit in this matter. In *Pygmalion*, Shaw made sociolinguistic issues a dramatic theme, yet this did not make him forget his other views on the Life Force. This is borne out by the ending of the play: Higgins is successful in his experiment, but apart from a sentimental attachment, he has been blind to Eliza as a person. So he is made to look on when a self-confident and ladylike Eliza turns him down for a genteel husband she has chosen for herself. A longer prose epilogue presents Shaw with the opportunity to comment on Eliza's married life in particular as well as on marriage in general. *Pygmalion*, which had been successful as a stage-play (1914) and in a film version (1938) for whom Shaw received an Academy Award, was finally immortalised through a further adaptation. *My Fair Lady* by Alan Jay Lerner (text) and Frederic Loewe (music) became one of the most famous musicals ever, both on stage (regularly revived since 1956) and on screen (1963).

|Fig. 4.15
First American serialised printing of Bernard Shaw's *Pygmalion*

Caesar and Cleopatra: A History was Shaw's answer to famous Roman plays by Shakespeare (*Julius Caesar*; *Anthony and Cleopatra*) and by Dryden (*All for Love*). With his choice of period (48/47 B.C.) and of Cleopatra's first enchantment of a Roman leader, Shaw avoided being seen as an imitator. Although two characters are dead by the end of Shaw's historical play, *Caesar and Cleopatra* is not constructed as a tragedy, but as a witty comedy. The constel-

Caesar and Cleopatra

lation of characters prefigured the situation in *Pygmalion/My Fair Lady*: a powerful, older man educates a young girl, falls sentimentally in love with her, but is left by her once her education is completed. When they meet for the first time in the desert in front of the Sphinx, Cleopatra does not recognise Caesar and appears naïve and innocent, so he begins to teach her, his principal lesson being how to behave as a queen. Later at Cleopatra's court, it is the Roman ruler who settles the power struggle between Cleopatra, her brother Ptolemy and his guardian Pothinus. Half a year later (Act IV–V), the situation has changed: Caesar leaves Egypt, triumphant in battle but disconcerted by the character of its queen. Cleopatra has developed into a charming woman, and into a more mature but also ruthless ruler: she orders the assassination of Pothinus, which occasions a further death (that of her nurse). By comparison with his royal apprentice, Caesar looks old and also naïve in his customary clemency to his opponents. Thus, in a self-ironic gesture on their farewell, Caesar promises to send her Mark Antony in return, instead of the 'old man' himself.

In a typically Shavian paradox, this 'Play for Puritans' (1901) was published years before Shaw could have it premiered in New York in 1906. Some 50 years later, Shaw returned to the matter and wrote the screenplay for a film version. This film of 1946, although the most expensive British movie ever made until that time, contrasts greatly with the lavish 1964 *Cleopatra* film that centres on Elizabeth Taylor as the man-eating pharaoh-queen. In all versions of his 'Play for Puritans', Shaw followed the events, but presented history on his own terms. Moreover, he presented himself, as usual, not only as a man of words, but of many words. In addition to a Prologue (in prose) and a second, Alternative Prologue (in dramatised form), the book version of the play is framed by notes on "Apparent Anachronisms", on Shaw's personal view of Caesar and of Cleopatra, and by a funny note on "Cleopatra's Cure for Baldness". In these notes, Shaw justifies his conscious use of anachronism (in speech and elsewhere) and his highly personal conception of Caesar (including Caesar's humour). In the play, Shaw introduced Britannus as Caesar's secretary and also as an alter ego for audiences in Britain. When the people outside Cleopatra's palace cried "Egypt for the Egyptians", this off-stage outburst of a nationalist and anti-colonial spirit was meant for the ears of Caesar and Britannus, and moreover directed at all those spectators who were likewise administrators of the modern British Empire, then in its prime.

Saint Joan: A Chronicle Play in Six Scenes and an Epilogue (premiered in New York 1923) centres on Joan of Arc/Jeanne d'Arc, the peasant girl who led the French troops to victory in the late medieval wars against the English. Half a millennium after the Maid of Orleans had been condemned as a witch and executed (1431), the Church of Rome canonised her as Saint Joan (1920). This instigated Shaw to write a history play *à la* Shakespeare, yet to write against the English-nationalist bias of the Bard (Jeanne *la Pucelle* is a prominent character in *1 Henry VI*) as well as against the romantic treatment in Schiller's tragedy *Die Jungfrau von Orléans* (1801). In Shaw's more general view, the woman warrior was a champion of the New vs. the Old, fighting for the liberating ideas of Nationalism and Protestantism, and against the combined establishment of both the feudal lords and the Catholic Church. Once again, Shaw explained his view in a long preface and dramatised his subject as 'a matter of debate', as in the following instances. After a series of defeats, the Earl of Warwick as commander of the English army exchanges summary views on the significance and on the future of his female opponent with a leader of the church (Peter Cauchon, the Bishop of Beauvais):

Saint Joan

> WARWICK: [...] These two ideas of hers are the same idea at bottom. It goes deep, my lord. It is the protest of the individual against the interference of priest or peer between the private man and his God. I should call it Protestantism if I had to find a name for it. [...]
>
> CAUCHON: [...] To her the French-speaking people are what the Holy Scriptures describe as a nation. Call this side of her heresy Nationalism if you will: I can find you no better name for it. I can only tell you that it is essentially anti-Catholic and anti-Christian; for the Catholic Church knows only one realm, and that is the realm of Christ's kingdom. Divide that kingdom into nations, and you dethrone Christ. Dethrone Christ, and who will stand between our throats and the sword? [...]
>
> WARWICK: Well, if you will burn the Protestant, I will burn the Nationalist, [...].
>
> (*Saint Joan*. Scene 4. Shaw 1960, 98–99.)

In an epilogue set a quarter of a century after Joan was burned on the stake, the annulling of her sentence marks her rehabilitation. Representatives of both sides meet again in an imaginary encounter, which is opened by the nobleman in polite fashion:

> WARWICK: Madam: my congratulations on your rehabilitation. I feel that I owe you an apology.
> JOAN: Oh, please don't mention it.
> WARWICK [*pleasantly*]: The burning was purely political. There was no personal feeling against you, I assure you.
> JOAN: I bear no malice, my lord.
> WARWICK: Just so. Very kind of you to meet me in that way: a touch of true breeding. But I must insist on apologizing very amply. The truth is, these political necessities sometimes turn out to be political mistakes; and this one was a veritable howler; for your spirit conquered us, madam, in spite of our faggots. History will remember me for your sake, though the incidents of the connection were perhaps a little unfortunate.
>
> (Epilogue, 1960: 154)

This exchange of pleasantries, at once polite and yet bitterly ironical, and in a language which speaks to a modern audience ("a veritable howler"), is a good example of Shavian wit and Shavian views on Woman as more vital than Man. *Saint Joan*, too, was made into a film based on a screenplay by Shaw (1927, with more film versions to follow). In 1925, two years after the premiere of this play, and likewise two years after Yeats, Shaw was 'canonised' by receiving the Nobel Prize for Literature.

John Bull's Other Island

Among the many provocative plays by 'G. B. S.', there was only one play that addressed the Irish Question. *John Bull's Other Island* (1904) was staged at London's Royal Court Theatre under the direction of Granville-Barker, who thus brought about Shaw's breakthrough and fame. The provocation in *John Bull's Other Island* was twofold. Shaw's "Preface for Politicians" rounded on all those (the politicians in England and the Church of Rome alike) who stood in the way of political autonomy or Home Rule for Ireland. Other passages of the preface (e. g. "The Curse of Nationalism") as well as the whole character of the stage-play proved unsatisfactory for the ideals of Irish Nationalism and in particular of W. B. Yeats, who had commissioned the play for the Irish Literary Theatre. (See below. Shaw's play was however annually revived at the Abbey Theatre between 1916 and 1931.) After not just autonomy but independence had finally been achieved (for the Irish Free State in 1922), Shaw, in a characteristic gesture, expanded his preface by a passage entitled "Twentyfour Years Later" (1929). There, he lamented the behaviour of both Irish Nationalists and the British government during the Easter Rising of 1916, and characterised the way to the Irish Free State with caustic wit: "And so we settled the Irish Question, not as civilized and reasonable men should have settled it, but as dogs settle a dispute over a bone."

In the performance text, the issue is still in the open. The functional characterisation of the *dramatis personae* determines them to be personifications of various aspects of Anglo-Irish relations; each of them a type, some of them involved in a paradoxical reversal of stereotypes, and none fit to be a 'hero'. In the first act, the two civil engineers and business partners Tom Broadbent and Larry Doyle – the first an English Liberal, the other an Irish Socialist – meet in their Westminster office and decide to make a joint business trip to Ireland. The partnership is implicated in a reversal of roles that holds good for the remaining three of four acts, which are set in Ireland and which are built around two strands of the plot: Tom's romance with the Irish 'heiress' Nora Reilly (who enjoys a fortune of £40 a year), and his ambitions to be elected in an Irish constituency as an MP for Westminster. Tom Broadbent is seen to be a romantic to boot, though not in love but in politics, where he is increasingly given to dreaming, to boasting and to bombast (all of them Irish stereotypes rather). On the other hand, Larry Doyle is made to present himself throughout as a passionately commonsensical analyst of Irish matters. He is a bitter realist untainted by nostalgia even after spending half of his life in exile (actually, to be far away from Nora, who was once in love with him). With a third character appearing right at the beginning of his play, Shaw calls up and at the same time deconstructs for good a lasting English stereotype of *John Bull's Other Island*, the **stage Irishman**. Tim Haffigan, who successfully applies to Tom Broadbent for a job, may be able to deceive Broadbent and an English audience by speaking a heavy Irish brogue and acting the bragging drunkard: "I'm Irish, sir: a poor aither [eater], but a powerful dhrinker. [...] Tay is a good dhrink if your nerves can stand it. Mine cant". However, the 'real' Irishman Larry Doyle is not taken in and reveals Haffigan to be no more than a stage Irishman from Glasgow, and a "seedy swindler". Further prejudices by Broadbent (read: the English) that relate to the politics, economy and cultural identity of Ireland, are refuted in the course of the play. Moreover, Larry Doyle also rounds on those romantic auto-stereotypes, myths and dreams propounded by cultural nationalists such as Yeats:

> "It's a l l dreaming, a l l imagination. [... An Irishman] cant be intelligently political: he dreams of what the Shan Van Vocht said in ninety-eight. If you want to interest him in Ireland you've got to call the unfortunate island Kathleen ni Hoolihan and pretend she's a little woman. It saves thinking. It saves working. [...] I want Ireland to be the brains and imagination of a big Commonwealth, not a Robinson Crusoe island." (To understand the literary context, see the remarks below on Yeats's play *Cathleen ni Houlihan*.)

Other typified characters such as Father Dempsey (a Protestant), the unfrocked Catholic priest Peter Keegan and, once again, the representatives of the upper, middle and lower classes in both of John Bull's isles complete the picture: Cornelius Doyle, a former landlord, and Matthew Haffigan, whose hard-working attitude made him rise above a tenant; not to forget the servants Hodson and Patsy Farrell – another Cockney and a Paddy. All of them have their share in the series of debates on the Irish Question that are at the heart of this play. Bitterness and Shavian wit apart, there is some hope left: both the partnership of Broadbent and Doyle and the marriage of Tom to Nora show the possibility of a union of the English and the Irish that are built on toleration and respect, and not on the ways dogs settle a dispute.

The Irish Renaissance:
W.B. Yeats

As a collector of folklore (*The Celtic Twilight*, 1893), as a poet and as a dramatist, William Butler Yeats (1865–1939) was instrumental in bringing about the **Irish Renaissance**. Together with Augusta, Lady Gregory (1852–1932) and with Edward Martyn (1859–1923), two other playwrights and cultural nationalists, Yeats launched the Irish Literary Theatre (1899–1901) as an antidote against the frequent revivals of Boucicault's plays and other melodrama. A patriotic self-image, the ideal of rural Ireland, found its dramatic expression in the **peasant play** (so-called even though the form was used by landowners like Martyn or Lady Gregory). The first productions signalled two possible ways for drama in this national spirit: while Martyn's *The Heather Field* (premiered on 9 May 1899) was influenced by Ibsen, Lady Gregory and Yeats favoured instead a **poetic drama** based on Irish mythology. Between the Romantic poets and Yeats, the tradition of poetic drama had been kept up – but also kept mainly to the closet – by Tennyson, Browning, Arnold and Swinburne (see chap. 4.4). Yeats's early plays (which were often written in blank verse) clearly affected Irish sensibilities even when they drew a mixed response. (This was one reason for his habitual revision of the text that resulted in competing versions of his plays.) In *The Countess Cathleen*, which is set in times of famine, the countess can save her peasants from starvation only by selling her soul to the devils, but apparently just because the soul of a Protestant aristocrat appears to be more valuable to God than those of her Catholic peasants. A Catholic audience protested against such morals in Yeats's verse play (which was premiered one day before Martyn's piece), and the cast received police protection for later productions in the same year. Another one-act play (in prose), *Cathleen ni Houlihan*, found more favour with Irish nationalists in 1902. Here, a particular tale of the 1798 Rebellion against the British in Ireland is fraught with perennial political symbolism and a topical Home Rule agenda. The preparations for a country wedding are interrupted by the visionary appearance of poor Cathleen ni Houlihan, a legendary personification of Ireland. "The Shan Van Vocht" (literally: old beggar-woman), as she is also called after an Irish peasants' song of around 1798, tells an allegorical story of rural Ireland: that she were bereft of her own house, which was occupied by strangers, and of her four beautiful green fields (provinces). With the promise of a hero's death and lasting fame, this Mother Ireland character persuades the bridegroom to leave his bride and fight for Cathleen and country. Thus, political history, Irish mythology and nationalist propaganda are interwoven into a patriotic call to arms. The play's success was partly due to Lady Gregory as a collaborator who helped Yeats in having the peasants' speech ring true, and to Maud Gonne, the English-born Irish nationalist and actress who stirred the audience when she played Cathleen. Maud Gonne continued to be Yeats's muse, even though she repeatedly rejected him as a lover. *Cathleen ni Houlihan* was criticised as unworldly and dangerous in Shaw's *John Bull's Other Island* (see the quotation above), but Yeats's ideological play found favour with Irish nationalists, and helped to pave the way for the abortive Easter Rising. Maud Gonne's divorced husband was among

|Fig. 4.16
W. B. Yeats (by George Charles Beresford)

those Irish rebels executed by the British in 1916, which ensured that Yeats would have to face the question of his own responsibility. Long after he had commemorated the dead in his poem "Easter 1916" (1920), he was to ask himself again in one of his last poems: "Did that play of mine send out/Certain men the English shot?" ("The Man and the Echo", 1939).

Abbey Theatre

The company that had been involved with the Irish Literary Theatre found a permanent home in 1904 at the **Abbey Theatre** in Dublin. Yeats and Lady Gregory (and J. M. Synge) were to remain artistic directors of this writers' theatre to the end of their lives; they contributed regularly to its productions and commissioned plays by other Irish playwrights. Peasant plays dominated the repertoire, while Frank and William Fay and the other Abbey players became known for their unadorned style of acting. Yeats followed up on his concern with Irish folklore in a series of plays centring on mythological characters from the medieval Ulster Cycle. The tragic tale of Deirdre who follows her lover Naoise (or Naisi) into death rather than marry his murderer, King Conchubar of Ulster, has been popular with many Anglo-Irish writers. In addition to Yeats's *Deirdre* (1906), there are other verse plays under that title by Samuel Ferguson (1880) and by George Russell a. k. a. AE (1902), there is J. M. Synge's *Deirdre of the Sorrows* as a tragedy in prose (Synge's fragment was posthumously produced in 1910), and there is the novella *Deirdre* by James Stephens (1923). Yeats was also attracted to the heroic warrior Cuchulain, who featured in a number of his plays, such as *On Baile's Strand* (1904), *At the Hawk's Well; or, Waters of Immortality* (1916), and *The Death of Cuchulain* (1939). *At the Hawk's Well*, like the other *Four Plays for Dancers* (1921), was conceived under the influence of the Japanese Nō theatre (in Ezra Pound's translations). The traditional Japanese form shows a similar concern with mythological and warrior heroes, and it is moreover characterised by a highly symbolical and stylised combination of dance and music, masks and mime. These later dance and dream plays by Yeats were first performed for the chosen few, and by design did not appeal to a larger audience.

While being in Paris in 1896, Yeats had met a wandering musician of Anglo-Irish Protestant stock, John Millington Synge (1871–1909), and mustered him in for the Gaelic revival. Over several years, Synge studied the Gaelic language and traditional

Irish culture in the remote Aran Islands. Afterwards, Yeats promoted him as a playwright and as a director at the Abbey Theatre. Here, Synge came out with original variations upon the peasant play that moreover defy conventional notions of comedy and tragedy. Synge's best-known play, *The Playboy of the Western World* (1907), is also the best example. This tragicomedy is set among peasants in a *shebeen* (a country pub) in the West of Ireland. Christy Mahon, a slight and frightened young man who is new to the village, arrives to tell the story of how he killed his overbearing father in the heat of the moment – and with this tale of manslaughter the anti-hero immediately becomes an attraction to old and young. Soon, the young man on the run from the police finds himself pursued by two women. Widow Quin, who is likewise responsible for the death of her husband, attempts to seduce Christy; and moreover young and wild Pegeen Mike is willing to leave her bridegroom Shawn Keogh for the love of this other, seemingly braver man. Christy does not accept Shawn's offer of a ticket for the USA, which would turn him out of the way. In view of this combined female pursuit of a single male, Synge's characterisation of Christy as a 'playboy' is clearly ironical and compares well with Shaw's handling of the Don Juan theme. Moreover, the dramatic irony consists in the fact that the audience soon comes to know that Old Mahon is alive and well, and also finds his way into the *shebeen*. For much of its course, this play appears to be a comic fusion of the Oedipus and the Don Juan themes. Yet in the latter half of this three-act play, Christy's reputation rises and falls in relation to a series of both farcical and fateful reversals. By winning in the village games, the 'playboy' justifies his nickname, before the truth about his father comes out and negatively affects Christy's standing. When Christy strikes home in earnest, Old Mahon appears to become the victim of a parricide for real. This time however the villagers turn against Christy in an attempt to lynch him, and Pegeen disavows him shortly after having become his fiancée. Synge's morally ambivalent tragicomedy ends with neither murder nor marriage. The second 'murder' turns out to be a fiction like the first: Old Mahon returns alive once more to save his son in time, yet the son makes him leave the village and go home together, so that a destitute Pegeen is thrown back on Shawn. The last words of the play, which are Pegeen's, proclaim anything but a happy

| Fig. 4.17
J. M. Synge

ending: "Oh, my grief, I've lost him surely. I've lost the only Playboy of the Western World."

Synge is nowadays seen as one of the greatest talents of the Irish literary revival, but there were some trademark features that initially did not endear his plays to nationalists in the audience (including Maud Gonne). Among those features was Synge's decision to elevate people from the margins of rural society to characters of great importance in his plays, such as beggars (*The Well of the Saints*, 1905), tinkers (*The Tinker's Wedding*, 1909), tramps (*In the Shadow of the Glen*, 1903) or a man on the run like Christy Mahon. With his disillusioning sketches of rural life – as for instance of the plight of fishermen and their wives in *Riders to the Sea* (1904) – Synge seemed to align himself with Naturalism (see Murray 2000: 69–74). Yet Synge also wanted to upstage the "joyless and pallid" manner of both Ibsen and Zola by a more "fully flavoured" dramatic language (as he wrote in the preface to *Playboy*). By his incorporation of the regional dialect and of Gaelic features into his prose dialogue, Synge achieved what looked like a fresh attempt at a literary representation of the 'language really used by men' a century after William Wordsworth (and Robert Burns). What his contemporary Irish audience received less favourably were Synge's iconoclasm in relation to moral institutions and his indifference towards sexual morality. Quite like some early plays by Wilde, Shaw and Yeats, Synge's *Playboy* met with a *succès de scandale*. In response to a passage in the dialogue that was seen as a defamation of the purity of Irish womanhood, the audience

Playboy Riots

on the first night started the 'Playboy Riots' that continued every evening for a whole week (see chap. 4.2.3). In repetition of what happened to Yeats's *The Countess Cathleen* in 1899, Synge's play could only be performed with police protection, while members of the Irish diaspora still called for a boycott when the Abbey players toured in the USA between 1911 and 1914. History would repeat itself once more when Sean O'Casey's *The Plough and the Stars* had a fiery welcome at the Abbey Theatre in 1926.

Guiding Questions and Exercises

1. The Anglo-Irish playwrights Boucicault, Wilde, Shaw, Yeats and Synge are related to distinct forms of drama in the century up to the 1920s. Summarise their most salient features.

2. Point out the way in which *Murder Most Foul* (1964), the film starring Margaret Rutherford as Miss Marple in an adaptation of Agatha Christie's crime novels, is related to Victorian and early twentieth-century conventions of stage drama and theatrical production.

3. Discuss the postcolonial play *Pantomime* (1978), in which the Caribbean playwright Derek Walcott fused the British traditions of music-hall comedy and the Christmas Pantomime with the distinct genre of the Jamaican Pantomime.

4. Compare G. B. Shaw's *Caesar and Cleopatra: A History* to the thematically related Roman plays by Shakespeare (*Julius Caesar, Anthony and Cleopatra*) and by Dryden (*All for Love*). Include in your comparison the playwright's period context, his treatment of history and the theme of love and honour.

5. *Saint Joan* is subtitled *A Chronicle Play*. Please situate Shaw's play in the tradition of historical drama.

6. With *Educating Rita* (1980), the dramatist Willy Russell provided a reworking of the Pygmalion myth that ties in well with both Shaw's *Pygmalion* and the musical *My Fair Lady*. Compare the three plays (and possibly their film versions) with regard to the handling of theme and form.

Poetry from Tennyson to Yeats: Forms and Themes | 4.4

Throughout the long reign of Queen Victoria, and well into the twentieth century, audiences were still used to hearing poems spoken or sung. The custom of reading aloud in private prevailed, and the range of performance included the public recital of 'parlour poetry' in the family circle or in the classroom, the singing of music-hall songs and of ballads in barrack-rooms and trenches. "The Land of Hope and Glory", A. C. Benson's triumphal hymn set to music by Edward Elgar for the coronation of Edward VII in 1902, has been sung up to today (at least on the Last Night of the Proms). Although Neoclassicist doctrines of a hierarchy and purity of genres had been contested by Romantic poets such as Keats or Shelley, whose original effort for example produced generic crossovers between ode and sonnet, their immediate successors were again working along conventional lines, if only up to a certain degree. There were interesting poetic experiments in this post-Romantic and pre-Modernist period, and there were also new genres introduced, such as the dramatic monologue. It makes sense, therefore, to group relevant poems from the period under review not primarily by poets, but again with regard to genres – from the long poem to the limerick – taking in thematic preoccupations and changes in versification along the way.

Fig. 4.18

Lord Tennyson

Readers of A. S. Byatt's half-Victorian novel *Possession* (1990), which includes a good amount of nineteenth-century poetic pastiche, will not be surprised by a predilection for the **long poem** written by poets from Tennyson to Yeats. Alfred (later Lord) Tennyson (1809–92) set out to write what Milton had originally considered as a subject fit for an epic before he decided to dictate *Paradise Lost*. Tennyson's *Idylls of the King* is an epic on King Arthur and the Knights of the Round Table, inspired by Thomas Malory's *Morte Darthur* (1470) and amounting to twelve books in blank verse written over a span of fifty years (1833–88; see part 1). An intertextual relation to the Arthurian legends is also the basis of "The Lady of Shalott" (1832; revised 1842, 1855), Tennyson's late-Romantic poem about a magic spell and tragic love that moreover shares the **medievalism** of Keats's "La Belle Dame sans Merci". The beautiful but lonely Lady of Shalott remains unseen in her island castle in the river leading to King Arthur's Camelot, and can only be heard singing a song. A curse hinders her to look directly towards Camelot: she can see the world only as reflected in her mirror, and then weaves these shadow-images into a colourful magic web. When the mirror shows Sir Lancelot arriving as a knight in shining armour, the Lady forgets all and looks directly out of the window. 'Better safe than sorry': the turn from an ideal world-picture to the direct experience of reality proves disastrous. It brings about the loss of both the mirror and her web, and later also of the Lady's life, when she transgresses further by taking a boat down the river to Camelot, singing her last carol. Tennyson's meta-poem about the relation of art and reality was an inspiration for many painters, and its ballad-like qualities come out well in versions set to music and sung by Loreena McKennitt (1991; 1998).

Shortly after "The Lady of Shalott", Tennyson began to funnel his devastation at the death of his close friend Arthur Hallam (†1833) into an elegy that he was to complete and publish only in 1850. *In Memoriam A. H. H.* comprises more than 130 sections, half-autonomous but consistently written in quatrains of iambic tetrameter and embracing rhyme – called the **"In Memoriam" stanza** (in distinction from the form of Thomas Gray's "Elegy Written in a Country Churchyard"). This long poem was as characteristic of Tennyson's private grief and insecurity as it caught on with a more widespread religious doubt among the poet's contemporaries (sect. 54–57, 95–96, 124).

In the year of publication, Tennyson succeeded Wordsworth after his brief spell (1843–50) as a Poet Laureate, to fill this post for nearly half a century. Tennyson thus acquired an honourable position for life which called for occasional verse such as the elegiac "Ode on the Death of the Duke of Wellington" (1852). This eulogy on 'the greatest soldier' (Wellington), who is to be united with 'the greatest sailor' (Nelson) in another world, is rather uninspired as a poem, but quite telling as a piece of public relations, taking pride that "in our fair island-story,/The path of duty was the way to glory" (refrain in part VIII of this ode).

Tennyson wrote more such 'newspaper verse' (his term) on events of the day, of which "The Charge of the Light Brigade" (1854, revised a year later) is the best-known example. Likewise based on the Horatian theme of *dulce et decorum est pro patria mori* ('it is sweet and proper to die for one's country'), this poem takes the praise of duty to an extreme by glorifying a military disaster, namely the utterly useless death of British soldiers in a mismanaged cavalry attack in the Crimean War:

> Half a league, half a league,
>   Half a league onward,
> All in the valley of Death
>   Rode the six hundred.
> "Forward, the Light Brigade!
> Charge for the guns!" he said:
> Into the valley of Death
>   Rode the six hundred.
>
> "Forward, the Light Brigade!"
> Was there a man dismay'd?
> Not though the soldier knew
>   Someone had blundered:
> Their's not to make reply,
> Their's not to reason why,
> Their's but to do and die:
> Into the valley of Death
>   Rode the six hundred. (Stanzas 1–2)

Quite effectively, Tennyson combined a reprehensible ideology with incremental repetition (as defined in chap. 3.3.2) and a catchy rhythm that imitates the horses' gallop (e.g. ll. 1–2). The poem's form made it particularly suited to public recital as 'parlour poetry'. By labelling such "a vulgar thought vigorously expressed [...] a good bad poem", George Orwell tried to account for Tennyson's gift to shape public memory by memorable poetry. This also goes a long way to explain why the Laureate became the most popular poet of his day, but posthumously as well as past the Empire's prime, like Kipling, an all-too-easy target for wholesale critical condemnation (see Orwell 1942). Yet Tennyson has not been lost on a postcolonial Caribbean-British poet such as Fred D'Aguiar:

> When Grandad recited the Tennyson learned at sea,
> [...] We'd sit tight,
> All eyes on our sweet seasalter, for that last-line-sound,
> Someone mistimed once, making him start again.
> These days the perfect-lined face of a blank page,
> Startles at first, like Papa-T's no-nonsense recitals;
> It has me itching to bring him reeling-off in that tongue –
> *Honour the charge they made! Honour the Light Brigade,*
> *Noble six hundred*: to hear, to disobey.
>
> ("Papa-T", 1985. D'Aguiar 2001: 19, ll. 1, 11–18.)

Here are the Laureate's lines again, and that mixed response of fascination and rejection, too.

A different kind of longish 'newspaper verse' came from Elizabeth Barrett Browning (1806–61). "The Cry of Children" (1843) was written in response to a parliamentary commission's report on child labour in factories and coalmines. The poem continued in the line of Blake's songs on chimney sweepers and on "London", and it moreover linked up with the social novels of its day. "The Runaway Slave at Pilgrim's Point" was an Abolitionist poem that connected with Harriet Beecher Stowe's anti-slavery novel *Uncle Tom's Cabin*. (The poem was first published in Boston, Mass. in 1847, to be revised for a London edition of 1850; the novel followed in 1851–52.) With *Aurora Leigh* (1857), her widely popular novel in blank verse, Barrett Browning produced a long poem on the growth of a woman poet's mind that can be seen as a companion-piece to *The Prelude* by Wordsworth. Barrett Browning herself was considered the foremost English woman poet of her

Fig. 4.19
Elizabeth Barrett
Browning

time, and was even considered as a successor of Wordsworth as Poet Laureate, before the post went to Tennyson.

After Tennyson, it was Algernon Charles Swinburne (1837–1909) – another eccentric Victorian, but of a more scandalous kind – who seemed most fascinated by the elegy as a genre. "Ave Atque Vale: In Memory of Charles Baudelaire" (1868) tells of the poet's classical learning (the title is taken from an elegy by Catullus), of the respect paid by one socially incompatible *poète maudit* to another (Baudelaire), and also of Swinburne's own poetic hallmark: hypnotic lines of chiming verse, not always infused with profound meaning (e.g. "O sleepless heart and sombre soul unsleeping,/That were athirst for sleep and no more life/ And no more love, for peace and no more strife!", ll. 34–36).

A.C. Swinburne

"Goblin Market" (1862) by Christina Rossetti (1830–94) compares well with Swinburne's exuberance. This non-elegiac long poem was the accomplished title piece of Christina Rossetti's first volume of poetry: a melodious poem of over 560, two- or three-stressed lines, rhymed throughout but to no continuous scheme. In a reversal of the Biblical story of the Fall, this long poem tells the story of how two sisters are approached by goblin men to buy and taste forbidden fruit. When Laura gives in to sweet-talk and seduction and sucks the fruit, this drains her vitality in much the same way as the close contact with *La Belle Dame sans Merci* (in Keats's ballad) had sucked the life out of men. Were it not for her brave and steadfast sister Lizzie, who can outwit the magic men and break the charm, Laura would have perished; yet so, there returns "Life out of death." (ll. 524). What shone through the fairy-tale setting and the seemingly simple diction was both a quasi-Biblical parable of temptation, sinning and repentance, and a more worldly fable of gender relations and sexual morality. In simple terms, the moral of the tale looked as much feminist as it was Victorian: never trust a charming man, and in case of temptation, fall back on female bonding or you are bound to become a fallen woman.

Christina Rossetti

In one last, and lasting, example of the elegy from the period of the Irish Renaissance, W. B. Yeats (1865–1939) combined 'newspaper verse' and poetry of mourning. "Easter 1916" was composed after the unsuccessful Easter Rising in Dublin against the British government (yet published not before 1921). The beginning of the rebellion on April 24, 1916, is enshrined in the poetic design (there are four stanzas of 24 and 16 lines in alternation), and the elegy was written in order to commemorate those rebel leaders who were executed by the British, among them the poets Patrick Pearse and Thomas MacDonagh. Although Yeats qualified his judgment on the dead while they were alive (in particular, but not surprisingly, with regard to the divorced husband of Maud Gonne, Yeats's militant muse), he saw them transformed by the events, a change for which he can account however only in oxymoronic form: "A terrible beauty is born." (refrain to stanzas 1, 2 and 4). The question "Was it needless death after all?" (l. 67), apart from providing martyrs for the Irish nationalist cause, is left unanswered, and so is a similar question in the later poem "The Man and the Echo" (1939, see chap. 4.3) which queried the Irish poet's own responsibility for the course of events.

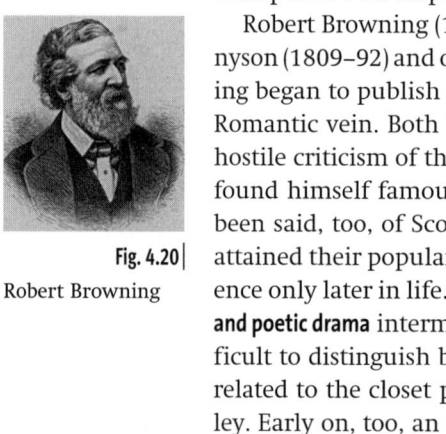

Robert Browning (1812–89) was a direct contemporary of Tennyson (1809–92) and of Dickens (1812–70). Like Tennyson, Browning began to publish his verse at around 1830, and likewise in a Romantic vein. Both Victorian poets moreover had to overcome hostile criticism of their early work: none of them 'woke up and found himself famous', as it was said of Byron, and could have been said, too, of Scott and of Dickens. Indeed, Browning never attained their popularity, and found a larger and respectful audience only later in life. Yet already in his early work, **dramatic poetry and poetic drama** intermingled, so much so that it is sometimes difficult to distinguish between the two. Clearly, these pieces were related to the closet plays of Romantic poets like Byron or Shelley. Early on, too, an interest in historical settings and historical persons is noticeable. This links Browning's poems and plays to some extent with the historical novels of Walter Scott. *Paracelsus* (1835) is such a hybrid of poetry and drama, written in blank verse and focused on the life of the Renaissance alchemist. *Strafford: A Tragedy* in blank verse, written in the year of Queen Victoria's accession (1837), concentrates on the powerful minister of the Stuart monarch Charles I, who preceded his king in laying his head on the block. More tragedies were to follow, and Browning did not remain alone. To name but a few contemporaries who likewise wrote poetic drama (mainly for the closet): Matthew Arnold centred on a Greek philosopher (*Empedocles on Etna*, 1852), and Alfred Tennyson wrote a history play on *Becket*, the murdered medieval Archbishop of Canterbury (1884). Both Algernon Charles Swinburne and Thomas Hardy composed whole trilogies of historical verse plays. Swinburne singled out Mary Queen of Scots (1865–81), while Hardy mixed historical personalities with ordinary 'Wessex' folk of his own imagination in *The Dynasts: A Drama of the Napoleonic Wars* (1904–08). The tradition of poetic drama continued with W. B. Yeats and T. S. Eliot (see the chapters below on drama and poetry after c. 1920).

In 1843, Robert Browning met and fell in love with fellow-poet Elizabeth Barrett, who was six years his senior. They became secretly married in September 1846, leaving for Italy soon after, and stayed in Florence for the rest of her life (†1861). Only after the death of his famous wife, and after his return to England, Robert Browning finally achieved wider recognition. *The Ring and the Book* is considered his most ambitious and most accomplished work, an epic poem in twelve books, running to 21,000 lines of blank verse. Interestingly enough, this poem was published, like the novels of Dickens, in monthly instalments (1868–69). Robert Browning continued to publish volumes of poetry with ever more outlandish titles, which already testify to his notorious leaning towards quaintness and obscurity. *Caliban upon Setebos* (1864), an intertextual adaptation of Shakespeare's *The Tempest* with Caliban, and not Prospero, in the centre, is a good example of such titles. The subtitle *Natural Theology in the Island* hints at the fact that Browning was not interested primarily in Shakespeare's play as such, but in a discussion of theological questions of his own day. *Caliban upon Setebos* is also characteristic of the genre that is prominently connected with Browning's name, the **dramatic monologue**, of which his "My Last Duchess" (1842) is perhaps the most frequently anthologised example. In this poem and in the genre as such prevails the extended monologue of a lyrical speaker who addresses an invisible and certainly inaudible audience. In its dramatic depiction of character and in its dramatised *personae*, the new poetic kind may be said to echo the Romantic cult of the individual. Arguably, one may go as far back as to Andrew Marvell's "To His Coy Mistress" (published 1681) for a poem that takes the form of a dramatised monologue. In "My Last Duchess" (but not necessarily in all instances) the lyrical speaker is clearly not identical with the poet. Browning's historical character sketch is set in the portrait gallery at a Renaissance court, where the Duke of Ferrara negotiates with an envoy from

My Last Duchess

another nobleman who offers his daughter as a marriage candidate. In his uninterrupted comment on a portrait of his recently deceased wife, the duke comes out as the villain in the piece. He is clearly conceited, and was therefore hurt when he could not secure the full interest of 'his last duchess' at all times. There is a strong hint that the duke's egotism and his suspicion of possible rivals in her affection proved fatal to his wife: "I gave commands;/Then all smiles stopped together. There she stands/As if alive." (ll. 45–47).

Fig. 4.21|
Ulysses and the Sirens by John W. Waterhouse (1891)

Within the same year, 1842, Tennyson published "Ulysses", a dramatic monologue that he had begun to compose nine years earlier. In Tennyson's version, the Homeric hero first reflects on his unpromising life after the return from the Trojan War and a long series of adventures. He sees himself as "an idle king [...] Matched with an aged wife", soon to be replaced by his son Telemachus as the epitome of an ideal ruler, and left without a purpose: "How dull is it to pause, to make an end,/To rust unburnished, not to shine in use!" (ll. 1–3, 22–23). However, there are ways of escape. What resembled a brooding soliloquy on stage turns into a proper monologue, into a clarion call to action sent out to Ulysses's old mariners in the poem, and certainly also to the young imperialists among Tennyson's readers:

> [...] Come, my friends,
> 'Tis not to late to seek a newer world.
> [...] that which we are, we are;
> One equal temper of heroic hearts,
> Made weak by time and fate, but strong in will
> To strive, to seek, to find, and not to yield.   (ll. 56–57, 67–70)

Tennyson's "Ulysses" not only exemplifies a new poetic sub-genre and the political context of Victorian poetry; it also provides a good occasion for a brief look at the fate of **Classical literature in post-Neoclassical times.** Swinburne's poetry (not just "Ave Atque Vale") was full of Classical allusions, and the learning of A[lfred]. E[dward]. Housman (1859–1936) as a Cambridge Professor of Latin did also show in his verse. Some Romantic and Victorian poets returned to the Greek dramatist Aeschylus, for example Percy Bysshe Shelley when he wrote his own play *Prometheus Unbound* (1819–20, a closet play). Elizabeth Barrett Browning later translated the source, Aeschylus's *Prometheus Bound* (she did so twice, in 1833 and 1850). Robert Browning continued in this vein, with his translation of Aeschylus's *Agamemnon* (1877) that deals with one of the Greek leaders in the Trojan War. The list of well-known British and American writers who engaged in adapting the Homeric epics for children includes Charles Lamb (*The Adventures of Ulysses*, 1811), Charles Kingsley (*The Heroes; or, Greek Fairy Tales for Children*, 1856) and Nathaniel Hawthorne (*A Wonder-Book for Girls and Boys*, 1851). The translations of Edward FitzGerald (1809–83) indicate a change in outlook under the impact of Orientalism and the overseas Empire. Far more than through his translations from the Greek, FitzGerald influenced his contemporaries by the exotic imagery and comforting philosophy of *The Rubáiyát of Omar Khayyám*, which he brought out in five successive and steadily revised editions (1859–89). FitzGerald freely translated and transformed the rhymed quatrains (*rubáiyát*) of the medieval Persian astronomer and poet into pentameter lines rhyming *aaba*, and he re-arranged them so as to follow the course of the day. Traces of this growing interest in the Orient are to be found later in the last lines (in Sanskrit) of T. S. Eliot's *The Waste Land* (1922). W. B. Yeats however (notwithstanding his interest in forms of Far Eastern theatre) returned in his poetry to Europe and its Classical tradition by "Sailing to Byzantium" (1927), and only so far. In addition to his concern with Irish folklore, the foremost poet of the Irish Renaissance used Greek mythology as a basis for poems like "No Second Troy" (1910) and "Leda and the Swan" (1924). In *Ulysses* (1922), James Joyce, no less prominent as a novelist from Ireland, adapted the Homeric epic to the Dublin of his day. In his concern with the restless Greek traveller, Joyce the Modernist followed upon Tennyson the arch-Victorian, and testified further to the fact that the legends and literature of Classical Antiquity continued to hold a strong interest for a nineteenth- and early twentieth-century literary public.

Matthew Arnold (1822–88), who had already written a poetic drama centring on a Greek philosopher (*Empedocles on Etna*), went on to make the dramatist Sophocles an explicit point of reference in "Dover Beach" (1867). Like Arnold's lectures (see chap. 4.5.1), this poem can be read as cultural criticism, too, and in this mono-logue, the lyrical speaker could indeed be equated with the poet. Apart from the speaker and his loving, but silent companion, both of whom look from Dover over the Channel towards France, and apart from the casual reference to Sophocles, there is no hu-man being present in the poem. However, this Victorian night-and sea-piece is neither another instance of the Romantic Sub-lime, nor is it a case of nature poetry proper. The sea functions as object of reflection, but not the actual subject of the poem. At ebb-time, the sea is calm, but there is "the grating roar/Of pebbles which the waves draw back" (ll. 9–10). This sound compares with "The eternal note of sadness" that Sophocles heard on the Ae-gean Sea and associated with "human misery" (ll. 14, 18). To the lyrical speaker, this is moreover associated metaphorically with the ebbed flow of "The Sea of Faith" which is now "withdraw-ing" and "Retreating" (21, 25–26). The last paragraph of the poem concludes with a Victorian World Picture in the negative. A faith-less world is seen as "a darkling plain" which offers "neither joy, nor love, nor light,/Nor certitude, nor peace, nor help for pain"; and such a world looks like a battlefield where "ignorant armies" are directed by "confused alarms" (ll. 33–37). In a strikingly ex-istentialist, even absurd picture before the terms were coined, Arnold presents a world devoid of security and meaning. The desperate cry for faithfulness and love in the private sphere ("Ah, love, let us be true/To one another!" ll. 29–30) appears to be the only remedy for such a general loss of Faith, of (Christian) reli-gion and of comforting ideals. This Victorian World Picture *ex negativo* could be explained as a lament on the harmful effect of the theory of Evolution on the observance of Christian doctrine. However, Matthew Arnold had written his dramatic monologue already in around 1851, at the time of publication of Tennyson's *In Memoriam*, and thus a good many years before Darwin's *The Origin of Species* (1859) came out.

Arnold's poem raises the terminological question as to what matters most in a dramatic monologue: the arbitrary rule that the poem should dramatise a character other than the poet, or the internal, communicative situation. The dramatic situation was generally the same in all three monologues under review, regardless of their differences as to metre, rhyme or stanza pattern. Browning's "My Last Duchess" was composed in heroic couplets, and thus in true Neoclassical fashion. Tennyson's "Ulysses" was presented in verse paragraphs without a consistent stanza pattern, but still in blank verse. Arnold's "Dover Beach" was quite free from conventions of metre and rhyme: these were still visible, but they were loosely applied. "Dover Beach" is an example of how these older conventions could still be used in an intricate and innovative way, but it was also going a long way towards **free verse**. The latter, together with the repetition of sound and phrases as a structuring device, was the new form that T.S. Eliot (1888–1965) later used for "The Love Song of J. Alfred Prufrock" (1915). This is another monologue-cum-meditation, yet *Prufrock* in a Modernist mode. Eliot's poem sets in with the description of the evening twilight as if "spread out against the sky/Like a patient etherised upon a table" (ll. 2–3, i.e. hovering between two states of existence), and it also ends with a sad reflection upon the sea:

> I have heard the mermaids singing, each to each.
>   I do not think that they will sing to me. [...]
>   We have lingered in the chambers of the sea
> By sea-girls wreathed with seaweed red and brown
> Till human voices wake us, and we drown.   (ll. 124–31)

Given out as the 'love-song' of an elderly and tired snob who is undecided as to ask some "overwhelming question" (i.e. to make a proposal of marriage? ll. 10, 93), this Modernist poem no longer shows a coherent action or train of thought. It is marked instead by association and by a juxtaposition of images and quasi-Metaphysical conceits such as "I have measured out my life with coffee spoons;" (l. 51) in short: by "a hundred indecisions,/ [...by] a hundred visions and revisions" (ll. 32–33). Though Eliot occasionally makes use of rhyme, this comes in various forms, and there is no consistent metrical pattern. Eliot's free verse is structured instead by verbal repetition: by anaphora and refrain.

Thus, some poetic traditions may go a long way, from Browning's scene of revenge and courtship at a Renaissance court to Eliot's hesitant coffee courtier who protests "No! I am not Prince Hamlet, nor was meant to be;/Am an attendant lord," (ll. 111–12).

In Janus-faced fashion, the chosen genre and the poetic design of "Prufrock" look back at the Victorian canon and ahead to Modernist experiment, both at the same time. However, the negotiation of "Tradition and the Individual Talent" (such is the title of Eliot's programmatic essay of 1920) was nothing new to the pre-Modernist period. A concern with demanding poetic form shows markedly in a **revival of Old French and Italian forms** other than the sonnet. From the 1870s through the 1890s, Austin Dobson (1840–1921), Edmund Gosse (1849–1928), W.E. Henley (1849–1903), Robert Bridges (1844–1930) and also Thomas Hardy produced *triolets*, *rondeaux*, *villanelles* or *sestinas*, or came up like Swinburne with original variations such as the *roundel*. As a consequence of the later shift towards Modernism, such poetry is only rarely represented in today's anthologies, even though it was not lost on W.H. Auden and Dylan Thomas (see *BCP* 154–56, and for the characteristics of each form, see Preminger and Brogan 1993 or the introductions to poetry listed at the end of this volume).

The much better represented development of the sonnet testifies to the fact that in its negotiation of "Tradition and the Individual Talent", the period under review was not at all free from poetic experiment. First of all, a number of **sonnet sequences** were composed, e.g. by Elizabeth Barrett Browning. There is a Romantic context to her 44 (Italian) *Sonnets from the Portuguese* (1850): she composed these intensely personal love poems during her courtship with Robert Browning (1843–46). Actually, the title is a trick: there are no Portuguese originals for these poems – they are only given out as translations to abstract from their autobiographical content. In recording the stages of the couple's courtship (which ended in a secret marriage to escape her tyrannical father), this sequence basically conforms to the tradition of the genre since the Renaissance, and in particular to Spenser's *Amoretti* (1595), which depict and celebrate a successful courtship, too.

Not very long afterwards, the novelist, poet and publisher's reader George Meredith (1828–1909) made a fresh attempt at love poetry, however with a sonnet sequence on the breakdown of a marriage. In 1849, Meredith had married the daughter of Thomas Love Peacock, a widow eight years his senior, and only for nine years his partner. Her elopement with an artist to Capri sealed their separation, and her death in 1861 made Meredith publish *Modern Love* (1862), a sequence of fifty sonnets that reads like a novel in verse (akin to Barrett Browning's *Aurora Leigh*, and to Meredith's other prose works). A husband and his wife are the two main characters in the sequence: both partners have extra-marital relations, and ultimately fail to become reconciled, so that in the end she commits suicide. These **Meredithian sonnets** are unconventional, first because they tell the story of an unhappy love, and second because they come in 16 lines. (A century later, Roy Fuller paid homage to this new variant in his own sequence of "Meredithian Sonnets", 1962.)

A third and last notable sequence came from Dante Gabriel Rossetti (1828–82). Together with the painters William Holman Hunt and John Everett Millais, he founded an artists' circle, the Pre-Raphaelite Brotherhood, in 1848. In painting and in poetry, **Pre-Raphaelite art** was an example of deliberate medievalism. With its sensuous imagery and anti-Realist attitude, this movement became a precursor of Symbolism and of Aestheticism. When initial repudiation had met with the favourable stance of John Ruskin, the pre-eminent art critic of the time, the new style of painting soon became fashionable, and it has been considered a characteristic feature of painting in Victorian Britain up to to-day. Also in 1848, D. G. Rossetti began to compose his sonnet sequence *The House of Life*, parts of which first appeared in the little magazine of the Brotherhood in 1850. The further history of this sequence is a morbid story: when his wife (a former model of his) died in 1862, Rossetti insisted that his poems were being buried together with her – later however he would revise his decision and had his poems disinterred. *The House of Life* was published in 1870, and again in an enlarged and completed version in 1881, shortly before Rossetti's death. The sequence consists of over 100 sonnets and is subdivided into two parts of equal length: "Youth and Change", followed by "Change and Fate". Once again, the themes are love and beauty, and the loss of love; however, in contrast to Browning and Meredith, Rossetti provided no con-tinuous narrative. "A Sonnet is a moment's monument" runs the first line of the introductory sonnet to the enlarged sequence

| Fig. 4.23
Dante Gabriel Rossetti (by George Frederic Watts)

(1881), and this poem has three points of interest: first, as **meta-poetry**; second, as an example of Pre-Raphaelite poetry; and third, as a remnant of the tradition of publishing poetry in manuscript form. As meta-poetry, the sonnet is rather disappointing: it is neither a factual definition in verse, nor a toying with the technicalities of the genre, as in the comparable meta-sonnet of John Keats, "If By Dull Rhymes Our English Must Be Chained". (Rossetti's sonnet takes the ambivalent form used by John Donne, *abba abba cdcdee*). The poem is however a good example of Pre-Raphaelite poetry, and obviously was considered as a programmatic piece. In this poem, which ends on a note of death, words were chosen for their sound effect and for their symbolic connotations rather than for a precise meaning. Lines like "Whether for lustral rite or dire portent,/Of its own arduous fulness reverent:" (ll. 4–5) moreover testify to Rossetti's medievalism, visible in his fondness of Latinised diction and archaisms. This shows, too, in the **combination of poem and illustration** that is typical of the work of this poet and painter. One point of reference (as for instance also in the initial sketches to Thackeray's novel *Vanity Fair*) are the illuminated manuscript books of the Middle Ages. Another influence came from William Blake's intermedial work and its manner of distribution, which bore **resemblance to the circulation of poetry in manuscript**. Just like with Blake's poetry, which was published in small editions individually coloured by the artist, Rossetti's sonnets and their illustration first appeared only in a limited edition directed at a circle of the chosen few. By comparison, the poems of Gerard Manley Hopkins (1844–89) were circulating in manuscript for three or four decades before a first edition was printed (1918). W. B. Yeats was circulating his poetry to a select circle in this manner and in similar forms alike. Yeats took part in the poetry recitals in a London pub among fellow poets of the Rhymer's Club (1891–94, they were sometimes joined by Oscar Wilde), and he presented his work to those subscribing to *The Yellow Book* (London, 1894–97). Equivalents to such a literary and art periodical can be seen later in **little magazines** such as *Poetry* (Chicago, 1912 ff.) and *The Egoist* (London, 1914–19), and also in the **small presses** of the period. The work of William Morris (1834–96) at the Kelmscott Press (from 1891) is a further example of the revival of the tradition of the medieval codex and of the early printed book of the Renaissance. The Hogarth Press, set up by Leonard and Virginia Woolf in 1917, published Modernist works such as T. S. Eliot's *The Waste Land*. Altogether, this partial return to pre-Victorian forms of distribution also demonstrated a re-opening of a gap between widely popular (and not just parlour) poetry – as exemplified by the work of Barrett Browning, Tennyson and Kipling – and various kinds of *l'art pour l'art* and avant-garde verse.

In addition to whole sequences, a good number of single sonnets were produced. Elizabeth Barrett Browning for example wrote Italian sonnets in praise of the female French novelist George Sand (1844), and Christina Rossetti's first volume of poetry (1862) contained counterparts such as "Cobwebs" (an exercise in *ex negativo* definition), "Dead Before Death" and "After Death" (the latter a vision of a lyrical speaker on his deathbed). Later sonnets of note can serve as an illustration of the **experimentation** that took place up to Modernism. Just like his predecessors Donne and Milton, Gerard Manley Hopkins (who had converted to Catholicism and become a Jesuit priest) used the form for religious verse. However, when his poetry was finally published in a collected edition, he was seen less as following tradition than as a prime example of a poet ahead of contemporary taste. To Modernist poets and their readers (who overall may not have shared his religious commitment), he appeared to be born before his time, which is reflected in his place in anthologies since the 1930s (see below). A comparison of two of his sonnets written in 1877 is helpful here. Where "God's Grandeur" ends, praising the Trinity in images of sunrise and birds at dawn, "The Windhover: To Christ Our Lord" continues with a joyful celebration of the flight of a falcon as a Sublime symbol. While "God's Grandeur", albeit strongly marked by alliteration and enjambment, basically follows in the 'Italian' tradition, "The Windhover" recognises this only with a nod on its way to an utterly unconventional form distinguished by distorted syntax, an intricate compounding of words, and the use of one rhyme only for the octave. Hopkins's poetry is also marked by his strong interest in stress patterns, in **sprung rhythm** (his term), which situates him on a line leading, if not all the way from Old English poetry, then from Coleridge's metrical experiments in *Christabel* (1816) to the accentual verse of Robert Graves (see the chapter on poetry after c. 1920).

G. M. Hopkins

Thomas Hardy (1840–1928) was altogether much more sceptical about religion than Hopkins, and his poetic experiments
were focused on complex stanza forms instead of stress patterns.
Both of this had already been signalled in his early sonnet "Hap"
(written in 1866). The title translates as 'Chance', and the poem
has religion as its theme, but recognises no god – not even "some
vengeful god" (l. 1). Instead, "Crass Casualty" (l. 11; in other
words: Chaos) reigns supreme. In this sonnet, the young Hardy
came up with a mix of Petrarchan and Shakespearean conventions, and with a poetic diction of his own ("unbloom", l. 10).
Hardy returned to his youthful interest in poetry after the increasingly hostile criticism of his later novels (see chap. 4.5.3),
and published his first collection, characteristically entitled *Wessex Poems* (1898), at the age of 58. Until the end of his life, his
poetic œuvre summed up to over 900 poems, besides the verse
play *The Dynasts*. The 'odd' sonnet is present in most of the other
collections published during his lifetime, too, leading to the reversal of the Italian form in "Shortening Days at the Homestead"
and further to the unconventional, seven-plus-seven-line poems
"Nobody Comes" and "The Sexton at Longpuddle", which testify
to Hardy's experimental vein (all three were first published in
1925). A few other poems (no sonnets) have to be mentioned,
too. "The Darkling Thrush" (dated 31 December 1900) is a pessimistic poem on the 'death' of the nineteenth century, ending on
a note of no hope left. "Drummer Hodge" (1901), which centres
on a soldier from 'Wessex' dying in the Boer War, to be buried
in the South African *veldt*, is a good example for the intrusion of
Afrikaans words and other non-English expressions into English
poetry in the colonial period. Later, Hardy commented upon the
sinking of the Titanic in "The Convergence of the Twain" (1912),
and on the Great War in "Channel Firing" and other often doubt-
ful "Poems of War and Patriotism" (1914–17). In response to the
signing of the Armistice in November 1918, 78-year-old Hardy
wrote "'And there was a Great Calm'", ending his poem on the
unanswered question "Why?"

Other, much younger poets who were actively involved in
the fighting, added more (anti-)war sonnets in response to their
experience. Up to the war, Rupert Brooke (1887–1915), Edward
Thomas (1878–1917) and others who were then labelled **Georgian Poets** (with reference to King George V, who was crowned

in 1911), had written pastoral poems that celebrated nature, and the English landscape in particular. In those pre-war years, Brooke had turned out a "Sonnet Reversed" (1911, in Amis 1987: 216) that gave a new twist to the traditional love theme. True to its programmatic title, this Shakespearean sonnet begins with an end couplet that tells of a couple of newly-weds in their ultimate hour of bliss. Then, in a sarcastic turn and tone, the everyday life of their marriage is rehearsed, up to the couple's death. And there is no other happy ending envisioned: this sonnet does not recognise any promise of an after-life, not even in the children who remain. Such a Hardyesque stance was however rare in the early *Georgian Anthologies* (1912–22). The war experience brought a change: in the poetry of Edward Thomas, nostalgic reminiscences of a pastoral world were now coloured by more sombre meditations on death. Rupert Brooke joined the Forces in the field much more willingly, and welcomed the opportunity to fight for King and Country. Brooke's sonnet "The Soldier" (1915) mirrors the poet's patriotism, and it foreshadows his early death in Flanders: "If I should die, think only this of me:/ That there's some corner of a foreign field/ That is for ever England." (ll. 1–3). Quite consciously, the sonnet's form is made to stress this point by incorporating the rhyming pattern of an English sonnet into an overall basically Italian design and 'foreign field'.

| Fig. 4.24
Rupert Brooke

That the world would not profit from such wars, but that they indeed resembled hell on earth, was to become Wilfred Owen's theme. Owen (1893–1918) took part in the murderous fight for minute and meaningless movements in the muddy fields of Flanders, and he became thoroughly disillusioned in the process. Owen's "Anthem for Doomed Youth" (written in the autumn of 1917) dedicates another sonnet amalgamating English and Italian patterns to those who "die as cattle" (l. 1). In "Dulce Et Decorum Est" (from the same period), the real experience of the Great War is shown to be far removed from the time-worn glorification of war that had informed Tennyson's and Brooke's poems, but which Owen's lyrical speaker calls simply an "old Lie" (l. 27). In Owen's anti-war poem, the situation is as follows: a group of soldiers retreats from the fighting zone to their own lines, slowly, lame, and bereft of their senses. An attack with poison gas changes the situation in an instant. All those who could don their gas masks in time are made to witness how the chemical weapon hits one

Wilfred Owen

comrade with full force, and with dreadful consequence. For his poem, Owen used an imagery of physical disability and disease throughout, but as if in search of the ultimate stretcher, he built an intricate stanza form to fixate the horrors of war. A first, regular and Shakespearean sonnet is glued together with another 'English sonnet reversed', so that the couplets in the centre of the double sonnet function as a joint. And at this joint, the concrete description of a particular situation turns into a general reflection on the bitterness and meaninglessness of the Great War, and in an advice from the front no longer to teach the "old Lie" to pupils back home.

As if he found it necessary to improve upon one of the most terrifying anti-war poems in the language, Owen soldiered on from a double sonnet to a fourteen-line poem that is split exactly in two halves. "Futility" (1918) resembled Hardy's later poems mentioned above, but Owen's lines of verse moreover came on half a rhyme. Owen paired "sun" with "sown", "seeds" with "sides" or "tall" with "toil", and used such **consonance, or para-rhyme** (his favoured term) for a front poem that tells of death, but knows no rebirth. With original experiments like these, Owen showed the potential to become an even greater poet, but he was killed in action, sadly, just one week before the Armistice.

In 1920, Owen's poems were brought out through the comrade and colleague who had inspired and assisted him when they met in hospital three years earlier. Siegfried Sassoon (1886–1967) bore an unlikely name for someone who was both a highly decorated British soldier and an anti-war poet. The two sonnets "Glory of Women" (1918) and "On Passing the New Menin Gate" (1928) tell of his uncompromising stance: the one written during the war is full of satirical quips against women's hero-worship, the other finds fault with a Brussels war memorial that lacks the names of "The unheroic Dead who fed the guns" (l. 2). The latter sonnet continues to attack the glorification of a botched war and industrialised slaughter, which Owen had also abhorred, but which can still be found in "Epitaph on an Army of Mercenaries" (1922) by the older poet A. E. Housman.

As editor of the 1936 *Oxford Book of Modern Verse, 1892–1935*, a prestigious anthology of post-Tennysonian poetry, W. B. Yeats paid homage to military bravery, but excluded the war poetry. Neither Brooke nor Sassoon had been represented with poems from the war (only "On Passing the New Menin Gate" found favour with the editor), and Owen's verse was excluded altogether simply because Yeats would not share its sympathetic stance to those who suffered: "passive suffering is not a theme for poetry" (Yeats 1936: xxxiv). On the long run, this eccentric judgment was overruled. In *War Requiem* (1962), Benjamin Britten was to set Wilfred Owen's poems to music, and in Pat Barker's *Regeneration Trilogy* of novels on the First World War (1991–95), Owen and Sassoon were to feature largely as characters. Other poets of the First World War, who were generally less well known in their time, are now regularly anthologised, such as Isaac Rosenberg (1890–1918) and Ivor Gurney (1890–1937).

With "Leda and the Swan" (1924), Yeats first of all produced (quasi as a counterpart to "The Soldier" and "Anthem for Doomed Youth") his elaborate specimen of an amalgamated sonnet on a martial theme: the origin of the war against Troy. Yeats even incorporated **half-rhymes** of his own (pairing "push" with "rush", and "up" with "drop"). His own experiments with dissonance during the war years (e. g. in "The Scholars", 1915) make for an interesting comparison with

|Fig. 4.25
Leda and the Swan (copy after Michelangelo, 1530). One copy was in Yeats's possession

Owen's treatment – however, readers of the 1936 *Oxford Book of Modern Verse* were not given such an opportunity. When his own verse, like his dramatic work, was concerned with struggle and strife, Yeats was indeed more interested in heroic suffering within a mythological context. The constellation of beauty and the beast in "Leda and the Swan" was connected with a whole string of Greek myths alluded to in the poem: by his rape of the queen of Sparta, Zeus (in animal shape) fathered Helena, who later became the ultimate cause for the war against Troy, which in turn led to the death of Agamemnon and the destruction of the city. Earlier on, in "No Second Troy" (1910, a poem which may, but must not be seen as a kind of clipped Shakespearean sonnet, bereft of its final couplet), Yeats had already referred to the Greek myth, but in a different context. In a series of rhetorical questions, the lyrical speaker tries to come to terms with a beautiful but agitating woman who makes his life miserable, and who instigates others to acts of violence: "Was there another Troy for her to burn?" (l. 12). It is not too far-fetched to equate the speaker with Yeats, and this *femme vitale* with both Helen of Troy and Maud Gonne, Yeats's distant muse – or, to give this comparison another twist, to equate ancient Greece with modern Ireland. In "A Coat" (1914), Yeats would renounce such mythological dress, but only for a time. (The poem is also interesting for its variation on the stanza of Keats's odes.) Later, in "Leda and the Swan", Yeats was to come up with a private mythology of his own, and to generalise even further. Indeed, Leda's suffering is not a point of pity in the poem. Yeats regarded the event within a larger world-historical scheme, and he used poems such as "Leda and the Swan" and "The Second Coming" (1920) to illustrate an apocalyptic scheme that he expounded at greater length in his book *A Vision* (1926; this, together with other poems by Yeats, will be dealt with in the chapter on Modernist poetry).

The name of Yeats is also linked to yet another **folk song revival** that occurred at the turn of the twentieth century and led to a new wave of collections of folk songs, folk tales and ballads. In the field of popular narrative verse, the interplay of performance and of print had become more marked since the appearance of printed collections in the eighteenth century. Among the best-known Victorian compilations are *English and Scottish Popular Ballads* (1882–98) by F. J. Child, Andrew Lang's *The Nursery Rhyme Book* (1897) and *The Blue Fairy Book* (which developed into a series, 1889–1910), and *The Celtic Twilight* (1893) by W. B. Yeats. In 1898, Cecil Sharp (1859–1924) founded the Folk Song Society, together with the composer Ralph Vaughan Williams (1872–1958), who either arranged the tunes for songs like "Greensleeves", or made such material the basis of his original work. The great number of versions collected of "Barbara Allen" and of other popular ballads testifies to the continuous exchange of oral ballads across the Irish Sea and across the Atlantic, which produced variation on either side. On the seven seas, sailors sang **shanties** keyed to the particular work to be done on a sailing ship. Both these songs for work and songs for pleasure continued to be sung for a long time, even though they were already much less heard in public by 1900.

Moreover, in order to add to the corpus of 'popular' songs and ballads, poets came up with original specimens of the 'literary' type. If the versatile, but minor poet Hilaire Belloc (1870–1953) – a friend of the novelist G.K. Chesterton, and like him a Catholic 'outsider' in British society – were to be remembered by one poem only, "Tarantella" would do the trick. This song for a dance translated the *sic transit gloria mundi topos* (the depressing theme of the world's decay) into a highly musical performance (Yeats 1936: 127–28). With W.B. Yeats, the impact of Irish folk songs is audible in "The Lake Isle of Innisfree" (1890). This lyrical poem also exemplifies the late-Romantic streak in his early poetry, as do "The Ballad of Moll Magee" and "The Stolen Child" (both published in 1889). "The Ballad of Moll Magee" is a specimen of the Chevy Chase type (as explained in chap. 3.3.2). In order to stop children from pelting her with stones, and make them commiserate her instead, old Moll Magee gathers them in a round to listen to her life. Even though the conventions of the genre seem to call for sadness, strains and misery, an exemplary life of rural Ireland shines out of the stories told by this poor Irish fisherwoman: of how she lost her baby to the cold winter, and in consequence was turned out by her husband; how she met with charity from just one kind person in the village, and thus has hopes for a better life only after death.

A glimpse of Naturalism can also be gained from two **'hanging ballads'** that come in different rhythmical form. "The Ballad of Reading Gaol" (1898) by Oscar Wilde sets in with the execution of a soldier in prison and turns into an extended lament of capital punishment, of the prison system, and of inhumanity in general:

Oscar Wilde

> With midnight always in one's heart,
>   And twilight in one's cell,
> We turn the crank, or tear the rope,
>   Each in his separate Hell,
> And the silence is more awful far
>   Than the sound of a brazen bell.
>
> And never a human voice comes near
>   To speak a gentle word:
> And the eye that watches through the door
>   Is pitiless and hard:
> And by all forgot, we rot and rot,
>   With soul and body marred.

[...]
And all men kill the thing they love,
    By all let this be heard,
Some do it with a bitter look,
    Some with a flattering word,
The coward does it with a kiss,
    The brave man with a sword! (parts 5–6)

Far from being 'Art for Art's Sake', Wilde's ballad shows the aesthete sobered by his personal experience of Victorian prisons. (After his trial for homosexuality in 1895, the poet was sentenced to hard labour.) Wilde's poem ends on a note of moral ambivalence: while it does not proclaim everyone to be graced by creativity, it conceives all men to be implicated in crime. In its mix of gruesome detail and psychological interest, Wilde's ballad connected with "Danny Deever" (1890) by Rudyard Kipling (1865–1936). This is one of his *Barrack-Room Ballads* (1892) that look at Empire-building from a common soldier's point of view. In dramatic form and in Cockney dialect, the ballad tells of the hanging of a soldier for murdering another, and of the way his comrades come to live with the experience of the death penalty used by the superiors as a way to enforce discipline among the rank and file. Even though George Orwell listed "Danny Deever" as another prime example of a "good bad poem" (Orwell 1942), it ties in nevertheless with Orwell's clearly anti-colonial prose account of "A Hanging" (1931).

Rudyard Kipling

Kipling's much-anthologised poem "If–" (1910), which was ranked by Orwell in the same category, originated also from a colonial context (an incident shortly before the outbreak of the Boer War). The anaphoric poem takes the form of a parental sermon to a son on how to become "a Man" (last line) by keeping a 'stiff upper lip'. In this sense, the West Indian poet Una Marson (1905–65) provided an answer to Kipling's poem from the point of view of a woman, and of a wife ("If", 1930, in Donnell and Welsh 1996: 129). However, Kipling's "If–" can also be read in a more general sense as advice on how to become self-confident and independent from others, on how to move as a free individual in society. If your poem can live for a century and still be voted the nation's favourite (BBC opinion poll, 1995), if your poem is quoted in *Bridget Jones: The Edge of Reason* (Helen Fielding's novel, 1999) and also at the Centre Court of Wimbledon (above the entrance), if your poem is performed by Benjamin Zephaniah

("What If", in *Too Black, Too Strong*, 2001) and by Joni Mitchell the singer (on the album *Shine*, 2007) – then who cares over 'good' or 'bad' in what is next to immortal.

In Kipling's gift of producing musical verse, his Methodist family background paid off, including the singing of Wesleyan hymns (see chap. 3.3.2). The tradition of the Protestant hymn also informed Kipling's "Recessional", written for the Queen's Diamond Jubilee (1897; see chap. 4.2.2). As Orwell had observed, too, Kipling's musicality and the stylised working-class idiom (with which Orwell found fault) rendered his ballads suitable for the **music hall** (see chap. 4.3). Indeed, during his schooling in Britain (before he went back to India, where he was born), Kipling had relished the London music halls, where singers like Marie Lloyd and Harry Lauder entertained their audiences. Some of the most popular music-hall songs have become signature tunes for their period: "Ta-ra-ra Boom-de-ay" (with lyrics by Henry Sayers, 1891), a risqué song about a "Belle of good society" who promises much to men, is a good example, and so is "It's a Long Way to Tipperary" (by Jack Judge, 1912), which was on many soldiers' lips in the First World War.

In addition to comic songs from the music halls or from the Savoy Operas (with lyrics by W. S. Gilbert, 1836–1911), there was a good deal of **parody and light verse** (see *BCP* 318–25; Amis 1987: 98 ff.). The founding of the comic magazine *Punch* in 1841 testified to the fact that the Victorian Age was not only a seemingly staid period. The *Punch* cartoonist John Tenniell illustrated both *Alice's Adventures in Wonderland* (1865) and its sequel, *Through the Looking-Glass* (1871). These books by Lewis Carroll (pseudonym for Charles Lutwidge Dogson, 1832–98) contain a number of parodies, of which "Jabberwocky" (1871) is the most famous. This mock-medieval ballad with its extravagant diction is characterised by the many instances where two expressions are blended into one. Some of these **portmanteau words** (Carroll's term) are 'explained' in the discussion upon the poem that ensues between Alice and Humpty Dumpty, others are left to the reader's imagination. J. K. Stephen (1859–92) gave a self-ironical twist to "Rule Britannia" in "On a Parisian Boulevard", and wrote "A Sonnet" on Wordsworth, while in "Variations on an Air", G. K. Chesterton (1874–1936) provided a funny set of literary parodies on poets from Tennyson to Swinburne (Amis 1987: 171–76, 201–03). Edward Lear (1812–88) became famous for his **limericks and nonsense verse**, with several collections following upon the first *Book of Nonsense* (1845), written for children and illustrated by the author. The best-known limericks passed over into the sphere of oral poetry, such as "There was a young lady of Niger" (attributed to William Cosmo Monkhouse, 1840–1901):

> There was a young lady of Niger
> Who smiled as she rode on a tiger;
>> They returned from the ride
>> With the lady inside,
> And the smile on the face of the tiger.

> THE STERN PARENT
> Father heard his Children scream,
> So he threw them in the stream,
> Saying, as he drowned the third,
> "Children should be seen, *not* heard!"

"The Stern Parent" is one of the *Ruthless Rhymes for Heartless Homes* (1909) by Harry Graham (1874–1936). Without spoiling the joke by too close a reading, one is tempted to see this comic poem also as an indicator of how much repressed feeling lurked behind the façade of the Victorian household and its Family Values – but this is a matter for another chapter (chap. 4.2.3).

Guiding Questions and Exercises

1. Sum up the use of medievalism and of the ballad form in Keats's "La Belle Dame sans Merci" and in Tennyson's "The Lady of Shalott". Moreover, discuss the relation of art and reality as a theme in Tennyson's poem and in Keats's "Ode on a Grecian Urn".

2. There are musical adaptations of Yeats's "The Second Coming" by Joni Mitchell (as "Slouching Towards Bethlehem" on the album *Night Ride Home*, 1991) and of "The Two Trees" by Loreena McKennit (*The Mask and the Mirror*, 1994). McKennit also set to music Tennyson's "The Lady of Shalott" (recorded in the studio for the album *The Visit* in 1991, and *Live in Paris and Toronto* in 1998). Compare the musical adaptations to each other and to their original sources. Which qualities of the poems come out best in adaptation? What is lost or done differently in the intermedial reworking?

3. The dramatic monologue was a new sub-genre of poetry that came up in the nineteenth century and continued in the twentieth century. Point out the most prominent features and summarise its variety of application by discussing relevant examples from Browning and Tennyson up to T. S. Eliot.

4. Compare Matthew Arnold's poem "Dover Beach" to Shakespeare's thematically related sonnet no. 60 ("Like as the waves make towards the pebbled shore"). How does the Renaissance and the Victorian poet handle theme and form?

The Development of Fiction from Dickens to Lawrence | 4.5

Charles Dickens and the Breakthrough of the Novel | 4.5.1

As a best-selling novelist and editor of popular magazines, Charles Dickens (1812–70) dominated the literary world during his lifetime. Yet one should be wary to fall back into a typically Victorian discourse on 'Heroes and Hero-Worship in Literary History' (to adapt the title of Thomas Carlyle's influential lectures of 1837–40, discussed in chap. 4.2.1). In all fairness, one should certainly mention, too, that critics disagreed at all times upon the merits of Dickens's works, and that perhaps even his best-known novels are more frequently quoted than actually read today. However, it is also true to say that he partook in crucial developments within the manner of literary communication, which was why he was put centre-stage in chap. 4.1.

|Fig. 4.26
Charles Dickens

Dickens had a miserable childhood: as a 12-year old boy, he started work in a shoe-blacking factory while the rest of his family joined his father in the Marshalsea debtors' prison. Child labour and the prison as setting or symbol were to become recurrent elements of his fiction, with the Marshalsea Prison featuring prominently in *Little Dorrit* (1855–57). At the age of 17, Dickens turned journalist, and as one of London's fastest shorthand reporters, he covered the courts and later parliamentary debates. The day after his 24th birthday, in 1836, he published a collection of his miscellaneous writings for newspapers and magazines, such as the prison piece "A Visit to Newgate". Together with the illustrations of George Cruickshank (1792–1878), they came out under the title *Sketches by 'Boz'*. In collaboration with

Pickwick Papers

another illustrator, namely 'Phiz' (Hablot K. Browne, 1815–82), Dickens followed up his first successful book with his first serial publication, *The Pickwick Papers* (1836–37). From the introduction of the comic Cockney character Sam Weller into this episodic narrative, sales of the monthly parts rose markedly. Dickens continued in this form of collaborative production for the rest of his life, at times writing two serial novels simultaneously, as with *Oliver Twist* (1837–39, illustrated by Cruickshank) and *Nicholas Nickleby* (1838–39, illustrated by 'Phiz'). *Oliver Twist* presents several **typical features of Dickens's style.** *First,* the plot involves a great number of characters, including very many minor, but memorable ones – memorable because they are eccentric (such as Bumble, the puffed-up beadle, and later Scrooge, the prototypical miser in *A Christmas Carol*) and because they are predictable with regard to repetitive gestures and habits. A *second* feature is the heightening of effect by means of a repetition of key words and key sentences. A *third* point concerns the effects of serialisation on the storyline: the monthly instalments frequently end on a note of suspense. Generally speaking, Dickens's serial novels became less episodic and more tightly crafted, and – even though the novelist went on to create a fair share of comic characters – less humorous and more pessimistic in outlook.

Social Criticism

Where Scott's formula of the historical novel looked for social and cultural conflict in the past, the 'social problem novel' of Dickens and of others laid the finger into the open wounds of the present. *Oliver Twist* is a ready example that combines the depiction of urban squalor, poverty and crime with a focus on childhood experience, and with a criticism of the workhouse system based on Utilitarian principles (see chap. 4.2.1). In their criticism, Dickens and his associates did not shy away from including the death of poor, innocent children as part of the stories told, and thereby could count on an even greater impact of their novels on the social conscience of their contemporary audiences. This helped to bring about, at last, the breakthrough of the novel, and its widespread acknowledgment and acceptance as a medium of both literary and social discourse, as a social document and as a work of art.

Hard Times

While *Hard Times. For These Times* (1854) is typical of Dickens's social realism, it is also a rare exception in his *œuvre* in that this novel is set entirely outside London, and that it lacked illustrations (which remained scarce even after the reprints of the 1860s). On the other hand, Dickens's graphic description of the fictional 'Coketown' – an industrial town much like Manchester or Preston (which had just seen a workers' strike and a lock-out) – as a "triumph of fact" could very well stand on its own:

> It was a town of red brick, or of brick that would have been red if the smoke and ashes had allowed it; but as matters stood, it was a town of unnatural red and black like the painted face of a savage. It was a town of machinery and tall chimneys, out of which interminable serpents of smoke trailed themselves for ever and ever, and never got uncoiled. It had a black canal in it, and a river that ran purple with ill-smelling dye, and vast piles of building full of windows where there was a rattling and a trembling all day long, and where the piston of the steam-engine worked monotonously up and down, like the head of an elephant in a state of melancholy madness. It contained several large streets all very like one another, and many small streets still more like one another, inhabited by people equally like one another, who all went in and out at the same hours, with the same sound upon the same pavements, to do the same work, and to whom every day was the same as yesterday and to-morrow, and every year the counterpart of the last and the next.
> [...] You saw nothing in Coketown but what was severely workful. [...] All the public inscriptions in the town were painted alike, in severe characters of black and white. The jail might have been the infirmary, the infirmary might have been the jail, the town-hall might have been either, or both, [...]. Fact, fact, fact, everywhere in the material aspect of the town; fact, fact, fact, everywhere in the immaterial. [...] everything was fact between the lying-in hospital and the cemetery, and what you couldn't state in figures, or show to be purchaseable in the cheapest market and saleable in the dearest, was not, and never should be, world without end, Amen. (Chap. 5. Dickens 1966: 16–17.)

This outcry at the de-humanising effects of pure rationality and industrialisation has to be compared to the initial and 'factual' description of a horse ("Quadruped. Graminivorous. Forty teeth [...]", chap. 2) called up by Mr Gradgrind, a schoolmaster who is out to instil a passion for Fact rather than Fancy in his pupils – a tendency that is clearly contradicted and subverted by the narrative voice. Taken together with Dickens's related and contemporary article "Frauds on the Fairies" (1853, see chap. 4.5.5), such passages vividly represent the novelist's ongoing assault on Utilitarianism. (*Hard Times* is dedicated to Thomas Carlyle, a fellow critic of that creed.) At the end of the novel, Gradgrind's former pupil Sissy Jupe – the fanciful 'girl number twenty' who could never be taught to define a horse 'factually', because the circus world of her father had made her immune against such an imaginative drain – is rehabilitated, and Gradgrind's educational principles are proven wrong in the fate of his own children. The arranged marriage between Louisa Gradgrind and Mr Bounderby, a coarse and self-styled self-made man of her father's age and intellectual mould, fails when she rediscovers her more emotional side. His son Tom Gradgrind meanwhile resorts to robbing Bounderby's bank to meet his expenses, for which someone else has to take the blame, namely Stephen Blackpool. This honest textile worker was dismissed by Bounderby (who is also a cotton-mill owner) in a labour dispute, and after he sought the advice of his employer on how to break free from an unhappy marriage in order to establish a more loving union. (In vain, and it is here that Dickens criticises contemporary divorce law, too.) There is no happy ending for Stephen Blackpool: while Tom is able to escape criminal prosecution, and Bounderby is finally exposed to be a fraud, Stephen has a fatal accident in the Old Hell Shaft (an unsecured part of an unused pit) and dies a melodramatic death. In the martyrdom and idolisation of devout Stephen, as in the moral conversion of Scrooge in A Christmas Carol (1843), Dickens presented Christianity and a compassionate Christmas Spirit as the best way out of class conflict and materialist mentality. But to make his point in a programmatic novel, Dickens for once relied too much on hallmark features of his style such as verbal repetition and typecasting (see the above quotation). For his negative portrayal of the trade union movement as part of the problem rather than the solution, he drew the criticism of G. B. Shaw, who was (like Orwell) generally sympathetic to Dickens's work.

Bleak House   The immediately preceding novel Bleak House (1852–53) was at once an institutional satire and an indictment of slum housing and social morality. The legal system is bitterly satirised in the perennial suit of 'Jarndyce and Jarndyce', which only comes to an end when the whole estate at issue has been absorbed in costs of the Court of Chancery (chaps. 1, 65). The case brings unhappiness to Richard Carstone and Ada Clare, the two cousins of John Jarndyce, who is also their benevolent guardian at Bleak House. Richard, who secretly marries Ada, but who could never decide on a profession as he has relied on inheriting the estate, does not survive the frustration of his hopes. That you stand little chance in the Court of Chancery is also borne out by the example of another suitor, Miss Flite, a poor, old and eccentric lady who keeps several birds in cages, as symbols of those entangled in the legal system: "With the intention of restoring them to liberty. When my judgment should be given. Ye-es! They die in prison, though. Their lives, poor silly things, are so short in comparison with Chancery proceedings, that the whole collection has died over and over again." (Chap. 5, Dickens 1977: 53) It is only after Richard's death that Miss Flite can give her birds their liberty; yet that Justice had turned a blind eye to those in need, this is an impression that is not lost on the reader.

Among the key themes and images in *Bleak House* are blindness and blackmail, detection and detention, duplicity, disease and death. In this novel, Dickens experiments with a shift between homo- and heterodiegetic narration, between fictional autobiography and a more wide-ranging view and criticism of social grievances. There is a regular alternation between the first-person retrospective narration of Esther Summerson and the ironical and occasionally enraged voice of an unnamed narrator talking in, and looking at, the present. Esther is an orphaned ward of John Jarndyce, and Ada's companion at Bleak House near St Albans (north of London). The pleasing irregularity of the house, together with the benevolence of John Jarndyce, create a place of comfort, which looks like a safe haven especially in comparison with the London slum of Tom-all-Alone's, prison rather than 'home' to Jo, a young crossing-sweeper (chap. 45–46). Before the ending of his life, which is brutish and short (see chap. 4.5.5), Jo accompanies a lady to an iron gate which secures the grave of her former lover, Nemo (a no-name used again later by Jules Verne). The woman who keeps her face hidden by a veil is no other than proud Lady Dedlock, a woman who had thought to have covered up a premarital affair ending in childbirth, but who recognises that she is locked in the past when she is being blackmailed by Mr Tulkinghorn, the family lawyer. Shortly afterwards, he is murdered at his home (which borders on a "little prison-like yard", chap. 48), and Lady Dedlock, now a suspect, flees. When Inspector Bucket solves the murder mystery, this comes too late for Lady Dedlock: her corpse is discovered at the gate to her former lover's grave by Esther Summerson, who has meanwhile recovered from a disease contracted from Jo, and from a temporary blindness in more than one sense (chaps. 32, 35–36, 59). At least for her, the novelist has a happy ending in store.

Problematic Families

The general outlook, however, remains bleak: apart from the surrogate family assembled by John Jarndyce at Bleak House (which also includes Harold Skimpole, a good-for-nothing, grown-up child, and the neighbouring friend Lawrence Boythorn), there is hardly a complete, or a completely happy family to be found in this novel. The marriage of Sir Leicester and Lady Dedlock remains an empty union of pomp and pride. From the likewise childless marriages of the Snagsbys and the Chadbands, Mrs Snagsby sticks out as the type of the jealous and inquisitive wife, and the table talk of Mr Chadband strikes the reader as an example of empty rhetoric. The poor Smallweed family lacks the father, while the Jellybys have to make do with an absent mother, who neglects her family in order to engage in the 'telescopic philanthropy' of Africa Projects, and later in the suffragettes' cause (chaps. 5, 8, 23, 30, 67). By contrast, Dickens's conviction that charity begins at home is illustrated with the example of Charlotte 'Charley' Coavins: the 13-year old girl, who in many ways compares with Esther (and with a younger 'Charley' Dickens), has to go to work to provide for her orphaned siblings – and thus serves for a critical look at child labour (chap. 15). From the myriad of minor characters, a further two are bound up with **elements of sensational and crime fiction**: the landlord of the lady's former lover, an eccentric loner tellingly named Krook, spectacularly vanishes into thin air in an incident of 'spontaneous combustion' (chap. 32, the end of an instalment). Furthermore, Inspector Bucket from the 'Detective Force' merits mention because he is the first detective inspector to appear in English fiction (to be followed by Sergeant Cuff from Scotland Yard in Wilkie Collins's *The Moonstone*, 1868). Dickens's last novel, *The Mystery of Edwin Drood* (1870), took the form of a murder mystery without a corpse, and ended – because of the novelist's death in the middle of serialisation – with his most suspenseful cliffhanger.

When *The Personal History of David Copperfield* (1849–50) is seen from the perspective of the later novels, some striking similarities will come more clearly into view. In this novel, too, we find legal satire, albeit intermittently and on a smaller scale (chaps. 23, 26, 33). Such satire extends also to the prison system (chap. 61), and it is certainly no coincidence that the magistrate in charge of the prison is a harsh former schoolmaster of David's, and that prisoners are numbered like the pupils in Mr Gradgrind's school. As to social and sexual morality: among the minor characters of the novel, there are two fellow schoolgirls who end up as fallen women – the one seduced (Little Em'ly), the other a streetwalker (Martha Endell, chaps. 22, 46–47, 50). Another immediately striking similarity lies in the fact that, already in this novel, Dickens tried out the form of fictional autobiography to great effect. Moreover, he incorporated much of his own life into that of the protagonist, who has a mixed educational experience, begins to work at the age of 10 in a warehouse, helps himself to a thorough grounding in eighteenth-century novels, before he then re-invents himself as a shorthand reporter and a novelist. The first third of this long novel can be subdivided into two stages, beginning with David's unhappy childhood (chaps. 1–12) in a patchwork family dominated by his new stepfather, Mr (Edward) Murdstone. Together with his sister Jane, 'a metallic lady', Murdstone advocates Firmness in education in as much the same way as Mr Gradgrind in *Hard Times* idolises Fact, and he moreover inflicts corporal punishment and 'imprisonment' on his stepson (chap. 4). Salem House, the private London school of Mr Creakle, is no improvement, but brings David into contact with James Steerforth, who impresses him, and with Tommy Traddles, who will become a lifelong friend. While working in Murdstone's London warehouse, David lodges with Mr Micawber, who lives perennially in debt, and sometimes in the debtors' prison, too, much like Dickens's father. On the rare side of emotional warmth, we find David's nurse (Clara) Peggotty and her orphaned nephew and niece, Ham and Little Em'ly. For David, half-orphaned and soon also bereft of his mother, Little Em'ly becomes the first object of love. The second and happier phase of David's adolescent life is spent at Dover and at the Canterbury school of Dr Strong (chaps. 13–18), where David travels under the new name and identity of Trot(wood) Copperfield. This is to honour his great-aunt Betsy Trotwood, whom Dickens portrays as a self-confident if also headstrong woman, as successful in reaching a separation from her violent husband as in helping David into a new life. During this second phase, David befriends Agnes, the daughter of lawyer Wickfield, and meets the lawyer's servant and later partner Uriah Heep.

Fig. 4.27
David Copperfield

The last two thirds of the novel tell of David's adult life: up to his marriage and to the start of a career (chaps. 19–43), during his marriage to Dora Spenlow (44–53) and beyond (54–64). With her cry, "Blind, blind, blind!" Aunt Betsy had struck a keynote for David's further education of the head and the heart. Uriah Heep is less of a creep than rather a malicious "monster of meanness" (chap. 54), professing love for Agnes while plotting against her father, and robbing Aunt Betsy of her property, too. David must also learn that Steerforth is no real gentleman, as he first abducts and then simply casts off Little Em'ly, and that Dora is no perfect lady, but really the spoiled "child-wife" as which she sees herself (chaps. 44, 48). The ending of the novel is a mixture of melodrama, merely a lucky escape, and merited happiness. Both Steerforth and Ham die during a climactic storm scene in a shipwreck (chap. 55), whereas Dora passes away with a deathbed monologue during a more sentimental scene (chap. 53). After Uriah Heep's schemes and machinations are laid bare, we meet him again as an unlikely model prisoner in the prison run by Creakle as a magistrate. Mr Micawber – who helped to bring Heep to book – finally turned the tables to become a respected magistrate 'down under', and Australia is shown to be kind alike to fallen women such as Little Em'ly and Martha Endell. And when David has recovered from the death of his wife and a depression during a time out on the Continent, he is then free to marry Agnes, his faithful friend and counsel, in a real love match.

Great Expectations   A comparison with *David Copperfield* is helpful to elucidate *Great Expectations* (1860–61), a major novel of Dickens's last phase. Obvious similarities include the rise of an orphaned boy from a surrogate family to success in society, linked up with a story of education of head and heart that takes the form of a fictional autobiography. This time, however, the focus rests throughout on the experiencing, not the (older) narrating self. The story begins eerily in a churchyard, where the boy Pip (Philip Pirrip) meets a convict rising as if from a grave, and helps him out with food before soldiers can again secure him (chaps. I.1–5). From then on, the story of Pip's material expectations and moral education in life are divided into three stages that are clearly marked out and also identical with the individual tomes of the novel when published as a three-decker. The first stage is set in rural Kent, where Pip lives with his older sister and is apprenticed to her husband, gentle Joe Gargery. Pip is also chosen by the local gentlewoman Miss Havisham to keep company with her ward Estella in run-down Satis House. Miss Havisham, who was deserted for good by her bridegroom on the day of her marriage, has trained Estella to be a cold-hearted and contemptuous seductress in order to revenge Miss Havisham on the male sex. Indeed, the boy Pip is soon torn between his affections for Biddy, a rural girl who moved into the Gargery household, and for Estella. With the announcement of Miss Havisham's London lawyer Jaggers that Pip has been adopted by an unnamed benefactor who wants him to be "brought up as a gentleman – in a word, as a young fellow of great expectations" (chap. I.18, Dickens 1994: 135), a new stage in Pip's life sets in. It is bound up with his move to lodgings in the London street called Little Britain, where Herbert Pocket, his friend and tutor in genteel manners, paradoxically indulges in grand projects of trading within the Empire. Soon, both live beyond their 'expectations' in amassing debts to cultivate a showy lifestyle in a snobbish circle that includes also Bentley Drummle, Pip's rival to Estella's love.

The Empire strikes back, however, when the convict met in the churchyard unexpectedly returns from Australia. The whole façade of Pip's bourgeois gentility is suddenly torn apart by the disclosure that no-one else but a transported convict turned successful sheep farmer 'down under' is Pip's anonymous benefactor. Abel Magwitch alias Provis repaid the boy's benevolence in providing him with the means to live as a gentleman in the metropolis. Pip receives the full force of this revelation after Dickens had already confronted his social snobbery with both the rural world of his childhood (chaps. I.19; II.8–9, 15–16) and the London underworld, in- and outside Newgate Prison (II.1, 5, 13). The further discoveries that Magwitch is also Estella's father, that Estella had married the arrogant Drummle, and that Magwitch's fellow-convict and enemy Compeyson is Miss Havisham's runaway husband, are even more humbling blows for Pip's (and also for Estella's) great expectations in life. But they also bring about Pip's recovery of his old, less materialist and more compassionate self. Pip and Herbert Pocket plan to smuggle Magwitch – who risked the death penalty for his return – out of the country. This leads to a suspenseful boat race on the Thames and a short courtroom scene that read not the worse for their similarities to earlier equivalents in Gaskell's *Mary Barton* (1848, chaps. 27–28, 32). Neither the individual fate of Magwitch, Compeyson and Miss Havisham shall be disclosed here, nor what became of Pip's divided feelings for Biddy and Estella. The ending of *Great Expectations* consists of a number of twists and turns, some more deliberately conceived than others, as Dickens had second and third thoughts about how to end his novel. His friend and fellow-novelist Bulwer Lytton had made him drop his original conclusion (which is preserved in the appendix to most modern editions) for a happier one. The revised ending came just in time for serialisation and first edition, but the ambiguous last sentence was rewritten once more for a reprint – and still hovers between the grave moral of *Hard Times* and the happy marriages that conclude *David Copperfield* and *Bleak House*.

There are many characters in *Great Expectations* that are either funny or grotesque, but in any way memorable in the eccentric sense mentioned above. Jaggers's clerk Wemmick is an outright model of benevolence: when working as a 'gardener among his plants' at Newgate Prison (II.13), and also in private at his home and 'castle' where he ever so often gives his Aged P[arent]. a gentle nod, to humour the old man in the dawn of his life. By contrast, Mr Jaggers, when he is not biting the side of his forefinger, is the incarnation of a lawyer who is equally fond of cross-examining others as of not committing himself by the use of hypothetical phrases like "Put the case ..." (III.12). In addition, Jaggers is recurrently associated with

Fig. 4.28

"Miss Havisham and Pip", illustration by F. A. Fraser for a reprint of *Great Expectations*, 1877

the scent of soap – from the habitual attempt to wash his hands in innocence? A more grotesque example is Miss Havisham, who still wears her bridal dress and lives on amidst the funereal remains of what should have been her marriage feast (I.8, 11). Satis House thus became a monument to dissatisfaction, and Miss Havisham appears as a personified Death-in-Life. To some extent, so does Magwitch the convict, who is characterised right from the start by something clicking in his throat – as when the hangman's noose snaps a neck. The convict and the "corpse-like" bride (Dickens 1994: 59) are reminiscent of melodrama, Newgate novels situated in the London under-world, Gothic and sensational fiction, and they might have won over thus inclined Victorian readers, too. They moreover inspired director David Lean to a congenial film version (1946), some novelists to continuations (see Nowak 1994), and poet Carol Ann Duffy to her dramatic monologue "Havisham" (*Mean Time*, 1993; see chap. 5.1). Elements of crime fiction abound in *Great Expectations*, not only as to the convicts Magwitch and Compeyson, but also in connection with Old Orlick, the porter at Satis House and at different times the scourge of both Pip's sister and of himself (I.15, III.14). Crime is however not just a means to create suspense. While the social criticism in the novel is directed first and foremost at the materialism of the Victorian middle classes, Dickens singled out unprofessional policemen and the police courts with their summary justice for satirical attacks (I.16, III.16).

History and Social Realism in Fiction by Dickens's Rivals and Contemporaries

4.5.2

Turning from the varied work of Dickens to the novels of his contemporaries, one should not expect to find much more uniformity. Kathleen Tillotson introduced her seminal study on the breakthrough of the novel in the 1840s with the candid statement that "It is now, I think, too late to talk about 'Victorian novels'; their range is too vast and vague to lead to any useful generalization." (1961: 1). Indeed, **there is not one 'Victorian novel'**. The following survey of fiction by Dickens's rivals and successors combines the different approaches of Michael Wheeler (1985), Robin Gilmour (1986) and Philip Davies (2002) in that it is subdivided into phases as well as into thematic groups, beginning with historical fiction.

In the wake of Sir Walter Scott (†1832), writers such as William Harrison Ainsworth (1805–82) and Edward Bulwer Lytton (1803–73) provided the public regularly and profitably with **historical romances** rather than with historical *novels* (see chap. 3.5.6 for more about this distinction). From the 1830s to the 1850s, they counted among the most popular authors of the day. In nearly forty romances and novels, Ainsworth romanticised English history, for instance in *The Tower of London* (1840), which centres on

Ainsworth and Bulwer Lytton

the short life and tragic fate of Lady Jane Grey, the rival to Maria Tudor ('Bloody Mary'). *Old St Paul's* (1841) is set a century later and deals with the Plague and the Great Fire of London in 1666. In *The Last Days of Pompeii* (1834), Bulwer Lytton extended the coverage of the historical novel or romance to include Ancient Rome. *The Last Days of Pompeii* combines the story of a love that overcomes obstacles with a narrative full of suspense, but uses the historical setting only as a background. Although this is a work of entertainment only, devoid of an additional didactic intention or a serious investigation into the past, this romance was a 'must' for every British tourist visiting Southern Italy throughout the nineteenth century, and it survived also as a popular children's book. Bulwer Lytton, who was for a time regarded as England's leading man of letters, and who was also active as a politician, still managed to write some two dozen books, including Newgate novels as well as high society **'silver-fork novels'**. (For both types, see below. The latter term was coined by William Hazlitt in his 1827 essay "The Dandy School", which also calls for a comparison with Oscar Wilde's dandyism.) Ainsworth and Bulwer Lytton were good friends of Charles Dickens, who likewise turned to the under-world and to prisons in his fiction. With Ainsworth, he moreover shared the collaboration with famous illustrators such as George Cruickshank or 'Phiz'; and from Bulwer Lytton, he took the advice to change the ending of his novel *Great Expectations*. Yet it is also a measure of success of Dickens and of his critical form of contemporary social realism, that it is his name that is still remembered, while their work of fiction is nowadays historical in a double sense of the word.

Lorna Doone

Before we approach those novels concerned with the contemporary 'condition of England', a few other works of historical fiction should be mentioned. They can conveniently be grouped with regard to their historical subject matter, beginning with the Long Eighteenth Century, Scott's original domain. By the 1860s, one generation after Scott's death, the historical novel was already firmly established, and the distinction from the historical romance was apparently already a household one, as is obvious from the preface by R. D. Blackmore (1825–1900) to *Lorna Doone* (1869). Subtitled *"A Romance of Exmoor"*, this long seller is set on the border between the counties of Somerset and Devon in the 'Wild West' of England (a remote area notorious for pirates, smugglers and highway robbers), and the narrative takes place in 1673–86, i. e. in the Restoration period. The key historical event in focus is the 1685 Monmouth Rebellion against the Stuart King James II, who ordered the 'hanging judge' Lord Jeffreys to exert a particularly cruel form of retribution. Apart from this historical and political strand to the plot, there is also the love story between farmer John Ridd (the narrator) and Lorna, a member of the Doone family. The problems their love has to overcome are, first, the class difference (she comes from a squire's family, albeit an impoverished one) and, second, the nature of the Doones: they are a Catholic family that originally lived in the North before its members migrated to the (Protestant and often Methodist) West of England and turned to Mafia-style robbers, terrorising the whole region until finally overcome by John Ridd and others. The generic classification of *Lorna Doone*, which tells an imaginary love story in a recognisably historical setting, is not an easy one. Contrary to the author's preface, this text is not simply a historical romance in the sense of a 'period piece', or the equivalent to a 'costume drama' in narrative form. *Lorna Doone* is perhaps best described as a combination of features pertinent to the historical romance, the historical novel and the regional novel. R. D. Blackmore was indeed interested in fact and not just fantasy, which came out in particular in his endeavour to render the rural dialect in a realistic fashion. His etymological research into the history of West English dialects surfaced in the novel, which includes words that have otherwise become extinct. In several instances, the *OED* cites *Lorna Doone* as the only extant source for words used by Blackmore. In this way, his piece of historical fiction has become a historical document itself, and it was successful in reviving the cultural record of a past time that would otherwise have been lost.

Between Scott and Blackmore, William Makepeace Thackeray (1811–63) had covered the early eighteenth century, but with a difference. In *The Luck of Barry Lyndon* (serialised 1844, rev. for book publication 1856), the protagonist relates his military and sexual adventures so as to have the novel turn essentially into a rogue's biography. In 1975, Thackeray's novel was successfully adapted for the screen by Stanley Kubrick, with a similar attention to historical detail. In the preface to *The History of Henry Esmond* (1852), Thackeray had explicitly spelt out his programme

Further Historical Fiction

for the historical novel, namely to oppose Carlyle's hero-worship (see chap. 4.2.1) and to present history 'familiar rather than heroic'. Thackeray's historical and autobiographical narrative does however not go all the way in the direction of a 'history from below', as it includes literary lions such as Addison, Steele and Swift. Their appearance as characters in the novel relates *Esmond* to Thackeray's lecture series on *The English Humourists of the Eighteenth Century* (1851; see here chaps. 4.1 and 4.2.3). In contrast to Thackeray, Charles Dickens was in favour of Carlyle's teaching. In writing about the 1790s Reign of Terror in *A Tale of Two Cities* (1859), Dickens let himself be inspired by Carlyle's *The French Revolution: A History* (1837), and he also observed Scott's original concept of refreshing collective memory of events occurring two generations ago (e.g. in *Waverley; or: 'Tis Sixty Years Since*). Much later, Baroness Orczy (1865–1947) returned to the same historical period in **swashbuckling or cloak-and-dagger romances** such as *The Scarlet Pimpernel* (1905), where the hero in disguise rescues aristocrats from the guillotine. Like Dickens, Baroness Orczy was unenthusiastic about the French Revolution, but laid a stronger stress on entertainment than on moral didacticism (see Hughes 1993).

George Eliot (1819–80) turned to Renaissance Florence in *Romola* (1863), while Charles Reade (1814–84) presented a portrait of fifteenth-century Holland in *The Cloister and the Hearth* (1861), for which he likewise engaged in painstaking research. It was Reade – a dramatist and theatre manager besides being a novelist – who followed up Thackeray's programme of presenting history 'familiar rather than heroic' when he dealt with the courtship of the parents of the humanist scholar Erasmus of Rotterdam. While his historical accuracy was widely acknowledged, Reade offended some Victorian readers by his comparatively uninhibited lingering on the sexual side of the love affair. Such readers objected also against the instances of nakedness in *Hypatia; or, New Foes with Old Faces* (1851), a historical novel by Charles Kingsley (1819–75, see chap. 4.2.1) about a Greek philosopher in fifth-century Alexandria who died an extremely violent death at the hand of (Christian) religious fanatics. Kingsley's other historical novels centred on patriotic English rebels that rose against the Norman Conquerors after 1066 (*Hereward the Wake*, 1866) as well as against the threatening Spaniards in Elizabethan times (*Westward Ho!*, 1855). In the late nineteenth-century era of Imperialism, G. A. Henty followed up that ideological manner of presentation in his juvenile historical fiction (see chap. 4.2.2).

Besides an interest in plausible stories set in the past, Victorian fiction was strongly marked by a social realism directed to the present situation. To access the full range and the diverse forms of social realism centring on the authors' society during the period under review, it is useful to arrange examples according to the layer of society on which they focus. A portrait of **Regency aristocracy** can be found in the **'fashionable novels'** from the 1820s to the mid-1840s that are also known as **'silver-fork novels'**. Such fiction that told of high society life certainly had a snob appeal for aspiring members of the middle classes that prospered economically, e. g. from trading within the Empire after the end of the Napoleonic Wars. The publisher Henry Colburn (Colburn & Co., 1808–53) was instrumental in the creation of 'silver-fork novels', which became a springboard for the careers of Benjamin Disraeli (*Vivian Grey,* 1826–27) and of Edward Bulwer Lytton – fellow novelists and fellow politicians that were to become joint members of the Cabinet in 1858 (see Davis 2002: 272–89). While most of these 'fashionable novels' were best sellers with a short shelf life, Bulwer Lytton's *Pelham* sticks out as a record long seller (with over 200,000 sold between first publication in 1828 and the 1890s). Yet *Pelham* is likewise of interest as an indicator of cultural trends rather than for its literary qualities, as Sutherland (1989: 577) observed: "This portrait of a modish 'gentleman' profoundly affected contemporary sensibility and fashion. (It led directly, for example, to the universal Victorian style of dark suiting for men.)"

Beginning with Jane Austen, a usually good-natured, only mildly satiric portrayal **of the (upper) middle class** occurred frequently in **novels of manners** connected with a love plot. In the expatriate American novelist Henry James (1843–1916), Austen found a critic that was full of praise for the scenic presentation of social interaction that is her hallmark, together with the use of Free Indirect Discourse for the representation of individual minds. In his otherwise quite comparable fiction, however, James includes darker aspects of life, too: *Daisy Miller* (1879) ends with the death of the protagonist, and *The Portrait of a Lady* (1881) with that of her husband. In both the novella and the full-length novel, James made use of his 'international theme', i. e. the experience of a

Range and Forms of Contemporary Social Realism

culture clash by US-American characters who made their way to Europe. *The Ambassadors* (1903) is one of James's later novels on that theme, and a good example for his use of 'reflector' characters (his term) as centres of consciousness. *A Room with a View* (1908) by E[dward]. M[organ]. Forster (1879–1970) varies upon James's international theme by describing a culture clash experienced by English travellers to Continental Europe. In this novel, Forster followed up Jane Austen's restriction to a social range of just 'two inches of ivory' (see chap. 3.5.4) and her mild form of *épater le bourgeois*, or 'beating the bourgeois'. In *Howard's End* (1910) and, most of all, in *A Passage to India* (1924, see chap. 5.3), Forster painted on a larger canvas. John Galsworthy (1867–1933) addressed the *bourgeoisie* in terms of its affluence and its artistic aspirations in his aptly entitled novel *The Man of Property*, which initiated *The Forsyte Saga* (1906–22). Apart from being a novelist given to social realism – for which he was awarded the Nobel Prize for Literature in 1923, and yet reproached by Virginia Woolf – Galsworthy was a playwright working along the same lines for the stage (see chap. 4.3). In *Love at Second Sight* (1916), Ada Leverson (1862–1933) does not only tell the story of a middle-class marriage ending in the wife's adultery and divorce, but also brings in the war experience that is absent from Austen's novels. In this respect, Ada Leverson – a novelist of the second rank that still waits to be discovered – looks ahead to Virginia Woolf's *Mrs Dalloway* (1925). Her narrative centres – quite like Austen's novels – on an evening party as a social event and as a means to unite and contrast characters, yet includes among them a shell-shocked man suffering from his war experience.

In her programmatic essays "Mr Bennett and Mrs Brown" (1924) and "Modern Fiction" (1925), Woolf castigated the 'materialist' social realism of Galsworthy, Arnold Bennett and H. G. Wells in order to promote the psychological realism and Modernist aesthetics that she subscribed to herself. Woolf's argument proved so persuasive that her rivals are not much read today, even though in contrast to her, they made an effort to reach further down the social scale. After his beginnings with *The Time Machine* (1895) and other 'science fiction', Wells returned to novels of society, but chose the **lower middle class** into which he was born as setting for *Kipps* and other novels (1905–10). In this, he can be seen together with Arnold Bennett, who came from the same background and turned to the same section of society in his *Clayhanger Trilogy* (1910–16), which is set in the provincial Staffordshire pottery area. **Rural society** had found its novelist earlier in the *Wessex Novels* of Thomas Hardy, of which *Tess of the d'Urbervilles* (1891) is the best known. **Romany people or gypsies** as outsiders of rural society are cited in the 1847 novels of the Brontës: Heathcliff in *Wuthering Heights* is said to resemble a gypsy in outlook, and Mr Rochester in *Jane Eyre* appears in the disguise of one (chaps. 18–19). In George Eliot's *The Mill on the Floss* (1860), Maggie Tulliver runs away to live with gypsies, but while lecturing them on Columbus, she learns a lesson herself on mistaken idealism (chap. I.11). Apart from such occasionally exotic effect, the life of the Romany people became a principal theme in the fiction of George Borrow (1803–81), e.g. in *Lavengro* (1851; the title reads 'he who is expert with words') and in its sequel *The Romany Rye* ('man of the gypsies', 1857), before it regained prominence in the contemporary novels of Louise Doughty (*Fires in the Dark*, 2003; *Stone Cradle*, 2006).

Apart from the 'silver-fork school' in fiction and the many novels of manners that depicted the (upper) middle class, we find especially in the 1840s and '50s novels with a marked interest in the 'condition of England', in particular in the effects of the industrial revolution on society. The great number of **'condition of England', 'industrial' or 'social problem novels'** – one of the most typical forms of nineteenth-century British fiction – turned to the plight of the urban working class and to the poor, as had Friedrich Engels in his pertinent study (*Die Lage der arbeitenden Klasse in England*, 1845). In addition to Dickens and his novel *Hard Times* (1854), the names of other novelists spring to mind, such as Benjamin Disraeli, Elizabeth Gaskell, Charlotte Brontë, and Charles Kingsley. In *Sybil; or, The Two Nations* (1845), Benjamin Disraeli (1804–1881), the dandyish Conservative politician who was to become Prime Minister in the following years, describes the class system brought along by the Industrial Revolution – the opposition between 'them' and 'us' – in a drastically realistic way that is far away from his beginnings as a 'silver-fork' novelist focused only on the fashionable set. In *Shirley* (1849) by Charlotte Brontë (1816–55), the social problems (a mill-owner's conflict with his workers over new machinery) are clearly contemporary, although the novel is set in 1811–12, at a time when the first

Social Problems in the Novel

machine breaking (Luddite Riots) took place that led to the Peter-loo Massacre at Manchester in 1819, where the militia attacked a peaceful protest rally. Poverty, poor sanitary conditions leading to epidemics, and the political upheaval related to Chartism (a re-formist movement, from 1836, calling for a People's Charter) are the topic of Charles Kingsley's *Yeast* (serialised 1848), *Alton Locke, Tailor and Poet* (1850) and *Two Years Ago* (1857) as well as of Eliza-beth Gaskell's novel *Mary Barton: A Tale of Manchester Life* (1848).

Fig. 4.29
Elisabeth Gaskell

Gaskell (1810–1865) was well informed about industrial pov-erty and working conditions in the textile mills. In the preface to her novel, which came out at the time when Heinrich Heine wrote his protest song of the weavers ("Das Weberlied"), Gaskell voices the workers' belief in the injustice and harshness of their treatment, too. The narrative is set in 1839, at a high time of Chartism, when the People's Charter is to be presented to the Westminster Parliament (chap. 8). The constellation of characters in the novel pits the working-class Bartons against a mill-owner's family, the Carsons. John Barton is a Chartist and a good example for the vicious effects of Manchester Capitalism, in which the increased use of machinery directly led to unemployment, pov-erty, political unrest and crime. Gaskell's novel includes graphic descriptions of the lack of hygiene in the slum dwellings which breeds the typhoid fever killing Ben Davenport in his cellar room (a subterranean image of hell) and also the twin children of George Wilson, a companion of John Barton (chap. 6). As a reaction to the loss of his job, Barton becomes increasingly vio-lent and addicted to opium. In a situation of strike and political confrontation, he is chosen to commit a murder on the mill-own-er's son Harry Carson. Harry's flirt with Barton's daughter Mary made the seamstress turn away from one of her peers, the honest worker Jem Wilson, who is indicted with the murder (chap. 10). The fate of Esther Barton, John's sister-in-law and Mary's aunt, is a warning, as Esther became first seduced and then a street-walking prostitute. Later, she finds out about John's involvement in the murder and before her death passes the information on to Mary (chaps. 1, 10, 14, 38). The ending of the novel involves much (melo-)dramatic action (for some similarities with *Great Ex-pectations*, see chap. 4.5.1). In *Mary Barton*, Gaskell's solution to the social problems – just like Dickens's in *A Christmas Carol* and *Hard Times* – lies in a revitalised Christian moral code (chap. 37),

and not in the Trade Union Movement that is presented negatively as just another interest group. In *North and South* (1855),
Gaskell was again concerned with class struggle in Manchester,
and in *Ruth* (1853, see chap. 4.2.3), the plight of a seduced and
fallen woman shifted centre stage.

As a prominent woman writer, 'Mrs Gaskell' is representative
in a gender context, too. "Unsex me here" (to quote Lady Macbeth): the public face of female authorship in Victorian times was
often characterised by a sort of **anonymity** that was found earlier
on the title pages of novels announced to have been written 'by
a Lady' (Austen) or 'by the Author of *Waverley*' (Scott). For male
authors, this eighteenth-century tradition died out with Scott's
generation, but for female writers, difficulties remained with regard to admitting authorship (see Showalter 1977; Berger 1987).
Therefore, we find this convention as late as 1853 in the best-
selling novel *The Heir of Redclyffe: By the Author of "Heartsease"* (Charlotte Yonge), and not only for the reason that the public view
of the novel as an undemanding, essentially low (and therefore
possibly vulgar) form of entertainment did not allow 'persons of
quality' to put their name to it. Dickens was very much involved
in a respective change of attitude (see Ford 1955). It is with regard
to the use of **pseudonyms** that the differences in the public standing of male and female authors became more evident. No doubt,
male authors on occasion made use of pseudonyms on the title
pages of their publications. 'Boz' (Dickens) springs to mind, but
also the instances of plagiarism and imitation of *The Pickwick Papers* where the fraud is offered to the public under cover of the
pseudonym 'Bos', 'Pos' or 'Poz'. Dickens's use of the pseudonym,
and his illustrator's similar masquerade as 'Phiz', are however to
be seen in a comic context. This playing with the reading public
lasted only for a certain time: already on the cover of the first
book edition of *Oliver Twist* (1838), Dickens is named explicitly
as author, and by the time of *Little Dorrit* (1855–57), both author
and illustrator do no longer use their by now well-deciphered
pseudonyms. Thackeray's use of the pen-name 'Mr Michael An-
gelo Titmarsh' and a series of other pseudonyms from 1838 up
to the publication of *Vanity Fair* nine years later can be similarly
explained. This is however true only for male authors. For female
writers, it was evidently still necessary to disclaim authorship, or
to hide under pseudonym. In 1846, the Brontë sisters Charlotte,

The Masks of Female
Novelists

Emily and Anne collectively published *Poems by Currer, Ellis and Acton Bell*. When *Jane Eyre: An Autobiography. Edited by Currer Bell* was published a year later, the mystery about the ambiguous name and sex of the author formed the basis for the critical evaluation of the novel. History repeated itself with the publication of *Adam Bede* by 'George Eliot' (Mary Ann Evans) in 1859, only with the difference that this time even the publisher John Blackwood was kept in the dark (see Sutherland 1989: 7, 211). Why did women novelists find it necessary to unsex them and to appear as male or possibly male writers? The answer lies very much in the interaction of female stereotypes and Victorian Values (see chap. 4.2.3). Apparently, Victorian views on femininity, mother-hood and the family pressed women to produce many children and care for them lovingly – that is, to prove their *reproductive* qualities – while the production of literature was evidently not thought fit for the female sex. Here lies, finally, the reason why other women writers, when they dared to put their name to fic-tion, often stressed marriage and family life, but 'unsexed' them-selves in signing as 'Mrs [Elizabeth] Gaskell', 'Mrs [Margaret] Oli-phant', and 'Mrs [Mary] Molesworth' (the writer of children's and Christmas Books), or still stronger by referring to themselves as 'Mrs Henry Wood' or 'Mrs Humphry Ward'.

The Brontë Sisters

Women writers such as Charlotte Brontë and George Eliot outwardly conformed to convention, but challenged such atti-tudes within their novels. Together with her younger sisters Em-ily (1818–48) and Anne (1820–49), Charlotte Brontë (1816–55) received her literary inspiration in her youth from Byron, Scott and *Blackwood's Magazine*, and collaboratively produced stories about the fantastic worlds of Angria and Gondal. All three sis-ters worked as governesses before they embarked on a novelist's career with the appearance of their first published works of fic-tion in 1847: Charlotte's *Jane Eyre*, Anne's *Agnes Grey* – both of them novels about governesses – and Emily's *Wuthering Heights*, which is spectacularly set in their native Yorkshire. Later novels (apart form Charlotte's 1853 industrial novel *Shirley* mentioned above) are also marked by autobiographical elements, which to-gether with the early death (due to tuberculosis) running in the family furthered a biographical reading of the novels, and the Brontë personality cult that has become a hallmark of British Heritage.

Fig. 4.30

Charlotte Brontë

Published a decade after *Oliver Twist*, *Jane Eyre* likewise sets in with a depiction of children and misery. Once again we find an orphan who has to come to terms with an alien world: this time it is an orphaned girl who must make her stand, first, against members of the Reed family (her step-mother and her step-brother) and then, second, in Lowood School. Once more, too, we read a vivid account of how poorly children were fed in these institutions; moreover, a typhoid epidemic breaks out which takes some children's lives. In successive episodes, however, the retrospective, fictional autobiography turns from social realism to a Cinderella plot. During her time as a governess at Thornfield Hall, Jane Eyre falls in love with her employer, Mr (Edward) Rochester, an ambivalent kind of fairy-tale prince whom she, like Cinderella, marries in the end, when he has been redeemed. The concluding chapter opens with the statement: "Reader, I married him" – yet the phrasing of the sentence stresses that Jane Eyre marries her former superior on her, not on his terms.

Jane Eyre

Plain Jane Eyre is a prime example of an emancipated female protagonist challenging stereotypical Victorian gender concepts. By contrast, the typified character of Bertha Mason, the madwoman locked away in the attic of Thornfield Hall (see Gilbert and Gubar 1979), comes straight from the Gothic romance and is explained by Brontë as the degenerated product resulting from a combination of sexual excess, alcohol abuse and hot climate (Bertha's native West Indies). All these characteristics may have been plausible to a Victorian audience cherishing instead chastity, temperance and the English weather, but they provoked the British-West Indian novelist Jean Rhys to produce a less stereotypical and psychologically more convincing motivation of the character in her novel *Wide Sargasso Sea* (1966; see chap. 5.3). This notwithstanding, *Jane Eyre* remains a notable example of the **novel of development** *(Bildungsroman)* – from orphaned girl to emancipated woman – that reaches back to Fanny Burney's *Evelina* (1778) and Jane Austen's *Emma* (1816), which also centred on *The History of a Young Lady's Entrance into the World* (as the subtitle to *Evelina* put it so memorably). Dickens's *David Copperfield* (1849–50) and *Great Expectations* (1860–61) as well as Thackeray's *The History of Henry Esmond [...]: Written by Himself* (1852) also belong into this category, as does George Eliot's *The Mill on the Floss* (1860).

In addition, both *Jane Eyre* and *Great Expectations* are good examples of the way in which the **publication as a three-decker novel** is replicated in the structure of the plot. At the *ending of the first volume*, Jane, who is already favourably impressed by Mr Rochester, can just save him when a fire breaks out around his bed. Later, it turns out to be the doing of the madwoman in the attic of Thornfield Hall. At the suspenseful *ending of the second volume*, when Jane Eyre and Mr Rochester are about to be married in church, it turns out that mad Bertha Mason really is Rochester's first wife, and that he is caught in the act of committing bigamy. The *last volume* brings about the atonement of Rochester, and the happy ending to the novel. The conclusion of *Jane Eyre* as well as the two more controversial, quite different endings to *Great Expectations* (see chap. 4.5.1) comply with the convention of the closed, and above all, **happy ending** – a convention that Paul Goetsch (1978) made out as typical for the years between 1840 and 1880. It was not only Dickens who took Bulwer Lytton's advice for a change, but also Thomas Hardy and George Gissing who had to change the endings of some of their novels because the publishers demanded it. Goetsch explained this convention with regard to the context of literary communication, and pointed to the influence that publishers and circulating libraries exerted in the maintenance of this convention. One could add that the Victorian novel compares to today's Hollywood films, where the convention of the happy ending is still vital, in that there is a line of development leading from serial publication (advance screening) to alterations demanded for a three-decker novel (commercial screening) up to the point where the author (director) steps in again to produce a final revision (director's cut) that reverses previous changes made under pressure from the publishers (producers).

Wuthering Heights   *Wuthering Heights* (1847) by Emily Brontë (1818–1848) relates the story of two families – the Earnshaws of Wuthering Heights, and the Lintons of Thrushcross Grange – and of an outsider named Heathcliff, who is slighted by members of both families, and swears to revenge himself. Heathcliff, another poor orphan taken from the streets of Liverpool and raised in Yorkshire in the Earnshaw family, experiences several rebuffs: first, Hindley Earnshaw, the heir to the property, hates him. Second, he overhears a conversation in which Catherine Earnshaw confesses to be passionately in love with Heathcliff, but at the same time states that she disapproves of his lack of wealth, and therefore has decided to embark on a marriage of convenience with her neighbour Edgar Linton, who is materially better off. Third and finally, Heathcliff is also looked down upon by just this rival, Edgar Linton, who treats him like a stable-boy. Heathcliff's revenge (on which he is always candid and outspoken, see Brontë 1981: 112, 208, 215) develops in three stages:

► When he returns transformed from a time spent on the Continent, Heathcliff has Hindley Earnshaw sink into drink and debts, and when he becomes master of Wuthering Heights on Hindley's death, Heathcliff degrades also Hindley's son Hareton Earnshaw, the rightful heir.

► Heathcliff's marriage to Isabella Linton, Edgar's sister and his heir-to-be, produces a son (Linton Heathcliff), but soon ends in the couple's separation. After Isabella's death, Heathcliff claims the ill-healthed son he abhors, only to wait for his premature death, in which case Heathcliff would also be master of Thrushcross Grange.

► To secure this union of estates, he plans to have his son be married in time to Edgar Linton's daughter Cathy, thereby bringing the offspring and the property of all the families permanently under his control.

While Heathcliff succeeds with the first two stages, and for a time also with the third, his scheme of revenge is ultimately frustrated when young Cathy turns to Hareton Earnshaw, and thus brings about a happier union than the one Heathcliff envisaged. His unexpected death helps this turn to a happier ending. The actual conclusion of the novel sees Heathcliff and Catherine Earnshaw/ Linton, the passionate lovers who could not live together in their lifetime, ultimately united in the grave, and their ghosts – as apparitions – walk together out there on the moor in rainy nights.

Clearly, *Wuthering Heights* stands out as a late Romantic novel, with its diabolic, revengeful outsider-protagonist; its gloomy, even spooky atmosphere; and its depictions of a sublime, superhuman and essentially antagonistic Nature. However, and at the same time, it can also be seen in terms of plotting as early Modernist in the way the narrative is broken down into the assembled stories of individual characters. These stories are nested like boxes within boxes, with each being told from a different, or sometimes from two overlapping points of view. The retrospective narration spans a period of about 20 years, but it is told or written down on two occasions in 1801 and 1802. The two principal components are the oral narrative of Heathcliff's old housekeeper Nelly Dean and the diary of his new tenant Mr Lockwood. Both of the two narrators look at events from the periphery, but enrich their narrative by quasi-documentary reports (i.e. reported stories or letters) from other characters that are more closely involved in the events, such as Heathcliff's wife Isabella or Catherine Earnshaw and Cathy Linton.

Both 1847 novels of the Brontë sisters fall back on Gothic and Romantic features, but in three respects there is a marked difference between them. In the handling of point of view, *Wuthering Heights* turns out to be ahead of its time, while *Jane Eyre* appears rather conventional. The other differences pertain to characterisation, and in particular to gender relations. Here it is *Wuthering Heights* that appears to take recourse to doomed lovers and evil fiends as stock characters of romances, and to adhere to the notion of poetic justice as another genre convention. By contrast, *Jane Eyre* – which seems to sport in Mr Rochester a likewise domineering male character – ultimately puts much stronger stress on the nature of its *female* protagonist as an emancipated woman: a woman who talks back, who takes her life into her own hands, and who is only willing to accept the man of her life on terms which are acceptable to her – and not just on his terms.

'George Eliot' (Mary Ann Evans, 1819–80), who was an intellectually ambitious woman ('bluestocking') with an unconventional private life, continued to feature such emancipated women in her regional novels. (See chaps. 4.2.3, 4.5.3, 4.5.5, and see Dolin 2005.) *The Mill on the Floss* (1860) consists of three strands to the plot: the intellectual and emotional development of Maggie Tulliver, the education of her brother Tom and the relationship between the siblings; and their father's road to ruin, which implicates the whole family living at the mill. Although none of the three Tullivers is consistently in the focus of the narrative, Maggie sticks out from childhood age because of her intellectual ambition and independence, and because she is torn between two lovers on her way to womanhood: between Philip Wakem, the deformed son of a lawyer, and Stephen Guest, the son of a rich businessman. The ending of *The Mill on the Floss*, like that

Fig. 4.31

George Eliot

of *Wuthering Heights*, flouts convention by showing the central characters happily united, yet in their death. The cosmos of provincial society in the novel is peopled with a great number of contrasting characters made up of relatives of the Tullivers, of representatives of various local professions, and of various off-stage characters. George Eliot's narrator casts no more than an ironical glance at "great men" and stresses instead: "I am telling the history of very simple people" (see chaps. V.6 and IV.2 in the novel, and for a comparison with Carlyle's heroic concept of history, see chap. 4.2.1). George Eliot had elaborated upon this, her own concept as a critic – years before she became a published novelist – in the *Westminster Review* article "The Natural History of German Life" (1856, in Eliot 1992: 260–95). There, she attested that a thorough knowledge of the life of ordinary people is needed to reform society, and that social novels contribute their share to such an understanding. Yet she also criticised Dickens for stopping short of a psychological realism:

> We have one great novelist who is gifted with the utmost power of rendering the external traits of our town population; and if he could give us their psychological character – their conceptions of life, and their emotions – with the same truth as their idiom and manners, his books would be the greatest contribution Art has ever made to the awakening of social sympathies. (Eliot 1992: 264)

Adam Bede, Eliot's first regional novel, includes a chapter *à la* Fielding "In which the Story Pauses a Little" (chap. 17) to give the narrator room to compare his narrative to the homely realism of a Dutch genre painting. *Silas Marner: The Weaver of Raveloe* (1861) is also endowed with such features. Eliot's masterpiece, *Middlemarch: A Study of Provincial Life* (1871–72), is a regional novel that in its portrait of Middlemarch (an imaginary town modelled on Coventry) attempts a social panorama of the English Midlands. There is a historical element, too, as the narrative is set forty years earlier, in 1829–32, at the time of the Reform Bill that boosted the democratic development in Britain. Eliot juxtaposed two originally distinct narratives, which still shows in the two strands to the plot of *Middlemarch* that run nearly independently along each other. One strand centres on Dorothea Brooke: her ideals and intellectual ambition, her emotional disillusionment in her marriage to the scholarly Edward Casaubon, and her rela-

Middlemarch

tionship to Casaubon's cousin, the artist Will Ladislaw. The other strand is focused on the physician Dr (Tertius) Lydgate: his innovations at the New Hospital (symbolic of an Age of Reform), his courting of and marriage with Rosamond Vincy, his incurrence of household debts and his resulting business relationship to Mr (Nicholas) Bulstrode. The influential banker and proud Dissenter personifies Max Weber's thesis about the intimate connection between Protestantism and Capitalism. However, this pillar of local society is being blackmailed for his behaviour in the past, and experiences a spectacular fall from grace. On Dorothea Brooke, Dr Lydgate and Mr Bulstrode hinge the novel's (and the author's) concerns with religion and science, faith and fact – two views on the world that became increasingly incompatible during the Victorian Era (see chap. 4.2.1). Dorothea's sister Celia and the families of the Vincys, the Garths and the Featherstones provide contrasting characters and additional interest. The well-informed and intrusive narrator's pen-portrait of Rosamond says as much about the character as it does about George Eliot's critical views on the 'perfect lady' and the 'angel in the house' in general:

> Rosamond never showed any unbecoming knowledge, and was always that combination of correct sentiments, music, dancing, drawing, elegant note-writing, private album for extracted verse, and perfect blond loveliness, which made the irresistible woman for the doomed man of that date. Think no unfair evil of her, pray: she had no wicked plots, nothing sordid or mercenary; in fact, she never thought of money except as something necessary which other people would always provide. (Chap. 27. Eliot 1965: 301)

George Eliot's hallmark style is a combination of such a **self-conscious and intrusive narrator** who frequently addresses the reader in a memorable way with a psychological realism that makes use of **Free Indirect Discourse**. One very instructive example of such inside views among many (e.g. chap. 37) is the scene after Dorothea Brooke's parting from Will Ladislaw, whom she had accidentally met at Rosamond Lydgate's when searching for Dr Lydgate herself (chap. 43, Eliot 1965: 471–73). The following two paragraphs present extended inside views first of Dorothea ("In the five minutes' drive to the Hospital [...]") and then of Will ("Will Ladislaw, meanwhile, was mortified [...]"). In each case, there are switches to and fro between heterodiegetic narration, direct and indirect representation of thought, and Free Indirect Discourse (e.g. "But

Will was Mr Casaubon's relative, and one towards whom she was bound to show kindness" and "Confound Casaubon!"). Right in the middle of the Victorian Period, this amounts altogether to a psychological realism that was highly esteemed (much more highly than Eliot's frequently intrusive narrator) by the contemporary novelist and critic Henry James and later by Modernists like Virginia Woolf.

A further **panorama of English society** in epic totality situated between Henry Fielding's *Tom Jones* (1749) and George Eliot's *Middlemarch* (1871–72) stems from the pen of William Makepeace Thackeray (1811–63). Thackeray, who was like Eliot seen as a serious rival to Dickens, emulated Dickens's manner by publishing *Vanity Fair* as a serial novel, illustrated by the author and subtitled *Pen and Pencil Sketches of English Society* (1847–48). Thackeray had tested out the form successfully in *The Snobs of England* (serialised in *Punch* magazine, 1846–47, and then published as *The Book of Snobs*). In *Barry Lyndon* (1844, see above), Thackeray had already given proof of his expertise in the eighteenth century, and in *Vanity Fair*, he applied the historical touch to the period from the Napoleonic Wars up to the Age of Reform (thus ending where *Middlemarch* would later set in). For the publication of *Vanity Fair* as a three-decker novel (1848), Thackeray changed the subtitle to *A Novel without a Hero* and added a new meta-literary frame in which the narrator and characters appear as a puppet-player and his puppets. In the final (new) paragraph of the novel, Thackeray's narrator complemented the theme of *theatrum mundi* or "All the world's a stage" (*As You Like It*) by a reference to vanity, a key concept in satirical tales of morality and mortality: "Ah! *Vanitas Vanitatum*! Which of us is happy in this world? Which of us has his desire? or, having it, is satisfied? – Come, children, let us shut up the box and the puppets, for our play is played out." (Thackeray 1983: 878). From John Bunyan's Puritan tale *The Pilgrim's Progress* (1678–84, see chap. 3.4.5), Thackeray took the title *Vanity Fair*, but as a satirist of society, he was less concerned with religious matter than with materialism and (the lack of) morals in late Georgian and early Victorian times. Moreover, when he published his *Novel without a Hero*, Thackeray acted as a literary parodist of romance, as again in his Christmas Book and comic continuation of Scott's *Ivanhoe* entitled *Rebecca and Rowena: A Romance upon Romance* (1850). In the two principal female charac-

Fig. 4.32
W. M. Thackeray

ters of *Vanity Fair*, schoolfellows Rebecca 'Becky' Sharp (a blonde beast rising in society) and Amelia Sedley (a virtuous brunette treated unfairly in life), the romance formula is reversed. Becky Sharp is a serial flirt who hunts men for their money and status. She rejects old Sir Pitt Crawley's proposal of marriage only to elope with his son Capt. Rawdon Crawley, a duelling dandy. Upwardly mobile, Becky goes on to entice Lord Steyne, and is even presented at court to King George IV. Becky's phenomenal rise in society is followed by a catastrophic fall when Rawdon surprises her with Lord Steyne, who has showered money and diamonds on her. Meanwhile, Amelia Sedley had already experienced such a fall from grace due to the bankruptcy of her father, and to her disastrous marriage to Lieut. George Osborne – which leads from his disinheritance to the progressive disintegration of the marriage, and ends ultimately in his death on the battlefield of Waterloo (1815). Amelia lives the life of a single mother without a fortune, until she learns to love Major William Dobbin of the Indian Army, and her fate turns for the better. This is a good occasion for Thackeray, who was born in Calcutta, to extend his panoramic novel with a humorous section (chap. 43) set "in the Madras division of our Indian empire". (Rudyard Kipling, born in Bombay a couple of years after Thackeray's death, would provide a broader social panorama of colonial India in his turn-of-the-century novel *Kim*. See chap. 4.2.2.) Thackeray's pseudo-romance ends 'happily', though in an ironical sense. Dobbin's qualities become apparent to Amelia only after she learns that her former schoolfellow Becky had also ensnared her husband, and that therefore Amelia's grief for George Osborne was quite unwarranted. Meanwhile, Becky continues to flirt with Amelia's brother, the stockbroker and merchant Jos Sedley. This brings about her rehabilitation, in particular after the death of Jos, in which she might have had a hand (as one of Thackeray's illustrations insinuates, see chap. 4.2.1).

4.5.3 | Regional and Sensational Elements in the Novel from Wilkie Collins and Thomas Hardy to D. H. Lawrence

The Beginnings of Crime Fiction

Nineteenth- and twentieth-century crime fiction is part of a long tradition that involves distinct phases and various sub-genres, including detective fiction and the thriller. (For a typology and history of crime fiction, see Cawelti 1976, Suerbaum 1984, Knight 2003 and Priestman 2003.) The beginning of that tradition dates back at least to the eighteenth century's **interest in exceptional criminals and outlaws**. Among those who were imprisoned at Newgate and hanged at Tyburn Tree, Jonathan Wild (executed 1725) is still the best known, because his exemplary story was seized by several leading writers of the day, starting with Daniel Defoe's *True and Genuine Account of the Life and Actions of the Late Jonathan Wild* (1725). The so-called 'Thieftaker-General' served as a vehicle of satire directed against great (but corrupt) politicians such as the first Prime Minister Robert Walpole. In John Gay's satiric portrait of Peachum, the king of thieves in *The Beggar's Opera* (1728), Wild and Walpole merged into one, as they did in Henry Fielding's novel entitled *History of the Life of the Late Mr Jonathan Wild the Great* (1743). It followed upon Fielding's ironical essay "Of True Greatness" (1741), where the outlaw is depicted in a sympathetic light. This tradition is continued in the historical fiction of Sir Walter Scott, with its Romantic portrayal of outlaws as essentially good, well-meaning individuals, e.g. 'Locksley'/Robin Hood (*Ivanhoe*) or the Highland robbers Fergus MacIvor (*Waverley*) and the eponymous hero in *Rob Roy*. In all these works, the timeless conflict between the individual and society is depicted as a conflict between the 'noble criminal' and a corrupt society.

Apart from this satiric reversal of good and evil, there is a more sensational interest in the depiction of crime and criminal individuals, which involves the extraordinary – and extraordinarily brutal – character of crime, its irrationalism and inhumanity. This, too, dates back to the eighteenth century, and can be seen as a counterpoint to more mainstream concepts such as Enlightened Rationalism, Sentimentalism and Benevolence, both in Britain and on the Continent. The amorality of the protagonists in *Les Liaisons dangereuses* (1782), the Sadistic sexual fantasies of the Marquis de Sade (*La Nouvelle Justine*, 1797–1801) and the exceptionally vicious characters in the Gothic romances of the day all belong to that irrational, **anti-Enlightenment counter-culture**. Vice is here no longer presented in order to cure the evils of society, but, more perversely, to conjure up sensual delight.

With the so-called Newgate novels and the mass-market fiction of the 'penny dreadfuls', this line of tradition continues well into the middle of the nineteenth century. Here, too, W. H. Ainsworth

Newgate Novels and
Penny Dreadfuls

and Edward Bulwer Lytton achieved prominence, with a type of fiction that succeeded the Gothic romance in its sensational aspect. The **Newgate novels** fleshed out the collection of criminal biographies entitled *The Newgate Calendar* (1773 ff.), and they exploited the sensational aspects of the London under-world and of the new Towers of London, such as Newgate and other prisons built to keep criminals in check. Ainsworth's depiction of eighteenth-century highwaymen such as Dick Turpin (in *Rookwood*, 1834) or *Jack Sheppard* (in his eponymous 1839 novel), together with Bulwer Lytton's novels *Paul Clifford* (1830) and *Eugene Aram* (1832), are the prime examples of an early form of crime fiction (c. 1830–50) which was highly controversial, but also a great sales success. The influence on Dickens's novels can be seen in his frequent prison settings or symbolism, and in characters such as Fagin the master criminal (*Oliver Twist*) or the convicts Magwitch and Compeyson (*Great Expectations*). Thackeray, on the other hand, began his career by writing parodies and satires of Newgate novels, pinpointing their morbid interest in the sensational aspects of crime. The **'penny dreadfuls'** (from the 1840s) followed upon the vogue of the Gothic and of the Newgate novel, but addressed a larger audience with even more sensational, luridly illustrated stories of crime and terror. *Varney the Vampire; or, The Feast of Blood* (1845–47) by James Malcolm Rymer is a telling example that predates Bram Stoker's *Dracula* by half a century. In the latter half of the Victorian Age, the 'penny dreadfuls' addressed themselves to a newly literate, juvenile audience. By contrast, many other tales of adventure were written, and several 'boy's weeklies' founded, just in order to keep adolescents away from that morally questionable reading matter. (See chap. 4.5.5)

Sensation Novels

What all these sub-traditions of crime fiction have in common is that those works – despite their sensational appeal – effectively keep crime at a distance from the middle-class audience. The stories of eighteenth-century highwaymen, and of outlaws such as Robin Hood or Rob Roy further in the past, deal with transgressive behaviour 'out there', against which one's own home is indeed a castle. However, in the middle of the nineteenth century there occurred a change: crime fiction conquered the domestic castle. The **sensation novels of the 1860s** brought crime back home, and so did the famous British tradition of detective fiction, which dates back to about the same time. Again, Dickens is involved in both cases of best-selling fiction: as the editor of the magazine *All the Year Round*, and as the writer of *Bleak House*, which is a precursor of the sensation novel and arguably the first detective novel in Britain (see above). Elementary plot summaries of major examples of sensation novels will serve to illustrate this sub-genre: *The Woman in White* by Dickens's friend Wilkie Collins (1824–89) is a tale of mystery (who is the Woman in White?), featuring abduction, intrigue, larger-than-life villains (e. g. Count Fosco) and surprise twists of the plot. The pseudo-documentary character of the narrative (which presents itself as an *assemblage* of diary entries, testimonial evidence etc.) was a new feature. Serialisation (in *All the Year Round*, 1859–60) enabled Wilkie Collins to make much use of the 'cliffhanger' technique, and thus contributed to the creation of suspense. In Collins's *The Moonstone* (serialised in *All the Year Round* in 1868), the plot revolves around the attempt of Indian 'thugs' (gangsters) to get hold of a great Indian diamond that was carried off to Britain (like the Kohinoor diamond that became the jewel in the crown of Queen and Empress Victoria). Thematically, this Indian and colonial element of plot links up with early instances of detective fiction such as the Sherlock Holmes stories *The Sign of Four* (1890) and "The Adventure of the Crooked Man" (1892/93). Commercial crime is addressed in *Hard Cash*, written by the above-mentioned Charles Reade (and also serialised in *All the Year Round* in 1863), a sensation novel that deals with a banker who tries to get hold of another person's fortune. To further his ends, the vicious banker manages to have the 'goodies' of the story secured in a lunatic asylum, and those madhouse scenes – in addition to the twist that one of the characters is nearly buried alive – are exploited by Reade to great effect. In *Uncle Silas* (1864), the Irish novelist Sheridan Le Fanu (1814–73), who is also famous for his ghost stories, cooked up a tale of intrigue, murder and suicide. By comparison, the plot of *Lady Audley's Secret* (1862) by M[ary]. E[lizabeth]. Braddon (1835–1915) can be summarised as follows: "Braddon's bigamous heroine deserts her child, pushes husband number one down a well, thinks about poisoning husband number two, and sets fire to a hotel in which her other male acquaintances are residing" (Showalter 1977: 163). However, Elaine Showalter points out that mid-Victorian fiction even in its most sensational aspect observed the limits of representation: "Braddon's novels

|Fig. 4.33
Wilkie Collins

had so little overt sexuality in them that they were paradoxically permitted in the Victorian schoolroom when [Gaskell's] *Ruth* and [Eliot's] *The Mill on the Floss* were excluded" (Showalter 1977: 161; see also Cruse 1935: 326).

Stoker's *Dracula* and Wilde's *Dorian Gray*

Towards the end of the century, there is a notable change in this respect. In *Dracula* (1897) by Bram Stoker (1847–1912), **the vampire theme** – a scarcely disguised way of showing and telling of sexual acts – found its most notable expression, after it had been brought up earlier by Lord Byron's personal physician John Polidori in *The Vampyre* (1819), in J. M. Rymer's 'penny dreadful' *Varney the Vampire* (1845–47), and by Stoker's fellow-Irishman Le Fanu in *Carmilla* (1871). In *Dracula*, the male predator's manner of seeking an intimate union with his female victims – which generally ends in an invigorating blood infusion for himself, and occasionally also in a fusion of his blood and that of his victims – clearly resembles a sexual assault. From more than 150 adaptations to the screen (including F. W. Murnau's *Nosferatu*, 1922), the plot of *Dracula* is too well known to need another rehearsal here, but it may still be useful to say a word about its fictional form. Stoker's sensational horror novel looks back to Wilkie Collins's *The Woman in White* (and further to the epistolary novel) as it is made up alike of journals, letters and telegrams by several homodiegetic narrators. Among them are Jonathan Harker (Count Dracula's legal adviser, and *de facto* his prisoner), Harker's fiancée Mina Murray, Mina's pen friend Lucy Westenra, three of Lucy's suitors, and Abraham Van Helsing, who is ultimately successful in tracking down and destroying the aristocratic vampire in his Transylvanian castle. Successful for a time, that is, because the neo-Gothic vogue initiated by *Dracula* regularly included attempts to bring the bloodthirsty Count back to life, in fiction and on screen. Count Dracula, who shows a different aspect of his character during the day and at night, is moreover one of a number of **split personalities** that hint at the new and increasing interest in psychological processes in *fin de siècle* science (Freud) and fiction. R. L. Stevenson's *The Strange Case of Dr Jekyll and Mr Hyde* (1886, see chap. 4.5.4) and Oscar Wilde's *The Picture of Dorian Gray* (serialised 1890, revised 1891) are further examples. Dorian Gray, an attractive young man, is seduced by the dandy Lord Henry Wotton to enjoy the lustful pleasures of seemingly endless youth. In Wilde's novel this is achieved not by the vampire's way

of regular blood infusion, but by the fantastic device of transferring the process of ageing and of physical decay from the human
body to a double. Basil Hallward's life-sized painting of Dorian
Gray has to bear the marks of the sitter's hedonistic, but also ir-
responsible life style that destroys other people's lives through
misery, suicide and murder. When Dorian Gray's feelings of guilt
can no longer be suppressed with opium, he stabs the painting in
a rage – and thus brings about his own death (and the restoration
of the painting to its original state). Quite like Wilde's comedies
of manners (see chap. 4.3), *The Picture of Dorian Gray* is full of witti-
cisms. They can be found in the narrator's intrusive commentary
("His principles were out of date, but there was a good deal to
be said for his prejudices", 1966: 38), in Lord Henry's conversation ("A man cannot be too careful in the choice of his enemies",
23) and in Oscar Wilde's preface to the novel, which is both an
epigrammatic and a programmatic piece of Aestheticism. "There
is no such thing as a moral or an immoral book. Books are well
written, or badly written. That is all" ("The Preface", 17). However, both the author's Aestheticist credentials and his character
Lord Henry's credo cannot easily be reconciled with the moral of
the tale, which unequivocally speaks out against a single-mind-
ed, anti-social pursuit of happiness.

Those works of fiction that have a **Portrait of the Artist** as a
central theme (*Künstlerromane*) are worth a short digression, as
they add up to a thematic subgenre of fiction, albeit realised
in different forms. Apart from Joyce's eponymous novel, this
subgenre comprises Oscar Wilde's *The Picture of Dorian Gray* and
Dickens's *David Copperfield* (1849–50). Further, minor examples
that are of interest for a comparison include Disraeli's *Contarini
Fleming: A Psychological Romance* (1832) and Charles Kingsley's *Alton Locke* (1850), the fictional autobiography of a working-class
poet. With *Sandra Belloni* and *Vittoria* (1864–66), George Meredith
(1828–1909) wrote two novels about the complicated love life of
an opera singer and her involvement in the 1860–61 Italian War
of Independence. In its development, the 'portrait of the artist'
as a fictional subgenre mirrors the rise and fall of the convention of the happy ending pointed out above. By comparison with
Meredith, Thomas Hardy casts a more critical look at the role of
society in *Jude the Obscure* (1895), the tragic story of a stonema-
son whose unconventional love life blocks his entrance into the

Portraits of the Artist

academic world. George Gissing's *New Grub Street* (1891) likewise ends unhappily, this time with the death of an ambitious novelist who does not compromise with a corrupted literary establishment. Gissing (1857–1903) wrote his novel in Naturalist fashion, which involves the representation of urban slum life. By contrast, *A Portrait of the Artist as a Young Man* (serialised 1914–15) by James Joyce (1882–1941) became a prime example of Modernist fiction. Despite its critical engagement with religion and politics in Ireland, this novel is characterised by a psychological rather than a social realism. This is apparent in the frequent use of Free Indirect Discourse to represent the intellectual development of artist Stephen Dedalus, who reappears as a character in Joyce's Modernist masterpiece *Ulysses* (1922).

New Genres: Spy Fiction and Thriller

Back on track with the more sensational narratives, we find that modern spy fiction was also born at the end of the Victorian Era, embedded into the political situation of the time. The British-Russian antagonism at the North-West Frontier of British India features as the 'Great Game' in *Kim* (1900–01) by Rudyard Kipling (1865–1936). *The Secret Agent* (1906–07) by Joseph Conrad (1857–1924) hints at a Russian connection, too, in its tale of anarchic terrorists who set out to explode a bomb at Greenwich. (For *Kim* and for Conrad, see chap. 4.2.2.) Other thrilling novels deal with spy scare in connection with Anglo-German competition in the running-up to the First World War. In *The Riddle of the Sands* (1903) by Erskine Childers (1870–1922) and in *The Thirty-Nine Steps* (1915) by John Buchan (1875–1940), British gentleman agents detect and rule out the threat of a German invasion. The success of *The Thirty-Nine Steps* (which is also mirrored in Alfred Hitchcock's 1935 film version and in further adaptations) made Buchan expand it into a series of altogether four novels about gentleman agent Richard Hannay. *Greenmantle* (1916), which was written before Buchan became the chief of British wartime propaganda, includes (in chap. 6) a meeting of Richard Hannay and the arch-enemy, namely Kaiser Wilhelm II. Ideologically, Buchan's best-selling Hannay novels present a mixture of social snobbery and national prejudices with the gentleman ideal and the public school spirit of fair play, the latter extending to the Great Game of espionage. *Mr Standfast* (1919) is moreover interesting for its extended portrait of the Cotswolds region as an epitome of rural England. (See Hindersmann 1995, with further reference.)

The **regional novel** had set in with Maria Edgeworth's novels on Ireland (*Castle Rackrent*, 1801) and experienced a shift of focus to Scotland and to the recent past in Sir Walter Scott's *Waverley Novels* (from 1814). Besides his work for the Post Office – which included the introduction of the pillar-box in the UK – Anthony Trollope (1815–82) began his career (unsuccessfully) as a writer with novels placed in Ireland, before he hit upon the imaginary West Country county of Barset and its chief town, Barchester (modelled e.g. on Winchester), for a setting. *Barchester Towers* (1857) is a prominent example of the *Barsetshire Novels* (1855–67), a series of regional novels connected by recurrent characters, with which Trollope established the novel-sequence in Britain. Trollope's close friend George Eliot favoured the Midlands as a setting for *Adam Bede* (1859), *The Mill on the Floss* (1860) and *Middlemarch* (1871–72), whereas R.D. Blackmore focused on Exmoor and Devon in *Lorna Doone* (1869, see above).

Regional Novel

For his *Wessex Novels*, Thomas Hardy (1840–1928) chose a fictionalised part of Southwest England as a setting. Although real locations in Dorset, Somerset and Devon appear under invented names (so that the regional novelist could occasionally take a creative license), Hardy himself indicated the relationship between topographical fact and fiction for a map that from 1895 adorned all editions. *Far From the Madding Crowd* (1874), *The Return of the Native* (1878), *The Mayor of Casterbridge* (1886) and *Jude the Obscure* (1894–95) are remarkable novels in this series, which also includes *Tess of the d'Urbervilles: A Pure Woman Faithfully Presented* (1891). As a regional novel, *Tess* stands out for the novelist's social realism in showing the rural population at work in the cowsheds and in the fields. (This holds also true for Roman Polanski's successful 1979 adaptation of *Tess* and rural England to the screen, which invites the comparison with the director's likewise faithful, 2005 representation of *Oliver Twist* as a social problem novel with an urban setting.) In contrast to other novelists depicting the life of the landed gentry, Hardy points to rural poverty as an incentive to work for a living (Tess works as a dairymaid), and he does not forget to mention the impact of the Industrial Revolution on agriculture (see the threshing-machine in chap. 45). In his depiction of the determining influence of rural milieu and morality on an individual's fate, Hardy is moreover close to Naturalism.

Hardy's Tess and the Wessex Novels

Fig. 4.34
Thomas Hardy

With its division into seven 'phases' (which compare to the three 'stages' in *Great Expectations*), *Tess* is marked out as a novel of development. However, Hardy dispenses with the conventional happy ending; instead, *Tess* moves, like a Greek tragedy, relentlessly towards catastrophe. Young and innocent Tess, who is throughout referred to as a 'pure' woman, is raped in her sleep by Alec Stoke-d'Urberville, and left as a single mother to bury her child called Sorrow soon after giving birth unattended. With the (veiled) depiction of the rape of Tess, and with the infant's Christian burial after an act of lay baptism, the novelist was out to provoke his more conventional Victorian readers so that those passages were censored and could not be published during serialisation. (They were reinstated in later editions that were further revised by the novelist.) Yet this is not the end of Tess's martyrdom. The ensuing romance with and marriage to Angel Clare fails spectacularly. Angel admits to a pre-marital bout of passion with a stranger, and asks for Tess's indulgence, but he is abhorred when he hears of his wife's pre-marital record. For 'Angel' Clare, who has been won over from a family and a rival lover that are likewise characterised by outward respectability, Evangelical religion and conventional morality, Tess is suddenly no more than a fallen angel – and therefore he has no qualms about proposing to another girl, Izz Huet, to replace Tess after their separation. Meanwhile, Tess meets Alec again, who returns as a convert to Evangelicalism, and who soon returns to his passionate self, too. The tragic "fulfilment" of the heroine (phase 7) occurs at Stonehenge, where Tess, after a final loving reunion with Angel Clare within the ancestral stone monument, is arrested for the murder of Alec. Hardy, who had so far already tried Victorian stereotypes of womanhood and the religious feelings of his more conventional readers, did not spare them the ultimate shock. On the last page of the novel, they encountered first the execution of a 'pure' woman for murder, and then the narrator's acerbic commentary upon such a judicial hanging: "'Justice' was done, and the President of the Immortals (in Æschylean phrase) had ended his sport with Tess." In a rejoinder to the outcry of (to him) bigot Christian critics who objected to such phrasing, the atheist Hardy did not relent and cited Gloucester's alike sarcastic remark from Shakespeare's *King Lear*: "As flies to wanton boys are we to the gods;/They kill us for their sport." (4.1.36–37, quoted from Hardy's preface to the 1892 fifth edition of *Tess*). When *Jude the Obscure* (1894–95) met with even more furious objections against its representation of marriage and divorce, Hardy quit as a novelist and turned to publishing *Wessex Poems* (1898) and other works of poetry.

An interest in the West Country is also shown by later writers such as John Cowper Powys (1872–1963), e.g. in *A Glastonbury Romance* (1932), and in the romances written by Daphne du Maurier (1907–89), such as *Jamaica Inn* (1936) and *Rebecca* (1938). The tradition of the regional novel was kept up, for the Staffordshire pottery district, by Arnold Bennett (1867–1931) in his *Clayhanger Trilogy* (1910–16, see above), and for Nottinghamshire and its mining communities in the novels and short stories by D[avid]. H[erbert]. Lawrence (1885–1930). Together with novelists as diverse as Joseph Conrad and E. M. Forster, Lawrence cannot easily be classified either as a pre-Modernist or as a Modernist writer. For the sake of his affiliation to the nineteenth-century regional novel, he is treated here; yet he can also be compared to Virginia Woolf in his use of Free Indirect Discourse as a means of psychological realism, or to James Joyce in the freedom taken with the literary representation of sexuality. Lawrence's manner to have "the stream of consciousness [...] turning downwards" (Lawrence 1961: 220) regularly led to the censorship of his fiction. *Sons and Lovers* (1913) came out only after having been heavily edited by the publisher's reader Edward Garnett (the original version was available again only in 1992). Lawrence's first novel (which bears some parallels to his own life) deals with the precarious relationship of Paul Morel, from a Nottinghamshire miners' family, to his possessive mother Gertrude. His further development is marked by his romantic feelings for Miriam Leivers, and by his adulterous affair with Clara Dawes, a married woman. *The Rainbow* (1915) and its sequel *Women in Love* (1920) stem from an original draft entitled "The Sisters", but *Women in Love* had to wait for four years after completion until it could be published, and still proved controversial. Both of Lawrence's novels concentrate on the search for true and lasting love in three generations of the Brangwen family that is connected with rural Nottinghamshire. In every generation, a longing for a spiritual union is interspersed by flashes of sexual passion. The increasingly more harmonious marriage between Tom Brangwen and the Polish

The Novels of
D. H. Lawrence

widow Lydia Lensky is juxtaposed with the match between two cousins from the next generation, Tom's stepdaughter Anna Lensky and his nephew Will Brangwen. Their marriage is soon characterised only by their sexual communion, which – although depicted in anything but Victorian fashion – is given out as a degeneration: "This was what their love had become, a sensuality violent and extreme as death. They had no conscious intimacy, no tenderness of love. It was all the lust and the infinite, maddening intoxication of the senses, a passion of death." (Chap. 10) In the second half of The Rainbow, the focus shifts to their daughter Ursula Brangwen, and in Women in Love also to her sister Gudrun. After two passionate but unfulfilled relationships, first to her schoolmistress Winifred Inger (who then marries another Brangwen) and then to Anton Skrebensky, Ursula – now a teacher herself – embarks on an affair with Rupert Birkin, a school inspector. Meanwhile, Gudrun Brangwen's fascination extends not only to her lover Gerald Crich, but increasingly also to the German sculptor Loerke. In both novels, the narrative is fused with a running discourse on vitality (and sterility) as a principle of life. This private philosophy bears resemblance to Henri Bergson's notion of élan vital as well as to G. B. Shaw's conception of a Life Force, and it informs also Lady Chatterley's Lover (1928). In this, Lawrence's most controversial novel, sexuality is represented utterly without any Victorian inhibition, but it is clad into a view of life made up of the contrasting pairs warmth vs. coldness, vitality vs. mechanisation, and organic growth vs. industry. Such a view extends, first of all, to the setting of this post-World War regional novel in the stately halls and mining villages of Nottinghamshire and Derbyshire, where

> One England blots out another. The mines had made the halls wealthy. Now they were blotting them out, as they had already blotted out the cottages. The industrial England blots out the agricultural England. One meaning blots out another. The new England blots out the old England. And the continuity is not organic, but mechanical. (Chap. 11, Lawrence 1961: 163. See also 123–25, 158–66.)

An exception from the common people at Tevershall village "in whom the living intuitive faculty was dead as nails, and only queer mechanical yells and uncanny will-power remained" (158) is (Oliver) Mellors, the gamekeeper at Wragby Hall, the seat of Sir

Clifford and Lady Connie Chatterley. Connie's marriage to Clifford, who survived the First World War only as a cripple in a (mechanical) wheelchair, becomes sterile in more than just the physical sense. Her vital self is reawakened through her sexual liaison with Mellors that is about to overcome the obstacles presented by both their marriages and by their different positions in society: the open ending of the novel sees Connie separated from Clifford and pregnant by Mellors. The class difference is accentuated by Mellors's use of the local dialect, though he is perfectly able to switch to 'good English' when he feels the need to, in conversation as well as in writing (chaps. 15–16, 19). While Connie's thoughts on her post-war generation and on gender relations are usually presented either in discussion within her social circle (chaps. 4, 6, 7) or in the form of Free Indirect Discourse (pp. 47, 64–67, 140–41, 258–59, 265–73), Mellors is made to speak his mind in conversation with her or in an occasional letter (chaps. 14, 15, 18, 19). Speaking in his own person, Lawrence continued to make his point in his essays "Pornography and Obscenity" (1929) and "A Propos of *Lady Chatterley's Lover*" (1930). In spite of such vigorous self-defence, *Lady Chatterley's Lover* remained banned in Britain for obscenity until 1961, when the novel was finally cleared in a trial at the Old Bailey in London. This signified a clear break with Victorian sexual morality, and the beginning of the Swinging Sixties. Among the witnesses who stood up for Lawrence's novel at that trial were notable academic critics from Oxford and Cambridge universities, and the novelist E. M. Forster.

Apart from a marked interest in the regions of the British Isles, there is also a concern with other worlds in the fiction of the period under review. Alice's Wonderland, Peter Pan's Never Land and Kipling's Jungle are fantastic worlds from children's literature that have been fondly stored in the adult's mind (see chaps. 4.3 and 4.5.4). In *Erewhon; or, Over the Range* (1872) and in *Erewhon Revisited* (1901; '*Erewhon*' is an anagram of 'nowhere'), Samuel Butler (1835–1902) revived **utopia** as a genre together with the satiric manner of *Gulliver's Travels*. William Morris (1834–96) – who was the driving force behind the Arts and Crafts movement, an enthusiast of handsomely produced books and a social reformer – envisaged in his utopia *News from Nowhere* (1890) a commonwealth where a brotherhood of men has been liberated from the restraints of industry and market economy to express their individual creativ-

Concern with Other Worlds

H.G. Wells

ity. With the Socialist H[erbert]. G[eorge]. Wells (1866–1946), uto-pian literature took a turn towards **dystopia** (or negative utopia) and to the **scientific romance** (a contemporary British term for what is now generally called **science fiction**). In Wells's novella *The Time Machine* (1895), the adventures of a time traveller are embedded into a narrative frame which consists of a more abstract discussion of Time as a fourth dimension of Space (questions that were famously treated ten years later by Albert Einstein in his Theory of Relativity). There is social criticism and a pessimistic view on evolution, too. The bipartite world of the year 802 701 comes to be seen as a transposition of the class-ridden Victorian society, and it is peopled by two degenerated humanoid beings. There are the Eloi, an aristocratic and beautiful people who enjoy a leisurely lifestyle on the surface in broad daylight, but who do no longer develop (physically and intellectually) beyond child-hood. They contrast starkly with the Morlocks, a blind working race who have to live and work in the darkness underground in a network of tunnels and machine rooms, from which they escape to haunt the Eloi at night. In all these respects, *The Time Machine* makes for an interesting comparison with Bulwer Lytton's *The Coming Race* (1871), where the dystopian world is presented from a politically conservative point of view, and also with its two se-quels *Die Reise mit der Zeitmaschine* (by Egon Friedell, 1946) and *The Space Machine: A Scientific Romance* (by Christopher Priest, 1976). Two other fantastic stories by Wells have continued to fascinate an audience. In the cruel vivisection and animal experiments that take place on *The Island of Doctor Moreau* (1896), evolution and scientific progress are once more presented in a negative light. *The War of the Worlds* (serialised 1897) became the model for sto-ries about an alien invasion of Earth, and its shock value was tested again successfully by the author's near-namesake Orson Welles, whose 1938 adaptation of the story as a radio play mask-ing as breaking news sent panic-stricken US-Americans packing.

4.5.4 | Devils, Doubles and Detectives: The Development of Short Fiction in Ireland, Scotland and England

The development of the short story has to be seen within the wider context of short narratives in Britain and Ireland. Their variety comprises Chaucer's *Canterbury Tales*, the ballad tradition, eighteenth- and nineteenth-century character sketches and story-essays, Gothic tales as well as those moral tales written to counter their allegedly harmful influence (see chap. 3.4.6). A new stage is reached with the great Irish and Scottish storytellers of the nineteenth and twentieth centuries that transformed the previous oral tradition. The magazine played an important part as a medium of distribution, both within Britain and (in particular after the Great Famine in the "Hungry Forties") for the Irish diaspora abroad. As with the serialisation of novels, the publication of stories in a magazine generally preceded their collection in volume form. Thematically, fresh manners of dealing with elements of mystery, fantasy and horror contributed their share to the acknowledgment of the short story as a genre of its own. (For greater detail, see Korte 2003, Löffler and Späth 2005.)

In *Traits and Stories of the Irish Peasantry* (1830–33, rev. 1843–44)   Ireland
by William Carleton (1794–1869) as well as in the stories by Gerald Griffin, an obvious effort is made to preserve features of an oral society in the printed text. Carleton's stories testify to the harsh reality of peasant life, and tell of its particularities, as e. g. in "The Hedge School". From the 1780s to the introduction of English-language National Schools (1831), hedge schools for Catholic Irish peasants formed a counterpart to English Sunday schools, and they were fondly remembered in Carleton's tales of the 1830s (as well as in Brian Friel's 1980 play *Translations*: see chap. 5.2). In "The Death of a Devotee" (in Trevor 1989), Carleton pointed to the oral tradition by his use of dialect for the dialogue in a story that contrasts the themes of true religion and superstition. Old Father Moyle is requested to perform the last rites on a religious 'devotee' or 'voteen' who in fact does not believe in Christianity, but in magic rites and objects. The struggle within the priest as to absolve an unrepentant sinner is heightened in true Romantic fashion by the rare Irish phenomenon of a hurricane. "The Brown Man" by Gerald Griffin (1803–40) is a related story about superstition, and an example of Irish Gothic: an unknown brown horseman, who is seen to visit the churchyard at night, fetches Nora to the wilderness to marry her – only to turn into a killer and cannibal who devours her in a different fashion. With *The Collegians* (1829), Griffin provided a novel about a murder case, which his Irish compatriot Dion Boucicault successfully

adapted for the stage under the title *The Colleen Bawn* (1860, see chap. 4.3).

Published a century later, "The Priest" (1929) by Daniel Corkery (1878–1964) rounds off those stories concerned with religious faith. Just like in "The Death of a Devotee", a Catholic clergyman, Father Reen, is called to a deathbed. He meets with indignation, which presents him with a moment of revelation regarding his bond to the congregation ('my people') for whom he fulfils his clerical duties, but whom he fails to inspire. Corkery, a professor of English at Cork, centred on rural Irish life and dialect, and exerted his influence as a mentor on younger writers such as Frank O'Connor and Sean O'Faolain. In their generation, the short story assumed a unique position within a national literature. In his use of Free Indirect Discourse and of moments of **epiphany** as a means of psychological realism, Corkery followed upon James Joyce who had earlier defined epiphany in his novel-fragment *Stephen Hero* as "a sudden spiritual manifestation, whether in the vulgarity of speech or of gesture or in a memorable phrase of the mind itself". Joyce (1882–1941) completed a sequence of 15 stories about middle-class Dublin in 1907, some years after he had left his native city for good to live for the rest of his life in Continental exile. Due to its rejection by altogether 40 publishers, the publication of *Dubliners* was delayed until 1914. Joyce revealed that

J. Joyce, *Dubliners*

> My intention was to write a chapter of the moral history of my country and I chose Dublin for the scene because that city seemed to me the centre of paralysis. I have tried to present it to the indifferent public under four of its aspects: childhood, adolescence, maturity and public life. The stories are arranged in this order. (Letter to his publisher Grant Richards, May 1906)

In "The Sisters" (aspect: childhood), a boy-narrator tells of his reaction to the death of the priest Father Flynn. "Eveline" (adolescence) shows a bipartite division: first, a young woman reflects on her childhood and on her lover Frank, a sailor, with whom she wants to emigrate from a stilted family life and the occasional bout of violence of her father. Later, at the docks and at the moment of departure, Eveline cannot bring herself to do the final step: she is suddenly paralysed – and thus exemplary. "Ivy Day in the Committee Room", one of the stories of public life, engages with Irish nationalist politics that at the time of publication had not brought about Home Rule. "The Dead" (another such novella of public life adapted for the screen by director John Huston in 1987) is set around an annual party. There, Gabriel Conroy vents his frustration over his country, and experiences a revelation about death when he learns of his wife that she still blames herself for the death of a teenager, thirty years ago, who was in love with her. In general, the stories are not endowed with a dramatic development, but lead to such moments of revelation, and Joyce's psychological realism extends (over and above his use of Free Indirect Discourse) to suiting the language of narration to the characters' state of mind.

Fig. 4.36

James Joyce by C. Ruf, Zurich, c.1918

Scotland

In Scotland, the transformation from oral traditional narratives to prose fiction revealed itself in Robert Burns's verse tale "Tam O'Shanter", in the ballads collected by Sir Walter Scott, and in the first specimens of Scottish short fiction in prose produced by Scott ("The Two Drovers", 1827) and his contemporaries James Hogg ("The Cameronian Preacher's Tale", 1828) and John Galt ("The Howdie: An Autobiography", 1833). "Then for the best part of fifty years the Scottish short story endured in a state close to torpor", states Douglas Dunn in his representative anthology (1995: xiv). *Blackwood's Edinburgh Magazine* however made an impact with their Gothic tales, for instance on Edgar Allan Poe (see Morrison and Baldick 1995, 1997). This situation lasted until Robert Louis Stevenson (1850–94) appeared on the scene. Apart from his traveller's tales and his children's books (see chap. 4.5.4), he was renowned in his own time (and is now being rediscovered) as a Scottish master of short fiction. In "The Merry Men" (1882), Stevenson combined elements of love, historical and Gothic romances with a tale of treasure hunt and shipwreck. The novella is vaguely set in the time before the 1745 Jacobite Rebellion and the narrative structure is informed by Scott's *Waverley Novels*, as here, too, a neutral hero and narrator takes his readers to the rough Scottish Highlands and their uncouth inhabitants. Charles Darnaway, an Edinburgh graduate, travels to the North Western coast of Scotland to seek a treasure-trove from the times of the Spanish Armada, and also the love of his cousin Mary Ellen. The real focus of the story, however, is on Gordon Darnaway, Mary's father and Charles's uncle: a loud-mouthed Calvinist, a plunderer of wrecked ships together with his servant Rorie, and eventually

Fig. 4.37

Robert Louis Stevenson by Girolamo Nerli

a murderer. Much of the novella's appeal lies in the detailed description of sublime land- and seascape, in particular of the tidal breakers 'dancing' around the Merry Men – a 'dance of death' that spells doom for any ship passing these great granite rocks in tempestuous tide. The miraculous appearance of a single Black sailor as sole survivor from such a sunken ship is more than an allusion to Man Friday in Defoe's famous tale of shipwrecking, *Robinson Crusoe*. With the Black Man who pursues Gordon Darnaway to death, Stevenson moreover evoked a Scottish legend about the Devil in disguise that is also central to "Thrawn Janet" (1881), as he explained in a footnote when this first Scottish tale of his became collected in *"The Merry Men" and Other Tales and Fables* (1887). "Thrawn Janet" tells of a Reverend who, as a young man in 1712, was confronted with the Devil and with Death-in-Life in the witch-like character of Janet M'Clour, whose crooked form looked as if her neck had been twisted by hanging on the gallows. This proper Gothic tale is also a linguistic experiment. In "The Merry Men", Stevenson limited the use of Scots to the dialogue passages involving Uncle Gordon and his servant Rorie, but in "Thrawn Janet", he went one step further. There, the narrator speaks in Standard English only in an introductory section, before he switches to the main body of the story that is told retrospectively and entirely in Scots. Death, a *Doppelgänger* or arguably the Devil also appear as characters in the short stories "Will O' the Mill" and "Markheim" (from the same collection), but then they are found to be involved in casual conversation rather than in an atmosphere of terror.

Stevenson's lasting fame rests on two books of juvenile adventure fiction with an eighteenth-century setting, namely *Treasure Island* and *Kidnapped: Being Memoirs of the Adventures of David Balfour in the Year 1751* (both of which were serialised in a boys' weekly entitled *Young Folks* in 1881 and 1886, respectively), and on *The Strange Case of Dr Jekyll and Mr Hyde* (1886). The story of *Kidnapped* was continued in *Catriona* (1893) and accompanied by *The Master of Ballantrae* (1889), an adult novel about a fraternal feud in an eighteenth-century setting. With "The Persons of the Tale" (published together with other "Fables" and *Dr Jekyll and Mr Hyde* in a posthumous collection in 1896), Stevenson had written a metafictional epilogue to *Treasure Island* that might have endeared him more to Modernists like Virginia Woolf who (other than her

father Leslie Stephen) looked down on Stevenson as a mere storyteller. *The Strange Case of Dr Jekyll and Mr Hyde* became the exception
in that it continued to fascinate twentieth-century critics because
of its fractured narrative, psychological aspects and *Doppelgänger*
theme, as well as most other readers (and many film directors)
because of its horror elements, too. The scientific ambition of Dr
Henry Jekyll bends towards a separation of the rational and the
irrational parts of his dual personality. He experiments with a
special drug in order to split up the two sides of his self, and to
be able to alternate between them. While the rational character
of Dr Jekyll continues to be seen in broad daylight, a more lusty
side of his personality appears, outwardly transformed, in the
form of Edward Hyde. Yet Dr Jekyll's experiment on himself goes
tragically wrong, as he cannot control the effects of his drug, and
cannot secure control over the increasingly violent Hyde. At the
end, Jekyll sees no other solution than to make a "Full Statement
of the Case" (chap. 10) before he kills off Hyde, and thus himself. Up to the point when Jekyll comes out in the open, the case
has been put together, within a heterodiegetic and extradiegetic
frame-narrative, through the interpolated stories and letters of
Jekyll's butler Poole and of his colleague Dr Lanyon (himself a
victim), and through the thoughts and conversation shared between Mr Utterson the lawyer and his cousin Mr Enfield. From
its first publication in a cheap and popular edition, this short
novel was seen as more than merely a 'shilling shocker'. It could
be read as a moral tale about the struggle between Good and Evil,
or alternatively between the Spirit and the Flesh. Actually, it was
more often read as a psychological narrative about instinctive
passions or subconscious drives lurking behind a mask of reason. The phrasing in Dr Jekyll's final statement, which comes to
speak on Jekyll's 'undignified pleasures' immediately after char-
acterising Hyde as a solitary specimen of 'pure evil', contributes
to such ambivalence. In his correspondence, Stevenson attempted to block a pre-Freudian reading of his tale that saw Hyde as
the personification of Jekyll's usually suppressed, sexual drive:

> Hyde [...] was not [...] a mere voluptuary. There is no harm in a volup-
> tuary; and none [...] in what prurient fools call 'immorality.' The harm
> was in Jekyll, because he was a hypocrite – not because he was fond
> of women; he says so himself; but people are so filled full of folly and
> inverted lust, that they can think of nothing but sexuality. The hypocrite

let out the beast Hyde – who is no more sensual than another, but who is the essence of cruelty and malice, and selfishness and cowardice: and these are the diabolic in man – not this poor wish to have a woman, that they make such a cry about. (Letter to John Paul Bocock, November 1887; quoted from Maixner 1981: 231).

All to no avail: from its first publication in the 1890s, Freudian psychoanalysis had an impact on the reading and on the screening of Stevenson's *Doppelgänger* tale.

After he had travelled to Hawaii and to the South Sea islands of Tahiti and Samoa, where he spent the rest of his life, Stevenson published a collection of short stories entitled *Island Nights' Entertainments* (1893). This collection included "The Bottle Imp", a Hawaiian tale of the supernatural and a former classroom classic, and "The Beach of Falesá", a decidedly realistic South Sea story. Stevenson's exotic settings inspired the novelist Joseph Conrad (see chap. 4.2.2), perhaps also Somerset Maugham, and surprisingly even the Welsh poet Dylan Thomas (who in 1948 turned "The Beach of Falesá" into the script for a film which however was never produced). When he was not of direct influence, as with *Treasure Island* on Rider Haggard's *King Solomon's Mines* (1885) and on *Moonfleet* by J. Meade Falkner (1898), then Stevenson at least paved the way for later writers of genre fiction. Story elements from "The Merry Men" were re-assembled and transferred to a Cornish setting by Daphne Du Maurier in her regional and historical romances *Jamaica Inn* (1936) and *Frenchman's Creek* (1941). As a crime story with a focus on the shoplifter and murderer rather than on detection, "Markheim" (first published in 1885) looks ahead to the sequence of Tom Ripley novels by the American crime writer Patricia Highsmith (starting off with *The Talented Mr Ripley*, 1955).

After Stevenson's death, local colour and homely regionalism became hallmarks of the **Kailyard School** of writers. The 1894 novel *Beside the Bonnie Brier Bush* by 'Ian MacLaren' (i. e. John Watson, 1850–1907) provided the term *Kailyard* with its motto, by quoting this Scots word for 'cabbage patch' from a poem by Burns.

England

In England, the development of the short story happened more slowly. Relevant examples from well-known novelists come e. g. in comic form (Thackeray, *The Book of Snobs*, serialised in *Punch*, 1846–47) or as Gothic stories (Dickens, "The Signal-Man", 1866). There are ghost stories in an imperialist vein (G. A. Henty, "A Pipe of Mystery", from *Tales of Daring and Danger*, 1890; repr. in Boehmer 1998) or with an experimental touch (see Henry James's novella *The Turn of the Screw*, 1898). Not very long after the establishment, in 1829, of the Metropolitan Police Force (commonly called Scotland Yard), **detective fiction** sprang up as a new subgenre. In "The Murders in the Rue Morgue" (1841), the US-American writer Edgar Allan Poe (1809–49) introduced the amateur detective and intellectual genius C. Auguste Dupin in combination with a nameless narrator, and thus produced the structural pattern for the detective stories by Arthur Conan Doyle (1859–1930).

|Fig. 4.38
Sherlock Holmes

Sherlock Holmes and Dr John Watson were first concerned with *A Study in Scarlet* (published in *Beeton's Christmas Annual*, 1887), and from 1891 regularly appeared as a double act in the pages of *The Strand Magazine* (in a short story sequence illustrated by Sidney Paget and others). Over 40 years, the 'canon' of spectacular case histories unearthed from Dr Watson's battered dispatch-box grew to altogether four novels (famously including *The Hound of the Baskervilles*, 1901–02) and 56 short stories. Even though Conan Doyle soon grew weary of his creation, it was no longer in his power to kill him off. "The Adventure of the Final Problem" (1893) closed with the apparent drowning of Holmes together with his archrival Prof. Moriarty in the Reichenbach Falls. This gave an opportunity to various writers to close the gap with their stories about Sexton Blake, who appeared as 'the office-boy's Sherlock Holmes' in boys' weeklies from 1893. Ten years later, however, Conan Doyle gave in to the constant nagging of his readers, and published the 1903 collection of stories entitled *The Return of Sherlock Holmes*. From this time onwards, Sherlock Holmes was never again lost to the world, and the "Thinking Machine" (as he is called in "A Scandal in Bohemia", the first of the short stories) remained a household word for rationality. It does not detract from the enduring appeal of Conan Doyle's stories to see that they are a piece of **'formula fiction'** (as described by Cawelti 1976: 80–98): while the focus rests on Holmes's manner of deduction, the narrative voice belongs to Dr Watson, who presents selected cases from his limited point of view, and thus figures as a mediator between the detective and his audience. "Elementary, my dear Watson": the exposition of the case histories regularly provides Holmes with an opportunity to show off his skills, before he embarks on the solution of a seemingly intractable mystery. The constellation of characters is tailor-made to see Sherlock Holmes in comparison with his likewise exceptionally bright brother Mycroft and with Prof. Moriarty, the 'Napoleon of crime', and against the much inferior abilities of Dr Watson and of Inspector Lestrade. Finally, Sherlock Holmes is an eccentric individual also in other matters than his intellectual brilliance. When he is not seen in his hallmark deerstalker hat and cape, Holmes appears as a lone professional in disguise. His bohemian lifestyle involves his virtuosity at playing the violin at uncommon times as well as an addiction to opium, and in these respects, Holmes is very much part of *fin de siècle* Aestheticism.

Gilbert Keith Chesterton (1874–1936) set his detective fiction within a very different framework. As a critic and essayist, Chesterton was known for his influential study of Dickens (1906) and for his works on religious subject matter, which resulted in his conversion to Roman Catholicism (1922). Starting with *The Innocence of Father Brown* (1911), Chesterton produced a series of detective stories centring on an unassuming Roman Catholic priest (serialised in magazines and collected in five books, 1911–35). The special feature of Chesterton's detective fiction is that the story is presented as a moral problem and not as an intellectual sport, and that the moral and religious implications of a crime dominate over the solution of a mystery. In this sense, Chesterton's Father Brown stories are less abstractly rational: they attempt to unite Rationalism and Religious Belief, and thus two tendencies that were opposed since the Enlightenment, and that appeared to be increasingly irreconcilable to nineteenth-century writers.

Among the late Victorian and early Modernist writers of short stories, we find writers as diverse as H. G. Wells (1866–1914), the humorist 'Saki' (Hector Munro, 1870–1916), and D. H. Lawrence (1885–1930). Lawrence's fame rests on his short stories as well as on his novels, poetry and travel writing. His general concern with love and marriage, with the individual and the family in rural and industrial Nottinghamshire, comes out e. g. in "Her Turn" and "Love Among the Haystacks" (both of them early stories composed around 1911/12, and collected by Edward Garnett for the posthumous 1930 collection *"Love Among the Haystacks" and Other Stories*). Moreover, some of Lawrence's best-known magazine stories, which he regularly revised for book publication, are distinguished by the theme of death. "Odour of Chrysanthemums" (1911, included in *"The Prussian Officer" and Other Stories*, 1914) is subdivided into two parts: one characterised by a looming death, the other by the reaction to fatal news. When Elizabeth Bates's husband, a miner, does not come home from Brinsley Colliery, she gets angry as she suspects him to have gone drunk at a pub while she looks after their children. On her return from a call to another miner's family (which gives Lawrence the opportunity to render the dialogue in dialect), her mother-in-law informs her of the husband's accident, and soon after his corpse is brought home: he was suffocated in the pit. While the two women wash the corpse, Elizabeth reflects on her married life. The pale, dead chrysanthemums – flowers connected with her marriage and childbirth – are used as a symbol throughout the story: when the corpse is brought, vase and flowers are shattered in the event. In the thematically related story "The Horse-Dealer's Daughter" (from *"England, My England" and Other Stories*, 1922), Free Indirect Discourse is frequently used, too, for psychological realism, a feature that relates Lawrence to Modernist short story writers such as James Joyce, Katherine Mansfield and Virginia Woolf. In the first of three parts, the story begins *in medias res*, showing four of the adult Pervin children together after their father's death. They receive notice that all is at an end: they have to move out soon, as the horse-dealer left them nothing but debts. When Jack Ferguson, the young country-doctor arrives and talks to Fred Henry and his sister Mabel Pervin, their conversation is marked by the recurrent question: "Mabel, what are you going to do with yourself?" The second part turns to narrate what happened before the event. It tells of Mabel's relationship to her mother who died 13 years earlier and to death in general, and of her subsequent role as housekeeper to a family that once had servants but later had to cope with a long period of poverty. After yet another time leap, the original situation is developed further in the third part: seeing no other way out than suicide, which also appears to her as a reunion with her dead mother, Mabel wants to drown herself in a nearby pond. However, she is being observed and then rescued by Ferguson, who brings her home. There, he is successful in revitalising the undressed woman, and she in bringing him round to love her (which he had not contemplated before), whereupon they spend the night together. The seemingly happy ending to this irrational affair remains open, as the reader is made to feel that they have merely been overcome by a sudden passion, but are still strangers to one another. Although sexuality is clearly part of the action, Lawrence did not depict it in explicit fashion – this he reserved for his later novel *Lady Chatterley's Lover*, which likewise treats passionate love together with poverty and futility in a coal-mining region (see chap. 4.5.3).

4.5.5 | **From Workhouse to Wonderland:**
The Child in Fiction, and Fiction for Children

The growing interest in children's education and the children's mind had led to moral tales and other children's books as new features on the eighteenth-century book market. Childhood became an important theme for Romantic poets such as Blake and Wordsworth, whereas the novel (just like sentimental drama) had hitherto concentrated on young adults. Samuel Richardson, Frances Burney and Jane Austen created heroines that were just of age, and became entangled in romantic love plots of matchmaking and marriage. Novels of development centred on the initiation into the world of adults, and on the mechanism of adaptation and resistance that leads to the formation of an individual character and a personal identity (an idea that was dear both to the Enlightenment and to Romanticism). Such a general outlook of fiction changed in Victorian times with the appearance of a great many works that had children as protagonists or childhood as a theme. (They were fleshing out the fifth category mentioned at the outset of chap. 3.4.6. For a more extended treatment of this complex theme, see Banerjee 1996.)

The School Experience   For children after infancy, school is a major experience, albeit sometimes a difficult one. In "Nicholas Nickleby at the Yorkshire School", Dickens's public reading version of the first part of his novel *Nicholas Nickleby* (1838–39), and in the first nine chapters of Charlotte Brontë's *Jane Eyre* (1847), the problems in Yorkshire schools are vividly illustrated. Dickens provided further (negative) examples of a boarding school in *Dombey and Son* (1847–48), and of an evening school in rural Kent in *Great Expectations* (1860–61, chaps. 7, 10). The foremost example of a school novel predating J.K. Rowling's Harry Potter series is however *Tom Brown's Schooldays* (1857) by Thomas Hughes (1822–96), which tells of Rugby public school under the headmastership of Dr Thomas Arnold (an educational reformer and the father of the poet Matthew Arnold). A prime feature of George Eliot's contemporary novel *The Mill on the Floss* (1860) is the different education allocated to boys and girls in Victorian times. The second 'book' of her novel is entitled "School-Time", and it deals critically with the strict regiment of an Evangelical Reverend at a boys' school attended by Tom Tulliver, while his sister Maggie – who has a far greater thirst for knowledge – has to see to her own education at home. In life and in literature, nannies (such as Mary Poppins in the eponymous 1934 children's novel by P. L. Travers) and governesses (such as Charlotte Brontë's Jane Eyre) were frequently employed to assist in the nursery and in female education. The exception from the rule, namely a 'finishing school' for girls, is represented by Miss Pinkerton's establishment in Thackeray's *Vanity Fair* (1847–48), which however had little influence on Becky Sharp's attitude to life. (For the context and development of the education system from the eighteenth-century Sunday school movement to Forster's Education Act of 1870, see Altick 1957: 141 ff. and McMurtry 1979: 189 ff.) One of the most ironical and amusing accounts of Victorian school-life, and of learning Latin in particular, stems from Winston Churchill (*1874), who included such reminiscences, a decade before he became wartime prime minister, in his 1930 autobiography *My Early Life*.

The miseries of his school-life notwithstanding, only a few children enjoyed such a privileged childhood as Churchill, who was born in Blenheim Palace as the grandchild of a duke. Over the whole of Queen Victoria's reign, the continuum of children presented as social outcasts in fiction stretched from Dickens's Oliver Twist in 1837–38, who is born into the workhouse as an orphan sustained by the parish, to Rudyard Kipling's Kim in 1900–01, who is characterised right away as "a poor white of the very poorest" (see chap. 4.2.2). From parish boy to pariah: by shifting the focus to such children of the poor, Victorian novelists tried to create an awareness of social grievances, at home and abroad. Charles Dickens was always eager to stress that charity begins at home, as can be gleaned from the following characterisation of Jo, a poor and ailing crossing-sweeper in the slum called Tom-all-Alone's, in his novel *Bleak House* (1852–53):

> [Jo] is not a genuine foreign-grown savage; he is the ordinary home-made article. Dirty, ugly, disagreeable to all the senses, in body a common creature of the common streets, only in soul a heathen. Homely filth begrimes him, homely parasites devour him, homely sores are in him, homely rags are on him: native ignorance, the growth of English soil and climate, sinks his immortal nature lower than the beasts that perish. [...] He is not of the same order of things, not of the same place in creation. He is of no order and no place; neither of the beasts, nor of humanity. (Chap. 47, Dickens 1977: 564)

A Poor Law for Poor Children: Dickens's *Oliver Twist*

Dickens's *Oliver Twist; or, The Parish Boy's Progress* (1837–38) may be regarded as one of the earliest examples of the social problem novel, and the scene in the workhouse (at the ending of chap. 2) where Oliver the orphan confronts Bumble the beadle by asking for more gruel "has become probably the single best-known scene in Victorian fiction" (Sutherland 1989: 478). This symbolical scene of 'asking for more' epitomised Dickens's criticism of the uncharitable side of Utilitarian work ethics (see chap. 4.2.1), and in particular of the New Poor Law of 1834 that condoned child labour. In the newly institutionalised workhouses, the poor and the parentless should make themselves useful to society – but they were accommodated like in prison, which might turn them to crime in the last resort, like Noah Claypole, another parish boy in the novel. The linkage between poverty and crime in *Oliver Twist* resumed the theme of John Gay's *The Beggar's Opera* a century earlier, and Oliver's progress through and out of a society of thieves provided just so much hope for improvement as it entailed a severe complaint against social conditions. The foundling Oliver, much like Tom Jones in Henry Fielding's eighteenth-century novel, can ultimately secure the affection of an adoptive father by averting the intrigue of a sinister rival, 'Monks', who contested Oliver's place in the heart of benevolent Mr Brownlow. For other memorable characters, Dickens had no such happy ending in store. In the last year of the novelist's life, the heavily melodramatic story of "Sikes and Nancy" became one of the most frightful (if also strenuous) pieces of his public reading repertoire. Nancy, the kind-hearted prostitute who means well for Oliver, also acts as a sick-nurse for the criminal Bill Sikes, who repays her cruelly with murder. Readers may not very much pity Nancy's killer when he afterwards accidentally inflicts capital punishment upon himself, yet they may have more ambivalent feelings about the man who had masterminded a gang of young thieves, and who had seen to Oliver's training as a pickpocket. Much like Shakespeare's Shylock, the Jewish Merchant of Venice, Dickens's Fagin the Jew is presented as both pitiless and as a figure of pity. The penultimate chapter of Dickens's serial novel, and the last of George Cruickshank's accompanying illustrations, focus

Fig. 4.39

"Fagin in the Condemned Cell", illustration by G. Cruickshank, 1838

on "Fagin in the Condemned Cell", sitting alone in utter darkness on his last night alive before his execution at the gallows. With this frightening spectacle of a tormented soul left alone to itself, both Dickens and his illustrator once again stressed, albeit in a different context, the complex motif of human solitude and imprisonment that was first related to Oliver.

As infant mortality rates, despite their decrease around 1800, were much higher in former centuries, the death of children occurred in novels, too. This was used to heighten the effect, including that of social criticism. The deaths of Mrs Wilson's twins in Gaskell's *Mary Barton* (1848, chap. 7) were used to cry out at the appalling misery of urban slums, as was the death of poor Jo, the above-mentioned crossing-sweeper in *Bleak House*: "Dead, your Majesty. Dead, my lords and gentlemen. Dead, Right Reverends and Wrong Reverends of every order. Dead, men and women, born with Heavenly compassion in your hearts. And dying thus around us every day." (ending of chap. 48, Dickens 1977: 572). With further such death scenes, Dickens knew, too, to hit home where it hurts: at the Victorian middle-class ideals of 'Home, Sweet Home' and cosy family life. The impact of his sentimental death scenes was increased through the mode of serial publication, which provided additional suspense on the outcome – and also readers with the opportunity to urge the serial novelist to avert an impending death and go for a lucky escape. To no avail: large numbers of the English reading public collectively went into mourning when a new number of Dickens's *The Old*

Infant Mortality in the Novel

Curiosity Shop (1840–41) opened with the fearfully awaited death of Little Nell. Some thirty years later, George MacDonald ended *At the Back of the North Wind* (serialised 1868–69), his fantasy novel for children, with a similar deathbed scene. However, there is an ambivalence: a morbid fascination with the death of children can be seen in the fact that Dickens successfully toured with "The Story of Little Dombey", his public reading version of a comparably tragic episode in his novel *Dombey and Son* (1847–48). (The phenomenon was not limited to Britain: in the 1852 best-selling American novel *Uncle Tom's Cabin* by Harriet Beecher Stowe, 'Little Eva' St Clare, whose life had been saved by Tom, also passes away in a highly sentimental death scene.)

Christmas Books and Christmas Spirit

Dickens's *A Christmas Carol in Prose: Being a Ghost Story of Christmas* (1843) summarily touches most of the points made so far. Like *Oliver Twist* and later *Great Expectations*, the moral of the *Carol* is tied up with a criticism of materialism in society, and a call for a change of mentality. In the tale, the old miser Ebeneezer Scrooge is confronted first with the ghost of his deceased business partner, and then successively with the three Ghosts of Christmas Past, of Christmas Present and of Christmas Yet to Come. They make him aware of his human deficiencies as they had shown in school and family life, in his behaviour to his clerk Bob Cratchit, and in his strict approval of the Poor Law. The impending death of Cratchit's son, Tiny Tim, brings about Scrooge's reformation to his former, more charitable self. Here, the infant's death can just be avoided, and Scrooge becomes a shining example for Dickens's reformist call for a charitable Christmas mentality all the year round: in the individual, in the family and in society. This book-length moral tale was eagerly seized by audiences of all ages, and its public reading version became part of Dickens's performance repertoire right from the start. The success made Dickens write four more Christmas Books in the years up to 1847, when the baton passed to W.M. Thackeray. His Christmas Books, which have a more ironical character and were illustrated by himself, include *Rebecca and Rowena: A Romance upon Romance* (1850, a comic sequel to Scott's *Ivanhoe*) and the fairy-tale fantasy *The Rose and the Ring* (1854).

General Tendencies in Children's Literature

When writers more frequently focused on children, they did not only make them out as literary characters, but also increasingly as readers of a literature of their own. In the long run, one can observe **three overlapping tendencies**, of which the first is a **shift away from didacticism**. Such a change of emphasis opened up new vistas, both for more realistic forms of entertainment and for a flight into fancy. One can see a second general tendency in the gradual **separation into juvenile and adult audiences**, and in a consequential diversification of texts and redistribution of genres. From there, it was only a third step to come to the **creation of literature first and foremost for a juvenile readership**. Such a corpus of literature for children became more marked out from the publication of *Alice in Wonderland* to *Winnie-the-Pooh*, which is why the period between the 1860s and the 1920s has been called "The Golden Age of Children's Literature" (Carpenter 1985).

Until the mid-nineteenth century, proper children's books explicitly came bound up with a moral, such as *The History of the Fairchild Family: A Child's Manual, Being a Collection of Stories Calculated to Show the Importance and Effects of Religious Education*. Mary Butt Sherwood (1775–1851) intermittently produced this best-selling narrative in three volumes (1817/[17]1848; 1842; 1847). While other **moral tales** usually were short on the side of entertainment, including such elements of suspense and of Gothic horror that were left to chapbooks and 'penny dreadfuls', Mrs Sherwood's three-decker novel for children combined morality with the macabre. Her gruesome tales were to be found on the shelves of most middle-class households during the author's lifetime, and continued to appear until the ending of our period (see Carpenter and Prichard 1984: 174; Gaull 1988: 53). The counter-movement away from explicit didacticism can be exemplified with the novels of Charlotte M. Yonge (1823–1901), which aimed at young girls in particular. For their very realism, they are sometimes used as a source of information on the life of Victorian middle-class families. In *The Heir of Redclyffe* (1853), Yonge managed to present a positively virtuous and charitable protagonist without outright moralising, and secured a great success. *Anne of Green Gables* (1908), the first of numerous novels by the Canadian writer L[ucy]. M[aud]. Montgomery (1874–1942) about her heroine Anne Shirley, also belongs into this context.

Shift Away from Didacticism

By contrast, boys of all ages were served with **serial novels and adventure stories** in book form and in **boys' weeklies** such as *Boys of England* (1866–99) and *The Boy's Own Paper* (1879–1967; see Turner 1948). *Masterman Ready; or, the Wreck in the Pacific* (1841) by Captain

[Frederick] Marryat as well as *The Coral Island* (1857) by R[obert]. M[ichael]. Ballantyne are sea novels of the *Robinsonade* type. In *The Coral Island*, three young boys manage – just like Robinson Crusoe – to survive as outcasts on a desert island and to rescue natives from cannibals before they receive a hero's welcome on their return to civilisation. With *The Coral Island*, Ballantyne (1825–94) made an impact on *Treasure Island* by fellow-Scotsman R[obert]. L[ouis]. Stevenson (1850–94) and, moreover, on *The Lord of the Flies* (1954), the much more pessimistic classroom classic by William Golding (1911–93). Having passed the test of being read aloud to the family during composition, *Treasure Island* was serialised in 1881 in a boys' weekly before it was published as a book in 1883. In Stevenson's novel, which is set in the eighteenth century, the boy Jim Hawkins and his older companions set out from a map to find the treasure of the pirate Capt. Flint. The suspense is heightened by the appearance of some of Flint's former crew as rival fortune hunters on the scene, including Long John Silver, the one-legged double-dealing pirate with a parrot. Stevenson's tale of a treasure hunt in turn provided the cue for J. Meade Falkner (1858–1932) to write a related tale of smuggling entitled *Moonfleet* (1898), and for H. Rider Haggard to come up with his imperial romance *King Solomon's Mines* (1885, discussed in chap. 4.2.2).

The shift away from a predominantly didactic form of early children's literature is also noticeable in a successful revival of folklore over the nineteenth century (see chaps. 3.4.6 and 4.4). Like its eighteenth-century precedent, this revival is marked by **fresh collections of oral literature**. *Popular Rhymes of Scotland* by Robert Chambers (1826 ff.) led to a collection of *The Nursery Rhymes of England* by the renowned Shakespeare scholar J[ames]. O[rchard]. Halliwell (1842), and later to *The Nursery Rhyme Book* edited by Andrew Lang (1897). In addition to the collections of nursery rhymes, some poets wrote **children's verse** of their own. Relevant examples are *The Book of Nonsense* (1845) and related collections written and illustrated by Edward Lear (see chap. 4.4), *Sing-Song: A Nursery Rhyme Book* by Christina Rossetti (1872), *A Child's Garden of Verses* by R. L. Stevenson (1885), *The Bad Child's Book of Beasts* by Hilaire Belloc (1896), *Puck of Pook's Hill* (1906) and *Rewards and Fairies* (1910) by Rudyard Kipling (see below), and *Peacock Pie* by Walter de la Mare (1913).

The Catnach Press (1813–c. 1883) supervised a related revival of **chapbooks for children**. Moreover, the renewed publication of **fairy tales** aimed first and foremost at children as readers. Hard on the heels of the *Fairy Tales* by Jacob and Wilhelm Grimm (1823, a translation of their *Kinder- und Hausmärchen*, 1812–15) followed T. Crofton Croker's *Fairy Legends and Traditions of the South of Ireland* (1825–28), a collection directly addressed to children. Such moral scruples as were to remain about the suitability of fairy tales, Charles Dickens countered in an 1853 article for his family magazine *Household Words* entitled "Frauds on the Fairies". In this article, Dickens turned against the practice of his former illustrator George Cruikshank in the *Fairy Library* (1853) and spoke out strongly against any editorial tampering with the source-texts. To make his point with a parody, Dickens included a 'politically correct' rewriting of the story of Cinderella as if edited by a Victorian travelling salesman. The full rehabilitation of the fairy tale came half a century later, when *The Blue Fairy Book* – a wide-ranging collection edited by Andrew Lang, mostly from rewritings by his wife Leonora – became as popular with children as to be made into a series (1889–1910).

The flight into fancy was not restricted to the fairy tale. Once successful, Leonora and Andrew Lang applied their approach also to the Oriental tales involving Ali Baba and the Forty Thieves, Aladdin, and Sindbad the Sailor. Those children's favourites were included in the Langs' *Arabian Nights Entertainments* (1898), after the – sexually more explicit – adult versions of such tales had already been published by Sir Richard Burton in *The Arabian Nights*, one of the most celebrated of Victorian translations (1885–88, see chap. 4.2.2). In the fact that entertainments originally meant for adults were increasingly adapted for children, one encounters the second general tendency mentioned. In particular for fiction, the reading audience that had consisted for a long time of both adults (parents) and children altogether, now split into two separate groups. They were served in turn by different versions of a given story, be it 'foreign-grown' or 'home-made' (to take up Dickens's distinction in *Bleak House*, quoted above). Several notable writers of adult fiction took it up to have Greek mythology sound less Greek to children. Following the precedent of Charles Lamb's rewriting of *The Adventures of Ulysses* (1811), the US-American writer Nathaniel Hawthorne produced *A Wonder-Book for Girls*

Diversification of Audiences and Texts

and Boys (1851), thus setting an example for the British novelist Charles Kingsley and his adaptation *The Heroes; or, Greek Fairy Tales for Children* (1856).

Among the household names in nineteenth-century British literature were Charles Dickens and Sir Walter Scott. According to an 1888 poll, Dickens (†1870) was considered to be the most-widely read author by boys and girls. Scott (†1832) ranked third with boys, and Shakespeare eighth (see Carpenter and Prichard 1984: 285). While Scott and Dickens already composed the original versions of their novels in a way that rendered them fit for reading aloud to the family, other and older texts were made available in adaptation, too. *The Riches of Chaucer, in which His Impurities Have Been Expunged* (by Charles Cowden Clarke, 1833; ²1877) was a likewise 'bowdlerised' and 'purified' companion volume to *The Family Shakespeare* by Thomas and Henrietta Bowdler (1807; ²1818). In *The Children's Shakespeare* (1897) by E. Nesbit (see below), a main feature of the adaptation is the way the illustrator depicted all characters as children, except King Lear.

Stories from history were dealt with in different ways. With his narrative poems and with his historical novels and romances (*Ivanhoe* in particular), Scott had produced historical fiction for both adults and adolescents, focusing on periods of conflict and change. Fellow-Scotsman R. L. Stevenson attempted to emulate him on his home ground of Scottish-English relations with the historical novel *Kidnapped: Being Memoirs of the Adventures of David Balfour in the Year 1751* (serialised in *Young Folks* in 1886) and a sequel, *Catriona* (1893). One of Scott's first successors that concentrated on children was Capt. Frederick Marryat, who wrote (as mentioned above) sea novels as well as a historical novel for children. Marryat, who lived his life (1792–1848) between two great European revolutions, began as a sailor (like Joseph Conrad) and served during the Napoleonic Wars (1799–1815). With *The Children of the New Forest* (1847), Marryat produced a historical novel that was set around the seventeenth-century Civil Wars, and thus in another period of national crisis. In Marryat's novel, the Royalist Beverley children have to take refuge from their Puritan oppressors in a forest, to be raised by a gamekeeper. Robinson-like, the young aristocrats have to adapt to the circumstances, before they can return into their family's possessions at the Restoration of Charles II. With its strong pro-Royalist and anti-Puritan bias,

Marryat's historical novel had an impact on later and likewise partial children's books.

In *A Child's History of England* (first serialised and then issued in three volumes just like his novels, 1851–53), Charles Dickens painted history on a much larger canvas – from the invasion of Julius Caesar in 50 B.C. to the accession of Queen Victoria and her marriage to Prince Albert (1840). Dickens was occasionally partial, too, in the negative – see e.g. his characterisations of the Tudor and Stuart kings Henry VIII and James I – as well as in the positive. A true Victorian, he finished with a flourish: "She [Victoria] is very good, and much beloved. So I end, like the crier, with GOD SAVE THE QUEEN". – When Rudyard Kipling set out to emulate Dickens after the ending of Victoria's long reign, he did so as a storyteller and as a poet. *Puck of Pook's Hill* (1906), which was designed for both adults and children, is a collection of ten stories and accompanying poems, framed by an intertextual narrative. The frame story sets in with Dan and Una, two children resembling Kipling's own, acting a scene from *A Midsummer Night's Dream*, before Shakespeare's Puck appears to tell them individual stories which are freely based on English history from Roman times through the Middle Ages to the Tudors. To be able to endow his tales with credibility, Kipling actually studied historical records. A sequel entitled *Rewards and Fairies* (1910) brought the historical record more up to date, and contained one of Kipling's best-known poems, "If". In 1911, Kipling collaborated with C. R. L. Fletcher on *A History of England*, again (but this time only) by contributing verse. In between Dickens and Kipling, the popular novelist G. A. Henty had written a large series of patriotic novels of adventure, mainly for boys, on decisive moments in the history of Britain and its Empire (see chap. 4.2.2).

The separation of adolescent from adult audiences had led to the adaptation of canonical texts and also of whole genres (such as the historical novel) for children. Moreover, a redistribution of genres had taken place, in which fairy tales had wandered into the children's domain. (Kipling's history book also gives an indication of the trend.) In the latter half of the nineteenth century, **animal stories**, too, began to be produced primarily for young readers. This involved a clean break with the hallowed tradition of satiric animal fables that had still been *en vogue* in the Age of Enlightenment. (Satirical texts of the twentieth century such

The Golden Age of Children's Literature

as George Orwell's *Animal Farm* and Erich Kästner's *Konferenz der Tiere* are exceptions that prove to the rule.) From the (dis-)appearance of the Cheshire Cat in *Alice's Adventures in Wonderland* over the threatening presence of Shere Khan the tiger in the Jungle to the hyper-active Tigger bouncing in the Forest, such perennially famous stories involving animals, together with other, more fantastic classics of the nursery, make up the "Golden Age of Children's Literature". (For further information on texts and contexts, see Carpenter and Prichard 1984, Carpenter 1985 and Gaschke 2002.)

Black Beauty

The most famous animal story from the nineteenth century is *Black Beauty: The Autobiography of a Horse* (1877), and it came from a writer who was an invalid from childhood. The realistic portrait of horses and their behaviour is therefore the more surprising, and it contributed as much to the success of the only novel by Anna Sewell (1820–78) as her idea to tell the story from the horse's mouth. When such realism includes incidents of cruelty against horses by their owners, the narrative is endowed with a didactic subtext that looks back to the moral tale. While Black Beauty, who passes through the hands of many owners, has a lucky escape from the wearisome work of pulling cabs in London to retirement in the country, his friend Ginger is less fortunate: when they meet again as cab-horses in London, Ginger is worn out and dies a short time later, to be carted away unceremoniously (chap. 40). In this novel, too, materialism, death and (un-)sentimentalism are part of the picture, and here they are used to make a point for animal rights.

Exotic Stories by Rudyard Kipling

With Rudyard Kipling, we move away from the streets of London to more exotic settings. In his two *Jungle Books* (1894–95) and in his *Just So Stories* (1902), Kipling had already experimented successfully with the combination of prose and poetry that was to be characteristic also of his later history books. Like his *Barrack-Room Ballads* and his novel *Kim* (see chap. 4.2.2), the *Jungle Books* breathe the exotic atmosphere of colonial India. Some stories from the collections that have also been published separately centre on the boy Toomai and the working elephants, and on Rickki-Tikki-Tavi, the mongoose who fends off heroically the attacks of cobras against an English family and itself. Or himself: like with so many other animal stories from the Golden Age, we deal with anthropomorphic animals that bear human character traits so as to be used for moral lessons. However, contrary to the fictional settings in the works of Beatrix Potter, Kenneth Grahame and A. A. Milne, Kipling's Jungle is no playground, but a contested place of power plays. The majority of stories deal with the boy Mowgli and his animal friends and foes in the Jungle. They are some of the best-known titles in Kipling's oeuvre, not least because of the 1967 Walt Disney movie, which became a classic in its own right, but also involved drastic changes of characterisation. (For the original texts, Kipling's father had provided most illustrations.) Raised by wolves (like the legendary Romulus and Remus) and supported by Bagheera the Black Panther and Baloo the bear, the boy Mowgli has to fend off and strike out against Shere Khan. This arrogant and ferocious Bengal tiger tries at all costs to maintain his position at the top of the pecking order, which also includes Hathi's Indian elephants, the Bandar-Log monkeys, and Kaa the python. By contrast, Kipling's double dozen of *Just So Stories* and related poems are much more humorous. In the way that they were illustrated by the author himself, though written to be read aloud in the family circle, the 1902 collection is still characteristic of the outgoing century in its design, and also in its concerns: the story "How the Leopard Got Its Spots", for instance, is a spoof on Darwin's Theory of Evolution.

| Fig. 4.40
Mowgli versus Shere Khan, clay bas-relief by John Lockwood Kipling

In comparison with Kipling's stories, the world of Beatrix Potter, Kenneth Grahame and A. A. Milne, though not entirely harmonious, presented quite a cosy picture of animals and of Englishness. As a hare's tale, *The Tale of Peter Rabbit* (1901) has no rival in the imagination of English-speaking children apart from the Brer Rabbit stories (in Black English) that the American writer Joel Chandler Harris included twenty years earlier in *Uncle Remus [...]: The Folk-Lore of the Old Plantation.* (As far as hare's tales for adults are concerned, one could also think of the exploits of the Rabbitte family in Roddy Doyle's *Barrytown Trilogy* and of the frequent coupling in the Rabbit series by John Updike.) With *The Tale of Peter Rabbit*, a small-sized picture book for nursery readers with carefully realistic portraits of animals done by herself, Beatrix Potter (1866–1943) landed a Christmas best seller. Together with Frederick Warne & Co. (now part of Penguin Books), a publishing firm which specialised on illustrated children's books, Beatrix Potter expanded her surprise success

Beatrix Potter

into a series of altogether 23 little books that, together with the related merchandising products, became collectors' items, and hallmarks of Englishness.

The Wind in the Willows   In his essays collected in *The Golden Age* (1895) and *Dream Days* (1898), Kenneth Grahame (1859–1932) had presented an unsentimental and disillusioned view on childhood before he published *The Wind in the Willows* (1908). This novel, which originated from the bedtime stories Grahame told, and the story-letters he sent to his son, had a slow start. Just like *Black Beauty* and *The Tale of Peter Rabbit*, Grahame's novel, too, was at first rejected by several publishers. It became more widely known only when A. A. Milne adapted it for the West End stage in a version entitled *Toad of Toad Hall* (1929), and when a new edition in 1931 came with the illustrations by the Punch cartoonist E[rnest]. H[oward]. Shepard (1879–1976). Apart from its status as a classic of children's fiction (and a Christmas treat in adaptation), Grahame's novel about the friendship and adventures of four humanised animals is also a historical (and now quite nostalgic) document of country-life in Edwardian England. The group of friends living along the banks of the River Thames includes the gentle Mole, the river-wise Water Rat, the unsociable but reliable Badger, and Toad of Toad Hall, a conceited squire mad about the modern motor car. The cast of bachelor animal characters can while away their leisure time without being bothered by too much work (much like their creator, after he had given up his position as Secretary of the Bank of England to live the life of a country gentleman). It is only when Toad Hall is taken over by the anarchic weasels from the Wild Wood, during the time Toad has to spend in prison for road rage, that the rather idyllic picture is tainted by an outbreak of class conflict. However, there is a happy ending in store for a reformed Toad.

With two more celebrated series from the 1920s that have originated from oral storytelling and story-letters, we can round the animal story off. When Hugh Lofting (1886–1947) sent illustrated story-letters home to his children from the trenches during the First World War, he did not want them to share in the brutality of modern warfare, but came up instead with nostalgic tales of his own invention. *The Story of Doctor Dolittle* (1922), which is set in a fictional West County village in Victorian times, initiated a series of altogether a dozen novels, illustrated by the author, about a medical doctor who turned away from humanity to talk to animals in their own languages. The Doctor Dolittle books were often adapted for stage and screen, but when the charm of the originals began to wear off, in the 1960s and '70s, criticism set in from Black Consciousness circles against racial stereotyping in the wording and the illustrations of some of the tales, so that newly revised editions were subjected to a contemporary form of bowdlerisation. Such censorship would be considered sacrilege were it exacted on *Winnie-the-Pooh* (1926) and *The House at Pooh Corner* (1928). With those two books of stories, A[lan]. A[lexander]. Milne (1882–1956) and his illustrator E.H. Shepard had already scored a great success before each of them on their own contributed to the breakthrough of Kenneth Grahame's *The Wind in the Willows*. In direct opposition to the books about the amiable eccentric Doctor Dolittle, it is the eccentric (toy) animals that take centre stage in the good-humoured Pooh stories: apart from the honey-hungry teddy bear Edward Bear alias Winnie-the-Pooh, we meet Piglet and Rabbit, wise Owl, Eeyore the melancholy donkey (tellingly named but often un-tailed), Kanga and Baby Roo, and later the ever-bouncing Tigger. In their peculiar narrative mode, the Pooh stories bear the mark of their composition. They originated from give-and-take between A.A. Milne and his son Christopher, who appears – under the name of Christopher Robin – as the only human character in the background of the story, and also as the 'you' listening to the narrator's monologue:

Winnie-the-Pooh

> So Winnie-the-Pooh went round to his friend Christopher Robin, who lived behind a green door in another part of the Forest.
> "Good morning, Christopher Robin," he said.
> "Good morning, Winnie-*ther*-Pooh," said you. (Milne 2002: 21)

Apart from situation comedy and character eccentricities, a large part of the fun lies in the verbal humour of unexpected conversational twists,

> "Hallo, Rabbit," he said, "is that you?"
> "Let's pretend it isn't," said Rabbit, "and see what happens."
> "I've got a message for you."
> "I'll give it to him." (Milne 2002: 112),

of nonce words ("Woozle" and "Heffalump"), and of non-sequential (if not outright nonsensical) sentences:

"He's Winnie-ther-Pooh. Don't you know what '*ther*' means?"
"Ah, yes, now I do," I said quickly; and I hope you do too, because it is all
the explanation you are going to get. (Milne 2002: 15)

Such comic features were already characteristic of *Alice's Adventures in Wonderland* (1865) and its sequel *Through the Looking-Glass and What Alice Found There* (1871). The two books by 'Lewis Carroll' (i. e. the Reverend Charles Lutwidge Dodgson, 1832–98) are not

Fig. 4.41

Alice's Adventures in Wonderland (by John Tenniel)

properly speaking the first, but they are still the best-known examples of nineteenth-century **fantasy fiction** for children and adults alike. Carroll's books were preceded by e. g. W. M. Thackeray's Christmas Book *The Rose and the Ring* (1854) and Charles Kingsley's *The Water Babies: A Fairy Tale for a Land Baby* (serialised 1862–63), which were already characterised by magic and supernatural features. Fantasy as a new genre is closely connected with the "revival of interest in, and admiration for, the orally transmitted fairy tale", and *Alice's Adventures in Wonderland* proved to be "at once revolutionary (in that it showed the limitless possibilities of fantasy) and inimitable" (Carpenter and Prichard 1984: 181). Inimitable in particular in its complex humour which further enlivens the story of a girl who enters a wonder world through a White Rabbit's hole. "A Mad Tea-Party" (chap. 7) is a good example, as it brings together a ridiculous situation, comic characters (both the Mad Hatter and the March Hare are personified proverbs), literary parody (e. g. of Jane Taylor's Romantic poem, "Twinkle, twinkle, little star") and quite nonsensical conversation (e. g. by starting the tea-party off with the offer of wine, and of wine which then turns out to be unavailable). Further unforgettable characters include the fading Cheshire Cat with the unfettered grin, and the Mock Turtle who once was a real turtle that called her old turtle schoolmaster punningly a "Tortoise because he taught us" (Carroll 1970: 127). There is the Ugly Duchess who is the only one trying to find a moral (120–21) in what was never meant to be a moral tale, and for the more sarcastically minded, the heartless Queen of Hearts who executes order through ordering executions. (A similarly grim kind of humour can be found in Thackeray's *The Rose and the Ring*, which includes the fencing master 'Count Kutasoff Hedsoff'.) Carroll's *Through the Looking-Glass* adds characters that come straight from the nursery rhyme, such as Humpty Dumpty or Tweedledum and Tweedledee. Moreover, with "Jabberwocky", Carroll provided a literary parody of the medieval ballads of chivalry, and the best-known nonsense poem in the language. Humpty Dumpty's explication within the running text of some **portmanteau words** (Carroll's term for the blending of two meanings into one word, as arguably in 'slithy', 270–72) makes the poem just slightly more meaningful, and Carroll's editor Martin Gardner did his best in trying to top rather than stop such nonsense by the inclusion of a further six pages of notes in small print (191–97).

At the Back of the North Wind (serialised 1868–69 before book publication in 1871) was the first children's book by Carroll's friend and mentor George MacDonald (1824–1905). Here, fantasy is brought together not with comedy but with consolation. The young coachman's son Diamond finds his adventures during nightly excursions in the company of the North Wind – at once a beautiful woman but also a harbinger of pain, destruction and death. The tale can be read as a Christian parable, with Diamond as a Christ-like figure and the North Wind (likewise cruel and kind) as a personification of God's will, which may work out in various ways. The tale ends in a sentimental death scene that is also an epiphany: once dead, Diamond will be able to clearly see the country 'at the back of the North Wind', no longer in shadowy outline but as a real paradise without pain and death. In *The Princess and the Goblin* (1872), MacDonald established once more a fusion of fantasy and faith, foreshadowing the *Narnia* novels of C. S. Lewis. In addition, the division of the fantastic realm into a world above and below lends itself to a political reading in terms of a class conflict. The subterranean world peopled by dissatisfied goblins working for a (proletarian) revolution foreshadows the realm and role of the Morlocks in *The Time Machine* by H. G. Wells (1895). Such subterranean machinations relate to subconscious fears of an end to stability for the middle classes, and thus introduce a political subtext into the fantastic context.

Oscar Wilde (1854–1900), too, wrote children's literature also read by adults; indeed, "The Canterville Ghost" (serialised 1887)

Fantasy and Faith: George MacDonald

Anglo-American Relations

was the first such story that he published at all. It was closely followed by two collections of original fairy tales, which did not always end on a happy note, but often enough in death: *"The Happy Prince" and Other Tales* (1888) and *A House of Pomegranates* (1891). As a literary parody, "The Canterville Ghost" makes fun of the ghost story, a customary Christmas treat that is represented by *A Christmas Carol in Prose: Being a Ghost Story of Christmas* by Charles Dickens (1843), and also by G. A. Henty's "A Pipe of Mystery" (1890; see chap. 4.2.2). As a mild satire, Oscar Wilde's "The Canterville Ghost" is directed likewise against a British sense of tradition and against American manners. The story appears, moreover, as a kind of warming-up for Wilde's subsequent career as a writer of comedies of wit and manners (see chap. 4.3). Sir Simon, the family ghost of Canterville Chase who has to atone for murdering his wife in 1575, is a stock character; but so are the new owners of the manor, the Otis family. In both his bluntness and his non-nonsense approach to the real and the surreal, Mr Hiram B. Otis personifies the pragmatic American businessman ("I come from a modern country, where we have everything that money can buy; [...] I reckon that if there were such a thing as a ghost in Europe, we'd have it at home in a very short time in one of our public museums, or on the road as a show." Wilde 1966: 193). Mrs Otis is ironically described by the (British) narrator as "an excellent example of the fact that we have really everything in common with America nowadays, except, of course, language" (194). If she is a failed Brit, the twin sons called "The Stars and Stripes" are spoiled brats. Their sister is patriotically called Virginia, and the eldest son named Washington. He is another specimen of the practical type that would apply a detergent to bloodstains on the carpet rather than getting frightened by their mysterious re-appearance. The confrontation between the ghost who tries to uphold a ghastly tradition, and the fearless Americans who show no sense of history, gives rise to a number of farcical and mock-Gothic situations. It also allows for witty repartee, as in this exchange between the Ghost and the girl:

> "I don't think I should like America."
> "I suppose because we have no ruins and no curiosities," said Virginia satirically.
> "No ruins! No curiosities!" answered the Ghost; "you have your navy and your manners." (207)

Virginia turns out to be the only approachable, and indeed sensible member of the family. It is she who saves the Ghost by making it possible for him to die, and paradoxically, this secures a happy ending for herself, too. In this, her marriage to a Duke, "which is the reward of all good little American girls" (213), is only an ironical bow to the conventions of romance. In her subsequent reminiscences on the Ghost, Virginia reveals to her husband that she has profited even more by learning a lesson for life: "He made me see what Life is, and what Death signifies, and why Love is stronger than both." (214). In such a sentimental, but far from ironical manner, Wilde provided a surprise moral to his story that otherwise confirms the overall trend by being a piece of entertainment rather than didacticism.

Prior to "The Canterville Ghost", the transatlantic (or, to speak with Henry James, international) theme had received a much more sentimental, and less fantastic treatment in *Little Lord Fauntleroy* (serialised 1885–86) by Frances Hodgson Burnett (1849–1924). She was born into the slums of Manchester but in her teens moved to Tennessee. Her Little Lord, a poor boy from New York City named Cedric Erroll, crosses the Atlantic in the other direction. On the death of his father, Cedric learns that he is in fact an expatriate English aristocrat and heir presumptive to the estate of his estranged grandfather, the Earl of Dorincourt. During an extended visit to Dorincourt Castle, the boy's charm and charitable behaviour win over the old Earl's anti-American prejudices, and prepare a happy ending for a re-united transatlantic family. Critics who were at first charmed, too, later transferred their approval to Burnett's *The Secret Garden* (which was serialised for adults in 1910, and published as a children's book a year later). This is again a proper fantasy novel, centring on the magic charm that exudes from a hidden Garden Eden in Yorkshire, and that transforms people by bringing out the best in them. In the episodic narrative, the charm is applied first to Mary Lennox, an expatriate British girl born in Imperial India, then to her invalid cousin Colin Craven, and finally to Mary's uncle and Colin's father Archibald Craven. At the happy ending of this tale of magic, Colin is again able to walk, and his father is joyfully re-united with all his family.

The next and last celebrated instances of fantasy fiction within the period under review are E. Nesbit's magic realism as well

The Magic Realism of E. Nesbit

as J.M. Barrie's 1904 fantasy play and the related novels about Peter Pan from Never Land (see chap. 4.3); not to forget *The Wonderful Wizard of Oz* (1900) by the American writer Frank L. Baum. After the publication of *The Children's Shakespeare* (1897), E[dith]. Nesbit (1858–1924) became a famous children's writer in her own right with some 40 other juvenile books to her credit, from which two trilogies stick out. *The Story of the Treasure Seekers: Being the Adventures of the Bastable Children in Search of a Fortune* (1899) and its sequels *The Wouldbegoods* (1899) and *The New Treasure Seekers* (1904) feature a group of siblings out for adventures on their own, in which some extra pocket money may count as a fortune. Together with G.B. Shaw (see chap. 4.3), Nesbit was a founding member of the reformist Fabian Society, and included elements of social realism in her works. Nesbit's ear for realistic dialogue between children and the absence of didacticism are again in evidence in the sequence comprising *Five Children and It* (serialised as *The Psammead* in 1900), *The Phoenix and the Carpet* (1904) and *The Story of the Amulet* (1906). This second trilogy tells of five brothers and sisters that, when separated from their parents, explore their native London (in the second book), the Kent countryside (in the first book) and locations elsewhere in space and time. The basically realistic framework is enriched by fantastic features such as the magic powers of a Phoenix and of the Psammead (an ugly pre-historic fairy-creature), and also a magic carpet and an amulet that allow for time-travel. The whole series foreshadows not only Enid Blyton's – less fantastic – adventure novels about the Famous Five, but also "established a pattern that was to be used by many later children's writers: the intrusion of magic into the real world, with alarming but usually comic consequences" (Carpenter and Prichard 1984: 181). Nesbit's *The Railway Children* (1906) includes elements of spy fiction rather than fantasy. Here we see three children who – once left to themselves – manage on their own to clear their imprisoned father from the alleged betrayal of state secrets to the Russians. If Family Values are stressed once more in this post-Victorian children's novel, they clearly do no longer include "The Stern Parent" and the children who 'should be seen, *not* heard', as they were referred to in the piece of light verse quoted at the ending of chapter 4.4.

1. Point out significant features of the development of fiction in the period under review, and exemplify them with reference to individual subgenres, authors and their works. Include the convention of the happy ending, and the device of Free Indirect Discourse in your summary discussion.

2. As a best-selling novelist, Charles Dickens (1812–70) dominated the literary world in his lifetime. Describe the ways in which he was involved in crucial developments in the manner of literary communication during the Victorian Age.
   [To check whether your answer comprises the most relevant details, take a look at the model answer on the publisher's website: http://utb-mehr-wissen.de]

3. Have a look at Dickens's fictional 'Coketown' in *Hard Times* (chap. 5) and compare it to the description of urban slums in *Oliver Twist* (chaps. 5 and 8) and in *Bleak House* (together with the illustration by H.K. Browne, chap. 46). Which stylistic devices does Dickens employ? Please comment upon the imagery used and its symbolic qualities, and relate the selected passages to Dickens's social criticism.

4. Compare the 1994 television miniseries of *Middlemarch* (based on the screenplay by Andrew Davies and directed by Anthony Page for the BBC) to the star-studded and highly visual 2004 adaptation of *Vanity Fair* as a movie (by the Indian director Mira Nair). How successful are these adaptations in revamping George Eliot's and W.M. Thackeray's panoramic portraits of metropolitan and urban society? Where do they reflect today's concerns with the Victorian Age, and where do today's issues come in?

5. Do women write differently about gender relations, and if so, how?

6. Give a short sketch of the development and forms of sensational and crime fiction.

7. In what ways do English, Irish and Scottish writers make use of short fiction? Where do you see thematic parallels, and where are telling differences?

8. Summarise the development of children's literature during its Golden Age.

Modernism and Beyond (c.1920 to the Present)

Summary

From the turn-of-the-century Irish Renaissance, we again find a parallel development in British and Irish literatures. Since the 1920s, the electronic media provide new opportunities for literature, but also pose a challenge. A radical break with literary conventions happens in the *free verse* of T.S. Eliot and Ted Hughes as well as in the *interior monologue* and further fictional experiments of James Joyce and Virginia Woolf. This is however no model for all. Poets such as Philip Larkin abstained from that free verse movement, others – most notably W.H. Auden and Dylan Thomas – tested out alternative forms such as *accentual* and *syllabic verse*. Writers of mainstream fiction successfully retained and entertained their audience not only with stories of crime, thrill and adventure, but also with psychological realism and (historical) novels of character. The multicultural character of postcolonial British society is reflected in poetry, fiction and stage-plays alike. Since the 1950s, a flowering of British and Irish drama occurred in various venues, from the West End stages to the Fringe, as well as in radio and television.

New Developments in Poetry

The years between Queen Victoria's Golden Jubilee in 1887 and the ending of the First World War appear in retrospect as a period of transition in the history of poetry. From the vantage point of Modernism, Hardy's creation of his own stanza forms, Hopkins's stressed verse, the experimentation of W.B. Yeats and Wilfred Owen with half- and para-rhyme, and Yeats's mythological symbolism all seem to point to Modernist experimentation, or to be already part of it. Indeed, the early ventures of T.S. Eliot into free verse ("Prufrock") and of Ezra Pound with Imagism date back to the 1910s (see below). On the other hand, Hardy's "Hap" (to begin with an extreme example) was published in 1898, but had already been written as long ago as 1866. Again, even though Hopkins's poetry became quite influential when it was first published in 1918, it had been written in the 1870s and '80s, and therefore Hopkins has been reclassified as a Victorian poet in more recent editions of *The Norton Anthology of English Literature*. The overlapping of old and new traditions renders a clear demarcation of periods difficult. But is it at all necessary? Basically, the situation is not much different from, say, that one a century earlier, when Neoclassicist and Romantic tendencies were visible alongside each other. There is however one striking difference: it may be said summarily that, when compared with former periods, the impact of conventional genres such as ode, elegy and dramatic monologue has been much less visible in poetry since the 1920s. Apart from keeping an eye open for the sonnet throughout and also at the end of this chapter, the presentation will be focused less on genre than on a gradual development, with a concentration on outstanding individual poets who put a stamp on their decade, and on the affiliations to a *Movement* or a *Group* (which are just two convenient designations from the 1950s and '60s).

5.1.1 | From Yeats's Later Poetry to Radical Modernism

Yeats's Later Poetry

Even if the name of W. B. Yeats (1865–1939) is strongly connected with that of other poets and playwrights of the Irish Renaissance, he himself is difficult to enlist under one period alone. In the time between the Armistice and the founding of the Irish Free State – a time that Yeats had spent in Oxford, but that in Ireland was characterised by heavy fighting – Yeats brought out a number of apocalyptic poems. "Nineteen Hundred and Nineteen" was composed in the self-same year, but was first published in 1921 under the title "Thoughts upon the Present State of the World". This long poem was subdivided into six parts of varying lengths and stanza forms. Such finger exercises included a variation upon the stanza Keats had devised for his odes, and that Yeats had taken up in his pre-war poem "A Coat" (a shortened Italian sonnet of ten lines, here in part III reversed), and also *ottava rima* (part I), the form that was to become the hallmark of Yeats's later poetry, as it had been of Byron's. Despite all this artifice, however, Yeats's post-war poem describes the world as a nightmare, full of the atrocities of war (ll. 25–48, 85–88, 113–30). Also related to terror and destruction is the rich animal imagery of the poem, including the swan as an image that can "bring a rage/To end all things" (ll. 80–81) at the time when the Platonic Year turns full circle (l. 54 and poet's note). The Platonic or Great Year, comprising a period of more than 25,000 years, is a concept more dear to astrologers than astronomers, and tells of Yeats's interest in the occult and in a cyclical view of history. He was to follow up both his peculiar animal imagery and his interest in a larger world-historical scheme in the blank-verse poem "The Second Coming" (also written in 1919, to be published in the following year) and in the sonnet "Leda and the Swan" (1924, see chap. 4.4). Both poems also served him as illustration when he dwelled at greater length upon his private mythology, in his book *A Vision* (1926). In his cyclical view of history, Yeats envisioned the rise and fall of historical movements as two intertwined, conical spirals he called 'gyres': one of them is expanding at the same time when the other's circle is narrowing down to a point that marks the end of one age and the flowering of another in a 'violent annunciation' or 'revelation'. To illustrate this idiosyncratic view, "The Second Coming" is best quoted in full:

> Turning and turning in the widening gyre
> The falcon cannot hear the falconer;
> Things fall apart; the centre cannot hold;
> Mere anarchy is loosed upon the world,
> The blood-dimmed tide is loosed, and everywhere
> The ceremony of innocence is drowned;
> The best lack all conviction, while the worst
> Are full of passionate intensity.
>
> Surely some revelation is at hand;
> Surely the Second Coming is at hand.
> The Second Coming! Hardly are those words out
> When a vast image out of *Spiritus Mundi*
> Troubles my sight: somewhere in sands of the desert
> A shape with lion body and the head of a man,
> A gaze blank and pitiless as the sun,
> Is moving its slow thighs, while all about it
> Reel shadows of the indignant desert birds.
> The darkness drops again; but now I know

> That twenty centuries of stony sleep
> Were vexed to nightmare by a rocking cradle,
> And what rough beast, its hour come round at last,
> Slouches towards Bethlehem to be born?

Yeats set in, like G. M. Hopkins in "The Windhover" (1918), with the flight of a falcon, but while Hopkins had presented this bird as a symbol for Divine creation, Yeats's millenarian poem makes use of it as a harbinger of Anarchy and Apocalypse, in a reversal of the Biblical stories of the birth and the Second Coming of Christ. Yeats had adjusted his figures, but not his general outlook: after 2,000 years, he foresaw the coming of a sphinx-like monster to announce a new age, which to Yeats was to break with Christianity, Scientific Rationalism and Democracy. While this prophecy still awaits fulfilment, the poem had an impact both on the African novelist Chinua Achebe (who used the phrase "Things fall apart" in 1957 as the title of his classic African novel) and on the American singer-songwriter Joni Mitchell (who in 1991 set the whole poem to music in her song "Slouching Towards Bethlehem").

Yeats's later, retro- and introspective poems "Sailing to Byzantium" (1927), "The Circus Animals' Desertion" and "The Man and the Echo" (both published in the year of his death, 1939) were more focused on the inner world of the poet. Although his poetic craft had not visibly diminished (the last poem is set in rhyming couplets, while the first two poems are laid out in *ottava rima*, with an abundance of half-rhyme), Yeats was now concerned with old age and with his artistic legacy. The aged speaker in "Sailing to Byzantium", regarding himself as little better than a scarecrow ("A tattered coat upon a stick", l. 10), wants to leave "That [which] is no country for old men" (l. 1) to arrive at a Byzantium of the mind – a holy city full of golden artefacts, an aesthete's paradise. "The Circus Animals' Desertion" was Yeats's variation upon the theme of, as it were, *sic vanitas gloriae poetae,* or the wane of the poet's craft, and as such, Yeats's poem could stand besides Wordsworth's and Coleridge's depressed odes on immortality and dejection. In the second part of his poem, Yeats came to speak again on his early, mythological poems and plays *The Wanderings of Oisin* (1889), *The Countess Cathleen* (1899) and *On Baile's Strand* (1904). "The Man and the Echo" is haunted by the impact of his nationalist play *Cathleen ni Houlihan* (1902) on the rebels of the Easter Rising: "Did that play of mine send out/Certain men the English shot?" (ll. 11–12). However, in "Under Ben Bulben" (1939), his poetic epitaph, Yeats admonished his successors to follow in his tracks, to continue his concern with both heroic legends and peasant themes, and with the poet's craft.

In order to account for the craft of other notable twentieth-century poets, one may distinguish between **three, at times overlapping, tendencies**. There are those radical Modernists who may have continued to be concerned with mythological themes, but who left conventional forms for free verse. This is a poetic design that at first must have looked indeed "out of shape from toe to top" ("Under Ben Bulben", st. V), but which soon became sanctioned by academic critics. Then there is a second tendency, represented by poets who negotiated between "Tradition and the Individual Talent" (to borrow the title of Eliot's programmatic essay) by opting for more moderate forms of experiment and innovation. The third tendency which in retrospect seems to be farthest away from the practitioners of free verse, and which became much less visible over time, comprises those poets that visibly stressed an ideal of craftsmanship by their attempt to excel in conventional but demanding forms such as the villanelle.

The foremost representatives of radical Modernism in poetry were two expatriate Americans who settled in London in the years before or during the First World War: Ezra Pound (1885–1972) and T.S. Eliot (1888–1965). Pound's early work as a poet and translator ("The Seafarer", 1911) is marked by his medieval interests, which soon broadened to include non-European forms of art such as traditional Japanese Nō theatre, a fascination which he could pass on to W.B. Yeats. Between 1912 and 1920, Pound was involved in a series of transatlantic avant-garde movements, before he himself moved on from London to Paris and then to Italy. In fact, the Anglo-American avant-garde was trailing behind the developments in nineteenth-century France. There, a break with conventional form and rhythm had led to the **prose poem** (e.g. Baudelaire's *Le spleen de Paris*, 1869) and to **free verse** (in Rimbaud's "Marine", 1872, and in the poetry of Jules Laforgue). The impersonal, abstract and **pure poetry** of Baudelaire, Mallarmé and Valéry was accompanied by a **Symbolism** that translated to Britain via Arthur Symons's *The Symbolist Movement in Literature* (1899). This French *fin de siècle* movement favoured ambivalent charac-

Radical Modernism: Free Verse from T.S. Eliot to Ted Hughes

ters such as Salomé and Hamlet (to reappear in Oscar Wilde's scandalous play and in T. S. Eliot's "Prufrock", respectively), furthermore journeys to exotic countries and foreign luxury (as in Yeats's "Sailing to Byzantium"), but also nebulous, dark, gloomy and labyrinthine settings (as in Yeats's apocalyptic poems). A significant impact on the new ideal of a 'hard, dry image' moreover came from relevant essays by Edgar Allan Poe ("The Poetic Principle", 1849) and by T[homas]. E[rnest]. Hulme ("Romanticism and Classicism", 1911). In consequence, **Imagism** as a movement in poetry (1912–17) wanted to cut back on decorative embellishments and proclaimed the single, concise and musical image as an ideal, which for instance can be found in the Japanese *haiku* (a three-line poem of 5-7-5 syllables). Pound's *haiku* "In a Station of the Metro" (1913) is built on such a spare and startling image. Together with the painter, poet, novelist and critic Wyndham Lewis (who was born into an Anglo-American marriage, 1882–1957), Pound engaged in *Vorticism*, another short-lived movement that centred on the *vortex* as an image of energy. It is remembered by its publication *Blast* (1914–15; see *NAEL* II, 2009–15), a programmatic manifesto that is not only typographically 'loud'. In its wilful rejection of any popular appeal in the sense of 'the People', it is moreover telling of the elitism of many of these avant-garde movements.

T.S. Eliot and "The Waste Land"

Blast also contained some early poetry of T. S. Eliot, who was born in St. Louis but became a British subject in 1927, and who exerted some influence as director with the publishing firm of Faber & Faber (1925–65). Starting with the publication of "The Love Song of J. Alfred Prufrock" (1915), Eliot had been promoted by Pound, and the two expatriate Americans collaborated on Eliot's draft of "The Waste Land". Eliot wrote his poem under the influence of comparative studies of anthropology and myth, such as James Frazer's *The Golden Bough* (15 vols., 1890–1915) – a phrase that appears also in Yeats's "Sailing to Byzantium" (l. 30) – and Jessie Weston's *From Ritual to Romance* (1920). Initially, Eliot had conceived of "The Waste Land" as a long poem built on a complex of allusions to primitive vegetation ceremonies as well as to medieval romances of the Holy Grail, both culminating in a symbolic imagery of fertility and sterility. Pound helped to bring "The Waste Land" into its final, fractured shape by cutting back on its Arthurian allusions and on its lines of iambic pentameter. Thus, the poem was reduced to half of its original length, and the internal connection between its individual parts became increasingly obscure. Such revision brought about the archetype of a Modernist and free-verse poem, but one where the grand original design arguably had been exchanged for "A heap of broken images" (l. 22). A comparison of Eliot's apocalyptic cityscape poem to Yeats's "Nineteen Hundred and Nineteen", which was composed and published around the same time, and which likewise envisioned a devastated world, is enlightening. Each poem consists of five or six sections of varying length, but while Yeats reined in Anarchy through a combination of several forms of rhyme and strophic design, Eliot was more radical and went the full way to free verse, held together only by the recurrent image of "Death by Water" (as the fourth part of his poem is aptly entitled). In the Symbolist tradition, each poet made use of exotic and esoteric imagery, but to a different degree: where Yeats alluded to Loie Fuller's troupe of Chinese dancers, to ancient Athens and to Platonism, Eliot's references stretch from Phoenicians to the Biblical procession to Emmaus and further to a Mme Sosostris and her Tarot cards, to end in Buddha's Fire Sermon and a few words in Sanskrit. Like contemporary Cubist and Surrealist painters, Eliot can be said to have created his own "heap of broken images" from an assemblage or collage of different source materials, thus fulfilling Pound's artistic imperative to 'Make it new!'

However, there are other sides to Eliot's poetry. In connection with his admission to the Church of England in 1927, his apocalyptic view made way for a desire for order in a Christian cosmos. "The Hollow Men" (1925) is a transitional poem that renders the two tendencies visible through having a bleak vision interspersed by words from the Lord's Prayer. Eliot's later poetry (such as "Ash-Wednesday", 1930, or the *Ariel Poems*, 1927–54) and also his verse plays (beginning with *Murder in the Cathedral*, 1935) were increasingly concerned with religious themes such as guilt, penitence and atonement. *Four Quartets* developed from a series of individual poems (1935–42) into a unified sequence (1943). "Burnt Norton" and "East Coker" are set in the West of England, "Little Gidding" in Cambridgeshire, and "The Dry Salvages" (which hovers between prose poem and verse essay) in New England. This trans-Atlantic sequence gains its unity from the recurrent meditation upon place, time (past, present, and future), and timelessness.

In addition to such sombre, metaphysical contemplation, Eliot wrote animal poems full of humour. "The Hippopotamus" was followed up by "Five-Finger Exercises" on cats and dogs, the last poem of which is both a playful imitation of Edward Lear's "How pleasant to know Mr. Lear!" and an ironic self-characterisation ("How unpleasant to meet Mr. Eliot!"). *Old Possum's Book of Practical Cats* (1939) continued in this tradition of light verse, with an occasional mock-heroic strain (in "Of the Awefull Battle of the Pekes and the Pollicles", Eliot wrote back to Jonathan Swift's satiric *Battle of the Books*). Eliot's sequence, which was originally composed for children, became even more popular when it was adapted by Andrew Lloyd Webber, together with unpublished verse by Eliot, and made into *Cats* (1981), one of the longest running of all West End musicals. Eliot himself became the object of good-natured parody in "Waste Land Limericks" (1986) by Wendy Cope (see below), who compressed the content of this icon of Modernism in a comical manner. The limerick parallel to part III, "The Fire Sermon", brings together slight criticism and light verse, to end with the remark "Wei la la. After this it gets deep." (l. 15). The final limerick continues in this manner:

Old Possum's Book of Practical Cats

> V
>
> No water. Dry rocks and dry throats,
> Then thunder, a shower of quotes
> From the Sanskrit and Dante.
> Da. Damyata. Shantih.
> I hope you'll make sense of the notes. (ll. 21–25)

Indeed, Eliot's own sense of humour could already be discerned in his mock-pedantic notes to *The Waste Land*. His tongue-in-cheek way of providing additional information to the obscure parts of the poem by what he referred to later as 'a remarkable exposition of bogus scholarship' led more than one critic up the garden-path.

In a more serious fashion, Eliot wrote essays that had a huge impact on literary criticism in his time. "Tradition and the Individual Talent" (1919) was a general reflection on ways of response to literature by writers and readers. "The Metaphysical Poets" (1921) led to a re-evaluation of the startling imagery used by Donne and Marvell (providing a model e.g. for Eliot's "Prufrock"). "Reflections on *vers libre*" (1917) together with "The Music of Poetry" (1942) defended the use of free verse, by Eliot and others, against contemporary critics. This issue bears some elaboration. In a speech made in 1935, the American poet Robert Frost (1874–1963) – an anti-Modernist poet who put his talent instead to the renewal of poetic tradition – had quipped: "Writing free verse is like playing tennis with the net down." In his essay "The Music of Poetry", Eliot retorted with a qualification:

> [N]o verse is free for the man who wants to do a good job. [...] a great deal of bad prose has been written under the name of free verse; [...]. But only a bad poet could welcome free verse as a liberation from form. It was a revolt against dead form, and a preparation for new form or for the renewal of the old [...]. Forms have to be broken and remade.

While pre-Modernist poetry relied on the regularities of metre and rhyme for its musicality, the rhythm of free verse is often established (as in Eliot's poetry) by verbal repetition. But how can a mere arbitrariness of lineation be avoided – and thus the impression that one deals with "mere chopped-up prose" (Fuller 1971: 62, 64)? When reflecting on the performance of his long poem "Howl" (1955), the American poet Allen Ginsberg (1926–97) defined a line of free verse as a single breath unit. This was taken up in turn by the British poet Roy Fuller (1912–91), who sided with Frost rather than with Eliot and Ginsberg when he summarised the argument in one of his lectures as an Oxford Professor of Poetry:

> Poetry cannot ignore all patterns: to do so would condemn itself to prose. Much so-called free verse – particularly that of the past and that now written by mediocre poets – is verse of iambic metre, irregularly lineated. [...] the rationale of such verse is often given as the poet's individual voice or breath.
>
> There seems little doubt that rhythm, alas, is the root of the matter in poetry. One accompanies the remark with a sigh because so many other elements in poetry seem more interesting [... than] the residual influence of the tom-tom or the capstan. Even the more complicated notion of the connection between the rhythms of poetry and of the human body, like breathing and heart-beats, lacks great appeal. [...] what prevents a poet from being a poet all the time – the business of inspiration – is not so much the lack of ideas or perceptions as the trickiness of casting them into rhythmical form.
>
> (Roy Fuller, "Fascinating Rhythm". (Fuller 1973: 89, 81–82.)

The discussion among poets of this central issue points out once again that radical Modernists such as Eliot represented only one

Fig. 5.1|

Edith Sitwell by
Roger Fry, 1915

Ted Hughes

tendency in twentieth-century poetry. However, before the focus shifts to competing lines of tradition, a few other notable practitioners of free verse have to be mentioned. Edith Sitwell (1887–1964) joined free verse with chiming sound effects in her poetic sequence "Façade", which was set to music by the composer William Walton and performed to a *succès de scandale* in 1922. With his long prose poem *In Parenthesis* (1937), David Jones (1895–1974) came up with a belated response to the wartime experience, but one that was informed by a varied tradition from the Arthurian epics up to *The Waste Land*. Another latecomer, *Briggflatts* (1966), the long autobiographical poem by Basil Bunting (1900–85) set in Northumbria, bore more resemblance to Eliot's *Four Quartets*.

Besides his vocation as a prose writer, D. H. Lawrence (1885–1930) was also a poet. "Cruelty and Love" (1913, re-titled "Love on the Farm" in 1928) echoed his concerns in fiction with rural life and death, with Classical mythology, with the metaphysics of vitalism, and with unrestrained sexuality as its form of expression. Such concerns re-appeared in later poems collected in *Birds, Beasts and Flowers* (1923), on "Bavarian Gentians" as harbingers of Hades and on Tuscan "Cypresses" as monuments to a lost Etruscan culture, on a (Biblical as well as phallic) "Snake" in Sicily and on a "Tortoise Shout" during the act of coition. For those poems on flora and fauna, however, Lawrence found a new shape, namely free verse run through and held together by various forms of verbal repetition.

Perhaps the most prominent successor, from the 1950s, to both T. S. Eliot and D. H. Lawrence in their metaphysical and mythological concerns, in their use of vegetation and animal imagery, and in their championing of free verse, was the Yorkshire-born poet Ted Hughes (1930–98, Poet Laureate since 1984). The beginning of "Crow's Last Stand" (1970) neatly ties in with the ending (and indeed the whole bleak setting) of *The Waste Land* by quoting the lines Eliot in turn had quoted from Buddha's Fire Sermon. The titles of Hughes's collections – from *The Hawk in the Rain* (1957) over *Crow* (1970; ext. 1972) to *Wolfwatching* and *Flowers and Insects* (both 1989) – testify to similar concerns, as do the titles of individual, much-anthologised pieces such as "Hawk Roosting" and "The Jaguar" (1957), "Pike" and "Relic" (1960), "Theology" (1967) and of the meta-literary poem "The Thought-Fox" (1957). However, when dealing with animals and nature, the poetry of

Hughes is characterised not only by vital forces but also by savage violence, the conceiving of evolution (in the rephrasing of Charles Darwin's views by the philosopher Herbert Spencer) as a brutal 'struggle for life' in a world essentially devoid of deity. "Hawk Roosting" as well as the sea-poems "Pike" (centring on an eventually cannibalistic killer-fish) and "Relic" (contemplating jawbones as the indigestible remains of such evolutionary struggle) exemplify this unrelenting world of predators.

In "Theology", the Biblical story of the beginning of human history was rewritten to conform to such cosmology ("Adam ate the apple./Eve ate Adam./The serpent ate Eve." ll. 5–8). "Crow's First Lesson" (1970) entailed not only yet another un- if not anti-Biblical act of Creation – Crow is shown to have created Man and Woman by retching at the word 'Love' – but also confronted directly the Flower-Power world of the Sixties as exemplified by the famous pop song of The Beatles, "All You Need Is Love" (which in 1967 was televised live by the BBC to the world). The private loves of Hughes became public when his stormy marriage to the American poet Sylvia Plath ended in Plath's suicide in 1963. In the year of his own death, Hughes answered to decades of public speculation about their marriage by publishing *Birthday Letters* addressed to his former wife, recounting their life together in a continuous dramatic monologue of epic length, broken into poems as if into chapters. Hughes himself is remembered also for two anthologies (*The Rattle Bag*, 1982, and *The School Bag*, 1997) that he edited together with the Irish poet Seamus Heaney to foster an interest in poetry. He also shared two other vocations – his many children's books, and his translations from Classical and Modern authors – with the older poet Robert Graves.

Tradition and the Individual Talent: More Moderate Forms of Experiment and Innovation

5.1.2

Much like Eliot, Lawrence and later Hughes, Robert Graves (1895–1985) had embarked on an eclectic study of Classical mythology and comparative anthropology. This led to his erudite study *The White Goddess: A Historical Grammar of Poetic Myth* (1948, rev. 1952), which was original in its accent on matriarchy and the Muse. Although Graves embraced experimentation as well as these other poets, he nevertheless differed from them in his

Robert Graves

reluctance to break radically with convention, and to commit himself to free verse as a poetic practice. When Graves, together with his own muse, the American poet Laura Riding, published *A Survey of Modernist Poetry* (1927), they managed to coin a broad term for the manner of Pound and Eliot and likewise to fire a broadside against their obscurity. Graves's own poetry, which had evolved from Georgian beginnings over an appraisal of the direct experience of trench warfare (*Fairies and Fusiliers*, 1917), was by the later 1920s already connected to a different beat.

Counting the Beats

You, love, and I,
(He whispers) you and I,
And if no more than only you and I
What care you or I?

Counting the beats,
Counting the slow heart beats,
The bleeding to death of time in slow heart beats,
Wakeful they lie.

Cloudless day,
Night, and a cloudless day,
Yet the huge storm will burst upon their heads one day
From a bitter sky.

Where shall we be,
(She whispers) where shall we be,
When death strikes home, O where then shall we be
Who were you and I?

Not there but here,
(He whispers) only here,
As we are, here, together, now and here,
Always you and I.

Counting the beats,
Counting the slow heart beats,
The bleeding to death of time in slow heart beats,
Wakeful they lie.   (Graves 1975: 165)

Graves's poem on the desire for endless love was cast as a whispered dialogue between lovers, overheard by the lyrical speaker and interspersed with his commentary. In the consistent use he made of identical rhyme, Graves apparently felt no longer bound by (Neoclassicist) 'rules' of versifying; and yet, the ragged look of his stanzas together with the frequent repetition of phrases should not suggest that the poet turned to free verse instead. The title "Counting the Beats" is programmatic not only for this love poem's theme (that the lovers' harmony becomes audible in their heartbeats striking in unison), but also and in a meta-poetical sense for Graves's habit of writing **accentual verse**. Such poetic innovation breaks with iambic pentameter and other accentual-syllabic conventions by 'counting the beats' only, regardless of the number of syllables per line. In Graves's poem, the corresponding lines of stanzas have the same number of stresses, so that the layout, perhaps inadvertently, resembles a cardiogram (in which case it would also link up with seventeenth-century shaped verse such as George Herbert's "Easter Wings", or the 'concrete poetry' mentioned below). In the likewise stress-timed, but slightly surrealist "Warning to Children" (1929; 1975: 30–31) – namely that the apparently limitless world is just an endless set of Chinese boxes and parcels, nested one inside the other – Graves had come up with a variation upon the Renaissance *topos* of *mundus inversus*, here presented as the world outside in. Despite of interests he shared with Eliot, Lawrence or Hughes, Graves brought his individual talent to original innovation rather than to a radical break with tradition, and he stands for a distinctly different (second) tendency among poets. If the Old English tradition is disregarded, Graves's accentual verse had its more immediate precursors in the nineteenth century in the metrical experiments of S. T. Coleridge (*Christabel*, 1816) and of G.M. Hopkins ('sprung rhythm'). Later, W. H. Auden used accentual verse for individual poems, and the Caribbean poet Derek Walcott made it a habit, too.

A logical counterpart to accentual verse is **syllabic verse**, which shows a regular pattern of syllables per line (as in the syllable-counting poetry in the Romance languages, or in the Japanese *haiku*), regardless of the number of accents. This had been tried out, too, in English-language poetry of the period under review, for instance in Ezra Pound's already quoted *haiku* "In a Station of the Metro" (1913) and in "Poetry" (1921, later revised) by fellow-American Marianne Moore (1887–1972). Much like in "Counting the Beats", Moore's syllabic verse consisted of lines of different syllable count organised into complex stanzas. With her model of syllabic verse, Marianne Moore influenced the poetry of W.H. Auden and of Dylan Thomas. By comparison, the related, but different attempt by the British poet Robert Bridges (1844–1930) to challenge metrical verse by a revival of the Classical tradition of **quantitative verse**, which was based on the perceived length of syllables rather than their stress pattern, did not find many followers.

A Synopsis of Twentieth-Century Experiments with Versification

markers within the line of verse		terminology: kind of verse
length of syllables: regular pattern of long and short syllables		*quantitative verse*
number of stresses per line	*number of syllables per line*	
regular pattern	regular pattern	*accentual-syllabic verse = metrical verse*
regular pattern	irregular pattern	*accentual verse*
irregular pattern	regular pattern	*syllabic verse*
irregular pattern	irregular pattern	vers libre/*free verse*

Fig. 5.2

W. H. Auden by Carl van Vechten, 1939

It was T. S. Eliot who accepted the early *Poems* (1930; rev, 1933) by W[ystan]. H[ugh]. Auden (1907–73) for publication with Faber & Faber. Auden was to remain close to Eliot's ironic and conversational manner, yet he turned away soon from free verse to write in a wide variety of different forms and styles. With equal ease, Auden took up Classical, medieval and modern forms, and he wrote light verse as well as politically charged poetry. In both its scale and quality, Auden's versatility compared well with that of predecessors such as Spenser, Milton or Keats, who had likewise attempted to reach across the range of poetic kinds. In an early volume such as *The Orators* (1932), a counting rhyme ('Last day but ten') rubbed shoulders with Chaucer's rhyme royal (in 'Beethamer, Beethamer, bully of Britain'), with a demanding form such as the sestina ('We have brought you, they said, a map of the country') and with "Six Odes" (Book III, all previously cited poems in Book II). Auden followed this up with more specimens of the sestina – "*Paysage Moralisé*" ('Hearing of harvests rotting in the valleys', 1933) and "Kairos and Logos" (1941) –, with sonnets and with sonnet sequences. One such sequence (comprising 27 sonnets and a long epilogue in triplets) was written in response to the direct experience of the Sino-Japanese War (1937–45) and entitled "In Time of War" (1939). A couple of years earlier, Auden had reacted to his observation of the Spanish Civil War (1936–39) with a poem that was simply called "Spain", but that was elaborately composed in accentual verse. Within this single productive year, from 1937 to early 1938, Auden brought out more anthology-pieces in a variety of forms. His adaptation of popular and oral forms ranged from a "Lullaby" ('Lay your sleeping head, my love') over love ballads ('As I walked out one evening') and further ballads in a more cruel and sarcastic vein ("Miss Gee", "James Honeyman" and "Victor") to include a "Passenger Shanty" and a "Funeral Blues". This last song, 'Stop all the clocks', was written for a play in 1937, published in 1940, and became even more popular through its inclusion in the 1994 film *Four Weddings and a Funeral*. The poet's long "Letter to Lord Byron", again from the year 1937, is another more elaborate example of Auden's intertextual response. Although written in rhyme royal, and not in the *ottava rima* of Byron's *Don Juan*, Auden's epistle and travelogue, which was written during a journey to Iceland, compares well with Byron's light and ironic manner. Auden turned to the Romantic poet "To chat about your poetry or mine" (l. 30), about writers from Austen to Joyce and Eliot, and about the spirit of the age.

The Thirties were a decade that brought the heated confrontation between the political Left and Right, between Democracy and Authoritarian or Totalitarian rule to a boiling point. In this confrontation, which had at its pivotal moments the outbreak first of the Spanish Civil War and then of the Second World War, writers visibly took sides. Auden's sonnet sequence "In Time of War" (1939) was dedicated to E.M. Forster, who was one of the few writers to come up with *Two Cheers for Democracy* (1930s essays collected in 1951). Interestingly enough, most of those poets who could have been seen to rally under Ezra Pound's cry of 'Make it new!' up to the point of breaking radically with past conventions of poetry, were now seen to side with extremely right-wing or, in some cases, even Fascist and anti-Semitic views. This included poets such as Yeats, Eliot, Pound and Wyndham Lewis, and it also applied to the expatriate South African poet Roy Campbell (1901–57), who supported the Spanish Right under General Franco. (Campbell's Fascist sympathies in *Flowering Rifle*, 1939, do however not extend to accomplished poems such as "The Zulu Girl", "The Zebras" and "Luis de Camoes".) A new British Left was also represented in the Spanish trenches: Auden stayed for several weeks at the front, whereas the novelist and essayist George Orwell actively fought for the Republican side. Orwell wrote about his experience in *Homage to Catalonia* (1938), and rounded on the politics of the poets of his generation in the second part of his essay "Inside The Whale" (1940).

Auden's oeuvre was to run to altogether about 400 poems that he continually revised and excised. His self-criticism did not stop short of his most pronounced political poems such as "Spain" (later revised and re-titled as "Spain 1937", then discarded altogether), "In Memory of W. B. Yeats" (1939, later pruned) and also "September 1, 1939" (deselected). Auden's elegy on Yeats is both an accomplished poem and a sceptical piece of politics. Each part of the poem was composed in a different style. The first part, in free verse, reflects on the last day in the life of Yeats as the beginning of his critical after-life and re-evaluation ("The words of a dead man/Are modified in the guts of the living." ll. 22–23). In the short, second part – composed in accentual verse, with both rhyme and half-rhyme – the lyrical speaker summarily rejects both a Romantic notion of the poet as a sage ("You were silly like us", l. 32) and the effectiveness of committed literature, stating bluntly: "For poetry makes nothing happen" (l. 36). In formal terms, the third part of Auden's elegy nods towards the quatrains of Gray's "Elegy Written in a Country Churchyard" as well as to the metre of Yeats's own poetic epitaph, "Under Ben Bulben". In this last part, Auden refers to the right-wing politics of old Yeats, but also forgives the Irish poet in the light of his poetic achievement – only to omit those indicting lines from later editions. "In Memory of W. B. Yeats" was written shortly before Auden's controversial move to the USA in the run-up to the outbreak of the Second World War. From the now more distanced point of view of a migrant in New York, Auden wrote "September 1, 1939" shortly after the event, and likewise as an obituary to "a low dishonest decade" (l. 5). In a *tour d'horizon* ranging from the wisdom of the ancient Greek historian Thucydides to the making of a modern "psychopathic god" (l. 18) such as Hitler, Auden disavowed ideologies celebrating "The strength of Collective Man," (l. 37), and he came up with a more positive answer on the purpose of poetry. The office of a poet were to "Show an affirming flame" in times of "Negation and despair" (ll. 98–99, quite like the Statue of Liberty), and to cherish the idea of a Brotherhood of Men.

Auden assumed US-American citizenship in 1946, but regularly returned to Italy and Austria, and to Oxford. In addition to "The Shield of Achilles" (1952), a poem that adapted an episode from *The Iliad* to talk on the brutality of totalitarian rule, he wrote whole sequences on the themes of humanity and nature ("Bucolics", 1955) and of history (*Homage to Clio*, 1960). Auden's versatility did not end, and his oeuvre began to resemble a primer on poetic forms. An "Epithalamion" or poem on marriage (written in September 1939, to start with the line "While explosives blow to dust") was succeeded by further elegies on Sigmund Freud (1940), and later on John F. Kennedy (1963). *The Age of Anxiety: A Baroque Eclogue* set in a wartime bar (1947) won him the Pulitzer Prize for Poetry. Besides, Auden tried out medieval forms, following up a "Madrigal" ('O lurcher-loving collier, black as night', 1940) with several instances of the villanelle, which earlier on had been favoured by those pre-Modernist poets who sought a revival of Old French and Italian forms (see chap. 4.3). The most prominent of Auden's villanelles is "Miranda's Song" in "The Sea and the Mirror: A Commentary on Shakespeare's *The Tempest*" (1944), which comes as a series of dramatic monologues given to characters from the play. With Auden, accentual verse – as in "Spain" and "September 1, 1939" – was matched first by longer forms of syllabic verse – as in the 1940 elegy on Freud, and "In Praise of Limestone" (1948) – and then by *haiku* poems. Among his collection of prose writings (*The Dyer's Hand*, 1962), he included the lectures he gave as an Oxford Professor of Poetry (1956–60).

A significant habit of Auden was his willingness to work in a team with other artists. Such collaboration stretched further than to the circle of fellow-poets who had met Auden at Oxford and who shared more or less Marxist sympathies at that time. Louis MacNeice (1907–63), Stephen Spender (1909–95) and C[ecil]. Day-Lewis (1904–72) were variously (but wrongly) perceived as fellows of a homogenous 'Auden Group', as 'MacSpaunday' (in Roy Campbell's deprecating conflation of their names), or as 'Pylon Poets', because of their initial fascination – evident from Spender's "The Pylons" (1933) – with such images of technological progress and modernity. Together with Louis MacNeice, Auden collaborated on the travel-book *Letters from Iceland* (1937, in prose and verse), and he teamed up with Christopher Isher-

'MacSpaunday'

wood (1904–86) on a similar travel-book, namely *Journey to a War* (1939). Auden and Isherwood had already cooperated on three plays (*The Dog Beneath the Skin*, 1935; *The Ascent of F6*, 1937; *On the Frontier*, 1939), and in 1939, they moved together from Britain to the USA. With the American poet Chester Kallman, Auden wrote libretti for operas by Igor Stravinsky (*The Rake's Progress*, 1951) and by Hans Werner Henze (1961), after he had already worked together with the composer Benjamin Britten on the opera *Paul Bunyan* (1941). MacSpaunday's other members are interesting poets over and above their association with Auden in the Thirties. Stephen Spender's "The Pylons" (1933) is a timepiece telling also of the poet's readiness to embrace assonance as well as accentual verse, while his "Fall of a City" (1939) comes as yet another poem on the war in Spain. (Together with further thematically related pieces, Spender's poems can be found in Skelton's anthology *Poetry of the Thirties*, 1964.) The Anglo-Irish poets C. Day-Lewis and Louis MacNeice distinguished themselves by verse translations of Aeschylus and Virgil, and in other ways, too. Day-Lewis had long assumed the pseudonym 'Nicholas Blake' for his literary mystery novels (centring on the amateur detective Nigel Strangeways) before he first preceded Auden as Oxford Professor of Poetry and then went on to become Poet Laureate (1968–72). MacNeice is best known as a poet for "Bagpipe Music" (1937) and for *Autumn Journal* (1939). As the work of an Irish-born poet, "Bagpipe Music" was endowed with a surprising number of *Scottish* references when it rounded on the blatant materialism, and correspondent decay of other standards, in the Thirties. Because of its prominent use of assonance, "Bagpipe Music" is indeed a highly musical piece, verging on performance poetry. With *Autumn Journal*, MacNeice created a poetical commentary on political developments during 1938, and on his personal experience of the war in Spain. From 1941, MacNeice worked for the BBC, where he pioneered the radio play.

Dylan Thomas

One of the actors in these radio plays was an unconventional, yet also very versatile, Welsh-born poet: Dylan Thomas (1914–53). In an extant verse-letter "To my Aunt, Discussing the Correct Approach to Modern Poetry" (written in 1933), this young poet had shown himself quite aware of Modernist experiments, yet also positioned himself at an ironical distance:

Fie on you, aunt, that you should see
[...]
No elemental form and sound
In T.S.E. and Ezra Pound.
Fie on you, aunt! I'll show you how
To elevate your middle brow,
And how to scale and see the sights
From modernist Parnassian heights.
[...]

Do not forget that 'limpet' rhymes
With 'strumpet' in these troubled times;
And commas are the worst of crimes;
Few understand the worst of [E.E.] Cummings,
And few James Joyce's mental slummings,
And few young Auden's coded chatter;
But then it is the few that matter.

(Thomas 1971: 83–85, ll. 7–14, 33–39)

As if to prove that he could stand the test himself, Dylan Thomas produced, during the same period, a poetic sequence without 'elemental form and sound'. "Altarwise by Owl-Light" (1935–36; 1971: 116–21) consisted of ten religious 'sonnets' in unevenly rhymed, partly half-rhymed or completely unrhymed form, with much dark imagery. Later on, Thomas turned to Marianne Moore's model of syllabic verse for some of his best-known, autobiographical poems. "Fern Hill" dealt with the innocent, 'green and golden' childhood holidays in rural Wales, "once below a time" (l. 7), while "Poem in October" celebrated the thirtieth birthday of the speaker/poet in a lyrically evoked landscape and harbour town. Both syllabic poems were published in Dylan Thomas's breakthrough collection *Deaths and Entrances* (1946), and indeed, apart from poems celebrating entrances into life, he composed others that memorably dealt with its exits. "A Refusal to Mourn the Death, by Fire, of a Child in London" was written, in accentual rather than syllabic verse, in March 1945 and published the week after VE-Day (Victory in Europe) in May. This anti-elegy is conspicuous for its acceptance, from a Christian point of view, of the unnatural situation, and ends in the line: "After the first death, there is no other." The unconventionality and versatility of Dylan Thomas showed also in "Do not go gentle into that good night" (1951), which by contrast admonished the dying father to struggle on against death. For this poem, Thomas chose the complicated, rhyming form of the villanelle. With this moribund poem, he might also have written, like Mozart, his own requiem. The short time that was left to him was filled with extensive reading tours of the USA (1950–53) that consolidated his public image as a Welsh bard and womaniser, resonantly reading from his own work, though seldom sober. Before he drank himself to death, Dylan Thomas could take part in the production of his radio play *Under Milk Wood: A Play for Voices* (1954), with which he created a model of his own.

In the poetry of W.H. Auden and Dylan Thomas, and also in the work of Roy Fuller (1912–91), the overlapping of the second and third tendencies within twentieth-century poetry became apparent. As Oxford Professor of Poetry (1968–73), Roy Fuller – who consistently deferred using free verse – lectured on accentual and on syllabic verse (Fuller 1971: 44–68; 1973: 81–97). He later partially aligned himself with this more moderate (second) tendency of poetic experimentation and was anxious at the same time to be seen as following an older ideal of craftsmanship (the third tendency). In "September 1939", his companion-piece to Auden's poem on the outbreak of the war, Fuller wrote accentual verse in combination with a double sonnet and a rhyme scheme of his own invention. Fuller produced "Meredithian Sonnets" and other sonnet sequences, too, and he strove to excel, just like W.H. Auden and Dylan Thomas (though with less impact), in older and technically more difficult forms such as the "Sestina" (1939) or the villanelle ("The Fifties", 1954). Moreover, Roy Fuller characteristically chose to combine syllabic verse with even more rare and demanding forms ("Cinquains" and "Six *stornelli*"; for all poems cited, see Fuller 1985). In testing his individual talent against tradition, John Fuller (*1939) followed in his father's footsteps, not least in his penchant for the sonnet, both as a poet and as a critic. The esteem in which poetical craftsmanship continued to be held, over and above the composition of free verse, comes out in the number of those introductions to poetic practice written by practising poets (see Hobsbaum 1995; Hollander 2001; Fenton 2002; Wainwright 2004).

Poetry on the Second World War

In addition to their tendency to approach form, poems can be sorted by theme or by the affiliation of poets to a group (such as MacSpaunday). The Second World War had not come up with war poetry on the scale of the Great War (see above), but produced enough specimens to enable latter-day readers to share in the collective experience of sailors, soldiers, and civilians. Moreover, those memorial poems that found their way into anthologies (e. g. recent editions of *NAEL*) also show the divergent tendencies well represented, from a linking up with conventional forms up to radical Modernism. "At the British War Cemetery, Bayeux" (1957) by Charles Causley (1917–2003) is a commemorative poem and a companion-piece to Siegfried Sassoon's sonnet "On Passing the New Menin Gate" (1928). Causley's poem takes the conventional ballad-form, like so many other pieces by this poet from Cornwall who wrote in an accessible manner and often on regional material. Causley's "Armistice Day" (1957) is a further poetic memorial to the dead, and the poem moreover preserves a good number of military terms that were in regular use among the Royal Navy during the Second World War. Keith Douglas (1920–44), who died on D-Day, likewise cast his poems "Gallantry", "Vergissmeinnicht" and "Aristocrats" in quatrains. By joining embracing rhyme and half-rhyme, these three poems (written in 1943) look back to Wilfred Owen's earlier, wartime experimentation with dissonance. Further down on the formal continuum we find "Naming of Parts" by Henry Reed (1914–86), who made use of accentual verse, occasionally rhymed. Reed's much-anthologised, first poem in his sequence *Lessons of the War* (1945) abounds, too, in military terminology. In "Still Falls the Rain" by Edith Sitwell, another kind of wartime sentiment is reached, together with the end of the formal continuum. Sitwell's free-verse poem was written in 1940 (to be published two years later), and it centres on a civilian's experience of the air raids on London during the Battle of Britain. To this may be added T. S. Eliot's commissioned poems "Defence of the Islands" and "A Note on War Poetry", which come from the same period. There is a shift of focus to another aspect of the war in "Annotations of Auschwitz" (1961, later set to music) by Peter Porter, a British poet born in Australia (in 1929), and also in "I Was Not There" by Karen Gershon. This Jewish poet (born Kaethe Loewenthal, 1923–93) tried to come to terms with the fact that she could escape from Nazi Germany on a *kindertransport*, but had to leave her parents behind to die in the Holocaust. Geoffrey Hill has contributed several poems on this theme, namely "Two Formal Elegies" (a double sonnet, 1959), "September Song" and "Ovid in the Third Reich" (1968). When James Fenton composed "A German Reqiem" (1980), he approched the topic from a different angle and focused on another natural urge in both victims and persecutors, namely not to commemorate the dead, but to forget the deed.

> It is not your memories which haunt you.
> [...]
> It is what you have forgotten, what you must forget.
> What you must go on forgetting all your life.　　　　(ll. 4–7)

By contrast, George Szirtes felt a responsibility, as a son and as a poet, to overcome his Jewish mother's lifelong reluctance and recreate her grave experience of persecution long after her death, in what became a sequence of sixty sonnets entitled *Metro* (1988). (A more detailed treatment of the last three poets will be found below.)

Besides memorial poems that preserve the grim reality of these years, there is, typically enough, also **humorous verse** on the war. "In Westminster Abbey" (1940) by John Betjeman (1906–84) was written in the ironical fashion characteristic of his work. The poem is a dramatic monologue by 'a lady' who had come to pray in an egotistic and self-serving manner. The poem includes, too, a brief catalogue of those essentials of Britishness that are worth fighting for:

Humorous Verse

Fig. 5.3

John Betjeman Statue in St Pancras Station, London by Martin Jennings, 2007

> Gracious Lord, oh bomb the Germans.
> 　　Spare their women for Thy Sake,
> And if that is not too easy
> 　　We will pardon Thy Mistake.
> But, gracious Lord, whate'er shall be,
> Don't let anyone bomb me.
>
> Think of what our Nation stands for,
> 　　Books from Boots' and country lanes,
> Free speech, free passes, class distinction,
> 　　Democracy and proper drains.
> Lord, put beneath Thy special care
> One-eighty-nine Cadogan Square.　　　　(ll. 7–12, 19–24)

In addition to a hypocritical attitude towards the Empire, and the idea of racial superiority that goes with it (ll. 13–18), the poem speaks of a mentality that prefers private profit over the public interest, and values a hedonistic lifestyle higher than any kind of obligation (ll. 19–30, 41–42).

Thus, in his poem from the year of the Battle of Britain, Betjeman singled out the same aspects of British mentality that George Orwell branded as destructive to society in his essay *The Lion and the Unicorn* (1941), though Betjeman addressed them in a lighter, ironical way. By contrast with Orwell, Betjeman's conception of Britishness was on the whole rather nostalgic, and that, as well as his adherence to metrical tradition, may have been part of his popular appeal. Betjeman began his career at the same time as the members of the Auden Group, and was equally able to display a mocking tone and a sarcastic humour, but he never really became a Pylon Poet. Betjeman soon enough was seen to lament the loss that especially modern architecture and town planning brought to English cities and the countryside, and to the customary way of life. For him, the cities and their historic buildings symbolised the historical bond that connected present Britishness with the past. Betjeman's notorious, pre-war poem "Slough" (1937) was in many ways typical of his negative view of modern society (which is also evident from his poems "The Planster's Vision", 1945, "Inexpensive Progress", 1966, and "Executive", 1974).

> Come, friendly bombs, and fall on Slough
> It isn't fit for humans now,
> There isn't grass to graze a cow
>   Swarm over, Death!
>
> Come, bombs, and blow to smithereens
> Those air-conditioned, bright canteens,
> Tinned fruit, tinned meat, tinned milk, tinned beans
>   Tinned minds, tinned breath.   ("Slough", ll. 1–8)

After the war, Betjeman became the most popular poet in his own day – and this popularity lasted: his *Collected Poems* (1958) were estimated to have sold close to a million copies by 1993. Betjeman's representative status as a poet was in many ways comparable to that of Tennyson a century earlier (if not among critics, then at least in society), and it was furthered first by a knighthood and then, in 1972, by the nomination as Poet Laureate.

Stevie Smith (1902–71) was another 'funny' poet who did not care for poetic fashions and yet became a popular favourite. When she wrote "Thoughts about the Person from Porlock" (1962) – who had allegedly interrupted Coleridge's dream vision

Stevie Smith

of Kubla-Khan's pleasure-dome – her answer poem struck a critical as well as a comic note, not the least by focusing on the visitor rather than on the visionary. Her best-known poem, "Not Waving but Drowning" (1957) proved that she could (as she often did) talk even about death with deadpan humour. Other notable writers of light verse and parody include Gavin Ewart (1916–95) and Wendy Cope (*1945). Ewart made his name in the Thirties with a parody on the poetry of Ezra Pound entitled "Phallus in Wonderland" (1933), before he was silenced by the war experience. He gained a new audience from the 1960s for both erotic and funny poems, ending his career with the parody "Auden's Juvenilia Revisited" (1996). Wendy Cope has the gift to turn forms as diverse as Shakespearean sonnets, triolets and villanelles, *rondeaux*, *rubáiyát* and *haiku* to comic purpose. She dedicated "A Poem on the Theme of Humour" (from her collection *If I Don't Know*, 2001) to Gavin Ewart. Such at times caustic wit can also be found in the parodies on Wordsworth and T.S. Eliot (such as "Waste Land Limericks", quoted above), or in the poems by and about Strugnell, a Totally Useless Male Poet of her own invention, all of which were included in her earlier collections, *Making Cocoa for Kingsley Amis* (1986) and *Serious Concerns* (1992).

The Movement and Other Circles of Poets

Besides John Betjeman and Charles Causley, there were other poets who made their names in the 1950s and who likewise sidestepped Modernism to continue writing in the tradition of rhymed metrical verse. The most prominent of these poets – commonly subsumed under the designation **The Movement**, and conveniently contained in the programmatic anthology *New Lines* (1956) – was Philip Larkin (1922–85). Larkin took the opportunity to delimit his own canon when being asked to edit *The Oxford Book of Twentieth-Century English Verse* (1973), in which both Yeats and Eliot were then less well represented than Thomas Hardy. What was characteristic of Larkin's own verse was its observation of ordinary life rendered in everyday language, but cast into elaborate form; and a general scepticism combined with a devaluation of older ideals. Larkin's "Church Going" (1955) was a disillusioned reflection on the function of religion, and of churches in particular. Both senses of the title are called up in the poem (which ties in well with Betjeman's "A Lincolnshire Church", 1948). Larkin's lyrical speaker wonders who is still going to service: he himself goes to 'another church' only as a tourist 'when there's nothing going on', and then leaves no more than 'an Irish sixpence' as a donation that is of no real value in an English context. With the title poem of his collection *The Whitsun Weddings* (1964), Larkin went on to take a disillusioned look at marriage, another institution that is said to be "wholly farcical", "like a happy funeral" (ll. 51, 53). "The Whitsun Weddings" shares its stanza form with Keats's odes, but not their idealism. In "Annus Mirabilis" (1967), Larkin commented upon the Sexual Revolution of the Swinging Sixties, while "This Be The Verse" (1971) with its pungent opening line "They fuck you up, your mum and dad." exploded the ideal of a nuclear family. In equally stark language, "Love Again" centred on sexual jealousy (this intensely personal poem on a lover's loss was written in 1979, yet not published within the poet's lifetime). In "Aubade" (1977), Larkin memorably linked a new day's dawn with death, and thus closed a circle with "Mr Bleaney" (1955), his earlier matter-of-fact reflection upon provincial life and death to which Larkin's editor Anthony Thwaite (*1930) had provided a companion-piece entitled "Mr Cooper" (1963).

The Movement was trailed by several other circles of poets, likewise brought together and branded by anthologists and journalists. **The Group** (c. 1955–65) featured largely in *The Group Anthology* (1963) and in *British Poetry since 1945* (1970; rev. 1985), both edited by Edward Lucie-Smith (*1933). This informal circle of discussion that however met regularly in London included, in addition to the editor, also Philip Hobsbaum (1932–2005), Peter Porter (mentioned above), George MacBeth (1932–92) and Martin Bell (1918–78). Under Bell's influence, *The Group* transmuted into the *Poets' Workshop*, while Hobsbaum was already under way to convene similar discussion groups first in Belfast (1962–66, with the poets Seamus Heaney, Michael Longley and Derek Mahon) and then in Glasgow (1966–75, including dramatists and novelists). George MacBeth was born in Scotland and educated at Oxford before he joined BBC Radio as a producer of poetry programmes, just like Louis MacNeice earlier on. MacBeth and the other members of *The Group* aligned with the committed poet Adrian Mitchell (1932–2008) and with the **Liverpool Poets** Adrian Henri (1932–2000) and Roger McGough (*1937) in their endeavour to produce poems that were accessible and meant for oral delivery. Adrian Mitchell coined the well-known aphorism "Most people ignore most poetry/because/most poetry ignores most people." Not

Fig. 5.4
Cover of *The Mersey Sound*, published by Penguin Books 1967

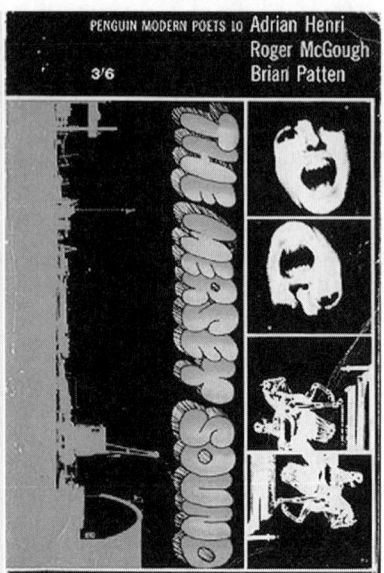

PENGUIN MODERN POETS 10 Adrian Henri
Roger McGough
3/6   Brian Patten

James Fenton

so with *The Mersey Sound*: with over a million copies sold, this 1967 Penguin Modern Poets selection of work by the *Liverpool Poets* made performance poetry popular in an age already dominated by another Liverpudlian pop group – *The Beatles*. Politically, all those British performance poets met in their protest against the US-American war in Vietnam (see MacBeth's "The Bamboo Nightingale" and Mitchell's "To Whom It May Concern"). James Fenton (*1949) had already won a prize as an Oxford undergraduate for his combined sequence of sonnets and *haikus* entitled "Our Western Furniture" (1968), on the set theme of the American opening of Japan in the nineteenth-century, when he followed the precedent of his mentor W. H. Auden in the Thirties to embark on his own 'journey to a war' in 1973. In his poetic collection *The Memory of War* (1982), Fenton re-worked his experience as a journalist who had spectacularly witnessed the ending and the aftermath of the war in Vietnam and Cambodia. (For his reportage, see the prose collection *All the Wrong Places*, 1988.) His narrative poem "A Staffordshire Murderer" (1983) blends an eerie atmosphere with an at times nonsensical plot peppered up by the unexpected turn. Such a combination of the tale of the unexpected with ballad elements, including an ingenious handling of incremental repetition, soon was to secure Fenton widespread popularity. According to hearsay, "Don't read after Fenton" was a piece of advice circulating among writers on the lecture circuit during the 1980s and '90s who thus acknowledged Fenton's extraordinary skill as a performance poet. The gift to combine a moribund theme with technical accomplishment to memorable effect is borne out by more ballads with a Far Eastern setting that were collected in *Out of Danger* (1993). "Out of the East" is a dramatic monologue given to a common soldier in the Cambodian war. "The Ballad of the Imam and the Shah: An Old Persian Legend" is actually a hanging ballad with scarcely veiled allusions to Imam Khomeini's 1979 Islamic Revolution in Iran. The suppression of the 1989 Chinese student revolution by the Communist authorities in Beijing's Tienanmen Square led Fenton to write "Tienanmen" (June 1989) immediately after the event. The most effective, albeit quite nonsensical, of his ballads is "Here Come the Drum-Majorettes!" Moreover, *Out of Danger* contains some chiming love-songs, also written to great effect, such as "In Paris with You", "I'll Explain", and "Hinterhof" (which begins thus: "Stay near to me and I'll stay near to you – /As near as you are dear to me will do,"). After having followed once more in Auden's footsteps, this time as Oxford Professor of Poetry (1994–99), Fenton shared his technical expertise in a lightly written *Introduction to English Poetry* (2002), and made his more general views on poetry available in *The Strength of Poetry* (2001).

Much earlier, Fenton had been involved in another promotional sorting of contemporary poets into convenient groups when he coined the term **Martian Poetry** for the work of Craig Raine (*1944) and Christopher Reid (*1949), in reaction to Raine's second collection, *A Martian Sends a Postcard Home* (1979). Raine's poetic sequence gave a new twist to the eighteenth-century fashion of humorous or satirical letters allegedly written by travellers who reported home to correspondents in their exotic countries of origin about everyday life and manners in Britain and Europe (see Montesquieu's *Lettres persanes*, 1721, and the 'Chinese letters' in Goldsmith's *The Citizen of the World*, 1762). Through its foregrounding of the familiar in unfamiliar ways, *Martian Poetry* also became a popular didactic tool in the classroom. Craig Raine not only published critical essays on T.S. Eliot, but also succeeded him as poetry editor at publishers Faber & Faber, to hand over to Christopher Reid.

After *The Group* and the *Martian Poets* came the *New Generation Poets* in 1994, duly followed a decade later by the *Next Generation* (of whom more below). However, and if the pun is excused, a *girls' group* with a bite of their own could also and easily have been formed, as Fleur Adcock (*1934) already proved by editing *The Faber Book of Twentieth-Century Women's Poetry* (1987). Adcock became a published poet soon after she had left her native New

Zealand for Britain in 1963, and her poetry is marked by an unsentimental and ironical treatment of love romance ("Against
Coupling", "Bed and Breakfast"). Apart from, say, Wendy Cope
("Two Cures for Love"), Selima Hill (*1945) might have joined
that imaginary circle of women poets, as she, too, can be said
to write love poetry with a difference ("Don't Let's Talk About
Being in Love", "The Unsuccessful Wedding-Night"), up to and
including the treatment of sexual abuse (*Bunny*, 2001). For several reasons, Carol Ann Duffy (*1955) is another prime candidate
for membership: for editing an anthology with the startling title
I Wouldn't Thank You for a Valentine (1992); for writing movingly,
in *Rapture* (2005), on the course of an intense love affair which
ended unhappily; for becoming Britain's first-ever female Poet
Laureate (2009); and for her hallmark, namely dramatic monologues written frequently in a colloquial (and sometimes even
slangy) style. The monologues in *The World's Wife* (1999) take
pride of place in this respect. They were given to real or imaginary women bypassed by history for their men, such as "Anne
Hathaway" (Shakespeare's wife, here recreated in a blank-verse
sonnet). Other successful impersonations which became set texts
in the classroom include "Havisham" (1993), which evokes sympathy for the grotesque female character from Dickens's novel
Great Expectations. Then there is "Warming Her Pearls" (1987), spoken by a (possibly black) servant girl who sees the necklace she
is warming for her mistress on her own skin as a bond between
the two women in more senses than one. Yet Duffy (like all other
women poets listed here) has not restricted herself to poems only
written from a feminist angle; her collections have also included
monologues on Englishness from an English perspective ("Translating the English", 1989) as well as from a migrant's point of
view ("Foreign", 1987).

Carol Ann Duffy, Poet Laureate

5.1.3 | Englishness in English Verse since the 1960s

Geoffrey Hill

In various other ways, Englishness has featured in English verse
since the 1960s. In addition to downright religious poems such as
"Genesis" (1958), and to his above-mentioned poems on the Third
Reich and the Holocaust, Geoffrey Hill (*1932) had composed poems that rounded on violence and war in a medieval English
setting. In his "Requiem for the Plantagenet Kings" (1959), Hill

looked beyond the royal repose of tomb effigies to remind the reader of the bloody battles of the past, which, even though covered by decay and dust, only wait for being re-counted on Judgement Day. Hill's "Requiem", in the form of an English sonnet, was trailed by a sequence of eight unrhymed sonnets entitled "Funeral Music" (1968) which took the story of bloodshed and beheading further into the period of the Wars of the Roses. *Mercian Hymns* (1971), a sequence of prose poems and Hill's best-known collection, were written in the memory both of an earlier medieval monarch, King Offa of Mercia, and of Hill's childhood in the Midlands. In view of his wide-ranging subject matter and his impacted syntax, Hill's poetry is not always easily accessible (this is also the point of Wendy Cope's parody on the *Mercian Hymns* in "Duffa Rex", 1986), but the poems are rewarding when reread. In an extraordinary outburst of energy, Hill followed up his *New and Collected Poems* of 1994 with seven further, individual collections. Their range stretches from Britain to the Biafran War, commemorating e.g. the poet Christopher Okigbo who was killed in that Nigerian civil war in the late 1960s.

By coincidence, Tony Harrison (*1937) lectured in Nigeria up to the outbreak of the civil war. Harrison first wrote poems on White expatriates' sensual experience of Black Africa, e. g. "The Heart of Darkness" (1970, with a nod to Joseph Conrad in the title, see chap. 4.2.2). Afterwards, he accentuated Englishness in terms of class, and revealed his Leeds working-class credentials more markedly in *The School of Eloquence* (1978; rev. 1981), an ongoing sequence of 'sonnets' in sixteen lines, variously rhymed. The elegiac sonnets Harrison had composed first on the death of his mother and later on the cremation of his father, "Book Ends I, II" and "Marked with D.", proudly if disconcertingly referred to his father's profession, a baker's, in their imagery. With other sixteen-line sonnets focused on mining, such as "National Trust", Harrison indeed presented social history from below, and his social realism pertained to language as marker of the regional and class divide in Britain. This was borne out by the occasional inclusion of a line of verse in the Cornish dialect, as in "National Trust", or by sonnets striking at linguistic variation right away, such as "On Not Being Milton", "The Queen's English", and "Them & [uz] I, II". The poet's personal command of languages enabled him to produce translations for the stage of

Tony Harrison

poetic drama from the Classical Greek canon and from French Neoclassicism. Harrison's politics and poetics continued to be controversial. He related to the divisive Miners' Strike of 1984/85 and to vandalism in his long poem *V.* (1985), which was set in Leeds cemetery and fittingly composed in the manner of Gray's famous *Elegy Written in a Country Churchyard*. The adaptation of *V.* for television, which had led to a heated debate in and outside parliament in 1987, also sparked Harrison's continuing interest in television film as a new medium for his verse. In *Prometheus* (1998, likewise adapted for television), the poet returned to the plight of mineworkers, while he also took issue with the Gulf War in poetry (*A Cold Coming*, 1991), with the Bosnian conflict (in the singular position of a poetic war correspondent for *The Guardian*) and with the invasion of Iraq (through his translation of Euripides's play *Hecuba*, 2005). "A Celebratory Ode on the Abdication of King Charles III" (1995, yet uncrowned) testified to Harrison's Republican views, and thus effectively ruled him out to succeed Ted Hughes as Poet Laureate.

Andrew Motion, Poet
Laureate

In the end, the honour – which in 1999 was no longer awarded for life, but limited to a period of 10 years – went first to Andrew Motion (*1952) and then to Carol Ann Duffy (see above). Motion linked himself to a particularly English tradition by writing his M. Litt. thesis on Edward Thomas and later by writing the official yet iconoclastic biography of Philip Larkin (1993). Motion's collection entitled *Independence* was published in the same year as Salman Rushdie's novel *Midnight's Children* (1981) and likewise centred on Indian Independence in 1947 – a seminal event in the history of the British Empire and of Decolonisation. Another recurrent concern has been the war experience, which he followed up in other poets' *First World War Poems* (Motion 2003) as well as in his own narrative poetry ("The Letter", 1980; "Joe Soap", 1994). In stark contrast to Tennyson ("The Charge of the Light Brigade"), this Laureate did not necessarily toe the line, and published what he called an anti-war poem on the campaign in Iraq ("Regime Change", 2003). Motion's later poetry outside his Laureate verse (which is available in the 2002 collection *Public Property* and on the Internet) became increasingly autobiographical. In 1982, Motion had edited *The Penguin Book of Contemporary British Poetry* together with the poet and critic Blake Morrison (*1950), who was like him interested in *The Movement* (Morrison 1980). Their anthology, which prominently included James Fenton as well as the *Martian Poets* Raine and Reid, was given out to survey the state of the art, yet ran into trouble when Seamus Heaney as an Irishman protested against his inclusion, although he had received pride of place in the opening section. (Poets' fighting when ended is soon mended: Motion was able to include Heaney in 2001 in a further anthology, partly with the same poems but under the unobjectionable title *Here to Eternity*.) Fellow-editor Blake Morrison, a Yorkshireman by birth, became otherwise known for his response to a spectacular series of murders in the region in *The Ballad of the Yorkshire Ripper* (1987). Morrison's use of the vernacular is not the only difference to Fenton's style in "A Staffordshire Murderer", which comes from the same decade.

Other institutions besides the Oxford Professor of Poetry, the Poet Laureate and the new National Poets (see below) that care for the public visibility of poetry are The Poetry Society (established in 1909) and The Poetry Book Society (founded by T. S. Eliot in 1953). Since 1993, The Poetry Book Society has awarded the prestigious T. S. Eliot Prize, which together with the Forward Poetry prizes (created in 1991) is the equivalent to the (Man) Booker Prize for Fiction. With the shortlists of such prizes, contemporary poetry in Britain and Ireland is sifted and canonised for the time being (thus a look at those lists provides one way of keeping up to date). The Poetry Society fosters British poetry through the thematically focused National Poetry Day (launched in 1994), through its online archive, and through its magazine *Poetry Review*. Glyn Maxwell (*1962) was one of twenty **New Generation Poets** whom *Poetry Review* had assembled in a promotional exercise in 1994. Andrew Motion's interest in the poetry of Edward Thomas and in the First World War is mirrored in Maxwell's collection *The Breakage* (1998), and Maxwell became known also as a writer of verse plays and of a novel in verse, *Time's Fool* (2000). Other poets included among this *New Generation* were Simon Armitage and Carol Ann Duffy, Lavinia Greenlaw and Michael Hofmann (born in Germany), Moniza Alvi (born in Pakistan) and David Dabydeen (born in Guyana), and the Scottish poets Robert Crawford, Kathleen Jamie and Don Paterson. One-sentence summaries could read as follows: science is a prominent feature of the poetry of Lavinia Greenlaw (*1962). Besides being a poet, Michael Hofmann (*1957) is a prolific translator from the Ger-

The 1994 New Generation Poets

man. Carol Ann Duffy and Simon Armitage were prime candidates for the succession to the Laureateship when Andrew Motion's term of office expired – but here we have to go into more detail. Simon Armitage (*1963) has the gift to make his lyrical speakers converse with the man on the street, unreservedly and colloquially. The metrical and rhymed form of his poems may further their accessibility, but Armitage does not feel forced to obey any rule, and therefore engages in irregular rhyme schemes and makes much use of half-rhyme. He writes and translates also for theatre, radio and television, and several of his poems have become set texts in English classrooms. Their tone varies: there are the both casual and morbid reflections of an organ donor ("I've made out my will; I'm leaving myself") that are typical of the sonnets and near-sonnets in Armitage's *Book of Matches* (1993). By comparison, the title poem from his collection *Kid* (1992) is a 'comic' dramatic monologue spoken by Batman's sidekick Robin the Boy Wonder, who thinks of the superhero in less glorifying terms after their separation. Due to the accessibility and to the prolific presence of his verse in different media, Armitage is one of the most-widely-known poets of this erstwhile *New Generation*, which he and his fellow-nominee Robert Crawford came to edit for a Penguin anthology (1998).

Together with Andrew Motion and Bernardine Evaristo – who has two novels in verse to her credit: *Lara* (1997; rev. 2009) and *The Emperor's Babe* (2001) – Simon Armitage was involved in drawing up the new promotional list of **Next Generation Poets** in 2004. One of those included is Alice Oswald (*1966). In the ecological anthology she edited (*The Thunder Mutters: 101 Poems for the Planet*, 2005) as well as in her own poetry so far, nature and region are predominant themes. Alice Oswald has consciously focused on her native Devon in a manner that evokes the comparison with Hardy's preoccupation with Dorset/'Wessex', and of Charles Causley with Cornwall. Oswald won the prestigious T. S. Eliot Prize for her book-length poem *Dart* (2002) that however circumvents the 'waste land' of the cities. During the composition of this long poem, Oswald interviewed many people living near the River Dart in Devon and then transformed the actual prose samples into "a sound-map of the river, a songline from the source to the sea" (poet's prefatory note). If pressed for a parallel, one may think less of Coleridge's "Sonnet to the River Otter" (1796) than of *Under Milkwood*, Dylan Thomas's 'play for voices', and also of the peculiar mapping of the world by Australian Aboriginals recounted by Bruce Chatwin in his travelogue *The Songlines* (1987). However, Alice Oswald's polyphonic poem remains as English as it could be with regard to its subject matter, and it is quite original in its design. The River Dart comes alive through an alternation of memories and voices, ranging from eel watchers over oyster gatherers to tin miners and sewage workers, taking in an otter, a water-nymph, a dreamer and a 'rememberer' along the way. These interlinked stories are presented in a great variety of forms, from the Chevy Chase ballad on an epic theme (Oswald 2002: 30–33) and the waternymph's song using the half-rhymed stanza of Yeats's "Under Ben Bulben" (11) over accentual and syllabic verse (5–7, 27–28) to examples of free verse (16–17) and of concrete poetry (23). In the accomplished and comprehensive design of a quintessentially English poem, *Dart* summed up, only a couple of years after the Millennium, the full formal variety of twentieth-century poetry from Hardy to Hughes, in order to move beyond. In 2009, Alice Oswald continued her poetic investigations into nature and region with the publication of *A Sleepwalk on the Severn*: a further dramatic poem for several voices that depicts the effect of the moon on the River Severn and the people living next to its estuary.

Post-war immigration to Britain from the Commonwealth after the dismantling of the Empire changed British society, but also British literature for good. Englishness and Britishness were now perceived and portrayed from a new migrants' perspective, and the language of poetry was extended to include not only regional registers, but also Black British or Asian British varieties of speech. Already before the war, the Jamaican-born poet Una Marson (1905–65) had published witty answer poems to Shakespeare ("To Wed or Not to Wed", in Burnett 1986: 161) and to Kipling ("If", 1930, in Donnell and Welsh 1996: 129) from a woman's, not yet from a West Indian point of view. Marson had also prepared the ground for the BBC radio programme *Caribbean Voices*, which was to exert a singular influence after 1946. A number of West Indian poets who had migrated to Britain after the war became important also for their landmark anthologies which promoted the new developments in poetry. These are *News for Babylon* (1984) by James Berry (*1924 in Jamaica, from 1948 resi-

Englishness from a Migrant's Perspective

dent in the UK) and *Hinterland* (1989) by E. A. Markham (*1939 in Montserrat, a UK resident since 1956). Poetry published in Britain gained a West Indian flavour in e. g. Amryl Johnson's *Tread Carefully in Paradise* (1991) and Grace Nichols's *Sunris* (1996), both of which contain poems on the Caribbean Carnival, which in the 1950s translated to London's Notting Hill, too. Amryl Johnson (1944–2000) was born in Trinidad and moved to London in 1955, while Grace Nichols (*1950) left Guyana for Britain in 1977. A harsher, postcolonial note was sounded in the poetry of David Dabydeen (*1955), who also hailed from Guyana. *"Turner": New and Selected Poems* (1994) includes besides the title-piece, which centres on the drowning of slaves during the Middle Passage over the Atlantic, also a recreation of the experience on the slave plantations in e.g. "Slavewoman's Song" (1984). Fred D'Aguiar (*1960), who was born of Guyanese parents in London, produced *An English Sampler: New and Selected Poems* (2001) partly along the same lines. D'Aguiar's personal selection from all his previous collections set in with the fourteen-line poem "Mama Dot", a re-writing in free verse and Black English of the well-known nursery rhyme of "Solomon Grundy" in terms of race and gender. (For comparison, see Alice Oswald's adaptation of this nursery rhyme in "Solomon Grundy", in *Woods etc.*, 2005.) D'Aguiar's *An English Sampler* concluded with "The Last Sonnet About Slavery", which is unlikely to remain the poet's last verse in this matter. With *Bloodlines* (2000), he had composed a long narrative poem in *ottava rima* dealing with the love between a slave-owner's son and a Black slave, set in the nineteenth century around the time of the Abolition of Slavery within the British Empire (1833) and during the US Civil War. However, D'Aguiar does not see the world (or Britain, for that matter) only in Black and White. Although he acted as editor of the "Black British Poetry" section in the revisionist anthology *The New British Poetry* (Allnutt 1988), D'Aguiar's introduction to that section showed his uneasiness with such a label. Little wonder then, that the 1993 collection of his own poetry was entitled *British Subjects*, without any further qualifier. This collection included "Sonnets from Whitley Bay", a sequence set in the North of England.

Those writers who descended from the African, Caribbean and South Asian parts of the former Empire are altogether the most numerous groups of migrant writers by far, but there have always been alternative migrant perspectives on Englishness and Britishness which should not be overlooked. George Szirtes, who considers himself a British writer of Hungarian extraction, is a case in point: he was born in Budapest in 1948 and arrived in London with his family after the Soviet suppression of the Hungarian Uprising in 1956. Szirtes received initial encouragement by *The Group* poet Martin Bell, and in 1988, he published *Metro*, a sequence of sixty sonnets on his Jewish mother's persecution during the Third Reich (1988, mentioned above). Thereafter and more by coincidence (he switched publishers) than by conscious choice, George Szirtes developed both sides of his story in the poetic collections *The Budapest File* (2000) and *An English Apocalypse* (2001). The 'English' collection, which also reprinted poems from previous volumes (such as the ironic/Byronic and at the same time very tender "Prayer for My Daughter"), had an idiosyncratic design. A first title sequence consisted of over sixty pages of sonnets (sometimes in sub-sequences), which recreated from memory the poet's own experience of growing up as a Hungarian refugee in suburban London in the later 1950s, including the confrontation with anti-Semitic violence. There was an underlying colour pattern, a continuous reference to music, and the occasional intertextual hint at either Matthew Arnold's "Dover Beach" (in "Payne's Grey") or "Fern Hill" by Dylan Thomas (in "Golden Boy"). The mini-sequence "Backwaters: Norfolk Fields" added a regional touch, while the second title sequence continued the story, yet in *terza rima*. The overall design was repeated in *Reel* (2004), a collection that was awarded the T.S. Eliot Prize.

Migration, ethnicity and identity have been recurrent themes of the **performance poetry** of John Agard (*1949), who left his native Guyana for Britain in 1977. "Listen Mr Oxford Don" (1985) has become a set text in numerous examinations, not least because the poem is set in an educational context itself. "I didn't graduate/I immigrate": the dramatic monologue of "a simple immigrant/from Clapham Common" (ll. 2–5), directed at a member of the cultural establishment, compares well with Tony Harrison's "Them & [uz] I, II", because its satire likewise thrives on its confrontation of Standard ('Oxford' or 'Queen's') English with the Black British variety ("Dem accuse me of assault/on de Oxford dictionary/", ll. 22–23). However, the educational establishment played fair with Agard. "Half-caste" (1988), a companion poem,

Performance Poetry

was conferred canonical status, too, as a set text for the GCSE examination in England and Wales, under the rubric 'Poems from Different Cultures'. Beginning with its title, "Half-caste" – another dramatic monologue in free verse – first plays around with different collocations (like 'half-caste canvas', 'half-caste weather' and 'half-caste symphony', ll. 4 ff.) before it addresses the notion of hybridity directly in its biological and ethnic sense in the second half of the poem (ll. 31 ff.). Through the inclusion of poems such as "From Britannia To Whom It May Concern" in We Brits (2006), Agard's most recent collection, matters of Englishness and Britishness are clearly made an issue. "Feeling the Whirlwind" and "Caribbean Eye over Yorkshire" abound with West Indian local colour, blended with streaks of England's grey. Then, matters of race are shifted into focus again: "Mr and Mrs Xenophobia" (65) addresses imperial nostalgia in combination with a distrust in anything foreign, and "Task of Spirit (in memory of Stephen Lawrence, 1974–93)" commemorates a prominent victim of present-day racism. "By Liverpool Docks I Sat Down" blends Liverpool's historical role in the triangular trade with the popular culture of the Swinging Sixties (ll. 10–14), and also the psalm "By the Rivers of Babylon" (alluded to in the poem's title) with Shelley's original sonnet stanza used for his "Ode to the West Wind". In We Brits, we find both vintage Agard humour and a new mix bringing together the media of performance and print, and a variety of poetic genres.

Building on diverse African and Afro-Caribbean cultural traditions, performance poetry has developed into a characteristic subgenre of Black British literature since the late 1970s. For some time, **Dub Poetry** came to stand for the whole, though it was only one particular kind of performance poetry that attempted to fuse committed literature written or spoken from a Black stance with the rhythm of Reggae Music, as a distinct part of Afro-Jamaican culture. 'Dub' referred to the alternative, all-rhythm version of a Reggae song usually recorded on the B-side of a single. Linton Kwesi Johnson (*1952) is the best known of these Dub Poets, and his erstwhile provocative song "Inglan is a Bitch" (1980), in which a Jamaican migrant tells in the vernacular about a series of disillusioning experiences in London, has become an anthology piece. Benjamin Zephaniah (*1958, "Dis Poetry"), who switched between Jamaica and his native Birmingham in his youth, and

Jean 'Binta' Breeze (*1956), who came to London from Jamaica in 1985, were also dubbed Dub Poets, though this designation did not agree with Breeze. She brought out her collection *Spring Cleaning* in 1992, and within the same year appeared the collection *Rotten Pomerack* by the Grenadian poet Merle Collins (*1950), who lived and worked in London (1984–95) before she moved on to the USA. Apart from the outstanding performance poem "Crick Crack", which offers a Black and feminist view on race relations in history in the form of an Afro-Caribbean folktale, *Rotten Pomerack* contains also the performance poems "When Britain Had Its GREAT" and "What Ting Is Dat", which question Empire and ethnicity from a postcolonial and a migrant's point of view. With "Celtic" (2003, setting in with the phrase "She was brought up to lie/back and think of England"), London-born Patience Agbabi (*1965) followed up on *Transformatrix* (2000), her collection of poems that she continues to present successfully in live performances, and that earned her the accolade of being a *Next Generation Poet*.

Performance poetry as the more neutral term is better suited to embrace all those poems primarily conceived for the stage rather than the page, which are usually performed by their creators themselves. Sixties poets such as George MacBeth, Roger McGough and Adrian Mitchell as well as the bravura performer James Fenton should therefore be mentioned in this performance context, too, as well as two Northern artists. Around 1980, John Cooper Clarke (*1949) was seen as the rightful heir to the *Liverpool Poets* since he began to appear on the scene at the advent of Punk Music, closing the gap between performance poetry, stand-up comedy and pop music. (His lyrics are available online.) Joolz Denby (*1955) came out in a similar environment and has catered to audiences in Britain and abroad as a 'spoken-word artist' since the early 1980s. Although there is a fuzzy border between performance poetry and pop music, the **singer-songwriters** and their lyrics rightfully belong here, too (in difference to mere musicians). To give but a few examples, one may think of the lyrics produced by John Lennon (1940–80) and Paul McCartney (*1942) for *The Beatles*, of Sting (Gordon Sumner, *1951) for *The Police* and for his solo career, of Bono (Paul Hewson, *1960) for the Irish band *U2*, of his older Irish colleague Van Morrison (*1945), and of Joan Armatrading (*1950), who migrated to Britain from her native

Caribbean island of St. Kitts in 1957, to come out in 1976 as the first Black British singer-songwriter to achieve major success.

5.1.4 | Scottish, Welsh and Irish Poetry since the 1960s

Scottish Poetry

Poetry in Britain and Ireland in the twentieth century has not only profited from new voices and new perspectives originating abroad, but has also seen a regional accentuation. Let us therefore take a closer look at the development in Scotland, Wales and Ireland. The cultural and political history of Scotland was marked by two interrelated developments: the Scottish Renaissance that set in during the 1920s, and the political movement for Devolution (and perhaps future Scottish Independence) which peaked around the Millennium, accompanied by yet another literary renewal. Poetry played its part in both developments. As troublesome in poetry as he was in politics, Hugh MacDiarmid (pseudonym for Christopher Murray Grieve, 1892–1978) was a foundational figure in the **Scottish Renaissance** (so-called in response to the somewhat earlier Irish Renaissance). In 1928, MacDiarmid, a card-holding Communist, became one of the founders of the Scottish Nationalist Party, too, only to be expelled from both parties during the Thirties. In the same patriotic spirit, MacDiarmid (who was also a translator of Scottish Gaelic) revived Scots as a language of poetry. To be exact: in contrast to Robert Burns over a century earlier, who could still feed on a lively oral tradition, MacDiarmid had to forge his **'synthetic Scots' or Lallans** to a great extent from dictionaries and other written sources. MacDiarmid's *A Drunk Man Looks at the Thistle* (1926) made a great impact, not least because the poet fused Celtic Revival with Modernist renewal. MacDiarmid himself abstained from the use of Scots in his later poetry, while again presenting his Modernist credentials in his long poem *In Memoriam James Joyce* (1955).

With regard to language use, the Scottish Renaissance turned out to be a 'broad kirk' that allowed for variety within. Its multilingualism embraced poets who wrote in English, such as Edwin Muir (1887–1959, "Scotland in 1941"), Norman MacCaig (1910–96, "Aunt Julia") or George Mackay Brown (1921–96, "Kirkyard"). There were others who decided for Scots/Lallans, such as Robert Garioch (1909–81, see his sonnet "I'm Neutral"); and there were also Gaelic poets such as Sorley MacLean (Somhairle MacGill-Eain, 1911–96, "Hallaig"). By the 1960s, the direct impact of the Scottish Renaissance was no longer strongly felt, yet Scottish poets were at the avant-garde of experimentation. Ian Hamilton Finlay (1925–2006) engaged in **concrete poetry** (shaped verse in print) as well as in assembling stones with inscriptions into poetic installations in a natural environment. Edwin Morgan (*1920) responded to the American avant-garde composer John Cage with a 'sonnet' entitled "Opening the Cage: 14 Variations on 14 Words", and he wrote if not exactly Martian Poetry, then a witty piece of science poetry in "The First Men on Mercury". (*From Glasgow to Saturn*, 1973. To compare, see three decades later "Excursion to the Planet Mercury" by Alice Oswald, in *Woods etc.*)

In 2004, Edwin Morgan was appointed the *Scots Makar*, or National Poet for Scotland, thus effectively becoming Scotland's first Poet Laureate. Such office includes writing verse for the opening of Parliament, and in this task, Morgan had a precedent in Iain Crichton Smith (1928–98). This other notable poet of the older generation, who wrote in English and Gaelic, was commissioned with "The Beginning of a New Song", a poem to be read as part of the opening of the devolved Scottish Parliament in 1999. The renewed reunion of the literary and political movements within the Scottish cultural revival (both started off by MacDiarmid) is also in evidence in "St. Kilda's Parliament: 1879–1979" by Douglas Dunn as well as in "On the Design Chosen for the New Scottish Parliament Building [...]" by Kathleen Jamie. And if the promotional lists of *New* and *Next Generation Poets* are anything to go by, then the Scottish poetry scene, which was well served, is very much alive. Besides Kathleen Jamie (*1962), there are others among those chosen few who likewise write in English and in Scots, e.g. Robert Crawford (*1959, *A Scottish Assembly*) and Don Paterson. In "Homesick Paterson, Live at the *Blue Bannock*, Thurso" (1996), Paterson (*1963), who is also a jazz musician, remembered one of his gigs in a fusion of standard and vernacular English. The promotional lists included moreover John Burnside (*1955, "Dundee"), Robin Robertson (*1955, winner of the Forward Poetry Prize in 1996 for *A Painted Field* and in 2006 for *Swithering*). In addition to those who enjoyed such promotion, there are others who have already arrived. In *Terry Street* (1969), Douglas Dunn (*1942) observed the everyday life of impoverished citizens in a way that looked both to Larkin and to Harrison. The minimalism and colloquialism of Tom Leonard (*1944) show in "Unrelated Incidents" (which is characterised by aural spelling) as well as in "Ghostie Men" and "Dripping with Nostalgia". In addition to poems such as "Scotch Mist", Liz Lochhead (*1947) produced "Dreaming Frankenstein" and "An Abortion" which stress her feminist angle. Meg Bateman (*1959) writes poems in Gaelic, and translates her own poems and those of others into English (*"Lightness" ["Aotromachd"] and Other Poems*, 1997). Novelist, poet and performer Jackie Kay (*1961), finally, forged *The Adoption Papers* (1991) from her own experience, while she exploited English as well as a Scottish Brogue for comic purposes in poems such as "Brendon Gallacher" and "The Broons' Bairn's Black" (the title of which calls up MacDiarmid's "The Bonnie Broukit Bairn"). Some of these poets have done their share recently in editing anthologies that allow seeing their contemporaries, and also those poets of preceding generations, under different thematic angles. (See e. g. Crawford and Herbert 1990, Kerrigan 1991, Dunn 1992, Watson 1995, Crawford and Imlah 2000, Gifford and Riach 2004.)

Poetry from Wales

In some ways, the course of **poetry in Wales** over the twentieth century paralleled the development in Scotland. A literary revival at the beginning of the century paved the way for a second one towards the century's end, and for the political momentum that led to Devolution and to a Welsh Assembly. Religious overtones are noticeable already in the poetry of Dylan Thomas, who is sure to remain the best-known twentieth-century poet to hail from Wales. However, yet likewise in the English language, it was his namesake and contemporary, the Anglican priest R. S. Thomas (1913–2000) who had concerned himself much more with "Welsh History", with the landscape and the people of his native region, including the work of "The Country Clergy", but also the deterioration and decay of "The Welsh Hill Country". "Ancient Monuments" by John Ormond (1923–90) is thematically related to his concerns. The experience of those others (including many poets) who could or would not live such a permanently reclusive life at home as did R. S. Thomas, was captured by T. H. Jones (1921–65) in "The Welshman in Exile".

Dannie Abse (*1923) is such a Welshman in exile. In his poetry, he falls back thematically on his work as a doctor in London, his Jewish family background, and his Welsh nationality. The professional concern with the human body, but also with the human 'soul', comes out in the poem "In the Theatre", where Abse recreates, from the notes of his brother who assisted the surgeon, a brain operation gone wrong. The free-verse poem "White Balloon" (1990) is indicative of the second concern and sets in abruptly with the lines: "Dear love, Auschwitz made me/more of a Jew than Moses did." Outside his own poetry, Abse engaged himself in editing an anthology on *Twentieth-Century Anglo-Welsh Poetry* (Abse 1997), a collection that usefully supplements other anthologies that also chart *The Bright Field* (Stephens 1991) of poetry from Wales, be it in English (Garlick and Mathias 1982) or in the Welsh language (Jones 1977; Elfyn and Rowlands 2003).

By comparison, (Robert) Bobi Jones (*1929) is an example of a Welsh nationalist who made himself at home in Welsh as a second language, relying on others to translate his poems, e.g. "Aber-Porth" (which deals with an epiphany in this coastal town). Among the poets of a younger generation, Menna Elfyn (*1951) has followed his example, and has relied for instance on Gillian Clarke (*1937) as a translator. Gillian Clarke herself, who writes in English, has seen a good number of her poems selected for the GCSE syllabus in England and Wales. Among those set texts are poems on mothers, daughters and granddaughters ("Baby Sitting", "Catrin", "Mali"), and there are others focused on animals and country life (e.g. "A Difficult Birth, Easter 1998"). "The Field-Mouse" begs the comparison with "To a Mouse" by the Scottish poet Robert Burns, while the title of "October" echoes "Poem in October" by Dylan Thomas. Stephen Knight (*1960), an experimental poet in the (Post-)Modernist tradition, also uses English for his tall columns of free verse in *Flowering Limbs* (1993) and *Dream City Cinema* (1996). Gwyneth Lewis (*1959), finally, is an example of a bilingual poet who bridges the language divide and writes in English as well as in Welsh (her first volume of poetry was a sonnet sequence in Welsh, *Sonedau Redsa*, 1990). As the equivalent to Edwin Morgan in Scotland, this member of the *Next Generation* was appointed the first National Poet for Wales in 2005.

Due to the political context, there is no Irish equivalent to those National Poets, although the position of a Professor of Poetry for Ireland has been created in 1998. Clearly, however, the unofficial national poet of the Green Isle is Seamus Heaney, who had filled the post of Oxford Professor of Poetry (1989–1994) be-

Poetry in Ireland since the 1960s

Fig. 5.5

Seamus Heaney (on the right hand side, here together with Antoni Milosz) by Mariusz Kubik, 2004

fore he went on to win the Nobel Prize for Literature in 1995. Over the last decades, Heaney came to dominate the Irish poetry scene as no other poet has done since Yeats; and it may therefore be permissible to make him a recurrent focus within this section. Heaney has lived in Northern Ireland (where he was born in 1939, and where he once more made his home) as well as in the Republic (where he settled in 1973) and among the Irish abroad (in the early 1980s, he began to spend part of each year at US-American universities). After he had come into contact with Philip Hobsbaum and the *Belfast Group*, Heaney published his first collection, *Death of a Naturalist*, in 1966 to great acclaim. Poems such as "At a Potato Digging" centred on rural working life and on the potato as an ambivalent symbol of Irish history (including the Great Famine of 1845–50). The meta-poetical poem "Digging" established a link between the turf-cutting and potato-digging done by the lyrical speaker's grandfather and father, and the use of the poet's pen instead of the farmer's spade in order to dig deep into memory. In the Windeby Girl and other archaeological finds from the Viking period preserved in the moors, Heaney found a poetical metaphor which he turned to good use in the Bog Poems spanning his next collections. "Punishment" (from *North*, 1975) linked the drowned and found body of a young 'adulteress' – an ancient victim of cruel justice – to the present IRA punishments (shaving, tarring, stripping) of such girls said to have fraternised with British soldiers. In accentual verse, "Casualty" (from *Field Work*, 1979) spoke directly of the victims of the bombings and shootings in Ulster after the Bloody Sunday in Derry in 1972. By contrast, the same collection contained love poems that celebrated sensual life, and at the same time signalled an interest in the natural world, too, through their startling animal imagery (an otter and a skunk). The sonnet sequences entitled "Glanmore Sonnets" (1979) and "Clearances" (1987) moreover involved a sounding out of poetic conventions by a writer who so far had made more use of accentual and of free verse, and thus had been more akin to Ted Hughes, with whom he teamed up twice as an anthologist (see above). Heaney had avoided following Yeats too far on his way into Irish legend, but then a concern with the mythological character Mad Sweeney made itself felt in the sequences *Sweeney Astray* (1983) and "Sweeney Redivivus" (1984). Finally, "From the Frontier of Writing" (1987, in tercets) can be seen as a variation upon the meta-literary theme of "Digging", as Heaney applied the theme of border inspections and of crossing boundaries to the act of writing. Heaney went on to publish altogether eleven collections between 1966 and 2006, the last of which (*District and Circle*) won the T. S. Eliot Prize.

In 1983, Heaney fuelled his anger over his (prominent) inclusion in Morrison and Motion's anthology of 'British' poetry into *An Open Letter* in verse, and that epistle printed as a pamphlet marked out the way to the Field Day Publishing cooperative that Heaney founded in 1984 together with the dramatist Brian Friel and others. This move in turn led to the re-canonisation of Irish literature in the two series of *The Field Day Anthology of Irish Writing*, which was first edited by Seamus Deane in 1991, and later supplemented with a view on *Irish Women's Writing and Tradition* by Angela Bourke and others in 2002. This, then, is the right moment to mention other notable poets, first those from the Republic of Ireland. Patrick Kavanagh (1904–67) was opposed to a false glorification of Irish peasant life for nationalist purposes, and approached his long narrative poem *The Great Hunger* (1942) with Social Realism in mind, yet as a Modernist in form. The best-selling poet Brendan Kennelly (*1936) centred on history in *Cromwell* (1983), while Eavan Boland (*1944), who is generally known for writing poetry from a woman's point of view (e.g. "The Oral Tradition"), addressed the 1916 Easter Rising in "The Doll's Museum in Dublin" (1994). Thomas Kinsella (*1928, "Ancestor") translated from the Gaelic. Nuala Ní Dhomhnaill (*1952) has published in Gaelic since 1981, and she found translators in the Northern Irish poets Medbh McGuckian (*1950) and Paul Muldoon (*1951).

The Northern Irish poet Louis MacNeice (1907–63, "Belfast") was mentioned already as a member of the Auden circle in Oxford. Other Ulster residents who came out as poets before the 1960s include John Hewitt (1907–87, "The Irish Dimension"). At Queen's University, Belfast, Seamus Heaney joined the *Belfast Group* assembled by Philip Hobsbaum between 1962 and 1966, which also included Derek Mahon (*1941) and Michael Longley (*1939). Much like Heaney in his "Digging" poems, Mahon unearthed hidden historical layers in "Lives" (dedicated to Heaney) and in "A Disused Shed in Co. Wexford" (dedicated to the historical novelist J. G. Farrell). In the title of Mahon's elegy "A Refusal to Mourn", there is an echo of Dylan Thomas's earlier piece. Longley's "Letter to Derek Mahon" talks about 'the Troubles', i.e. the sectarian conflict in Northern Ireland, which Ciarán Carson (*1948) moved centre-stage in *Belfast Confetti* (1990). After Carson in his turn had written back to MacNeice in his poem "Bagpipe Music" (1993), he focused again on his hometown in *The Ballad of HMS Belfast: A Compendium of Belfast Poems* (1999). In recent years, Carson had turned his energy to translating first the French poets Baudelaire, Rimbaud and Mallarmé (*The Alexandrine Plan*, 1998), then *The Inferno of Dante Alighieri* (2002), and finally the medieval Irish epic *Táin Bó Cúailnge* (*The Táin*, 2007). In this, Carson invited the comparison with Kinsella's *The Táin* (1969), and perhaps also with Heaney's Modern English version of the Anglo-Saxon epic *Beowulf* (1999).

One of the teachers, when Paul Muldoon (*1951) read English at Queen's University, Belfast, was Seamus Heaney, whom Muldoon succeeded later as Oxford Professor of Poetry. In between, Muldoon had worked as a producer for the BBC (much like MacNeice). In "Anseo" (from the collection *Why Brownlee Left*, 1980), Muldoon jumps from a schoolboy's memory of corporal punishment to the discipline among IRA irregulars during 'the Troubles', by introducing the Gaelic word in the title (which translates as 'here, I'm present') as a narrative link. The casual introduction of Gaelic words into an English context as well as the testing out of the sonnet form (in a triple sonnet in free verse) are both hallmarks of Muldoon's style. Shortly before he left Ireland to teach as a professor at US-American universities (again, like Heaney), Muldoon published *Meeting the British* (1987). This time, the title poem to the collection serves as an introduction to Muldoon's obliquely referential manner, which is not always easy to disentangle. "Meeting the British" is set during the eighteenth-century French and Indian Wars in America, but it seems to equate Indian-British relations then with Irish-British relations then and now. In this bitterly sarcastic poem, personal contact leads to contact disease, and in consequence to physical and cultural annihilation. "Incantata" (from *The Annals of Chile*, 1994) is one of Muldoon's more accessible long poems, yet laden with references ranging from Samuel Beckett's *Waiting for Godot* over the IRA victims Airey Neave and Lord Mountbatten to painters and pop musicians. Muldoon's collection *Hay* (1998) included a sequence on various pop musicians entitled "Sleeve Notes" and a great number of sonnets and poems in fourteen lines, e.g. the title poem; the funny schoolroom reminiscence called "The Point"; the likewise humorous sonnet "Symposium" which consists of a list of cliché phrases given an extra twist; a sequence of 30 sonnets entitled "The Bangle (Slight Return)" and a further series of 110 "Hopewell Haiku". With such credentials, Muldoon was elected Oxford Professor of Poetry (1999–2004).

When Muldoon left that post, the *Next Generation* of poets was promoted. The list included Leontia Flynn (*1974), who had published *These Days*, her first collection, in 2004. To keep up to date on the island's poetry scene and on the various literary festivals that also serve as venues for readings and performances of poetry, see the website of the national organisation *Poetry Ireland/Éigse Éireann*.

Summing Up a Century in Sonnets | 5.1.5

Looking back on the poetry produced in Britain and Ireland during the twentieth century, one may say indeed that there was a multifarious development – not only in the diverse regions of the British Isles, but also with regard to the three, at times overlapping tendencies marked out for the sake of presentation. While free verse for the first time has become a widely used form of poetic expression, it never reigned supreme. Generally speaking, the movement towards free verse was held in check not only by ongoing innovation in the field of metrical verse, but also by the alternative yet likewise 'new', accentual and syllabic forms of verse. On the individual level, too, the use of free verse was tampered in the work of most poets by the parallel use of alternative forms of expression: Auden's elegy on Yeats is a case in point. Yet although this century provided enough occasions for elegies in various churchyards, there was no pressure to take Gray's model as a pattern (as Tony Harrison did for *V.*). The conscious urge to excel in, or perhaps to further develop one or more poetic kinds also seems to have been the exception rather than the rule. The ode as a once highly esteemed poetic kind definitely appears to have suffered in the period under review. It may be that in times of totalitarian propaganda abroad and of "blood, toil, tears and sweat" at home (as Winston Churchill offered a nation at war), songs in praise of outstanding contemporaries or ideals lost much of their appeal to English-speaking poets and their audiences. "Epilogue to an Empire, 1600–1900: An Ode for Trafalgar Day" by Jon Stallworthy (1969; in Baker 1988: 423–24) and Tony Harrison's "Celebratory Ode on the Abdication of King Charles III" (1995) did not disprove this rule.

However, as Auden's example proves, too, a likewise time-honoured and technically demanding kind such as the villanelle did not vanish once Modernism had entered the scene. It was again loaded up with new meaning when used for light verse (e.g. by Wendy Cope) as well as for deadly earnest matter (e.g. by Dylan Thomas). The sonnet tradition at first looked to be discontinued by Modernism, as already before during the Age of Neoclassicism. When he collected his own poetry, Eliot as much as his predecessors Dryden and Pope did not wish to be seen as having dabbled with the form. Yet the sonnet did not become outmoded through Modernism. A perhaps surprising fact is the frequency in which poets up to and including those of the *New* and of the *Next Generation* have attested to the liveliness of the sonnet tradition. Therefore, a summary look at this development will round off the present chapter.

After the sonnets written by poets of the Great War such as Wilfred Owen, the form continued to be used, single and in sequences (as was pointed out in each case above), by Yeats and Auden (on the theme of war), by both Roy and John Fuller (on any theme), by Dylan Thomas and Geoffrey Hill (in unrhymed manner), and by Wendy Cope (on rhyming men). There are sonnets from all regions of the British Isles: Seamus Heaney trailed his single sonnets "Requiem for the Croppies" (1969) and "Act of Union" (1975) first with "Glanmore Sonnets" (1979) and then with the elegiac sonnet sequence "Clearances" (1987). Edwin Morgan, the *Scots Makar*, followed up his *Glasgow Sonnets* (1972) with *Sonnets from Scotland* (1984), while his Welsh counterpart Gwyneth Lewis embarked on her career with the Welsh sequence *Sonedau Redsa* (1990). And they did not remain alone: Don Paterson tested out the form himself (e.g. in the sequence "Exeunt", 1993) before he edited an anthology entitled *101 Sonnets: From Shakespeare to Heaney* (1999) and then translated Rilke's *Sonnets to Orpheus* (2006). By this time, Paul Muldoon had already come up with "Rainer Maria Rilke: *The Unicorn*" (for Ted Hughes, 1995), with the sonnets lending their titles to *Why Brownlee Left* (1980) and *Quoof* (1983), and with the many further sonnets and fourteen-line poems in *Hay* (1998). In turn, Muldoon had Ciarán Carson's collection *The Twelfth of Never: Seventy-Seven Sonnets* (1998) dedicated to him.

In *We Brits* (2006) by performance poet John Agard, there is surprisingly also a good number of proper sonnets or variations upon that form. "Ave Eliza" comes as a recollection of Queen Elizabeth I, who fended off the Spanish Armada, only to find herself surprised by another invasion, which saw her "realm growing motley with Blackamoors." (l. 14). "Newton's Amazing Grace" is spoken by another historical, eighteenth-century character: John Newton had been the captain of one of those slave ships embarking on the Middle Passage, before he was seized by religious fervour and became the composer of "Amazing Grace" and other hymns. "Toussaint L'Ouverture Acknowledges Wordsworth's Sonnet 'To Toussaint L'Ouverture'" (44) is an answer poem and a postcolonial counter-discourse, spoken by the leader of the slave rebellion that brought about the first Black republic in Haiti. Finally, the Caribbean flavour of "Chilling Out Beside the Thames" (45) lies in the use made of Caribbean Creole to render the voice of a present-day immigrant in London.

Some traits of the sonnet tradition were singled out for further use. Carol Ann Duffy referred to Shakespeare in person in "Anne Hathaway" (1999), and she evoked a seventeenth-century religious tradition in "Prayer" (1993), though this is a poem for faithless times (much like Auden's "Lullaby"). The Miltonian tradition of the political sonnet came alive again, at a high point of the Vietnam War, in James Fenton's prize-winning sequence "Our Western Furniture" (1968) on the confrontation between East and West a century earlier. A shift to Black and White race relations in history occurred in Fred D'Aguiar's irregular poem "Mama Dot" (1985) and in "The Last Sonnet About Slavery" (2001). A mix of the political and the personal can be found in the two long sequences by George Szirtes that were already mentioned, namely in *Metro* (1988) and in "An English Apocalypse" (2001).

Finally, unconventional variations upon the established models abound. Alice Oswald's collections *The Thing in the Gap-Stone Stile* (1996) and *Woods etc.* (2005) contain a greater number of fourteen-line poems, some of which are simply called "Sonnet", and there is also "Another Westminster Bridge" (in *Woods etc.*) to compare to Wordsworth's precedent. Douglas Dunn's "Little Rich Rhapsody" and "Modern Love" come as unrhymed accentual verse. The latter takes up the title, but not the form of George Meredith's 1862 sequence, nor do the sixteen-line 'sonnets' in

Tony Harrison's ongoing sequence *The School of Eloquence* conform to Meredith's variant pattern. For further examples of irregular sequences, see Simon Armitage's *Book of Matches* (1993) and Fred D'Aguiar's "Sonnets from Whitley Bay" as well as "Frail Deposits" (from the same year). Clearly, four centuries after the first Elizabethan 'Sonnet Craze', this poetic tradition has not phased out. In this second Elizabethan Age, there continue to be sonnets galore – for this and the *Next Generation*.

Guiding Questions and Exercises

1. Try to summarise distinctive features of the poetry of W. B. Yeats, T. S. Eliot, D. H. Lawrence and Ted Hughes by comparing their use of animal imagery.

2. Discuss in more detail Hughes's poems "Hawk Roosting" (1957), "The Jaguar" (1957) and "Pike" (1960) with reference to respective counterparts such as "The Windhover" by G. M. Hopkins (1877/1918), "Der Panther" by Rainer Maria Rilke (in German, 1902), and "The Pike" by Edmund Blunden (1919).

3. Together with "The Circus Animals' Desertion", "The Man and the Echo" and "Under Ben Bulben", "Sailing to Byzantium" forms a series of retro- and introspections by W. B. Yeats in advanced age. The poet's metaphor of a boat-trip into another world can be found, too, in Lord Tennyson's "Crossing the Bar" (1889), a shorter, lyrical poem that the Laureate wanted to stand as his poetic epitaph. Moreover, these poems compare to the poetical 'last words' and epitaphs of Lord Byron ("January 22nd [1824]. Missolonghi. On this day I complete my thirty sixth year"), of Emily Brontë ("No coward soul is mine", 1850), of Gerard Manley Hopkins ("Thou art indeed just, Lord", 1889/1918) and of Thomas Hardy ("He Never Expected Much", 1928). How do all these poems (in theme and form) deal with individually variant views on life, death and Deity?

4. Relate Dylan Thomas's poems "A Refusal to Mourn the Death, by Fire, of a Child in London" (1945) and "Do not go gentle into that good night" (1951) to "A Child Ill" (1954) and "On a Portrait of a Deaf Man" (1940), both by John Betjeman, to account for the individual habits of the two contemporary poets.

5. In their poems "Leda and the Swan" (1924) and "The Shield of Achilles" (1952), W. B. Yeats and W. H. Auden, respectively,

used the Homeric epics to conceive of politics and war in their own time. Compare the two poems as to their line of argument in relation to their poetic form.

6. After his death, W.H. Auden became the addressee both of the commemorative "Eulogy to W.H. Auden" by the Caribbean poet Derek Walcott (1983, included in *The Arkansas Testament*, London: Faber, 1988, 61–65), and of "Memo to Auden" (1997) by Anne Rouse, a poet who was born in the USA but went to live to Britain, thus reversing Auden's own migration. In "Memo to Auden" (which can be found in *Making for Planet Alice: New Women Poets*, ed. Maura Dooley, Newcastle upon Tyne: Bloodaxe Books, 1997, 153–55), Anne Rouse alluded to Auden's poems "In Memory to W.B. Yeats" and "September 1, 1939" (ll. 27–33, 43–48). Discuss Walcott's and Rouse's answer poems, together with relevant poems by Auden, in the light of their poetics and politics.

7. Try to account for the development of the sonnet, and for the character of sonnet sequences, in the poetry of Wilfred Owen, W.H. Auden, Dylan Thomas, Roy Fuller, Edwin Morgan, Tony Harrison, Seamus Heaney, Wendy Cope and Simon Armitage. If this list does not sound too long already, you might further like to include the Black Jamaican-American poet Claude McKay (1890–1948) in the comparison.

8. Have a look at the section on Romantic poetry (chap. 3.3) for a suggested comparison (first) between P.B. Shelley's "Ode to the West Wind" and the thematically related poems "Why east wind chills" by Dylan Thomas and "Facing North" by Tony Harrison, and (second) between Harrison's "A Kumquat for John Keats" and the "Ode on Melancholy" by Keats.

Drama and Theatre | 5.2

New Spaces for Performance and New Media | 5.2.1

Since the mid-nineteenth century, theatre in Britain had been dominated by the long-run system, which favoured the production of a few long-running plays with star actors over a playbill which listed a greater variety of plays performed *en suite* over a period. Annie Horniman, who was also giving her financial backing to Dublin's Abbey Theatre, brought about a change in

The Repertory Theatre Movement and the West End Theatreland

1908, when she founded the first provincial repertory theatre in England at the Gaiety in Manchester. Other **'provincial reps'** followed at Glasgow (1909–15), Liverpool (1911) and Birmingham (1913). The Old Vic in London was also turned into a repertory-style theatre in 1914, when it began to stage all of Shakespeare's plays over a period of nine years. Further to that, repertory theatres provided opportunities to see the work of promising British playwrights and of renowned dramatists from the Continent. By comparison, the mainstream **West End** theatres in London's 'Theatreland' have continued to rely on long-running shows. Agatha Christie's criminal play *The Mousetrap* set the record with more than 23,000 performances since 1952. Between the two world wars, the typical ingredients of music hall and variety entertainment – the combination of songs and dance, sketches and stand-up comedy – found a new expression in the **revues** produced by Charles Cochran. Noël Coward (see below) proved to be a successful scriptwriter, and Ivor Novello (1893–1951) a gifted composer for such revues. A decided break with Victorian Values occurred in the nude revues staged by Laura Henderson at the Windmill Theatre in the 1930s and throughout the Second World War, which made streetwise Londoners turn the theatre's slogan "We Never Closed" more directly on the Windmill Girls, as "We Never Clothed". (In *Mrs Henderson Presents*, the 2005 movie on this revue theatre, Judi Dench impersonated the impresario.) The West End – like its New York equivalent, the Broadway – also became the home of the **musical**. Long-running shows include the Cockney musical *Me and My Girl* by Noel Gay (1937), and also *My Fair Lady* (1956, film version 1963), an adaptation of Shaw's *Pygmalion* by the American team of Alan Jay Lerner (lyrics) and Frederick Loewe (music). Since the 1970s, the musicals of Andrew Lloyd Webber (*1948) have also held sway in the West End. In collaboration with lyricists such as Tim Rice or Trevor Nunn, Lloyd Webber produced record-breaking shows that drew on a variety of sources and themes, ranging from secular saints such as Evita Perón (*Evita*, 1976) to the Biblical Messiah (*Jesus Christ Superstar*, 1970), and from the light verse of T.S. Eliot (*Cats*, 1981) to a heavily melodramatic French novel (*The Phantom of the Opera*, 1986).

Actors and Directors

In both commercial theatres and in those playhouses subsidised by the tax-payer, you will still find the traditional system of star actors and actresses: from John Gielgud and Laurence Olivier to Michael Caine and Ian McKellen, and from Peggy Ashcroft to Judi Dench and Diana Rigg, to name but a few. From the 1930s to the 1960s, Gielgud and Olivier revived the tradition of actor-managers in Shakespeare productions on the stage and on the screen. Since the 1960s at the latest, such an **actors' theatre** has been paralleled and replaced by a **directors' theatre** that created a new type of stardom for influential *stage directors* such as Peter Brook (*1925) and John Barton (*1928) who were in control of an individual production, as well as for *artistic directors* such as Tyrone Guthrie (1900–71), Peter Hall (*1930), Trevor Nunn (*1940), Adrian Noble (*1950) and Nicholas Hytner (*1956) that moreover were in charge of a theatre's or a company's entire programme.

A proper British counterpart to the Abbey Theatre, which had begun to be subsidised by the Irish Free State in 1924, had to wait until the establishment of the **(Royal) National Theatre** at Chichester Festival Theatre and at the Old Vic (1962). The NT as another repertory theatre had its first artistic directors in Laurence Olivier and then in Peter Hall (1973–88). With Hall, who had earlier on (1960–68) founded and directed the **Royal Shakespeare Company** (RSC, see chap. 5.2.3), the NT moved into its new permanent building on London's South Bank (1976). Yet perhaps the single most influential production space in Britain in the latter half of the twentieth century was another London playhouse: the **Royal Court Theatre**. There, in Sloane Square, Harley Granville-Barker had made Shaw's name famous a decade before the first of two world wars. Exactly eleven years after the ending of the second, on 8 May 1956, the Royal Court's artistic director George Devine (1910–66) once again wrote theatrical history when he premièred John Osborne's play *Look Back in Anger*. Ever since, the Royal Court has taken pride in being a **writers' theatre**, as Dublin's Abbey Theatre had been when managed by Lady Gregory, Yeats and Synge. During the 1960s, the theatre and the playwrights John Osborne and Edward Bond ran into persistent conflict with the Lord Chamberlain as official censor, a process that led – after more than 400 years – to the **abolition of stage censorship** in Britain with the 1968 Theatres Act. (The situation in Ireland differed from that in Britain – because the Lord Chamberlain's powers had not extended to Ireland.) A year later, the smaller Theatre Upstairs opened as the Royal Court's studio theatre. Devine's successor as artistic director was Max Stafford-Clark (*1941), who

The NT and the Royal Court Theatre

successfully and over a long period (1979–93) found in Sloane Square a public for the avant-garde. Stafford-Clark's name is linked, too, with his direction of new writing for the stage at the Traverse Theatre, Edinburgh (Scotland's equivalent to the Royal Court, established in 1963), and with the foundation of two renowned London-based companies. With their workshops and productions, both the Joint Stock Theatre Company (1974–89) and the touring company Out of Joint (from 1993) have made an impact on young dramatists and their audiences.

Theatre Festivals and Other Venues

Outside the repertory, theatre festivals have provided a good opportunity to see new writing for the stage. The Malvern Festival (1929–49, revived in 1977) prominently included the work of Shaw among that of other contemporaries, and thus set an example for the creation of the **Edinburgh International Festival** in 1947. Together with other Edinburgh festivals taking place annually in August, this became the world's largest arts festival, breaking ground for the Dublin Theatre Festival (from 1957) and the London International Festival of Theatre (since 1981). The exclusion of more radical and also Scottish companies from the first Edinburgh Festival led to the creation (within the same year) of the Edinburgh Festival Fringe – or just **The Fringe** – as a venue for **alternative or fringe theatre**. Throughout the year, such plays by new playwrights addressing contemporary issues in unconventional ways, can be seen in studio theatres such as Edinburgh's Traverse Theatre or in The Bush Theatre, which opened above a West London pub in 1972. To round the story off, one should mention two other London theatres that distinguished themselves in their own way. At the Theatre Royal Stratford East, artistic director Joan Littlewood (1914–2002), together with the Theatre Workshop, pioneered **community theatre** between 1953 and 1975, and moreover employed the improvisation by actors as a method of production. Under Littlewood's successors, the focus of productions shifted from the experience of local East Enders to that of the new immigrant communities. Since 1980, Irish, Jewish, Black and Asian communities and their experience have also been targeted in plays staged at the Tricycle Theatre, which has moreover become renowned for **documentary theatre** based on public inquiries, such as *Guantánamo* (2004, see below). Documentary theatre contests the coverage of the news in print as well as in radio and television, and thus tips the scales between the media.

Altogether, the impact of the new media on stage drama has been an ambivalent one, implying a serious threat and likewise more security, as well as an opportunity for the creation of something "fresh". In 1896, only one year after its invention, the Lumière brothers brought the *cinématographe* to London. In the next decades, British actors and directors such as Charlie Chaplin and Alfred Hitchcock were to excel in 'silent movies' and in 'talking pictures', or 'talkies' – but not to everyone's delight:

Literature and the Movies

> The cinema, more than any other cultural phenomenon, was seen as the greatest threat to theatre. [...] The new form cut across class barriers. Almost everyone went to the cinema, largely seeing the same films, [...]. By 1929 there were some 3,300 cinemas in Britain, [...]. By the late 1930s some 20 million British people attended the cinema weekly, with an estimated 25 per cent going twice or more each week. [...]
> Inevitably, the popularity of cinema worried theatre managements, but it also provided a new avenue of expression for playwrights and more lucrative work for actors and actresses. The cinema industry borrowed, absorbed and exploited the star system, feeding on popular stage successes by making them into films for mass distribution. The rise of cinema, though, hardly depleted London theatre audiences in this period (Thomson 2004: III, 154).

The theatre's response to the movies was manifold. The musical revues that became so popular after the First World War were Theatreland's answer to the film industry. A war later, this can be said of other successful West End shows. The satirical revue *Oh! What a Lovely War* (by Joan Littlewood and the Theatre Workshop, 1963) used a First Wold War setting to question the mechanisms of social conformity (see Thomson 2004: III, 397–411). The nude revue *Oh! Calcutta!* (1969) – an icon of the Swinging Sixties with over 2,400 West End performances to its credit – was arranged by the drama critic Kenneth Tynan from sketches written by Samuel Beckett, Sam Shepard, Edna O'Brien and John Lennon, all of which exploited the new liberties to express the libido after the ending of stage censorship. Andrew Lloyd Webber's musicals are another good but quite different example, as they have been made available simultaneously in several media: they were pre-released as a soundtrack record and then reworked into a film version that however rather stimulated the interest in the live performance on stage, in the West End and elsewhere. (For theatrical history, see Thomsen 1980, Thomson 2004 and Richards 2004.)

It is not easy to tell stimulus and response apart in these intermedial exchanges, and it is certainly not only the cinema, but also such popular stage revues and musicals that by their sheer success constantly narrow the space for more serious dramatic entertainment. However, even here we find crossover developments. Celebrated actors were involved in the creation of ambitious films that, far from doing disservice to earlier stage productions, rather preserved and heightened the effect of the original effort. Laurence Olivier for example directed and took the lead in three adaptations of Shakespeare for the screen. "Once more unto the breach, dear friends" (III.1): Olivier's 1944 colour film *Henry V*, with its scenes of fighting in medieval France, was a patriotic war effort explicitly dedicated to the Allied Forces that had landed on the Normandy beaches barely a month before the film's release. In 1948, Olivier followed this up with an expressive psychological study (in black and white) of an Oedipal *Hamlet*, and then with his colourful portrait of a black villain: *Richard III*. Based on the celebrated 1944 Old Vic production, this 1955 movie reached an even greater audience a year later, when it was released in the USA simultaneously through cinema and television. In 1995, actor Ian McKellen wrote the script for a fresh film version of *Richard III* (dir. Richard Loncraine) that adapted the 1992 NT stage production (dir. Richard Eyre) in which McKellen had already taken the lead. In this modernisation of a classic as a piece of alternative history, King Richard appears (plausibly) as a Fascist dictator in a 1930s Britain that never was. Olivier found another successor in Kenneth Branagh, who first formed his own company of actors before he contested Olivier in the cinema as actor and director: in the anti-war movie *Henry V* (1989), in the delightful comedy *Much Ado About Nothing* (1993), and in a *Hamlet* film that proclaimed to conflate all textual versions (1996; see Helbig 1999: 194–202).

Further than to actors and directors, the cinema presented a welcome opportunity to playwrights to develop another side of their talent, and "put money in thy purse" (*Othello*, I.3.340/342). John Osborne adapted Henry Fielding's novel *Tom Jones* for the screen (1963); Tom Stoppard wrote the screenplays for *Brazil* (1983, realised 1985) and for *Shakespeare in Love* (1998); while David Hare's script (2002) added an intermedial side to Michael Cunningham's intertextual novel *The Hours* (1998), which includes a portrait of Virginia Woolf. The screenplays by Harold Pinter,

Christopher Hampton and Hanif Kureishi were later published in collections of their own. His own plays apart, Pinter's intermedial adaptations range from the thriller *The Quiller Memorandum* (1965/66) over John Fowles's experimental novel *The French Lieutenant's Woman* (1969, film 1981) and Margaret Atwood's dystopia *The Handmaid's Tale* (1985/90) to Ian McEwan's disturbing novella *The Comfort of Strangers* (1981/90), while Christopher Hampton provided the shooting script for the filming of McEwan's *Atonement* (2001/07). Hanif Kureishi's fame as a writer of screenplays (*My Beautiful Laundrette*, 1985) preceded that as a novelist who adapted himself (*The Buddha of Suburbia*, 1990/93). Other novelists turned their colleagues' novels into screenplays, too: McEwan himself adapted Timothy Mo's *Sour Sweet* (1982/88), and Ruth Prawer Jhabvala even won two Academy Awards ('Oscars') for her screenplays based on E. M. Forster's *A Room with a View* (1908/86) and *Howard's End* (1910/92) that were at the heart of the nostalgic Heritage Cinema genre.

A further effect of the new media was that they led to the creation of new dramatic kinds. Within a year after its initial radio broadcasts of 1922, the British Broadcasting Corporation pioneered **radio drama** with the first Shakespeare adaptations, followed up by the first original radio play in 1924. Together with the radio plays of Louis MacNeice (who began to work for the BBC in 1941), *Under Milk Wood: A Play for Voices* by Dylan Thomas (1954) constituted a breakthrough. Among those who later successfully produced drama for the new electronic medium are Tom Stoppard and Caryl Churchill. (See Thomsen 1985 and Crook 1999.) Comparatively early, namely in the 1950s, the **television play** was institutionalised with series such as *Armchair Theatre* (ABC, 1956–74), *The Wednesday Play* (BBC, 1964–70) and *Play for Today* (BBC, 1970–84). The class of TV dramatists includes the names of, again, Harold Pinter (from *A Night Out*, 1960), Alan Bennett (appropriately continuing with *A Day Out* in 1972), David Mercer (*A Suitable Case for Treatment*, 1965) and Dennis Potter (*Stand Up, Nigel Barton*, 1965). The 'classic' piece from the era of the **single play** is *Cathy Come Home* (directed by Ken Loach from a script by Jeremy Sandford, 1966). Since the 1970s, the single play had to compete with an increasing number of serials and mini series. "Radio and television drama borrowed the serial from the magazine and the series from the novel and developed an array of new dramatic

Literature for Electronic Media: Radio Play and Television Play genres to fit them, from soap opera and sitcom to the police and hospital drama" (Edgar 2008a: 105). They are exemplified by long-running (albeit intermittent) **serials** such as *Rumpole of the Bailey* (by John Mortimer, ITV, 1978–92), by situation comedies or *sitcoms* such as *Yes, Minister* and *Yes, Prime Minister* (by Jonathan Lynn and Anthony Jay, BBC, 1980–88), and by *soap operas* such as *Brookside* (Channel 4, 1982–2003) and *EastEnders* (BBC, from 1985). In addition, one finds politically committed **mini series** such as Alan Bleasdale's *Boys from the Blackstuff* (BBC, 1982) and *GBH* (Channel 4, 1991), or genre parodies such as *The Singing Detective*. This six-part series by Dennis Potter (BBC, 1986) veered between a parody of Raymond Chandler's crime fiction and a psychological interest of its own. Potter's Philip Marlow as a re-incarnation of Chandler's gumshoe Marlowe is not the only example of **intertextuality and intermediality**. If already the onset of the radio play was marked by Shakespeare adaptations, British television soon followed suit in what became a tradition of its own. When classics were adapted for the TV screen, canonisation worked in both ways:

> The adaptation of classic literature, or more precisely the construction of certain literary works as classic – the classic serial – has been a characteristic of British television almost since television began. Certainly, since television resumed its normal service in 1946, the novels of Jane Austen, the Brontë sisters, Conrad, Dickens, Hardy, and Henry James, have been adapted and sometimes readapted. (Caughie 2000: 207, with further details)

Irish Television Play

As the beginnings of broadcasting coincided with the partition of Ireland, we find a parallel development of the new electronic media in the British province of Ulster and in the Irish Free State (later the Republic of Ireland). The first broadcasts of BBC Radio Ulster in 1924 were swiftly answered by the Free State's establishment of Radio Éireann two years later. However, Irish politicians greeted television with scepticism for a long time. This is why Telefis Éireann (RTÉ) went on air not before 1961 – once again trailing by two years the establishment of its counterpart, the private Ulster Television station (UTV) – and additional programmes (including an Irish-language TV channel) made themselves felt only after 1996. As a consequence, the television play in Ireland became marked out at a later date, too. Initially, the playbill was dominated by the adaptations of stage-plays: a piece by J. M. Synge was shown within the first week of television broadcasting. In the Republic, the religious themes and the high ratio of Catholic priests and nuns among the characters was characteristic of many early television plays. What paved the way for contemporary realism and also working-class life on the screen were the long-running Irish soap operas such as *Tolka Row* (1964–68) and *The Riordans* (1965–79), that RTÉ included in its programme to counter British serials such as *The Archers* (BBC Radio, from 1950), *Coronation Street* (ITV, from 1960) and *Crossroads* (ITV, 1964–88). Both Irish single plays and serials countered the global influence of serials produced in the USA, and transmitted to Ireland via British television stations. (For the development of the television play, see Brandt 1993, Bignell et al. 2000, Caughie 2000, Krewani 2001, Sheehan 2001 and Duguid 2005.)

Well-Made Plays and Verse Plays

| 5.2.2

Apart from its response to the new media and from its re-negotiation of performance space, the theatre cherished its own traditions, too. The drama presented on London stages between the 1890s and the 1950s showed much continuity. (When there is no other venue indicated, all plays mentioned throughout this chapter premièred in the West End.) In both its comic and its more serious forms, the outlook of these well-made plays was predominantly realistic, domestic and middle-class. Oscar Wilde's successful negotiation of the Restoration comedy of wit with Victorian values continued in **drawing room plays** that probed bourgeois manners and morality. In the plays by William Somerset Maugham (1874–1965), the drawing room was put to various uses. With its temporary return of a 'woman with a past' into the family, Maugham's *The Circle* (1921) compares to *Lady Windermere's Fan* and it is likewise more of a comedy of manners than a problem play. Just when the grandmother returns with the lover for whom she left her husband, her granddaughter begins to follow in her tracks, and to start the circle anew. Through many entertaining twists of dialogue and of plot, *The Circle* runs its course, touching upon the poles of romantic and of pragmatic love, and of faithfulness inside and outside of marriage. Marital in/fidelity was again a theme in *The Constant Wife* (premièred on Broadway, 1926), where Somerset Maugham played around with the notion of 'constancy' in a way that was reminiscent of Wilde's *The Importance of Being Earnest*

| Fig. 5.6
W. Somerset Maugham by Carl van Vechten, 1934

(up to the echo of the play's title and theme in the name of the female lead, Constance Middleton). In *The Letter* (1927), Somerset Maugham adapted one of his own short stories with an exotic South East Asian setting (a companion-piece to "The Force of Circumstance", 1926) to tell a melodramatic tale of adultery and murder, inter-racial and homosexual desire. While the many film versions of *The Letter* focused on the murder mystery related to the female lead character (impersonated by star actresses such as Bette Davis), the most recent 1995 and 2007 London revivals of this stage-play stressed either its colonial and racial or its homosexual subtext. A more sombre than melodramatic drawing room play was *For Services Rendered* (1932), which depicted the experience and effects of the First World War on various members of a middle-class family. The bitterness with which human sacrifice and patriotic propaganda were targeted compared well with Wilfred Owen's anti-war poem "Dulce Et Decorum Est", which did not appeal to the likes of Yeats, and this may also explain why Somerset Maugham's piece was originally less well received, and is only now seen as one of his dramatic achievements.

20th-Century Comedies of Manners

In their witty dialogue, the drawing room comedies of Noël Coward (1899–1973) – up to *Suite in Three Keys* (1966), his final trilogy set in a penthouse suite – were even more congenial to those of Oscar Wilde. *Hay Fever* (1925) is a farcical comedy of bad manners, in which the members of an eccentric family called Bliss first invite weekend guests independently of each other, only to irritate them altogether. In his treatment of sexual morality and marriage, Coward was increasingly less in conformity with Victorian values. Together with Somerset Maugham and Terence Rattigan, Noël Coward shared Oscar Wilde's homosexual orientation; yet though their plays may include oblique references to 'the love that dare not speak its name' (as in Coward's *The Vortex*, 1924), none of these playwrights chose to confront the taboo topic in their time. Instead, Noël Coward likewise turned to marital in/fidelity as a comic theme. In *Private Lives* (1930), a divorced couple reunites while on honeymoon with their new partners, then separates anew, only to reunite once more ... Everlasting love or falling in love again? The problems of bringing a *ménage à trois* to life were at the heart of *Design for Living* (premièred on Broadway, 1933), while the wartime comedy *Blithe Spirit* (Manchester Opera House, 1941) centred on such a threesome arrangement after death. In this spooky comedy, a writer married twice meets the ghost of his first wife – a ghost that remains visible to him only. His second wife remains oblivious of this spectre until she becomes its victim, and then joins it/her as a blithe spirit – whereupon the former husband happily makes his exit from the ghosts of his two marriages.

In his patriotic attitude to Britain and the war, Noël Coward differed markedly from Somerset Maugham. Coward's *Cavalcade* (1931) presented memorable scenes from the last thirty years of British history, with a running commentary from members of an upper middle-class family and their servants, and interspersed by many period pieces and some songs of his own invention. *Cavalcade* was a mixture of musical revue and historic pageant, full of nostalgia and even jingoism, to cater for a nation struck by the world economic crisis and the decline of the Empire. Coward wrote and performed patriotic songs with an ironic note, such as "Mad Dogs and Englishmen" (1931). The sentimental song "London Pride" (1941) boosted morale in the metropolis by pointing to the example of the eponymous "flower that's free" and that stubbornly survived bombings during the Blitz. Coward also contributed to the war effort by scripting and starring in the meticulously detailed naval war film *In Which We Serve* (1942). His song "Don't Let's Be Beastly to the Germans" (1943) looked ahead to the time "when our victory is ultimately won", and satirised rather than condoned a too tolerant view of the enemy. Once the war was over, Coward envisaged what an alternate outcome might have been: his stage-play *Peace In Our Time* (1947) was set in 1940, imagining the Germans had won the Battle of Britain.

Another prolific playwright and novelist, J[ohn]. B[oynton]. Priestley (1894–1984), contributed his share to the war effort as a broadcaster. During the Battle of Britain, Priestley's voice was perhaps as popular as that of Winston Churchill with millions of BBC listeners, and within a short time, his wartime broadcasts appeared in book form, too (*Postscripts* and *Britain Speaks*, both 1940, were later followed by the selection *All England Listened*, 1968). In the inter-war period, Priestley had already made highly subjective investigations into the English national character in essayistic books such as *English Humour* (1929; rev. 1976) or in his travelogue *English Journey* (1934). He never lost that interest in *The English* (1973).

J.B. Priestley

In his drawing room plays, Priestley made good use of the theory of simultaneity, rather than linearity, of time past, present and future, as expounded in J.W. Dunne's theoretical essay *An Experiment with Time* (1927) and reiterated in the opening lines of T.S. Eliot's poem "Burnt Norton" (1935, the first of Eliot's *Four Quartets*). Priestley's stage experiments with the relativity of time began with *Dangerous Corner* (1932), in which the ending of a dramatic murder mystery returns to the beginning, begging the question if the revelations in all intervening scenes are meant as actual or merely hypothetical developments of the initial situation. Priestley's stage-play (like those of his peers) is also notable for the far from Victorian treatment of hetero- and homosexual love affairs, and also because it refers to the new media by including a radio play within the play. In *Time and the Conways* (1937), Priestley explicitly referred to Dunne's theory and used a similarly disruptive sequence of events in order to stage the (possible) disintegration of a Yorkshire family, and in a wider sense the (definite) decline of other than material values in the interwar period.

An Inspector Calls (premièred in Moscow, 1946) summed up decisive features of its two predecessors. This is once again a murder mystery located in a domestic and family setting in the North of England, with acts arranged in a non-linear temporal sequence, and with much criticism of the real amorality hidden behind the outward façade of bourgeois respectability. After intense interrogation through Inspector Goole, the surprise guest at a family celebration, the various members of the well-to-do Bingley family have to confess to their moral guilt in the downfall and death of Eva Smith, a working-class girl who is said to have committed suicide. When the family has barely begun, after the inspector's departure, to gloat over the communicated information that there were neither a record of the inspector nor of the suicidal girl, there's a final twist to the plot, announcing the impending visit of just such an inspector investigating a recent suicide ... *An Inspector Calls* is not merely a cleverly constructed piece of dramatic irony and suspense, but also an indictment of the morals of its time (and there is only little consolation in the fact that events were set more than thirty years earlier). As an Everyman figure, Eva Smith is a female counterpart to Winston Smith in George Orwell's *Nineteen Eighty-Four* (1948), the dystopian novel by a fellow-Socialist, and the fact that Priestley's working-class girl is made to remain off-stage, voiceless and invisible, and only as an object of others, has to do as much with the playwright's criticism of society as it does with the plotting of his play.

The Winslow Boy (1946) by Terence Rattigan (1911–77) is another well-crafted and successful, analytical play that moreover shared a contemporary audience and a common setting prior to the First World War with Priestley's classroom classic. Rattigan adapted an actual legal case fought between a banker and the military establishment for the stage. When the teenage cadet and banker's son Ronnie Winslow is expelled from a Royal Naval College on alleged theft of money, his father Arthur Winslow asks an expert advocate, Sir Robert Morton, to cleanse his son's and the family's honour. Having convinced himself of Ronnie's innocence through intense interrogation, Sir Robert fights for the individual's right against the Admiralty and the government, and ultimately succeeds in getting the boy's name cleared. Justice has been done, but at a price: the outcome involves great loss of wealth, health and happiness for various members of the family. The Winslow Boy was successfully filmed twice, in 1948 (dir. Anthony Asquith) and in 1999 (dir. David Mamet), with more room given to the climactic courtroom drama than in the stage-play. In The Deep Blue Sea (1952), Rattigan further developed his skills in pitting the individual against society, in the psychological motivation of his characters, and in generating suspense. In the delineation of the milieu and its impact on the characters, Rattigan's well-made play was visibly influenced by nineteenth-century Naturalism. The audience is presented with a female lead character that can hardly come to terms with the breaking-down of her extra-marital affair to a semi-alcoholic. The Deep Blue Sea sets in with a failed suicide attempt by Hester Collyer, and ends with an aborted second effort. Hester Collyer's final decision to live instead of die is due to the humanitarian effort and comfort offered by a neighbour, who was made to leave the medical profession for what appears to have been a homosexual offence. Once again, the treatment of gender issues in this problem play was much less concerned with such a taboo topic than with the more frequently dramatised theme of marital infidelity.

Noël Coward can be said to follow on the comedy of Wilde, and Priestley and Rattigan to follow on Ibsen and occasionally   Verse Plays

Shaw in their indictment of social morals and the class system. T. S. Eliot (1888–1965) linked up with Yeats in his persistent effort to put his individual talent to the hallowed tradition of poetic drama. Eliot's *The Family Reunion* (1939), *The Cocktail Party* (1949), *The Confidential Clerk* (1953) and *The Elder Statesman* (1959) are all drawing room plays in verse for West End audiences, endowed with a contemporary domestic setting, but also with plots that are indebted to the work of Aeschylus, Sophokles and Euripides. Once again, marital infidelity serves as an element of plot and as a topic of conversation in *The Family Reunion* and *The Cocktail Party*, yet as soon as this and other skeletons have made their way out of the family's cupboard, the plays approach another thematic level, and deal with the Christian theme of guilt and atonement. In *The Family Reunion*, this theme is connected with the Greek myth of Orestes and with the Biblical parable of the Lost Son. Harry, Lord Monchensey returns to the family fold, confesses to have killed his wife – what may be untrue – only to be told that his father had likewise attempted to murder his mother during her pregnancy and while he had an affair with her sister. As an act of atonement for the family's sins, Harry resigns from his position and decides to spread the Holy Word as an antidote against "death in life" (II.2). The intertextual mix in *The Family Reunion* is however problematic. Some of the elements taken from Classical Greek drama, such as the Chorus's intrusive commentary upon the action, seem more artificial than artful. Moreover, the Lost Son motif and Harry's missionary vocation do not convincingly go together with his typified characterization as a Byronic Hero, as a bored and bitter type of the better classes; and perhaps the social setting chosen is generally too narrow for staging such existential conflicts. Eliot included some self-criticism in his lecture and essay upon "Poetry and Drama" (1951), yet continued to use the verse play to promote Christian belief. In *The Cocktail Party*, just like in Priestley's *An Inspector Calls*, a mysterious guest is actively involved in dismantling the outward façade of a happy home, and to lay bare the reality of the failed marriage of the Chamberlaynes. Here, the mysterious guest turns out to be a psychotherapist for the couple and a kind of confessor for the husband's mistress, Celia. To atone for her guilt, he can lead her to adopt a Christian belief, and she is said to have later died a martyr's death in Africa.

Another Christian martyr's death, that of Thomas à Becket (†1170), the medieval Archbishop of Canterbury who was assassinated after a power-struggle with the king, is central to the plot of Eliot's *Murder in the Cathedral* (1935). Fifty years earlier, this event had already been the subject of a history play in blank verse by Lord Tennyson (*Becket*, 1884), and much earlier still, it had provided Chaucer with the motivation for his *Canterbury Tales*, as told by pilgrims on their way to the tomb of the martyr and saint. In Eliot's play, where passages in rhyme and in free verse alternate with prose, the Chorus of poor women represents such common people: those who go on suffering passively, in resistance to any form of change. The other characters are types, too, representing various forms of temptation (in the first part of the play) or the hollowness of secular political rhetoric at all times. This comes out at the ending of the play, when the four murderous knights turn *ad spectatores* and embark on a set of concerted and suddenly prosaic speeches in their defence. Here, they do not only tempt the audience into taking part in a trial by jury, by means of a national stereotype: "you are Englishmen, and therefore your sympathies are always with the underdog. It is the English spirit of fair play." Since some spectators might answer themselves to this characterisation, "We are four plain Englishmen who put our country first", they are moreover implicated in the deed itself:

> if you have now arrived at a just subordination of the pretensions of the Church to the welfare of the State, remember that it is we who took the first step. [...] We have served your interests; we merit your applause; and if there is any guilt whatever in the matter, you must share it with us.

In view of the whole drift of this religious play that ends in a *Te Deum*, the first sentence here is clearly ironical. When compared to G.B. Shaw's *Saint Joan* (1923, see chap. 4.2), another contemporary play on a historical character that the church made a saint, *Murder in the Cathedral* will be seen to celebrate the Church rather than the State or the Nation.

Eliot's religious play had been commissioned for the 1935 Canterbury Festival and was first produced in the Cathedral. During his lifetime, his other verse plays could be seen in likewise prominent and also popular locations. Beginning with *The Cocktail Party*, Eliot's last plays were premièred at the Edinburgh Festival (established only in 1947) before becoming a West End

Eliot, *Murder in the Cathedral*

| Fig. 5.7
Earliest known portrayal of Thomas Becket's murder in Canterbury Cathedral

success. However, they have seldom been revived after Eliot's death. This may have to do with the many ways in which Eliot had loaded his plays with references to Classical Greek drama and with a Christian subtext. Eliot had his followers, such as Christopher Fry (1907–2005), who succeeded in the West End and on Broadway with *The Lady's Not For Burning* (1948). Yet with the advent of John Osborne's *Look Back in Anger* in 1956, religious verse plays, and soon also any upper middle-class setting, went out of fashion.

However, this should not lead to overlook the fact that other poets and dramatists had engaged with poetic drama in interesting ways prior to and after 1956. W. H. Auden had begun early on with *Paid on Both Sides* (written in 1928) and *The Dance of Death* (1933) before he went on to script a verse commentary for the documentary film *Night Mail* (1935). Louis MacNeice wrote radio plays in verse, to be followed in memorable fashion by Dylan Thomas in *Under Milk Wood* (1954). In addressing contemporary politics – the confrontation between Communist and Fascist movements – in the form of poetic drama (*Trial of a Judge*, 1938), Stephen Spender had set an example for a younger generation of political playwrights. In *Dick Deterred* (1974), David Edgar (*1948) adapted Shakespeare's *Richard III* to satirise the Watergate scandal, with US-President Richard Nixon as the villain in the piece. At about the same time, the dramatist, actor and director Steven Berkoff (*1932) began a series of verse plays for the fringe theatre including *Sink the Belgrano!* (1986), which attacks the political and military leadership that had fought the Falklands War a few years earlier. The play's title refers to the order, endorsed by prime minister Margaret Thatcher herself, to sink an Argentine warship, the *General Belgrano*: a decision which involved great loss of life, undermined ongoing international peace initiatives, and at the home front led to the infamous jingoist headline of *The Sun*, "Gotcha". The political play suggests that such consequences were not unwelcome to Thatcher's government. Berkoff had embarked upon poetic drama with *East* (Edinburgh Festival, 1975), a play that uses Cockney rhyming slang in its presentation of scenes of sex and violence in the East End.

Two other political as well as poetical playwrights, Tony Harrison (*1937) and Caryl Churchill (*1938), attacked the Thatcherite spirit of the times in the economic arena. Following Auden's precept in *Night Mail*, Harrison also wrote verse commentary for television films, including the adaptations of his own long poems *V.* (screened in 1987) and *Prometheus* (1998), both of which addressed the Miners' Strike of 1984–85 and the closing of coalmines in Britain. In addition to his adaptation of English Medieval Mystery Plays in *The Mysteries* (1985), Harrison produced translations for the stage of poetic drama from the Classical Greek canon (Aeschylus, Euripides and Aristophanes) and from French Neoclassicism (Molière and Racine). Harrison's translation of *Hecuba* (2005) relates Euripides's play to the Iraq War. In addition to such freshening-up of plays from the Greek canon, the playwrights Caryl Churchill and Sarah Kane were commissioned to do the same for the Classical Roman dramatist Seneca, which resulted in Churchill's translation of *Thyestes* (1994) and in Kane's reworking of *Phaedra's Love* (1996). In *Serious Money: A City Comedy* (Royal Court Theatre, 1987), Churchill couched her satire on the London Stock Exchange in the form of rhyming couplets. This award-winning verse play, which 'deals' with intrigue and unfriendly takeover in the corporate world, with high-risk investments and insider trading, made it to Broadway in the year of the 1987 American Stock Market Crash.

Auden's and Harrison's works in verse for different media find their equivalent in the poetic works of Simon Armitage (*1963) and Glyn Maxwell (*1962). Together, these two poets collaborated on a poetic reiteration of Auden's and MacNeice's 1936 visit to Iceland sixty years after the event, which was published under the title *Moon Country* before it was adapted in turn as a BBC radio series under the title *Second Draft from Saga Land* (1996). On his own, Simon Armitage produced further film-poems and, just like Tony Harrison, translated Classical Greek literature as well as medieval English literature for the stage (e.g. *The Odyssey*, 2006; *Sir Gawain and the Green Knight*, 2007). In the three verse plays that Glyn Maxwell collected under the title *Gnyss the Magnificent* (1993), the poet and playwright translated his political theatre (with hardly veiled references to Stalinism) into a fairy tale context. Later, in *The Lifeblood* (likewise produced on an alternative stage, 2004), Maxwell turned to a rift in English-Scottish relations in the past when he dramatised – like Liz Lochhead in a different way in 1987 (see below) – the last days of Mary Queen of Scots.

Absurdity, Anger and After

Several discrete theatrical events during the 1950s and '60s, even though they may now be seen to have been less momentous individually than they appeared to contemporary audiences and critics, altogether created the feeling of a new phase in the development of British and Irish drama. Among the contemporary catchphrases coined to mark out such turning points were: The Theatre of the Absurd and The Theatre of Cruelty, The Angry Young Men and Kitchen Sink Drama.

Theatre of the Absurd

The Theatre of the Absurd involved the most radical break with dramatic conventions. Yet if it were a movement, then a French one (involving the dramatists Eugène Ionesco and Arthur Adamov), in Britain and Ireland, it was a one-man show: Samuel Beckett (1906–89) came from a Protestant family in Dublin. As a student, he was present on the tumultuous opening night of O'Casey's *The Plough and the Stars*, and soon was hooked by the theatre. From 1928, he went to live and teach on the Continent, and in 1937 he finally settled in Paris. In 1948, Beckett wrote – in French – the two-act play that was to make him famous: *En attendant Godot* (publ. 1952, premièred Paris January 1953). The first German production and translation followed in the autumn of 1953, before Beckett rewrote rather than translated the play into English, where it appeared as *Waiting for Godot* (Arts Club, London, 1955). The Irish critic Vivian Mercier, reviewing the play in the *Irish Times* (18 Feb. 1956), "coined the most quotable one-line account of *Waiting for Godot*: 'A play in which nothing happens, *twice*.'" (Morash 2002: 207). Vladimir ('Didi') and Estragon ('Gogo'), two tramps reminiscent of early Charlie Chaplin films, are passing away the time waiting for a Mr Godot (God?) who does not show up, but who sends a boy (towards the ending of each act) with the message that he "won't come this evening but surely tomorrow". Who does arrive on each of two evenings is Pozzo, leading his servant Lucky on a rope. The only recognisable change is that from one evening to another, Pozzo has gone blind, while Lucky – who had entered into a long monologue before – now appears to be mute.

What is recognisable, too, is that the hallmark of **Beckett's conception** (here and in his subsequent plays) is the **reduction of all dramatic means**, up to the point where this type of play may be defined by what it is not. Beckett's set is stripped down to the bare stage of Shakespeare's times; the circular action of his play is devoid of real development (there is no linear plot); there is no real social interaction between the rather isolated characters, and the character's speech is sometimes incoherent (as in Lucky's monologue), often illogical, and generally inconsequential (the dialogue leads nowhere). In his subsequent plays *Fin de Partie* (*Endgame*, premièred in French at the Royal Court Theatre, 1957), *Krapp's Last Tape* (originally written in English, Royal Court Theatre, 1958) and *Happy Days* (New York 1961), Beckett engaged in further and increasingly more radical reduction. In 1969, he was awarded the Nobel Prize for Literature. Perhaps because they asked for an interpretation, rather than came with one ready-made, Beckett's plays found an interested audience, and they fascinated the critics, who found themselves called up to provide an interpretation. The world on stage seems to make sense only in an Existentialist sense, which is why Martin Esslin entitled his pertinent study *The Theatre of the Absurd* (1961) and pointed to the contemporary Existentialist philosophy of Jean-Paul Sartre and Albert Camus for an explanation.

Look Back in Anger by John Osborne (1929–1994) was another momentous play of the 1950s that was hailed by the critic Kenneth Tynan as "a minor miracle [...] the best young play of its decade" (in Tynan's review in *The Observer*). The Royal Court production of *Look Back in Anger*, which premièred in May 1956, was made available to millions of TV viewers by both the BBC and ITV in the autumn of 1956, and as a movie two years later. This increased the impact of Osborne's play, which was widely seen as revolutionising the English stage, even though it also showed much continuity with theatrical conventions. Osborne kept the basic framework of the well-made problem play, and set his play apart from either Epic Theatre or the Theatre of the Absurd. Unlike Beckett's pieces, Osborne's play is laid out in three acts and five scenes; it is based on a plausible plot, with a dramatic conflict that leads to a 'solution'; and it is peopled with psychologically motivated characters (most of them in their twenties). For this play that deals with the disillusionment of a younger generation, Osborne does not make use of Brechtian techniques of disillusionment of the audience: there is neither a central character who functions as narrator of events nor are the other actors

John Osborne, *Look Back in Anger*

speaking out of character, and there are no songs or posters which comment upon the dramatic action. Among the unconventional features of *Look Back in Anger* – in distinction from the tradition of the drawing room play (which is acknowledged by an occasional reference to Oscar Wilde's character of Lady Bracknell, Osborne 1960: 51) – are the working-class and lower middle-class setting in a Midlands bedsit, and the domestic realism, which involves the ironing of clothes at the outset of the play, but also marital bouts, extra-marital affairs, and a miscarriage. Moreover, there is the unrestricted and disillusioned manner in which the characters talk about sex, death and the end of the Empire (in the year of the Suez Crisis, when the imperial-style British and French invasion of the canal zone was unceremoniously halted by the USA as the new super-power). In one of the best-known passages from the play, the protagonist Jimmy Porter complains: "I suppose people of our generation aren't able to die for good causes any longer. We had all that done for us, in the thirties and the forties, when we were still kids. (*In his familiar, semi-serious mood.*) There aren't any good, brave causes left." (Osborne 1960: 84). In the end, the play's success was made out to depend less on its storyline, but on the way Jimmy vented his anger about lost causes, a lost generation (his own), and a general lack of perspective. The play was soon seen to express the frustration of a post-war generation of Angry Young Men, among writers and in the audience.

Revivals of Music Hall Comedy

Jimmy Porter returned in Osborne's last play, aptly entitled *Déjà Vu* (1992). In between, the playwright had produced an Academy Award winning screenplay (*Tom Jones*, 1963) and a couple of historical plays (*Luther*, 1961), one of which provoked the Lord Chamberlain to ban it because of its explicit treatment of homosexuality (*A Patriot for Me*, 1965). The music-hall act included in *Look Back in Anger* (1960: 81–82) was extended into a full-length play about the dying-out of this form of popular entertainment. *The Entertainer* premièred in 1957 at the Royal Court Theatre, transferred to the West End, and was made into a film in 1960. In all productions, Laurence Olivier had successfully acted in the title role – the theatre establishment bestowed approval on the generation of angry young playwrights. An updating of the theme occurred in *Comedians* (1975) by Trevor Griffiths (*1935, see below), and also in *Not Only But Always* by Terry Johnson (*1955), which is a 2004 television play centring on the disintegrating relationship between two actual British TV comedians, Peter Cook and Dudley Moore. Their double act in the comedy series *Not Only ... But Also* (hence the title of Johnson's piece) had been popular with British TV audiences in the 1960s and '70s. (See Davison 1982 and Raab 1989.)

Like Beckett, Harold Pinter (1930–2008), who was born as the son of a Jewish tailor in the East End, secured for himself an international reputation that is mirrored in the 2005 Nobel Prize. In 2006, Pinter – who trained and toured as an actor in repertory before he turned dramatist – performed *Krapp's Last Tape*, Beckett's one-man play about memory. However, the similarities between Beckett's Theatre of the Absurd and Pinter's own 'comedies of menace' and 'memory plays' seemed to be greater for then-contemporary critics than they nowadays appear to us. Beckett, though he occasionally inspired other dramatists such as Pinter or Tom Stoppard (in *Rosencrantz and Guildenstern are Dead*, 1966), did not find real followers, and the political turn in Pinter's later work clearly marks a difference. From the beginning of his career as a dramatist, Harold Pinter simultaneously wrote plays for the stage as well as for radio and television, and he later wrote screenplays that adapted other writers' works (such as John Fowles's *The French Lieutenant's Woman* in 1982 and Anthony Shaffer's *Sleuth* in 2007).

By calling Pinter's early stage-plays 'comedies of menace' (not manners), the theatre critic Irving Wardle (in a 1958 review) coined a label that stuck. *The Birthday Party* (Lyric Theatre Hammersmith, 1957) as well as *The Dumb Waiter* (Hampstead Theatre Club, January, 1960; transferring to the Royal Court Theatre, in March 1960) and *The Caretaker* (Arts Theatre, April 1960, transferring to the West End in May) involved a limited number of characters isolated in a single room that provides no shelter against threats from the outside. In *The Dumb Waiter*, two killers are shown 'waiting for a murder' in a windowless room in Birmingham – until it is revealed that one of them will be the victim. How Pinter created tension in plays that are short on action, and that show a lack of logical explanation, brought up the comparison to the Theatre of the Absurd. Pinter's signature style of a dialogue replete with repeated phrases, *non-sequiturs* and 'pregnant pauses', was delightfully parodied by A. A. Gill in

Harold Pinter

a sketch involving the dramatist and his wife ("Harold Pauses, Antonia is Silent", 1996).

For the plays written in the middle of Pinter's career, such as *The Homecoming* (1967), *No Man's Land* (1975) and *Betrayal* (1980), critics have coined the vague term 'memory play' because of their subject matter. A third and so far last phase, beginning with his short play *One for the Road* (1984, in Geisen 1999), is characterised by a more overtly political approach. In *One for the Road*, the scene is a prison-room in which a self-assured official called Victor afflicts psychological torture upon a marital couple, separated from each other. Pinter's more radical engagement with contemporary politics culminated in his controversial Nobel Prize acceptance speech of 2005, which entailed a harsh criticism of U.S. foreign policy.

Osborne's domestic realism showed in the **Kitchen Sink Drama**, a catchphrase that hinges on the play *The Kitchen* (Royal Court Theatre, 1959) by Arnold Wesker (*1932). All the world's a kitchen: in much detail, the Marxist playwright presented the routine work in a restaurant kitchen as paradigmatic of Capitalist society. Wesker's *Chips with Everything* (Royal Court Theatre, 1962) turned to the Royal Air Force for another dramatic analysis of social hierarchies, by making much more use of techniques from the Epic Theatre (see the above discussion of *Look Back in Anger*). In the trilogy *Chicken Soup with Barley/Roots/I'm Talking about Jerusalem* (Belgrade Theatre, Coventry, 1958–60), Wesker displayed British working-class history from participation in the Spanish Civil War (1936) to the disillusionment after the Russian Communist suppression of the Hungarian Revolution (1956). In this trilogy and in his Shakespeare adaptation *The Merchant* (1977), Wesker addressed his own Jewish background, too.

In London's East End, Joan Littlewood (1914–2002) and the Theatre Workshop also put a stress on dramatic subjects relevant to working-class audiences (see above). Among the plays first produced by these pioneers of **Community Theatre** was *A Taste of Honey* (1958) by Shelagh Delaney (*1939). In characteristic fashion, Delaney's script of the play was altered during rehearsals through collaboration with director Joan Littlewood and the actors of the Theatre Workshop (a treatment that was also given to the plays of Brendan Behan mentioned below). Delaney's *A Taste of Honey* (1958) successfully transferred to the West End before it was

Arnold Wesker

Joan Littlewood, Shelagh Delaney and Ann Jellicoe

made into a film based on Delaney's screenplay (1962), although it confronted stage and film conventions by addressing teenage pregnancy and single motherhood, inter-racial friendships and homosexuality as themes. Rather than following in the new wave of social realism, *The Sport of My Mad Mother* (Royal Court Theatre, 1958) by Ann Jellicoe (*1927) can be seen as a continuation, in a feminist context, of both Yeats's concern with mythological themes and Beckett's experiments with non-linear plot structures (see Lacey 1995; Rabey 2003: 42–46). In her later plays, such as *The Rising Generation* (1969), Jellicoe attempted to fuse social realism and formal experimentation in her concept of Community Plays which were performed by great casts of local amateurs in a non-theatrical, communal space. This concept (see Jellicoe's *Community Plays: How to Put Them On*, 1987) relates to other, ongoing developments within the new Alternative or Fringe Theatre tradition in the purposeful crossing and dissolution of the boundaries separating the cast of performers from its audience.

With his scandalous play *Saved* (Royal Court Theatre, 1965), in which the stoning of a baby in a pram was mimed on stage, Edward Bond (*1934) challenged the Lord Chamberlain's Office, and with *Early Morning* (1968), he was ultimately successful to bring about the abolition of statutory theatre censorship in Britain. As in his reworking of Shakespeare in *Lear* (Royal Court Theatre, 1971), the key to Bond's drama was Antonin Artaud's idea of a **Theatre of Cruelty**, which attempts to unsettle the audience with shock tactics, with scenes of verbal and physical brutality. In *Lear*, this involves arbitrary executions, scenes of torture, the blinding not only of Gloucester but also of Lear, and the rape of Lear's daughter Cordelia – all in view of the audience. Bond's purpose was to foreground the mechanisms of social violence in order to further a discussion about them. This aim is also apparent in *Black Mass* (1970), a commemoration of the 1960 Sharpeville Massacre in South Africa, to be performed at demonstrations of the Anti-Apartheid Movement in Britain. In *Bingo: Scenes of Money and Death* (Exeter 1973, Royal Court Theatre, 1974) and in *The Fool: Scenes of Bread and Love* (Royal Court Theatre, 1975), Bond threw a Marxist's eye on the lives of Shakespeare and of the Romantic poet John Clare.

There were more left-wing dramatists and political plays in the generation of Pinter, Wesker and Bond. For instance, there

Edward Bond and the Theatre of Cruelty

Look Left: Other Plays about Class

are three remarkable plays that share both the classroom as set and the class struggle as a theme. In *Comedians* (Nottingham Playhouse, 1975; rev. 1979) by Trevor Griffiths (*1935), we witness the warming-up of a group of music-hall trainees with their teacher (Act I) before they deliver their individual acts full of controversial jokes in terms of race, class and gender (II). In the third and last act, they briefly return to the classroom to review the evening before they go their own ways. Griffiths's play implies a critical look at the controversial jokes included. *Class Enemy* (Royal Court Theatre, 1978) by Nigel Williams (*1948) is a problem play set in a deprived, run-down Inner City school near Brixton in South London. The general layout – a circular two-act play in which pupils are waiting for a new teacher who apparently does not come – is inspired by *Waiting for Godot*, while the pupils' series of imitation of their former teachers recalls a 'numbers' revue in a music hall. *Educating Rita* (RSC, 1980) by Willy Russell (*1947) is a variation upon the theme of Shaw's *Pygmalion*. Russell himself adapted his play for the screen (1983, starring Julie Walters and Michael Caine). Among other playwrights whose names should be mentioned in this context are Howard Brenton (*1942), David Hare (*1947) and David Edgar (*1948). Brenton's *The Romans in Britain* (NT, 1980), set during Caesar's invasion of Britain and also in contemporary Northern Ireland amidst the Troubles, is an attempt at showing 'history from below'. The enactment of the homosexual rape of a British Celt by Roman soldiers, meant to serve as an image of power relations, came close to Bond's Theatre of Cruelty, and was no less controversial.

Historical Plays   In addition to the guest appearance of Julius Caesar in *The Romans in Britain*, there were more plays on historical characters in the period. Osborne's *Luther* (1961) belongs here, and it ties in nicely with *A Man for All Seasons* by Robert Bolt (1924–95). In a series of re-productions, *A Man for All Seasons* became a play for all media (and thus a good example for the many options now available to playwrights). It was first produced as a *radio play* (BBC, 1954) before it was turned into a *television play* (BBC TV, 1957). Only the third version was meant for the stage (West End, 1960), and this was rewritten in 1966 into a screenplay for Fred Zinnemann's award-winning film. (Robert Bolt had also written the *screenplays* for the two blockbuster movies *Lawrence of Arabia*, 1962, and *Doctor Zhivago*, 1964.) Bolt's popular play dealt with the life and death of Sir Thomas More, the Chancellor of King Henry VIII, who was made to see the other face of royalty when he steadfastly remained a conscientious objector to Henry's plans for a royal divorce and remarriage that in the end led to the establishment of the Church of England. None of Bolt's many versions of his play is a nostalgic period piece: instead, they all deal with the theme of an individual against authority and society.

The contrast between pre- and post-1956 British drama can be exemplified with two plays on Lord Nelson: on the politics and military pursuits of this naval hero, up to his death in the Battle of Trafalgar (1805), and on his extra-marital affair with Lady Hamilton. Terence Rattigan, who had made his name before 1956, took a consistently patriotic and romantic approach when he dramatised Nelson's last days and the fate of his mistress in turns as a television play (*Nelson*, 1966), stage-play (*A Bequest to the Nation*, 1970) and screenplay (for a film under the same title, 1973). All three versions make for an interesting comparison with *The Hero Rises Up* (1968), one of the many plays that John Arden (*1930) and his wife Margaretta D'Arcy (*1934) have written in collaboration. Their historical play is heavily indebted to the Epic Theatre of Brecht, both in its questioning of heroic ideology and in the use of techniques of disillusionment.

Kindertransport (1993) by Diane Samuels (*1960) addressed the experience of Jewish children who could be brought out of Nazi-Germany just in time. More recently, Michael Frayn (*1933) has distinguished himself with historical plays focused on war and post-war events. *Copenhagen* (NT, 1998) deals with a historical 1941 meeting and fall-out of the nuclear physicists and long-time friends Werner Heisenberg and Niels Bohr in the Danish capital. Both are involved in competing programmes that aim at the construction of an atomic bomb as the cruel weapon that will ultimately end the Second World War. In the structure of his play, Frayn reflects important notions of theoretical physics, such as Heisenberg's uncertainty principle. Frayn's play cannot solve the mystery that still hovers over this meeting of physicists, but it sparkled a new public interest in what was actually discussed at Copenhagen. (In his usual witty way, Tom Stoppard had dealt with modern physics, too, in his 1988 and 1993 plays *Hapgood* and *Arcadia*.) In his likewise successful play *Democracy* (NT, 2003), Frayn concerned himself with a piece of Cold War history, and a story of personal and political betrayal. Frayn made a stage-play out of the real-life drama surrounding the decision of West German chancellor Willy Brandt to retire over the discovery that one of his political aides, Günter Guillaume, was a Communist undercover agent.

Farce

'*History* repeats itself, first as tragedy, second as *farce*', said Karl Marx. With *Noises Off* (Lyric Theatre Hammersmith, 1982), Michael Frayn had earlier on written a repetitive and yet most effective farce, and also a piece of meta-drama. In the first of three acts, the audience witnesses a touring company's dress rehearsal of a farce within the farce entitled *Nothing On*, which also tells about the sexual relations and tensions within the company. The fun of the second act consists in viewing the now well-known play in performance, but from behind the scenes, including all mistakes and undisciplined behaviour. The final act comes to climax, paradoxically through another performance towards the close of the tour. The funny variation between individual performances of the play within the play may have been increased over the years in Frayn's continual rewriting of passages. Other notable examples of farce are *What the Butler Saw* (West End, 1969) by Joe Orton (1933–67) and *Bedroom Farce* (NT, 1977) by Alan Ayckbourn (*1939). Ayckbourn, who runs his own theatre, the Scarborough Theatre-in-the-Round, is well known for the ingenuity and dexterity with which he handles complicated setups, mostly for a comic effect. *The Norman Conquests* (Scarborough, 1973) is not a history play, it is a trilogy of plays. They can be put up in any order, as they tell of what happened in three different rooms over a weekend. In Alan Bennett's stage- and screenplays, finally, comedy and history come together. Bennett (*1934) adapted his own successful play *The Madness of George III* (1991) for the screen, where it came out to great acclaim in 1994 as *The Madness of King George*. In occasionally very moving, and often quite funny terms, this award-winning history play and film dealt with the king's illness and with the schemes at court. *The History Boys* is another example where the playwright turned his successful play (NT, 2005) into a film (2006) that tells of the clandestine relations between teachers and pupils preparing for an history exam at a boys' grammar school in Sheffield in 1983.

Peter Shaffer (*1926), who was born into a Jewish family in Liverpool, received his training in history at Cambridge University, before he came out with a television play on the BBC (*The Salt Land*, 1954). In the wake of Osborne's angry revolution of the London stage, Shaffer could first win the star actor John Gielgud as a director for a drawing room play, and then won over West End audiences. Everything about *Five-Finger Exercise* (1958), and about *Black Comedy* (1965) – a play in which the characters are made to come to terms with a black box (on a clean, well lighted stage) – signalled the playwright's interest in stagecraft, and also his lack of enthusiasm for the new dramatic fashion. This did not endear him to those critics who made anger and political protest into desirable qualities of the New British Drama, as well as for those who patiently joined the characters on a bare stage in their waiting for Godot, once again in vain. For them, Shaffer was simply the wrong man at the right time. Late in his career, Shaffer paid back for such criticism by quipping: "I am tired of seeing a one-set play with two people whining at each other all night or delivering a sequence of lectures to the audience. It doesn't seem to me to be what the theatre is for" (Interview with *The Times*, 28 April 1980). Indeed, his stagecraft and themes found more favour with other audiences, so much so that Shaffer was to become one of the most successful of New British Dramatists (see Kerensky 1977: 50–58). His National Theatre plays were such that could compete with popular musicals: they broke box-office records in the West End and on Broadway when they came out, and they were frequently revived and made into films.

|Fig. 5.8
Peter Shaffer
© Topix

With plays like *The Royal Hunt of the Sun* and *Amadeus*, Shaffer may look more like another contributor to the time-honoured genre of the history play, but such an impression were not entirely correct. Shaffer did first conceive of *The Royal Hunt of the Sun* as a chronicle play about 'the conquest of Peru by the Spaniards' (updating Dryden's heroic play of that title). The final product that was presented at the 1964 Chichester Festival by the National Theatre company (and made into a movie in 1969), integrated elements of music and pantomime into a kind of total theatre that actually highlighted the complex interaction of religious worship, faith and doubt. These themes were to reappear prominently in *Equus* and *Amadeus*, Shaffer's subsequent two-act plays. In the analytical and psychoanalytical play *Equus* (NT, 1973; film version 1977), the psychiatrist Dr Martin Dysart is professionally concerned with Alan Strang, a teenage stable boy who has ritually blinded six horses. As a result of therapy sessions, Dysart finds out more than he originally bargained for about Alan's sexualised cult of the horse god Equus as well as about his own disillusioned self. In his introduction/postscript, Shaffer states laconically: "In London *Equus* caused a sensation because it displayed cruelty to horses; in New York because it allegedly displayed cruelty to psychiatrists." (Shaffer 1983: viii) *Equus* is moreover interesting for Shaffer's mix of modern dramatic modes. By contrast with the more lavish set of *The Royal Hunt of the Sun*, Shaffer used "A square of wood set on a circle of wood" as a bare stage for *Equus*, and indicated changes of time and place on this simultaneous stage by characters entering the square room (e.g. Dysart's office) from the circle. Other anti-illusionary features come from the Epic Theatre (e.g. that the horses are visibly impersonated by actors in track-suits, and that Dysart acts as narrator), and there are scenes of nudity and violence reminiscent of the Theatre of Cruelty.

In each case of theatrical reference, here and in *Amadeus*, this was done for Shaffer's own dramatic purposes rather than to proclaim an allegiance to theorists. *Amadeus*, too, was premièred at London's prestigious National Theatre (1979), and likewise ran over a thousand performances on Broadway (in a revised version), before it was made into a successful film (1984). On the one hand, this play looks like an analytical play that tries to investigate the alleged murder of Wolfgang Amadeus Mozart by the hands of Antonio Salieri, a rival composer at Vienna's Imperial Court. On the other hand, Shaffer's play gathers momentum in the second act when everything drives towards Mozart's death during the composition of his *Requiem* as a work commissioned by a patron who will not reveal his identity (staple food for any conspiracy theorist). Salieri himself leads as master of ceremonies through the play that (like *Equus*) combines a series of flashbacks to a consecutive story. The contrast between Salieri and Mozart is dramatised to great effect: here the figure of the establishment (Salieri), the court composer of limited talent, but of an insatiable ambition to be a Divine darling – only to be utterly disillusioned when a natural genius appears on the scene that must really be beloved by God ("Ama-Deus" Mozart), despite his vulgar speech and other breaches of decorum. Was this motivation enough, the audience soon wants to know, to turn Salieri into Mozart's murderer?

The tradition of the murder mystery that is called up, amongst others, in *Amadeus* was more fully exploited by Peter's twin brother Anthony Shaffer (1926–2001). *Sleuth*, his play based on the tradition of the mystery and the thriller, became a West End success in 1970 and lasted for five years before the production successfully transferred to Broadway with the original cast. Meanwhile, Shaffer had turned his stage-play into a screenplay for the successful 1972 film version directed by Joseph L. Mankiewicz, starring Laurence Olivier as country squire Andrew Wyke who was cuckolded by the hairdresser Milo Tindle, played by Michael Caine. The two men are testing out their wits in a murderous game with many twists and turns. A new adaptation for the screen came out in 2007, directed by Kenneth Branagh and based on Harold Pinter's script, now starring an older Michael Caine in the opposite role of Andrew Wyke. Anthony Shaffer's other screenplays include *Frenzy* (dir. Alfred Hitchcock, 1972) and adaptations of Agatha Christie's crime novels featuring Hercule Poirot as a detective (*Death on the Nile*, 1978, and *Evil under the Sun*, 1982, both with Peter Ustinov in the role of the Belgian detective). J.B. Priestley's *An Inspector Calls* (1946) and Dennis Potter's *The Singing Detective* (BBC TV, 1986) were further plays that fell back on mystery and thriller conventions. (For Potter, see above, and see also Thomson 2004: III, 159–60.) Another convention from crime fiction appeared in Agatha Christie's *Witness for the Prosecution*. In the memorable movie starring Marlene Dietrich and Charles Laughton (1957), much more room was given to the climactic courtroom drama than in Christie's short story, as had also happened to the adaptations of Terence Rattigan's *The Winslow Boy* for the screen. For the sake of comparison, one may also note Denis Johnston's *Blind Man's Buff* (Abbey Theatre, 1936) as another play about a murder trial. Agatha Christie's long-running play *The Mousetrap* (1952) was parodied in Stoppard's *The Real Inspector Hound* (1968), while in *Hapgood* (1988), Stoppard turned the well-known thriller element of the double agent to new use. (More plays by Stoppard will be mentioned below in connection with his Shakespeare adaptations and his other intertextual plays.)

At the beginning of the twentieth century, both the production and the critical attitude to Shakespeare's plays took a new turn. A.C. Bradley's Oxford lectures on *Shakespearean Tragedy* (publ. 1904) are commonly labelled 'character criticism' but were

Crime and Detection on Stage

Shakespeare on Stage (not just by the RSC)

actually shrewd readings of the play-scripts in more than this respect. They found their complement in *Prefaces to Shakespeare* (1927–48), Harley Granville-Barker's essays in 'performance criticism' by the hand of an experienced actor-manager. In his revolutionary productions at the Savoy Theatre (1912–14), Granville-Barker had replaced a declamatory by a more naturalistic style of acting on an open stage. In seamless succession to his own productions, Lilian Baylis put all of Shakespeare's plays on the stage of the Old Vic over a period of nine years, beginning in 1914. The annual festival productions in the Shakespeare Memorial Theatre (1879, rebuilt 1932) in Stratford-upon-Avon set in about the same time, to be followed in 1953 by a Canadian equivalent, the annual Shakespeare Festival in Stratford, Ontario. Festival Shakespeare was transformed into an all-year-round cycle of productions in Stratford and in London by Peter Hall's formation of the **Royal Shakespeare Company** in 1960. The successors to Hall as artistic director of the RSC (1960–68) were Trevor Nunn (1968–86) and Adrian Noble (1991–2003). The formation of a company permanently devoted to the works of the Bard (and to new writing, too), together with the opening of the reconstructed Shakespeare's Globe Theatre on London's Bankside in 1997, put the final seal of approval on the Bard's status as Britain's most prominent playwright, then and now.

If any further proof were needed, this would have been provided by the many instances of **intertextual and intermedial reference to Shakespeare and his works** in the twentieth century. A short list will serve to indicate the variety of approaches taken outside the burlesque skit. The Shakespearean original (which in itself was usually based on a compilation of sources) may have been cited

Play within the Play

as a play within the play, as e.g. in Cole Porter's adaptation of *The Taming of the Shrew* as a Broadway musical (*Kiss Me, Kate*, 1948), in Derek Walcott's relocation of *Antony and Cleopatra* to a Caribbean theatrical context (*A Branch of the Blue Nile*, 1983, rev. 1985), or in Tom Stoppard's screenplay for the film *Shakespeare in Love* (1998, dir. John Madden), which involves a production of *Romeo and Juliet*. In other instances, Shakespeare's *Romeo and Juliet* appeared in

Modern Dress

modern dress, and in modern conflicts. In *Mixed Marriage* (Abbey Theatre, 1917), the Irish dramatist St. John Ervine adapted Shakespeare's plot for a tragic problem play on the impact of class and sectarianism on the common people. *Mixed Marriage* tells of the love relationship between Hugh, the son of a Protestant working-class family in Belfast, and Nora, a Catholic girl. At the end, Nora leaves the Protestant home, only to be killed in a shipyard strike that turned into a riot. Forty years later, the American composer and conductor Leonard Bernstein, together with the librettist Stephen Sondheim, made *Romeo and Juliet* into a tragic musical set amidst warring youth gangs in contemporary New York (*West Side Story*, 1957). And in the same year, the multi-talented actor Peter Ustinov reworked Shakespeare's tragedy into a West End comedy of Russian-American relations during the Cold War (*Romanoff and Juliet*, 1957). A different kind of modernisation may be perceived **Theatrical Fashions** in dressing the source-text in a contemporary theatrical fashion. Tom Stoppard's *Rosencrantz and Guildenstern are Dead* (Edinburgh Festival Fringe, 1966; adapted for the screen in 1990) fleshed out two minor characters from *Hamlet* yet limited their human agency in a manner reminiscent of the Theatre of the Absurd, whereas Edward Bond's *Lear* (Royal Court Theatre, 1971) brought *King Lear* in line with a Theatre of Cruelty. In other cases, modern dramatists (and also poets and novelists, see Auden and chap. 5.3.6) may have been interested in relating Shakespeare's constellation of characters to contemporary issues such as Feminism or (nega-   **Contemporary Issues** tively speaking) Racism and anti-Semitism. Anti-Racism has been at the base of every reworking of the Prospero/Caliban/Miranda constellation in a spirit of *Négritude*, Black Consciousness or Post-colonialism. Aimé Césaire's stage-play *Une Tempête: Adaptation de "La Tempête" de Shakespeare pour un théâtre nègre* (1969) is still the classic example. However, see also the novels *Water with Berries* by George Lamming (1971) and *Indigo; or, Mapping the Waters* by Marina Warner (1992), or the "Caliban" poems in the collections of the Barbadian poet Edward Kamau Brathwaite (*Islands*, 1969) and of the Guyanese-born poet and novelist David Dabydeen (*Coolie Odyssey*, 1988). By freely addressing anti-Jewish feeling in his play *The Merchant* (first produced in English in New York, 1977), and by making Shylock a sympathetic character outright, Arnold Wesker gave a new twist to the critical discussion about Shakespeare's ambivalent characterisation in *The Merchant of Venice*. As the last of an open-ended list of approaches, one may think of the inclusion of Shakespeare himself among the characters. Be-   **Enter Shakespeare** fore the screening of *Shakespeare in Love*, the 1964 novel *Nothing Like the Sun: A Story of Shakespeare's Love-Life* by Anthony Burgess had devoted itself to the Bard and his Dark Lady, while Edward Bond's 1973 stage-play *Bingo: Scenes of Money and Death* focused on the last rather than the lost years in Shakespeare's life, but from a Marxist angle.

(Intertextual) Stage
Biographies

The Bard apart, other stage biographies included real-historical artists and also scientists, often in intertextual plays. In *The Invention of Love* (NT, 1997), Tom Stoppard concerned himself with the remembrances of the poet and classical scholar A.E. Housman (†1936), splitting the character up into an older self who reviews his life from the other side of death, and a younger Housman involved in scenic action. Among the topics discussed are Housman's repressed homosexuality and his unrequited love for another man, and also the Aestheticism of the 1890s, which is why Oscar Wilde makes a guest appearance. Earlier on, in Stoppard's *Travesties*, a production of Wilde's play *The Importance of Being Earnest* at the ending of the First World War had provided the playwright with an opportunity to team James Joyce with Lenin and the Dadaist Tristan Tzara in Zurich. The fun of watching *Travesties* (in both its original 1974 version and in the 1993 revision, each produced by the RSC in the West End) consists in the skilful manner in which Stoppard intertwines Wilde's dialogue with his own plot as well as with the personalities and writings of his famous characters. The same holds true when applied to *Arcadia* (NT, 1993), which includes Lord Byron's life, loves and poetry, the Neoclassicist and Romantic aspects of English landscape gardening as well as Newtonian Physics and Chaos Theory among its subject matter – all of it organised into a complex and entertaining mystery plot. Stoppard is perhaps the most witty and clever playwright of his generation, combining the qualities of Shaw's drama of ideas with Wilde's comedies of wit.

Plays featuring real-life characters have also become a trademark of Terry Johnson (*1955) since he made a Marilyn Monroe look-alike explain special relativity theory to Albert Einstein in *Insignificance*, a stage-play that was first produced at the Royal Court (1982) before it was made into an equally successful film (dir. Nicholas Roeg, 1985). In his subsequent play *Hitchcock Blonde* (2003), Johnson investigated the famous filmmaker's relationship to women on and off the set, a theme that was enhanced by the extraordinary special effects in the première at the Royal

Court. The television play *Not Only But Always* (2004, see above) cast a new look at the partnership of two well known British TV comedians, yet Johnson does not concern himself only with TV and film celebrities. The protagonist of *Hysteria; or, Fragments of an Analysis of an Obsessional Neurosis* (1993) is Sigmund Freud, who, in his London exile at the end of his life, is brought together with the painter Salvador Dalí and with Jessica, the daughter of one of his early patients. True to Freudian psychoanalysis, Johnson's analytic play involves the decoding of traumatic dreams and childhood memories, to come up with a re-appreciation of Freud's early work, and with a story of sexual abuse within the family. In *Hysteria*, Johnson followed upon Shaw and Stoppard in his successful combination of a drama of history and ideas with elements of farce.

Irish Drama and Theatre since the 1920s

5.2.4

In the 1920s, the Irish cause, Irish drama and the Dublin stage took a great leap forward, and then developed along different lines from Britain. Within five years after the ending of the First World War, Ireland had not just secured Home Rule, but a Free State (1922); W. B. Yeats had been awarded the Nobel Prize for Literature (1923); and the Abbey Theatre had become the **first subsidised repertory theatre** in the English-speaking world (1924). Twenty years earlier, productions at the Abbey were initially made possible by the financial backing of Annie Horniman, the driving force behind the repertory movement. Yet this resolute Englishwoman, who had always demanded that (Nationalist) politics be kept out of the Abbey, withdrew her annual subsidy in 1910 when the disrespectful directors Yeats and Lady Gregory decided to open the theatre on the day of King Edward's funeral. After years of financial insecurity, the Irish Free State stepped in with regular funding for what had in fact become the National Theatre of Ireland. In 1926, such subsidies were helpful, too, when the Abbey was also furnished with an experimental space by the opening of the Peacock Theatre as its annexe. In 1928, Hilton Edwards and the actor and playwright Micheál MacLíammóir co-founded the Gate Theatre in Dublin, which readily embraced the work of Oscar Wilde, and more experimental plays by Irish and Continental dramatists.

The Dublin Stage in the 1920s and '30s

Up to this time, the Dublin Drama League (1918–28) run by the Abbey's manager Lennox Robinson (1886–1958) had complemented the Abbey's home-grown repertoire with plays of the Continental avant-garde, to which Robinson himself subscribed as a playwright in his later years. Robinson's *The Big House* (1926) takes place in the formative but also confrontational period between the ending of the Great War and the Irish Civil War (1918–23). The play is both topical as well as historically significant in its exemplary depiction of this final stage in the downfall of the Anglo-Irish Protestant Ascendancy from its established social position. This important development was taken up again in Brendan Behan's radio play *The Big House* (1957) and Brian Friel's *Aristocrats* (1979). With its episodic structure and open ending, Robinson's *The Big House* was already one step removed from his penchant for the well-made play. In *Church Street* (1934), Robinson went further and, inspired by Luigi Pirandello's anti-illusionism in *Six Characters in Search of an Author* (1921), came up with a meta-dramatic play within the play. (For these and more details, see Vormann 2001.) When Pirandello's experimental novel was adapted and produced as an opera (New York, 1959), the Dublin playwright Denis Johnston (1901–84) wrote the script for Hugo Weisgall's score. With his stage-play *The Old Lady Says 'No!'* (1929), Johnston helped to establish the reputation of the Gate Theatre. For this play, he had found no favour at the Abbey, which however premièred *The Moon in the Yellow River* (1931). After 1939, Johnston made a career move and distinguished himself as a BBC war correspondent.

The confrontational politics in early twentieth-century Ireland were also mirrored in the Dublin Trilogy for which Sean O'Casey (1880–1964) is best known. In contrast to Robinson's *The Big House*, they were seen together with the bitter social realities of slum life. *The Plough and the Stars* (1926) takes its title from the banner of the socialist Irish Citizen Army that took part in the Easter Rising 1916, which is the setting of the second half of the play. The aptly titled play *The Shadow of a Gunman* (1923) takes place among Irish Nationalists and British paramilitary troops in the middle of the Anglo-Irish War or Irish War of Independence (1919–21) that led to the establishment of the Irish Free State (with Northern Ireland remaining an integral part of the United Kingdom). *Juno and the Paycock* (1924) looked to the Irish Civil War (1922–23)

Fig. 5.9

Sean O' Casey, 1924

and, like the Trilogy throughout, is set in the Dublin tenements. O'Casey's agenda (like Shaw's) was a Socialist rather than a Nationalist one: the urban slum context of his early plays rendered them distinct from other contemporary plays that were set either (like Wilde's) in the bourgeois drawing room or (like Yeats's) in the rural peasant hut. O'Casey's social realism extended to the working-class Dublin English spoken by his characters (with peacock pronounced 'paycock'), and his Naturalism foresaw no way out of a life of dreariness, hard drinking and determination by others. However, in addition to its elements of tragedy, the Dublin Trilogy has a considerable comic potential and is at the same time one of the prime examples of twentieth-century farce. The first two plays drew the crowds and provided much-wanted financial relief to the Abbey, before another scandal occurred, as had before with Synge's *The Playboy of the Western World* (1907).

The similarities between Synge's play and *The Plough and the Stars* do not only involve their tragicomic ambivalence; O'Casey, too, provoked the Nationalists in the audience by denouncing their ideals of Irishness. In the second act of the play, a vainglorious speech is delivered at a rally outside a pub: this is based on authentic documents of one of the rebel leaders, but relegated to the theatrical space off-stage. Moreover, the patriotic and heroic words of the rabble-rouser ring hollow, as they are juxtaposed against the comic and unromantic action on stage, which consists of the hard drinking and quarrelling among regulars in a pub, and of a prostitute's attempt to find a client among the locals. Here, the contrast between Nationalism and Naturalism can hardly be greater. Heroic patriotism receives a further blow later, when the locals are shown to go looting during the rebellion, and when Irish soldiers in British service take some of their countrymen as hostages against a sniper. In *The Plough and the Stars*, nothing good comes out of the Easter Rising, and it is primarily Irish womanhood that is made to suffer. Nora Clitheroe first loses her husband Jack to the rebels' cause and then her mind, when she is left alone with the experience of stillbirth during the abortive rebellion. During Easter Week, another girl dies of consumption, and Bessie Burgess, a fruit-vendor, is shot dead – accidentally – in the really brave and charitable act of giving help to Nora. Such a presentation of the historical event gave rise to scandal. W.B. Yeats stood up for the playwright on

The Plough and the Stars

the tumultuous opening night of *The Plough and the Stars*, and as a director of the Abbey confronted the audience that had returned to riot, as it had earlier on the occasion of Synge's *Playboy* (see Morash 2002: 163–71).

After the scandal, O'Casey left the country and settled in Britain for good. He found himself out of tune with his audience, with the moral and political outlook in Ireland, and soon also with the theatre management. With the new Irish Free State came new regulations for many areas of culture, as in the establishment of the Irish Film Censors Office in 1923 and the passing of the 1929 Censorship of Publications Act. Other legislation passed to prohibit the sale of contraceptives (1935) as well as divorce (1925) tell of the long and strong impact of the Catholic Church on sexual morality in general (divorce became legalised not before 1995). Although the Dublin stage was exempt from statutory theatre censorship, there were other restrictions. The subsidised Abbey was well on its way to become a conservative cultural institution, and altogether more notorious for rejecting promising new playwrights (from Denis Johnston to Tom Murphy) than for risking another riot. O'Casey broke with the Abbey Theatre after Yeats had rejected *The Silver Tassie* (1928), a pacifist play about the First World War, on much the same grounds as he would later reject the disillusioned war poetry of Wilfred Owen (see chap. 4.3). *The Silver Tassie* was typical of a second, more ideological phase in the work of O'Casey, a phase that was also characterised by an interest in Expressionism and in the Epic Theatre of Brecht. *Red Roses for Me* (1942), which deals with the strike in Dublin in 1913, belongs to the same group of didactic and experimental plays.

Post-War Developments   The distribution of peasant plays and more experimental pieces between the Abbey and the Peacock Theatre developed into a permanent arrangement that survived the demolition of the original Abbey Theatre after a fire in 1951. The new playhouse was opened not before 1966, and in the meantime other institutions had established themselves beside the Abbey, Peacock and Gate theatres. The Pike Theatre in Dublin (1953), which cared for the avant-garde, premièred Beckett and Brendan Behan, while the Lyric Players' Theatre in Belfast (1951) became best known for producing the work of Brian Friel. In 1957, the **Dublin Theatre Festival** began to showcase Irish and international plays alongside each other, and immediately ran into problems with the authorities. The first Irish production of *The Rose Tattoo* by the American playwright Tennessee Williams at the Pike Theatre was suppressed already during the 1957 Festival, as one scene entailed the (mimed) dropping of a condom onto the stage. This led to a prosecution for obscenity, and to the short imprisonment of the director. Even though the theatre won the case, the court costs enforced its closing down. O'Casey was the next to be involved. In the plays of his last phase, O'Casey had returned to tragicomedy. *Cock-a-Doodle-Dandy* (first produced in Newcastle, 1949) is a satire on the outlook and morals of Irish provincial society. This and O'Casey's other anticlerical plays were not allowed a production in Ireland, and in 1958, the Archbishop of Dublin himself intervened to have the Dublin Theatre Festival cancelled so that *The Drums of Father Ned* could not be produced. When the Festival organisers complied, both O'Casey and Beckett protested by forbidding all productions of their plays in Ireland for the next years.

To some, Samuel Beckett – a Nobel Prize laureate like Yeats and Shaw – is the greatest of twentieth-century Irish playwrights, and his self-imposed exile in Paris (where he met Joyce, another Irishman in exile) may paradoxically rather further than harm his Irish credentials. Beckett's dramatic conception, however, does not principally endear him to a 'national' theatre. In significant fashion, the director of the first Irish production of *Waiting for Godot* (Pike Theatre, 1955) added local colour in costume and in the spoken dialogue. Yet the increasingly more radical reduction in Beckett's subsequent plays rendered such a practice less feasible. By contrast, the particularly Irish character of the plays of Brendan Behan (1923–64) has never been in doubt. In his autobiographical writings (*Borstal Boy*, 1958; *Confessions of an Irish Rebel*, 1965) as well as in his stage-plays *The Quare Fellow* and *The Hostage*, Behan drew on his personal involvement with the IRA as a young man that led to a prolonged prison experience. For a first version of *The Quare Fellow* (Pike Theatre, 1954) as a one-act play in Irish, the Dublin-born playwright borrowed the title *Casadh an tSúgáin*, or 'The Twisting of Another Rope', from Douglas Hyde's pioneering peasant play that moreover was one of the first pieces ever staged in Irish. After the Abbey manager turned it down, *The Quare Fellow* premièred at the newly opened Pike Theatre in 1954 as a three-act play in English, set in Dublin's Mount-

Beckett and Behan

|Fig. 5.10
Brendan Behan by Phil Stanziola, 1960

joy Prison 24 hours before the execution of a man who killed and dissected his own brother. The Biblical motif is linked with the theme of judicial hanging that featured before (and just as negatively) in the ballads and stories of Kipling, Wilde and Orwell (see chap. 4.3), whereas the time frame of Behan's play is reminiscent of classic Modernist novels such as *Ulysses* and *Mrs Dalloway*. The audience is made to look at the prisoners on stage who themselves can only comment on the drama within the condemned cell which they witness from the outside. (The title reflects the expression from prison slang for such an inmate awaiting capital punishment.) The make-up of the play goes a long way to explain its built-in suspense as well as its success: after the initial Dublin run of six months, *The Quare Fellow* was brought out by Joan Littlewood's Theatre Workshop in Stratford East in 1956 before the play transferred to the West End. Littlewood was also instrumental in the production of *The Hostage*, which is likewise indebted to the Workshop's signature revue style. Behan's impersonation of the stage Irishman *cliché* certainly helped, too. (He was drunk during TV interviews and occasionally interrupted his own plays by singing songs from the audience.) Behan's best-known play is a good example for the crossover between languages and the media. *The Hostage* is another experiment in extended foreshadowing, which again features an impending prison execution, but in addition reflects the basic situation of Frank O'Connor's short story "Guests of the Nation" (1931): the detention (in a brothel) of a British soldier who converses with the Irish on a level of general humanity while his fate is in the hands of his captors. Behan's play was first produced in Dublin in an Irish version (*An Giall*, 1958) and then in variant English versions related to London productions that were favourably received. Joan Littlewood revised the script for the Theatre Workshop production, which was then reworked again for mounting the play in the West End. After a further adaptation as a television play, *The Hostage* was presented by RTÉ in 1968 (and again in 1973). However, as no other but the English stage versions are extant, the entire and telling complexity of this production process across the language and the media divide can easily fall out of view.

Irish Television Drama

Another piece of dramatic realism made an impact, too, in the medium of television. *Tolka Row: A Play of Dublin Life* (1951; see Deane 2002: V, 1247–49) was further developed by its creator, the minor novelist and playwright Maura Laverty (1907–67), into the first Irish soap opera (1964–68). Just like Roddy Doyle's *Barrytown Trilogy*, this serial was set in the working-class homes of Dublin's Northside. The setting contrasted with that of Wesley Burrowes's competing soap opera *The Riordans* (1965–79) that dealt with family life in a rural village, the fictionalised 'Leestown' in Kilkenny. In this, *The Riordans* did not only tie in with its British counterpart *The Archers*, but also with the tradition of the *peasant play*. In the television drama by Ulster playwrights, Irish politics became a topic, too. Sam Thompson (1916–65), who had advanced from the Belfast shipyards to the dramatic profession, addressed the sectarian politics in Northern Ireland several times, and not without difficulty. The Ulster Group Theatre rejected Thompson's stage-play *Over the Bridge* (1959) – in which a Protestant worker defends and protects a Catholic colleague against a mob – as too controversial, but when the play was produced at another venue, it drew a record-breaking audience of more than 40,000 people over a six-week run. By now it was accepted and even transmitted twice in different media: by BBC Radio Belfast as a radio play and by Granada TV as a television play. However, *Cemented with Love*, which was conceived right from the start as a play for television, had to wait for a production until the year of Thompson's death. This satirical comedy includes among its characters both a Unionist and a Nationalist candidate contesting a parliamentary election, which ends in a surprise result. The reason for the delay in transmission was that *Cemented with Love* had given rise to a controversy between the BBC's London headquarters and its Belfast branch, which initially saw the piece as too provoking – only to be disproved once more by the audience's positive response. The renewed outbreak of violence in Ulster a few years later made the matter even more urgent. A general estimate said that Northern Ireland and the Troubles featured in some 70 single plays and series episodes – many of them controversial – on British television since 1980 (Bignell 2000: 110; see also Sheehan 2001).

The Troubles featured, too, in Neil Jordan's memorable 1992 movie *The Crying Game*, where the basic situation of O'Connor's "Guests of the Nation" and Behan's *The Hostage* was further developed. One of the actors who made his mark by playing an ex-IRA man in this movie was Stephen Rea, who had worked with the

Brian Friel

dramatist Brian Friel (*1929 as a Catholic in Northern Ireland). In 1980, both men had co-founded the **Field Day Theatre Company** near the border to the Republic of Ireland, at Derry – or Londonderry, to those Northern Irish Unionists loyal to Britain. (This purposeful move away from the two cultural centres of Dublin and Belfast echoed the earlier foundation of the Druid Theatre Company in Galway in 1975, which successfully toured in Ireland and abroad.) Earlier still, in 1972 – after the renewed outbreak of **'Troubles'** in Northern Ireland between the (Catholic) Irish Republican Army (IRA), the Protestant Unionists and their loyalist paramilitary affiliations, and regular British troops – Derry had been the site of the 'Bloody Sunday' when British soldiers killed fourteen Civil Rights demonstrators. This decisive political event was mirrored in Brian Friel's most overtly political play, *The Freedom of the City* (Abbey Theatre, 1973).

Friel had begun with radio plays for the BBC before he turned to write for the stage, and to make Baile Beag/Ballybeg (literally 'small town', an invented Irish-speaking community in County Donegal) the location for many of his stage-plays. In *Aristocrats* (Abbey Theatre, 1979), Friel continued the story of the decline of the Big House from where Lennox Robinson and Brendan Behan had left off up to the 1970s, but gave it a twist by focusing on a highborn *Catholic* family. In Friel's play, Chopin's music and the characters' memories make them tell themselves in turn the history of the O'Donnells (namesakes of which people most of his plays), of their servants and their guests (including Yeats and O'Casey) at Ballybeg Hall.

Together with the Field Day Theatre Company, Friel produced further plays of history and cultural memory. *Making History* (1988) takes the audience back to Hugh O'Neill's abortive rebellion against the early English colonisation of Ireland in the last years of the reign of Elizabeth I (1595–1603). Friel's history play suggests a comparison with the works of both Shakespeare and Scott. Unlike Shakespeare's English history plays, *Making History* cannot be said to propagate a Tudor Myth, but – quite like Scott's Waverley Novels – deals with the defeat and suppression of a Gaelic culture on the Celtic Fringe. In Friel's play, the aftermath of the decisive Battle of Kinsale (1601) is told in messenger's reports as a bloody story of executions ordered by the English victors. However, Friel is by no means deaf to the disharmonies in the Irish cultural record. In his image of Pre-Ascendancy society, there is already a pronounced social spread, with Catholic Primate Peter Lombard and chieftains like the earls Hugh O'Neill and Hugh O'Donnell on top. The outlook of this Gaelic elite is marred by national and religious prejudices. They become audible when O'Neill – who is made to speak with an upper-class English accent – announces his marriage to Mabel, a member of the family of the Queen's Marshal, and meets with strong anti-English and anti-Protestant resentment among his peers. However, O'Neill's nonconformity in these respects does not translate to gender relations: a true patriarch, he makes both his wife and his mistresses live uneasily with him under the same roof. In addition to its ambivalent and far from Nationalist picture of Irishness in the past, *Making History* provides the audience also with a very contemporary reflection about history and ideology. O'Neill's talks with Archbishop Lombard about the latter's projected history of Ireland, and about the role of truth and myth in the fabrication of historical narratives, always ascend to a meta-historical level (Friel 1989: 8–9, 15–16, 66–67).

In Friel's earlier play *Translations*, language had taken the place of history as a meta-discursive subject. *Translations* (Field Day's first production at the Guildhall, Derry, 1980) came from the pen of a man who is himself noted for his translations and adaptations of Chekhov and Turgenev. In this play, modernity and change arrive in 1833 in two expressions of standardisation and uniformity that come as a threat to the traditional life of the Irish Gaelic community: the Irish Survey and the English-language National School.

Emigration was at the centre of Friel's breakthrough play, *Philadelphia, Here I Come!* (a variation upon the often covered song, "California, Here I Come"), where a young man called Gareth O'Donnell is about to move away from provincial Ireland to a New World. This early and experimental play (produced by the Gate at the Gaiety Theatre, Dublin, in 1964) was placed in contemporary Ballybeg, and to dramatise the protagonist's inner conflict, his personality was split into Private Gar, a personified soliloquy or aside, and Public Gar (played by different actors). This allowed for a continuous, often ironic comment of Private Gar on the utterances of both his public self and of his friends. In the course of their conversation, hidden emotions are uncovered behind outward appearances, and emigration looks less and less like a solution. When he responded to the Troubles in *The Freedom of the City* (1973), Friel joined political commitment with formal experiment by splitting up the action into several, simultaneous and intertwined strands of the plot. In only slightly veiled fashion, this analytical play deals with the 1972 Bloody Sunday, and with different versions of the 'truth' in the 'making of history'. At the opening of the play, the audience encounters three bodies lying dead on stage. Several versions of the last hours and the deaths of these working-class characters are given by others and themselves, in a series of concerted speeches *ad spectatores* at the beginning of the second act. *Faith Healer* (1979) and *Molly Sweeney* (Gate Theatre, 1994), two plays that consist of a series of parallel monologues spoken by characters on an empty stage, were further experiments with dramatic interaction. Since his success with *Dancing at Lughnasa* (Abbey Theatre, 1990), his play about five sisters in 1930s Ballybeg (made into a film in 1998), Friel enjoys international renown, with few peers in his generation.

Tom Murphy

The controversial plays of Tom Murphy (*1935) have regularly been produced at the Abbey Theatre, from *A Whistle in the Dark* (1961) up to *The Alice Trilogy* (2005). *A Whistle in the Dark* was first rejected by the Abbey's director, who objected to its unwanted portrait of a violent family and criminal gang of Irish immigrants in Coventry. From this controversial start, Murphy's standing with the Abbey improved so significantly that he was honoured in October 2001 by a retrospective season of six of his plays, a singular event which attracted large audiences. Murphy's dramatic work includes two history plays: *Famine* (1968), referring to the Irish Potato Famine of 1845, and *The Patriot Game* (1991), keyed to the Easter Rising 1916; and moreover *The Sanctuary Lamp*, which was premièred in 1975 but considerably revised in 2000 after much criticism of its anti-Catholic features. *Conversations on a Homecoming* (1985) deals with the exchanges of a returned emigrant and regulars in a pub (and involved, true to stereotype, really hard drinking of the Irish actors on stage).

Martin McDonagh and Conor McPherson

In the 1990s, a younger group of Irish playwrights made their mark with plays whose setting in the West of Ireland is reminiscent (but no copy) of the early twentieth-century peasant play. Much like Yeats before him, Martin McDonagh (*1970) became acquainted with the West of Ireland during his holidays away from London, where he was born to Irish parents. *The Beauty Queen of Leenane* is set throughout in the living-room/kitchen of a rural cottage in County Galway (and was first produced at Galway Town Hall Theatre and at the Royal Court Theatre Upstairs, 1996). McDonagh's combination of a parent-child-relationship that went sour with stage Irishness and black humour looks back to Synge. However, here we deal not with a *Playboy* but with a virgin beauty of the Western World: it is when her domineering mother Mag threatens to spoil her last chance of lasting love, and of emigration to America, that Maureen Folan, the unmarried middle-aged daughter, retaliates fiercely. After McDonagh had achieved his international breakthrough with this play, he completed two trilogies set in the West of Ireland: *The Leenane Trilogy* (1996–97) and *The Aran Islands Trilogy* (best known for *The Lieutenant of Inishmore*, 2001). The movie *In Bruges*, which McDonagh directed for release in 2008, is based upon his own script (and on analogies to Pinter's *The Dumb Waiter*). With the 1997 first production of his award-winning play *The Weir* at the Royal Court, Conor McPherson (*1971) joined the circle of contemporary playwrights with an international audience. In *The Weir*, those characters assembled in a country pub in the West of Ireland tell themselves stories of the supernatural, and thereby reveal some hidden side of their personal selves.

The theatre in Northern Ireland had been enriched by community plays from a women's angle that were produced by Marie Jones (*1951) in collaboration with the Charabanc Theatre Company (1983–95; see Harris 2007). Among other plays of note are the stage biographies of Stewart Parker (1941–88). *Northern Star* (Lyric Theatre, Belfast, 1984) is a mixture of history play and dramatic pastiche. The life of a Belfast rebel who took part in the 1798 rebellion is told from the gallows, with different scenes presented in the manner of Boucicault, Behan and Beckett. Parker's *Heavenly Bodies* (premièred in Birmingham, 1986) concentrates on the Irish-American melodramatist Dion Boucicault, and as a retrospective play about a playwright's life and work for the stage, bears some general resemblance to Peter Shaffer's *Amadeus* (1980). The Northern Irish playwright himself is commemorated by the Stewart Parker Award set up in the year after his death to encourage young Irish dramatists. The extreme case of one of the recipients of the award, who likewise hailed from the

The Belfast Scene

Protestant working-class community in Belfast, provided proof that such encouragement is indeed necessary. The Good Friday Agreement (1998) may have signalled the ending of the Troubles in Northern Ireland, but did not stop internal violence within the Protestant community. In a series of stage and screenplays that were produced by the Abbey Theatre's Peacock Stage and by the Royal Court Theatre Upstairs (e. g. *As the Beast Sleeps*, 1998; *The Force of Change*, 2000; *Remnants of Fear*, 2006), Gary Mitchell (*1965) addressed the controversial role of loyalist paramilitary groups in Northern Ireland. Shortly before Christmas 2005, such paramilitaries from the neighbourhood who felt provoked by the playwright, forced him and his family to flee their homes and go into hiding. Sometimes, the unforeseen events of real life drama rival any writing for the stage.

5.2.5 | **Drama and Theatre since the 1980s**

Caryl Churchill's Feminist Plays

The plays of Caryl Churchill (*1938) have been produced on stage as well as on radio (BBC Third Programme, 1962–73) and television (1972ff.). After her stint as a resident dramatist (1974–75), the prestigious Royal Court Theatre regularly premièred her plays, which however were also produced by the Joint Stock Theatre Group for Alternative Theatre venues and in lunchtime productions. Churchill's political outlook is Feminist and anti-Capitalist, her plots are often non-linear and less and less realistic, and she sometimes provokes by stark language, but generally refrains from the more brutal shock tactics of the Theatre of Cruelty. The two-act play *Cloud Nine* (1979, revival 1980), which is set first in Victorian times and then in contemporary London, questions colonialism and patriarchy at the same time. The constellation of characters includes a colonial administrator and his family, his widowed mistress, his black servant, a governess, and an explorer. Each of the characters represents a position on a continuum of colonial and gender roles that however are subverted. During the first act, various heterosexual and homosexual liaisons are formed, a process that continues in the second act, where many of the characters re-appear, but now played by different actors. In an unconventional dramatic experiment, Churchill had used cross-gender and cross-ethnic casting in the first act, reverting to a more conventional casting in the second act, which is however more loosely structured. In the all-female play *Top Girls* (1982), both the non-linear structure and the feminist agenda are more marked. In the opening scene, Marlene, a career woman working for the Top Girls employment agency, meets a series of famous women from history in a restaurant. Female icons among the dinner guests include Pope Joan and the explorer Isabella Bird, but also the character of Patient Griselda from one of Chaucer's *Canterbury Tales*. In the next scenes of the play, the similarities between these characters from history and some of Marlene's colleagues at the agency are stressed, for instance by doubling the roles. The constellation of the characters and the quarrels between the women invite the audience to compare and qualify their gender roles. Caryl Churchill's later plays for the Royal Court Theatre included her verse play *Serious Money* (1987, see chap. 5.2.2), *Blue Heart* as well as *This is a Chair* (both 1997) and *Far Away* (2000).

The 1990s saw a new shock wave of drama that combined the themes of violence or materialism with a provocative treatment of sexuality. Royal Court audiences have been used to such provocation at least since the staging of Bond's *Saved* (1965). Nevertheless, the 1994 stage adaptation of Irvine Welsh's novel *Trainspotting* (1993) set the scene for an ongoing series of stage-plays that were bound to the moment, in their attempt to catch up with the *Zeitgeist* as well as in their episodic structure and their sensational effects. The work by the two young dramatists Mark Ravenhill and Sarah Kane could be promoted as **'In-Yer-Face Theatre'** and successfully be transferred to Continental stages, where they may have been produced more often than in Britain (see Sierz 2001, but also his and other more distanced views in D'Monté and Saunders 2008). Due to the shortness of a troubled life ending in suicide, the name of Sarah Kane (1971–99) remains primarily linked with *Blasted* (1995). In its investigation of personal relationships through enactments of physical and emotional cruelty, Kane's first stage-play was reminiscent of Pinter's 'comedies of menace', Bond's form of the Theatre of Cruelty, and Brenton's *The Romans in Britain*. Kane combined a domestic but increasingly claustrophobic setting (a hotel room in apparently war-torn Leeds, blasted by a mortar bomb in the middle of the play) with conversational breaks and with acts and images of violence committed against others and oneself. It was less the thematic link-

'In-Yer-Face Theatre'

ing of racism, sadism and sexuality that made for Kane's *succès de scandale* rather than the nature of sexual gratification and the offensive degree of verbal and physical brutality the audience was made to view. In addition to much explicit language, and to a baby coming to harm, this involved a soldier who first told in detail about war crimes, then raped and blinded another male character on stage, before he blasted his own brains out with a gun. Kane's plays *Cleansed* (1998) and *Phaedra's Love* (1996, after Seneca) continued in this vein, while her last plays *Crave* (1998) and *4:48 Psychosis* (posthumously produced 2000) were more experimental, by dispensing with plot and stage directions altogether.

The plays by Mark Ravenhill (*1966) have likewise been sensational and offensive. *Shopping and Fucking* (1996) includes both heterosexual and homosexual acts as well as violence and vomiting on stage. It is tempting to shift attention to the seemingly less offensive first word in the title of Ravenhill's coming out as a playwright, and to investigate his ambivalent treatment of a consumer culture, here and likewise in *Some Explicit Polaroids* (1999). The dialogue of Ravenhill's plays involves instances of a critique of materialism, yet Ravenhill quite consciously evaded a real debate on political, social or economic issues in the line of G. B. Shaw's *Mrs Warren's Profession* or of successive political playwrights. Male and female prostitutes as well as junkies may regularly feature in Ravenhill's cast, yet those characters from the margins of society are likewise trying to get their share in the consumption of sex, drugs and rave music. The style and vision of Ravenhill's more recent plays saw some adjustment and extension. The wish for instant fame and celebrity was made a topic in *Totally Over You* (2002), yet in this play for teenagers (inspired by a piece of Molière), Ravenhill for once cut back on expletives. Other plays of his came with a new historic dimension: *Mother Clap's Molly House* (2001) took turns between the contemporary gay scene in London and an eighteenth-century setting (in a brothel), while *Ripper* (2007) engaged with the Victorian serial murderer as a sensational icon of sexual violence.

Documentary Theatre However, what was sometimes referred to as a New Brutalism on stage was overtaken by the reality of war in the former Yugoslavia, in Iraq and elsewhere. As a result, the committed playwright and critic David Edgar made out a new wave of **docudrama**, of factual plays based on actual and controversial events or inquiries (see Edgar 2008 a/b). The Tricycle Theatre under its director Nicolas Kent took a lead in the production of documentary theatre with *The Colour of Justice* (1999) by Richard Norton-Taylor, a journalist for *The Guardian*. His play was a verbatim reconstruction from official records of the public inquiry into a spectacular case of racial violence in the UK, namely the death of black teenager Stephen Lawrence. *Stuff Happens* (2004) by David Hare (*1947) brought the way into the Iraq War to the National Theatre stage, with leading politicians from the US and the UK appearing as characters in the play. In the same year 2004, audiences in the Tricycle Theatre, in the West End and on Broadway applauded *Guantánamo: Honor Bound to Defend Freedom*. This collaboration between the South African born novelist and playwright Gillian Slovo (*1952) and the journalist Victoria Brittain is based on interviews with relatives of those detained in the US-American prison. In similar fashion, the Scottish playwright Gregory Burke (*1968) detained his audience at the 2006 Edinburgh Festival with *Black Watch*, a docudrama based on interviews with soldiers in the British Army's eponymous Highland regiment. The play mixes scenes covering their experience of the Iraq Invasion with others depicting the regimental history of the legendary Black Watch.

Burke's play was first produced by the company of the National Theatre of Scotland (NTS). Since its foundation in 2006, this new cultural institution has performed at a variety of venues, as it is not based at a single playhouse – much like the Edinburgh Festival. Straight from the 2006 Festival, *Black Watch* went to be produced at the opening of the Scottish Parliament, the first with a Nationalist majority. The cultural nationalism that led to Devolution and the establishment of both a parliament and a 'national' theatre for Scotland, but also to a renewed interest in regional history, was one influence on *Mary Queen of Scots Got Her Head Chopped Off*, premièred at the 1987 Edinburgh Festival in the quatercentenary of the execution of Mary Stuart. Another influence on the play written and produced by Liz Lochhead (*1947) and Communicado Theatre Co. was Feminism.

A different approach to the dramatic presentation of Scottish history was taken before by John McGrath and his 7:84 Theatre Company who had originally devised *The Cheviot, the Stag and the*

The Scottish Scene

Black, Black Oil (1974) as a history play for the Alternative Theatre. This ended up in an experiment with different media.

> [T]he television adaptation brought together elements of recorded theatre (the performance by McGrath's 7:84 Theatre Company of the original stage version before an audience in the West Highlands), music hall (set pieces and songs), historical reconstruction of the Highland Clearances of the eighteenth and nineteenth centuries, and television documentary footage on the current working condition in the North Sea Oil industry. The elements are not integrated to confirm and support each other, but are clearly separated out. [...] In the Brechtian terminology which became almost formulaic in the 1970s, the viewer could not simply consume meanings which were already integrated, but had to become active as a producer of meaning, working to produce her own understanding of the relationships between the elements of the drama. (Caughie 2000: 113–14. For a short survey of the twentieth-century development of theatre and drama in Scotland and Wales, see Thomson 2004: III, 195ff., 470ff.; Holdsworth and Luckhurst 2008: 107–45.)

Black British and Asian British Plays and Films

The development towards a multi-ethnic and transcultural British society has also been reflected on stage and screen. Farrukh Dhondy was very influential in this respect. He was born in India in 1944 and has lived in the UK since 1964 as a teacher, playwright and writer of fiction, as well as beeing a scriptwriter and producer for television. With *Come to Mecca*, he wrote the first TV series set among the British-Asian group, and based it on his short fiction. His plays include *Mama Dragon* (1980), *Romance, Romance* (1985) and *Vigilantes* (1988). Hanif Kureishi (*1954) made his name by writing the screenplays for Stephen Frears's films *My Beautiful Laundrette* (1986) and *Sammy and Rosie Get Laid* (1987). These films, which were commissioned by Farrukh Dhondy as executive producer at Channel 4 TV, presented the problems of a multicultural Britain. In 1993, Kureishi adapted his own novel *The Buddha of Suburbia* (1990) into a TV miniseries. As an actor, Ayub Khan-Din (*1954), who likewise was born into a mixed marriage with a British Pakistani father, had taken the role of Sammy in Frears's film. His own family setup is mirrored in his play *East is East* (Royal Court Theatre, 1996), which he adapted himself for the screen (1999), where it met with great success.

Mustapha Matura (*1939) hailed from Trinidad, from where he arrived in Britain in 1961. By co-founding the Black Theatre Co-operative, he paved the way for other Black companies. The

Trinidad Carnival and Calypso is reflected in the plays entitled *Play Mas* (1974) and *Rum an' Coca Cola* (1976, both premièred at the Royal Court Theatre). In his topical play *The Coup* (NT, 1991), he addressed an attempted overthrow of the Trinidad government by a radical Muslim group. *The Playboy of the West Indies* (Oxford Playhouse, 1984) looked back to Synge's *Playboy*. Among a younger generation, Caryl Phillips (*1958) and Winsome Pinnock (*1961) came out with the Black version of a problem play. Phillips's *Strange Fruit* (Crucible Theatre, Sheffield, 1980) compares well with Pinnock's stage-play *Leave Taking* (Liverpool Playhouse Studio, 1988). Both deal with inter-generational problems, with single motherhood and the absence of fathers in Afro-Caribbean-British families, and with the clash between the lifestyles and cultural habitat of immigrant parents and their British-born children. Kay Adshead (*1954) co-founded Mama Quillo Productions as a feminist company producing plays for stage, radio and television. Adshead's *The Bogus Woman* was the first play produced by the company, and it made its way directly from the Edinburgh and London fringe to BBC Radio 3 in the years 2000–02. The play deals with asylum seekers as another group of migrants in a Britain that at the turn to the new millennium looked less centralised and much more multicultural than ever before.

Guiding Questions and Exercises

1. Summarise the overall development of theatre and drama in twentieth-century Britain and Ireland before and after the 1950s.
2. The twentieth century has seen two world wars, a number of other armed conflicts in which British troops were involved, and a perennial series of 'Troubles' in and about Ireland. Compare the attitude towards war in the work of British and Irish dramatists since the ending of the First World War and of the Anglo-Irish War.
3. Have a closer look at the different ways in which G. B Shaw's *Saint Joan*, T. S. Eliot's *Murder in the Cathedral* and Robert Bolt's *A Man for All Seasons* deal with the relationship of the religious individual to God, King and Country. How does Peter Shaffer's *Amadeus* come in to the comparison?

4. Priestley's *An Inspector Calls*, Eliot's *The Cocktail Party* and Pinter's *The Birthday Party* develop from a similar situation, namely the contribution of uninvited or unidentified guests in wrecking a party. Compare the dramatic presentation in each case and locate these plays in the context and development of twentieth-century drama.

5. Describe the central elements of plot and of dramatic conflict in Peter Shaffer's *Equus*, and point out those features in the play that are characteristic of his dramatic work in general. Moreover, compare Shaffer's play to Eliot's *The Cocktail Party* in its treatment of sexuality, religion and the role of psychotherapy.

6. There are a number of twentieth- and twenty-first century plays that have been concerned with the prison as a setting and with punishment as a theme. Compare the individual treatment and dramatic presentation in John Galsworthy's *Justice* (1910, mentioned in chap. 4.3) and Brendan Behan's *The Quare Fellow* (1954), in Caryl Churchill's two plays *Crimes* (BBC TV, 1982) and *Softcops* (RSC, 1984), in Harold Pinter's *One for the Road* (1984) as well as in *Guantánamo* by Gillian Slovo and Victoria Brittain (2004).

7. Modern physics play a prominent part in Tom Stoppard's *Hapgood* (1988) and *Arcadia* (1993) as well as in *Copenhagen* by Michael Frayn (1998). Discuss the way in which those playwrights deal with this subject matter, and extend your discussion to include Friedrich Dürrenmatt's *Die Physiker* (1962).

8. Sarah Kane's *Blasted* is in many ways reminiscent of earlier provocative plays by Harold Pinter (*The Dumb Waiter* and *The Birthday Party*), by Edward Bond (*Saved* and *Lear*), and by Howard Brenton (*The Romans in Britain*). Compare these plays with regard to their setting and atmosphere, to their engagement with violence and sexuality as a theme, and to their dramatic form of presentation.

5.3 | Fiction

With a view to the sheer number of works of fiction published since the 1920s, novels as well as short stories, any survey runs the risk of dropping authors' names only, and of unfairly treating others that necessarily have to be left out. If one accepts that any treatment will consequently be sketchy, it will be more fruitful to mark out some general tendencies, and to restrict oneself to a few select examples discussed in greater detail. The 1969 essay "The Novelist at the Crossroads" by the critic and novelist David Lodge, together with its 1992 update "The Novelist Today: Still at the Crossroads?" are helpful in this respect. Whereas other critics from the 1960s to the '90s set out from the fictional experiments of Modernists such as Joyce and Woolf in order to promote a single and seemingly continuous line of aesthetic progress culminating in the anti-realist 'fabulation' of their own 'Post-Modernist' times, Lodge made out several parallel traditions instead. Looking back from 1992, Lodge summarised his earlier argument and likewise the development since:

> The contemporary novelist was therefore in the situation of a man (or woman) at a crossroads. Before him stretched the way of traditional realism, now alleged to be a very boring route, and possibly a dead end. To the left and right were the ways of fabulation and non-fictional narrative. Many writers, I suggested, unable to choose between these three routes, built their hesitation into their fiction, made the problems of writing a novel the subject of the novel. I called this the problematic novel; later it was christened [...] metafiction: a name that achieved wider currency. [...] There was, I argued, no dominant style or *écriture* [...]. 'We seem to be living through a period of unprecedented cultural pluralism which allows, in all the arts, an astonishing variety of styles to flourish simultaneously.'
>
> Twenty years later, I think that generalisation still holds good; but I am struck by how sturdily traditional realism has survived [...], and how clearly it remains a serious option for the literary novelist today. (By realism I mean not only a mimetic representation of experience, but also the organisation of narrative according to a logic of causality and temporal sequence.) [...]
>
> Fabulation [a heading under which Lodge includes also Salman Rushdie's Magic Realism] has certainly flourished in the last twenty years, but it has not conquered the fictional scene. It remains a marginal form of fiction, at least in Britain.   (Lodge 1992: 205–06)

Following up on Lodge's argument (which statistically cannot be disproved), it seems adequate to start the survey with forms of fictional realism that stem from earlier periods, but that are still an option for contemporary novelists. (Apart from Connor 1996 and Head 2002, see moreover Shaffer 2005 and V. Nünning 2007, which provide information on the context of production and distribution of contemporary fiction, too.)

5.3.1 | **Mainstream Writing up to the 1960s, and a Concern with History Well Beyond**

Evelyn Waugh and
Graham Greene as
Catholic Novelists

In *Brideshead Revisited* (1945, rev. 1960), Evelyn Waugh (1903–66) chose the decline of a family of rural, Catholic aristocrats, the Marchmains at Brideshead, to illustrate the clash between tradition and modernity. In its wide-ranging portrait of upper middle-class society in London and in the country in the interwar period, *Brideshead Revisited* compares well with Victorian and Edwardian novels. Its distinctive feature, however, is Waugh's concern with Roman Catholicism as the religious belief of a minority of Christians in Britain. Here lie the similarities with the

Graham Greene

work of Graham Greene (1904–91), who had converted to Roman Catholicism in 1926 and who explored the moral dilemma of Catholic characters in a number of widely read novels. *Brighton Rock* (1938) relates the short and brutal life of Pinkie, whose criminal career as a teenage gangster in contemporary Brighton leads from blackmail over gang wars to murder. Along the way, Pinkie tries to find his identity in a religious framework that is marked by the poles of sin and punishment, and the possibility of salvation that might lie in his relationship to Rose, a teenage waitress whom Pinkie seduces and marries (in order to prevent her from testifying against him). Among the remarkable features of Naturalism in *Brighton Rock* are Greene's realistic portrait of characters and their milieu, which includes the language spoken. In the alike suspenseful plots and in the more exotic settings of Greene's further Catholic novels and 'entertainments' (his designation for thrillers) lay part of their appeal to contemporary audiences, including those that went to see their adaptation for the screen. For *Brighton Rock* as a movie (1947) as well as for successful adaptations of his other works of fiction, such as *The Third Man* (1949, set in post-war Vienna), *Our Man in Havana* (1958/59, set in Cuba before Castro's revolution) and *The Comedians* (1966/67, set in violence-torn Haiti), Greene also wrote the screenplays. His novel *The Power and the Glory* (1940) is set in post-revolutionary Mexico, in a situation where religious faith competes with revolutionary politics as means of salvation (in a material as well as idealistic sense). Greene's novel centres on a Whiskey Priest who is inwardly torn between his religious doubts and duties, at a time when he is being pursued by a police officer as powerful personification of an atheist state. In Greene's *The Heart of the Matter* (1948, set in West Africa), it is just such a police officer whose faithfulness is put to the test: Major Scobie's charitable endeavours are frustrated by fate (as when he cannot help a ship-wrecked boy to survive), a love born out of the same compassion leads him into adultery and thus into a conflict with his Catholic creed, and his trust into a dubious diamond dealer entangles him in a net of corruption and murder. In a tragic denouement the protagonists in all three novels mentioned die of unnatural causes. Despite his interest in the psychology of his characters, Greene the novelist valued his thematic concerns higher than a participation in the stylistic experiments of Modernism with the representation of the human mind. The turn from a sense of duty to disloyalty, in a conflict between compassion and other obligations, is also at the heart of the matter in *The Quiet American* (1955) and *The Human Factor* (1978), two further novels by Greene set in Vietnam and South Africa, respectively. (See chaps. 5.3.2 and 5.3.5.) After Waugh and Greene, Catholicism and disbelief as topics reappear in various ways in the work of other novelists, e.g. in the Scottish writer Muriel Spark's parable *The Comforters* (1957) and in *The Abbess of Crewe* (1974), a political satire on the Watergate Scandal that is set in a convent. In a mix of fiction and non-fiction entitled *1985* (but published in 1978), Anthony Burgess provided a theological interpretation of his own work, including his earlier dystopia *A Clockwork Orange* (1962). Finally, the academic novelist David Lodge combined Catholic concerns with comedy in his novels *The British Museum Is Falling Down* (1965) and *How Far Can You Go* (1980). Over and above faithfulness and (dis-)loyalty as themes, Greene's *The Power and the Glory* (1940) suggests a comparison with *Under the Volcano* (1947) by Malcolm Lowry (1909–57) as another character study within an exotic setting, centring on a British consul and alcoholic in Mexico.

The exotic locations alone distinguish Lowry's novel as well as the later novels by Graham Greene from other post-war fiction whose authors combined narrative realism with social realism when they took a disillusioned view on the class-ridden society

Social Realism

of 1950s Britain. This often happened from the point of view of working-class or lower middle-class characters, and with an un-inhibited interest in their sexual relations. Prominent examples are *Lucky Jim* (1954) and *Take a Girl Like You* (1960) by Kingsley Amis (1922–95), *Saturday Night and Sunday Morning* (1958) as well as *The Loneliness of the Long-Distance Runner* (1959) by Alan Sillitoe (*1928), and *Room at the Top* (1957) by John Braine (1922–86). Together with the dramatist John Osborne (see chap. 5.2), those novelists were soon spoken of as **Angry Young Men**, and the epithet **'kitchen sink'** was applied to such Naturalist novels and their adaptations for the screen because of their mode of realism that looked be-yond the bourgeois drawing room. In *Absolute Beginners* (1959), Colin MacInnes (1914–76) focused on teenage subculture and on racial violence in London's Notting Hill in the summer of 1958. The novels *Up the Junction* (1963) and *Poor Cow* (1967) by Nell Dunn (*1936), which were as successful as they were controversial be-cause they featured an abortion and prostitution, also belong into this context of social and sexual realism. Related examples from Scotland comprise the 1990s novels by Jeff Torrington, James Kel-man and Irvine Welsh (see chap. 5.3.4) that were likewise contro-versial, but also stylistically more experimental.

Historical Novels and
Novels about History

History as such and British history in particular are further topics that have frequently been dealt with in a realistic mode, in single novels as well as in larger series. A few select and popular examples may suffice. *Restoration* (1989) by Rose Tremain (*1943) is a good example of historical fiction that is more than just a costume piece (which may not always be said of its 1995 adap-tation for the screen). Tremain's **historical novel of character**, which was popular with a large readership and found critical acclaim, too, catches the atmosphere of the 1660s, but also reflects the interests of the time when and for which it was conceived – more than 300 years after the events. *Restoration* reminds its readers of the diary of Samuel Pepys as one of the great authentic period documents that covered the same time-span as the novel (see chap. 3.4.4). Tremain's protagonist Robert Merivel is a tool and a fool. He is useful to King Charles II who presents this capable surgeon with a Manor House for an arranged marriage with the King's mistress – on the condition that Merivel shall never en-joy sexual relations with his nominal wife, although Merivel's insatiable sex drive leads him to go to bed with women from all stations of society. With his clumsiness and coarse manners, Merivel in any case makes a strange bedfellow, but the King's order effectively turns him into a cuckold and a joke at Court. When Merivel transgresses his orders and attempts to make love to the King's mistress, he is punished and loses all possessions. In a humbler station, working together with Quakers for the mentally ill, Merivel develops a more responsible attitude to life and love, and distinguishes himself during the Great Plague and the Fire of London in 1665/66. His behaviour *restores* him to the King's favour (hence the title), albeit within certain limits. The reader's interest throughout the colourful and changeable life of the protagonist is kept up by Tremain's choice of first-person narration which guarantees sympathy for the 'King's Fool': he is a reliable narrator just because he is naïve, and his career break ensures the reader's pity. In some ways, Robert Graves's historical novels which are set in Rome under Emperor Augustus and his later successor Claudius (*I, Claudius* and *Claudius the God and his Wife Messalina*, both 1934) may have provided a model for Tremain, as they, too, employ homodiegetic narration about an age of loose morals. In his coarseness, indeed, Merivel seems much more typical of this later Augustan Age – which like its namesake in Graves's novels is presented not at all as an age of politeness and refinement – than appeared at first sight. Against the decadence at Court and in the city of London, the Quakers' mental hospital in the country represents not a safe haven, but at least a social alternative.

In a time of peril, shortly before the Second World War, C[ecil]. S[cott]. Forester (1899–1966) had begun to produce a series of sea novels that transcended the nineteenth-century example of Capt. Marryat, and in turn provided a model for later writers who also dealt with historical development in **multi-volume series keyed to one central character**. Forester's sea novels about Horatio Hornblower returned to the then most glorious period of the Royal Navy, in its fight against Revolutionary and Napoleonic France (1793–1815). Between 1945–62, the initial *Captain Hornblower* trilogy (*The Happy Return, A Ship of the Line, Flying Colours*, 1937–39) was made into a film starring Gregory Peck (*Captain Horatio Hornblower*, 1951, dir. Raoul Walsh) while it was expanded into a series of altogether ten novels and two books of short stories. Hornblower's career as an officer in the Royal Navy who is promoted from midshipman to

Admiral of the Fleet is based throughout on his abilities, and not on the social privilege of a gentleman's purchase of a commission. The similarities to the career of Horatio (!) Viscount Nelson are obvious, as are the similarities between the fictional South American tyrant El Supremo, Hornblower's antagonist who is as much a look-alike of Napoleon as of the right-wing dictators of the 1930s. Yet Forester did more than contribute his share of patriotism to the war effort. In his own account of "Me and My Books", the writer stated that he was concerned with the characterisation of his protagonist: Hornblower should be seen as a man of action who was at the same time his most severe critic. In some respects, Hornblower is indeed conceived as an anti-hero: he cannot fight with a sword and is as much afraid of climbing a mast as of going into a battle from which he might return maimed, like Nelson. Shy and reticent by nature, Hornblower is nevertheless extremely gifted as leader of a crew and as a professional sailor, and he overcomes his natural inhibition in his love affair with Barbara Wellesley, the fictional sister of the Duke of Wellington. With all his ambivalence, Hornblower proved to be a memorable character, so much so that the German writer Sten Nadolny included a reference to the subject matter of Forester's initial trilogy and its film adaptation in *Die Entdeckung der Langsamkeit* (1987: 158–59), another historical novel of character that deals with the nineteenth-century British explorer John Franklin as a likewise handicapped person. To name but a couple of related examples: George MacDonald Fraser (1925–2008) gave an ironic twist to the genre in *The Flashman Papers* (12 novels, 1969–2005, see chap. 5.3.5). *Ross Poldark: A Novel of Cornwall* was the first of a dozen novels in the Poldark series (1945–2002), a family saga conceived by Winston Graham (1908–2003) which spawned in 1975–77 one of the most successful BBC television dramas with an audience of c.15 million.

Graham Swift, *Waterland*

Apart from historical novels proper, single or in series, there are also **novels about history** written in a realistic mode. *Waterland* (1983) by Graham Swift (*1949) is a regional novel that deals with history on a personal, general and meta-historical level. The narrative voice belongs to Tom Crick, a history teacher about to retire in 1980 after more than 30 years of teaching, who gives his last lesson in the form of an oral tale told to 'Children' (i.e., the readers). On a personal level, the central element of the story (which is set in the war years 1940–43) deals with the death of Freddie Parr and the involvement of Mary Metcalf and of Crick's retarded brother Dick. The events in the past partly explain why Mary, now Tom Crick's wife, abducted a child in 1979, before the teacher's retirement. A more general outlook is provided with the family histories of the Cricks and of the Atkinsons, a dynasty of beer brewers: this account is sprinkled with historical reminiscences from the time of the French Revolution up to 1940. All this is bound up with the River Leem in the Fens as a setting that evokes an atmosphere of fairy tale and magic (Swift 1999: 1–2, 101) and thus explains the paradoxical fusion of land and water in the title (7, 11, 163). In his manner of "telling stories" about history (a phrase repeatedly stressed throughout the narrative), Tom Crick the teacher defends his view on history not only against myth and magic, but also against the view of his headmaster Lewis Scott, who – just like his counterpart Mr Gradgrind in Dickens's novel *Hard Times* (1854, see chap. 4.5.1) – recognises the 'real world' merely through "Facts. Facts" (Swift 1999: 48, 76). A meta-historical level is moreover reached when Crick's stories and Swift's novel are compared to more recent theories of historiography, the key features of which they are seen to illustrate well. In *Waterland*, we find the historical process represented in terms of a *longue durée* rather than as a series of incidents. We find the 'micro-history' along the 'grand narrative' of the French Revolution (chap. 25), yet with the stress on the life of the common people rather than the high and mighty – truly a 'history from below'. And we find, finally, human history contrasted with "Natural History" (1999: 119) in memorable passages that deal with water, silt and eels (chaps. 26–28). For *Last Orders*, a novel of character told from multiple points of view, Swift went on to win the Booker Prize in 1996 (see chap. 5.3.3).

Angus Wilson (*Anglo-Saxon Attitudes*, 1956), Sybille Bedford (*A Legacy*, 1956), Penelope Lively (*Moon Tiger*, 1987), Julian Barnes (*A History of the World in 10½ Chapters*, 1989), Peter Ackroyd (in more than one instance, see chap. 5.3.6), Pat Barker (*Regeneration Trilogy*, 1991–95), Sebastian Faulks (*Birdsong*, 1993) and Hilary Mantel (Booker Prize 2009 for *Wolf Hall*) – to name but a few – are among those writers that have in various other ways been concerned with historical characters and themes. (For more examples of historical fiction concerned with the history of the

Empire, see chap. 5.3.5, and for stage-plays on historical subject matter, see chap. 5.2.3.) Despite its title, *The History Man* (1975) by Malcolm Bradbury (1932–2000) deals less with views on history than with academic life and teaching outside Oxford and Cambridge in a post-1960s context of political and sexual revolution. *Lucky Jim* (1954) by Kingsley Amis as well as the trilogy of

Campus Novel

campus novels by David Lodge (*1935) – *Changing Places* (1975), *Small World: An Academic Romance* (1984) and *Nice Work* (1988) – compare with Bradbury's comic as well as disillusioned portrait of academia. *Possession* (1990), the novel which won A[ntonia]. S[usan] Byatt (*1936) the Booker Prize, tells the story of a contemporary pair of scholars investigating the mysterious relationship between two Victorian poets through their poems and letters. Besides, *Possession* is an instructive example of how publishers and commercial editors (from within the same publishing group) today sometimes and silently alter the text and design of a published novel to suit different audiences in Britain and in America (see Nowak 1997 and Mühleisen 2009).

5.3.2 | Forms of Popular Fiction

The Golden Age of Detective Fiction

Crime fiction is one among the many genres of twentieth-century fiction that found a particularly wide readership. The **murder mystery presented as a 'clue-puzzle'** that awaits a solution by detective and reader alike had an extraordinarily popular appeal in Britain. (For a typology and history of crime fiction, see Cawelti 1976, Suerbaum 1984, Knight 2003, Priestman 2003, Forshaw 2007.) The first **whodunit** proper was *Trent's Last Case* (1913) by E[dmund]. C[lerihew]. Bentley. The Golden Age of Detective Fiction between the two World Wars contains the work of several women writers or 'Queens of Crime'. When Allen Lane founded Penguin Books in 1935 and thus initiated a publishing revolution by putting the **paperback** on the market as a new affordable format that replaced magazine serialisation, the murder mysteries by Agatha Christie and Dorothy Sayers were among the first new titles on his list. Christie (1890–1976) is best known for two series, one featuring the Belgian sleuth Hercule Poirot (1920–75) and the other the amateur detective Miss Jane Marple (1930–76). Both series with their plots full of suspense were successfully adapted for the screen, which provided additional **royalties** for the writer. Margaret Rutherford became famous as Miss Marple (in four films, 1962–64), and a series of actors played Hercule Poirot, namely Albert Finney (*Murder on the Orient Express*, 1974), Peter Ustinov (1978–88) and David Suchet (ITV, 1989ff.), either in star-studded films with extravagant sets or in television plays. Christie's stage-play *The Mousetrap* is still running in London, with a record of more than 23,000 performances since 1952 (see chap. 5.2.3). Apart from *Murder on the Orient Express* (1934), other Christie mysteries with an exotic setting such as *Death on the Nile* (1937), *Murder in Mesopotamia* (1936) and *They Came to Baghdad* (1951) draw on Christie's first-hand experience of the region as the wife of an archaeologist. *A Caribbean Mystery* (1964) is one of Christie's murder mysteries featuring the elderly spinster Miss Jane Marple as shrewd amateur detective. This time, Christie transferred the setting from the English provincial village of St. Mary Mead, where Miss Marple is at home, to the likewise fictional West Indian island of St. Honoré, a tourist resort in late colonial times. However, despite its exotic locale, this is essentially another clue-puzzle and **country-house murder mystery**, marked by habitual features such as a limited set of characters (victims, suspects and assistants in the investigation) and a place of middle-class comfort sealed off from the rest of the world. Part of the entertainment, as with the many titles of Christie's novels that are based on nursery rhymes or proverbs, is the casual literary allusion; e.g. in the description of a valet-attendant ("He was also a man of extreme muscular development heightened by his training. His not to reason why, his but to do." Chap. 24) which is spiced with an ironic reference to Tennyson's poem "The Charge of the Light Brigade". What is different from earlier Christie mysteries is the stronger accentuation of changing sexual mores in this novel from the Swinging Sixties.

Between 1923 and 1937, amateur sleuth Lord Peter Wimsey, his manservant Bunter and his fiancée Harriet Vane (a writer of detective fiction) featured in a series of novels and short stories written by Dorothy L. Sayers (1893–1957). The appeal of Sayers's fiction lies as much in the murder mystery as in the developing relationship between her characters and in the locale. The plot of *The Nine Tailors* (1934) is based upon the English tradition of change ringing of church bells, and the murder mystery is solved amidst a climactic flood threatening a Fenland village.

Gaudy Night (1935) is a campus crime novel that thrives upon its setting in an Oxford college for women. Sayers's novels were adapted as radio and television plays for the BBC in three series (BBC TV, 1972–75; 1987; BBC Radio 4, 1973–83 and 2005). Later, Jill Paton Walsh completed a fragmentary Sayers novel (*Thrones, Dominations*, 1998) and provided a sequel of her own (*A Presumption of Death*, 2002). A third Queen of Crime from the Golden Age is Margery Allingham (1904–66) who found a devoted readership for her long-running series about detective Albert Campion (1929–68, with a completion and sequels by her husband, Philip Youngman Carter). *The Crime at Black Dudley* (1929) is a countryhouse murder mystery, whereas *Tiger in the Smoke* (1952) features a psychopathic killer.

Detective Inspectors and Police Procedural

Two other women writers, Ngaio Marsh, a native New Zealander (1895–1982), and 'Josephine Tey' (Elizabeth Mackintosh, 1896–1952) were instrumental in presenting a new type of detective. Notwithstanding the early introduction of members of the police force in Charles Dickens's *Bleak House* and in Wilkie Collins's *The Moonstone* (see chaps. 4.4.1 and 4.4.3.), the proper arrival on the scene of crime of the taxpayer's **detective inspector** as a rival to the amateur detective had to wait until the 1920s. Tey's Inspector Alan Grant from Scotland Yard made the start in a series (1927–51) that culminated in *The Daughter of Time* (1951), where he 'solves' (in hospital, and 400 years after the event) the mystery whether King Richard III murdered his nephews, the Princes in the Tower. Ngaio Marsh's contribution consisted in Inspector Roderick Alleyn from the Criminal Investigation Department (CID), who starred in novels and TV series (1934–82). A similar series about Inspector Appleby of Scotland Yard (1936–86), published by the Scottish literary critic and Oxford don J[ohn]. I[nnes]. M[acintosh]. Stewart (1906–94) under the pseudonym 'Michael Innes', contained many literary allusions. In the **police procedural**, the stress falls on teamwork rather than on individual genius. 'J.J. Marric' (John Creasey, 1908–73) is credited with the introduction of the form to Britain (popularised by the US-American writer 'Ed McBain' around the same time) with a series of 21 novels on Commander Gideon and his team at Scotland Yard (1955–76), beginning with *Gideon's Day*. After Creasey's death, William Vivian Butler continued the series about a team of detectives through five sequels (1978–90). On a seemingly endless list of further police investigators, those that mustered a special circle of fans among reading and television audiences since the 1960s number Scotland Yard Commander Adam Dalgliesh (P. D. James, since 1962), Inspector Reginald Wexford (Ruth Rendell, since 1964) and Chief Superintendent Charles Wycliffe (W. J. Burley, 1968–2000). Inspector/Superintendent Richard Jury and his aristocratic friend Melrose Plant (Martha Grimes, 1981 ff.) as well as Inspector Thomas Lynley (Lord Asherton) and Detective Sergeant Barbara Havers (Elizabeth George, 1988 ff.) are Scotland Yard detectives that were conceived by US-American writers.

A decentralisation and move away from Scotland Yard, and a stress on regions outside London, is increasingly apparent in post-war crime fiction as it is in other genres. Perhaps the best-known examples are two caustic Detective Chief Inspectors, namely Morse in Oxford (Colin Dexter, 1975–2000) and Barnaby in the fictional county of Midsomer somewhere in the Home Counties (Caroline Graham, 1987 ff.). Beginning with *An Air That Kills*, the Lydmouth Series is set in an imaginary village on the Anglo-Welsh borders in the 1950s, and features Detective Inspector Richard Thornhill (Andrew Taylor, 1994 ff.). In addition to unconventional novels about Yorkshire police detectives Dalziel and Pascoe (Reginald Hill, 1970ff.) there are further series about Detective Inspectors Charlie Resnick in Nottingham (1989–98) and Frank Elder in Cornwall (2004–6, both by John Harvey). Scotland is being policed in a trilogy featuring eccentric Detective Inspector Jack Laidlaw in Glasgow (by William McIlvanney: *Laidlaw*, 1977; *The Papers of Tony Veitch*, 1983, and *Strange Loyalties*, 1991) and in a series about Detective Inspector John Rebus in Edinburgh (Ian Rankin, 1987 ff.). Outside Britain, readers sustained an interest in the work of Inspector Van der Valk in Amsterdam (Nicolas Freeling, 1962–72) and of Inspector Ghote in Bombay/ Mumbai (H. R. F. Keating, 1964–2000).

There is also **crime fiction with a transnational and multicultural angle**. Large-scale migration to Britain from its former colonies set in with the docking of the *SS Empire Windrush* and the embarkation of its Caribbean passengers at Tilbury in 1948. In the long run, such migration effected a marked change. Mike Phillips, who was born in Guyana but grew up in London, addressed the ethnic diversity of postcolonial Britain in two popular forms. Together with his brother and fellow-journalist Trevor Phillips, he col-

Regionalisation

Multicultural Crime Fiction

laborated on the television series *Windrush: The Irresistible Rise of Multi-Racial Britain* (1998), after he had already made a name for himself as a writer of crime fiction. *Blood Rights* (1989, adapted for television, too) introduced the Black journalist-investigator Sam Deane, who featured also in *The Late Candidate*, *Point of Darkness* and *The Dancing Face* (1990–97). With his 'Yardie Trilogy' (*Yardie*, *Excess* and *Yush!*, 1992–94) which chronicles the rise and fall of a Jamaican drug ring leader, Jamaican-born Victor Headley (*1959) launched his own career and that of X Press alike as a leading London publisher of Black popular fiction. Courttia Newland (who was born to Caribbean parents in 1973) came out with two crime novels that address an adolescent audience, too. In *The Scholar: A West-Side Story* (1997) Newland deals with two young Black cousins from Greenside Estate, West London, who originally set out for different career options – education for a job vs. drug dealing and crime – until fate intervenes, and they run along parallel paths. Newland followed up his debut with *Snakeskin* (2002). In *City of Tiny Lights* (2005), Patrick Neate (*1970) is nodding to the (American) tradition of the hard-boiled detective novel, but strikes an original note with its protagonist-narrator, its multicultural setting and its topical politics. Tommy Akhtar is a private detective in London who was born into a family of Ugandan-Indian immigrants and who has a peculiar record as an Afghanistan warrior, switching from the Mujahideen to the side of the CIA. Hired by one call girl to rediscover another Russian one, wisecracking Tommy Akhtar is suddenly involved once more in international terrorism and secret service operations, without so much as detecting the difference. If Patrick Neate plays a variation upon the hard-boiled detective novels of Dashiell Hammett and Raymond Chandler, Alexander McCall Smith (*1948) calls up Agatha Christie's Miss Marple as a more homely precedent for Mma Precious Ramotswe, a female private detective in Botswana. McCall Smith – who was born in neighbouring Rhodesia (now Zimbabwe) and lives in Scotland – found an international audience for his *No 1 Ladies' Detective Agency* series which set in with the eponymous novel in 1998. The charm of these episodic novels, which seem to do well without a murder mystery and violent crime, lies in their female protagonist, their Botswanan setting and their general humanity.

Gender Aspects   **Female investigators** were rare in Miss Marple's time, but their number does increase, as in the several series written by 'Liza

Cody' (i.e. Liza Passim, 1980–97), Val McDermid (since 1987) and 'Frances Fyfield' (i.e. Frances Hegarty, since 1988). Lynda La Plante's screenplays and successive novelisations related to *Prime Suspect* (1991–2006, starring Helen Mirren as Detective Superintendent Jane Tennison) combine social realism with a study in character. Likewise on the increase is the number of non-professional detectives such as investigative journalists (Antonia Fraser's Jemima Shore, 1977–95; Val McDermid's Lindsay Gordon, 1987ff.) A few detectives are outside the norm, if only for the reason that they come from the pens of writers who usually do not engage with crime fiction. Both Graham Swift (in *The Light of Day*, in 2003) and Julian Barnes alias 'Dan Kavanagh' (with his quartet of novels centring on Duffy, a bi-sexual gumshoe, 1980–87) came up with unconventional portraits of a private eye. Some writers fused historical and crime fiction, such as Jake Arnott in his trilogy about London's gangland from the 1960s to the '90s, with a focus on homosexual protagonists (*The Long Firm*, *He Kills Coppers*, and *Truecrime*, 1999–2003). Umberto Eco translated the Sherlock Holmes/Dr Watson configuration back into the year 1327 in *Il nome della rosa* (1980, featuring monk-detectives Guglielmo da Baskerville and Adso de Melk). There is a counterpart in Brother Cadfael who is at the centre of the medieval murder mysteries by 'Ellis Peters' (i.e. Edith Pargiter, 1977–94).

Not only some investigators, but also a few crime writers are unusual, but for a different reason, namely because they delve into crime fiction with a psychological moment, or full of suspense, but do not commit themselves to a series. Daphne du Maurier (1907–89) set an example with her **Neo-Gothic romance** *Rebecca* (1938), in which the unnamed female narrator tries to find out about the mysterious death of her husband's first wife Rebecca de Winter. (*Mrs de Winter*, a sequel to du Maurier's best-selling romance and to Hitchcock's 1940 film adaptation, was published by Susan Hill in 1993.) After du Maurier and, occasionally, Ruth Rendell, Minette Walters (*1949) began with *The Ice House* (1992) to write **psychological crime fiction** with different protagonists. With a view to how suspense is created, such fiction may not be far from the **thriller**, but this genre is generally less marked by an interest in character. Through *The Ringer* (1926, developed from a stage-play) and its mystery about the identity of a serial killer in disguise, Edgar Wallace (1875–1932) achieved his breakthrough

Thrilling Fictions

on an international scale. With *The Four Just Men* (1905) who announce that they would assassinate the British Foreign Secretary in order to maintain the right to political asylum, Wallace had written the prototype of a suspenseful narrative based on a run against time, ending in a climax. This provided the model for later political thrillers based upon a combination of fact and fiction. In *Rogue Male* (1939) by Geoffrey Household (1900–88), a British hunter tells of his decision to assassinate a contemporary European dictator (unnamed but clearly meant to be Hitler), of the would-be sniper's capture and torture, and of his escape. With *The Eagle Has Landed* (1975), 'Jack Higgins' (Harry Patterson, *1929) wrote a companion-piece that tells of a German attempt to kidnap Prime Minister Winston Churchill during World War II. In *The Day of the Jackal* (1971), Frederick Forsyth (*1938) spectacularly focused on a contract killer out to assassinate French President and wartime hero General de Gaulle in 1963.

Spy Fiction

Fig. 5.11
John Buchan, 1936

At another point on the continuum, the thriller blends over into **spy fiction**, which had made a proper start prior to and during the First World War, especially with the work of John Buchan (1875–1940, see chap. 4.5.3). The development continued with a short story sequence by W. Somerset Maugham (1874–1965): *Ashenden; or, The British Agent* (1928) features a writer turned secret agent, who is non-heroic, seldom in the know and constantly fighting against boredom. The sequence, which is endowed with a psychological interest rather than with an eye on suspense, inspired Hitchcock's movie *The Secret Agent* (1936) and looked ahead to Graham Greene and John Le Carré. In between, however, began the ongoing success story of a modern Ulysses, of a superhero who travels around the globe to rid the world from existential threats. In *Casino Royale* (1953), Ian Fleming (1908–64), a writer with wartime Naval Intelligence record, introduced the British Secret Service agent James Bond alias 007. This cultural icon appeared in an original series of altogether 13 novels and nine short stories. Written from Fleming's luxurious Jamaican residence, the novels uphold a colonial framework and ideology: a British agent is instrumental in deciding world history, even in the period of Decolonisation and of the Cold War between the two super-powers USA and USSR. Single-handedly, Bond fights against Russian Intelligence (*Casino Royale*, 1953; *From Russia With Love*, 1957), villainous egomaniacs (e. g. *Dr No*, 1958; *Goldfinger*,

1959) or organised crime on a global scale (*Thunderball*, 1961). Apart from this, Bond's hedonistic lifestyle was wishful thinking for the Swinging Sixties. After Fleming's death, the series was continued by a number of other writers, who either wrote possible screenplays for Bond films, or turned actual screenplays into novels, such as John Gardner and Raymond Benson. In the meantime, the world has changed, and so has James Bond: the Bond films (starting with *Dr No*, 1962) present the British agent and the British Secret Service in a more and more un-imperial light.

Ian Fleming's portrait of Secret Service operations is qualified in the novels by Graham Greene, Len Deighton, and John Le Carré. (Dis-)Loyalty is one of the major themes of Graham Greene (1904–91, see chap. 5.3.1), who returns to this theme repeatedly in *Why Do I Write?* (1948), his exchange of letter-essays with Elizabeth Bowen and V.S. Pritchett after the experience of the totalitarian state. Moreover, Greene puts it into the mouth of Javitt, one of the characters in the 1963 short story "Under the Garden", who is made to say:

> Be disloyal. It's your duty to the human race. The human race needs to survive and it's the loyal man who dies first from anxiety or a bullet or overwork. If you have to earn a living, boy, and the price they make you pay is loyalty, be a double agent – and never let either of the two sides know your real name (*Collected Stories*, 1972: 215–16).

This utterance is less provoking when it is seen against E.M. Forster's similarly anti-totalitarian statement made in his 1938 essay "What I Believe": "if I had to choose between betraying my country and betraying my friend I hope I should have the guts to betray my country" (*Two Cheers For Democracy*, 1972: 66), and also against Ingeborg Bachmann's poem "Alle Tage" (1952). Greene wrote a novella as preparation for his screenplay to Carol Reed's film *The Third Man* (1949), set in post-war Vienna. His other works of fiction related to investigation and espionage include *The Quiet American* (1955, see chap. 5.3.5), set in Vietnam; *Our Man in Havana* (1958), set in Cuba before Castro's revolution; and *The Human Factor* (1978). In the latter novel, Greene does several things at the same time. He takes stock of the literary myth (much of Fleming's making) surrounding the British Secret Intelligence Service by pointing to the double agent or 'mole' as a traitor within the ranks. Greene could refer to the spectacular defection of Kim Philby, his former superior during his work for the Secret

Service, in 1963. In the novel, this leads to a 'mole' hunt that ends in the elimination of a false suspect. Greene combines this strand of the plot with another that concerns the international collaboration between British and South African intelligence services despite the official politics of isolating South Africa because of its Apartheid politics. This brings up a dilemma for Maurice Castle, a British agent who lives in a patchwork family with his Black South African wife Sarah and her son Sam from a previous relationship. The link between the two strands of the plot is therefore Greene's preoccupation with the theme of loyalty in private and disloyalty towards institutions. This is highlighted in the novel in Sarah Castle's answer to her husband's admitting to his betrayal: "'Who cares?' she said [...] 'We have our own country. You and I and Sam. You've never betrayed that country, Maurice.'" (Greene 1978: 263–64).

Whereas Greene loads spy fiction with moral dilemma, Len Deighton (*1929) attempts to brush away the snobbery in Fleming's portrait of 007 for more social realism, and comes up instead with a working-class agent. As the narrator-agent of *The IPCRESS File* (1962) and three sequels, he remains unnamed, but is given the name Harry Palmer in three subsequent films (1965–67). The spy fiction by 'John Le Carré' (David Cornwell, *1931) is strong on the psychology of character, and stresses the moral ambivalence and callousness of espionage work. This is most famously done so in *The Spy Who Came In From The Cold* (1963, filmed 1965), where agent Alec Leamas and the girl he fell in love with are deceived and betrayed by British Counter-Intelligence. George Smiley, a minor character in this novel, is central to Le Carré's fiction right from his debut novel *Call for the Dead* (1961) up to *Smiley's People* (1979), and perhaps most notably in *Tinker Tailor Soldier Spy* (1974). A successful spymaster, Smiley – middle-aged, unassuming in outlook and duped by his wife – is another contrasting character to James Bond. The plot of *Tinker Tailor Soldier Spy* is based upon the hunt for a mole, just like that of Greene's *The Human Factor* later, while in *The Tailor of Panama* (1996), Le Carré pays homage to Greene's earlier *Our Man in Havana*.

Fantastic Worlds

Another group of popular fiction is related to the creation of fantastic worlds, over and above the fantasies indulged in by Ian Fleming and the directors of James Bond movies. There are utopias and dystopias, science fiction and fantasy romances, sometimes separated only by a fuzzy border. The classroom classics of twentieth-century utopian literature are negative utopias or **dystopias**, as was *The Time Machine* by H. G. Wells (see chap. 4.5.3). *Brave New World* (1932) by Aldous Huxley (1894–1963) is set in a World State in the year 632 "after Ford" (i.e. after the fabrication of Henry Ford's first Model T car in 1908) and depicts a world in which technology and efficiency reign supreme, to the disadvantage of free will and choice as elements of individualism and humanity. Social life is streamlined by way of reproductive technology and selective breeding resulting in functional castes, conditioning centres for children and the indoctrination of adults during their sleep. Emotions are regulated through "feelie" (instead of talking) movies and the availability of the hallucinogenic Soma drug. The ideal product of such a totalitarian version of the welfare state (which was yet to be created in Britain) is the thoughtlessly happy consumer of material goods as well as of sex, which is encouraged as a form of recreation rather than reproduction. Outsiders and individualists with suggestive names such as Bernard Marx, Helmholtz Watson and John the Savage, even though they successfully make an impact for a time, stand no chance against the World State, a fact for which the suicide of the Savage is a striking symbol and final act of recognition. In his 1949 preface to *Brave New World* and in his 1958 essay "Brave New World Revisited", Huxley kept his criticism of social developments up to date. Huxley's shorter dystopia *Ape and Essence* (1948), which is presented in the form of a screenplay-within-the-novel, compares with *Lord of the Flies* (1954) by William Golding (1911–93). This story is also related to a nuclear war and sees humanity and civilisation rather as wishful thinking. *Lord of the Flies* is a dystopian adaptation of R. M. Ballantyne's Victorian juvenile book *Coral Island* (1857). With Golding, the Robinson-like survival of a group of boys degenerates into a murderous story of 'survival of the fittest', measured against a world without morality.

In *Nineteen Eighty-Four* (1949) by 'George Orwell' (Eric Arthur Blair, 1903–50), the world is not much braver. After the experience of Hitler and Stalin, and of the atrocities committed by the Right and the Left alike during the Spanish Civil War in which he fought for the Republican side, Orwell's criticism of totalitarian parties, e.g. in his political satire on Russian Communism entitled *Animal Farm* (1945), was devastating and indiscriminate.

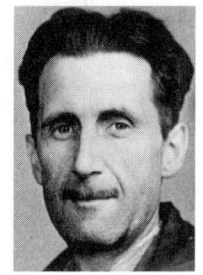

|Fig. 5.12
George Orwell,
1933

He had argued for a democratic Socialism as an alternative in his book-length essay *The Lion and the Unicorn: Socialism and the English Genius* (1941), and this is not necessarily opposed to his portrait of a totalitarian brand of 'Ingsoc' or English Socialism in power in *Nineteen Eighty-Four*. Here, Orwell's reference to Huxley extended the creative use of a suggestive name for his protagonist Winston Smith, who is an Everyman figure with half of Churchill's name, and some of his resilience (which seems to make more sense as an interpretation than to implicate the wartime Prime Minister in dictatorial politics). The hierarchical society of Orwell's Oceania (competing with the two other super-states Eurasia and Eastasia) is divided into castes much like Huxley's World State. In *Nineteen Eighty-Four*, however, this occurs in relation to the share of political power, ranging from Big Brother and the Inner Party to the Thought Police exerting control over the Outer Party, and then down to the majority of the *proles*. Orwell, too, most famously depicts brainwashing as an element of political stability, but in several different forms. First, the Ministry of Truth ("Minitrue") is responsible for nonsensical "doublethink" slogans such as "War is Peace – Freedom is Slavery – Ignorance is Strength". Outside the narrative, in an appendix to the book, Orwell elaborates upon "The Principles of Newspeak" as the politically correct form of English at the time. Brainwashing extends, secondly, to 'information' channelled to the people via telescreens that can transmit and receive at the same time, and thus function also as surveillance mechanism. Truly, "Big Brother Is Watching You", as the slogan in Orwell's narrative ran that has become proverbial. Thirdly, Ingsoc also exerts control over the past, that is continuously made to serve present needs: Winston Smith is employed in altering the historical record to fit the latest political development. Finally, and most bitterly, the protagonist himself is made a victim of such methods. Out of his (illicit) love for Julia, a comrade, Winston Smith stages a rebellion but is deceived by a senior party member called O'Brien, who changes from the role of Winston's guardian to his torturer in the Ministry of Love. Clearly, love and friendship is alien to this dystopian world. For Winston, brainwashing ends in his betrayal and loss of Julia, and in his conditioned redirection of emotion. The last sentences of the text run: "the struggle was finished. He had won the victory over himself. He loved Big Brother." (Such a form of re-education is at the centre of the 1962 dystopian novel *A Clockwork Orange* by Anthony Burgess, see chap. 5.3.3. For Orwell's *Burmese Days*, see chap. 5.3.5.)

The pessimistic outlook in the dystopian fiction from Wells to Golding is also typical of the **British tradition of scientific romances** between the wars. With his speculative novels, Olaf Stapledon (1886–1950) had an impact on later writers because of his combination of a grand cosmological vision with accuracy in scientific detail. *Last and First Men* (1930) deals with man's descendants, while *Star Maker* (1937) tells of an intergalactic journey through space and time that results in the view of a disinterested God experimenting with new worlds that are likewise prone to end in war and destruction. The works of the American writer Ray Bradbury (*1920) such as *The Martian Chronicles* (1950, about the colonisation of the planet while a nuclear war rages on Earth) and *Fahrenheit 451* (1953, the story of resistance against a totalitarian state that burns books) are not too far away from the catastrophic vision of their British counterparts. However, an **American brand of science fiction** (SF) that entertained with less serious concerns became established in Britain from the 1940s, too, distributed in magazines and paperbacks alike. Successive British writers did their best to react to both traditions and to raise critical esteem for the genre. Arthur C. Clarke (1917–2008) famously collaborated with director Stanley Kubrick both on the novel and the film entitled *2001: A Space Odyssey* (1968, followed up by three sequels written entirely by Clarke). Michael Moorcock (*1939) promoted a New Wave during his editorship (intermittently 1964–96) of the magazine *New Worlds* that was funded by the Arts Council. J. G. Ballard (1930–2009) became a prominent part of that New Wave, although his work defies easy categorisation and includes also *The Empire of the Sun* (see chap. 5.3.5). In *Canopus in Argos: Archives* (1979–83), her five-volume-series of 'space fiction', Nobel Prize winner Doris Lessing (*1919) was concerned with social issues, but looked at the Earth from outside. By contrast, space fiction with a comic angle was the domain of Douglas Adams (1952–2001): the BBC had developed a radio series from his script for *The Hitchhiker's Guide to the Galaxy* that turned into a cult, and spawned a series of five novels (1979–92).

Brian Aldiss (*1925) became known for his intertextual reference to popular classics by Mary Shelley, H. G. Wells and Bram

Stoker (*Frankenstein Unbound*, 1973; *Moreau's Other Island*, 1980; *Dracula Unbound*, 1991) as well as for his chronicle of an **alternate world** in *The Helliconia Trilogy* (1982–85). *The Colour of Magic* (1983) is the first of by now close to 40 novels in which Terry Pratchett (*1948) created an alternate 'Discworld'. Pratchett sided with Douglas Adams in bringing a comic angle to the genre, and this applies also to his cultural and intertextual references which take the form of a good-natured parody of writers such as Shakespeare or Tolkien. Pratchett's *Wyrd Sisters* (1988) adapts the plot of *Macbeth*, while *Lords and Ladies* (1992) contains allusions to *A Midsummer Night's Dream*. Since *Consider Phlebas* (1987), Iain M. Banks (*1954) has been concerned with another alternate world called 'the Culture' (for a different line of fiction published under the name Iain Banks see chap. 5.3.4).

J[ohn]. R[onald]. R[euel]. Tolkien (1892–1973) brought the expertise of an Oxford Professor of medieval English language and literature to his works of fantasy, for which he created in Middle-earth a prime example of an alternate world, and even invented Elvish as the language of the elves. (Tolkien himself recited and recorded two specimens of Elvish, namely "A Elbereth Gilthoniel" and "Namárië; or, Galadriel's Lament".) Tolkien's works of fantasy invite comparison to the Arthurian romances and to medieval epics such as *Beowulf* or *The Ring of the Nibelung*. In *The Hobbit* (1937), which he intended for children, Tolkien gives an introduction to the Shire, the idyllic land of the hobbits, and to Bilbo Baggins as the singular hobbit who is in possession of one of three powerful rings. In *The Lord of the Rings* (1954–55), Tolkien continued the story in a trilogy that he had likewise written immediately before and during the Second World War, yet for a wider audience. To extend and secure his power over the whole of Middle-earth, Sauron, the Lord of the Rings and tyrannical ruler of the land of Mordor, needs the third ring that meanwhile has passed from Bilbo's hands into those of Frodo Baggins. With the help of Gandalf the Grey, a powerful wizard, and the Fellowship of the Ring (a multi-ethnic band of human and humanoid friends from the ranks of hobbits, elves and dwarfs), Frodo takes up the fight with Sauron and his fearful monsters, the orcs. Other characters of note include Saruman, an evil wizard; Gollum, a creepy being who desires to repossess the ring he once owned; Sam Gamgee, Master Frodo's loyal servant; and Aragorn, a heroic fighter of royal blood. Frodo successfully defies all enemies including his own drive to keep the ring he actually means to destroy. Tolkien himself denied a topical interpretation of his fiction. However, the political context of the period of composition – from the 1930s over the World War to the Cold War – nevertheless shows in the fight of the few good and honest against a dictatorship that is totalitarian and imperialist at the same time. For his trilogy of epic length, Tolkien evoked a strong contrast between light and darkness that looks back to the Bible as well as to Milton's *Paradise Lost*. *The Lord of the Rings* was adapted twice for the screen: first in a 1978 animated version of the first volume only, and then in Peter Jackson's blockbuster adaptation of the whole trilogy (2001–03), which raised a new interest in Tolkien's original, and in those places in New Zealand which he chose to illustrate the Shire (originally an idyllic version of Southern England).

C[live]. S[taples]. Lewis (1898–1963), a friend of Tolkien and a Professor of English at Cambridge, created an alternate world of his own, yet endowed with many Christian overtones, in *The Chronicles of Narnia* (1950–56). Much like in E. Nesbit's and Enid Blyton's novels of adventure, we are presented with a group of altogether five boys and girls as protagonists: the four Pevensil children and their cousin Eustace Scrubb. Moreover, *The Lion, the Witch, and the Wardrobe* (1950) – the first of the seven Narnia books to be published – hints at the beginning of Lewis Carroll's *Alice in Wonderland*, as the parallel world of Narnia is entered through a wardrobe (a counterpart to Alice's descent into Wonderland through a rabbit's hole). However, the magical land of Narnia can only be discovered by the sheer belief in its existence as such – and belief is a key to the understanding of the whole series as a Christian allegory. The shadow of an evil White Witch looms over Narnia, but Evil is redeemed through the self-sacrifice of Aslan the great lion, a Christ-like figure who gives his life for others, to be resurrected after death. The remaining books tell of several more trips by some of the children, e. g. to help Prince Caspian of Narnia in various ways, and about earlier events. (This is why the exact ordering of the series is in question, and why the 1955 volume *The Magician's Nephew* sometimes takes precedence.) In addition to his Narnia books, C. S. Lewis had also written a series of Christian science fiction, from *Out of the Silent Planet* (1938) over *Pelendra* (1943) to *That Hidden Strength* (1945). More recently, Philip Pullman (*1946) raised some eyebrows when he positioned himself decidedly against the Christian subtext of *The Chronicles of Narnia*. Pullman found a large audience for *His Dark Materials*, a fantasy trilogy built upon a different ideological framework, and consisting of *Northern Lights* (1995), *The Subtle Knife* (1997) and *The Amber Spyglass* (2000).

Children's Literature Children's literature after its Golden Age (see chap. 4.5.5) had its fair share of the fantastic, but this was not the rule. Most of the 800 titles by best-selling author Enid Blyton (1897–1968) stay on the realistic side, without a dash of the supernatural. Several series of her children's books became classics of the nursery not only in Britain. The St. Clare series and the Malory Towers series (6 novels each, 1941–45 and 1946–51, respectively) are **boarding school stories** with a special interest for girls. Year by year, they follow their heroines through school: the twins Pat and Isabel O'Sullivan (in German translation: *Hanni und Nanni*) in St. Clare, and Darell Rivers in Malory Towers. Other series are **tales of adventure, mystery and detection** in which a mixed group of boys and girls (often together with a dog) succeed on their own in the world of adults outside their middle-class homes. Just like in Ballantyne's *Coral Island*, Stevenson's *Treasure Island* and in E. Nesbit's stories, this happens without the help of their parents. *The Island of Adventure* started off Blyton's Adventure series (8 novels, 1944–55), while *Five on Treasure Island* introduced the Famous Five in a series (21 novels, 1942–63) that ran parallel with another one about the Secret Seven (15 novels, 1949–63).

In her efforts at creating historical fiction for children, Rosemary Sutcliff (1920–92) went further back in time than her predecessors Marryat and Stevenson. Whereas they set their stories amidst seventeenth- and eighteenth-century political conflicts in Britain, Sutcliff focused on Roman Britain instead, as in *The Eagle of the Ninth* (1954). This novel about a soldier in a Roman legion was made into a series that blended over into Sutcliff's Arthurian novels, such as *The Sword at Sunset* (1963). Joan Aiken (1924–2004) is the author of six Jane Austen continuations (1984–2000) set firmly in the Regency period. By contrast, Aiken introduced her juvenile readers to a Britain in which the Hanoverian Succession of 1714 that led to the Georgian Age simply did not occur, and thus to a piece of **alternate history** (in distinction from alter-

nate or parallel worlds). In *Wolves of Willoughby Chase* and successive volumes of Aiken's Wolves Chronicles series (1963–2005),
nineteenth-century Britain is ruled instead by a King James III
and then by his successor, Richard IV. Bonnie Willoughby and
her poor London cousin Sylvia Green are meant to be educated on the estate of Bonnie's uncle. In the absence of Bonnie's
parents, the girls meet with the intrigues of Miss Slighcarp, the
scheming governess who tries to seize the property herself. The
adventures of the two girls are dressed up with mild forms of
sensation: first in the howl of hungry wolves that have arrived
in England from the Continent through a (then imaginary) Channel Tunnel, and then in the cruel manner in which the girls are
treated in a school that suggests a comparison with the institution where readers first meet Dickens's Oliver Twist. In a series of
further juvenile novels with the same invented historical setting,
Aiken relates the adventures of Dido Twite, another London girl
who is actively involved in fending off assassination plots, one
of which is timed for the coronation of Richard IV, for instance.
Further pieces of alternate history – meant for a more mature
audience – include those fictions that envisage a successful invasion of Britain by the Germans under the Kaiser or under Hitler,
namely *When William Came: A Story of London under the Hohenzollerns*
by 'Saki' (H. H. Munro, 1914) and the thrillers *SS-GB* by Len Deighton (1978, set in 1941) and *Fatherland* by Robert Harris (1992, set
in 1964).

In addition to spy thrillers of his own, Ian Fleming wrote one
children's book about a magic car, *Chitty Chitty Bang Bang* (1964).
This was successfully adapted as a film musical (1968) based on
the screenplay by Roald Dahl (1916–90), who made his name as
a writer of short stories and children's books with a very special
humour. The film scene and the song "Toot Sweets" that are related to a candy maker overlap with the plot of Dahl's *Charly
and the Chocolate Factory* (1967). In his later children's book *Matilda* (1988), Dahl tells the story of Matilda Wormwood who practices her magic powers at school. From here, it is but one step to
the **Harry Potter series** by the Scottish novelist J[oanne]. K[athleen].
Rowling (*1965). Her career is certainly the most extraordinary
success story of a writer in recent years, in terms of both personal fortune and literary significance. The publication of each of
her seven novels in the series (1997–2007) was accompanied by

J. K. Rowling's
Harry Potter Novels

a global frenzy, not only among juvenile audiences. The clever marketing in juvenile and adult, British and American editions (with different covers and sometimes variant wording, see Mühl-eisen 2009), together with the adaptation as movies trailing each single volume while the series was still in the state of completion, contributed to a 'media hype' on an unprecedented scale, yet cannot explain Rowling's singular success with audiences of all ages. The series combines features from a whole range of traditional genres of children's literature. There is the parallel and **fairy-tale world** of witches and wizards, together with the **moral tale** of perseverance in the fight of the Good against the Powers of Evil in the person of the Dark Wizard, Lord Voldemort, and his followers. Even though the curriculum at Hogwarts School of Wizardry is a very special one, the whole series looks back to a tradition of **boarding school stories** that includes *Tom Brown's Schooldays* by Thomas Hughes (1857) as well as Enid Blyton's St. Clare and Malory Towers series. Blyton's spirit is evoked once more when the group of friends around Harry Potter, an orphaned wizard reared in a surrogate family of non-wizards or 'muggles', face mysteries and adventures. The elements of **magic and supernaturalism** are reminiscent of the fiction of E. Nesbit, C.S. Lewis and J.R.R. Tolkien. The whole combination, however, is unique. Rowling's success with adult readers alike is due to her gift of writing subtle and realistic dialogue. In her narrative presentation, mental processes included, Rowling generally opts for what Lodge called 'traditional realism' in distinction from the experiments of (Post-)Modernism. Rowling's major and minor characters react in very different but always plausible ways to situations that range from pressure at the working place over social ostracism to full-blooded terror.

5.3.3 | Modernist and Postmodernist Experiments

In 1922, two key works of **Modernism,** namely James Joyce's novel *Ulysses* and T.S. Eliot's long poem *The Waste Land*, appeared in print. For this reason alone (and not in the coming of the electronic media, as signalled by the establishment of the BBC within the same year), many twentieth-century critics have seen 1922 as an *annus mirabilis*, ringing in "the dream of a movement that would never age and never end" – as Michael Levenson put it before he continued to point out that "[t]he influence of the first thirty years of the century over the next fifty was so great that the achievement of a distance from Modernism remains an event in contemporary culture. We are still learning how not to be Modernist" (1999: 1). At the same time it is not only true to point at the continuity of earlier forms of realism (as has been done so far within this chapter), but also to say that hardly any other movement in literary history has been so vaguely defined. The beginnings of Modernism are sometimes marked out already in the 1880s and '90s, and there is no proper consensus whether the Modernist period of experimentation has reached its end so far – a view that entails obvious problems for the definition and delimitation of **Postmodernism**, too. The most common, indeed the only widely consensual view of (Post-)Modernism as a movement that was far from being uniform, points to its break with convention as a hallmark.

Virginia Woolf (1882–1941) broke with convention in several ways, in her private life as well as in her writing. In addition to her fiction, her work also comprises lectures and essays of a more general nature, such as "How Should One Read a Book" (1926, collected in *The Common Reader*, 1925–32), as well as two key works of feminist criticism, namely *A Room of One's Own* (1929) and *Three Guineas* (1938). "Mr Bennett and Mrs Brown" (1924) and "Modern Fiction" (1925) are programmatic essays in which Woolf attempted to mark out the difference between the 'materialist' social realism of John Galsworthy, Arnold Bennett and H. G. Wells and the Modernist aesthetics of writers such as James Joyce, Katherine Mansfield and herself (see chap. 4.5.2). In difference to D. H. Lawrence, their contemporary, both Woolf and Mansfield abstract in their short stories from the social realities of the day, and often also from plot, to make psychological realism their predominant concern (see Korte 2003, Löffler and Späth 2005). "Mrs Dalloway in Bond Street" (1923) was a first draft of the beginning of Woolf's 1925 novel, published separately but characterised, like her novels at that stage, by the extensive use made of Free Indirect Discourse to represent the reflector character's consciousness. The novel *Mrs Dalloway* was originally envisaged under the working title "The Hours", and its narrative is structured by the sound of Big Ben striking the hours on an ordinary day in London in June 1923, the day Mrs Dalloway, the wife

The Modernist Short Stories of V. Woolf and K. Mansfield

of a Conservative MP, wants to give a dinner party. Guests of note include Clarissa's old friend Peter Walsh, whose offer of marriage she once rejected; Sally Seton, another loving friend with whom Clarissa embarked on what might have become a lesbian relationship; and Miss Kilman, who in turn may be the lover of Clarissa's daughter Elizabeth. A parallel strand of the plot focuses on Septimus Warren Smith, who returned from active service in the Great or First World War with all the symptoms of shell shock that ultimately bring him to take his own life. It is in this character's tragic fate that Woolf transcends the homely upper middle-class setting of Mrs Dalloway's world.

In the train of association that takes its origin from the reflection upon "The Mark on the Wall" (1917), Woolf the stylist had already gone further by using the fresh form of Interior Monologue. While Woolf still observes punctuation, and the sentence as a semantic unit, this plot-less story (which does not render itself easily to a generic classification) looks out to Molly Bloom's soliloquy at the ending of Joyce's *Ulysses* (1922) in particular, and to Modernist aesthetics in general:

> As we face each other in omnibuses and underground railways we are looking into the mirror; that accounts for the vagueness, the gleam of glassiness, in our eyes. And the novelists in future will realise more and more the importance of these reflections, for of course there is not one reflection but an almost infinite number; those are the depths they will explore, those the phantoms they will pursue, leaving the description of reality more and more out of their stories, taking a knowledge of it for granted (*NAEL* II, 2084).

The New Zealand-born writer Katherine Mansfield (1888–1923) conformed to Woolf's Modernist credo, and her stories "Bliss" (1918), "Sun and Moon" (1920) and "The Garden-Party" (1922, all in Mansfield 1984) moreover tie in with the social and festive setting of *Mrs Dalloway*. In the first story, 30-year-old Bertha Young experiences a blissful feeling before returning to her middle-class home and a dinner party. Bertha has fallen in love with Pearl Fulton, one of the guests, but her bliss is soon over when she comes to see, at the breaking up of the party, that Bertha's husband and Miss Fulton are not the antagonists she believed them to be, but seem to have an affair instead. In "Sun and Moon", the preparation for a dinner party, and the event itself, is seen with the eyes of two children. In typical **'slice of life'** fashion, their disillusionment with the world is symbolised by their discovery that an ice-cake in form of a little house is now shattered, which leads to an angry scene between Sun (the boy) and his father. The build-up of "The Garden-Party" is quite comparable, only that it is a fatal accident in the neighbourhood that tarnishes the mood of a party in the afternoon, and that Laura, the young daughter, is personally confronted with class differences and death. When she pays a call of condolence to the workers' families, their coarse behaviour does not fit with Laura's ideals, and she more-over sees the corpse. This momentous experience is what Joyce called an **epiphany** (see chap. 4.5.4), and Mansfield a 'glimpse'. In "The Doll's House" (1922), class differences are again presented through the mind of children. Mansfield's "The Daughters of the Late Colonel" (1921) compares to Lawrence's "The Horse-Dealer's Daughter" (1922, see chap. 4.4.1), and were it only for the way that both stories start off with an impending funeral, and then include extended passages of characters' reflection rendered in Free Indirect Discourse.

In Virginia Woolf's novel *To the Lighthouse* (1927), the stress falls once more on psychological impressionism rather than on significant action. The first of two longer sections is entitled "The Window" and takes place in a seaside village over one day in about 1908, when an excursion is planned by the Ramsay fam-ily and their circle of friends. Instead, the highlight of the day is a dinner party that, typically enough, is represented through the thoughts of each participant, interrupted by a short part of the table talk (chap. 17). In an interlude with the heading "Time Passes", the death of Mrs Ramsay as the central character within the first section and what happened else over the course of the next ten years is related retrospectively and in poetic prose. A third section entitled "The Lighthouse" takes place after the Ar-mistice, when the surviving characters return to the village af-ter the Great War, and successfully embark on the long-planned excursion. In this section, the focus is on the artist Lily Briscoe, whose extended reflections on Mrs Ramsay and, more generally, on the meaning of life, culminate in a moment of epiphany that enable her to finish the painting she had been working upon ten years earlier (in the first part of the novel).

In *The Waves* (1931), Woolf went further and abstained from a division into parts or chapters and, in their stead, made use of a

| Fig. 5.13
Virginia Woolf by George Charles Beresford, 1902

feature that E. M. Forster had earlier employed for the beginning of each part of his novel *A Passage to India* (1924, see chap. 5.3.4). Likewise, each section of *The Waves* is introduced by a descriptive passage (in italics and poetic prose), in which impressions of cyclical Nature (e. g. the course of the sun, and the tides) appear without the intrusion of human beings. Heterodiegetic narration is being restricted to those passages; in the remainder of the narrative, where dialogue alternates with the rendering of characters' thoughts, Woolf creates the illusion of unmediated representation. Anaphoric repetition is used as a signal for the beginning of descriptive passages ("The sun […]") as well as for the segmentation of the dialogue ("Now […]"). As the most prominent image of eternal repetition, the waves are meant to signify the stream of thought as well as the flow of life. Like in *Ulysses* and in Woolf's *Mrs Dalloway*, the action is restricted to one day, from before dawn to nightfall. (For the very different approach Woolf took in *Orlando*, see chap. 5.3.4.) This single day nevertheless equals the whole life of each character in the novel, from the time when Bernard met with Neville and Louis (an Australian), and with the girls Susan, Jinny and Rhoda at Elvedon, a boarding-school, up to a reunion at Hampton Court in middle age and to the ending of Bernard's life, when he still (as throughout) ponders his identity. Each of the six characters is reduced to a telling set of features, told by him- or herself, while a seventh person, a mute character named Percival who dies early, remains a common point of reference for all of them (akin to Mrs Ramsay before in *To the Lighthouse*). A stylistic progress in Woolf's writing can be observed when the dinner party in the centre of the narrative (Woolf 1943: 84–105), which is presented as a series of Interior Monologues (albeit brought into the form of direct *speech*), is measured against its counterpart in *To the Lighthouse* (chap. 17), where Woolf had used the more conventionalised technique of Free Indirect Discourse instead.

James Joyce (1882–1941), too, had made use of such conventions in two works published at the beginning of the First World War, namely *Dubliners* and *A Portrait of the Artist as a Young Man* (see chaps. 4.5.3 and 4.5.4). In *Ulysses*, Joyce (who now lived in exile) returned to his native Dublin but took a more innovative approach and thus created his Modernist masterpiece. It was unrivalled in its attention to psychological detail, while being

Fig. 5.14

James Joyce, painted by Patrick Tuohy in Paris in 1924

provocative in its form and in its sexually explicit manner. Parts of *Ulysses* appeared in a little magazine in New York in 1918–20 before the completed novel was published as a book in Paris in 1922, and it had an impact on Virginia Woolf as well as on T. S. Eliot who was working on *The Waste Land*. It takes no more than a comparison with the 1967 adaptation for the screen (dir. by Joseph Strick) – which was banned in Ireland until 2000 for the verbal obscenities inherent in Joyce's text – to observe that Joyce's novel is indeed built upon a consecutive story set in Dublin on the single day of 16 June 1904 ('Bloomsday'), but that the author did his best to obscure the impression of a linear narrative. In the first three of altogether 18 episodes, the focus is on Stephen Dedalus (the protagonist of Joyce's earlier *Portrait of the Artist*). Leopold Bloom, the Ulysses of this modern *Odyssey*, appears in the fourth episode that at the same time introduces the second part of the novel. Mr Bloom's work as an advertisement-canvasser means that he spends his day walking the streets of Dublin, and visiting the city's taverns. In the third part of the novel, which again comprises three episodes, Mr Bloom returns home at night, together with Stephen whom he had met in a hospital later in the evening. To provide for coherence over and above the unity of place and the mythological reference to the 24 books of the *Odyssey*, Joyce encouraged the critic Stuart Gilbert to come up with a synoptic table of further correspondences (see Gilbert 1963: 38). The fact that such an effort was made at all, and that Joyce obscured the reference to Homer when he cut out again the titles of his episodes, goes a long way to explain why *Ulysses* is such a 'difficult' novel that readers may need a page-by-page commentary (see also Blamires 1988). Apart from a high degree of intertextual references, Joyce's readers are confronted with a continuous change of perspective and styles of narration. This may be the cause of entertainment, as when an episode set in a newspaper office is interspersed with headlines (no. 7, "Aeolus"), while others are presented in dramatic form (no. 15, "Circe") or as a series of questions and answers (no. 17, "Ithaca"). On the other hand, the episode which deals with Bloom's and Stephen's meeting in a lying-in hospital (no. 14, "Oxen of the Sun") testifies to Joyce's skilful use of pastiche as well as to his obscurity. This story of childbirth is submerged under layers of imitations of English prose, starting with an exercise in Old English (in the alliterative sentences "Before born babe bliss had. Within womb won he worship.") and ending in contemporary varieties of colloquial English (as in the last sentences of this episode). When Leopold Bloom is asleep beside his wife at the end of the day (episode 18, "Penelope"), the reader partakes in the train of thought of Marion 'Molly' Bloom, a sensuous woman who can look back on an adulterous encounter in the afternoon. This last episode caused offence for its sexual frankness yet it is actually the most impressive of Joyce's achievements. The author manages to present a 'stream of consciousness' in the form of a long Interior Monologue that in spite of all twists and turns of association remains readable even though the author refrains from punctuation and uses the word Yes instead. Joyce put an even greater experimental effort into his last novel *Finnegan's Wake* (1939), but also lost his audience outside academia on the way.

After Joyce

There were only a few novelists before the Second World War that continued along the lines of Joyce, Woolf and Mansfield, e. g. the Caribbean-British writer 'Jean Rhys' (Ella Gwendolen Rees Williams, ?1890/94–1979) in novels such as *Voyage in the Dark* and later *Wide Sargasso Sea* (see chaps. 5.3.5 and 5.3.6). Joyce's play with (mythological) pre-texts, and a play with Joyce's texts, can be discerned in the intertextual and meta-fictional novel *At Swim-Two-Birds* (1939) written by the Irish novelist 'Flann O'Brien' (Brian O'Nolan, 1911–66). In *The British Museum Is Falling Down* (1965), an early novel by David Lodge (*1935) that is characterised by its pastiche of the styles of other writers, many elements of *Ulysses* (from the setting within one day up to the Interior Monologue at the end of the novel) are taken up again in a comic context. At about the same time, the novelists 'Anthony Burgess' (John Wilson, 1917–93) and John Fowles succeeded in interesting a larger audience for their experimental works of fiction.

A. Burgess, *A Clockwork Orange*

Before he introduced Joyce first to the 'ordinary reader' (*Here Comes Everybody*, 1965) and then to students (*Joysprick*, 1973), and well before he adapted *Ulysses* as a musical entitled *Blooms of Dublin* (1986), Anthony Burgess had made a name for himself as experimental and dystopian novelist with *A Clockwork Orange* (1962). In a tripartite structure, the novel relates the trail of violence, rape and murder left by 15-year-old Alex and his teenage gang of 'droogs' (chaps. 1–7), before Alex is forcefully re-conditioned through the application of the 'Ludovico technique'. This entails the confrontation with scenes of extreme brutality, in which Beethoven's Ninth Symphony perversely serves as a stimulus that shall lead to aversion to violence as intended response (chaps. 8–14). Individual brutality is thus answered by state terror in a novel that upholds the ideal of free will in a dystopian world – a freedom of choice that paradoxically includes wilful violence as an option, too. In the last part of the narrative (chaps. 15–21), Alex returns from the institution only to experience acts of retaliation by his former victims that make him attempt to take his own life. This undercuts the government's interest in him as a shining example of re-education. On its publication, critics were not well pleased with the strangeness of the language in the novel, for which Burgess had created a juvenile slang called Nadsat (based upon Cockney English and Russian). The real breakthrough for Burgess came in 1971 when director Stanley Kubrick turned his novel into a film that however met with a *succès de scandale*. Kubrick had based his film on the US-American edition that lacked the last chapter of the novel in which Alex sets a positive example when he renounces his earlier life of violence. Contrary to Burgess's ethical intentions (which he elaborated upon in *1985*, a hybrid of fiction and non-fiction published in 1978), Kubrick's film was said to condone such violence because graphic scenes of brutality were left uncommented.

If *A Clockwork Orange* can be said to look back to Joyce's word-play, *The French Lieutenant's Woman* (1969) is characterised by its toying with the expectations of a reading audience. The story told in this historical and meta-fictional novel by John Fowles (1926–2005) takes place in 1867, a century before publication. Each chapter sets in with a motto taken from Mid-Victorian literature that makes the period come alive, as does Fowles's heterodiegetic narrator that spices the narrative with historical information. However, the narrator writes from a twentieth-century stance, and is not only self-conscious and intrusive, but also a prime example of unreliability. After a cliff-hanger ending that leaves the reader speculating whether Sarah Woodruff will throw herself out of a window, the narrator readily begins the next chapter with the admission:

John Fowles

> I do not know. This story I am telling is all imagination. These characters I create never existed outside my own mind. If I have pretended until now to know my characters' minds and innermost thoughts, it is be-

cause I am writing in (just as I have assumed some of the vocabulary and 'voice' of) a convention universally accepted at the time of my story: that the novelist stands next to God. He may not know all, yet he tries to pretend that he does. But I live in the age of Alain Robbe-Grillet and Roland Barthes: if this is a novel, it cannot be a novel in the modern sense of the word. (Chap. 13. Fowles 1977: 85)

Over 30 chapters later, but with still 100 pages to go, when the male protagonist Charles Smithson has managed to fend off Sarah's seductive charm to return to his wife Ernestina, the reader is suddenly addressed alike again by the narrator who confesses, "And now, having brought this fiction to a thoroughly traditional ending, I had better explain that although all I have described in the last two chapters happened, it did not happen quite in the way you may have been led to believe." (Chap. 45, 1977: 295). What is immediately afterwards given out as merely wishful thinking by a love-torn Charles turns out to be only the first of altogether three alternative and not always happy endings. In the novel, Fowles uses his romantic plot built upon a love triangle to play around with conventions and taboos of Victorian fiction. While Sarah, the discarded mistress in the title, veers between the gender stereotypes of the fallen woman and the *femme fatale*, Fowles discards Victorian Prudery when he depicts the sexual union of her and Charles (chap. 46). Their loving union brings about a second ending that could have been 'real' – were it not for the last chapter of the novel, which sets in with yet another meta-fictional commentary and ends with a third alternative conclusion to the story, which sees Charles as positively thrown upon himself. Drawn to the Victorian Age yet not to Victorian Values, this novel by John Fowles is Post-Victorian in spirit while at the same time marked out as a major example of **Postmodernism**: the way in which Fowles deals with narrative conventions (e.g. reliability, omniscience and happy ending) and socio-cultural stereotypes, the playful manner in which he cites pre-texts and suits them to new contexts, became a hallmark of intertextual and intermedial fiction from the 1970s that was alike subsumed under that provisional heading.

Postmodernist or not, those novels written by authors whose adolescence fell in the Swinging Sixties were even less characterised by Victorian Prudery. Indeed, a common reaction in the 1970s to the first published works of Ian McEwan and Martin

Amis was that of shock. Just like the collections of macabre short stories by Ian McEwan (*1948) entitled *First Love, Last Rites* (1975) and *In Between the Sheets* (1978), so is his novel *The Comfort of Strangers* (1981) marked by a concern with adolescence and (aberrant) sexuality. This comes out, too, in its screen version, for which Harold Pinter wrote the screenplay. Such a concern is much less visible in McEwan's later fiction. His Booker Prize winning novel *Amsterdam* (1998) is marked by occasionally bizarre twists of the plot: here, a woman's funeral reunites her three former lovers, before two of them think about doing themselves a favour by murdering the other one. *The Atonement* (2001) fits perhaps more easily into the Modernist tradition, because of its combination of psychological realism and meta-fiction. In the first three parts of this novel, which veer between 1935 and the 1941 Dunkirk evacuation, we are told about the thwarted love affair between Cecilia Tallis and Robbie Turner, and also about the rape of Cecilia's cousin Lola that ends in her marriage to the rapist. In a fourth part set in 1999, the full extent of the involvement of Cecilia's sister Briony Tallis in those past events comes out, and it transpires that Briony the novelist has not only reason for atonement, but has also authored the preceding parts of McEwan's novel which thus is made out to be hers, too. Following upon Fowles's precedent in *The French Lieutenant's Woman*, McEwan begins by telling the story of romantic love (gone wrong) only to change soon to the level of narrative discourse, in order to subvert the conventional view of a narrator standing next to God in the context of his own creation. In 2007, this meta-fictional novel was also successfully translated to the screen. In between, McEwan had published *Saturday* (2005), which – true to its title, and reminiscent of the novels by Joyce and Woolf – is limited to the course of one day in the life of a middle-aged London surgeon.

Fig. 5.15
Ian McEwan, 2006

Martin Amis (born in 1949 as the son of Kingsley Amis) started his career early with *The Rachel Papers* (1973) and the novel *Dead Babies* (1975), which sparked controversy due to its treatment of sex, drugs and violence. However, because of his expressive albeit slangy style – visible for instance in *Success* (1978) and *London Fields* (1989) – Amis became a fashionable novelist for a younger audience. *Money: A Suicide Note* (1984), which is set in London and New York at the time of the 1981 Royal Wedding, presents a satirical portrait of society in the early years of the Conservative

Martin Amis

government under Prime Minister Margaret Thatcher. John Self is a name that fits a highly unsympathetic narrator and protagonist who is an embodiment of materialism and greed, economic as well as sexual. There are many playful references to literature (e.g. connected to a character called Martina Twain, who brings John Self to read Orwell). The meta-fictional features of *Money* begin with the introductory "suicide note" and include the appearance of Martin Amis as a character in his own novel. *Time's Arrow* (1991) is a notable experiment with a reverse plot: the story is told backwards until it reaches the Holocaust.

Julian Barnes

Martin Amis and Julian Barnes (*1946) are erstwhile friends, fellow journalists (e.g. for *The Observer* and *The New Statesman*) and fellow novelists. Julian Barnes made his name with *Flaubert's Parrot* (1984), which is arguably either a witty biography of the pre-Modernist French writer, or a highly intertextual and Postmodernist novel about randomness and construction as elements in the formation and representation of a character. Individual chapters, when they are not written from the point of view of Geoffrey Braithwaite (a fan of Flaubert investigating his life and works) or from that of Louise Colet (Flaubert's mistress, chap. 11), are presented either in chronological or thematic fashion. In neat symmetry, Barnes's narrator comes up with three alternative ways to write a *curriculum vitae* chronologically (chap. 2) before he embarks upon a thematic approach, again in three different fashions, one of which is ironically labelled "The Train-spotter's Guide to Flaubert" (chaps. 4, 8, 12). All this is achieved by Barnes with much *jeu d'esprit*, occasionally dressed with an aside on the choice of endings offered by John Fowles in *The French Lieutenant's Woman* or an annotated list of Ten Commandments for fellow novelists (all in chap. 7). Barnes's exercise in writing an experimental writer's life in a congenial spirit is rounded off with an "Examination Paper" that awaits his readers (chap. 14). Julian Barnes's ironical sense of humour shows also in his later novels that were well received. *A History of the World in 10½ Chapters* (1989) is an episodic narrative (or a collection of short stories), introduced by a first piece entitled "The Stowaway" which tells the story of Noah's Ark from the point of view of a woodworm. By contrast, *England, England* (1998) looks into the future and – in a satirical encounter with Englishness – envisages the country as no more than a theme park. Intertextuality and history come together again in the novel *Arthur & George* (2005), where Barnes relates the true story of how Sir Arthur Conan Doyle in 1906 solved a mystery in the manner of his own creation, the detective Sherlock Holmes. Earlier on, but under the pseudonym Dan Kavanagh, Barnes had written a trilogy of detective fiction with a bisexual private eye as protagonist (1980–87).

To come back to David Lodge's summary view on the contemporary novel: when novelists today gather at a crossroads, they may not always look into different directions. On a more modest level of experimentation, Julian Barnes meets with e. g. Graham Swift, the author of *Waterland* (see chap. 5.3.1). In Barnes's *Talking It Over* (1991) and its sequel *Love, Etc.* (2000), we deal with confessional novels about love and infidelity that are narrated by several voices and from multiple points of view. Such a change of perspective is also central to *Last Orders*, the novel for which Graham Swift (*1949) won the Booker Prize in 1996. At the outset of Swift's novel – which is confined as so many Modernist novels to the events of one day – four regulars come together in a pub to take the ashes of their friend Jack on a last pub crawl before they are scattered into the sea. On their day trip from London to Margate, each of the four and Jack's widow Amy, too, is given his or her say, and thereby the opportunity to reveal their past. *Ulverton* (1992) by Adam Thorpe (*1956) is structurally based upon the same premise, but realised on a more ambitious scale. In its focus on a fictional village placed in Thomas Hardy's 'Wessex', rather than on a constant set of characters, Ulverton is a regional novel and also a novel about time. In twelve chapters, each of them set a generation apart, readers are told about life and loves within the village and about its development from the age of Cromwell and the Puritans to 1989. In this recreation of (English) rural history from multiple points of view, all strata of society are represented, from the barely literate up to the letter-writing lady. Thorpe's accomplished pastiche of prose styles includes the West Country dialect as well as the formal diction of a sermon, and his *assemblage* of texts over time ranges from a diary to the transcript of a broadcast and further to the 'post production script' of a feature film for television. In his command of narrative modes and in his impressive attempt to create a language that is both in character and of the period, Adam Thorpe's *Ulverton* invites the comparison with Joyce's *Ulysses*. Jonathan Coe (*1961) combined

Multiple Points of View

textual collage with a satire on the spirit of the 1980s in his portrait of an upper-class family, the Winshaws, and their dealings in *What a Carve Up!* (1994). Much like Martin Amis in *Money*, Coe subverted the call of the Thatcher government for a return to Victorian Values to present a world in which materialism met with a lack of morals. With its many instances in which the narrative is broken up by the insertion of journalism and advertisements, diary entries and transcripts from broadcasts, the fractured form of Coe's novel made it another prime example of 1990s experimentation in fiction.

Alasdair Gray (*Lanark*, 1981) and Irvine Welsh (*Trainspotting*, 1993) also belong into this picture, but are treated together with other Scottish novelists (in chap. 5.3.4). The great number of further examples of intertextuality and intermediality likewise merits a chapter of their own (see chap. 5.3.5).

5.3.4 | Gender and Region

The Sexual Revolution in Fiction

Let's talk about sex. One of the ways in which (Post-)Modernist works of fiction transgressed cultural boundaries in their time was in their liberal attitude to middle-class sexual mores. Likewise, one possible way to talk about those novels that, since the 1920s, have addressed gender relations in an unconventional manner, is to arrange the examples chosen not in chronological but in erotological order, that is with regard to their individual concern with hetero- or homosexual, bi- or transsexual love and identity formation. At the one end of a continuum, one could situate Joyce's *Ulysses* (1922) and *Lady Chatterley's Lover* by D. H. Lawrence (1928). In the openness of their depiction of **heterosexual** love and lust, those two novels confronted what still remained of Victorian Prudery (see chaps. 4.1 and 4.5). As a consequence, Joyce's and Lawrence's novels – which were also distinguished by the special effort their male creators took in the representation of female desire – were duly banned from British bookshops after they had been printed abroad. The ban on *Ulysses* was lifted in Britain and the USA in the 1930s, but while Joyce's novel (surprisingly) was never suppressed in the Republic of Ireland, the 1967 adaptation for the screen was, and this ban was lifted not before 2000. *Lady Chatterley's Lover* was banned in Britain until it was spectacularly cleared at the Old Bailey in 1960.

At this trial, fellow-novelist E.M. Forster spoke out in Lawrence's favour. In an act of self-censorship, however, Forster withheld his own novel *Maurice*, which he had completed in 1912, from publication during his lifetime, so that this novel on male homosexual desire could appear only posthumously, in 1971. The outcome of two earlier trials – of Oscar Wilde in person for homosexual acts, and of Radclyffe Hall's 1928 novel *The Well of Loneliness* for its depiction of lesbianism – may have convinced Forster that he trod on dangerous ground. In 1895, Wilde was sentenced to hard labour in prison, while Hall's novel was suppressed in Britain in the year of publication, and became widely available only after 1949. Despite or perhaps just because of such an atmosphere, one could place those novels that showed a **relaxed view on homosexuality**, and ventured to prominently address this as a topic, at the other end of the continuum. In Woolf's *Mrs Dalloway* (1925), such openness pertains to Clarissa's memory of a once seemingly attainable lesbian relationship to her friend Sally Seton (yet there is also the rather negative portrait of Doris Kilman, a Lesbian and the tutor of Clarissa's daughter Elizabeth). Three years later, Radclyffe Hall (1880–1943) produced *The Well of Loneliness*, her only novel of note yet one that became a classic of Lesbian literature. Writers like Forster and Woolf drafted a letter of protest to support Radclyffe Hall against prosecution, but they might have silently objected – on aesthetic as well as on ideological grounds – to Hall's appeal to convention. This pertains to Hall's pre-Modernist form of presentation as well as to her controversial portrait of the Lesbian protagonist Stephen Gordon as masculine in name and manner, as an example of 'sexual inversion' in the simple sense of a role reversal.

It is therefore tempting to go on by saying that with *Oranges Are Not the Only Fruit* (1985), Jeanette Winterson (*1959) submitted the experimental novel of development and Lesbian love that Radclyffe Hall would or could not write. Winterson's debut novel (which she successfully adapted for BBC Television in 1990) tells about the preoccupations of a writer who is as much given to formal experimentation as to homosexuality and gender relations as a theme. The Lesbian coming out of Winterson's narrator Jeannette provides liberation from the rigid and repressive life she has experienced in a foster-family under the influence of Christian fundamentalism. To make her point, Winterson

Jeanette Winterson

positively and unabashedly contrasts Lesbian love with other options, and moreover sets Jeannette's pursuit of happiness against
the teachings of her mother and of the Pentecostal Church, both
of which are portrayed as inflexible and intolerant. In addition
to her sexual frankness, Winterson gained a reputation as a Postmodernist writer because of the intertextual play with Biblical
books in the chapter headings of her novel, and because of her
combination of a realistic narrative with elements of fairy tale,
myth and meta-fiction. Such a combination is also characteristic of Winterson's historical novel *Sexing the Cherry* (1989), which
takes place in the time of the Civil Wars and the Restoration.
This novel, which is told from multiple points of view, is perhaps
even stronger marked by a non-linearity of narration and by the
appearance of fantastic female characters such as mermaids,
witches, and a Dog-Woman as one of the narrators. For good examples of Winterson's toying with other texts, one has to look no
further than to the story of the Twelve Dancing Princesses: after
the eldest has struck the note of self-characterisation by saying
that they have "lived happily ever after [...], but not with our husbands", the second princess joins in with the remark "'That's my
last husband painted on the wall, [...] looking as though he were
alive.'" (thereby adapting a phrase from Robert Browning's dramatic monologue "My Last Duchess", Winterson 1990: 48, 49).

V. Woolf, Orlando

Between the two poles of provocatively portrayed heterosexual and homosexual desire, one can situate those novels that are
concerned with bi- and transsexuality, with **sexual ambivalence and
sex change**. The peculiarity of *Written on the Body*, Winterson's 1992
novel on sexuality and textuality, is that the novelist refrains
from specifying the narrator's sex, which adds ambivalence to
her tragic love with Louise who is destined to die, but whose
erotic attraction is kept alive in prose poems as poetic re-imagi-
nations of her body. In this group of novels, Virginia Woolf set
the theme with *Orlando: A Biography* (1928), which originally was
conceived as the fictionalised life of Woolf's friend and lover,
the writer Vita Sackville-West. The three outstanding features of
the finished novel are Woolf's handling of gender, of time, and
of period language. The story of Orlando begins in Elizabethan
times, where the reader meets him as a 16-year-old courtier in
1586. In the two and a half centuries till the novel ends, Orlando
is constantly involved though he ages only by twenty years, yet

changes his sex half-way, in Restoration times. From now on, s/he lives through the centuries as a woman, meeting poets such as Alexander Pope while in every age concerned with a long poem of her own, until the androgynous s/he ends as an accomplished poet in the year of publication. In addition to references to literature and *literati*, the language spoken in Woolf's novel is often modelled on the prose style of the period. (For similar uses of pastiche, see the treatment of *Ulysses* and of *Ulverton* in chap. 5.3.3).

In two later novels by Patricia Duncker (*1951) and by the Black Scottish poet Jackie Kay (*1961), the theme of gender reversal is further explored. Kay's *Trumpet* (1998) sets in with the death of the famous Scottish jazz trumpet player Joss Moody in 1997, and then relates his life and after-life from multiple points of view, alternating between them from chapter to chapter. In contrast to what rumour has about the American pianist Billy Tipton (a real-life counterpart, †1989), the 'male' musician of Kay's invention is seen to have revealed his woman's body to his wife Millie, but not to their adopted son Colman, who therefore feels hurt and estranged from both foster-father and -mother. What Joss Moody was like is revealed in turn by Millie in those chapters entitled "House and Home", as well as by other "People" such as one of his musicians or the cleaner. Those memorial accounts are supplemented by the story of how Colman Moody tries to overcome his crisis of identity, part of which is his exclusive interview given to journalist Sophie Stones. The "Last Word" is the dead wo/man's own, telling a tale about the Black Diaspora. Duncker's *James Miranda Barry* (1999) covers much of the same ground, but adds a historical dimension. Her subject is the Victorian military surgeon James Barry (†1865), who served the Empire in various stations around the Globe, likewise passing for a man. His female body was discovered only at the time of his death. In her historical novel of character, Duncker alternates between Barry's voice and that of a heterodiegetic narrator, and sticks to those two inside and outside points of view (with the exception of a few letters written by other characters). The peculiarity of the situation is moreover fleshed out through Barry's interaction with his lifelong friend and lover Alice Jones, a decidedly female but entirely fictional character. Patrick McCabe's novel *Breakfast on Pluto* (1998, see below) also belongs into this context.

Doris Lessing

Writers who, like Patricia Duncker, were feminist critics, too, have concentrated on gender relations from a woman's point of view. In two classic pieces of feminist criticism entitled *A Room of One's Own* (1929) and *Three Guineas* (1938), Virginia Woolf concerned herself with the material and the intellectual circumstances that had hampered women's writing in the past (illustrated with reference to an imagined "Judith Shakespeare"), and with the need for a change. With her sketch of a history of women's writing in *A Room of One's Own*, Woolf also paved the way for a revision of the canon (see her view on Aphra Behn quoted in chap. 3.5.4). In the 1960s, other feminists quickly added *The Golden Notebook* (1962) by Doris Lessing (*1919) to such a revised canon because of its representation of the female experience in a work of psychological realism. Lessing's work, for which she received the Nobel Prize in 2007, comprises also 'space fiction' (see chap. 5.3.2) and many short stories (of which those early ones with a setting in Southern Africa were collected in 1973). Set in the 1950s, *The Golden Notebook* centres on Anna, a character with many autobiographical traits that is often seen in relation to her friend Molly. Anna is at once presented from a third-person point of view as the protagonist in a novel-within-the-novel entitled "Free Women", and at the same time (and in the first person) as a writer of fiction as well as of four notebooks, the differently coloured covers of which denote their variety of subjects, from Anna's South African background (black) over her political commitment (red) and her sketches of prose fiction (yellow) to her private life (blue). "Free Women" as well as the four notebooks are not presented consecutively, but cut up into sections. A fifth, the 'Golden Notebook', tells about how a new loving relationship did help her to overcome personal grief and a writer's block, and moreover provides the missing link to understand that "Free Women" is a novel written by Anna, too. Very soon after publication, feminists embraced *The Golden Notebook* as a Bible of the Women's Liberation Movement – to the surprise of Lessing, who felt she had to explain more than the complex structure of the novel in a long preface written for a 1972 re-issue.

Fay Weldon and
Angela Carter

The novelist and critic A. S. Byatt (*1936, see chap. 5.3.1), her sister Margaret Drabble (*1939) and the Irish author Edna O'Brien (*1932, see below) are writers that have also represented the female experience in fiction without taking a decidedly feminist

stance, in difference to e.g. Fay Weldon (*1931). The title of Weldon's 1975 novel *Female Friends* is paradigmatic for this and other
novels such as *Down Among the Women* (1971), *Praxis* (1978) and *Life
Force* (1992) which give a portrait of patriarchal gender relations
in working-class and middle-class Britain since the 1930s, seen
from a female and often feminist point of view. With *The Life and
Loves of a She-Devil* (1983), Weldon caught the spirit of the times:
this novel about a betrayed woman's revenge on her adulterous
husband and his lover was twice adapted for the screen, first
for the BBC (1986) and then in Hollywood (1989). With Angela
Carter (1940–92), feminist criticism of patriarchy expressed itself
differently, namely in connection with fairy myth and magic realism, with Gothic and sexual fantasies. Melanie, the orphaned
protagonist in *The Magic Toyshop* (1967), has to break free from the
torment and sexual degradation inflicted upon her by the shop's
owner, her Uncle Philip. In *The Infernal Desire Machines of Doctor
Hoffman* (1972), the title character likewise is a patriarch to boot.
Here, Carter revamps eighteenth-century Gothic romances and
the sexual fantasies of the Marquis de Sade, which she criticised
from a feminist point of view in her study *The Sadeian Woman*
(1979). In the same year, she published *"The Bloody Chamber" and
Other Stories*, a series of feminist rewritings of the classic fairy
tales about Bluebeard, Beauty and the Beast and Little Red Riding Hood. The title story of *Black Venus* (1985), a subsequent collection, refers to both Baudelaire's poems and to his Black mistress Jeanne Duval, whose rise and fall as a sexually emancipated
woman in Paris and on the island of Martinique is vividly depicted. This collection also includes a rewriting of Shakespeare's
fairy comedy entitled "Overture and Incidental Music for *A Midsummer Night's Dream*".

Besides a revision of gender roles and gender relations, **regional affiliation** is another feature that became increasingly more
marked over the twentieth century, in poetry and drama as well
as in fiction, where it traversed the divide between realism and
experimentation, and between high and low brow. (For crime
fiction related to gender as well as to region, see chap. 5.3.2.)
The supernatural element in Irish short fiction (see Trevor
1989) comes out again in "The Demon Lover" (1941) by Elizabeth Bowen (1899–1973), whose mastery of the short story is
as widely acknowledged as that of 'Frank O'Connor' (Michael

Region: Irish Masters of
the Short Story in the
Twentieth Century

Francis O'Donovan, 1903–66). O'Connor was more impressed by Daniel Corkery (1878–1964) and nineteenth-century realism than by Joyce's *Dubliners*. "Guests of the Nation", the title story of O'Connor's first collection (1931), takes place in the time of the Anglo-Irish War or Irish War of Independence (1919–21), in which O'Connor had fought in the ranks of the IRA. His story centres around two English mercenaries of the Black and Tans that have been taken hostages by the IRA. A regular game of cards seems to establish a common bond of humanity between the formerly powerful English, who (in a general sense) are no more than guests on the Green Isle, and their Irish captors. However, the awakening nation shows itself to be far from hospitable: an order arrives that the Englishmen are to be shot as reprisal for the death of IRA prisoners at the hand of the British. The stark realism in which the execution of the hostages is presented, and the contrast between the emotional involvement of the Irish narrator and the cold ferocity of his fellow IRA men during the event, mark the climax of O'Connor's deeply disturbing story, which inspired Brendan Behan's stage-play *The Hostage* (1958, see chap. 5.2.3) and Neil Jordan's film *The Crying Game* (1992). O'Connor's "The Majesty of the Law" (from his second collection of 1936) reiterates the theme of personal morality vs. depersonalised law.

Like Frank O'Connor, 'Seán O'Faoláin' (John Francis Whelan, 1900–91) had fought for the IRA before he turned a writer under the influence of Daniel Corkery. From 1932, O'Faoláin's short stories appeared in individual volumes before they were collected in 1980. The first published volume, *"Midsummer Madness" and Other Stories* (1932) centres on the 'Troubles'. With stories such as "The Faithless Wife" (1961), which explicitly cites Joyce's Molly Bloom when it tells the tale of an Irishwoman's adultery, O'Faoláin confronted the oppressive side of Irish Catholicism and its sexual taboos. In his later volumes of short stories, O'Faoláin increasingly abstracted from the situation in Ireland and turned to more universal themes. With the foundation of the magazine *The Bell* (1940–54), O'Faoláin had provided a new forum of publication, and in *The Short Story* (1948), he concerned himself with the genre as such. In its testing out of conventional morality, "The Faithless Wife" keeps good company with "Sarah" (1943) by Mary Lavin (1912–96), which refers to a single unmarried mother of four children from different fathers, and also with "Sister

Imelda" (1981) by Edna O'Brien, which tells about love between two women in a Catholic convent.

Edna O'Brien (*1932) had already left Ireland for London in 1959, when she began to criticise Catholic morality in Ireland first with a trilogy of novels and then with numerous short stories. *The Country Girls* (her first novel, 1960, which the author adapted herself for the screen in 1964), *Girl With Green Eyes* (1962) and *Girls in Their Married Bliss* (1964, updated with an additional epilogue in 1987) tell of Caithleen and Baba, two Irish girls from O'Brien's native County Clare whose sexual emancipation includes extra-marital relations of their own or of their partners (which is why the novels were banned in the Republic). The 1974 collection *"A Scandalous Woman" and Other Stories* is characteristic of Edna O'Brien's further interest in the theme. In a second trilogy of novels comprising *House of Splendid Isolation* (1994), *Down by the River* (1997) and *Wild Decembers* (1999), O'Brien continued to address a whole number of taboo topics: sectarian violence in Ireland as well as sexual violence in the family, together with incestuous rape and abortion.

The Novel in Ireland since the 1960s

With *Strumpet City* (1969), James Plunkett (1920–2003) produced a historical novel of epic length, whose social realism vividly recreated the poverty in the tenements and the industrial dispute in the years between 1907 and the Dublin Lockout of 1913/14. In 1980, *Strumpet City* was successfully adapted for Irish television. The story of working-class life in Dublin is continued in his novels *Farewell Companions* (1977) and *The Circus Animals* (1990). In Roddy Doyle (*1958), Plunkett found a worthy successor. Doyle's *The Last Roundup* series, which set in with *A Star Called Henry* (1999) and continued with *Oh, Play that Thing!* (2004), presents the fictional autobiography of Henry Smart, who is born in Dublin in 1901, distinguishes himself during the 1916 Easter Rising, and tells about his life in the Irish Diaspora in the USA in the Roaring Twenties. Before he wrote those historical novels about a working-class character (who encounters a great number of real historical characters along the way), Roddy Doyle secured fame with another series: *The Barrytown Trilogy* – made up of *The Commitments* (1987), *The Snapper* (1990) and *The Van* (1991) – centres on the life of individual members of the Rabbitte family living in 'Barrytown', a fictionalised working-class area of Northside Dublin. All novels in the trilogy have successfully been made into movies, of which Alan Parker's adaptation of *The Commitments* (1991) found the greatest acclaim. (For a discussion of novel and film in the context of intermediality, see chap. 5.3.6.)

With another Irish writer's trilogy of novels, we turn to the treatment of **the 'Troubles'**, that is the intermittent periods of armed conflict within the British Isles in the twentieth century. The eponymous novel *Troubles* (1970) by J[ames]. G[ordon]. Farrell (1935–79), which dealt with the Civil War period in Ireland between 1919 and 1921, became the first part of his *Empire Trilogy* that also includes *The Siege of Krishnapur* (1973) and *The Singapore Grip* (1978, for both of which see chap. 5.3.5). During the composition of the first novel in the series, a second major bout of 'Troubles' broke out (in 1969), which turned Farrell's prize-winning historical novel suddenly into a very topical one. The Northern Irish writer Bernard MacLaverty (*1942), who left Belfast for Glasgow in the early 1970s, made the new round of sectarian violence the central theme of *Cal* (1983). The five chapters of this novel are reminiscent of the act division of a tragedy. 19-year-old Cal, who lives on the dole and has only his widowed father Shamie McCluskey left in the family, is isolated not only on an estate dominated by Protestants but also within the Catholic community, because he wants to quit their underground militia for which he agrees to do one last job only. In the meantime, Cal is given work by a family of Protestant farmers, the Mortons, whereas other Protestants beat him up on the estate. The climactic third chapter of the novel relates how Cal takes a minor part in an armed robbery, which calls up the memory of another raid a year ago in which a fellow-Catholic killed the son of the Mortons, who accidentally was also the husband of Marcella, an Italian Catholic librarian with whom Cal has fallen in love. While the Mortons' farm, the library and Marcella's love altogether point to the possibility of a safe haven from sectarian violence, Cal's home is burnt down and his father is hospitalised. After he found sexual initiation and loving comfort with Marcella, Cal breaks the circle of violence and turns informer to save the library from a bomb attack. The ambivalent ending of the novel sees Cal being arrested by the police for complicity in the murder of Marcella's husband, as his former fellows must have informed on him, too. MacLaverty's novel of initiation and of tolerance became a classroom classic and, just like his earlier novel *Lamb* (1980), was successfully adapted for the screen from the author's script (1984). For an extended discussion of more examples of the 'Troubles novel', see Head (2002: 129–44), and for thematically related stage-plays from O'Casey to the present day, see chap. 5.2.4.

Three other Irish writers may stand as representative examples for all those whose fiction could not be mentioned in relation to the themes discussed above. John Banville (*1945) distinguished himself with a trilogy of fiction on science (*Doctor Copernicus*, 1976; *Kepler*, 1981; *The Newton Letter*, 1982) before he went on to win the Man Booker Prize for his 2005 novel of memory entitled *The Sea*. Patrick McCabe (*1955) wrote about violence and violent fantasies in rural Ireland in *The Butcher Boy* (1992), and with *Breakfast on Pluto* (1998) produced a novel of development about a transgender woman. Finally, Colm Tóibín (*1955) found an adequate form of psychological realism when he approached the novelist and critic Henry James in *The Master* (2004). As in the novel *The Blackwater Lightship* (1999) and in the stories collected in *Mothers and Sons* (2006), Tóibín also took the opportunity to address one of his favourite topics, namely homosexuality, which had been formally decriminalised in Ireland only in 1993.

The Scottish Renaissance (see chap. 5.1) is represented in fiction by the work of 'Lewis Grassic Gibbon' (James Leslie Mitchell, 1901–35). For typical features of his work, one has to look no further than to his short story "Smeddum", which is characterised by its depiction of the hardship of rural life in Scotland and by Gibbon's endeavour (together with that of the poet Hugh MacDiarmid) to revive Scots or Lallans as a literary language. The story of how Meg Menzies as a single mother takes care of her nine children, and of how her daughter Kath emancipates herself as a woman, illustrates that it needs 'smeddum' (meaning 'spirit' or 'spunk') to be able to lead a self-determined life. A trilogy that comprised the novels *Sunset Song* (1932), *Cloud Howe* (1933) and *Grey Granite* (1934) was later collected under the title *A Scots Quair* (1946). While being focused throughout on the protagonist Chris Guthrie and her ambivalent attitude to Scotland, Gibbon's trilogy moreover aspires to a chronicle of Scottish society in the period from 1911 to 1932.

Chronologically speaking, *The Prime of Miss Jean Brodie* (1961) follows suit, as it is set between 1930 and 1939. This novel by Mu-

Scottish Fiction

riel Spark (1918–2006) is regarded as another landmark of Scottish fiction because of its experimentation with narrative time and point of view. Spark relates how a teacher at an Edinburgh girls' school attempts to dominate the life of her adolescent pupils, in love as well as in politics. In her last novella entitled *The Finishing School* (2004), Spark returned to the school setting, after she had distinguished herself elsewhere as a Catholic novelist, as a satirist and – with her meta-literary parable *The Comforters* (1957) – as an early Postmodernist (see chap. 5.3.1). Edinburgh and especially the nearby Forth Bridge take pride of place in *The Bridge* (1986) by Iain Banks (*1954), the plot of which is alike built upon an intricate structure. The most easily accessible strand is a heterodiegetic narrative of development written in Standard English. Spanning the period from the 1960s to the 1980s, this strand focuses on the student life of an unnamed male in Edinburgh and on the open relationship (with affairs on both sides) to his girlfriend Andrea Cramond. His drunken driving ends in a road accident in view of the Forth Bridge. A logical connection might thus be made to the second, homodiegetic narrative that intermittently runs from "Coma" to "Coda" and deals with the stream of consciousness of a comatose patient who wakes up only on the novel's last page. A third and complex strand takes place within a futuristic setting that however in its references to war suggests earlier periods of the twentieth century, too. Central to this utopian setting is the Bridge, an apparently self-contained world that does not connect any land. Readers are told about John Orr, who lives under the supervision of Dr Joyce because he has forgotten his past, and about Orr's dreams. These are accompanied by another's Barbaric fantasies of sex and cruelty, rendered in a phonetically spelt Scots. Such a parallel world entitled 'the Culture' is developed in greater detail in other novels published, in alternation with his mainstream fiction, under the name of Iain M. Banks (see chap. 5.3.2).

The city of Glasgow as another Scottish centre of culture featured in experimental novels by e.g. Alasdair Gray (*1934) and James Kelman. Gray's novel *Lanark: A Life in Four Books* (which are presented in non-chronological order, 1981) combines a novel of development (books I and III) with a dystopian narrative set in a fantastic version of Glasgow (II and IV). Gray's novel was soon made out as an example of Postmodernist fiction because of its fractured form, its intermedial combination of the text with Gray's own illustrations, and its meta-fictional features (Gray appears as the character Nastler in the Epilogue to comment upon his own novel). Language is an issue again in *How Late It Was, How Late* (1994), a novel which fuses social and psychological realism and for which James Kelman (*1946) received the Booker Prize. Within a Glasgow setting, the focus is on Sammy (Mr Samuels), an alcoholic who has served a prison sentence, is left by his girlfriend Helen after he admitted to his criminal past, and turns blind after a confrontation with the police. Sammy's experience is rendered in a book-long stream of consciousness in Free Indirect Speech, which is only rarely interrupted by a narrator's commentary or by more dramatic scenes like a police interrogation. Kelman's social realism became controversial where it pertained to language: the narrative is not only rendered in the local dialect, but also strewn with expletives. Related examples of such (often controversial) social realism from Scotland comprise the Glasgow novel *Swing Hammer Swing!* (1992) by Jeff Torrington (1935–2009) as well as *Trainspotting* (1993) by Irvine Welsh (*1958), which centres on Edinburgh's drug subculture. In Welsh's fractured narrative, which includes dialogue in phonetically spelt Scots, many voices and many inside views come together to tell a tale of addiction to sex, drugs and fashionable music. The 1996 movie helped to make the novel a cult book, and most of its characters reappeared in a sequel conspicuously entitled *Porno* (2002).

A[lison]. L. Kennedy (*1965), who lives and works in Glasgow, and Ali Smith (*1962) are two Scottish writers that also made an impact in recent years. Smith's *Hotel World* (2001) pays homage to Joyce: all parts of her experimental novel are headed by tense (past, present historic, future conditional, perfect, future in the past, present), and the section entitled "future in the past" includes an Interior Monologue in imitation of *Ulysses*. A.L. Kennedy's novel with the ironical title *Paradise* (2004) is reminiscent of both Joyce and Kelman when it delves into an alcoholic's experience. Kennedy's dark humour shows in the title story to her collection *Night Geometry and the Garscadden Trains* (1990) – where a woman tells about her way into marriage, and how she nearly killed her husband – as well as in the stories collected in *Original Bliss* (1997). "Groucho's Moustache" is a woman's account of her flirtation and 'psycho-sexual debate' with a man that reveals himself as an embalmer, and the novella that provides the title to the collection engages in similarly deadpan humour. In the introductory story "Rockaway and the Draw", the woman in focus reflects, upon meeting the friends of her American partner, whether she had better dressed 'as a British citizen in the costume of a former British colony'. Reminiscences of the Empire, though, did not always go together (as here) with fantasies of inflicting cruelty – which remains to be demonstrated.

5.3.5 | Residues of Empire and Transcultural Fiction in Britain

W. Somerset Maugham

The years between the First and Second World Wars saw the climax and close of the British Empire. Several notable writers of fiction dealt with the waning of Empire, and with the problems of interethnic love and understanding in a South Asian setting. During his lifetime, W[illiam]. Somerset Maugham (1874–1965, see chap. 5.2.2) was widely regarded as one of the masters of the short story, because of his craftsmanship and psychological interest, and perhaps also because of the exotic locations of his stories. "The Force of Circumstance" from *The Casuarina Tree*, a 1926 collection of stories set in contemporary Malaya and Borneo, is a good example in all these respects. In the story, the marriage between Guy, a Malayan-born expatriate, and his English wife Doris breaks down when she finds out about what Guy calls 'only a temporary arrangement' under 'peculiar circumstances'. His earlier relationship to a Malayan woman, the mother of his children, is swiftly resumed under 'the force of circumstance', that is after Doris has left him to return to Britain. In his colonial story told with a series of flashbacks and with the use of Free Indirect Speech, Somerset Maugham engages with the notion of 'home', with the differences between colonial centre and periphery, and with the issue of interethnic (love) relationships. E. M. Forster, George Orwell, Paul Scott and Ruth Prawer Jhabvala (all of whom wrote with a similar first-hand experience) have been concerned with the same complex theme in their novels with an Asian setting.

E[dward]. M[organ]. Forster (1879–1970) travelled to India twice before and after the First World War, with a spell as private secretary to a Maharaja in the 1920s. In *A Passage to India* (1924), Forster's masterpiece, two Englishwomen – old Mrs Moore and her prospective daughter-in-law, Adela Quested – who embark on the journey from Britain to its 'Jewel in the Crown' are confronted with the narrow-mindedness of expatriate Anglo-Indians in 'Chandrapore' (the fictional counterpart of Bankipur in Northern India). The scenes in the Chandrapore Club, which remains reserved to White Anglo-Indians only, are symbolic of the failure to come to an understanding with the millions of colonial subjects in British India. David Lean's widely popular 1984 adaptation of Forster's novel for the screen recreated the splendour of the *British Raj* or British rule on the subcontinent together with the racism that went with it. This includes Adela's fiancé Ronny Heaslop, the City Magistrate who keeps his distance to native Indians, physically and mentally, and thereby shocks Mrs Moore, his much more tolerant mother. The exception to the rule in Forster's satirical panorama of expatriate society is Cyril Fielding, the principal of a college, who is on friendly terms with Dr Aziz, a Muslim Indian physician who moves in Indian nationalist circles, and also with Prof. Godbole, a Hindu Brahman. Together with Mrs Moore, who voices her discomfort with the racial prejudices rife among colonial servants and their wives, Fielding functions as a **go-between character** in a society which abhors nothing more than **going native**, i.e. the ultimate crossing of the colour bar. Therefore, the Englishwomen's readiness to embark on a trip to the (fictionalised) Marabar Caves organised by Dr Aziz causes eyebrows to be raised. The Caves are integral to the novel's symbolism and syncretism that also includes Mosque and Temple: they are likewise used as titles for each of its three parts. Forster's use of the Caves moreover suggests a reference to Plato's 'Allegory of the Cave' (which stresses the impossibility to attain to reality directly and securely). Adela's allegation that Aziz may have used the situation in the Caves for an indecent assault leads to his imprisonment and trial. Later on, however, Adela (who has dithered before in her commitment to marry Ronny Heaslop) retracts her charge during a climactic courtroom scene. When Indian nationalists organise a triumphal return for Aziz, havoc breaks loose, and formerly friendly relations break down, as Aziz disapproves of the gentlemanly manner in which Fielding sees to Adela's security. One of the central questions raised in the novel is whether Englishmen and Indians really can become friends, and the ultimate answer is 'not yet': even when they

Fig. 5.16

E. M. Forster by Dora Carrington, 1924/25

George Orwell,
Burmese Days

meet again years after the event, Fielding and Aziz cannot really renew what has been lost. This indicates that Forster the novelist had his doubts about the future of the *Raj* in the early stage of Gandhi's campaign for decolonisation.

Certainly no less pessimistic were the views of George Orwell and Paul Scott on interethnic relations. Orwell (1903–50, see chap. 5.3.2), who had been born in Bengal, was a member of the Imperial Police in Burma until his increasing dissatisfaction with his job, and his dislike of being involved with Imperialism, brought him to resign from office. In 1931, he published "A Hanging", a story essay set in British Burma that relates the hanging of a Hindu prisoner from the point of view of a White policeman. Over and above its autobiographical implications, the story suggests a comparison with Rudyard Kipling's 'barrack-room ballad' entitled "Danny Deever" as well as with Oscar Wilde's "Ballad of Reading Gaol" (both mentioned in chap. 4.4). In another clearly autobiographical story essay entitled "Shooting an Elephant" (1936), Orwell addresses the theme of Kipling's poem "White Man's Burden" through a disillusioned police officer introducing the story with the confession that "I was all for the Burmese and all against their oppressors, the British. [...] In a job like that you see the dirty work of Empire at close quarters." *Burmese Days* (1934) is a novel that also tells of the writer's indignation over political injustice and the role of the British in Asia. In this novel which is set in a fictional provincial town (based upon the location where Orwell served as a policeman) Orwell, too, tried his hand at a panorama of expatriate society. Some of the colonial officers and managers in the timber trade who frequent the European Club are characterised by overt racism, the exception being John Flory (a counterpart to Forster's Cyril Fielding) who is anti-Empire and who has 'gone native', e.g. by keeping a Burmese mistress. One strand of the plot follows Flory's increasingly strained relations to Ma Hla May, his mistress, because of his infatuation with Elizabeth Lackersteen, despite the fact that this superficial newcomer does not share Flory's fondness for Burma and the Burmese. Elizabeth Lackersteen, who has escaped attempted rape by her uncle and who remains evasive about Flory's proposal of marriage, becomes attracted to another new member of the Club, namely arrogant Lieut. Verrall. This (more or less) romantic strand of the plot is balanced by the intrigues of U Po Kyin, a corrupt and violent magistrate who seeks native membership in the Club. U Po Kyin plots against Flory's friend Dr Veraswami, whom he considers a rival to his career, and he even instigates a rebellion that leads to the siege of the Club, to the killing of Whites, and in the end to Flory's suicide.

Paul Scott (1920–78) got to know India and Malaya as a soldier in the Second World War, and those last years before Indian Independence in 1947 he also chose as a setting for his fiction, which in 'Mayapore' once more features a fictionalised location. In contrast to the novels by Forster and Orwell, Paul Scott decided for a multiple point of view. In this way, he developed the two main incidents told in *The Jewel in the Crown* (1966) over three further novels, before he followed up *The Raj Quartet* (1976) with the Booker Prize winning sequel *Staying On* (1977). One of these incidents is connected to the taboo of interethnic love, and moreover to the gang rape of a newly arrived White woman: when Indian youths surprise the journalist Hari Kumar with his English lover Daphne Manners, they first beat him up and then rape her. The other and no less violent incident concerns Edwina Crane, a missionary schoolteacher whose love for India turns sour when she witnesses the murder of an Indian colleague, which depresses her so much that she sets fire to herself. (This fatal act of self-violence refers to *suttee* or burning of widows. British colonialists took pride in having terminated that tradition in the name of humanity.) The other novels of the quartet are related either to those incidents or the characters mentioned. The scheming police superintendent Ronald Merrick appears in all four novels as a colonial *vice* character.

Paul Scott,
The Raj Quartet

In 1984, *The Raj Quartet* saw a successful adaptation as a television series in Britain. One year before, the filmmakers Ismail Merchant and James Ivory had produced an adaptation of Ruth Prawer Jhabvala's 1975 novel *Heat and Dust* from the author's screenplay. (See also chap. 5.2.1.) Migration and a transnational identity are the hallmarks of her life: born in Cologne as the daughter of German Jews who migrated to Britain in 1939, Ruth Prawer became a British citizen in 1948 and a resident in New Delhi after her marriage in 1951. She adopted US-American citizenship, too, some time after her move to New York in the year when *Heat and Dust* won the Booker Prize. The novel consists of two interlinked stories with many parallels: the frame narrative

Ruth Prawer Jhabvala,
Heat and Dust

is set in the 1970s, and the enframed story is set in 1923, when the *British Raj* began its decline. The locations in both stories are the town of Satipur in Northern India, and the nearby palace of the Nawab of Khatm (a local prince). Each of the two stories tells of interethnic and extra-marital love between a White British woman and a local Indian, so that the recurrent theme of 'going native' is here brought together with the colonial taboo of miscegenation. The link between the stories is achieved in that the homodiegetic narrator of the 1970s frame narrative is the granddaughter of Olivia Rivers, whose scandalous elopement with the Nawab is told heterodiegetically. Both interethnic love affairs lead to pregnancies, and eventually to one abortion – that of Olivia's child with the Nawab, whereas her granddaughter decides against such a termination. In this way, *Heat and Dust* gives at least a partially positive answer to Forster's question about the possibility of interethnic relations in colonial and postcolonial times.

From the Indian Mutiny to the Handover of Hong Kong

Upon Britain's victory in the Second World War, in Europe as well as in East Asia, followed the dismantling of its overseas empire and the loss of its status as a global power. Decolonisation properly began with the Independence of India and Pakistan in 1947, 90 years after the Indian Mutiny, that ultimately unsuccessful 1857 rebellion of native Indian troops (*sepoys*) against the *British Raj*. For the time being, the process of Decolonisation came to an end with the handover of Hong Kong in 1997. Meanwhile, large-scale migration to Britain from its former colonies in the Caribbean, in Asia and in Africa had led to the formation of a multicultural society in Britain. These colonial and postcolonial developments are reflected in a number of novels that are best seen in groups. (For crime fiction, see chap. 5.3.2.)

The **1857 Indian Mutiny or Sepoy Rebellion** led to atrocities on both sides. They involved the slaughter of British women and children after the surrender of their garrison-cities under siege, but also the summary execution of rebels who were either hanged or 'blown from cannons'. Twentieth-century representations of this key event in colonial history differ markedly from earlier treatments such as Lord Tennyson's poem "The Defence of Lucknow" (1880) and G. A. Henty's Christmas ghost story "A Pipe of Mystery" (1890). They took a patriotic British point of view (as mentioned in chap. 4.2.2) that became qualified in the 1970s in popular entertainment and in a prize-winning novel alike. In his comic and historical novel *Flashman in the Great Game* (1975), George MacDonald Fraser (1925–2008) blends a detailed account of events (and additional historical notes) with a plot of adventure and sexual trysts. For the anti-hero and narrator of this and the other novels in his popular series of *Flashman Papers* (1969–2005), Fraser took Harry Flashman, the bully from *Tom Brown's Schooldays* by Thomas Hughes (a Victorian novel that was published in the year of the Mutiny, and thus can be given Fraser's protagonist to read in *Flashman in the Great Game*). Fraser revived and revamped Flashman as a flirtatious agent employed in Her Majesty's Service, a kind of historical James Bond who is far from being a Victorian prude, yet is a coward and a braggart. The more astonishing is his fictional career at the hotspots of Empire, while the self-ironical form of presentation makes it possible to look at Imperial history not only in detail, but also from a distance (as when the atrocities of both sides are made part of the plot).

Two years earlier, the Booker Prize went to another historical novel that is more seriously inclined. *The Siege of Krishnapur* (1973) is part of the *Empire Trilogy* by J. G. Farrell (1935–79, see chap. 5.3.4 and below). In the novel's representation of colonial India, there are a number of resemblances to E. M. Forster's *A Passage to India*. They include the opening description of a landscape without figures (hinting at the comparative insignificance of human endeavour and strife in view of natural history), a fictionalised setting (based upon Lucknow under siege) that is still recognisable but lends itself to generalisation, and a satirical presentation of colonial expatriates. Farrell's interest in his characters, in their intellectual background and their degree of intercultural competence, make for a slow pace at the beginning of the novel which then steadily accelerates towards its climactic ending. In sharp contrast to Tennyson's poem "The Defence of Lucknow", the civil defence of 'Krishnapur' organised by the Collector Mr Hopkins (a positive representative of civilised manners) is given out as a Pyrrhic victory. Civilisation does not survive the siege, which is a symbol for the breakdown of interethnic relations under colonial rule. In a last and successful attempt at fending off a major assault, every specimen of technology and art is made to serve the defence, so that nothing remains from the Collector's collection of exhibits of the 1851 Great Exhibition. Shakespeare's great value consists in his well-rounded statue-head being more useful than those of his peers when fired from a mortar. When the relief troops finally arrive, the surviving defenders look like Untouchables to them. In a casual reunion between the Collector and a dandyish character some time later, the siege appears as an insignificant event (just like in the opening landscape description). Moreover, in the Collector's bitter dictum that "Culture is a sham", there is the recognition of the utter failure of the Imperialist mission to spread Civilisation. Indian treatments of this historical theme that offer themselves for comparison, not just for their look towards oral narrative and meta-fiction, include Shashi Tharoor's *The Great Indian Novel* (1989) and Vikram Chandra's *Red Earth and Pouring Rain* (1995). Mangal Panday, the first mutineer, appears in Zadie Smith's *White Teeth* (2000) and, much more prominently, in the 2005 film *Mangal Panday/The Rising*, directed by Ketan Mehta from the screenplay of British-Indian writer Farrukh Dhondy.

Apart from the group of novels about the 1857 Rising, there is a corresponding set of **novels dealing with South East Asia and the Far East at other times**. Some of those are keyed to another traumatic experience for British expatriates: the Fall of Singapore to the Japanese in 1942 and the successive treatment of the prisoners of war (POW) in Japanese camps. *The Singapore Grip* (1978) by J.G. Farrell is the last historical novel in his *Empire Trilogy* and relates the story of the fictitious rubber trade company of Blackett & Webb and of various members of the families of its owners, from the outbreak of the Sino-Japanese War in 1937 to the events in 1942. Through the inclusion of a French and a US-American character and their views on colonialism, of a Eurasian woman's varied experience of racism, and even of chapters focusing on Japanese soldiers and their war experience, Farrell avoids a one-sided picture of what wartime Prime Minister Winston Churchill branded as "the worst disaster and the largest capitulation in British history" (1959, chap. 7). From several interpretations of the ambivalent phrase *The Singapore Grip* suggested within Farrell's novel, one stands out that is made by Matthew Webb at a point of climax:

> It's the grip of our Western culture and economy on the Far East ... It's the stranglehold of capital on the traditional cultures of Malaya, China, Burma, Java, Indo-China and even India herself! It's the doing of things *our way* ... I mean, it's the pursuit of self-interest rather than of the *common* interest! (Farrell 1979: 498).

In this general sense, a comparison suggests itself not only with another historical novel about Burma and Singapore, *The Glass Palace* (2000) by the Indian writer Amitav Ghosh (*1956), and with the earlier *Malayan Trilogy* (1956–59) by Anthony Burgess (1917–93), but also with a number of other novels. In *Empire of the Sun* (1984), J[ames]. G[raham]. Ballard (1930–2009) drew upon his autobiographical experience of the Japanese occupation of the International Settlement in Shanghai in 1942, and of his detainment in a prison camp thereafter. Jim Graham, Ballard's *alter ego* in the novel, witnesses the cruelty afflicted upon the interned civilians, but also a certain fascination with the enemy. In 1987, the novel was successfully adapted for the screen by director Steven Spielberg from a script by Tom Stoppard. (For a comparison between fact and fiction, see Ballard's 2008 autobiography *Miracles of Life*. Kazuo Ishiguro's *When We Were Orphans*, mentioned below, is another novel partly set in historical Shanghai.) In the *Asian Saga* (1962–93), a blockbuster series of six novels some of which were likewise successfully adapted to the screen, James Clavell (1924–94) had dealt with a Japanese POW camp in Singapore (*King Rat*, 1962), and also with the history of Hong Kong (*Tai Pan*, 1966; *Noble House*, 1981). In his best-known novels Timothy Mo, who was born in Hong Kong in 1950, made much of the history of Britain's last Crown Colony, and of his own Chinese-English background. The intrusive heterodiegetic narration of *An Insular Possession* (1986) corresponds to its nineteenth-century setting in colonial Canton and Macao in the 1830s. The often humorous tone is balanced, towards the ending of this historical novel, by fictional newspaper reportage of the 1841 Opium War that made Hong Kong a British possession. In *The Monkey King* (1978), Mo recreated colonial Hong Kong a century later, by telling – again in humorous fashion – the story of an interethnic and bicultural family much like his own, in the period between 1937 and the years after 1945. In *The Quiet American* (1955), Graham Greene (1904–91) took a much more serious approach and provided a moral interest to a novel set in the early stages of the war fought first by the French and then by the USA in Vietnam. The narrator of Greene's novel, middle-aged British journalist Thomas Fowler, is in love with Phuong, a young Vietnamese woman, and likewise with her country. He therefore runs into conflict with Alden Pyle, an American agent with whom Fowler sympathises at first. Yet through his acts of subversion, Pyle becomes responsible for the deaths of civilians witnessed by Fowler. He is also Fowler's rival in love – a chain of events that prompts Fowler to question his own position, and to search for an adequate solution to the moral dilemma.

V.S. Naipaul

Among those transcultural British prose writers with an Asian background, V[idiadhar]. S[urajprasad]. Naipaul sticks out, not least because this widely travelled writer (who was born in 1932 into an Indo-Caribbean family in Trinidad, but left for Britain in 1950) received the Nobel Prize for Literature in 2001. In Naipaul's œuvre, works of fiction alternate with semi-autobiographical writings such as *The Enigma of Arrival* (1987) and with travel literature, often on an acerbic note. *The Middle Passage* (1962), Naipaul's otherwise quite readable account of his native Caribbean, is still notorious for his verdict that 'nothing was created in the West Indies'. Others found fault with his critical encounter with Islamic countries made in the year of the 1979 Iranian Revolution (*Among the Believers: An Islamic Journey*, 1981). For the time being, *India: A Million Mutinies Now* (1990) remains the last part of a trilogy that also includes *An Area Of Darkness* (1964) and *India: A Wounded Civilization* (1977). This last part is particularly to be recommended for the manner in which Naipaul steps back to listen to his conversational partners in India. Naipaul's novel *The Mimic Men* (1967) compares well with other postcolonial novels about migration and the search for identity from the pens of Caribbean-British writers such as Jean Rhys, Sam Selvon, George Lamming and David Dabydeen (see below). However, Naipaul's first-person narrator Ranjit Kripalsingh alias Ralph Singh is unusual in being a political refugee who has seen high life. In a London hotel, this ousted and exiled colonial politician writes his autobiography, telling about his Indian upbringing on the fictional Caribbean island of Isabella; about the behaviour of the British abroad in colonial times as well as of immigrants in Britain later; about his loss of power to a Black politician in a time of racial tension and violence on the island; and, throughout, about his mixed marriage to an Englishwoman as well as about his search for sexual adventures elsewhere. The title of Naipaul's novel has become a household word for a subservient attitude that welcomes rather than opposes cultural imperialism.

A generation younger than Naipaul, Salman Rushdie (*1947) is counted as one of the best-known contemporary writers worldwide – albeit sometimes only for the reason that his novel *The Satanic Verses* (1988) provoked Iran's Ayatollah Khomeini into pronouncing a *fatwa* (a religious edict, practically a death sentence). However, over and above the controversy about *The Satanic Verses*, Rushdie is of high interest for his peculiar blend of magic realism, for the way in which he combines older traditions of story-telling and (Post-)Modernist experiments in fiction, and for the insights that can be gained from his pointed essays and reviews (collected in *Imaginary Homelands*, 1992, and *Step Across This Line*, 2002). Both *Midnight's Children* (1981), which was singled out twice (in 1993 and 2008) as the best novel ever to have received the Booker Prize, and *The Moor's Last Sigh* (1995) combine family histories with the political history of the Indian subcontinent in the twentieth century. Saleem Sinai, the narrator of *Midnight's Children*, is "handcuffed to history" because he was born on 14/15 August 1947 on the stroke of midnight that brought the Independence of India and of Pakistan. (Rushdie himself was born in Bombay two months earlier.) What distinguishes Rushdie's novel from a mere fleshing out of a timeline of events between 1915 and 1978 (although such a timeline may come handy) are its intertextual as well as meta-historical character, and its spells of magic. Saleem's digressive and unreliable narration calls up Cervantes's *Don Quixote*, Sterne's *Tristram Shandy* and *The Tin Trum* (*Die Blechtrommel*) by Günter Grass as **intertextual precedents**. Moreover, Rushdie's self-confidence shows in his adoption of stylistic devices from Joyce's *Ulysses*, such as extra-long sentences, often without punctuation, and the repeated use of rhetorical questions (see chaps. 6–7, 10–11, 23, 26–27). In addition, there is a frequently ironical indebtedness to Indian mythology and story-telling conventions. In one form or another, cult figures such as Ganesha the elephant-god and his parents Shiva and Parvati appear in the novel: Aadam, the son from Saleem's first marriage to another Midnight's Child called Parvati-the-witch (actually the fruit of Parvati's previous affair with a Major Shiva) is born with elephant's ears, while Saleem shares his trunk-like "cyranose" (1995: 13) with the gifted wordsmith Cyrano de Bergerac from Edmond de Rostand's eponymous stage-play. Saleem's unreliability (see esp. chaps. 12, 14, 15) contributes to the **meta-historical character** of Rushdie's novel. Saleem recalls the family's history and narrates the story of his own life to Padma, his second wife,

| Fig. 5.17
Salman Rushdie by
Tim Ross, 2008

in a chutney factory. For this 'chutneyfication of history', in which each new chapter forms the counterpart of a newly bottled preserve, Saleem can fall back only on the truth of memory (chap. 15). The India of *Midnight's Children* – like that of other Indian novels, historical or otherwise – is an 'India of the mind', as Rushdie pointed out in the introductory essay to his 1992 collection *Imaginary Homelands*. To the same effect, his narrator Saleem Sinai states that India is "a collective fiction" (chap. 8). Moreover, he confesses freely that "in all autobiography, as in all literature, what actually happened is less important than what the author can manage to persuade his audience to believe" (chap. 19) – and Saleem's version of real historical events is spiced up with many elements of **magic realism**. Prominent instances are the telepathic connection between the 1,001 Midnight's Children, which Saleem eventually uses against them, and Saleem's fantastic experience in the Sundarbans, as a "forest of illusions" and a "jungle of dreams" (chap. 25). The manner in which Indira Gandhi – the Indian Prime Minister who became notorious in 1975/76 for her authoritarian rule and campaign for enforced sterilisations – is depicted as a witch-like Widow in the novel also belongs into this context.

The Satanic Verses (1988) opens right away with such a spell of magic. The star-actor Gibreel Farishta and the voice imitator Saladin Chamcha miraculously survive their fall from an airplane that was first hijacked and then destroyed, to land as Muslim Indian immigrants in London – with Farishta assuming traits of the Archangel Gibreel during the fall, while Saladin is metamorphosed into a goat (i.e. the Devil). There are two parallel strands of the plot. Chaps. 1, 3, 5, 7, 9 of the novel rehearse the personal life and love relations of both immigrants before and after their arrival in London. They culminate in Saladin's revenge upon Gibreel for his lack of intervention after the fall, to be followed by an outbreak of racial violence in London, and Gibreel's suicide back in Bombay. The remaining four chapters form a sequence of dream visions by Farishta in the character of the Archangel Gibreel (which suggests a case of schizophrenia). There are more inferred personalities or even doubles: the Imam as a radical religious leader in exile seems to be modelled on the Ayatollah Khomeini; the Prophet Muhammad appears under the name of Mahound; and readers may be puzzled to find two different characters appearing alike under the name of Ayesha (one of them a false prophet). The depiction of Muhammad in connection with the use of the apocryphal Satanic Verses as a plot device sparked a controversy that is certainly a prime example of the timeless conflict between literary satire and censorship. Rushdie, a Cambridge-educated Indian Muslim with a British passport and a postcolonial agenda, could only continue to work for more than a decade in various sheltered 'homes' and under the protection of British and other Western security forces. The dire consequences for his life and for others involved (such as his translators, who were attacked, one of them fatally) visualise what is at stake in the confrontation between a secular and a radically religious understanding of society and morality. In his collection of short stories entitled *East, West* (1994, a reference to Kipling's "Ballad of East and West"), Rushdie showed himself undaunted by the ayatollah's *fatwa*: there is an ironical reference to Muhammad in "The Prophet's Hair", while other hardly-veiled references to religious fundamentalism and to Rushdie's personal fate can be found in "At the Auction of the Ruby Slippers". This story moreover relates to the film version of *The Wizard of Oz* (based on Frank L. Baum's children's fantasy), whereas "Yorick" is a rewriting of Shakespeare's *Hamlet* in the style of Laurence Sterne's *Tristram Shandy*. "Chekov and Zulu" continues the intertextual and intermedial reference to popular culture, this time to the *Star Trek* series. Most of the story is set in the Indian diaspora in London in 1984 – only a short time after the assassination of Indira Gandhi. An epilogue is set in India in 1991, and involves the assassination of her son Rajiv Gandhi. For *The Moor's Last Sigh* (1995), Rushdie returned to the combination of family histories with political history known from *Midnight's Children*. This time, he singled out radical Hindu Nationalism as the object of political satire. Moreover, he stretched the angle of vision to include the expulsion of Moors (and Jews) from Spain in 1492 as well as the successive history of the Jewish diaspora in India. In *The Enchantress of Florence* (2008), his latest novel to date, Rushdie works again on such a broad historical canvas.

In *A Suitable Boy* (1993), poet and novelist Vikram Seth (*1952) put Rushdie's intertwining of Indian political history (here: of the formative period between Independence and the first national elections of 1952) with the narration of several family histories to

More British-Asian Writers

his own uses. Seth found critical acclaim for his mastery of detail and of dialogue that remains true to character. In his non-fictional family memoir entitled *Two Lives* (2005), which is set in 1930s Berlin, Seth tells an extraordinary story of interethnic love and marriage between his Indian great-uncle and his German-Jewish great-aunt. The 1930s are also part of the political background to *The Remains of the Day* (1989), for which the Japanese-British novelist Kazuo Ishiguro (*1954) won the Booker Prize. Yet this is essentially a novel of character, in which Stevens – the epitome of an English butler full of appropriate self-restraint – gives voice to his reflections about his loyalty to Lord Darlington, his erstwhile employer, and about his unacknowledged love to the former housekeeper Miss Kenton, whom Stevens revisits in 1956. (This is the year of the Suez Crisis, which brought the reduction of British influence overseas into the open.) In both cases, Stevens's version of events must not be taken as the last word in the matter. By reading between the lines, readers will detect the pro-Nazi sympathies of Lord Darlington as well as the full extent of the romantic attachment between butler and former housekeeper at Darlington Hall. (For the 1993 Merchant Ivory movie *The Remains of the Day*, Ruth Prawer Jhabvala adapted both Ishiguro's novel and Harold Pinter's original screenplay.) In Ishiguro's *When We Were Orphans* (2000), some of the characteristic features of *The Remains of the Day* can be found again. This time, they are mixed up with conventions of detective fiction: the narrator, a British private detective, learns much about his family history when he delves into the Shanghai International Settlement and war-torn 1930s China to unravel the mysterious disappearance of his parents.

Other British-Asian writers have concerned themselves less with history than with the multicultural society of post-war Britain. Hanif Kureishi (*1954), who was born in London to an English mother and a Pakistani father, made his name with screenplays for director Stephen Frears's films *My Beautiful Laundrette* (1986) and *Sammy and Rosie Get Laid* (1987), both of which deal with interethnic (and sometimes also homosexual) partnerships. Then Kureishi adapted his own successful novel *The Buddha of Suburbia* for television (1990/93) as well as his short story "My Son the Fanatic" (1994/98). *The Buddha of Suburbia* is a novel of development that opens with the memorable phrase: "My name is Karim Amir, and I am an Englishman born and bred, almost." The Buddha in the title is the narrator's Indian father Haroon, who left India for a South London suburb in 1950, and much later his English wife for his mistress Eva Kay, an arts enthusiast. With her, Haroon Amir moves to 1970s Inner London where he self-confidently embraces a racial stereotype, as he successfully remakes himself as a teacher of Eastern wisdom, as the Buddha of Suburbia. In contrast to his father, Karim appears in stereotyped roles forced upon him by others, professionally as an actor as well as in private. In a stage production of Kipling's *Jungle Book*, Karim is cast as an exotic Mowgli, painted brown and in a loincloth, and made to overdo an Indian accent in order to sound 'authentic'. Karim's sexual life lacks clear direction, too. He probes his bisexuality with various partners ranging from Jamila, a political radical and feminist, over Eva Kay's son Charlie to the overbearing stage director Matthew Pyke, and is often at the mercy of others. Kureishi's work is generally marked by post-1960s Pop Culture in the writer's sexual licence, in his engagement with multiculturalism and in his many references to pop music. So it is no coincidence that he became the editor of *The Faber Book of Pop* (1995). Yet there is also an engagement with topical politics outside race and gender, such as in his 1994 short story about Islamic Fundamentalism entitled "My Son the Fanatic" (Korte and Sternberg 1997: 147–65). In this heterodiegetic narrative, Kureishi focussed not on the son but on his Pakistani father, a taxi driver that wants to avert the worst (his son turning into a suicide bomber) and takes advice from a kind-hearted prostitute, but can no longer reach his son. In Kureishi's novel *The Black Album* (1995), which is set in the year of the *fatwa* against Rushdie (1989), the issue of Islamic Fundamentalism is given even more room.

Kureishi's work for different media is well matched by that of women writers who have addressed Asian British culture from a female point of view. The well-known television comedian and writer Meera Syal (*1961) did so successfully in the form of a screenplay (*Bhaji on the Beach*, 1993), in a novel of initiation (*Anita and Me*, 1996), and in a novel about a group of friends out of their twenties (*Life Isn't All Ha Ha Hee Hee*, 1999). *Brick Lane* (2003), the debut novel of Monica Ali (*1967) about the arranged marriage of a Bangladeshi woman in London, was adapted for the screen in 2007. With *Bend It Like Beckham*, it worked the other way round:

the 2003 novelisation by Narinder Dhami (*1958), a children's author, followed upon the successful 2002 film that dealt with the soccer enthusiasm and precarious friendship of the two teen-age girls Jess (from a traditional Indian family) and Jules (from the White middle-class).

The Middle Passage and the Black Atlantic

In the same way that novels have been written about the *British Raj* and its aftermath, there are also twentieth-century rec-reations of the experience of **Slavery and the Slave Trade**. In 1992, Barry Unsworth (*1930) won the Booker Prize for *Sacred Hunger*, a meticulously researched novel about the involvement of Liv-erpool merchants in the Atlantic Trade Triangle, and about **the Middle Passage** as the most savage part of the journey. The title of Unsworth's historical novel hints at its main theme, namely the 'pursuit of happiness' understood in the sense of the above quotation from Farrell's *The Singapore Grip*, i.e. in the radically capitalist and egotistic sense of maximising profit regardless of human costs. In addition to Unsworth, a Yorkshireman, younger British-Caribbean writers have written novels that exemplify a concern with Pan-Africanism and the Black Diaspora: a concern that has been theorised by the critic Paul Gilroy in his studies *There Ain't No Black in the Union Jack* (1987) and *The Black Atlantic* (1993).

In the 1980s, Caryl Phillips (*1958) began to script plays for the stage, for radio and television (see chap. 5.2.5) before he turned to writing essays (*The European Tribe*, 1987; *A New World Order*, 2001) and fiction. A thematic focus on both memory and history is in evidence in most of Phillips's novels, and the former dramatist's handling of point of view is generally marked by changes of fo-calisation. Events are presented from several points of view, with narrative voice characteristically given to both Black and White characters. *Higher Ground* (1989), *Cambridge* (1991) and *Crossing the River* (1993) are engaged with the recovery and preservation of the historical Black experience of migration, denigration and diaspora. *Cambridge* (1991) is set in the period between the Abo-lition of the Slave Trade (1807) and the Emancipation of Slaves within the British Empire (1833, with the last 'apprentices' freed in 1840). In an alternation of narrative voices, the novel's pro-logue and epilogue inform about the embarkation, return and pregnancy of Emily Cartwright, an Englishwoman and heiress to a West Indian estate. The first of three parts consists of Emily's journal of her stay on the slave plantation. Recurrent characters are Mr Brown, the overseer who is later killed; Hercules alias Cambridge, a Black slave; and Christiania, a black magic (*obeah*) woman. The third part gives a 'factual' report of the killing of Brown, of Cambridge's trial for murder, and of his execution, while the second part is reserved for a **neo-slave narrative**, namely the story of Cambridge's life as written by himself. The many changes of narrative voice and focus ensure that the presentation covers both Black and White perspectives, while Phillips's use of language, which is generally true to characters and period, shows his peculiar gift at writing pastiche.

These characteristics are found again in *Crossing the River* (1993), which Phillips extended from an earlier radio play into a historical and transnational novel, the four parts of which are set in three continents over two centuries. The narrative voice in the introduction and epilogue is at once the reader's contemporary and also belongs to a West African father who over 200 years earlier sold his children Nash, Martha and Travis into slavery. The four parts within this frame are told in non-chronological order. The third part entitled "Crossing the River" contains the journal of James Hamilton, the captain of a slave ship embarking on the Middle Passage in 1752. Part I is set again in West Africa in the years 1834–42 and tells of how ex-slave Nash Williams tries to settle down in Liberia (the territory marked out for repatriation of freed slaves) and how his ex-master follows him. Part II relates the experiences of another ex-slave, Martha Randolph, who travels from Kansas to California in 1865, after the American Civil War. Finally, Part IV is set "Somewhere in England" before and during the Second World War (1936–45). In this section, Joyce, a young White working-class woman, tells how she fell in love with Black G.I. Travis and had a child by him at the end of the war, and how she met her son again only in 1963. In what critics have called a 'chronicle of the Black Diaspora', Phillips circles the Black Atlantic, touching upon all stations of the former Trade Triangle.

In *The Nature of Blood* (1997) Phillips returns to his socio-cultural commitments while at the same time bringing his stylistic credentials into new shape, now making use of (Post-)Modernist forms of presentation throughout. The novel presents itself as an interweaving of three historical narratives: first, the story of the persecution of Jews in Portobuffole, near Venice, in 1480; then, the intertextual reworking of the story of Shakespeare's 'Moor of Venice' as told by Othello; and finally, the experience of Eva Stern and that of her Jewish family in the 1930s and '40s. While the focus in this third strand of the plot is generally on Eva, her individual story and the whole novel are framed by the account of Uncle Stephan, who in the end has an affair with Malka, a young Black nurse who has migrated from Africa. What distinguishes this novel by Caryl Phillips from those of his contemporaries that also turn to historical settings is the combination of the Black experience and the Jewish experience into one 'grand narrative' of suffering from racism and persecution.

Fig. 5.18

W. Hogarth,
A Harlot's Progress,
Scene 2 (1732)

Feeding the Ghosts (1997) by the Guyanese-British poet and novelist Fred D'Aguiar (*1960) chimes in well with Phillips's interests and style. D'Aguiar bases his novel on an authentic story of mass murder on the Middle Passage in the year 1783, when the captain of the slave ship *Zong* ordered the crew to throw over 130 slaves overboard, after calculating their falling monetary value against compensation from shipping insurance for their loss. While the narrative is ultimately focused on Black people's experience of the Middle Passage, its shifting point of view looks at the matter with the eyes of Blacks as well as Whites. In three parts, framed by Prologue and Epilogue, readers are told by a heterodiegetic narrator about the crime against humanity and about the trial of Capt. Cunningham for embezzling insurance money, before they get to know in an Interior Monologue about the fate of Mintah. This female slave managed to climb back aboard from the sea, and ended her life at the time of Emancipation. When Mintah together with her wooden idols that commemorate the dead perish in a fire, the novel read is seen to be the ultimate memorial. D'Aguiar's concern with slavery continued in his poetic narrative *Bloodlines* (2000). David Dabydeen (*1955), a fellow Guyanese-British poet, novelist and scholar of Indo-Caribbean stock, had already written a long poem about the inhumanity of the Middle Passage in response to J. M. W. Turner's painting *Slave Ship* (*Turner,* 1994, for which see also chap. 5.1) before he followed up his postcolonial agenda in his historical novels. In *A Harlot's Progress* (1999), Dabydeen writes back to William Hogarth's eponymous 1732 series of prints in which a Black servant boy – here called Mungo – features as a minor character. In Dabydeen's novel, which is marked by an overlapping of several narrative voices and silent thoughts, Mungo comes centre-stage in the 1760s to tell his life to an Abolitionist campaigner, Mr Pringle. Mungo's reliability as an oral storyteller, and the veracity of such (neo-)slave narratives that were taken down by Whites, is at stake in a novel with Modernist and meta-fictional credentials. Dabydeen's historical novel *The Counting House* (1996) deals with Indian indentured labourers who replaced the slaves on the sugar plantations in post-Emancipation British Guiana.

The formation of a Caribbean and an African Diaspora in twentieth-century Britain has been addressed by a number of notable writers – in the case of 'Jean Rhys' (Ella Gwendolen Rees Williams) well before the docking of the *SS Empire Windrush* in 1948 (see chap. 5.3.2). Rhys was born on the Caribbean island of Dominica in 1890 or 1894 and saw herself as a 'Creole' of White descent (an ambivalent designation claimed by Afro-Caribbean people, too). In 1907, she moved first to England, where she experienced several unhappy love affairs as a chorus girl, before she moved on to live in Paris in artists' circles from 1919 up to the publication of her first collection entitled *"The Left Bank" and Other Stories* (1927). Upon her return to Britain, Rhys published four novels influenced by her own experience and by Modernist forms of expression, before the outbreak of the World War sent her into oblivion. *Voyage in the Dark* (1934) is quite typical of the early novels, and at least to a certain extent an autobiographical narrative. Anna Morgan, the protagonist and narrator, tells of her migration from the West Indies to Britain, and of her time as a chorus girl. As the mistress of an older man, Anna experiences her sexual initiation, but is later cast off and left alone with the experience of an abortion. The novel follows up such a frank treatment of abortive love with an open ending. *Voyage in the Dark* is interesting for the contrast made between the West Indies and England in Anna's reminiscences of her youth, and for the impact of Modernism on the novel's scenic presentation and on its

The Caribbean and African Diaspora in Britain

use of Interior Monologue (trailing *Ulysses* by only eleven years). In 1966, Rhys had a sensational comeback with *Wide Sargasso Sea* (see chap. 5.3.6). She died in 1979, after the publication of further short stories from the Caribbean and from Britain.

In her short story "Let Them Call It Jazz" (1962, in Korte and Sternberg 1997), Rhys followed closely on the heels of Sam[uel] Selvon (1923–94) by focusing on the (female) Black experience in Britain, and by using Caribbean Creole consistently for both dialogue and narration. Selvon was born in Trinidad in 1923, of "East Indian" descent like V.S. Naipaul, and like Naipaul and many other Caribbean writers of his generation he achieved recognition after his emigration to Britain. Selvon stayed in London from 1950 to 1978, only to move on once more to Canada for the next 15 years. His life came full circle when, after a final reading back in London in 1993, he died in Trinidad in the following year. Of his ten novels published altogether since 1952, the so-called *Moses Trilogy* sticks out, spanning Selvon's entire career as a novelist. Over the years, the comic trilogy that increasingly centred on Moses Aloetta as protagonist and narrator, has circumscribed a cycle of migration: starting with the experiences of West Indians immediately after their emigration to Britain (*The Lonely Londoners*, 1956), it moved on to the conflict between the gradual establishment in middle-class comfort and values of some immigrants and the radical Black Power stance of others (*Moses Ascending*, 1975). *Moses Migrating* (1983), the final novel in this series and Selvon's last altogether, addresses return migration as a theme. Selvon's short stories, such as "Obeah in the Grove" (1958, in Korte and Sternberg 1997) show the same features as his novels, and were collected in *Ways of Sunlight* (1958) and *Foreday Morning* (1989). George Lamming (*1927) from Barbados entered Britain in 1950 on the same ship as Selvon. Emigration and exile are the themes of Lamming's novel *The Emigrants* (1954), which follows a group of Barbadians on their passage to Britain on the boat, their train journey upon arrival (stylistically a good example of Lamming's Modernism) and their attempt at integration, with varying luck. In his collection of essays under the ironical title *The Pleasures of Exile* (1960) Lamming reflects upon migration and integration in non-fictional form.

The writers of the Windrush Generation, such as Selvon, Lamming and Naipaul, were later joined by a younger generation dealing with multicultural Britain. David Dabydeen's *The Intended* (1991) is a first novel by the Indo-Caribbean-British writer, based on his autobiographical experience of growing up in two worlds. With *White Teeth* (2000), Zadie Smith (*1975) landed both a critical and a popular success. Her novel follows the wartime friendship and later lives of White Englishman Archie Jones and of Samad Iqbal, a Bangladeshi, and their families up to the present. Besides the Iqbals (Samad, Alsana and their twin sons) in their arranged marriage and the Jones's (Archie, his Jamaican wife Clara and their daughter Irie), there is also a Jewish family (the Chalfens) that are connected with genetic engineering. The fun with Zadie Smith's novel begins with the punning chapter headings and leads on to many humorous commentaries and comic situations. In the novel *Small Island* (2004), Andrea Levy (*1956) recreates with hindsight both the immigrant and the war experience. With a regular alternation of time-levels, shifting between 1948 (the year of the *SS. Empire Windrush*) and the years before and during the Second World War, the intertwining stories of Queenie Bligh, a White Englishwoman, her husband Bernard and her Jamaican lodgers Hortense and Gilbert Joseph are told in a variety of voices. The birth of Queenie's baby, which is also the climax of the novel, speaks of an interethnic love that is apparently no option for the year 1948, but a vision for a multicultural society in 2004.

There is a number of other notable Black British writers which merit more than passing attention. Buchi Emecheta (*1944) wrote novels about the role of women in postcolonial Nigeria (*The Joys of Motherhood*, 1979) as well as about the experience of African women in Britain (*Kehinde*, 1994). Ben Okri (*1959) won the Booker Prize for *The Famished Road* (1991), an epic novel set in a Nigerian village that was extended into a trilogy that also includes *Songs of Enchantment* (1993) and *Infinite Riches* (1998). Okri's use of oral storytelling and of magic realist traditions suggests a comparison with Rushdie's fiction. Diran Adebayo (*1968) is a younger writer of Nigerian descent who wrote about the search for identity among his generation of Black Britons in *Some Kind of Black* (1996). Likewise associated with the role of music (here: Jazz music) within Black culture is the novel *Trumpet* (1998) by the Black Scottish poet and novelist Jackie Kay (*1961), which moreover stands out for its treatment of trans-sexuality. (See chaps. 5.1 and 5.3.4. For crime fiction with a multicultural angle, see chap. 5.3.2.)

5.3.6 | Intertextuality and Intermediality in Contemporary Fiction

Let us come back to David Lodge's summary review of the state of the novel cited in the introduction to this survey of contemporary fiction. In one instance, Lodge qualified his original thesis by switching from the crossroads of fiction to 'crossover' fiction:

> Indeed I would say that my model or metaphor of the crossroads now seems to me inadequate chiefly because it doesn't allow for such mixing of genres and styles within a single text. Such mixing, what one might call 'crossover' fiction, seems to me to be a salient feature of writing today. That is to say, relatively few novelists are wholly and exclusively committed to fabulation or the non-fiction novel, or metafiction. Instead they combine one or more of these modes with realism, often in a startling, deliberately disjunctive way. [...] Foregrounded intertextuality, the overt citation or simulation of older texts in a modern text, has frequently been used to achieve the crossover effect in this period, from John Fowles' *The French Lieutenant's Woman* at the beginning of it, through Peter Ackroyd's *Hawksmoor* and *Chatterton*, to Antonia Byatt's *Possession*. My own *Small World* might be mentioned in this context. (Lodge 1992: 207–08)

Shakespearean Fictions The present context has thus far allowed only a passing acknowledgment of intertextuality and intermediality. However, because of the great number and varied nature of recent and relevant examples, such phenomena deserve more attention. At the end of this literary history, it seems reasonable to conclude, first, with examples of **intertextuality** as keyed to their historical reference in the literature of Britain and Ireland. (For a complementary typological approach, see Genette 1983.) The most prominent link between Shakespeare and a postcolonial agenda has been established with regard to *The Tempest* (see chap. 5.2.3), as for instance in *Water with Berries* (1971) by the Caribbean-British novelist George Lamming (*1927). By giving voice to Caliban's mother Sycorax in her novel *Indigo; or, Mapping the Waters* (1992), Marina Warner (*1946) read and rewrote *The Tempest* from a feminist angle. In his Venice novel *The Nature of Blood* (1997, see chap. 5.3.5), Caryl Phillips (*1958) included as one strand of the complex plot a retelling of the story of 'the Moor of Venice' from Othello's point of view.

There is an abundance of further examples, of which Angela Carter's "Overture and Incidental Music for *A Midsummer Night's Dream*" (from *Black Venus*, 1985) was mentioned already (in chap. 5.3.4). Shakespeare and *Hamlet* are prominent points of reference in *The Black Prince* (1972), a prize-winning novel by Iris Murdoch (1919–99) that is more experimental than her other fiction. The main part of Murdoch's novel focuses on an ageing writer named Bradley Pearson who becomes entangled in a network of (homosexual) love, suicide and murder, which alone bears some resemblance to Shakespeare's play. Further references are spelt out in a meta-fictional frame narrative that relates the response of other characters to Bradley and to the novel's action. There are more instances in which the police was concerned with criminal case histories hinged upon one of the Bard's plays. In *Hamlet, Revenge!* (1937) by Michael Innes (1906–94), Inspector Appleby solves a country-house murder related to a performance of Shakespeare's tragedy. His colleague Inspector Roderick Alleyn is called upon the scene when a performance of *Macbeth* ends in a real murder (in *Light Thickens*, published by Ngaio March in the year of her death, 1982). The historical murder mystery *A Dead Man in Deptford* (1993) about the death of Shakespeare's contemporary Marlowe was to be the last published novel of Anthony Burgess (1917–93). Years before, Burgess had already offered a solution to the mystery about Shakespeare's lost years and the Dark Lady of his sonnets: in *Nothing Like the Sun: A Story of Shakespeare's Love-Life* (1964), he presents the Bard and his Dark Lady in a less romantic light (and in a pastiche of Early Modern English). The subject was also treated by John Mortimer (1923–2009) in *Will Shakespeare: The Untold Story* (1977, made into a television miniseries in 1978) and by Tom Stoppard (*1937) in his screenplay for the film *Shakespeare in Love* (1998).

The Story of Marie Powell: Wife to Mr Milton (1943), a fictional recreation by the poet and historical novelist Robert von Ranke Graves (1895–1985), may be compared to *Milton in America* (1996), a historical fantasy which brings the Puritan poet to New England. Its creator, the novelist and historian Peter Ackroyd (*1949), engaged with the literature and the arts of previous centuries in further novels such as *Chatterton* (1987, on the eighteenth-century forger mentioned in chap. 3.3.2), *The Great Fire of London* (1982, which adapts Dickens's *Little Dorrit* to the twentieth century), *The*

Peter Ackroyd

Last Testament of Oscar Wilde (1983, purportedly written by Wilde himself), *The Casebook of Victor Frankenstein* (2008) and *Hawksmoor* (1985). Together with the playwright and fellow-architect Sir John Vanbrugh (see chap. 3.2.1), Nicholas Hawksmoor was engaged by the Duke of Marlborough to build Blenheim Palace (1705–16), one of *the* Baroque monuments in England meant to contend with Versailles. In 1986, Vanbrugh's ingenuous partner re-appeared as not one, but two literary characters in Ackroyd's novel *Hawksmoor*, a blending of historical novel, Gothic romance and murder mystery together with a pastiche of period diction. *English Music* (1992) is a novel that is steeped in extended references to more than one canonical author. In addition, Ackroyd is known for his skilful biographies of Thomas More (1998), William Blake (1995), Charles Dickens (1990), Ezra Pound (1981), T. S. Eliot (1984), and not to forget *London: The Biography* (2000).

Adapting Austen

Other canonical texts from the nineteenth century have also been given the crime fiction treatment, and thus an overhaul in popular form. *Darkness at Pemberley*, T. H. White's 1932 locked-room mystery with intertextual references to Austen's *Pride and Prejudice*, is only one among many sequels, 'prequels' and rewritings of Jane Austen's fiction (see Nowak 1994 and Breuer 1999). And there is of course the unending series of adaptations of Austen's novels for radio, television and the cinema, sometimes competing directly with one another. In 1995, the Hollywood film *Sense and Sensibility* (dir. Ang Lee, starring Emma Thompson, who also wrote the screenplay) ran against *Pride and Prejudice* as a BBC TV series (dir. Andrew Langton). A year later, the public had the choice between two blockbuster versions of *Emma*: either as an ITV series (likewise adapted by Andrew Davies, dir. by Diarmuid Lawrence) or as a British-American film (adapted and directed by Douglas McGrath). In the same year 1996, Helen Fielding (*1958) came out with her best seller *Bridget Jones's Diary*, which referred directly to *Pride and Prejudice* both as a novel (in Fielding's character Mark Darcy) and to its 1995 adaptation for television (with Colin Firth impersonating Mr Darcy). The iconic, ironic and intermedial treatment of Jane Austen reached a new level when Helen Fielding adapted her diary-novel for the screen (in collaboration with Andrew Davies; dir. Sharon Maguire). Helen Fielding followed up her success in the sequel *Bridget Jones: The Edge of Reason* (1999).

Charlotte Brontë's *Jane Eyre* has been revived in many different forms, most recently in *The Eyre Affair* (2001). The first novel by Jasper Fforde (*1961) is a comic piece of crime fiction with intertextual reference throughout to *Jane Eyre*, and at the same time a piece of fantasy set in an alternate world where England is a republic. The dissolution of the borderline between fiction and reality – a meta-fictional feature – gives the 'literary detective' Thursday Next the opportunity to change the 'original' ending of *Jane Eyre* into the actual one that readers know. (Fforde's 2005 novel *The Big Over Easy: An Investigation with the Nursery Crime Division* is a literary parody independent of the *Thursday Next Series*.) The best known reworking of *Jane Eyre* however remains *Wide Sargasso Sea* (1966) by Jean Rhys (?1890/94–1979), and not only because it is connected with the spectacular rediscovery of a lost Modernist writer (see chaps. 5.3.3 and 5.3.5). Out of disappointment with Brontë's delineation of the West Indian character Bertha Mason as a Gothic stereotype (as Mr Rochester's 'Indian Messalina' and a madwoman in the attic), Rhys – who hailed from the West Indies herself – set out to provide more psychological depth and motivation, and a different historical and cultural context to what she occasionally described as "Jane Eyre, leaving out Jane". Such a re-creation includes the social alienation of Rochester's first wife-to-be, here called Antoinette and depicted as a White Creole daughter of plantation owners, in post-Emancipation society (after 1833). Moreover, the increasingly strained relationship between both partners is explained from a culture clash that is symbolised in the way they see one another's world. 'Rochester' (who, though he does not appear under his own name, is made to speak his mind, too) feels oppressed by the exotic strangeness of his West Indian estate where "[e]verything is too much, [...]. Too much blue, too much purple, too much green. The flowers too red, the mountains too high, the hills too near" (Rhys 1966: 70). Antoinette, on the other hand, is frustrated when the England which she expected to be "rosy pink [as] in the geography book map" turns out to be a "cardboard world where everything is coloured brown or dark red or yellow that has no light in it" (111, 181). For her, the red dress that she brought from the Caribbean to her confinement in the attic makes all the difference:

Jean Rhys,
Wide Sargasso Sea

> I saw it hanging, the colour of fire and sunset. The colour of flamboyant flowers. [...] The scent that came from the dress was very faint at first, then it grew stronger. The smell of vetivert and frangipanni, of cinnamon and dust and lime trees when they are flowering. The smell of the sun and the smell of the rain. (185)

Such colour symbolism forms the grid of Rhys's Modernist masterpiece, the individual scenes of which are presented in a mix of narration and Interior Monologue, and from multiple points of view.

M. Cunningham,
The Hours

Intertextual acknowledgement of Modernism and its transgressions, intermedial reference to television and film, and the 'death and return of the author' (to borrow the title of Burke's 1998 study) are prime features of *The Hours* (1998). This profoundly intertextual novel by the US-American author Michael Cunningham (*1952) is not afraid of Virginia Woolf: it refers back to her as one of the most prominent writers of literary Modernism, and to her novel *Mrs Dalloway* (1925) as one of its key texts. Taking Woolf's working title "The Hours" as his cue, Cunningham's novel is focused on the passing of time on a single day in the life of not just one but three women. The first of three strands of the plot of *The Hours*, which are presented in alternating chapters, is entitled "Mrs Woolf" and centres on that day in the summer of 1923 when the writer begins the first manuscript pages of what is to become *Mrs Dalloway*. In the course of the day, Virginia Woolf ponders her own life, and she will make up her mind on the fate of both Mrs Dalloway and of the yet unnamed Septimus Warren Smith, who is going to die. A second, intermittent sequence of chapters is entitled "Mrs Brown", in allusion to Virginia Woolf's essay "Mr. Bennett and Mrs. Brown" (1924) in which she had expounded her views on 'modern fiction' at the time of writing *Mrs Dalloway*. This sequence within *The Hours* is set in Los Angeles on another June morning in 1949, and it sets in with Laura Brown reading the beginning of the novel *Mrs Dalloway*, that is those sentences Woolf was just shown to compose, and which are here presented in their finished form. At the end of the third, intermittent sequence of chapters, readers learn that Laura later had first unsuccessfully attempted suicide, and then left her family, only to return on the day her son had committed suicide himself. It is another day in June, this time in New York at about the time of the novel's publication, when Clarissa Vaughan organises a party for Richard Brown who has just won a literature prize. Richard's nickname for Clarissa is "Mrs Dalloway", which is also the title for this third sequence of chapters, one that engages in a great number of intertextual resemblances to and variations upon Woolf's novel. In 2002, Cunningham's *The Hours* received an additional accolade when it was made into a successful film. The film was achieved in collaboration with the dramatist David Hare, who was responsible for the screenplay – which is a good example of the profitable side-line that the electronic media opened up for writers of stage plays.

Apart from audiobooks and adaptations for the screen (see also chap. 5.2), **intermediality** comprises the combination of the literary text with other media or forms of art, or the incorporation of such media and forms into the literary text. The combinatory mode, which is known from illustrated novels of the nineteenth century, gained new prominence in Alasdair Gray's self-illustrated novel *Lanark* (1981, see chap. 5.3.4) and in comic books or 'graphic novels' by e.g. Alan Moore (*1953) and Neil Gaiman (*1960). *The League of Extraordinary Gentlemen*, an ongoing series that set off in 1999 as a collaboration between Moore and the illustrator Kevin O'Neill, thrives upon its revival of characters from nineteenth-century fiction in a new context of adventure (Mina Murray/Harker from *Dracula*, Allan Quatermain, Captain Nemo, Dr Jekyll and Dr Moreau, Professor Moriarty and Sherlock's brother Mycroft Holmes). Together with illustrator Melinda Gebbie, Alan Moore continued his intertextual pursuit in *Lost Girls*, which brings together Lewis Carroll's Alice, Dorothy Gale from *The Wizard of Oz* and Wendy Darling from *Peter Pan*, who meet as adults in the year 1913 to engage in their memories of childhood. Some readers of this graphic novel (published in 2006 after the serialisation of parts in 1991) took offence because of the graphic depiction of sexual encounters that indeed mark the difference to the original, late Victorian and turn-of-the-century context. A friend of Moore's, Neil Gaiman, collaborated with the fantasy writer Terry Pratchett (see chap. 5.3.2) on his first novel *Good Omens* (1990), and made a name for himself with *The Sandman* (1989–96). Within this highly intertextual series of comic books, Gaiman pays tribute to the authors Chaucer and Shakespeare, who appear as characters in *The Sand-*

'Graphic Novels'

Fig. 5.19
Alan Moore by Vëon Menelion, 2008

man, and plays with the reader's literary knowledge, as when some characters from *A Midsummer Night's Dream* are taken over, too.

Roddy Doyle,
The Commitments

A good and last example for intermedial and transcultural developments comes from Ireland: it is Roddy Doyle's novel *The Commitments* (1987). This was the first novel in what was to become his *Barrytown Trilogy* (1992, see chap. 5.3.4), a series which focuses on the lives of various members of the Rabbitte family living in 'Barrytown', a fictionalised working-class area of Dublin. *The Commitments* follows a group of young, unprofessional, but easily excited musicians from the early days of forming their band over the rehearsal stage to their ever more successful concerts in Dublin, until on the verge of break-through, the band breaks up. The basic element of the plot is the attempt, initiated by Jimmy Rabbitte, to transplant the Soul Music culture of Black America to the Republic of Ireland in order to invigorate the way of life in Dublin. Indeed, if the 'slanguage' and the frequent *double entendre* of band members are things to judge by, then at least talking about sex in public, frequently and with gusto, is no longer taboo among Dublin's youngsters who have stopped to follow a conventional code of sexual conduct. This is why the band takes the name of "The Commitments": they feel committed to creating a "Dublin soul" (14). This cultural hybrid should be nursed by the songs of Black America, but one should also feel free to "to make the words more Dubliny" (50; also 22), to extend the original lyrics by adding remarks of local and of historical interest for an Irish audience.

As an intermedial novel, *The Commitments* is characterised by the integration of pop songs into the printed text, and it is moreover characterised by a re-import into the electronic media of film, audio-recording and DVD. Roddy Doyle's novel (like those of Jane Austen) consists to a large extend of dialogue, which made matters easier when director Alan Parker made it into a movie in 1991. The most astonishing deviation, paradoxically, concerns the music included in the film, as none of the songs mentioned in the novel is actually part of the soundtrack. Regardless of changes in the repertoire, it was the soundtrack that turned the film into a 'cult movie'. Roddy Doyle's novel about "The Hardest Working Band In The World, The Saviours Of Soul" is a good example of a transcultural text, and it is moreover characterised by the way it crosses the borders between various media repeatedly and in more than one direction.

1. Both *Restoration* by Rose Tremain and *Sexing the Cherry* by Jeanette Winterson were published in 1989 as historical novels that are set alike in the seventeenth century. Compare those two novels with regard to their portrait of English history and of gender relations, and their manner of presentation.

2. See Peter Costello's *Leopold Bloom* (1981) in relation to James Joyce's *Ulysses* (1922), and Robin Lippincott's *Mr Dalloway* (1999) and Michael Cunningham's *The Hours* (2000) in their relation to Virginia Woolf's *Mrs Dalloway* (1925). In what manner of form and content do those later writers pay homage to their Modernist predecessor? Can you speculate on why their intertextual novels were written at all?

3. Please distinguish the Interior Monologue in fiction from the Dramatic Monologue as a genre of poetry and from monologues and soliloquies in stage-plays. Give examples from twentieth-century literature for each category.

4. In his *Asian Saga* (1962–93), James Clavell, a British novelist and screenwriter who was born in Australia and later became a US-American citizen, dealt with the meeting of East and West in six historical romances set in Japan, Hong Kong (*Tai Pan*, 1966; *Noble House*, 1981), Singapore (*King Rat*, 1962) and Iran between 1600 and 1979. Compare this best-selling form of popular entertainment to the thematically related *Malayan Trilogy* (*Time for a Tiger*, 1956; *The Enemy in the Blanket*, 1958; *Beds in the East*, 1959) by Anthony Burgess and moreover to the novels by J. G. Farrell (*The Singapore Grip*, 1978), J. G. Ballard (*Empire of the Sun*, 1984), Timothy Mo (*An Insular Possession*, 1986) and Amitav Ghosh (*The Glass Palace*, 2000, as well as his *Ibis Trilogy*, started off with *Sea of Poppies* in 2008). Please include the individual treatment of intercultural encounters and the style of narration in your comparison.

5. In the 1990s, Nick Hornby (*1957) became a best-selling writer with his non-fictional work on soccer entitled *Fever Pitch* (1992), which he followed up with his novels *High Fidelity* (1995) and *About a Boy* (1998). Situate Hornby's style of writing

within the main currents of fiction described in this chapter. Moreover, relate his works to e. g. those of Hanif Kureishi and Diran Adebayo as writers who have likewise engaged with popular culture.

7. Describe the ways in which original texts have been used in a feminist and a postcolonial context in the twentieth and twenty-first centuries.

References and Further Reading

Comprehensive Anthologies

BCP Meller, Horst, and Rudolf Sühnel, eds. 1966. *British and American Classical Poems: In continuation of Ludwig Herrig's "Classical Authors"*. Braunschweig: Westermann. Repr. with corrections. Heidelberg: Winter, 1999. [Subdivision into genres of poetry.]

Black, Joseph, et al., eds. 2006. *The Broadview Anthology of British Literature*. 6 vols. Peterborough, Ont.: Broadview Press. Related material online: http://www.broadviewpress.com/babl/.

Borgmeier, Raimund, ed. 1982–86. *Die englische Literatur in Text und Darstellung*. 10 vols. Stuttgart: Reclam.

Clark, Robert, and Thomas Healy, eds. 1997. *The Arnold Anthology of British and Irish Literature in English*. London: Arnold.

Damrosch, David, ed. 2006. *The Longman Anthology of British Literature*. 3rd, rev. ed. in 2 vols. New York: Longman.

NAAL Baym, Nina, et al., eds. 2003. *The Norton Anthology of American Literature*. 6th, rev. ed. in 2 vols. New York: Norton.

NAEL Abrams, M.H., and Stephen Greenblatt, eds. 2006. *The Norton Anthology of English Literature*. 8th, rev. ed. in 2 vols. New York: Norton.

NALW Gilbert, Sandra M., and Susan Gubar, eds. 1996. *The Norton Anthology of Literature by Women: The Traditions in English*. 2nd, rev. ed. New York: Norton.

OAEL Kermode, Frank, and John Hollander, ed. 1973. *The Oxford Anthology of English Literature*. 2 vols./6 vols. New York: Oxford UP.

Trapp, J.B., Douglas Gray and Julia Boffey, eds. 2002. *The Oxford Anthology of English Literature. Vol. 1: Medieval English Literature*. 2nd, rev ed. Oxford: Oxford UP.

Other Anthologies

Amis, Kingsley, ed. 1978a. *The New Oxford Book of Light Verse*. Repr. with corrections. Oxford: Oxford UP, 1987. ed. 1978b. *The Faber Popular Reciter*. London: Faber.

Baker, Kenneth, ed. 1988. *The Faber Book of English History in Verse*. London: Faber. [Poetry keyed to historical periods.]

Blishen, Edward and Brian Wildsmith, eds. 1984. *Oxford Book of Poetry for Children*. Oxford: Oxford UP.

Boehmer, Elleke, ed. 1998. *Empire Writing. An Anthology of Colonial Literature. 1870–1918*. Oxford: Oxford UP.

Burnett, Paula, ed. 1986. *The Penguin Book of Caribbean Verse in English*. Harmondsworth: Penguin Books.

Craig, Patricia, ed. 2000. *The Oxford Book of Detective Stories: An International Selection*. Oxford: Oxford UP.

Craig, Patricia, ed. 2002. *The Oxford Book of English Detective Stories*. 1990. Oxford: Oxford UP.

Craig, Patricia. 2003. *The Oxford Book of Ireland*. 1998. Oxford: Oxford UP.

Craig, Patricia, ed. 2006. *The Ulster Anthology*. Belfast: Blackstaff Press.

Crawford, Robert, and W.N. Herbert, eds. 1990. *Sharawaggi: Poems in Scots*. Edinburgh: Polygon.

Crawford, Robert, and Mick Imlah, eds. 2000. *The New Penguin Book of Scottish Verse*. Harmondsworth: Penguin Books.

Deane, Seamus, ed. 1991–2002. *The Field Day Anthology of Irish Writing*. 5 vols.

Vol. 1–3. Derry: Field Day Publications, distr. by W.W. Norton (New York), 1991.

Vol. 4–5: *Irish Women's Writing and Tradition*. Ed. Angela Bourke et al. Cork: Cork UP in assoc. with New York UP, 2002.

Donnell, Alison, and Sarah Lawson Welch, eds. 1996. *The Routledge Reader in Caribbean Literature*. London: Routledge.

Dunn, Douglas, ed. 1995. *The Oxford Book of Scottish Short Stories*. Oxford: Oxford UP. Repr. 2008.

Dunne, Seán, and George O'Brien, eds. 1999. *The Ireland Anthology*. Dublin: Gill & Macmillan.

Finnegan, Ruth, ed. 1978. *The Penguin Book of Oral Poetry*. Harmondsworth: Penguin.

Friedman, Albert B., ed. 1961. *The Viking Book of Folk Ballads of the English-Speaking World*. 1956. 2nd ed. New York: Viking Press.

Garlick, Raymond, and Roland Mathias, eds. 1982. *Anglo-Welsh Poetry 1480–1990 [sic: 1980]*. Bridgend: Seren Books/Poetry Wales Press.

Gifford, Douglas, and Alan Riach, eds. 2004. *Scotland's Poets and the Nation*. Manchester: Carcanet Press and Edinburgh: Scottish Poetry Library.

Gross, John, ed. 1991. *The Oxford Book of Essays*. Oxford: Oxford UP.

Gross, John, ed. 1998. *The New Oxford Book of English Prose*. Oxford: Oxford UP.

Haining, Peter, ed. 1993. *Great Irish Detective Stories*. London: Souvenir Press.

Harrison, Michael, and Christopher Stuart-Clark. 2007. *The Oxford Book of Children's Poetry*. Oxford: Oxford UP.

Heaney, Seamus, and Ted Hughes, eds. 1982. *The Rattle Bag*. London: Faber. [English-language poems in non-chronological order.]

Heaney, Seamus, and Ted Hughes, eds. 1997. *The School Bag*. London: Faber. [English-language poems in non-chronological order.]

Hillerman, Tony, and Rosemary Herbert, eds. 2005. *A New Omnibus of Crime*. Oxford: Oxford UP.

Jones, Edmund D., ed. 1961. *English Critical Essays (Sixteenth, Seventeenth and Eighteenth Centuries)*. 1922. New ed. 1947. Repr. London: Oxford UP.

Jones, Gwynn, ed. 1977. *The Oxford Book of Welsh Verse in English*. Oxford: Oxford UP.

Kendall, Tim, ed. 2006. *Modern English War Poetry*. Oxford: Oxford UP.

Kennelly, Brendan, ed. 1988. *Landmarks of Irish Drama*. London: Methuen.

Kerrigan, Catherine, ed. 1991. *An Anthology of Scottish Women Poets*. With Gaelic Translations by Meg Bateman. Edinburgh: Edinburgh UP. Repr. 2003.

Kinsella, Thomas, ed. 2005. *The New Oxford Book of Irish Verse*. Oxford: Oxford UP.

Korte, Barbara. 2003. *The Short Story in Britain: A Historical Sketch and Anthology*. Tübingen: Francke.

McCormack, W[illiam]. J[ohn]., ed. 2000. *Irish Poetry: An Interpretive Anthology from before Swift to Yeats and After*. New York: New York UP.

Motion, Andrew, ed. 2001. *Here to Eternity: An Anthology of Poetry*. London: Faber. [Thematic sections.]

Noçon, Peter, ed. 1979–83. *The English Sonnet: An Introduction to the Study of Poetry*. 2 vols.: *Students' Book* (1979) and *Teacher's Book* (1983). Paderborn: Schöningh.

Oswald, Alice, ed. 2005. *The Thunder Mutters: 101 Poems for the Planet*. London: Faber. [Nature poetry.]

Regan, Stephen, ed. 2008. *Irish Writing: An Anthology of Irish Literature in English 1789–1939*. Oxford: Oxford UP.

Rosengarten, Herbert, and Amanda Goldrick-Jones, eds. 2008. *The Broadview Anthology of Poetry*. 2nd, rev. ed. Peterborough, Ont.: Broadview Press.

Stallworthy, Jon, ed. 1987. *The Oxford Book of War Poetry*. Oxford: Oxford UP.

Thieme, John, ed. 1996. *The Arnold Anthology of Post-Colonial Literatures in English*. London: Arnold.

Thomas, Keith, ed. 2001. *The Oxford Book of Work*. Oxford: Oxford UP.

Tóibín, Colm, ed. 1999. *The Penguin Book of Irish Fiction*. Harmondsworth: Penguin Books.

Trevor, William, ed. 1989. *The Oxford Book of Irish Short Stories*. Oxford: Oxford UP. Repr. 2001.

Vallance, Rosalind, ed. 1936. *A Hundred English Essays*. London: Nelson. Repr. 1938.

Wain, John, ed. 2003. *The Oxford Anthology of English Poetry*. 2 vols. Oxford: Oxford UP.

Watson, Roderick, ed. 1995. *The Poetry of Scotland: Gaelic, Scots and English 1380–1980*. Edinburgh: Edinburgh UP.

Williams, W. E., ed. 1951. *A Book of English Essays*. 1942. Enl. ed. Harmondsworth: Penguin Books. Repr. 1980.

Wright, Julia M., ed. 2008. *Irish Literature 1750–1900: An Anthology*. Oxford: Blackwell.

General Histories of English Literature

Alexander, Michael. 2000. *A History of English Literature*. Basingstoke: Palgrave Macmillan.

Bate, Jonathan, ed. 2002 ff. *The Oxford English Literary History*. 13 vols. Oxford: Oxford UP.

Birch, Dinah, ed. 2009. *The Oxford Companion to English Literature*. 7th, rev. ed. Oxford: Oxford UP. [Previous, 6th ed. by Margaret Drabble.]

Borgmeier, Raimund, ed. 1982–86. *Die englische Literatur in Text und Darstellung*. 10 vols. Stuttgart: Reclam.

Carter, Ronald, and John McRae. 2001. *The Routledge History of Literature in English: Britain and Ireland*. 1997. 2nd, rev. ed. London, New York: Routledge.

Conrad, Peter. 1985. *The Everyman History of English Literature*. London: Dent.

Erlebach, Peter, Bernhard Reitz and Thomas Michael Stein. 2004. *Geschichte der englischen Literatur*. Stuttgart: Reclam.

Fabian, Bernhard, ed. 1991. *Die englische Literatur*. 2 vols. München: Deutscher Taschenbuch Verlag.

Gelfert, Hans-Dieter. 1997. *Kleine Geschichte der englischen Literatur*. München: Beck.

Head, Dominic, ed. 2006. *The Cambridge Guide to Literature in English*. 3rd, rev. ed. Cambridge: Cambridge UP.

Rogers, Pat, ed. 1987. *The Oxford Illustrated History of English Literature*. Oxford: Oxford UP. Repr. 1990.

Nünning, Ansgar, and Eberhard Kreutzer, eds. 2006. *Metzler Lexikon englischsprachiger Autorinnen und Autoren*. Stuttgart: Metzler.

Sanders, Andrew, 2000. *The Short Oxford History of English Literature*. 1994. 2nd, rev. ed. Oxford: Oxford UP.

Seeber, Hans Ulrich, ed. 2004. *Englische Literaturgeschichte*. 1991. 4th, enl. ed. Stuttgart: Metzler.

Thies, Henning, ed. 1995. *Hauptwerke der englischen Literatur: Einzeldarstellungen und Interpretationen*. 2 vols. München: Kindler.

Wagner, Hans-Peter. 2003. *A History of British, Irish and American Literature*. Trier: Wissenschaftlicher Verlag Trier. [Ill. incl. on CD-ROM.]

Ward, W., and A.R. Waller, eds. 1907–1921. *The Cambridge History of English and American Literature. An Encyclopedia in Eighteen Volumes*. 18 Vols. Cambridge: Cambridge UP. http://www.bartleby.com/cambridge/

Overall Surveys of Individual Regions, Genres or Groups of Writers

Arana, R. Victoria, and Lauri Ramey, eds. 2004. *Black British Writing*. Basingstoke: Palgrave Macmillan. Repr. 2009.

Banham, Martin, ed. 1995. *The Cambridge Guide to Theatre*. Cambridge: Cambridge UP.

Berger, Dieter A. 2008. *Englischer Humor – literarisch*. Trier: Wissenschaftlicher Verlag Trier.

Blain, Virginia, Patricia Clements and Isobel Grundy. 1990. *The Feminist Companion to Literature in English: Women Writers from the Middle Ages to the Present*. London: Batsford.

Bold, Alan. 1983. *Modern Scottish Literature*. London: Longman.

Breuer, Rolf. 2003. *Irland: Eine Einführung in seine Geschichte, Literatur und Kultur*. München: Beck.

Briggs, Asa, and Peter Burke. 2010. *A Social History of the Media: From Gutenberg to the Internet*. 2002. 3rd, rev. ed. Cambridge: Polity Press.

Brown, Ian, ed. 2007. *The Edinburgh History of Scottish Literature*. 3 vols. Edinburgh: Edinburgh UP.

Bushnell, Rebecca W., and Deborah Boedeker, eds. 2005. *A Companion to Tragedy* (Blackwell Companions to Literature and Culture). Oxford: Blackwell.

Byrne, Ophelia. 1997. *The Stage in Ulster from the Eighteenth Century*. Belfast: Linen Hall Library.

Carpenter, Humphrey, and Mari Prichard, eds. 1984. *The Oxford Companion to Children's Literature*. Oxford: Oxford UP. Repr. 1999.

Carpenter, Humphrey. 1985. *Secret Gardens: A Study of the Golden Age of Children's Literature*. London: Allen & Unwin.

Carruthers, Gerard. 2009. *Scottish Literature*. Edinburgh: Edinburgh UP.

Cawelti, John G. 1976. *Adventure, Mystery and Romance: Formula Stories as Art and Popular Culture*. Chicago: Univ. of Chicago Press.

Churchill, Winston S. 1956–58. *A History of the English-Speaking Peoples*. 4 vols. London: Cassell. Pb. repr. 1974.

Couturier, Maurice. 1991. *Textual Communication: A Print-Based Theory of the Novel*. London and New York: Routledge.

Craig, Cairns, et al. 1987–88. *The History of Scottish Literature*. 4 vols. Aberdeen: Aberdeen UP.

Craik, T. W., Clifford Leech and Lois Potter, eds. 1975–83. *The Revels History of Drama in English*. 8 vols. London: Methuen. Repr. London: Routledge, 1996.

Crawford, Robert. 2007. *Scotland's Books: The Penguin History of Scottish Literature*. Harmondsworth: Penguin Books.

Cruse, Amy. 1927. *The Shaping of English Literature and the Readers' Share in the Development of its Forms*. London: Harrap.

Cruse, Amy. 1930. *The Englishman and his Books in the Early Nineteenth Century*. London: Harrap.

Cruse, Amy. 1935. *The Victorians and their Books*. London: Allen & Unwin.

Daiches, David, ed. 1993. *The New Companion to Scottish Culture*. Edinburgh: Polygon.

Davies, Norman. 2000. *The Isles: A History*. London: Papermac.

Deane, Seamus. 1986. *A Short History of Irish Literature*. London: Hutchinson.

Devine, T. M. 2006. *The Scottish Nation, 1700–2007*. Harmondsworth: Penguin.

Eagles, Robin. 2002. *The Rough Guide History of England*. London: Rough Guides.

Edwards, Ruth Dudley. 1973. *An Atlas of Irish History*. London: Methuen.

Eliot, Simon. 1994. *Some Patterns and Trends in British Publishing, 1800–1919*. London: Bibliographical Society.

Eliot, Simon, and Jonathan Rose, eds. 2007. *A Companion to the History of the Book*. Oxford: Blackwell.

Forshaw, Barry, comp. 2007. *The Rough Guide to Crime Fiction*. London: Rough Guides.

Foster, Roy F., ed. 1989. *The Oxford Illustrated History of Ireland*. Oxford: Oxford UP. Repr. 2000.

Gaschke, Susanne. 2002. *Hexen, Hobbits und Piraten: Die besten Bücher für Kinder*. Stuttgart: Deutsche Verlagsanstalt.

Genet, Jacqueline, et al., eds. 2006. *The Book in Ireland*. Newcastle: Cambridge Scholars Press.

Genette, Gérard. 1983. *Palimpsestes: La littérature au second degré*. 1982. Corr. and enl. ed. Paris: Seuils.

Gillespie, Raymond, and Andrew Hadfield, eds. 2006. *The Oxford History of the Irish Book. Vol. III: The Irish Book in English, 1550–1800*. Oxford: Oxford UP.

Gonzalez, Alexander G, ed. 2005. *Irish Women Writers: An A–Z-Guide*. Westport, Conn.: Greenwood Press.

Haan, Heiner, and Gottfried Niedhart. 2002. *Geschichte Englands vom 16. bis zum 18. Jahrhundert*. 1993. 2nd ed. München: Beck.

Hart, Francis Russell. 1978. *The Scottish Novel: A Critical Survey*. London: John Murray.

Harte, Liam. 2009. *The Literature of the Irish in Britain: Autobiography and Memoir, 1725–2001*. Basingstoke: Palgrave Macmillan.

Hartnoll, Phyllis, ed. 1983. *The Oxford Companion to the Theatre*. 4th, rev. ed. Oxford: Oxford UP. Repr. 1995.

Helbig, Jörg. 1999. *Geschichte des britischen Films*. Stuttgart: Metzler.

Hindersmann, Jost. 1995. *Der britische Spionageroman: Vom Imperialismus bis zum Ende des Kalten Krieges*. Darmstadt: Wissenschaftliche Buchgesellschaft.

Hogan, Robert, ed. 1996. *Dictionary of Irish Literature*. 2nd, rev. ed. 2 vols. Westport, Conn.: Greenwood Press.

Houston, Rab. 2009. *Scotland: A Very Short Introduction*. Oxford: Oxford UP.

Hughes, Helen. 1993. *The Historical Romance*. London: Routledge.

Hunter, Adrian. 2007. *The Cambridge Introduction to the Short Story in English*. Cambridge: Cambridge UP.

Imhof, Rüdiger. 2002. *A Short History of Irish Literature*. Stuttgart: Klett.

Ingman, Heather. 2009. *A History of the Irish Short Story*. Cambridge: Cambridge UP.

Innes, Catherine Lynette. 2004. *A History of Black and Asian Writing in Britain, 1700–2000*. Cambridge: Cambridge UP.

Kelleher, Margaret, ed. 2006. *The Cambridge History of Irish Literature*. 2 vols. Cambridge: Cambridge UP.

Kent, Alan M. 2000. *The Literature of Cornwall: Continuity – Identity – Difference, 1000–2000*. Bristol: Redcliffe Press.

Kiberd, Declan. 2000. *Irish Classics*. London: Granta.

Knight, Stephen. 2003. *Crime Fiction, 1800–2000: Detection, Death, Diversity*. Basingstoke: Palgrave-Macmillan.

Korte, Barbara. 2000. *English Travel Writing from Pilgrimages to Postcolonial Explorations*. Enl. ed. of *Der englische Reisebericht* (Darmstadt: Wissenschaftliche Buchgesellschaft, 1996), transl. Catherine Mathias. London: Palgrave.

Korte, Barbara. 2003. *The Short Story in Britain: A Historical Sketch and Anthology*. Tübingen: Francke.

Kosok, Heinz. 1990. *Geschichte der anglo-irischen Literatur*. Berlin: Schmidt.

Lindsay, Maurice. 1977. *History of Scottish Literature*. London: Hale. Repr. 1992.

Lloyd, Matthew, comp. 2008. *The Music Hall and Theatre Site.* http://www.arthurlloyd.co.uk/index.html

Löffler, Arno, and Eberhard Späth, eds. 2005. *Geschichte der englischen Kurzgeschichte.* Tübingen: Francke.

Lownie, Andrew. 2000. *The Literary Companion to Edinburgh.* London: Methuen.

Lyons, Martyn. 2009. *A History of Reading and Writing.* Basingstoke: Palgrave Macmillan.

Mathias, Roland. 1992. *Anglo-Welsh Literature: An Illustrated History.* 2nd ed. Bridgend: Seren Books.

Mc Mahon, Sean, ed. 1998. *The Mercier Companion to Irish Literature.* Cork: Mercier.

Moody, T[heodore]. W[illiam]., et al., eds. 1982 ff. *A New History of Ireland.* 10 vols. Oxford: Oxford UP.

Morash, Christopher. 2004. *A History of Irish Theatre 1601–2000.* Cambridge: Cambridge UP. [With a "Bibliographic essay" included in the appendix.]

Murray, Isobel, and Bob Tait. 1984. *Ten Modern Scottish Novels.* Aberdeen: Aberdeen UP.

Neuburg, Victor E. 1977. *Popular Literature: A History and Guide. From the Beginning of Printing to the Year 1897.* Harmondsworth: Penguin Books.

Nicholson, Colin, and Matthew McGuire. 2009. *The Edinburgh Companion to Scottish Poetry.* Edinburgh: Edinburgh UP.

Nicoll, Allardyce. 1959. *A History of English Drama 1660–1900.* 6 vols., vol. 5. 2nd ed. Cambridge: Cambridge UP.

Nilsen, Don L. F. 1996. *Humor in Irish Literature: A Reference Guide.* Westport, Conn.: Greenwood Press.

Noçon, Peter, ed. 1979–83. *The English Sonnet: An Introduction to the Study of Poetry.* 2 vols.: *Students' Book* (1979) and *Teacher's Book* (1983). Paderborn: Schöningh.

Nowak, Helge. 1994. *"Completeness Is All": Fortsetzungen und andere Weiterführungen britischer Romane als Beispiel zeitübergreifender und interkultureller Rezeption.* Frankfurt a. M.: Peter Lang.

Nünning, Ansgar, ed. 1998. *Eine andere Geschichte der englischen Literatur: Epochen, Gattungen und Teilgebiete.* 1996. 2nd, corr. ed. Trier: Wissenschaftlicher Verlag Trier.

Nünning, Vera, ed. 2005. *Kulturgeschichte der englischen Literatur: Von der Renaissance bis zur Gegenwart.* Tübingen: Francke.

Ó hÓgáin, Dáithí. 2006. *The Lore of Ireland: An Encyclopedia of Myth, Legend and Romance.* Cork: Collins Press.

Powell, Kersti Tarien. 2004. *Irish Fiction: An Introduction.* New York: Continuum.

Priestman, Martin, ed. 2003. *The Cambridge Companion to Crime Fiction.* Cambridge: Cambridge UP. [With further reference.]

Richetti, John, ed. 1994. *The Columbia History of the British Novel.* New York: Columbia UP.

Royle, Trevor, comp. 1993. *The Mainstream Companion to Scottish Literature.* Rev. ed. Edinburgh: Mainstream.

Rzepka, Charles J. 2005. *Detective Fiction. Cultural History of Literature.* Cambridge: Polity Press.

Sage, Lorna, ed. 1999. *The Cambridge Guide to Women's Writing in English.* Cambridge: Cambridge UP.

Scaggs, John. 2005. *Crime Fiction. New Critical Idiom.* London: Taylor & Francis.

Schabert, Ina. 1997. *Englische Literaturgeschichte: Eine neue Darstellung aus der Sicht der Geschlechterforschung.* Stuttgart: Kröner.

Schabert, Ina. 2006. *Englische Literaturgeschichte des 20. Jahrhunderts: Eine neue Darstellung aus der Sicht der Geschlechterforschung.* Stuttgart: Kröner.

Schama, Simon. 2000–02. *A History of Britain.* 3 vols. London: BBC.

Schirmer, Gregory A. 1998. *Out of What Began: A History of Irish Poetry in English.* Ithaca: Cornell UP.

Schlueter, Paul, and June Schlueter, eds. 1998. *An Encyclopedia of British Women Writers.* 2nd, rev. ed. New Brunswick, N.J.: Rutgers UP.

Schoene, Berthold. 2007. *The Edinburgh Companion to Scottish Literature.* Edinburgh: Edinburgh UP.

Shattock, Joanne, ed. 1993. *The Oxford Guide to British Women Writers.* Oxford: Oxford UP.

Showalter, Elaine. 1977. *A Literature of Their Own: British Women Novelists from Brontë to Lessing.* Princeton: Princeton UP.

Smith, Donald. 2001. *Storytelling Scotland: A Nation in Narrative.* Edinburgh: Polygon.

Spiller, Michael R. G. 1992. *The Development of the Sonnet.* London: Routledge.

Stephens, Meic, ed. 1998. *The New Companion to the Literature of Wales.* Cardiff: University of Wales Press.

Stewart, William, ed. 2007. *British and Irish Poets: A Biographical Dictionary, 449–2006.* Jefferson, N.C.: McFarland.

Suerbaum, Ulrich. 1984. *Krimi: Eine Analyse der Gattung.* Stuttgart: Reclam.

Summers, Claude J. 2002. *The Gay and Lesbian Literary Heritage: A Reader's Companion to the Writers and Their Works, from Antiquity to the Present*. 1995. 2nd, rev. ed. London and New York: Routledge.

Thomson, Peter, ed. 2004. *The Cambridge History of British Theatre*. 3 vols. Cambridge: Cambridge UP. [With an extensive bibliography in each vol.]

Trussler, Simon, ed. 1994. *The Cambridge Illustrated History of British Theatre*. Cambridge: Cambridge UP.

Turner, E[rnest]. S[ackville]. 1948. *Boys Will Be Boys: The Story of Sweeney Todd, Deadwood Dick, Sexton Blake, Billy Bunter, Dick Barton, et al*. London: Michael Joseph. [On boys' weekly magazines.]

Vance, Norman. 2008. *Irish Literature since 1800*. Harlow: Longman.

[Victoria and Albert Museum: Theatre Collections.] *PeoplePlay UK: Theatre History Online*. http://www.peopleplayuk.org.uk/

Weekes, Ann Owens. 1990. *Irish Women Writers: An Uncharted Tradition*. Lexington: Univ. of Kentucky Press.

Weekes, Ann Owens. 1993. *Unveiling Treasures. The Attic Guide to the Published Works of Irish Women Literary Writers: Drama, Fiction, Poetry*. Dublin: Attic Press.

Welch, Robert and Bruce Stewart, eds. 1996. *The Oxford Companion to Irish Literature*. Oxford: Oxford UP.

Glossaries of Literary Terms, Introductions to Poetry, and Theories of Narrative and Drama

Abrams, M.H., and Geoffrey Galt Harpham. 2005. *A Glossary of Literary Terms*. 8th, rev. ed. Boston, Mass.: Thomson Wadsworth.

Birch, Dinah, ed. 2009. *The Oxford Companion to English Literature*. 7th, rev. ed. Oxford: Oxford UP. [Previous, 6th ed. by Margaret Drabble.]

Bode, Christoph. 2001. *Einführung in die Lyrikanalyse*. Trier: Wiss. Verlag Trier.

Bode, Christoph. 2005. *Der Roman: Eine Einführung*. Tübingen: Francke.

Booth, Wayne C. 1952. "Tristram Shandy and Its Precursors: The Self-Conscious Narrator in Comic Fiction Before *Tristram Shandy*." *PMLA* 67: 163–85.

Booth, Wayne C. 1991. *The Rhetoric of Fiction*. 1961. 2nd, rev. and enl. ed. Harmondsworth: Penguin Books.

Childs, Peter, and Roger Fowler, eds. 2005. *The Routledge Dictionary of Literary Terms*. London: Routledge.

Fenton, James. 2002. *An Introduction to English Poetry*. London: Viking. Repr. Harmondsworth: Penguin, 2003.

Fielitz, Sonja. 1999. *Drama: Text und Theater*. Berlin: Cornelsen.

Fielitz, Sonja. 2001. *Roman: Text und Kontext*. Berlin: Cornelsen.

Forster, E.M. 1976. *Aspects of the Novel*. 1927. Ed. Oliver Stallybrass. Harmondsworth: Penguin Books. Repr. 2000.

Genette, Gérard. 1988. *Narrative Discourse Revisited*. Ithaca, N.Y.: Cornell UP.

Head, Dominic, ed. 2006. *The Cambridge Guide to Literature in English*. 3rd, rev. ed. Cambridge: Cambridge UP.

Hobsbaum, Philip. 1995. *Metre, Rhythm and Verse Form*. London: Routledge.

Hollander, John. 2001. *Rhyme's Reason: A Guide to English Verse*. 1981. 3rd, enl. ed. New Haven: Yale UP.

Ingarden, Roman. 1968. *Vom Erkennen des literarischen Kunstwerks*. Tübingen: Niemeyer.

Iser, Wolfgang. 1976. *Der Akt des Lesens: Theorie ästhetischer Wirkung*. München: Fink.

Leech, Geoffrey N. 1969. *A Linguistic Guide to English Poetry*. Harlow: Longman. Repr. 1996.

Ludwig, Hans-Werner. 2005. *Arbeitsbuch Lyrikanalyse*. 1979. 5th, enl. ed. Tübingen: Narr.

Meller, Horst. 1985. *Zum Verstehen englischer Gedichte*. München: Fink.

Meyer, Michael. 2008. *English and American Literatures* (UTB Basics). 2004. 3rd, rev. ed. Tübingen: Francke.

Pfister, Manfred. 2001. *Das Drama: Theorie und Analyse*. 1977. 11th ed. München: Fink.

Preminger, Alex, and T.V.F. Brogan, eds. 1993. *The New Princeton Encyclopedia of Poetry and Poetics*. 3rd, rev. ed. Princeton: Princeton UP.

Raith, Joseph. 1962. *Englische Metrik*. München: Hueber. Repr. 1980.

Simpson, James, comp. 2006. "Literary Terminology". Appendix in *NAEL* A74–95.

Standop, Ewald. 1989. *Abriß der englischen Metrik*. Tübingen: Francke.

Stanzel, Franz K. 2001. *Theorie des Erzählens*. 1979. 7th ed. Göttingen: Vandenhoeck & Ruprecht.

Wainwright, Jeffrey. 2004. *Poetry. The Basics*. London: Routledge.

Medieval Literature

Anthologies

Trapp, J.B., Douglas Gray and Julia Boffey, eds. 2002. *The Oxford Anthology of English Literature. Vol. 1: Medieval English Literature*. 2nd, rev ed. Oxford: Oxford UP.

Works by Individual Writers

Anon. 2000. *Beowulf*. Transl. Seamus Heaney. 1999. New York: Farrar, Straus & Giroux. Repr. New York: Norton, 2001. [Bilingual ed. with Old English text. For Heaney's transl. only, see also *NAEL* I, 29–100.]

Surveys of the Period and Studies in Individual Genres or Notable Writers

Bjork, Robert E., and John D. Niles, eds. 1997. *A Beowulf Handbook*. Lincoln, Nebr.: Univ. of Nebraska Press.

Davenport, Tony. 2004. *Medieval Narrative: An Introduction*. Oxford: Oxford UP.

Dillon, Janette. 2006. *The Cambridge Introduction to Early English Theatre*. Cambridge: Cambridge UP. [Medieval and Renaissance periods.]

Fulk, R.D., and Christopher M. Cain. 2002. *A History of Old English Literature*. Oxford: Blackwell.

Godden, Malcolm, and Michael Lapidge, eds. 1986. *The Cambridge Companion to Old English Literature*. Cambridge: Cambridge UP.

Greenfield, Stanley B., and Daniel G. Calder. 1986. *A New Critical History of Old English Literature*. New York: New York UP.

Harris, John Weley. 1992. *Medieval Theatre in Context: An Introduction*. London: Routledge.

Lapidge, Michael, et al., eds. 1999. *The Blackwell Encyclopedia of Anglo-Saxon England*. Oxford: Backwell.

Meid, Wolfgang. 1997. *Die keltischen Sprachen und Literaturen: Ein Überblick*. Innsbruck: Institut für Sprachwissenschaft.

Milfull, Inge B., and Hans Sauer. 2003. "Seamus Heaney: Ulster, Old English, and *Beowulf*". *Bookmarks from the Past*. Eds. Lucia Kornexl and Ursula Lenker. Frankfurt a.M.: Lang. 81–141.

Obst, Wolfgang, and Florian Schleburg. 1999. *Die Sprache Chaucers: Ein Lehrbuch des Mittelenglischen auf der Grundlage von "Troilus and Criseyde"*. Heidelberg: Winter.

Obst, Wolfgang, and Florian Schleburg. 2004. *Lehrbuch des Altenglischen*. Heidelberg: Winter.

Ó hÓgáin, Dáithí. 2006. *The Lore of Ireland: An Encyclopedia of Myth, Legend and Romance*. Cork: Collins Press.

Orchard, Andy. 2003. *A Critical Companion to "Beowulf"*. Cambridge: Brewer.

Pehnt, Annette. 1997. *Mad Sweeney: Eine mittelalterliche Figur in der irischen Literatur des 19. und 20. Jahrhunderts*. Phil. Diss. Freiburg.

Porter, James. 2009. *Genre, Conflict, Presence: Traditional Ballads in a Modernizing World*. Trier: Wissenschaftlicher Verlag Trier.

Pulsiano, Phillip, and Elaine Treharne, eds. 2001. *A Companion to Anglo-Saxon Literature*. Oxford: Blackwell.

Richmond, Velma Bourgeois. 1996. *The Legend of Guy of Warwick*. New York: Garland.

Scraggs, Donald G., and Carole Weinberg, eds. 2000. *Literary Appropriations of the Anglo-Saxons from the Thirteenth to the Twentieth Centuries*. Cambridge: Cambridge UP.

Shields, Kathleen. 2000. *Gained in Translation: Language, Poetry and Identity in Twentieth-Century Ireland*. Frankfurt a.M.: Lang.

Szarnack, Paul E., M. Teresa Tavormina and Joel T. Rosenthal, eds. 1998. *Medieval England: An Encyclopedia*. New York: Garland.

Renaissance Literature (c.1500–1660)

Anthologies

Salzman, Paul. 2000. *Early Modern Women's Writing: An Anthology, 1560–1700*. Oxford: Oxford UP.

Works by Individual Writers

Donne, John. 1986. *The Complete English Poems*. Ed. A.J. Smith. 1971. Harmondsworth: Penguin Books.

Milton, John. 1966. *Poetical Works*. Ed. Douglas Bush. Oxford: Oxford UP.

Shakespeare, William. 1976. *The Sonnets*. Ed. M.R. Ridley. London: Dent.

Shakespeare, William. 1982. *Hamlet*. Ed. Harold Jenkins (Arden Shakespeare). London: Routledge.

Shakespeare, William. 1999a. *Othello*. Ed. E.A.J. Honigmann (Arden Shakespeare). London: Nelson/Thomson.

Shakespeare, William. 1999b. *The Tempest*. Ed. Virginia Mason Vaughan and Alden T. Vaughan (Arden Shakespeare). London: Nelson/Thomson.

Shakespeare, William. 2000. *Romeo and Juliet*. Ed. Jill L. Levenson (Oxford Shakespeare). Oxford: Oxford UP.

Surveys of the Period

Briggs, Julia. 1997. *This Stage-Play World: Texts and Contexts, 1580–1625*. 1983. 2nd, rev. ed. Oxford: Oxford UP.

Corns, Thomas. 2007. *A History of Seventeenth-Century English Literature*. Oxford: Blackwell.

Hattaway, Michael. 2005. *Renaissance and Reformations: An Introduction to Early Modern English Literature*. Oxford: Blackwell.

Loewenstein, David, ed. 2002. *The Cambridge History of Early Modern English Literature*. Cambridge: Cambridge UP.

Schoenbaum, S[amuel]. 1979. *Shakespeare: The Globe and the World*. New York: Oxford UP. [Many illustrations.]

Suerbaum, Ulrich. 2003. *Das elisabethanische Zeitalter*. 1989. With updated bibliography. Stuttgart: Reclam.

Tillyard, E[ustace].M.W. 1943. *The Elizabethan World Picture*. London: Chatto & Windus.

Wynne-Davies, Marion, ed. 1992. *The Renaissance: A Guide to English Renaissance Literature, 1500–1660*. London: Bloomsbury.

Studies in Individual Genres or Notable Writers from the Period

Bate, Jonathan, and Russell Jackson, eds. 1996. *Shakespeare: An Illustrated Stage History*. Oxford: Oxford UP.

Bradley, A[ndrew].C[ecil]. 1905. *Shakespearean Tragedy*. 1904. 2nd, corr. ed. London: Macmillan.

Braunmuller, A.R., and Michael Hattaway, eds. 1990. *The Cambridge Companion to English Renaissance Drama*. Cambridge: Cambridge UP.

Clemen, Wolfgang. 1964. *Shakespeares Monologe*. Göttingen: Vandenhoeck & Ruprecht.

de Grazia, Margareta, and Stanley Wells, eds. 2001. *The Cambridge Companion to Shakespeare*. Cambridge: Cambridge UP.

Dillon, Janette. 2006. *The Cambridge Introduction to Early English Theatre*. Cambridge: Cambridge UP. [Medieval and Renaissance periods.]

Dobson, Michael, and Stanley Wells, eds. 2001. *The Oxford Companion to Shakespeare*. Oxford: Oxford UP. Repr. 2005.

Elsky, Martin. 1989. *Authorizing Words: Speech, Writing, and Print in the English Renaissance*. Ithaca, N.Y.: Cornell UP.

Erne, Lukas. 2003. *Shakespeare as Literary Dramatist*. Cambridge: Cambridge UP. [Provocative re-view of Shakespeare on stage and in print.]

Fielitz, Sonja, ed. 2004 ff. *Shakespeare und kein Ende*. [7] Bde. Bochum: Kamp. [Every vol. dedicated to a single play.]

Greenblatt, Stephen. 1980. "The Improvisation of Power". *Renaissance Self-Fashioning: From More to Shakespeare*. Chicago: Chicago UP. 222–54, 296–307.

Greenblatt, Stephen. 1988. "Shakespeare and the Exorcists". 1984. *Shakespearean Negotiations: The Circulation of Social Energy in Renaissance England*. Oxford: Clarendon Press. 94–128, 184–92.

Greenblatt, Stephen. 1990. "The Cultivation of Anxiety: King Lear and his Heirs". *Learning to Curse: Essays in Early Modern Culture*. London: Routledge. 158–79.

Hattaway, Michael, ed. 2004. *The Cambridge Companion to Shakespeare's History Plays*. Cambridge: Cambridge UP.

Hunter, G.K. 1997. *English Drama 1586–1642: The Age of Shakespeare* (The Oxford History of English Literature, 6). Oxford: Oxford UP.

Kullmann, Thomas. 2005. *William Shakespeare: Eine Einführung*. Berlin: Erich Schmidt Verlag.

Leavis, F[rank].R[aymond]. 1952. "Diabolic Intellect and the Noble Hero". *"Othello": A Casebook*. Ed. John Wain. Basingstoke: Macmillan, 1971. 123–46.

Leggatt, Alexander. 1988. *English Drama: Shakespeare to the Restoration, 1590–1660*. Harlow: Longman.

Love, Harold. 1993. *Scribal Publication in Seventeenth-Century England*. Oxford: Clarendon Press.

Marotti, Arthur F. 1995. *Manuscript, Print, and the English Renaissance Lyric*. Ithaca, N.Y.: Cornell UP.

Mehl, Dieter. 1983. *Die Tragödien Shakespeares: Eine Einführung*. Berlin: Schmidt.

Rankin, Deana. 2005. *Between Spenser and Swift: English Writing in Seventeenth-Century Ireland*. Cambridge: Cambridge UP.

Schabert, Ina, ed. 2000. *Shakespeare-Handbuch: Die Zeit – der Mensch – das Werk – die Nachwelt*. 1972. 4th, rev. ed. Stuttgart: Kröner. [Earlier editions retain their usefulness.]

Schaffeld, Norbert, Hg. 2005. *Shakespeare's Legacy: The Appropriation of the Plays in Post-Colonial Drama*. Trier: Wissenschaftlicher Verlag Trier.

Spurgeon, Caroline. 1935. *Shakespeare's Imagery and What It Tells Us*. Cambridge: Cambridge UP. Repr. 1971.

Styan, J[ohn].L. 1967. *Shakespeare's Stagecraft*. Cambridge: Cambridge UP.

Suerbaum, Ulrich. 2001. *Shakespeares Dramen*. 1996. 2nd, rev. and enl. ed. Tübingen: Francke.

Taylor, Gary. 1989. *Reinventing Shakespeare: A Cultural History from the Restoration to the Present*. London: Hogarth Press, New York: Weidenfeld & Nicolson.

Transl. into German by Helga Schwalm as: *Shakespeare – wie er euch gefällt: Eine Kulturgeschichte von der Restauration bis zur Gegenwart*. Hamburg: Kellner, 1992. Repr. Reinbek: Rowohlt, 1994.

Tillyard, E[ustace].M.W. 1944. *Shakespeare's History Plays*. London: Chatto & Windus.

Weimann, Robert. 1967. *Shakespeare und die Tradition des Volkstheaters: Soziologie, Dramaturgie, Gestaltung*. Berlin: Henschelverlag.

Wells, Stanley, and Sarah Stanton, eds. 2002. *The Cambridge Companion to Shakespeare on Stage*. Cambridge: Cambridge UP.

The Long Eighteenth Century: Neoclassicism and Romanticism

Anthologies

Ashfield, Andrew, ed. 1993. *Women Romantic Poets, 1770–1838: An Anthology*. Manchester: Manchester UP.

BWP Fullard, Joyce, ed. 1990. *British Women Poets 1660–1800: An Anthology*. Troy, N.Y.: Whitston.

Carretta, Vincent, ed. 1996. *Unchained Voices: An Anthology of Black Authors in the English Speaking World of the Eighteenth Century*. Lexington: UP of Kentucky.

ECCO Eighteenth Century Collections Online. Detroit: Thomson-Gale. [More than 150,000 works from all kinds of literature published in the United Kingdom between 1801 and 1800 accessible online.]

ECP Fairer, David, and Christine Gerrard, eds. 1999. *Eighteenth-Century Poetry: An Annotated Anthology*. Oxford: Blackwell. 2nd, rev. ed. 2004.

Edwards, Paul, and David Dabydeen, eds. 1991. *Black Writers in Britain 1760–1960*. Edinburgh: Edinburgh UP. [Extracts with biographical notes.]

EWP Lonsdale, Roger, ed. 1990. *Eighteenth-Century Women Poets: An Oxford Anthology*. 2nd, corr. ed. Oxford: Oxford UP.

Gates, Henry Louis, ed. 1987. *The Classic Slave Narratives*. New York: Mentor.

Hamden, John, ed. 1928. *"The Beggar's Opera" and Other Eighteenth-Century Plays* (Everyman's Library). London: Dent. Repr. 1962.

Jain, Nalini, and John Richardson, eds. 1994. *Eighteenth-Century English Poetry: The Annotated Anthology*. New York: Harvester Wheatsheaf.

Jeffares, A[lexander]. Norman, ed. 2006. *Irish Literature: The Eighteenth Century: An Annotated Anthology*. Dublin: Irish Academic Press.

Kent, David A., and D.-R. Ewen, eds. 1992. *Romantic Parodies, 1797–1831*. Rutherford, NJ: Fairleigh Dickinson UP.

Kitson, Peter J., and Debbie Lee, eds. 1999. *Slavery, Abolition and Emancipation: Writings in the British Romantic Period*. 8 vols. London. Pickering and Chatto.

McMillin, Scott, ed. 1997. *Restoration and Eighteenth-Century Comedy* (Norton Critical Editions). 2nd, enl. ed. New York: Norton.

Neuburg, Victor E., ed. 1968. *The Penny Histories: A Study of Chapbooks for Young Readers over Two Centuries*. Oxford: Oxford UP, 1968. [For *Guy of Warwick*, see pp. 8–11, 81–104.]

NOBEV Lonsdale, Roger, ed. 1984. *The New Oxford Book of Eighteenth Century Verse*. Oxford: Oxford UP.

NOBRV McGann Jerome J., ed. 1993. *The New Oxford Book of Romantic Period Verse*. Oxford: Oxford UP.

NWP Armstrong, Isobel, and Joseph Bristow with Cath Sharrock, 1998. *Nineteenth Century Women Poets: An Oxford Anthology*. 2nd rev. ed. Oxford: Oxford UP.

RWP Wu, Duncan, ed. 1997. *Romantic Women Poets: An Anthology*. Oxford: Blackwell.

WSO Bernikow, Louise, ed. 1974. *The World Split Open: Four Centuries of Women Poets in England and America, 1552–1950*. New York: Vintage Books, 1974.

Wu, Duncan, ed. 1994. *Romanticism: An Anthology*. Oxford: Blackwell.

Wheatley, Christopher, and Kevin Donovan, ed. 2003. *Irish Drama of the Seventeenth and Eighteenth Centuries*. 2 vols. Bristol and Tokyo: Thoemmes Press.

Works by Individual Writers

Blake, William. 1981. *The Paintings and Drawings*, ed. Martin Butlin. 2 vols. New Haven: Yale UP.

    1991–95. *Blake's Illuminated Books*, ed. David Bindman. 6 vols. Princeton: Princeton UP.

Byron, George Gordon, Lord. 1980–93. *The Complete Poetical Works*, ed. Jerome J. McGann. 7 vols. Oxford: Clarendon Press.

Coleridge, Samuel Taylor. 1969 ff. *The Collected Works*, ed. Kathleen Coburn. 16 vols. London: Routledge; Princeton: Princeton UP.

    Stillinger, Jack. 1994. *Coleridge and Textual Instability: The Multiple Versions of the Major Poems*. Oxford: Oxford UP. [Critical edition combined with textual criticism.]

Defoe, Daniel. 1986. *The Life and Adventures of Robinson Crusoe*, ed. Angus Ross. 1965. Harmondsworth: Penguin Books.

Dryden, John. 1984. *All for Love; or, The World Well Lost: A Tragedy, [...] Written in Imitation of Shakespeare's Style*. 1678. *The Works of John Dryden*. Ed. Alan Roper. 19 vols. Berkeley, Univ. of California Press, 1956 ff. Vol. 13 (1984), 1–111.

Edgeworth, Maria. 1893. "The Grateful Negro". 1802. *Tales and Novels* (Longford Edition). 10 vols. London: Routledge. Repr. New York: AMS Press, 1967. II, 397–419. Also incl. in Kitson and Lee 1999, VI.

Fielding, Henry. 1986. *The History of Tom Jones*, ed. R. P. C. Mutter. 1966. Harmondsworth: Penguin Books.

Kant, Immanuel. 1784. "Beantwortung der Frage: Was ist Aufklärung?" *Werke*, ed. Ernst Cassirer, 11 vols. Berlin: Cassirer, 1922–23. IV, 167–76.

Keats, John. 1978. *The Poems*, ed. Jack Stillinger. Cambridge, Mass: Belknap Press; London: Heinemann.

Lamb, Charles and Mary. 1903–5. *The Works of Charles and Mary Lamb*, ed. E. V. Lukas. 7 vols. London: Methuen. Incl. "Mrs Battle's Opinions on Whist" (II, 32–37) and "Elinor Forester: The Father's Wedding-Day" (III, 302–5).

More, Hannah. 1830. "Betty Brown, the St. Giles's Orange Girl". 1801. *The Works of Hannah More*. 11 vols. London: Cadell. IV, 99–114.

Richardson, Samuel. 1985. *Pamela; or, Virtue Rewarded*, ed. Peter Sabor with an Introduction by Margaret A. Doody. 1980. Harmondsworth: Penguin Books.

Scott, Walter. 1893. *Rob Roy*, ed. Andrew Lang (Waverley Novels, Border Edition). 2 vols. London: Nimmo.

Scott, Walter. 1937. *Ivanhoe*, ed. Andrew Lang (Waverley Novels, Border Edition). 1893. London: Macmillan, 1900. Repr. 1937.

Shelley, Percy Bysshe. 1977. *Shelley's Poetry and Prose*, eds. Donald H. Reiman and Sharon B. Powers. New York: Norton.

Smith, Stevie. 1985. *Collected Poems*, ed. James MacGibbon. Harmondsworth: Penguin Books.

Sterne, Laurence. 1975. *A Sentimental Journey through France and Italy*, ed. Graham Petrie. 1967. Repr. Harmondsworth: Penguin Books.

Sterne, Laurence. 1983. *The Life and Opinions of Tristram Shandy, Gentleman*, ed. Graham Petrie with an Introduction by Christopher Ricks. 1967. Harmondsworth: Penguin Books.

Woolf, Virginia. 2000. *"A Room of One's Own"* – *"Three Guineas"*, ed. Michèle Barrett. 1993. Harmondsworth: Penguin Books.

Wordsworth, William. 1952–59. *The Poetical Works*, eds. Ernest de Selincourt and Helen Darbishire. 5 vols. Oxford: Clarendon Press. Repr. 1963–66. [Last revised versions.] 1975 ff. *The Cornell Wordsworth*, eds. Stephen Parrish and Marc L. Reed. Ithaca, N.Y.: Cornell UP. [Early versions.]

Surveys of the Period
Butler, Marilyn. 1981. *Romantics, Rebels and Reactionaries: English Literature and its Background, 1760–1830*. Oxford: Oxford UP.
Corns, Thomas. 2007. *A History of Seventeenth-Century English Literature*. Oxford: Blackwell.
Curran, Stuart, ed. 1993. *The Cambridge Companion to British Romanticism*. Cambridge: Cambridge UP.
Dabundo, Laura, ed. 1992. *Encyclopedia of Romanticism: Culture in Britain, 1780s–1830s*. London: Routledge.
Gaull, Marilyn. 1988. *English Romanticism: The Human Context*. New York: Norton.
Loewenstein, David, ed. 2002. *The Cambridge History of Early Modern English Literature*. Cambridge: Cambridge UP.
McCalman, Iain, ed. 1999. *An Oxford Companion to the Romantic Age: British Culture, 1776–1832*. Oxford: Oxford UP.
Müllenbrock, Heinz-Joachim, and Eberhard Späth. 1977. *Literatur des 18. Jahrhunderts*. Düsseldorf: Bagel.
Müllenbrock, Heinz-Joachim, ed. 1984. *Europäische Aufklärung*, vol. 2 (*Neues Handbuch der Literaturwissenschaft*, 12). Wiesbaden: Athenaion/Aula.
Nünning, Vera, and Ansgar Nünning. 1998. *Englische Literatur des 18. Jahrhunderts*. Stuttgart: Klett.
Rafroidi, Patrick. 1980. *Irish Literature in English: The Romantic Period*. 2 vols. Gerrards Cross: Colin Smythe.
Rankin, Deana. 2005. *Between Spenser and Swift: English Writing in Seventeenth-Century Ireland*. Cambridge: Cambridge UP.
Raimond, Jean, and John R. Watson, eds. 1992. *A Handbook to English Romanticism*. Basingstoke: Macmillan; New York: St. Martin's Press.
Ray, Gordon N. 1976. *The Illustrator and the Book in England from 1790–1914*. New York: The Pierpont Morgan Library and Oxford: Oxford UP.
Speck, W. A. 1998. *Literature and Society in Eighteenth-Century England 1680–1820: Ideology, Politics and Culture*. Harlow: Longman.
Womersley, David, ed. 2000. *A Companion to Literature from Milton to Blake* (Blackwell Companions to Literature and Culture, 7). Oxford: Blackwell.
Wu, Duncan, ed. 1995. *Romanticism: A Critical Reader*. Oxford: Blackwell.
Wu, Duncan, ed. 1997. *A Companion to Romanticism*. Oxford: Blackwell.

Studies in Individual Genres or Notable Writers from the Period
Abrams, M. H. 1953. *The Mirror and the Lamp: Romantic Theory and the Critical Tradition*. New York: Oxford UP.
Adams, Percy G. 1962. *Travelers and Travel Liars, 1660–1800*. Berkeley: Univ. of California Press.
Backscheider, Paula R. 2009. *Reading the Eighteenth-Century Novel*. Oxford: Blackwell.
Berger, Dieter A. 1990. *Die Parodie in der Dichtung der englischen Romantik*. Tübingen: Francke.
Bevis, Richard W. 1988. *English Drama: Restoration and Eighteenth Century, 1660–1789* (Longman Literature in English Series). Harlow: Longman.
Bode, Christoph, ed. 1997. *West Meets East: Klassiker der britischen Orient-Reiseliteratur*. Heidelberg: Winter.
Bode, Christoph. 1996. *John Keats: Play on*. Heidelberg: Winter.
Bremen, Thilo v. 1977. *Lord Byron als Erfolgsautor: Leser und Literaturmarkt im frühen 19. Jahrhundert*. Wiesbaden: Athenaion.
Breuer, Rolf, comp. 1999. "Jane Austen etc. The Completions, Continuations and Adaptations of Her Novels. Bibliography". *EESE Resources* http://webdoc.sub.gwdg.de/edoc/ia/eese/breuer/biblio.html. [For another and similar online bibliography, see http://www.pemberley.com/janeinfo/austseql.html.]
Carruthers, Gerard. 2009. *The Edinburgh Companion to Robert Burns*. Edinburgh: Edinburgh UP.
Curran, Stuart. 1986. *Poetic Form and British Romanticism*. New York: Oxford UP.
Davie, Donald. 1993. *The Eighteenth-Century Hymn in England*. Cambridge: Cambridge UP.
Fischer, Hermann. 1964. *Die Romantische Verserzählung in England: Versuch einer Gattungsgeschichte*. Tübingen: Niemeyer.
Friedman, Albert B. 1961. *The Ballad Revival: Studies in the Influence of Popular on Sophisticated Poetry*. Chicago: Chicago UP.

Fry, Paul H. 1980. *The Poet's Calling in the English Ode*. New Haven: Yale UP.

Gilbert, Sandra M., and Susan Gubar. 1979. *The Madwoman in the Attic: The Woman Writer and the Nineteenth-Century Literary Imagination*. New Haven, Conn.: Yale UP.

Hill, Errol. 1992. *The Jamaican Stage, 1655–1900. Profile of a Colonial Theatre*. Amherst: University of Massachussetts Press.

Hoffmeister, Gerhart. 1983. *Byron und der europäische Byronismus*. Darmstadt: Wissenschaftliche Buchgesellschaft.

Hopkins, David 2000. "Classical Translation and Imitation" and "John Dryden, *Fables*" in Womersley (2000: 76–93, 232–37).

Hume, Robert D., ed. 1980. *The London Theatre World, 1660–1800*. Carbondale: Southern Illinois UP.

Jack, Ian. 1952. *Augustan Satire: Intention and Idiom in English Poetry, 1660–1750*. Oxford: Oxford UP. Repr. 1970.

Kalb, Gertrud. 1981. *Bildungsreise und literarischer Reisebericht: Studien zur englischen Reiseliteratur (1700–1850)*. Nürnberg: Carl.

Kalb, Gertrud. 1985. *Daniel Defoe*. Heidelberg: Winter.

Konigsberg, Ira. 1985. *Narrative Technique in the English Novel: Defoe to Austen*. Hamden, Conn.: Archon Books.

Laqueur, Thomas. 1990. *Making Sex: Body and Gender from the Greeks to Freud*. Cambridge, Mass.: Harvard UP.

Laws, George Malcolm. 1972. *The British Literary Ballad: A Study in Poetic Imitation*. Carbondale: Southern Illinois Press.

Levinson, Marjorie. 1986. *The Romantic Fragment Poem: A Critique of a Form*. Chapel Hill: Univ. of North Carolina Press.

Lodge, David. 1984. *Language of Fiction: Essays in Criticism and Verbal Analysis of the English Novel*. 1966. 2nd, enl. ed. London: Routledge & Kegan Paul. Repr. 2001.

Love, Harold. 1993. *Scribal Publication in Seventeenth-Century England*. Oxford: Clarendon Press.

Marotti, Arthur F. 1995. *Manuscript, Print, and the English Renaissance Lyric*. Ithaca, N.Y.: Cornell UP.

Mehl, Dieter. 1977. *Der englische Roman bis zum Ende des 18. Jahrhunderts*. Düsseldorf: Bagel, Bern: Francke. [Also on Bunyan and Swift.]

Mulvey, Laura. 1975. "Visual Pleasure and Narrative Cinema", *Screen* 16,3: 6–18. Repr. in *Film and Theory: An Anthology*, eds. Robert Stam and Toby Miller. Oxford: Blackwell, 2000. 483–94.

Neuburg, Victor E., ed. 1968. *The Penny Histories: A Study of Chapbooks for Young Readers over Two Centuries*. Oxford: Oxford UP, 1968. 81–104.

Omasreiter, Ria. 1982. *Travels Through the British Isles: Die Funktion des Reiseberichts im 18. Jahrhundert*. Heidelberg: Winter.

Petzold, Dieter. 1982. *Daniel Defoe: "Robinson Crusoe"*. München: Fink.

Possin, Hans-Joachim. 1972. *Reisen und Literatur: Das Thema des Reisens in der englischen Literatur des 18. Jahrhunderts*. Tübingen: Niemeyer.

Probyn, Clive T. 1987. *English Fiction of the Eighteenth Century, 1700–1789*. Harlow: Longman.

Real, Hermann J., and Heinz J. Vienken. 1984. *Jonathan Swift: "Gulliver's Travels"*. München: Fink.

Richetti, John. 1996. *The Cambridge Companion to the Eighteenth-Century Novel*. Cambridge: Cambridge UP.

Rogers, Pat. 1979. *Robinson Crusoe*. London: Allen & Unwin.

Rogers, Pat. 1985. "Classics and chapbooks". In his *Literature and Popular Culture in Eighteenth Century England*. Brighton: Harvester Press. 162–82.

Russell, Gillian. 1999. "Theatre". In McCalman (1999: 223–31).

Sherbo, Arthur. 1969. *Studies in the Eighteenth-Century English Novel*. East Lansing: Michigan State UP.

Spencer, Jane. 1986. *The Rise of the Woman Novelist: From Aphra Behn to Jane Austen*. Oxford: Blackwell.

Spender, Dale. 1986. *Mothers of the Novel: 100 Good Women Writers before Jane Austen*. London: Pandora.

Sühnel, Rudolf. 1984. "Pietas Litterata: Das Vorbild der Antike". In Müllenbrock (1984: 55–90).

Thomson, Peter. 2006. *The Cambridge Introduction to English Theatre, 1660–1900*. Cambridge: Cambridge UP.

Thorslev, P.C. 1962. *The Byronic Hero: Types and Prototypes*. Minneapolis: Univ. of Minnesota Press.

Todd, Janet. 1989. *The Sign of Angellica: Women, Writing and Fiction, 1660–1800*. London: Virago.

Watt, Ian. 1963. *The Rise of the Novel: Studies in Defoe, Richardson and Fielding*. 1957. Harmondsworth: Penguin Books, 1963.

Watt, Ian. 1968. "Second Thought Series: Serious Reflections on *The Rise of the Novel*". *Novel* 1: 205–18.

Weber, Ingeborg. 1983. *Der englische Schauerroman: Eine Einführung*. München: Artemis.

Weiss, Wolfgang. 1992. *Swift und die Satire des 18. Jahrhunderts: Epoche – Werk – Wirkung*. München: Beck.

Williams, Raymond. 1973. *The Country and the City*. London: Chatto & Windus.

Wiseman, S. J. 1996. *Aphra Behn* (Writers and their Work). Plymouth: Northcote House.

Woolf, Virginia. 1993. *"A Room of One's Own", "Three Guineas"*. Ed. Michèle Barrett. Repr. Harmondsworth: Penguin, 2000.

The Literature of the Victorian Age and of the Early Twentieth Century

Anthologies

Armstrong, Isobel, Joseph Bristow and Cath Sharrock, eds. 1996. *Nineteenth-Century Women Poets: An Oxford Anthology*. Oxford: Oxford UP. 2nd, rev. ed. 1998.

Boehmer, Elleke, ed. 1998. *Empire Writing: An Anthology of Colonial Literature, 1870–1918* (Oxford World's Classics). Oxford: Oxford UP.

Collins, Thomas J., ed. 1999. *The Broadview Anthology of Victorian Poetry and Poetic Theory*. Ontario: Broadview Press. Concise Edition 2000.

Cox, Michael, ed. 2003. *The Oxford Book of Victorian Detective Stories*. Oxford: Oxford UP, [Originally published under the title: *Victorian Tales of Mystery and Detection*, 1992.]

Harrington, John P., ed. 2009. *Modern and Contemporary Irish Drama* (Norton Critical Editions). 1991. 2nd, rev. ed. New York: Norton. [14 plays, from W.B Yeats to Conor MacPherson and Marina Carr, together with historical contextualisation in a section on "Backgrounds and Criticism".]

Jeffares, A[lexander]. Norman, and Peter van de Kamp, eds. 2006. *Irish Literature: The Nineteenth Century*. 3 vols. Dublin: Irish Academic Press.

Leighton, Angela, and Margaret Reynolds, eds. 1995. *Victorian Women Poets: An Anthology*. Oxford: Blackwell.

Morrison, Robert, and Chris Baldick, eds. 1995. *Tales of Terror from "Blackwood's Magazine"*. Oxford: Oxford UP.

Morrison, Robert, and Chris Baldick., eds. 1997. *John Polidori, "The Vampyre", and Other Tales of the Macabre*. Oxford: Oxford UP. Repr. 2008.

Palgrave, Francis Turner, ed. 1861. *The Golden Treasury of the Best Songs and Lyrical Poems in the English Language*. Cambridge: Macmillan. Repr. 2002.

Pearson, Richard, and Heike Bauer, comps. 2003–07. *The Victorian Plays Project. "Lacy's Acting Edition of Victorian Plays": Electronic Catalogue of Lacy's Collected Volumes of Victorian Plays* [1848–74]. Birmingham Central Library. http://www.worc.ac.uk/victorian/victorianplays [Electronic texts of individual plays made available.]

Ricks, Christopher, ed. 1987. *The New Oxford Book of Victorian Verse*. Oxford: Oxford UP. Repr. 2002.

Turner, Michael R. ed. 1992. *Victorian Parlour Poetry: An Annotated Anthology*. New York: Dover Publications.

Wu, Duncan, and Valentine Cunningham, eds. 2002. *Victorian Poetry*. Oxford: Blackwell.

Yeats, W. B., ed. 1936. *The Oxford Book of Modern Verse, 1892–1935*. Oxford: Oxford UP.

Works by Individual Writers

Austen, Jane. 1983. *Emma*. 1816. Ed. Ronald Blythe (Penguin English Library). Harmondsworth: Penguin Books.

Benson, A[rthur]. C. 1978. "Land of Hope and Glory". 1902. *The Faber Popular Reciter*. Ed. Kingsley Amis. London: Faber. 213–214.

Breen, Henry H[egart]. 1857. *Modern English Literature: Its Blemishes and Defects*. London: Longman. [Available online.]

Brontë, Charlotte. 1996. *Jane Eyre: An Autobiography*. 1847. Ed. Michael Mason. Harmondsworth: Penguin Books.

Brontë, Emily. 1981. *Wuthering Heights*. 1847. Ed. Ian Jack (Oxford World's Classics). Oxford: Oxford UP. Repr. 1991.

Carroll, Lewis. 1970. *The Annotated Alice: "Alice's Adventures in Wonderland"* [1865] *and "Through the Looking-Glass"* [1871]. Ill. by John Tenniel. Ed. Martin Gardner. 1960. Rev. ed. Harmondsworth: Penguin Books.

Conrad, Joseph. 1984. *Heart of Darkness*. 1899/1902. Ed. Bernhard Reitz. Stuttgart: Reclam.

D'Aguiar, Fred. 2001. "Papa-T. (For Reginald Messiah)". First publ. in *Mama Dot*, 1985. Repr. in D'Aguiar's *An English Sampler: New and Selected Poems*. London: Chatto & Windus, 2001. 19.

Darwin, Charles. 1982. *The Origin of Species by Means of Natural Selection; or, The Preservation of Favoured Races in the Struggle for Life*. 1859. Ed. J.W. Burrow, 1968 (Penguin English Library). Harmondsworth: Penguin Books.

Dickens, Charles. 1966. *Hard Times*. 1854. Eds. George Ford and Sylvère Monod (Norton Critical Editions). New York: Norton.

Dickens, Charles. 1977. *Bleak House*. 1852–53. Eds. George Ford and Sylvère Monod. (Norton Critical Editions). New York: Norton.

Dickens, Charles. 1994. *Great Expectations*. 1860–61. Ed. Margaret Cardwell. Introduction by Kate Flint (Oxford World's Classics). Oxford: Oxford UP.

Dickens, Charles. 1997. *David Copperfield*. 1849–50. Ed. Nina Burgis. With an Introduction and Notes by Andrew Sanders (Oxford World's Classics). Oxford: Oxford UP.

Eliot, George [Mary Ann Evans]. 1965. *Middlemarch: A Study of Provincial Society*. 1871–72. Ed. W.J. Harvey (Penguin English Library). Harmondsworth: Penguin Books.

Eliot, George [Mary Ann Evans]. 1979. *The Mill on the Floss*. 1860. Ed. A.S. Byatt (Penguin English Library/Penguin Classics). Harmondsworth: Penguin Books. Repr. 1985.

Eliot, George [Mary Ann Evans]. 1992. *Selected Critical Writings*. Ed. Rosemary Ashton (Oxford World's Classics). Oxford: Oxford UP.

Gaskell, Elizabeth, and Robert Leeson. 2000. *Ruth*. 1853. Adapted by Robert Leeson. Resource Material by Cecily O'Neill (Collins Classics Plus). London: HarperCollins.

Haggard, H[enry]. Rider. 1989. *King Solomon's Mines*. 1885. Ed. Dennis Butts (Oxford World's Classics). Oxford: Oxford UP.

Joyce, James. 1977. *The Essential James Joyce*. Ed. Harry Levin. 1948. London: Granada.

Kipling, Rudyard. 1987. *Kim*. 1900–01. Ed. Alan Sandison (Oxford World's Classics). Oxford: Oxford UP.

Lawrence, D[avid]. H[erbert]. 1961. *Lady Chatterley's Lover*. 1928. Harmondsworth: Penguin Books. [Richard Hoggart's "Introduction" comments upon the 1961 trial at the Old Bailey in London.]

McKay, Claude. 1999. "The Dominant White". 1919. *Selected Poems*. Ed. J.R. Sherman. Mineola, N.Y.: Dover. 24–25.

Milne, A[lan]. A[lexander]. 2002. *The Complete Winnie-the-Pooh: Containing "Winnie-the-Pooh"* [1926] *and "The House at Pooh Corner"* [1928]. Ill. by E.H. Shepard. London: Dean/Egmont Books.

Rhys, Jean. 1968. *Wide Sargasso Sea*. 1966. Harmondsworth: Penguin Books.

Ruskin, John. 1900. *Sesame and Lilies*. 1865. London: Allen. [Excerpt in *NAEL* II, 1587–88.]

Shaw, George Bernard. 1960. *Saint Joan*. 1923. Harmondsworth: Penguin Books.

Synge, John Millington. 1961. *The Playboy of the Western World*. 1907. Ed. T.R. Henn. London: Eyre Methuen.

Thackeray, William Makepeace. 1983. *Vanity Fair*. 1847–48. Ed. John Sutherland, with 193 ills. by the author (Oxford World's Classics). Oxford: Oxford UP.

Wilde, Oscar. 1893. *Lady Windermere's Fan: A Play About a Good Woman*. London: Bodley Head.

Wilde, Oscar. 1894. *Salome: A Tragedy in One Act*. Transl. from French by Lord Alfred Bruce Douglas. London: Elkin Mathews & John Lane.

Wilde, Oscar. 1966. *Complete Works*. With an Introduction by Vyvyan Holland. 1948. New ed. London and Glasgow: Collins.

Woolf, Virginia. 1966–67. *Collected Essays*. 4 vols. London: Hogarth Press.

Surveys of the Period

Altick, Richard D. 1957. *The English Common Reader: A Social History of the Mass Reading Public 1800–1900*. Chicago: Univ. of Chicago Press.

Altick, Richard D. 1969. "Nineteenth-Century English Best-Sellers: A Further List". *Studies in Bibliography* 22: 197–206.

Altick, Richard D. 1973. *Victorian People and Ideas: A Companion for the Modern Reader of Victorian Literature*. London: Dent.

Altick, Richard D. 1986. "Nineteenth-Century English Best-Sellers: A Third List". *Studies in Bibliography* 39: 235–41.

Auerbach, Nina. 1982. *Woman and the Demon: The Life of a Victorian Myth*. Cambridge, Mass.: Harvard UP.

Cevasco, George. A., ed. 1993. *The 1890s: An Encyclopedia of British Literature, Art, and Culture*. New York: Garland.

Cox, Don Richard, ed. 1984. *Sexuality and Victorian Literature*. Knoxville: Univ. of Tennessee Press.

Davis, Philip. 2002. *The Victorians*. The Oxford English Literary History, vol. 8: 1830–1880. Ed. Jonathan Bate. Oxford: Oxford UP.

Flint, Kate. 1993. *The Woman Reader, 1837–1914*. Oxford: Oxford UP.

Gilbert, Sandra M., and Susan Gubar. 1979. *The Madwoman in the Attic: The Woman Writer and the Nineteenth-Century Literary Imagination*. New Haven, Conn.: Yale UP.

Gilmour, Robin. 1993. *The Victorian Period: The Intellectual and Cultural Context of English Literature, 1830–1890*. London: Longman.

Harvey, J. R. 1970. *Victorian Novelists and Their Illustrators*. London: Sidgwick & Jackson.

Houghton, Walter E. 1957. *The Victorian Frame of Mind, 1830–1870*. New Haven: Yale UP.

Landow, George P., et al., comps. 1993 ff. *The Victorian Web: Literature, History and Culture in the Age of Victoria*. http://www.victorianweb.org/index.html

Leerssen, Joep. 1996. *Remembrance and Imagination: Patterns in the Historical and Literary Representation of Ireland in the Nineteenth Century*. Cork: Cork UP.

Marcus, Steven. 1964. *The Other Victorians: A Study of Sexuality and Pornography in Mid-Nineteenth-Century England*. New York: Basic Books.

Mason, Michael. 1994. *The Making of Victorian Sexuality*. Oxford: Oxford UP. Repr. 1995.

McMurtry, Jo. 1979. *Victorian Life and Victorian Fiction: A Companion for the American Reader*. Hamden, Conn.: Archon Books.

Pearsall, Ronald. 1969. *The Worm in the Bud: The World of Victorian Sexuality*. London: Weidenfeld & Nicolson. Repr. Stroud: Sutton Publ., 2003.

Ray, Gordon N. 1976. *The Illustrator and the Book in England from 1790–1914*. New York: The Pierpont Morgan Library and Oxford: Oxford UP.

Reed, John R. 1975. *Victorian Conventions*. Athens, Ohio: Ohio UP.

Stonyk, Margaret. 1983. *Nineteenth Century English Literature*. London: Macmillan.

Sutherland, John. 1976. *Victorian Novelists and Publishers*. Chicago: Univ. of Chicago Press.

Sutherland, John. 1989. *The Longman Companion to Victorian Fiction*. Harlow: Longman. Repr. as *The Stanford Companion to Victorian Fiction*. Stanford, Cal.: Stanford UP.

Sutherland, John. 1995. *Victorian Fiction: Writers, Publishers, Readers*. Basingstoke: Macmillan.

Thomson, F[rancis]. M[ichael]. L[ongstreth]. 1988. *The Rise of Respectable Society: A Social History of Victorian Britain, 1830–1900*. Cambridge, Mass.: Harvard UP and London: Fontana.

Webb, R. K. 1980. "The Victorian Reading Public". *The Pelican Guide to English Literature*. Ed. Boris Ford. 7 vols. Harmondsworth: Penguin Books, 1958. Repr. with revisions, 1980. Vol. 6, 205–26.

Young, G[eorge]. M[alcolm]. 1977. *Portrait of an Age: Victorian England*. 1936. Ed. George Kitson Clark. London: Oxford UP.

Studies in Individual Genres or Notable Writers from the Period

Andrews, Malcom. 2006. *Dickens and the Public Readings*. Oxford: Oxford UP.

Banerjee, Jacqueline. 1996. *Through the Northern Gate: Childhood and Growing Up in British Fiction, 1719–1901*. Frankfurt a. M. and New York: Lang.

Berger, Dieter A. 1987. "Die Erzählerin im Spannungsfeld gesellschaftlicher Vorurteile des 19. Jahrhunderts". *Erstarrtes Denken: Studien zu Klischee, Stereotyp und Vorurteil in englisch-sprachiger Literatur*. Ed. Günther Blaicher. Tübingen: Narr. 228–40.

Belanger, Jacqueline, ed. 2005. *The Irish Novel in the Nineteenth Century: Facts and Fictions*. Dublin: Four Courts Press.

Boch, Gudrun. 1976. *Studien zum englischen Provinzroman: Eine Untersuchung zur Entstehung des Genres und seiner Entwicklung im Romanwerk George Eliots und Arnold Bennetts*. Heidelberg: Winter.

Boehmer, Elleke. 1995. *Colonial and Postcolonial Literature: Migrant Metaphors*. Oxford: Oxford UP.

Boehmer, Elleke. 2002. *Empire, the National, and the Postcolonial, 1890–1920*. Oxford: Oxford UP.

Bolton, H. Philip, comp. 1987. *Dickens Dramatized*. London: Mansell.

Bolton, H. Philip, comp. 1992. *Scott Dramatized*. London: Mansell.

Booth, Michael R. 1991. *Theatre in the Victorian Age*. Cambridge: Cambridge UP.

Bratton, J. S., ed. 1986. *Music Hall: Performance and Style*. Milton Keynes: Open UP.

Butt, John, and Kathleen Tillotson. 1957. *Dickens at Work*. London: Methuen.

Cheshire, D. F. 1974. *Music Hall in Britain*. Newton Abbott: David & Charles.

Chrisman, Laura. 2000. *Rereading the Imperial Romance: British Imperialism and South African Resistance in Haggard, Schreiner, and Plaatje*. Oxford: Oxford UP.

Colman, Anne Ulry, ed. 1996. *Dictionary of Nineteenth-Century Irish Women Poets*. Galway: Kenny's Bookshop and Art Gallery.

Collins, Philip. 1975. *Charles Dickens: The Public Readings*. Oxford: Oxford UP.

Demasters, William W., and Katherine E. Kelly, comps. 1996. *British Playwrights, 1880–1956: A Research and Production Sourcebook*. Westport, Conn.: Greenwood Press.

Demastes, William W., and Bernice Schrank, comps. 1997. *Irish Playwrights, 1880–1995: A Research and Production Sourcebook*. Westport, Conn.: Greenwood Press.

Dolin, Tim. 2005. *George Eliot* (Oxford World's Classics). Oxford: Oxford UP.

Ford, George H. 1955. *Dickens and His Readers: Aspects of Novel-Criticism since 1836*. Princeton, N.J.: Princeton UP. Repr. New York: Norton, 1965.

Ford, Richard, comp. 1979. *Dramatisations of Scott's Novels: A Catalogue*. Oxford: Oxford Bibliographical Society.

Foster, John Wilson. 2008. *Irish Novels 1890–1940: New Bearings in Culture and Fiction*. Oxford: Oxford UP.

Gilmour, Robin. 1982. *Thackeray: "Vanity Fair"*. London: Arnold.

Gilmour, Robin. 1986. *The Novel in the Victorian Age: A Modern Introduction*. London: Arnold.

Goetsch, Paul. 1978. "Literatursoziologische Aspekte des viktorianischen Romanschlusses". *Poetica* 10: 236–61. [Follows the changing nature of the ending of novels, and at the same time summarises the history of the novel in the Victorian period.]

Goetsch, Paul. 1986. *Dickens: Eine Einführung*. München: Artemis.

Gymnich, Marion. 1996. "Von *Greater Britain* zu *Little England*: Konstruktion und Dekonstruktion imperialistischer Denkweisen in Rudyard Kiplings *Kim*, E. M. Forsters *A Passage to India* und Joseph Conrads *Heart of Darkness*". *Anglistik und Englischunterricht* 58: 149–66.

Hewitt, Douglas. 1988. *English Fiction of the Modern Period 1890–1940*. Harlow: Longman.

Katz, Wendy R. 1987. *Rider Haggard and the Fiction of Empire: A Critical Study of British Imperial Fiction*. Cambridge: Cambridge UP.

Keating, Paul. 1989. *The Haunted Study: A Social History of the English Novel 1875–1914*. London: Secker & Warburg.

Kift, Dagmar. 1991. *Arbeiterkultur im gesellschaftlichen Konflikt: Die englische Music Hall im 19. Jahrhundert*. Essen: Klartext Verlag.

Korte, Barbara. 1996. *Der englische Reisebericht: Von der Pilgerfahrt bis zur Postmoderne*. Darmstadt: Wissenschaftliche Buchgesellschaft.

Landow, George P., comp. *The Victorian Web*. http://www.victorianweb.org/. [Web site with encyclopaedic information on all aspects of Victorian culture.]

[Lewes, George Henry]. 1859. "The Novels of Jane Austen". *Blackwood's Edinburgh Magazine* 68: 99–113. Repr. in *Jane Austen: The Critical Heritage*. Ed. B[rian]. C. Southam. 2 vols. London: Routledge & Kegan Paul, 1968–87. I, 148–66.

Lloyd, Matthew, comp. 2008. *The Music Hall and Theatre Site*. http://www.arthurlloyd.co.uk/index.html

Luckhurst, Mary, ed. 2006. *A Companion to Modern British and Irish Drama, 1880–2005*. Oxford: Blackwell.

Maack, Annegret. 1991. *Charles Dickens: Epoche – Werk – Wirkung*. München: Beck.

Mack, Douglas S. 2006. *Scottish Fiction and the British Empire*. Edinburgh: Edinburgh UP.

Mander, Raymond, and Joe Mitchenson. 1965. *British Music Hall: A Story in Pictures*. Foreword by John Betjeman. London: Studio Vista.

Müllenbrock, Heinz-Joachim. 1980. *Der historische Roman des 19. Jahrhunderts*. Heidelberg: Winter.

Müllenbrock, Heinz-Joachim. 1992. "Literatur als Politik: Zur Funktion imperialistischer Lyrik im viktorianischen England". *Anglia* 110: 119–42.

Murray, Christopher. 2000. *Twentieth-Century Irish Drama: Mirror Up to Nation*. 1997. Syracuse, N.Y.: Syracuse UP.

Nünning, Ansgar. 1998. "Metaphors of Empire: Victorian Literature and Culture, and the Making of Imperialist Mentalities". *Anglistentag 1997 Giessen: Proceedings*. Eds. Raimund Borgmeier et al. Trier: Wissenschaftlicher Verlag Trier. 348–67.

Orwell, George. 1940. "Boys' Weeklies". *Horizon* (March 1940). Repr. in *The Collected Essays, Journalism and Letters of George Orwell*. Eds. Sonia Orwell and Ian Angus. 4 vols. London: Secker & Warburg, 1968. I, 460–84.

Orwell, George. 1940. "Charles Dickens", in *"Inside the Whale" and Other Essays*. London: Gollancz. 9–85. Repr. in *The Collected Essays, Journalism and Letters of George Orwell*. Eds. Sonia Orwell and Ian Angus. 4 vols. London: Secker & Warburg, 1968. II, 413–60.

Orwell, George. 1942. "Rudyard Kipling". *Horizon* 5: 111–25. Repr. in *The Collected Essays, Journalism and Letters*. Eds. Sonia Orwell and Ian Angus. 4 vols. London: Secker & Warburg, 1968. II, 184–97.

Ovenden, Graham, ed. 1979. *The Illustrators of "Alice in Wonderland"*. 1972. Rev. ed. London: Academy Editions and New York: St. Martin's Press. [Numerous ills.]

Page, Norman. 1984. *A Dickens Companion*. London: Macmillan.

Patten, Robert L. 1978. *Charles Dickens and His Publishers*. Oxford: Clarendon Press.

Patteson, Richard F. 1978. "*King Solomon's Mines*: Imperialism and Narrative Structure". *Journal of Narrative Technique* 8: 112–23.

Powell, Kerry, ed. 2004. *The Cambridge Companion to Victorian and Edwardian Theatre*. Cambridge: Cambridge UP.

Pratt, Mary Louise. 1992. *Imperial Eyes: Travel Writing and Transculturation*. New York: Routledge.

Quinn, Justin. 2008. *The Cambridge Introduction to Modern Irish Poetry, 1800–2000*. Cambridge: Cambridge UP.

Ramazani, Jahan. 1994. *Poetry of Mourning: The Modern Elegy from Hardy to Heaney*. Chicago: Chicago UP.

Richards, Shaun, ed. 2004. *The Cambridge Companion to Twentieth-Century Irish Drama*. Cambridge: Cambridge UP.

Sadrin, Anny. 1988. *Great Expectations*. London: Unwin Hyman.

Sacks, Peter. 1985. *The English Elegy: Studies in the Genre from Spencer to Yeats*. Baltimore, Md.: Johns Hopkins UP.

Said, Edward W. 1978/1995. *Orientalism*. 1978. Repr. with a new Afterword. Harmondsworth: Penguin.

Said, Edward W. 1993. *Culture and Imperialism*. New York: Knopf, London: Chatto & Windus.

Schefold, Florian. 1999. *Koloniale Mythenbildung und ihre literarische Dekonstruktion: Britische Kolonialliteratur von Kipling bis Farrell*. Göttingen: Cuvillier.

Schlicke, Paul, ed. 1999. *Oxford's Reader's Companion to Dickens*. Oxford: Oxford UP.

Schneider, Ulrich. 1984. *Die Londoner Music Hall und ihre Songs 1850–1920*. Tübingen: Niemeyer.

Shillingsburg, Peter L. 1992. *Pegasus in Harness: Victorian Publishing and W.M. Thackeray*. Charlottesville: UP of Virginia.

Steig, Michael. 1978. *Dickens and Phiz*. Bloomington: Indiana UP. Extracts on *The Victorian Web* http://www.victorianweb.org/art/illustration/phiz/steig/1.html.

Stephens, John Russell. 1992. *The Profession of the Playwright: British Theatre 1800–1900*. Cambridge: Cambridge UP.

Strachey, Ray. 1928. *The Cause: A Short History of the Women's Movement in Great Britain*. London: Bell. Repr. Bath: Chivers, 1974.

Sutherland, John. 1989. *The Longman Companion to Victorian Fiction*. Harlow: Longman. Repr. as *The Stanford Companion to Victorian Fiction*. Stanford, Cal.: Stanford UP.

Thomson, Peter. 2006. *The Cambridge Introduction to English Theatre, 1660–1900*. Cambridge: Cambridge UP.

Tillotson, Kathleen. 1961. *Novels of the Eighteen-Forties*. 1954. Repr. with corrections. Oxford: Oxford UP.

Turner, E[rnest]. S[ackville]. 1948. *Boys Will Be Boys: The Story of Sweeney Todd, Deadwood Dick, Sexton Blake, Billy Bunter, Dick Barton, et al*. London: Michael Joseph. [On boys' weekly magazines.]

Wheeler, Michael. 1985. *English Fiction of the Victorian Period 1830–1890*. London: Longman.

Modernism and Beyond

Anthologies

[Various eds.] 1992 ff. *New Writing*. [Annual anthology published in assoc. with the British Council].

[Various poets.] 1992 ff. *The Forward Book of Poetry*. [Annual anthology publishing the best shortlisted poems for the Forward Poetry Prize.]

Abse, Dannie, ed. 1997. *Twentieth-Century Anglo-Welsh Poetry*. Bridgend: Seren Books.

Allnutt, Gillian, et al., eds. 1988. *The New British Poetry, 1968–88*. London: Paladin Grafton Books.

Armitage, Simon, and Robert Crawford, eds. 1998. *The Penguin Book of Poetry from Britain and Ireland since 1945*. Harmondsworth: Penguin Books.

Bolger, Dermot, ed. 1999. *The Picador Book of Contemporary Irish Fiction*. London: Picador.

Burnett, Paula, ed. 1986. *The Penguin Book of Caribbean Verse in English*. Harmondsworth: Penguin Books.

Caddel, Richard, and Peter Quatermain, eds. 1999. *Other: British and Irish Poetry since 1970*. Hanover, N.H.: Wesleyan UP.

Crotty, Patrick, ed. 1995. *Modern Irish Poetry: An Anthology*. Belfast: Blackstaff Press.

Dawe, Gerald, Noel Duffy and T. Dorgan, eds. 1999. *Watching the River Flow: A Century in Irish Poetry*. Dublin: Poetry Ireland.

Dawe, Gerald, ed. 2008. *Earth Voices Whispering: An Anthology of Irish War Poetry; 1914–1945*. Belfast: Blackstaff Press.

Donnell, Alison, and Sarah Lawson Welch, eds. 1996. *The Routledge Reader in Caribbean Literature*. London: Routledge.

Dunn, Douglas, ed. 1992. *The Faber Book of Twentieth-Century Scottish Poetry*. London: Faber.

Elfyn, Menna, and John Rowlands, eds. 2003. *The Bloodaxe Book of Modern Welsh Poetry: Twentieth-Century Welsh-Language Poetry in Translation*. Tarset: Bloodaxe Books.

Erzgräber, Willi, and Ute Knoedgen, eds. 1994. *Moderne englische Lyrik: Englisch und Deutsch*. 3rd ed. Stuttgart: Reclam.

Fallon, Peter, and Derek Mahon, eds. 1990. *The Penguin Book of Contemporary Irish Poetry*. Harmondsworth: Penguin.

Fairleigh, John, and Daragh Carville, eds. 1998. *Far from the Land: New Irish Plays*. London: Methuen Drama.

Featherstone, Simon, ed. 1995. *War Poetry: An Introductory Reader*. London: Routledge.

Fitzmaurice, Gabriel, ed. 1993. *Irish Poetry Now: Other Voices*. Dublin: Wolfhound.

Geisen, Herbert, ed. 1999. *Five English Short Plays*. Stuttgart: Reclam. [Includes plays produced and published between 1970 and 1990, by Edward Bond, Howard Brenton, Caryl Churchill, Harold Pinter and Tom Stoppard.]

Grant, David, Dermot Bolger and Marina Carr. 1994. *The Crack in the Emerald: New Irish Plays*. 2nd ed. London: Hern. [Incl. e.g. Bolger's *The Lament for Arthur Cleary* and Carr's *Low in the Dark*.]

Hamilton, Ian, ed. 1999. *The Penguin Book of Twentieth-Century Essays*. London: Penguin Books.

Harrington, John P., ed. 2009. *Modern and Contemporary Irish Drama* (Norton Critical Editions). 1991. 2nd, rev. ed. New York: Norton. [14 plays, from W.B Yeats to Conor MacPherson and Marina Carr, together with historical contextualisation in a section on "Backgrounds and Criticism".]

Harris, Claudia, ed. 2007. *Four Plays by the Charabanc Theatre Company: Reinventing Woman's Work*. Gerrards Cross, Bucks.: Colin Smythe. [Plays produced 1985–87.]

Kennedy, Thomas E., and John F. Deane, eds. 1997. *Small Gifts of Knowing: New Irish Poetry and Prose*. Madison: Fairleigh Dickinson UP.

Kennelly, Brendan, ed. 1988. *Landmarks of Irish Drama*. London: Methuen.

Korte, Barbara, and Claudia Sternberg, eds. 1997. *Many Voices – Many Cultures: Multicultural British Short Stories*. Stuttgart: Reclam.

Kureishi, Hanif, and Jon Savage, eds. 1995. *The Faber Book of Pop*. London: Faber.

Larkin, Philip, ed. 1973. *The Oxford Book of Twentieth-Century English Verse*. Oxford: Oxford UP.

Leeney, Cathy, ed. 2001. *Seen and Heard: Six New Plays by Irish Women*. Dublin: Carysfort.

Longley, Michael, ed. 2002. *Twentieth-Century Irish Poems*. London: Faber.

Lucie-Smith, Edward, ed. 1985. *British Poetry since 1945*. 1970. 2nd, rev. ed. Harmondsworth: Penguin Books.

McGuinness, Frank, and Jimmy Murphy, eds. 1996. *The Dazzling Dark: New Irish Plays*. London: Faber.

Markham, E.A., ed. 1989. *Hinterland: Caribbean Poetry from the West Indies and Britain*. Newcastle upon Tyne: Bloodaxe.

Moran, James, ed. 2007. *Four Irish Rebel Plays*. Dublin: Irish Academic Press. [Incl. e.g. Thomas MacDonagh: *When the Dawn is Come*; Pádraic Pearse: *The Master*; James Connolly: *Under Which Flag?*; Terence MacSwiney: *The Revolutionist*.]

Morrison, Blake, and Andrew Motion, eds. 1982. *The Penguin Book of Contemporary British Poetry*. Harmondsworth: Penguin Books.

Motion, Andrew, ed. 2003. *First World War Poems*. London: Faber.

O'Brien, Peggy, ed. 2000. *The Wake Forest Book of Irish Women's Poetry 1967–2000*. Winston-Salem, N.C.: Wake Forest UP.

Ormsby, Frank, ed. 1992. *A Rage for Order: Poetry of the Northern Ireland Troubles*. Belfast: Blackstaff Press.
Owens, Coilin D., and Joan N. Radner, eds. 1990. *Irish Drama 1900–1980*. Washington, D.C.: Catholic University of America Press.
Parkinson, Siobhán, ed. 1996. *Home: An Anthology of Modern Irish Writing*. Dublin: Farmar.
Paterson, Don, ed. 1999. *101 Sonnets: From Shakespeare to Heaney*. London: Faber.
Pierce, David, ed. 2000. *Irish Writing in the Twentieth Century: A Reader*. Cork: Cork UP.
Skelton, Robin, ed. 1964. *Poetry of the Thirties*. Harmondsworth: Penguin Books. [Thematic sections.]
Stephens, Meic, ed. 1991. *The Bright Field: An Anthology of Contemporary Poetry from Wales*. Manchester: Carcanet.
Tuma, Keith, ed. 2001. *Anthology of Twentieth-Century British and Irish Poetry*. Oxford: Oxford UP.
Walsh, Caroline, ed. 2003. *Dislocation: Stories from a New Ireland*. New York: Carroll & Graf.
Whybrow, Graham, ed. 2001. *The Methuen Book of Modern Drama*. London: Methuen. [Includes plays produced and published between 1982 and 1996, by Caryl Churchill, Terry Johnston, Sarah Kane, Mark Ravenhill and Martin McDonagh.]
Yeats, W. B., ed. 1936. *The Oxford Book of Modern Verse, 1892–1935*. Oxford: Oxford UP.

Works by Individual Writers

A note on drama: since about 1960, the interest that the new British drama has created for itself is mirrored also on the book market. Hitherto, Samuel French Ltd. had specialised on acting editions of contemporary plays. Nowadays, playscripts and screenplays are readily available from other publishers, too, such as Methuen, Faber & Faber, Penguin Books, Nick Hern Books, or Colin Smythe (with a special interest in Irish drama). Readers should however be aware that the printed text that is perhaps available during the first run of a play may not yet reflect the alterations made during rehearsals, to be incorporated later in a revised version of the play-script (as in the case of Tom Stoppard's plays, or of Peter Shaffer's *Amadeus*). The same applies for screenplays, where there may be variation between shooting scripts and post-production scripts. For details of production, see the following three sources of reference:

Demastes, William W., and Katherine E. Kelly, comps. 1996. *British Playwrights, 1880–1956: A Research and Production Sourcebook*. Westport, Conn.: Greenwood Press.
Demastes, William W., and Bernice Schrank, comps. 1997. *Irish Playwrights, 1880–1995: A Research and Production Sourcebook*. Westport, Conn.: Greenwood Press.
Doollee.com: The Playwright's Database. http://doollee.com.

Agard, John. 2006. *We Brits*. Tarset: Bloodaxe Books.
Auden, W. H. 1988 ff. *Complete Works*. Ed. Edward Mendelson. [8] vols. Princeton: Princeton UP.
Berry, James, ed. 1984. *News for Babylon: The Chatto Book of Westindian-British Poetry*. London: Chatto & Windus.
Betjeman, John. 1970. *Collected Poems*. Ed. the Earl of Birkenhead. 1958. 3rd, enl. ed. London: Murray.
    1982. *Uncollected Poems*. Ed. Bevis Hillier. London: Murray.
Bond, Edward. 1978. *Plays: Two. "Lear", "The Sea", "Narrow Road to the Deep North", "Black Mass", "Passion". With an Introduction by the Author*. London: Eyre Methuen.
Churchill, Winston S. 1959. *The Second World War and an Epilogue on the Years 1945 to 1957*. London: Cassell.
D'Aguiar, Fred. 1993. *British Subjects*. Newcastle upon Tyne: Bloodaxe Books.
    2001. *An English Sampler: New and Selected Poems*. London: Chatto & Windus.
Doyle, Roddy. 1992. *The Barrytown Trilogy: "The Commitments"* [1987], *"The Snapper"* [1990], *"The Van"* [1991]. London: Secker and Warburg.
Eliot, T. S. 1969. *The Complete Poems and Plays*. London: Faber.
Farrell, J[ames]. G[ordon]. 1979. *The Singapore Grip*. 1978. London: Fontana.
Fenton, James. 1993. *Out of Danger*. Harmondsworth: Penguin.
    2006. *Selected Poems*. Harmondsworth: Penguin.
Fowles, John. 1977. *The French Lieutenant's Woman*. 1969. London: Triad Granada.
Friel, Brian. 1984. *Selected Plays*. London: Faber.
Friel, Brian. 1989. *Making History*. London: Faber.

Fuller, Roy. 1971. *Owls and Artificers: Oxford Lectures on Poetry*. London: Deutsch.

1973. *Professors and Gods: Last Oxford Lectures on Poetry*. London: Deutsch.

1985. *New and Collected Poems 1934–84*. London: Secker & Warburg.

Graves, Robert. 1975. *Collected Poems*. London: Cassell. Repr. 1987.

Greene, Graham. 1978. *The Human Factor*. London: The Bodley Head.

Harrison, Tony. 2007a. *Collected Poems*. London: Viking.

2007b. *Collected Film Poetry*. London: Faber.

Heaney, Seamus. 1995. *The Redress of Poetry*. London: Faber; New York: Farrar, Straus & Giroux, 1995. [Lectures as Oxford Professor of Poetry.]

1998. *Opened Ground: Selected Poems, 1966–1996*. New York: Farrar, Straus & Giroux.

Hughes, Ted. 1995. *New Selected Poems 1957–1994*. London: Faber.

1998. *Birthday Letters*. London: Faber, 1998.

Larkin, Philip. 1993. *Collected Poems*. Ed. Anthony Thwaite. 1988. London: Noonday Press.

McGrath, John, and Nadine Holdsworth. 2005. *John McGrath: Plays for England* (Exeter Performance Studies). Exeter: Exeter UP.

Mansfield, Katherine. 1984. *The Stories*. Ed. Anthony Alpers. Auckland: Oxford UP.

Nadolny, Sten. 1987. *Die Entdeckung der Langsamkeit*. 1983. München: Piper.

Osborne. John. 1960. *Look Back in Anger*. 1957. London: Faber. Repr. 1969.

Oswald, Alice. 2002. *Dart*. London: Faber.

2005. *Woods etc*. London: Faber.

2009. *A Sleepwalk on the Severn*. London: Faber.

Rhys, Jean [Ella Gwendolen Rees Williams]. 1966. *Wide Sargasso Sea*. London: Deutsch.

Rushdie, Salman. 1995. *Midnight's Children*. 1981. London: Vintage.

Shaffer, Peter. 1980. *Amadeus: A Play*. [First version.] London: Deutsch.

Repr. in: *Amadeus: A Play*. Ed. Rainer Lengeler. Stuttgart: Reclam. 1981.

Amadeus: A Play. [Revised version.] Harmondsworth: Penguin Books.

Shaffer, Peter. 1983. *Equus* [1973]. *With a Personal Essay by Peter Shaffer* ("An Introduction to three plays: *The Royal Hunt of the Sun*, *Equus* and *Amadeus*", vi–x., followed by "Author's notes on the play", xxv–xxvii). Ed. T. S. Pearce. Harlow: Longman.

Swift, Graham. 1999. *Waterland*. 1983. London: Picador.

Szirtes, George. 2001. *An English Apocalypse*. Tarset: Bloodaxe Books.

Thomas, Dylan. 1971. *The Poems*. Ed. Daniel Jones. London: Dent.

Winterson, Jeanette. 1990. *Sexing the Cherry*. 1989. London: Vintage.

Woolf, Virginia. 1943. *The Waves*. 1931. Uniform Edition. London: The Hogarth Press.

Woolf, Virginia. 1993. "*A Room of One's Own*", "*Three Guineas*". Ed. Michèle Barrett. Repr. Harmondsworth: Penguin, 2000.

Yeats, W. B. 1966. *The Variorum Edition of the Poems of W. B. Yeats*. Eds. Peter Allt and Russell K. Alspach. 1957. 3rd, corr. ed. New York: Macmillan.

Surveys of the Period and Studies in Individual Genres or Notable Writers

Achilles, Jochen. 1996. *Irische Dramatiker der Gegenwart*. Darmstadt: Wissenschaftliche Buchgesellschaft.

Alderman, Nigel. 2009. *A Concise Companion to Postwar British and Irish Poetry*. Malden, Mass.: Wiley-Blackwell.

Arana, R. Victoria, ed. 2007. *Black British Aesthetics Torday*. Newcastle: Cambridge Scholars Press.

Arana, R. Victoria, ed. 2009. *Twenty-First Century "Black" British Writers* (Dictionary of Literary Biography, 347). Detroit: Gale.

Aston, Elaine, and Janelle Reinelt, eds. 2000. *The Cambridge Companion to Modern British Women Playwrights*. Cambridge: Cambridge UP.

Aston, Elaine. 2003. *Feminist Views on the English Stage: Women Playwrights 1990–2000*. Cambridge: Cambridge UP.

Attridge, Derek, ed. 1990. *The Cambridge Companion to James Joyce*. Cambridge: Cambridge UP.

Barker, Jonathan, *comp*. 1995. *Poetry in Britain and Ireland since 1970*. London: The British Council. [Select bibliography.]

Barnes, Philip, comp. 1986. *A Companion to Post-War British Theatre*. Totowa, NJ: Barnes & Noble.

Bartels, Anke. 1996. *Judiths erfolgreiche Schwester: Die Stücke Caryl Churchills im theater- und dramengeschichtlichen Kontext*. Frankfurt a. M.: P. Lang.

Berney, K. A., and N. G. Templeton, eds. 1994. *Contemporary British Dramatists*. London and Detroit: St. James Press.

Beyer, Manfred. 1996. *Das englische Drama des 20. Jahrhunderts*. Tübingen: Francke.

Bignell, Jonathan, Stephen Lacey and Madeleine Macmurraugh-Kavanagh, eds. 2000. *British Television Drama: Past, Present and Future*. Basingstoke: Palgrave Macmillan.

Billington, Michael. 1993. *One Night Stands: A Critic's View of Modern British Theatre*. London: Nick Hern Books.

Blamires, Harry. 1988. *The New Bloomsday Book. A Guide through "Ulysses": Rev. Ed. Keyed to the Corrected Text*. London: Routledge.

Bloom, Clive. 2002. *Bestsellers: Popular Fiction since 1900*. Basingstoke: Palgrave Macmillan.

Bode, Christoph, and Ulrich Broich, eds. 1998. *Die Zwanziger Jahre in Großbritannien: Literatur und Gesellschaft einer spannungsreichen Dekade*. Tübingen: Narr.

Boltwood, Scott. 2007. *Brian Friel, Ireland, and The North*. Cambridge: Cambridge UP.

Bort, Eberhard, ed. 1996. *The State of Play: Irish Theatre in the 'Nineties*. Trier: Wissenschaftlicher Verlag Trier.

Brandt, George W., ed. 1993. *British Television Drama in the 1980s*. Cambridge: Cambridge UP.

Broom, Sarah. 2006. *Contemporary British and Irish Poetry: An Introduction*. Basingstoke: Palgrave Macmillan.

Brown, Ian, and Alan Riach. 2009. *The Edinburgh Companion to Twentieth-Century Scottish Literature*. Edinburgh: Edinburgh UP.

Burke, Sean. 1998. *The Death and Return of the Author: Criticism and Subjectivity in Barthes, Foucault and Derrida*. 2nd ed. Edinburgh: Edinburgh: UP.

Byrne, Ophelia. 1997. *The Stage in Ulster from the Eighteenth Century*. Belfast: Linen Hall Library.

Cahalan, James M. 1993. *Modern Irish Literature and Culture: A Chronology*. New York: G. K. Hall.

Carlson, Julia, ed. 1990. *Banned in Ireland: Censorship and the Irish Writer*. London: Routledge.

Caughie, John. 2000. *Television Drama: Realism, Modernism, and British Culture*. Oxford Television Studies. Oxford: Oxford UP.

Cheshire, D. F. 1974. *Music Hall in Britain*. Newton Abbot: David & Charles.

Childs, Peter. 1998. *The Twentieth Century in Poetry*. London: Routledge.

Childs, Peter, and Michael Storry, eds. 1999. *Encyclopedia of Contemporary British Culture*. London: Routledge.

Connor, Steven. 1996. *The English Novel in History, 1950–1995*. London: Routledge.

Corcoran, Neil, ed. 2008. *The Cambridge Companion to Twentieth-Century Poetry*. Cambridge: Cambridge UP.

Corcoran, Neil. 1993. *English Poetry since 1940* (Longman Literature in English). Harlow: Longman.

Crook, Tim. 1999. *Radio Drama: Theory and Practice*. London: Routledge.

Crawford, Robert, and Thom Nairn. 1991. *The Arts of Alasdair Gray*. Edinburgh: Edinburgh UP.

Davis, Geoffrey V., and Anne Fuchs, eds 2006. *Staging New Britain: Aspects of Black and South Asian British Theatre Practice*. Frankfurt a. M.: Lang.

Davison, Peter. 1982. *Contemporary Drama and the Popular Dramatic Tradition in England*. London: Macmillan.

D'Monté, Rebecca, and Graham Saunders, eds. 2008. *Cool Britannia: British Political Drama in the 1990s*. Basingstoke: Palgrave Macmillan. [Includes essays on Scottish, Feminist and In-Yer-Face Theatre.]

Draper, R. P. 1998. *An Introduction to Twentieth-Century Poetry in English*. Oxford: Blackwell.

Duguid, Mark [2005]. "The Television Play: The Rise and Fall of the Single Drama". *Screenonline*. Ed. British Film Institute. http://www.screenonline.org.uk/tv/id/445349.

Edgar, David. 2008a. "Too True? The Achievements and Limitations of Fact-Based Theatre". Part of "Section II: The Documentary Turn", ed. by Christiane Schlote and Eckart Voigts-Virchow for *Anglistentag 2007 Münster: Proceedings*. Ed. Klaus Stierstorfer. Trier: Wissenschaftlicher Verlag Trier. 103–14. [The whole section, pp. 95–178, deals with documentaries and 'mockumentaries' or fakes on stage and screen.]

Edgar, David. 2008b. "Doc and Dram". *The Guardian* 27 September 2008.

Ellmann, Richard. 1983. *James Joyce*. 1959. 2nd, rev. ed. 1982, repr. with corrections. Oxford: Oxford UP.

Erzgräber, Willi. 1993. *Virginia Woolf: Eine Einführung*. 2nd, rev. and enl. ed. Tübingen: Francke.

Erzgräber, Willi. 1999. *Der englische Roman von Joseph Conrad bis Graham Greene*. Tübingen: Francke. [Incl. an extensive bibliography.]

Fitz-Simon, Christopher. 2004. *Players and Painted Stage: Aspects of the Twentieth-Century Theatre in Ireland*. Dublin: New Island.

Forshaw, Barry. 2007. *The Rough Guide to Crime Fiction*. London: Rough Guides.

Füger, Wilhelm. 1994. *James Joyce: Epoche – Werk – Wirkung*. München: Beck.

Fussell, Paul. 1975. *The Great War and Modern Memory*. Oxford: Oxford UP.

Gardiner, Michael, and Willy Maley. 2009. *The Edinburgh Companion to Muriel Spark*. Edinburgh: Edinburgh UP.

Gilbert, Stuart. 1963. *James Joyce's "Ulysses"": A Study*. 1930. Harmondsworth: Penguin Books.

Gill, A. A. 1996. "Harold Pauses, Antonia is Silent. A. A. Gill studies a Pinteresque husband and wife in the Ivy, and Mr. Pinter's new play on the printed page". *The Spectator* 28 September 1996, 31.

Godiwala, Dimple, ed. 2006. *Alternatives within the Mainstream: British Black and Asian Theatres*. Newcastle: Cambridge Scholars Press.

Gonzalez, Alexander G., ed. 1997. *Modern Irish Writers: A Bio-Critical Sourcebook*. Westport, Conn.: Greenwood Press.

Grene, Nicholas, ed. 1999. *The Politics of Irish Drama: Plays in Context from Boucicault to Friel*. Cambridge: Cambridge UP.

Griffin, Gabriele. 2003. *Contemporary Black and Asian Women Playwrights in Britain*. Cambridge: Cambridge UP.

Griffiths, Trevor R., and Margaret Llewellyn-Jones, eds. 1993. *British and Irish Women Dramatists since 1958: A Critical Handbook*. Buckingham: Open UP.

Haberstroh, Patricia Boyle, ed. 1996. *Women Creating Women: Contemporary Irish Women Poets*. New York: Syracuse UP.

Hagemann, Susanne. 1996. *Studies in Scottish Fiction: 1945 to the Present*. Frankfurt a. M.: Lang.

Hamilton, Ian, ed. 1994. *The Oxford Companion to Twentieth-Century Poetry in English*. Oxford: Oxford UP.

Hanke, Michael, ed. 1997. *Englische Gedichte des 20. Jahrhunderts*. Stuttgart: Reclam.

Harrington, John P. 1999. *Politics and Performance in Contemporary Northern Ireland*. Amherst: Univ. of Massachusetts Press.

Harte, Liam, and Yvonne Whelan, eds. 2007. *Ireland Beyond Boundaries: Mapping Irish Studies in the Twenty-First Century*. London: Pluto.

Head, Dominic. 2002. *The Cambridge Introduction to Modern British Fiction, 1950–2002*. Cambridge: Cambridge UP.

Hewitt, Douglas. 1988. *English Fiction of the Modern Period 1890–1940*. Harlow: Longman.

Hogan, Robert, et al., eds. 1975–92. *The Modern Irish Drama: A Documentary History*. 6 vols. Dublin: Dolmen Press.

Holdsworth, Nadine, and Mary Luckhurst, eds. 2008. *A Concise Companion to Contemporary British and Irish Drama*. Oxford: Blackwell.

Hühn, Peter. 1995. *Geschichte der englischen Lyrik*. 2 vols. Tübingen: Francke.

Imhof, Rüdiger. 2002. *The Modern Irish Novel: Irish Novelists after 1945*. Dublin: Wolfhound Press.

Innes, Christopher. 1992. *Modern British Drama 1890–1990*. Cambridge: Cambridge UP.

Jordan, Eamonn, ed. 2000. *Theatre Stuff: Critical Essays on Contemporary Irish Drama*. Dublin: Carysfort Press.

Jordan, Eamonn. 2010. *Dissident Dramaturgies: Contemporary Irish Theatre*. Dublin: Irish Academic Press.

Kendall, Tim, ed. 2007. *The Oxford Handbook of British and Irish War Poetry*. Oxford: Oxford UP.

Kennedy-Andrews, Elmer. 2003. *Fiction and the Northern Ireland Troubles since 1969: (De-)Constructing the North*. Dublin: Four Courts Press.

Kennedy-Andrews, Elmer. 2008. *Writing Home: Poetry and Place in Northern Ireland, 1968–2008*. Cambridge: Brewer.

Kerensky, Oleg. 1977. *The New British Drama: Fourteen Playwrights since Osborne and Pinter*. London: Hamish Hamilton.

Kift, Dagmar. 1991. *Arbeiterkultur im gesellschaftlichen Konflikt: Die englische Music Hall im 19. Jahrhundert*. Essen: Klartext Verlag.

Kirkland, Richard. 1996. *Literature and Culture in Northern Ireland since 1965: Moments of Danger*. Harlow: Longman.

Klaus, H. Gustav. 2004. *James Kelman*. Tavistock: Northcote House and The British Council.

Korte, Barbara, and Claudia Sternberg. 2004. *Bidding for the Mainstream? Black and Asian British Film since the 1990s*. Amsterdam: Rodopi.

Kövesi, Simon. 2007. *James Kelman*. Manchester: Manchester UP.

Krewani, Angela. 2001. *Hybride Formen: New British Cinema – Television Drama –Hypermedia*. Trier: Wissenschaftlicher Verlag Trier.

Krieger, Gottfried. 1998. Das englische Drama des 20. Jahrhunderts. Stuttgart: Klett.

Lacey, Stephen. 1995. *British Realist Theatre: The New Wave in Its Context 1956–1965*. London: Routledge.

Levenson, Michael, ed. 1999. *The Cambridge Companion to Modernism*. Cambridge: Cambridge UP.

Lloyd, Matthew, comp. 2008. *The Music Hall and Theatre Site*. http://www.arthurlloyd.co.uk/index.html

Lodge, David. 1971. *"The Novelist at the Crossroads"* [1969] *and Other Essays on Fiction and Criticism*. London: Routledge & Kegan Paul. [Title essay on pp. 3–34.]

Lodge, David. 1992. "The Novelist Today: Still at the Crossroads?". *New Writing [1]*. Eds. Malcolm Bradbury and Judy Cooke. London: Minerva. 203–15.

Lonergan, Patrick. 2010. *Theatre and Globalization: Irish Drama in the Celtic Tiger Era*. Basingstoke: Palgrave Macmillan.

Low, Gail Ching-Liang, and Marion Wynne-Davies, eds. 2006. *A Black British Canon?* Basingstoke: Palgrave Macmillan.

Luckhurst, Mary, ed. 2006. *A Companion to Modern British and Irish Drama, 1880–2005*. Oxford: Blackwell.

Maack, Annegret, and Rüdiger Imhof, eds. 1993. *Radikalität und Mäßigung: Der englische Roman seit 1960*. Darmstadt: Wissenschaftliche Buchgesellschaft.

Mc Cormack, W[illiam]. J[ohn]., ed. 1999. *The Blackwell Companion to Modern Irish Culture*. Oxford: Blackwell.

McCulloch, Margery. 2009. *Scottish Modernism and its Contexts, 1918–1959: Literature, National Identity and Cultural Exchange*. Edinburgh: Edinburgh UP.

McGlynn, Mary M. 2008. *Narratives of Class in New Irish and Scottish Literature: From Joyce to Kelman, Doyle, Galloway, and McNamee*. New York: Palgrave Macmillan.

McGuire, Matt. 2009. *Contemporary Scottish Literature*. London: Palgrave Macmillan.

Mack, Douglas S. 2006. *Scottish Fiction and the British Empire*. Edinburgh: Edinburgh UP.

Mander, Raymond, and Joe Mitchenson. 1965. *British Music Hall: A Story in Pictures*. London: Studio Vista.

Mengel, Ewald. 2004. Das englische Drama des 20. Jahrhunderts: Eine Einführung in seine Klassiker. Tübingen: Stauffenburg.

Miller, Jane Eldridge, ed. 2001. *Who's Who in Contemporary Women's Writing*. London: Routledge.

Mitter, Shomit, and Maria Shevtsova, eds. 2005. *Fifty Key Theatre Directors*. London: Routledge.

Monahan, Barry. 2009. *Ireland's Theatre on Film: Style, Stories and the National Stage on Screen*. Dublin: Irish Academic Press.

Morrison, Blake. 1980. *The Movement: English Poetry and Fiction of the 1950s*. Oxford: Oxford UP. New ed. London: Routledge, 1986.

Mühleisen, Susanne. 2009. "American Adaptations: Language Ideology and the Language Divide in Cross-Atlantic Translations". *Americanisms: Discourses of Exception, Exclusion, Exchange*. Ed. Michael Steppat. Heidelberg: Winter. 377–93.

Müller, Klaus Peter, ed. 1993. *Englisches Theater der Gegenwart: Geschichte(n) und Strukturen*. Tübingen: Narr.

Murphy, Neil. 2008. *British Asian Fiction: Framing the Contemporary*. Amherst, N.Y.: Cambria Press.

Murphy, Paula. 2008. *The Shattered Mirror: Irish Literature and Film, 1990–2005*. Newcastle upon Tyne: Cambridge Scholars.

Murray, Christopher. 2000. *Twentieth-Century Irish Drama: Mirror Up to Nation*. 1997. Syracuse, N.Y.: Syracuse UP.

Murray, Isobel, ed. 1996–2008. *Scottish Writers Talking*. 4 vols. East Linton: Tuckwell Press.

Nightingale, Benedict. 1982. *A Reader's Guide to Fifty Modern British Plays*. London: Heinemann.

Norris, Margot. 1998. *A Companion to Joyce's "Ulysses"*. Boston, Mass.: Bedford Books of St. Martin's Press.

Nowak, Helge. 1997. "A. S. Byatt's *Possession* for British and for American Readers". *Erfurt Electronic Studies in English*. http://webdoc.sub.gwdg.de/edoc/eese/artic97/nowak/8_97.html.

Nünning, Ansgar. 1998. *Der englische Roman des 20. Jahrhunderts*. Stuttgart: Klett.

Nünning, Vera, ed. 2007. *Der zeitgenössische englische Roman: Genres – Entwicklungen – Modellinterpretationen*. Trier: Wissenschaftlicher Verlag Trier.

O'Neill, Maggie. 2009. *Twentieth-Century British and Irish Poetry*. Oxford: Blackwell.

Oppel, Horst, ed. 1976. *Das englische Drama der Gegenwart: Interpretationen*. Berlin: Schmidt.

Owusu, Kwesi, ed. 2000. *Black British Culture and Society: A Text Reader*. London: Routledge.

Page, Norman. 1990. *The Thirties in Britain*. London: Macmillan.

Parker, Michael. 2007. *Northern Irish Literature, 1956–2006: The Imprint of History*. 2 vols. Basingstoke: Palgrave Macmillan.

Perkins, David. 1976–87. *A History of Modern Poetry*. 2 vols. Cambridge, Mass.: Harvard UP.

Peters, Susanne, Klaus Stierstorfer and Laurenz Volkmann, eds. 2006. *Teaching Contemporary Literature and Culture: Drama*. 2 vols. Trier: Wissenschaftlicher Verlag Trier.

Pierce, David. 2005. *Light, Freedom and Song: A Cultural History of Modern Irish Writing*. New Haven: Yale UP.

Plett, Heinrich, eds. 1982. *Englisches Drama von Beckett bis Bond*. München: Fink.

Porter, James. 2009. *Genre, Conflict, Presence: Traditional Ballads in a Modernizing World*. Trier: Wissenschaftlicher Verlag Trier.

Powell, Kerry, ed. 2004. *The Cambridge Companion to Victorian and Edwardian Theatre*. Cambridge: Cambridge UP.

Press, John. 1969. *A Map of Modern English Verse*. London: Oxford UP.

Quinn, Justin. 2008. *The Cambridge Introduction to Modern Irish Poetry, 1800–2000*. Cambridge: Cambridge UP.

Raab, Michael. 1989. *"The music hall is dying": Die Thematisierung der Unterhaltungsindustrie im englischen Gegenwartsdrama*. Tübingen: Niemeyer.

Rabey, David Ian. 2003. *English Drama since 1940*. Harlow: Longman/Pearson Education.

Richards, Shaun, ed. 2004. *The Cambridge Companion to Twentieth-Century Irish Drama*. Cambridge: Cambridge UP.

Roche, Anthony. 2009. *Contemporary Irish Drama: From Beckett to McGuinness*. 2nd, rev. ed. Basingstoke: Palgrave Macmillan.

Roe, Sue, and Susan Sellers, eds. 2000. *The Cambridge Companion to Virginia Woolf*. Cambridge: Cambridge UP.

Rothkirch, Alyce von. 2007. *The Place of Wales: Staging Place in Contemporary Welsh Drama in English*. Trier: Wissenschaftlicher Verlag Trier.

Ryan, Ray, ed. 2000. *Writing in the Irish Republic: Literature, Culture, Politics, 1949–1999*. Basingstoke: Macmillan.

Sabo, Gabi. 1995. *Das alternative Theater in Thatchers Großbritannien*. Frankfurt a.M.: Lang.

Saunders, Graham, and Rebecca D'Monte, eds. 2007. *Cool Britannia: Political Theatre in the 1990s*. Basingstoke: Palgrave.

Schneider, Ulrich. 1984. *Die Londoner Music Hall und ihre Songs 1850–1920*. Tübingen: Niemeyer.

Shaffer, Brian W., ed. 2005. *A Companion to the British and Irish Novel, 1945–2000*. Oxford: Blackwell.

Sheehan, Helena. 2001. *Irish Television Drama: A Society and Its Stories*. 1987. Revised version Dublin: Radio Telefis Éireann. For extracts, see http://www.comms.dcu.ie/sheehan/60s-itvd.htm.

Shepherd, Simon. 2009. *The Cambridge Introduction to Modern British Theatre*. Cambridge: Cambridge UP.

Shiach, Morag, ed. 2007. *The Cambridge Companion to the Modernist Novel*. Cambridge: Cambridge UP.

Shields, Kathleen. 2000. *Gained in Translation: Language, Poetry and Identity in Twentieth-Century Ireland*. Frankfurt a.M.: Lang.

Sierz, Aleks. 2001. *In-Yer-Face Theatre: British Drama Today*. London: Faber. Updated on the website http://www.inyerface-theatre.com/.

Stein, Mark. 2004. *Black British Literature: Novels of Transformation*. Columbus: Ohio State UP.

Sternlicht, Sanford V. 1998. *A Reader's Guide to Modern Irish Drama*. Syracuse: Syracuse UP.

Szabo, Carmen. 2007. *"Clearing the Ground": The Field Day Theatre Company and the Construction of Irish Identities*. Cambridge: Cambridge Scholars Publishing.

Thomsen, Christian W. 1980. *Das englische Theater der Gegenwart*. Düsseldorf: Bagel.

Thomsen, Christian W. 1985. "Weil doch die inneren Bilder viel schöner sind: Das englische Hörspiel". *Grundzüge der Geschichte des europäischen Hörspiels*. Eds. C.W. Thomsen and Irmela Schneider. Darmstadt: Wissenschaftliche Buchgesellschaft. 7–44.

Thomson, Brian Lindsay. 2009. *Graham Greene and the Politics of Popular Fiction and Film*. Basingstoke: Palgrave Macmillan.

Thwaite, Anthony. 1996. *Poetry Today: A Critical Guide to British Poetry 1960–1995*. Harlow: Longman.

Tönnies, Merle, ed. 2008. *Das englische Drama der Gegenwart: Kategorien – Entwicklungen – Modellinterpretationen*. Trier: Wissenschaftlicher Verlag Trier.

Vormann, Hartmut. 2001. *The Art of Lennox Robinson: Theoretical Premises and Theatrical Practice*. Trier: Wissenschaftlicher Verlag Trier.

Wallace, Gavin. 1994. *The Scottish Novel since the Seventies: New Visions, Old Dreams*. Edinburgh: Edinburgh UP.

Welch, Robert. 1999. *The Abbey Theatre 1899–1999: Form and Pressure*. Oxford: Oxford UP.

Worth, K. J. 1973. *Revolutions in Modern English Drama*. London: Bell. [With a survey of pre-1956 dramatic realism.]

Wu, Duncan. 1995. *Six Contemporary Dramatists: Bennett, Potter, Gray, Brenton, Hare, Ayckbourn*. Basingstoke: Macmillan.

Index

Subject Index

Abbey Theatre 320, 324–26, 471, 501–05, 510, 512

accentual verse 6, 341, 433–41, 462, 467

actor-manager 147, 304–05

adaptation (of a literary work in another literary work) *see* intertextuality

Aestheticism 137, 312, 339, 383, 398, 500

air 79–80, 86, 349

allegory 13–14, 109–10, 177, 208, 539

Alliterative Revival 9, 10, 14

Angel in the House 292–93, 297, 376

Angry Young Men 488, 522

answer poem 81, 183–91, 192, 453

Arthurian literature 7, 9–12, 23, 108–10, 328, 426, 540

assonance 438

autobiography 18, 119, 204–07, 274, 401, 505, 573

Augustan Age 128, 151–52, 163

ballad 8, 12–13, 79, 131, 175–78, 248, 266, 282, 346–48, 393, 415, 435, 446–47; *see also* ballad opera, Chevy Chase stanza, hanging ballad

ballad opera 131, 154–56, 176

Beautiful, the *see Sublime* 111, 136–38, 170, 171, 201, 209, 245

Beowulf 3–6

Benevolence 124, 200, 201, 232

biography 118, 202–06, 294, 450, 500–01, 588

Black British literature *see* postcolonial literature and criticism

blank verse 51, 55–62, 65, 68, 88–89, 96, 115, 151–54, 170, 175, 187, 190, 205, 317, 323, 328–37, 423, 439, 448–49, 466–67, 483

blazon 86, 92, 95, 101

Book of Common Prayer 32, 34, 35, 113

bluestocking 188, 294, 297, 374

'bowdlerise, to' 150, 159, 261, 408, 413

boys' weeklies 397, 405

Breton lay 10, 13, 16

burlesque *and* burletta 131, 146, 309

Byronic Hero 167, 208, 243, 246, 482, 606

canonisation 17, 82–83, 129–30, 206, 237, 263–64, 451, 463, 476, 558

Cavalier Poets 85, 92

censorship 19, 39, 83, 86, 120–21, 143, 145, 263–64, 386–87, 504, 539, 554–55; *stage censorship* 35, 38–39, 146, 154–56, 302–05, 314, 471–73, 488, 491, 505

circulating libraries 143, 262–63, 372

chapbook 12, 144, 220–21, 407

Chevy Chase stanza (ballad metre) 176, 282, 347

children's literature 400–18, 540–42

Christmas books 404

chronicle play *see* history play

city comedy 77–78, 485

class, treatment of 31, 317, 367–69, 390, 415, 449, 488, 491–92, 503, 521–22, 561

closet play 88, 89, 159, 203, 315

codex 2, 340

colonial, colonialist, anti-colonial fiction 283–91

comedy *see* city comedy, comedy of errors, comedy of humours, comedy of manners, romantic comedy, satiric comedy, sentimental comedy

comedy of humours 75–76, 148

comedy of manners 124, 147–150, 300–01, 312, 478

'comedy of menace' 489

comic relief 37, 59, 203

'comic epic poem in prose' 231

community theatre 472, 490

conceit 82, 87–88, 91, 95, 337

concrete poetry/shaped verse 90, 433, 453, 459

Condition of England novel 271, 367–69

consonance, half-rhyme and para-rhyme 344–45, 424, 436, 439, 441, 452–53

copyright 143, 265–66, 308

country-house poem 85, 108

court masque 37, 66, 77

crime fiction 356, 361, 378–84, 497, 526–34; *spy fiction and thriller* 280, 287, 384, 418, 475, 497, 520, 531–34, 541

De casibus tragedy 55–57

decorum 138, 152

detective fiction *see* crime fiction

diary 203, 204–05

Diaspora *see* postcolonial literature and criticism

didactic literature 38–39, 76, 134, 152–52, 164, 216–19, 231, 405

documentary theatre/docudrama 472, 514–15

domestic tragedy 65–66, 153

drama *see* comedy, docudrama, drama of ideas, drawing room play, heroic play, history play, legitimate drama, melodrama, memory play, miracle play, morality play, mystery play, peasant play, poetic drama, problem play, television play, tragedy, tragicomedy *and* well-made play

drama of ideas 303, 314–15

dramatic monologue 328, 333–34, 336–38, 361, 422, 431, 442, 446–47, 452, 455–56, 593

drawing room play 477–81

dream vision 14–15, 25

Dub Poetry 456–57

dumb show *see* pantomime

dystopia *see* utopia

elegy 4, 82, 86, 106–07, 168–69, 328–32, 436, 465

Elizabethan World Picture 33

empiricism 33

Englishness 152–53, 159–61, 411, 448–58, 552

epic 4–5, 12, 105–12, 129, 328, 333; *see also* long poem, mock-epic

epigram 85, 166

epiphany 392, 545

epistle *see* letter writing

epistolary novel/novel-in-letters 199, 227–30

epithalamion 25, 84, 97, 106, 437

essay 198, 200–03

Evangelicalism 174, 238

fable 76, 129

fabliaux 16

fairy tale 217, 407, 409, 414, 416, 559

fallen woman 298–300

fancy *see* imagination

fantasy literature 12, 214–25, 310, 389–90, 414–18, 534–42, 556; *see also* science fiction *and* utopia

farce 75, 294, 310–11, 494

femme fatale 52, 53, 110, 153, 177, 286

Field Day Theatre Company 463, 508

film version (of a literary work) 43–47, 59, 65, 251, 290–91, 372, 473–77, 497, 516, 549, 588, 591–92

folk literature 21–23, 79, 131, 175–76, 217, 324, 346–47, 406; *see also* orality

forgery 22–23

formal realism *see* realism

formula fiction 397

free indirect discourse 241, 365, 376, 384, 387, 389, 392, 399, 543, 546

free verse 337, 425–31, 434, 465

Fringe theatre 472, 491

gender relations 17, 38, 75, 93, 149, 155, 182–91, 225–30, 291–304, 310, 311, 316, 331, 369–70, 512–13, 530–31, 554–9

Gentleman, ideal of the 117

Georgian Poets 342–43
Gothic literature 59, 142, 242–47, 379–82, 391–94, 531, 559; see also vampire stories
Grand Tour 197, 208–9, 210, 213, 246, 278
graphic novel 196, 591
Group, The 445
Grub Street 141

haiku 426, 433, 465
half-rhyme see consonance
hanging ballad 347–48, 447
heroic couplet 16, 108, 140, 151, 163, 166, 167, 186, 337
heroic play 151, 153–54
heroic poetry 4–5; see epic
historical fiction 239, 247–53, 361–65, 408–09, 522–26, 540–41, 570–74
historiography 116, 128, 272, 524
history play 41–55, 317–20, 332–33, 492–94, 495, 508–09, 516
Home Tour 21, 213–14
homosexuality 100, 104, 229, 263–64, 295, 302, 478–81, 491–92, 500, 514, 531, 555–57, 563, 578
Humanism 115–18
humours, theory of the 33–34, 75–76, 124
hymn 89, 173–5, 281–82, 349

illuminated printing 194–96
imagination 134–36
Imagism 426
imitation 17, 64, 95, 106, 129, 133, 158, 162–64; see also pastiche
imperial romance see romance
incremental repetition 330, 446, 176
industrial novel 367–69
'In Memoriam' stanza 329
interior monologue 544, 546, 548, 565, 582, 584, 590
interlude 73
intermediality 147, 155, 194, 196, 473–77, 550, 591–93; see also film version
'international theme' 266, 365–66, 417
intertextuality 328, 333, 409, 435, 498–501, 511, 586–93; see also answer poem, imitation, parody, pastiche
Ireland, literature from or about 6, 21–3, 36, 44, 198, 215, 239, 303–04, 320–26, 391–93, 461–466, 476–77, 501–12, 559–63, 592; see also Irish Renaissance, Stage Irishman
Irish Renaissance 22, 322–6

Kailyard School 396
Kitchen Sink Drama 490, 522
Künstlerroman 383–84

Lake School Poets 177
Lallans ("synthetic Scots") 458, 563
letter writing 183–86, 192–194, 196–199
light verse 349–50, 428, 444
literacy and illiteracy 144, 259
literary communication 1, 34–6, 127–44, 192–221, 255–68
literary criticism 123–24, 142, 190–01, 193, 202–03, 232, 258, 290, 428–29
Liverpool Poets 445–46, 457
long poem 14–17, 105–08, 167–69, 176–77, 281, 328–31, 408, 422, 426–29, 446, 450–54, 458, 463–64, 485, 557, 582–83

madrigal 79–80, 95, 437
Madwoman in the Attic 252, 297, 372, 589, 606
magic realism 245, 417–18, 519, 559, 575–77
manuscript system (circulation of MSS.) 79, 81, 91, 98, 103, 112, 185–86, 192–94, 221, 340
melodrama 146–47, 151, 159, 177, 299–300, 304–17, 322, 354, 358–61, 402, 470, 478, 511
memory play 489–90
Metaphysical Poetry 82, 85–92, 102, 337, 428, 430
meta-literature 44, 62, 72, 74, 179, 181, 202, 311, 328, 340, 377, 394, 430–33, 462–63, 494, 502, 509, 519, 524–25, 548–52, 556, 564–65, 572, 575–76, 583, 586–89
migration (of writers and characters) 436, 448, 453–57, 467, 472, 510, 517, 530, 574–77, 584–85, 609; see also travel
miles gloriosus or military braggart 45, 72–73, 571
mimesis 133, 140
miracle play 19, 24
mock epic/mock-heroic poem 110, 129–31, 138–39, 153–54, 158, 162, 166–68, 182–83, 231, 234, 237, 349, 428
Modernism 6, 88, 235, 247, 289, 337–38, 341, 366, 373, 377, 384, 387, 398–99, 421 ff.
moral tale 144, 218–19, 228, 286, 391, 395, 400, 404–05, 410, 414, 542
morality play 19–20, 25, 39, 41, 57, 73
Movement, The 445–45, 450, 617
'Mrs Grundy' 264, 295, 301
Mudie's 262–64
multicultural literature 1–2, 7, 25, 206–07, 285–86, 453–58, 516–17, 529–30, 570, 578–79, 585–86, 612; see also postcolonial literature and criticism
musical drama 146, 151, 309; opera 12, 68, 146–47, 151–59, 162, 209, 237, 251, 253, 299, 302, 304, 309–10, 349, 383, 438, 502; musical 12, 65, 317, 327, 428, 470, 473–74,

479, 495, 498–99, 541, 548; see also burletta and melodrama
music hall 304–06, 327, 349, 470, 488–89, 492, 516, 599, 610–11, 618
mystery play 19, 24, 485

narrative poem see long poem, ballad, epic, mock-epic and verse romance
Naturalism 311–12, 326, 347, 384–85, 481, 503, 520, 522; see also Ibsen
Neoclassicism 53, 70, 84, 127–45, 150–57, 162–92, 201–02, 209, 213, 216, 231, 244, 327, 426, 432, 450, 466, 485, 500, 603–07
New Criticism and New Historicism 67–69, 269, 602
New Woman 263, 293, 303, 316
Newgate Prison and Newgate Novel 11, 226, 307, 351, 359–62, 379–80
New Generation and Next Generation Poets 447, 451–53
nonsense verse 256, 278, 350, 406, 415
novel 121, 124, 142–44, 199, 222–54, 256, 261–67, 283–91, 295–99, 351–419, 518–94; novel of development (Bildungsroman) 238, 371, 386, 555, 563, 564, 578; novel of manners 150, 239–42, 293, 365–67; see also Condition of England novel, crime fiction, epistolary novel/novel in letters, historical fiction, Künstlerroman, Newgate novel, sensational novel, social novel
novella 63–64, 265–66, 279, 288–90, 324, 365, 390, 393–94, 397, 475, 533, 564–66
nursery rhyme 217–19, 346, 406, 415, 434, 454, 527

ode (Pindaric and Horatian) 23, 29, 82, 85, 89, 106, 115, 160–161, 169–75, 181, 191–93, 197, 216, 327, 329, 346, 350, 422, 424, 434, 445, 450, 456, 465–66, 469; see also hymn
opera see musical drama
orality and oral literature 2–5, 12–13, 22–23, 79–80, 131, 139, 144, 155–56, 159–61, 175–76, 195, 206–07, 216–17, 221, 266, 269, 289, 346, 350, 374, 391, 393, 406, 412–14, 435, 445, 458, 463, 524, 583, 585, 596; see also folk literature
Orientalism 211–12, 242–44, 279–80, 284–86, 334, 407, 611
originality 64, 88, 95–96, 109–10, 134–36, 140, 172, 174, 179–81, 194, 299, 325, 327, 338, 344, 346, 416, 431–33, 453
ottava rima 16, 95, 106, 244, 422, 424, 435, 454
Oxford Professor of Poetry 269, 273, 429, 437–38, 440, 447, 451, 461–65

pantomime 146–47, 225, 310, 327, 495; *dumb show* 58, 62, 63

pastiche 328, 511, 547–48, 553, 557, 581, 587–88

pastoral literature 62, 74–75, 82, 84, 88–91, 98, 106–09, 121–22, 136, 169, 182, 342–43

para-rhyme *see* consonance

'parlour poetry' 327, 330, 341, 607

parody 16, 78, 101, 129, 146, 153–55, 163, 167, 179, 183–84, 215, 223, 228–33, 238, 245, 247, 253, 267, 309, 349–50, 377, 380, 407, 411, 414–16, 428, 444, 449, 476, 489–90, 497, 538, 589, 603, 605; *see also* mock epic

patent house 145–47, 304–05

patronage 24, 38, 81, 85, 93, 99, 108, 139–41, 145–46, 197, 496

peasant play 322–25, 504–07, 510–11

'penny dreadfuls' 258, 379–82, 405

performance poetry 83, 277–78, 438, 446–47, 455–57, 467; *see also* Dub Poetry

periodicals, literary 142, 145, 197, 200–03, 218, 256–58, 265, 268, 298, 306, 339–41, 349, 370, 375, 377, 381, 391, 393, 397–98, 451, 537, 547, 560, 600, 607

periodisation, problem of 127–31, 140, 421–22, 519, 542–43

Petrarchism 80, 85–86, 94–95, 101

picaresque narrative 122, 229

Picturesque, the 136–40, 170, 177–78, 209, 213

playhouses 18–19, 36–41, 145–47, 159, 162, 304–10, 320–26, 469–73, 490, 494, 498, 501–12, 515

poetic diction 138–39, 152, 170, 180, 187, 231, 342

poetic drama 323–24, 332–33, 336, 342, 427, 449–51, 481–85, 513

poetic justice 51, 69, 76, 152, 154, 226–27, 257, 299, 308–09, 374

Poet Laureate 6, 12, 17, 141, 167, 248, 280–81, 329–31, 430, 438, 443, 448, 450–51, 459

Poets' Corner 17, 83

Poets' groups *and* poetry societies 24–25, 81–82, 85, 95, 97, 247, 312, 314, 339, 425–26, 437–38, 444–47, 451, 458, 462–63; *see also* Cavalier Poets, Dub Poetry, Georgian Poets, Irish *and* Scottish Renaissance, Lakes School, Liverpool Poets, Metaphysical Poets, New Generation *and* Next Generation Poets, Pre-Raphaelites

popular fiction 8–9, 12–13, 218–19, 284–88, 293, 307, 526–42, 571, 588, 593

postcolonial literature and criticism *see also* multicultural literature 66–67, 72, 192, 206–07, 224–25, 272, 327, 330, 453–

58, 467, 499, 516–17, 529–30, 566–86, 587–90, 603, 609, 614, 617–18

Postmodernism 235, 519, 543, 550, 552, 556, 564–65

Pre-Raphaelite Brotherhood 196, 256, 276, 339–40

problem play 40, 70, 300, 311, 477, 481, 487, 492, 498–99, 517

prose poem 194, 425, 427, 430, 449, 556

psychological realism *see* realism

public readings 267–68, 272, 400, 402, 404, 609

publisher's reader 257, 338, 387

Punch 256, 258, 306–07, 349, 377, 412

quantitative verse 80, 124, 434

radio drama 438–40, 475–77, 480, 484–85, 489, 492, 502, 507, 508, 512, 517, 528, 537, 581, 615, 618

realism 16, 19, 65–66, 76–78, 186–87, 252, 271, 298–301, 311, 330, 352–56, 362–71, 375, 385, 405, 410, 418, 449, 463, 488–91, 503, 506–07, 519–22, 531, 534, 561, 565, 586; *formal realism* 223, 236–37, 245, 519, 586; *psychological realism* 233, 375–77, 384, 387, 392–93, 399, 543–44, 551, 558, 563, 565; *see also* magic realism

regional literature 239, 362–63, 374–76, 384–89, 451–53, 455, 524–25, 529, 553; *Cornwall* 24, 396, 441, 449, 524, 529, 598; *see also* Home Tour, Ireland, Scotland *and* Wales

religious concerns 4–5, 13–15, 18–19, 28, 31–32, 35, 38–39, 85, 88–91, 102–04, 110–114, 120, 137–38, 160, 173–75, 188, 195, 205, 208, 217–18, 223–234, 235, 238, 258, 262, 273–74, 336, 339, 342, 364, 376, 384, 386, 391–92, 398, 425, 427, 439, 444–45, 448, 460, 467, 483–84, 495, 509, 517, 520–21, 576–77

repartee 75, 148–49, 182, 185, 242, 416

repertory theatre 38, 469–72, 501

rewriting *see* intertextuality

revenge tragedy 50, 57–59, 62–63, 66

rhyme 6, 9–10, 15–19, 23, 25, 68, 84, 90, 94–97, 101, 103, 108, 124, 151, 153, 163, 168, 176, 181, 329, 335, 337, 340–41, 344–45, 350, 429, 432, 444, 484, 600; *see also* alliteration, assonance, consonance, blank verse, *terza rima, ottava rima,* and nursery rhyme

rhyme royal 15–17, 24–25, 95, 105, 434–35

Robinsonade 225, 406

Roman play 38, 40, 45–55, 151–53, 317–19, 492

Romance *in dramatic form* 40, 64–65, 70–74 (Shakespeare), 306–09, 316–17, 516; *as a narrative in verse* 10–17, 24, 98, 203, 426;

in prose 83, 121–22, 199, 237–38, 242–47, 374, 380–83, 387, 393, 526, 531, 538, 559, 588, 597; *historical romance* 251–54, 262–64, 361–64, 377, 396, 593, 598; *imperial romance* 283–86, 610; *scientific romance* 390, 537; *see also* Gothic literature

romance *vs.* novel 202–03, 223, 245, 252, 371, 374, 377–78; *see also* formal realism

romantic comedy 40, 44, 74–75

Romanticism 127–40, 168–217, 400, 426

satire *types and definition* 164–65, 606–07; *in verse* 14, 24, 81, 83, 91, 93, 95, 110, 121, 138, 160, 165–67, 175, 180–85, 191–92, 244, 344, 455, 479; *in prose* 121, 198, 214–16, 228–31, 256, 354–57, 361, 377–80, 389, 409–10, 416–17, 521, 535–36, 551–54, 567, 571, 576–77; *on stage* 25, 38–39, 66, 76–78, 148, 153–56, 473, 484–85, 505, 507

science in fiction 118, 215, 390, 537–40, 563

scientific concerns in poetry and drama 102, 106–07, 190, 451, 459, 493, 500, 518

Scotland, literature from/about 6, 24–25, 41, 44–47, 57, 78, 80, 103–04, 115, 118–19, 139, 175–76, 189, 198, 200, 205–06, 213–14, 239, 247–54, 260, 270–71, 279, 333, 346, 393–96, 406, 408, 438, 445, 451, 458–60, 466, 472, 485, 515–16, 528–30, 541–42, 557, 563–66

Scots Makar 6, 24–25, 459, 466

Scottish Renaissance 458–59, 563

screenplay 44, 318, 474–75, 489, 492–98, 512, 516, 520, 530, 535, 591

sensational novel 356, 380–82

Sensibility *and* Sentimentalism 128, 134, 156–59, 169, 210–11, 219, 228, 236, 238, 242, 245–46, 400

sentimental comedy 156–59

serial publication 256–64, 288, 317, 352, 372, 377, 381, 403–06, 475–76, 591

sermon *see* religious writing

sestina 338, 434, 440

sexuality, depiction of 66, 68, 78, 86–87, 101, 110, 117, 148–50, 155–57, 166, 177, 204, 226–30, 234, 246, 263–64, 285, 294–304, 326, 357, 363–64, 382, 387–89, 395–96, 400, 430, 445, 448, 478, 484, 488, 492, 496, 505, 513–14, 522, 526–27, 531, 535, 548–65, 578–79, 583, 591–92

silver-fork novel 362, 365, 367

shanty 346, 435

shaped verse *see* concrete poetry

short fiction 15–17, 25, 142, 218–19, 235, 249, 265–66, 286–87, 290, 390–419, 497, 527,

532–33, 541, 543–45, 551–52, 558–63, 566, 577–79, 584

Skeltonics 83

slavery 30, 72, 157, 160–61, 188, 206–07, 218, 224–25, 232, 237, 240, 266–67, 271, 283, 307–08, 330, 454, 467, 580–83, 603; *(neo-) slave narrative* 212–22, 581–83

soliloquy 60–62, 190, 334, 509, 544

song 65, 79–80, 96, 115, 131, 139, 155–56, 159–61, 174, 176, 189, 194–96, 346–49, 424, 431, 434, 456–57, 479, 592; see also *epithalamion*

Spectator, The 142, 200–01, 237

speeches 45, 50–52, 79, 119, 125, 161, 280, 490, 503

Spenserian stanza 84, 129, 244

sprung rhythm 341, 433

spy fiction *see* crime fiction

social novel 271, 298–99, 311, 330, 352–56, 367–71, 375

social realism *see* realism

sonnet 44, 64, 82–88, 93–105, 108, 112–13, 132, 138, 164, 169, 172–73, 178–81, 187, 338–45, 424–25, 434–35, 439–49, 452–56, 459–69, 599, 613

stage forms *see playhouses*

Stage Irishman 157–58, 308, 321–22, 506, 510

stock character (stereotype) 19, 30, 72–75, 157–58, 224, 237, 243, 290, 293–94, 308, 374, 416, 550; see also Angel in the House, Bluestocking, Byronic Hero, comedy of humours, Fallen Woman, *femme fatale*, Madwoman in the Attic, *miles gloriosus*, New Woman, Stage Irishman; Vice

stream of consciousness 366, 387, 543, 548, 564–65; see also free indirect discourse *and* interior monologue

Sublime, the 111, 131, 136–40, 170–72, 179, 190, 195, 209, 245–46, 341, 373, 394; *see also* the Beautiful *and* the Picturesque

subscription 139, 141, 186, 340

syllabic verse 23, 433–34, 437–40, 453

Symbolism 339, 421, 425–26

television play 309, 419, 450, 475–77, 485, 506–07, 516, 524, 528–30, 588, 615–88

terza rima 95, 172, 455

theatre *see* censorship, drama, *and* playhouses

theatre companies 38, 62, 146, 156, 324, 427, 471–74, 494–95, 498, 508, 511, 515–17, 612, 618

theatre festivals 18, 20, 130, 147, 471–72, 483–84, 495, 498, 504–05, 515

Theatre Acts (1737–1968) *see* censorship

Theatre of Cruelty 491–92, 496, 499, 512–13

Theatre of the Absurd 69, 337, 486–89, 499

three-decker novel 144, 251, 262–63, 358, 372, 377, 405

thriller *see* crime fiction

topos aere perennius 97–98, 100; *carpe diem* 91–92; *hortus conclusus* 80, 91; *mundus inversus* 433; *sic transit gloria mundi* 89, 107, 181, 347; *theatrum mundi* 75, 81, 97–98

Tottel's Miscellany 35, 82, 95–96

tragedy 9, 35, 38–42, 45–70, 88, 100, 131, 146, 151–53, 158, 162, 203, 231, 269, 301–02, 306, 324, 332, 386, 494, 503, 562, 597, 602; see also *De casibus* tragedy, domestic tragedy, revenge tragedy and Roman play

tragicomedy 40, 63, 70–72, 311, 325, 503, 505

translation 2–9, 18, 22–23, 25, 32–35, 50, 57, 64, 83, 90, 96, 105, 113–118, 123, 125, 153, 156, 163–65, 175, 180, 199, 243, 270, 280, 302, 324, 335, 338, 407, 431, 438, 449–50, 485–86, 509, 601, 606

travelogue and travel as a theme 15–18, 21, 106, 114–16, 122, 138, 193, 205–16, 221–25, 235–36, 244, 256, 278–80, 288, 334–35, 366, 390, 393, 398, 418, 435–38, 447, 453, 479, 567, 574, 598, 605–06, 611

Tudor myth 28, 42–45, 109, 508

unity of time, place and action 76, 130, 135, 152, 545–48, 506, 551, 553

Utilitarianism 271, 352–54, 402

utopia and dystopia 34, 116–20, 123, 196, 214–16, 283, 389–90, 475, 521, 534–37, 548–49, 564

vampire stories 247, 296, 380, 382, 538, 591

verse 3–6, 9–17, 21–25, 51, 55–61, 68, 79–116, 129–40, 151–56, 159–96, 208, 216–21, 243–44, 248, 73, 280–83, 291–93, 327–51, 415, 421–69, 481–85; *see also* accentual verse, free verse, quantitative verse *and* syllabic verse

verse play *see* poetic drama

Vice character 19, 41, 43, 57, 58, 67–68, 73, 111, 306, 379, 569

Victorian Values/Family Values 238, 251, 263, 268–304, 311, 350, 370, 418, 477–78, 550, 554

villanelle 338, 437, 440, 444, 466

Wales, literature from/about 2, 9, 10, 21, 23–24, 34, 44, 90, 105–06, 175, 213–14, 396, 438–40, 460–61, 466, 516, 529, 596, 599, 612–13, 618

war, depiction of 15, 41–55, 79, 120, 125, 151, 161, 202, 234, 280–81, 284, 286, 291, 329–30, 334–35, 342–45, 348–49, 366, 383–84, 390, 412, 422–24, 434–51, 454, 466–69, 473–74, 478–81, 484–85, 490, 493, 499, 502–04, 513–17, 521–25, 532–39, 544, 560, 562, 564, 569–73, 578, 581, 585, 596, 612–13, 616

well-made play 310–15, 477–502

West End theatres 412, 428, 469–73, 477, 482–501, 506, 515

Windrush Generation 529–30, 583–85

wit 73, 75, 78, 106–07, 121, 132–34, 148–50, 157–58, 182, 188–89, 207, 268, 309, 312–14, 320–22, 416–17, 444, 477, 500

'Woman with a Past' 297–301, 311, 477

Name Index

Abse, Dannie (*1923) 460–61

Ackroyd, Peter (*1949) 175, 306, 525, 587–88

Adams, Douglas (1952–2001) 537–38

Adcock, Fleur (*1934) 447–48

Addison, Joseph (1672–1719) 49, 137, 141, 151–53, 200–1, 209

Adebayo, Diran (*1968) 585, 594

Adshead, Kay ((*1954) 517

Agard, John (*1949) 455–56, 467

Agbabi, Patience (*1965) 457

Aiken, Joan (1924–2004) 241, 540–41

Ainsworth, William Harrison (1805–82) 361–62, 379–80

Aldiss, Brian (*1925) 537–38

Alfred (*849, King 871–99) 3, 5

Ali, Monica (*1967) 579

Amis, Kingsley (1922–95) 522, 526

Amis, Martin (*1949) 551, 554

Andrewes, Lancelot (1555–1626) 114

Arden, John (*1930) 493

Armatrading, Joan (*1950) 457–58

Armitage, Simon (*1963) 451–52, 485

Arnold, Matthew (1822–88) 272–74, 336–37

Ascham, Roger (1515–68) 117

Auden, W[ystan]. H[ugh]. (1907–73) 433, 434–438

Austen, Jane (1775–1817) 236, 239–42, 245, 247, 293–94, 365–66, 369, 400 *intertextual and intermedial response* 540, 588

Ayckbourn, Alan (*1939) 494

Bacon, Sir Francis (1561–1626) 32–33, 82, 118, 122–23, 200

Baillie, Joanna (1762–1851) 189

Ballantyne, R[obert]. M[ichael]. (1825–94) 406
Ballard, J[ames]. G[raham]. (1930–2009) 537, 573
Banks, Iain [M.] (*1954) 538, 564
Banville, John (*1945) 563
Barbauld, Anna Laetitia (1743–1825) 186–87, 190, 218, 219
Barbour, John (c.1320–95) 24
Barker, Pat (*1943) 345, 525
Barnes, Julian (*1946, pseud. 'Dan Kavanagh') 531, 552–53
Barrie, J[ames]. M[atthew]. (1860–1937) 305, 310
Beaumont, Francis (1584–1616) 70, 85
Beckett, Samuel (1906–89) 486–87, 489, 504–5
Beckford, William (1759–1844) 243, 244
Bede (672/73–735) 2, 3, 5
Behan, Brendan (1923–64) 490, 502, 504, 505–6, 507
Behn, Aphra (c.1640–89) 30, 149, 157, 182, 199, 223, 236–37, 253
Belloc, Hilaire (1870–1953) 278, 347, 406
Bennett, Alan (*1934) 475, 494
Bennett, Arnold (1867–1931) 366–67, 387
Benson, A[rthur]. C[hristopher]. (1862–1925) 281
Bentley, Richard (publisher, 1794–1871) 256, 258, 264
Berkoff, Steven (*1932) 484
Berry, James (*1924) 453–54
Betjeman, John (1906–84) 442–43, 444, 468
Blackmore, R[ichard]. D[oddridge]. (1825–1900) 262, 362–63, 385
Blake, William (1757–1827) 25, 105, 194–96, 216, 221, 588
Blyton, Enid (1897–1968) 540, 542
Boland, Eavan (*1944) 463
Bolt, Robert (1924–95) 117, 280, 492–93, 517
Bond, Edward (*1934) 471, 491, 499, 500, 513, 518
Borrow, George (1803–81) 367
Boswell, James (1740–95) 205, 206, 214
Boucicault, Dion(ysius) (1820–90) 307–9, 326, 391, 511
Bowdler, Thomas (1754–1825) and Henrietta (1754–1830), editors ('bowdlerise') 159, 220, 408
Bowen, Elizabeth (1899–1973) 533, 559
Bowles, William Lisle (1762–1850) 178
Bradbury, Malcolm (1932–2000) 526
Braddon, Mary Elizabeth (1835–1915) 381–82
Bradley, A[ndrew].C[ecil]. (critic, 1851–1935) 56–57, 67, 203, 269–70, 273, 497, 602
Braine, John (1922–86) 522
Branagh, Kenneth (actor and director, *1960) 45–46, 68, 474, 497

Brecht, Berthold 46, 156, 314, 487, 490, 493, 496, 504, 516
Brenton, Howard (*1942) 48, 49, 492, 518
Bridges, Robert (1844–1930) 338, 433–34
Brontë, Charlotte (1816–55) 252, 260, 262, 297, 367–68, 369–72, 374, 400, 401, 589
Brontë, Emily (1818–48) 367, 369–70, 372–74
Brooke, Rupert (1887–1915) 342–43, 344
Brown, George Mackay (1921–96) 6, 458
Browne, Sir Thomas (1605–82) 114
Browning, Elizabeth Barrett (1806–61) 266, 330–331, 335, 338, 341
Browning, Robert (1812–89) 332–334, 335
Buchan, John (1875–1940) 384, 532
Buchanan, George (1506–82) 118
Bulwer Lytton, Edward (1803–73) 48, 253, 264, 360, 361–62, 365, 372, 380, 390
Bunting, Basil (1900–85) 430
Bunyan, John (1628–88) 25, 205, 208, 377
Burgess, Anthony (John Wilson, 1917–93) 521, 548–49, 573, 587, 593
Burke, Edmund (1729–97) 131, 137, 161, 198, 248
Burke, Gregory (*1968) 515
Burnett, Frances Hodgson (1849–1924) 266, 417
Burney, Frances "Fanny" (1752–1840) 199, 205, 236, 238, 294, 400
Burns, Robert (1759–96) 139, 176–77, 169, 393, 396, 458, 461
Burnside, John (*1955) 459
Burton, Sir Richard (1821–90) 279–80, 407
Burton, Robert (1577–1640) 34, 124–25
Butler, Samuel (1835–1902) 110, 389
Byatt, A[ntonia]. S[usan]. (*1936) 328, 526, 558, 586
Byron, George Gordon, 6th Baron (1788–1824) 84, 95, 130, 132, 143, 159, 167–68, 180, 193–94, 197, 208, 243–44, 247, 332, 370, 435, 468, 500

Cædmon (fl. 670) 3
Campbell, Roy (1901–57) 435, 437
Campion, Thomas (1567–1620) 77, 80, 124
Carew, Thomas (1595–1640) 80, 82, 85, 92, 108
Carleton, William (1794–1869) 259, 391
Carlyle, Thomas (1795–1881) 265, 270–71, 276, 290, 295, 353, 364
Carroll, Lewis (Charles Lutwidge Dogson, 1832–98) 295, 349, 414–15, 539, 591
Carson, Ciarán (*1948) 22, 464, 466
Carter, Angela (1940–92) 559, 587
Caxton, William (?1422–91) 8, 11, 15, 17, 34, 115
Causley, Charles (1917–2003) 441, 452

Chapman, George (c.1559–1634) 78, 105, 116, 180
Chatterton, Thomas (1752–70) 175, 587
Chaucer, Geoffrey (c.1342–1400) 7–8, 14–17, 24–27, 34, 55, 82–84, 95, 105, 109, 129, 208, 390, 408, 434, 483, 513, 591–92, 601
Chesterfield, Philip Dormer Stanhope, Earl of (1694–1773) 197, 217
Chesterton, Gilbert Keith (1874–1936) 347, 349, 398
Childers, Erskine (1870–1922) 384
Christie, Agatha (1890–1976) 62, 326, 497, 526–7
Chudleigh, Mary Lady (1656–1710) 188–90
Churchill, Caryl (*1938) 475, 484–85, 512–13, 518
Churchill, Sir Winston (1874–1965) 125, 161, 311–12, 401, 465, 532, 536, 572
Clare, John (1793–1864) 491
Clarke, Arthur C. (1917–2008) 537
Clarke, Gillian (*1937) 461
Clavell, James (1924–94) 573, 593
Cleland, John (1710–89) 199, 229–30
Coe, Jonathan (*1961) 553–54
Coleridge, Samuel Taylor (1772–1834) 67, 130, 132, 135–36, 139, 161–62, 171–72, 173, 176–77, 178–79, 190–91, 193, 205, 246, 247, 269, 341, 433, 443–44, 452
Collier, Mary (?1690–1762) 186–87
Collins, Merle (*1950) 457
Collins, Wilkie (1824–89) 258, 263, 268, 295, 381
Collins, William (1721–59) 170
Combe, William (1741–1823) 138, 213
Conan Doyle, Sir Arthur (1859–1930) 397–98, 553
Congreve, William (1670–1729) 149–50
Conrad, Joseph (Józef Konrad Korzeniowski, 1857–1924) 257, 283, 288–291, 384, 396, 449
Cope, Wendy (*1945) 428, 444, 448, 466, 469
Corkery, Daniel (1878–1964) 392, 560
Coward, Noël (1899–1973) 150, 470, 478–79, 481
Cowley, Abraham (1618–67) 83, 106, 110, 200
Cowper, William (1731–1800) 174–75
Cranmer, Thomas (Archbishop, 1489–1556) 32, 113
Crashaw, Richard (c.1613–49) 90–91
Crawford, Robert (*1959) 451–52, 459–60, 595, 598, 612
Cumberland, Richard (1732–1811) 157
Cunningham, Michael (*1952) 590–91, 593

D'Aguiar, Fred (*1960) 222, 330, 454, 467, 468, 582
Dahl, Roald (1916–90) 541

Dabydeen, David (*1955) 222, 451–52, 499, 582–83, 585
Daniel, Samuel (1562–1619) 77, 98, 106, 124
Darwin, Charles (1809–82) 273, 274–76, 279, 315, 411, 431
Davenant (or D'Avenant), Sir William (1606–68) 110, 151
Day-Lewis, C[ecil]. (1904–72) 437–38
Defoe, Daniel (1660–1731) 142, 175, 213, 215, 220, 221, 222–227, 229, 230, 236–37, 250, 253, 285, 310, 379, 394, 406
Deighton, Len (*1929) 534, 541
Dekker, Thomas (?1572–1632) 77–78, 122
Delaney, Shelagh (*1939) 490–91
Deloney, Thomas (c.1543–1600) 122
Denham, Sir John (1615–69) 83, 108
De Quincey, Thomas (1785–1859) 142, 200, 203
Dhondy, Farrukh (*1944) 516, 572
Dickens, Charles (1812–1870) 143, 240, 255–73, 277–78, 283, 292–98, 306–08, 351–64, 367–77, 380–86, 396–404, 407–09, 416, 419, 448, 476, 525, 528, 541, 587–88, 608–11
Disraeli, Benjamin (Prime Minister, 1804–1881) 259, 280, 365, 367, 383
Donne, John (1572–1631) 80–82, 85–88, 89–90, 92, 93, 101–3, 106–7, 114, 118, 121, 128, 206, 428
Douglas, Gavin (c.1475–1522) 25, 115
Douglas, Keith (1920–44) 441
Doyle, Roddy (*1958) 411, 561–62, 592–93
Drabble, Margaret (*1939) 558
Drayton, Michael (1563–1631) 98, 105–6, 115
Drummond of Hawthornden, William (1585–1649) 80, 103–4
Dryden, John (1631–1700) 12, 54, 55, 129, 141, 151–53, 163–64, 165, 166, 169, 170, 202, 327, 495
Duffy, Carol Ann (*1955) 361, 448, 467
Du Maurier, Daphne (1907–89) 387, 396, 531
Dunbar, William (c.1460–1513) 24–25
Duncker, Patricia (*1951) 557
Dunn, Douglas (*1942) 393, 459, 467
Dunn, Nell (*1936) 522

Edgar, David (*1948) 484, 492, 514–15
Edgeworth, Maria (1767–1849) 218–19, 239, 250, 254, 385
Eliot, T[homas]. S[tearns]. (1888–1965) 88, 267, 306, 335, 337–38, 425–29, 434, 435, 441, 444, 451, 466, 468, 480, 483–84, 517, 518, 547, 588
Eliot, George (Mary Ann Evans, 1819–80) 257, 260, 261, 294, 295, 364, 367, 370, 374–77, 382, 385, 401, 419

Elizabeth I. (*1533, Queen 1558–1603) 28, 29, 30–32, 39, 42, 47, 73, 81, 93, 96, 109, 115, 118–19, 125, 467, 508
Elyot, Sir Thomas (c.1499–1546) 117
Emecheta, Buchi (*1944) 585
Equiano, Olaudah (1745–97) 207
Etherege, Sir George (1635–91) 148
Evelyn, John (1620–1706) 204

Falkner, J. Meade (1858–1932) 396, 406
Farquhar, George (1678–1707) 149–50
Farrell, J[ames]. G[ordon]. (1935–79) 463, 562, 571–72, 580
Fenton, James (*1949) 273, 442, 446–47, 451, 457, 467
Fforde, Jasper (*1961) 589
Fielding, Helen (*1958) 253, 448, 588
Fielding, Henry (1707–54) 77, 121, 131, 146, 153–54, 158, 200, 202–05, 210–11, 228, 231–32, 234, 237, 242, 253–54, 379, 474
Fielding, Sarah (1710–68) 237
Finlay, Ian Hamilton (1925–2006) 459
FitzGerald, Edward (1809–83) 335
Fletcher, John (?1579–1625) 38, 40, 42, 47, 70, 85
Fleming, Ian (1908–64) 532–34, 541
Ford, John (1586–?1640) 58
Forester, C[ecil]. S[cott]. (1899–1966) 523–24
Forster, E[dward]. M[organ]. (1879–1970) 226, 257, 263, 282, 366, 387, 389, 546, 555, 566–568
Forsyth, Frederick (*1938) 532
Fowles, John (1926–2005) 548–50, 586
Foxe, John (1516–87) 118
Fraser, George MacDonald (1925–2008) 524, 571
Frayn, Michael (*1933) 493–94, 518
Friel, Brian (*1929) 47, 463, 504, 507–08, 510
Frost, Robert (1874–1963) 429
Fry, Christopher (1907–2005) 484
Fuller, John (*1939) 440, 466
Fuller, Roy (1912–91) 339, 429, 440, 466, 468

Gaiman, Neil (*1960) 6, 591
Galsworthy, John (1867–1933) 257, 311, 366
Garioch, Robert (1909–81) 458
Garnett, Edward (publisher's reader, 1868–1937) 257, 387, 398
Garrick, David (actor-manager, 1717–79) 130, 147, 157, 207, 305
Gascoigne, George (1539–78) 83
Gaskell, Elizabeth (1810–1865) 240, 258, 298–99, 367–70
Gay, John (1685–1732) 154–55
Geoffrey of Monmouth (c.1100–c.1155) 9
Gerald of Wales (c.1146–1223) 21

Gibbon, Edward (1737–94) 48, 141, 205
Gibbon, Lewis Grassic (James Leslie Mitchell, 1901–35) 563
Gilbert, W[illiam]. S[chwenck]. (1836–1911) 309–10, 317, 349
Gissing, George (1857–1903) 372, 384
Golding, Arthur (1536–1605) 105, 115, 163
Golding, William (1911–93) 406, 535, 537
Goldsmith, Oliver (?1730–74) 121, 157, 201, 243
Gower, John (c.1330–1408) 7, 15, 17
Graham, Winston (1908–2003) 524
Grahame, Kenneth (1859–1932) 411–12
Granville-Barker, Harley (actor, director and critic, 1877–1946) 69, 305, 316, 320, 471, 498
Graves, Robert (1895–1985) 48, 273, 341, 431–33
Gray, Alasdair (*1934) 196, 554, 564
Gray, Thomas (1716–71) 23, 137–38, 168–69, 175, 197
Greene, Graham (1904–91) 520–21, 532–34, 573
Greene, Robert (1558–92) 122
Greenlaw, Lavinia (*1962) 451
Gregory, Lady Augusta (1852–1932) 322–24, 471, 501
Greville, Fulke (1554–1628) 89, 97
Griffin, Gerald (1803–40) 308, 391
Griffiths, Trevor (*1935) 306, 488, 492
Gurney, Ivor (1890–1937) 345

Haggard, H[enry]. Rider (1856–1925) 283–86, 288, 406
Hakluyt, Richard (c.1552–1616) 114
Hall, Joseph (1574–1656) 85, 121
Hall, (Marguerite) Radclyffe (1880–1943) 263, 555
Hampton, Christopher (*1946) 150, 475
Hardy, Thomas (1840–28) 5, 169, 258, 263, 238, 299, 333, 338, 342, 367, 372, 383, 385–87, 453, 468, 476
Hare, David (*1947) 492, 515, 591
Harris, Robert (*1957) 48, 541
Harrison, Tony (*1937) 191–92, 449, 459, 469, 484–85
Haywood, Eliza (c. 1693–1756) 237
Hazlitt, William (1778–1830) 69, 127, 142, 158–59, 200, 202–03, 362
Heaney, Seamus (*1939) 6, 22–23, 25, 273, 441, 445, 451, 461–64, 466, 469
Henri, Adrian (1932–2000) 445
Henryson, Robert (c.1425–1506) 25
Henty, G[eorge]. A[lfred]. (1832–1902) 283–84, 365, 409
Herbert, George (1593–1633) 85, 88, 90, 104, 206

Herrick, Robert (1591–1674) 82, 85, 92

Heywood, Thomas (?1573–1641) 63, 66

Hill, Geoffrey (*1932) 448, 466

Hill, Selima (*1945) 448

Hobbes, Thomas (1588–1679) 120–21, 124, 155

Hobsbaum, Philip (1932–2005) 445, 462–63

Hoby, Sir Thomas (1530–66) 117

Hoccleve, Thomas (c.1369–1437) 17

Hofmann, Michael (*1957) 451

Hogarth, William (artist, 1697–1764) 147, 154, 582–83

Hogg, James (1770–1835) 393

Holcroft, Thomas (1745–1809) 306, 309

Holinshed, Raphael (d.?1580) 41, 43, 106, 116

Hooker, Richard (1554–1600) 114

Hopkins, Gerard Manley (1844–89) 196, 340–42, 421–22, 424, 468

Horace (65–8 BC) 95, 106, 121, 131, 152, 163, 165, 169–72, 184–85, 193, 216, 329

Hornby, Nick (*1957) 593–94

Housman, A[lfred]. E[dward]. (1850–1936) 335, 344, 500

Hughes, Ted (1930–98) 430–31, 462, 466, 468

Hughes, Thomas (1822–96) 261, 273, 400, 542, 571

Hulme, T[homas]. E[rnest]. (1883–1917) 426

Hume, David (1711–76) 143, 200, 202, 205

Huxley, Aldous (1894–1963) 535–36

Ibsen, Henrik (1828–1906) 293, 303, 309, 311, 314, 322, 326, 481

Innes, Michael (J[ohn]. I[nnes]. M[acintosh]. Stewart, 1906–94) 528, 587

Isherwood, Christopher (1904–86) 438

Ishiguro, Kazuo (*1954) 573, 578

James, Henry (1843–1916) 266–67, 365–66, 377, 397, 417, 563

Jamie, Kathleen (*1962) 451, 459

Jellicoe, Ann (*1927) 490–91

Jerrold, Douglas (1803–57) 306

Jhabvala, Ruth Prawer (*1927) 475, 566, 569, 578

Johnson, Amryl (1944–2000) 454

Johnson, Linton Kwesi (*1952) 456

Johnson, Samuel (1709–84) 21, 88, 130–31, 135, 141–42, 158, 165–66, 197, 202–207, 214, 243

Johnson, Terry (*1955) 488–89, 500–01

Johnston, Denis (1901–84) 497, 502

Jones, Bobi (Robert, *1929) 461

Jones, David (1895–1974) 430

Jones, Henry Arthur (1851–1929) 299–300, 309, 311

Jonson, Ben (1572–1637) 31, 34, 38–39, 45, 48, 75–82, 84–85, 92, 103, 106, 108, 118, 121, 169

Joyce, James (1882–1941) 235, 263, 309, 335, 383–84, 392–93, 439, 458, 505, 542, 544–49, 554, 560, 564–65

Julian of Norwich (1342–c.1416) 18

Juvenal 121, 163–166

Kane, Sarah (1971–99) 485, 513–14, 518

Kavanagh, Patrick (1904–67) 463

Kay, Jackie (*1961) 460, 557, 585

Keats, John (1795–1821) 164, 171–73, 176–81, 191–94, 350, 469

Kempe, Margery (c.1373–1438) 18

Kelman, James (*1946) 522, 564–65

Kennedy, A[lison]. L. (*1965) 565

Kennelly, Brendan (*1936) 463, 596, 612

Khan-Din, Ayub (*1954) 516

Kingsley, Charles (1819–75) 273–74, 335, 364, 368, 383, 408, 414

Kingsley, Mary (1862–1900) 280

Kinsella, Thomas (*1928) 22, 463–64

Kipling, Rudyard (1865–1939) 282–83, 286–88, 341, 348–49, 378, 401, 409–11, 506, 568, 577, 579

Knight, Stephen (*1960) 461

Kureishi, Hanif (*1954) 475, 516, 578–79, 594

Kyd, Thomas (1558–94) 55, 58

Lamb, Charles (1775–1834) and Mary Lamb (1764–1847) 68, 121, 142, 158–59, 202–03, 218–20, 335, 407

Lamming, George (*1927) 499, 574, 584

Lang, Andrew (1844–1912) and Leonora Blanche Lang (1851–1933) 407

Langland, William (c.1330–87) 14, 25

Lanyer, Aemilia (1569–1645) 93, 108

Larkin, Philip (1922–85) 444–45

Laverty, Maura (1907–67) 507

Lavin, Mary (1912–96) 560

Lawrence, D[avid]. H[erbert]. (1885–1930) 229, 263, 279–80, 387–89, 398–400, 430, 468, 554–55

Lawrence, T[homas]. E[dward]. (1888–1935) 280

Le Carré, John (David Cornwell, *1931) 532–34

Le Fanu, Sheridan (1814–73) 247, 381–82

Lear, Edward (1812–88) 256, 278, 406

Lennon, John (1940–80) 457, 473

Lennox, Charlotte (1720–1804) 238

Leonard, Tom (*1944) 460

Lewes, George Henry (1817–87) 260, 295

Lessing, Doris (*1919) 537, 558

Leverson, Ada (1862–1933) 263, 366

Levy, Andrea (*1956) 585

Lewis, C[live]. S[taples]. (1898–1963) 113, 539, 542

Lewis, Matthew Gregory (1775–1818) 246

Lewis, Wyndham (1882–1957) 426, 435

Lillo, George (1693–1739) 47, 65, 153, 158

Lindsay, Sir David (c.1490–1555) 25, 39

Littlewood, Joan (1914–2002) 472–73, 490, 506

Locke, John (1632–1704) 198, 200, 217, 233

Lodge, David (*1935) 519, 521, 526, 548, 553, 586

Lodge, Thomas (c.1558–1625) 121

Lofting, Hugh (1886–1947) 412–13

Longley, Michael (*1939) 445, 463

Lovelace, Richard (1618–57) 92

Lowry, Malcolm (1909–57) 521

Lydgate, John (?1370–1449) 17

Lyly, John (1553/54–1606) 73, 121

Macaulay, Thomas Babington, Lord (1800–59) 161, 260, 272

Macaulay, Catharine (1731–91) 199

MacBeth, George (1932–92) 445–46

MacDiarmid, Hugh (Christopher Murray Grieve, 1892–1978) 458–60, 563

MacDonald, George (1824–1905) 404, 415

MacInnes, Colin (1914–76) 522

Mackenzie, Henry (1745–1831) 236

MacLaverty, Bernard (*1942) 562

MacLean, Sorley (Somhairle MacGill-Eain, 1911–96) 458

MacNeice, Louis (1907–63) 437–38, 463–64, 475, 484–85

Mahon, Derek (*1941) 445, 463–64

Malory, Sir Thomas (c.1405–71) 11–12, 328

Mansfield, Katherine (1888–1923) 399, 543–45

Marlowe, Christopher (1564–1593) 31, 45–46, 55–56, 62–63, 79, 81, 84, 105

Marryat, Captain Frederick (1792–1848) 406, 408–09, 523

Marsh, Ngaio (1895–1982) 528

Marson, Una (1905–65) 189–90, 192, 348, 453

Marston, John (1576–1634) 58, 78, 121

Martyn, Edward (1859–1923) 322–23

Marvell, Andrew (1621–78) 29, 88, 91–92, 106–08, 115, 117, 169, 182, 191, 333

Mary Stuart (Queen of Scots 1542–67, †1587) 29–30, 32, 45, 47, 90, 119, 333, 485, 515

Massinger, Philip (1583–1640) 48, 78

Matura, Mustapha (*1939) 516

Maturin, Charles Robert (1780–1824) 246

Maugham, William Somerset (1874–1965) 477–79, 566

Maxwell, Glyn (*1962) 451, 485

McCabe, Patrick (*1955) 557, 563

McCall Smith, Alexander (*1948) 530
McDonagh, Martin (*1970) 510–11
McEwan, Ian (*1948) 457, 550–51
McGough, Roger (*1937) 445, 457
McGuckian, Medbh (*1950) 463
McKay, Claude (1889–1948) 283, 469
McPherson, Conor (*1971) 510–11
Meredith, George (1828–1909) 263, 269, 298, 338–39, 383
Middleton, Thomas (1580–1627) 58, 66, 77–78
Mill, John Stuart (1806–73) 127, 271–73, 292, 295
Milne, A[lan]. A[lexander]. (1882–1956) 411–13
Milton, John (1608–74) 12, 27, 77, 82–83, 85, 88–89, 104–05, 108–10, 112–14, 119–20, 129–30, 141, 178–79, 194–95
Mitchell, Adrian (*1932) 445, 457
Mitchell, Gary (*1965) 512
Mo, Timothy (*1950) 475, 573, 593
Montagu, Lady Mary Wortley (1689–1762) 166, 181, 183–86, 197, 211, 243
Morgan, Sydney Owenson, Lady (c.1775–1859) 239–40, 254
Moorcock, Michael (*1939) 537
Moore, Alan (*1953) 591
Moore, Marianne (1887–1972) 433
Moore, Thomas (1779–1852) 143, 176, 244, 263
More, Hannah (1745–1833) 144, 218, 238, 294
More, Sir Thomas (1478–1535) 31, 34, 43, 47, 115–18, 493
Morgan, Edwin (*1920) 6, 459, 469
Morris, William (1834–96) 256, 277, 283, 340, 389
Morrison, Blake (*1950) 450–51
Mortimer, John (1923–2009) 476, 587
Motion, Andrew (*1952) 450–52
Muir, Edwin (1887–1959) 458
Muldoon, Paul (*1951) 273, 463–66
Murdoch, Iris (1919–99) 587
Murphy, Tom (*1935) 510

Nashe, Thomas (1567–1601) 89, 121–122
Nesbit, E[dith]. (1858–1924) 408, 417–18
Naipaul, V[idiadhar]. S[urajprasad]. (*1932) 272, 574, 584
Neate, Patrick (*1970) 530
Newbery, John (publisher, 1713–67) 142, 219
Newland, Courttia (*1973) 530
Newman, John Henry (Cardinal, 1801–90) 274, 295
Nichols, Grace (*1950) 454

O'Brien, Edna (*1932) 473, 558, 561
O'Brien, Flann (Brian O'Nolan, 1911–66) 22, 235, 548
O'Casey, Sean (1880–1964) 326, 502–05

O'Connor, Frank (Michael Francis O'Donovan, 1903–66) 392, 506–07, 559–60
O'Faoláin, Seán (John Francis Whelan, 1900–91) 392, 560
Okri, Ben (*1959) 585
Olivier, Laurence (actor and director, 1907–89) 43–46, 59, 68, 470–71, 474, 488, 497
Orczy, Baroness (1865–1947) 364
Orton, Joe (1933–67) 494
Orwell, George (Eric Arthur Blair, 1903–50) 348, 410, 436, 443, 535–37, 566, 568
Osborne, John (1929–94) 253, 306, 471, 474, 484, 487–88, 522
Oswald, Alice (*1966) 453–54, 467
Otway, Thomas (1652–85) 151
Ovid (43 BC–AD 17) 86, 92, 97, 105, 115, 129, 163, 193
Owen, Wilfred (1839–1918) 343–45, 421, 441, 466, 469, 478, 504

Parker, Stewart (1941–88) 511
Pater, Walter (1839–94) 295
Paterson, Don (*1963) 451, 459, 466
Patmore, Coventry (1823–96) 292
Peacock, Thomas Love (1785–1856) 130–31, 247, 339
Pembroke, Mary Herbert, Countess of (1562–1621) 83, 113, 122
Pepys, Samuel (1633–1703) 204, 522
Percy, Thomas (Bishop, 1729–1811) 131, 175
Petrarca (or Petrarch), Francesco (1304–74) 15, 27, 94–98, 112, 175
Philips, Katherine (1632–1664) 93, 188
Phillips, Caryl (*1958) 517, 580–82, 586
Pinero, Arthur Wing (1855–1934) 300, 310–11
Pinnock, Winsome (*1961) 517
Pinter, Harold (1930–2008) 474–75, 489–91, 497, 511, 518, 551, 578
Plath, Silvia (1932–63) 431
Plunkett, James (1920–2003) 561
Poe, Edgar Allan (1809–49) 142, 393, 397, 426
Polidori, Dr John (1795–1821) 247, 382
Pomfret, John (1667–1702) 162–63
Pope, Alexander (1688–1744) 129, 131, 133–38, 145, 151, 153, 163–67, 180, 183–86, 192–93, 196, 202
Porter, Peter (*1929) 441, 445
Potter, Beatrix (1866–1943) 256, 411
Potter, Denis (1935–97) 475–76, 497
Pound, Ezra (1885–1972) 6, 267, 324, 422, 425–27, 432–35, 439
Powys, John Cowper (1872–1963) 387
Pratchett, Terry (*1948) 538, 591
Priestley, J[ohn]. B[oynton]. (1894–1984) 479–81, 497, 518

Prior, Matthew (1664–1721) 166
Pullman, Philip (*1946) 540

Radcliffe, Ann (1764–1823) 143, 212, 238, 245–47
Raine, Craig (*1944) 447, 451
Ralegh (or Raleigh), Sir Walter (1552–1618) 81–84, 98, 109, 115–17
Rattigan, Terence (1911–77) 478, 481, 493
Ravenhill, Mark (*1966) 513–14
Reade, Charles (1814–84) 364, 381
Reed, Henry (1914–86) 441
Reeve, Clara (1729–1807) 244–45
Reid, Christopher (*1949) 447, 451
Rhys, Jean (Ella Gwendolen Rees Williams, ?1890/94–1979) 371, 548, 583–84, 589–90
Richardson, Samuel (1689–1761) 199, 213, 217, 227–28, 236, 253, 400
Robinson, Lennox (1886–1958) 502, 508
Robinson, Mary (1758–1800) 179, 190, 193
Rochester, John Wilmot, Earl of (1647–80) 92, 149, 165, 182, 192
Rosenberg, Isaac (1890–1918) 345
Rossetti, Christina (1830–94) 331, 341, 406
Rossetti, Dante Gabriel (1828–82) 196, 256, 339–40
Rowe, Nicholas (1674–1718) 153, 158
Rowling, J[oanne]. K[athleen]. (*1965) 541–42
Rushdie, Salman (*1947) 235, 282, 450, 574–77
Ruskin, John (1819–1900) 277, 280, 291, 293, 295, 339
Russell, Willy (*1947) 327, 492

Sackville, Thomas (1536–1608) 58
Saki (Hector Munro, 1870–1916) 398, 541
Samuels, Diane (*1960) 493
Sancho, Ignatius (1729–80) 207
Sassoon, Siegfried (1886–1967) 344–45
Sayers, Dorothy L. (1893–1957) 526–28
Schreiner, Olive (1855–1920) 283–84
Scott, Paul (1920–78) 569
Scott, Sir Walter (1771–1832) 13, 29, 143, 176, 198, 206, 239, 243, 247–53, 362, 364, 369, 379, 385, 393, 408
Selvon, Sam[uel] (1923–94) 584
Seth, Vikram (*1952) 577–78
Seward, Anna (1742–1809) 179
Sewell, Anna (1820–78) 410
Shadwell, Thomas (?1642–92) 166
Shaffer, Anthony (1926–2001) 489, 497
Shaffer, Peter (*1926) 494–96, 517, 518
Shaftesbury, Anthony Ashley Cooper, 3rd Earl of (1671–1713) 200
Shakespeare, William (1564–1616) *life and career* 31, 40, 85, 99–100, 448, 499–500,

587; *sources* 15–16, 19, 41, 50, 53–54, 57–58, 64, 72–73, 116, 121; *sonnets and short epics* 16, 78–85, 93–106, 112, 166, 179, 351; *Roman and history plays* 29, 41–55, 79, 125, 508; *comedies* 72–76, 148, 162, 182; *tragedies* 55–70; *tragicomedies* 30–31, 70–72, 167, 403; *stage and film productions, radio plays* 37–39, 44–48, 52–53, 58, 65, 69–70, 71, 147, 158–59, 305, 470–71, 474–76, 498; *editions* 39–41, 99–100, 141, 158–59, 164, 408, 602; *canonisation* 17, 82–83, 129–30, 141, 158–59; *criticism* 42, 53–54, 58, 66–69, 131, 135, 158, 203, 220, 225, 269–70, 311, 497–98, 602–03; *intertextual response* 62, 65, 69, 71, 72, 151–53, 179, 190, 192, 225, 235–37, 311, 317–20, 327, 333, 386–87, 406–09, 437, 448, 484, 490–91, 498–500, 538, 558–59, 571–72, 577, 582, 586–87, 591–92

Shaw, G[eorge]. B[ernard]. (1856–1950) 293, 302–3, 305, 313–22, 326–27, 354, 470, 471, 472, 492, 517

Shelley, Mary (1797–1851) 193, 246–47, 537

Shelley, Percy Bysshe (1792–1822) 131, 132, 136, 138, 159, 164, 169, 172, 175, 181, 191, 193, 247, 335, 456, 469

Sheridan, Richard Brinsley (1751–1816) 147, 157–58

Sherwood, Mary Butt (1775–1851) 405

Shirley, James (1596–1666) 78

Sidney, Sir Philip (1554–1586) 81, 83–84, 96–98, 108, 113, 117, 121–22, 123–24, 206

Sillitoe, Alan (*1928) 522

Sitwell, Edith (1887–1964) 430, 441

Skelton, John (c.1460–1529) 83

Slovo, Gillian (*1952) 515, 518

Smith, Ali (*1962) 565

Smith, Charlotte (1749–1806) 169, 173, 178

Smith, Iain Crichton (1928–98) 459

Smith, Stevie (1902–71) 190–91, 443–44

Smith, Zadie (*1975) 572, 585

Smollett, Tobias (1721–71) 143, 199, 209–11, 213–14

Southey, Robert (1774–1843) 167, 177, 206

Southwell, Robert (1561–95) 89–90

Spark, Muriel (1918–2006) 521, 564

Spender, Stephen (1909–95) 437–38, 484

Spenser, Edmund (1552–99) 28, 83–84, 89, 93, 97, 108–10, 112, 117, 129, 175, 338

Steele, Sir Richard (1672–1729) 142, 147, 156–57, 200–1

Sterne, Laurence (1713–68) 124–25, 141, 160, 200, 204, 209–11, 233–36, 296, 577

Stevenson, Robert Louis (1850–94) 262, 279, 393–96, 406, 408

Stoker, Bram (1847–1912) 296, 382, 538

Stoppard, Tom (*1937) 474, 475, 489, 493, 497, 498, 499, 500, 518, 573

Suckling, Sir John (1609–42) 80, 85, 92

Sullivan, Arthur (1842–1900) 309–10

Surrey, Henry Howard, Earl of (1517–47) 95–96, 103, 115, 117, 122

Sutcliff, Rosemary (1920–92) 540

Swift, Graham (*1949) 524–25, 531, 553

Swift, Jonathan (1667–1745) 129, 143, 165, 183–86, 196–97, 198, 204, 214–16, 428

Swinburne, Algernon Charles (1837–1909) 331, 333, 335

Syal, Meera (*1961) 579

Synge, John Millington (1871–1909) 22, 303–4, 313, 324–26, 476, 511, 517

Szirtes, George (*1948) 442, 455, 467

Tate, Nahum (1652–1715) 70

Taylor, Tom (1817–80) 306–7

Tennyson, Alfred, Lord (1809–92) 6, 12, 280–81, 293, 295, 328–30, 332, 334–35, 337, 350, 468, 483, 527, 570–71

Thackeray, William Makepeace (1811–63) 234, 253, 256–57, 268, 283, 295–96, 297, 298, 363–64, 369, 377–78, 380, 396, 401, 404, 414–15

Thomas, Brandon (1856–1914) 310

Thomas, Dylan (1914–53) 396, 433, 438–40, 455, 460, 463, 466, 468, 469, 475

Thomas, Edward (1878–1917) 342–43, 450

Thomas, R[onald]. S[tuart]. (1913–2000) 460

Thompson, Sam (1916–65) 507

Thomson, James (1700–48) 160–61, 169, 170, 175

Thorpe, Adam (*1956) 553

Thwaite, Anthony (*1930) 445, 619

Tóibín, Colm (*1955) 563

Tolkien, J[ohn]. R[onald]. R[euel]. (1892–1973) 538–39

Tonson, Jacob, the Elder (bookseller, 1655/56–1736) 141–42, 164

Torrington, Jeff (1935–2009) 565

Traherne, Thomas (1637–74) 90–91, 114

Tremain, Rose (*1943) 150, 522–23

Trollope, Anthony (1815–82) 278–79, 385

Trollope, Frances (1780–1863) 278

Twain, Mark (1835–1910) 266, 552

Tyndale, William (c.1490–1536) 113, 114, 115

Udall, Nicholas (?1504–56) 73

Unsworth, Barry (*1930) 20, 580

Ustinov, Sir Peter (actor and adaptor, 1921–2004) 48, 497, 499, 527

Vanbrugh, Sir John (1664–1726) 147, 149, 588

Vaughan, Henry (1621–95) 80, 90–91

Virgil (70–19 BC) 9, 84, 105, 108, 115, 163, 438

Wakefield Master 19

Walcott, Derek (*1930) 165, 168, 192, 225, 327, 469, 498

Wallace, Edgar (1875–1932) 531–32

Waller, Edmund (1606–87) 80, 82–83, 108

Walpole, Horace (1717–97) 137, 196–97, 244–45

Walpole, Sir Robert (Prime Minister, 1676–1745) 146, 154–56, 165, 379

Walton, Izaak (1593–1683) 118, 206

Warner, Marina (*1946) 499, 586

Watts, Isaac (1674–1748) 174

Waugh, Evelyn (1903–66) 520–21

Webster, John (c.1580–1625) 58, 78

Wells, H[erbert]. G[eorge]. (1866–1946) 263, 283, 366, 390, 415, 535, 537

Weldon, Fay (*1931) 558–59

Welsh, Irvine (*1958) 513, 522, 554, 565

Wesker, Arnold (*1932) 71, 490, 499

Wesley, Charles (1707–88) and John (1703–91) 174, 205

White, T[erence]. H[anbury]. (1906–64) 12, 588

Whitney, Isabella (*fl*. 1567–73) 93

Wilde, Oscar (1854–1900) 99, 149–50, 264, 266, 268, 295, 300–02, 311–14, 326, 340, 347–48, 382–83, 415–17, 426, 477–78, 500–01, 555, 588

Williams, Nigel (*1948) 492

Winchilsea, Anne Finch, Countess of (1661–1720) 183, 186

Winstanley, Gerrard (1609–?76) 120–21

Winterson, Jeanette (*1959) 555–56, 593

Wollstonecraft, Mary (1759–97) 187, 199, 212, 238, 292

Woolf, Virginia (1882–1941) 236, 257, 292, 341, 366, 474, 543–48, 555–58, 590–91, 593

Wordsworth, William (1770–1850) 105, 130–39, 144, 167, 170–71, 176–81, 205, 216, 221, 400

Wroth, Lady Mary (née Sidney, 1587–?1651) 103, 122

Wyatt, Sir Thomas (1503–42) 80, 82, 95–97, 112

Wycherley, William (1640–1716) 148

Yeats, W[illiam]. B[utler]. (1865–1939) 22–23, 95, 196, 313–14, 320–35, 340, 344–47, 350, 421–27, 436, 468, 471, 501, 503–504, 508

Yonge, Charlotte M. (1823–1901) 369, 405

Young, Edward (1683–1765) 134, 173

Zephaniah, Benjamin (*1958) 348, 456